Raising Finance

From Traditional to New Forms of Entrepreneurial Finance

Transformations in Banking, Finance and Regulation

Print ISSN: 2752-5821
Online ISSN: 2752-583X

Series Editors: Sabri Boubaker
(*EM Normandie Business School, France*)
Duc Khuong Nguyen
(*EMLV Business School, France*)

Presently, the banking and finance sectors evolve within a globalized and highly uncertain environment. Each business and financial decision requires careful consideration of country-specific and international factors due to high levels of shock transmission and volatility spillovers. Furthermore, it would be remiss to omit the COVID-19 health crisis, which caused harmful effects to all areas of the real economy and made profound changes in the way our firms, economies, and markets used to function.

Many other already well-known aspects, including the repercussions of quantitative easing policies, disruptive technologies in finance (e.g., FinTech, Big Data, Data Analytics, Artificial Intelligence, and Blockchains), as well as innovative financing instruments for startups (e.g., ICOs and crowdfunding) are currently revolutionizing banking and finance and posing numerous challenges to regulatory bodies and policymakers. Climate change emergencies also put pressure on governments and firms worldwide to improve policy on governance, corporate social responsibility, and sustainability practices.

This book series "Transformations in Banking, Finance and Regulation" attempts to address these issues by focusing on transformative perspectives in banking and finance. Accordingly, it provides evidence-based guidance, recommendations, and pathways to assist businesses and policy decision-makers through an interdisciplinary and in-depth understanding of ongoing changes in the behavior of economic agents.

Published

Vol. 18 *Raising Finance: From Traditional to New Forms of Entrepreneurial Finance*
edited by Douglas Cumming, Hafiz Hoque and Eilnaz Kashefi-Pour

Vol. 17 *Digital Banking and Finance: A Handbook*
edited by Christopher E. C. Gan, Nirosha Hewa-Wellalage and Ahmed Imran Hunjra

Vol. 16 *Handbook on Data Envelopment Analysis in Business, Finance, and Sustainability: Recent Trends and Developments*
edited by Sabri Boubaker and Thanh Ngo

Vol. 15 *Artificial Intelligence and Beyond for Finance*
edited by Marco Corazza, René Garcia, Faisal Shah Khan, Davide La Torre and Hatem Masri

For the complete list of volumes in this series, please visit
www.worldscientific.com/series/tbfr

Transformations in Banking, Finance and Regulation
Volume 18

Raising Finance

From Traditional to New Forms of Entrepreneurial Finance

Editors

Douglas Cumming
Stevens Institute of Technology School of Business, USA

Hafiz Hoque
Swansea University, UK

Eilnaz Kashefi-Pour
University of Birmingham, UK

World Scientific

NEW JERSEY • LONDON • SINGAPORE • BEIJING • SHANGHAI • HONG KONG • TAIPEI • CHENNAI • TOKYO

Published by

World Scientific Publishing Europe Ltd.

57 Shelton Street, Covent Garden, London WC2H 9HE

Head office: 5 Toh Tuck Link, Singapore 596224

USA office: 27 Warren Street, Suite 401-402, Hackensack, NJ 07601

Library of Congress Cataloging-in-Publication Data

Names: Cumming, Douglas editor | Hoque, Hafiz editor | Kashefi-Pour, Eilnaz editor.

Title: Raising finance : from traditional to new forms of entrepreneurial finance / editors, Douglas Cumming, Stevens Institute of Technology School of Business, USA, Hafiz Hoque, Swansea University, UK, Eilnaz Kashefi-Pour, University of Birmingham, UK.

Description: New Jersey : World Scientific, [2026] | Series: Transformations in banking, finance and regulation, 2752-5821 ; vol. 18 | Includes bibliographical references and index.

Identifiers: LCCN 2024056865 | ISBN 9781800617025 hardcover | ISBN 9781800617032 ebook | ISBN 9781800617049 ebook other

Subjects: LCSH: Venture capital--Europe | Business enterprises--Finance--Europe

Classification: LCC HG4751 .R355 2026 | DDC 658.15/224094--dc23/eng/20250502

LC record available at https://lccn.loc.gov/2024056865

British Library Cataloguing-in-Publication Data

A catalogue record for this book is available from the British Library.

For any available supplementary material, please visit
https://www.worldscientific.com/worldscibooks/10.1142/Q0502#t=suppl

Desk Editors: Kannan Krishnan/Gabriel Rawlinson

Typeset by Stallion Press
Email: enquiries@stallionpress.com

https://doi.org/10.1142/9781800617032_fmatter

About the Editors

Douglas Cumming, JD, PhD, CFA, is Professor of Finance and Steven Shulman '62 Endowed Chair for Business Leadership, Stevens Institute of Technology School of Business, United States and Research Member, European Corporate Governance Institute. Douglas has published over 240 articles in leading journals (including 45 in *Financial Times* top 50 journals) and 21 books with Oxford, Wiley, and others. His work spans topics that include entrepreneurial finance, crowdfunding, venture capital, private equity, hedge funds, mutual funds, crypto funds, fintech, securities regulation, climate finance, and ESG. Douglas' work has been cited over 29,000 times. He is also the managing editor-in-chief of *Review of Corporate Finance*. Douglas' work has been reviewed in *The Economist*, *The New York Times*, the *Chicago Tribune*, *The Wall Street Journal*, *The Globe and Mail*, *Canadian Business*, the *National Post*, and *The New Yorker*.

Hafiz Hoque is a Professor of Finance at Swansea University, UK. Before that, he was an Associate Professor at the University of York, UK. Professor Hafiz Hoque's research focuses on the intersection of real-world problems and corporate finance issues. He has an extensive publication record with over 25 publications in 4* and 3* ABS-listed journals, along with over 1,300 citations. He is the director of the Hawkes Centre for Empirical Finance. His current research interests include directors' networks, credit default swaps, green innovation, corporate misconduct, pay transparency, climate change and finance, and ESG. He has attracted significant grant incomes over the past 10 years. His research work has been presented at various conferences worldwide. He serves as an *ad hoc* referee for many journals, including the *Journal of Banking and Finance*, *European Financial Management*, and the *Journal of Corporate Finance*. He is an associate editor of the *Journal of International Finance and Economics*. He has supervised more than 10 PhD students to completion and welcomes interesting PhD applications. Hafiz Hoque holds a PhD degree in finance from Bayes (formerly Cass) Business School, University of London, UK.

Eilnaz Kashefi-Pour is an Associate Professor of Finance at the University of Birmingham, UK, holding a PhD in finance from Bayes (formerly Cass) Business School, University of London, UK with extensive experience in academic research, education, and leadership. Her current research interests focus on empirical issues in corporate finance, particularly capital structure, debt maturity, IPOs, and delistings. She also explores green finance, corporate social responsibility, and national culture. Dr. Kashefi Pour has a strong record of publications in peer-reviewed journals (ABS 4 and 3). She is a member of several professional organisations, including the European Finance Association (EFA) and the European Financial Management Association (EFMA). Additionally, she serves as an *ad hoc* reviewer for leading finance journals, such as *Entrepreneurship, Theory and Practice* (ABS 4) and the *British Journal of Management* (ABS 4). Dr. Kashefi Pour has presented her work at various prestigious international conferences and is an associate editor of the *International Review of Economics and Finance*. She has received research funding from NERC and the British Academy.

https://doi.org/10.1142/9781800617032_fmatter

Contents

https://doi.org/10.1142/9781800617032_fmatter

Introduction

This book comprises fourteen chapters. In the first part of the book, we have covered topics related to *traditional finance*. The first chapter is about What Drives a Firm's Debt Choice. The chapter focuses on the choice between bank debt and public debt. The authors review empirical evidence and the main methodologies employed in this field. In the second chapter, the authors ask, Is Firm Leverage Target Adjustment Mechanically Determined by Other Financial Behaviours? This study examines how adjustments about leverage are influenced by various financial behaviours, such as investment, cash holdings, equity issuance, and profitability. It also assesses whether the adjustment of the leverage target is established automatically. In order to account for the impacts of other financial habits, the authors incorporate interaction terms into the traditional partial adjustment model. In the third chapter, the authors address Corporate Innovation and IPO Survival: Evidence from the UK Alternative Investment Market (AIM). The impact of business innovation on the longevity of initial public offerings (IPOs) on the London Stock Exchange's AIM is examined in this chapter. According to findings, pre-listing innovation, as measured by the number of patent applications, has a favourable and significant impact on IPO firms' ability to survive after going public.

The second part of the book covers *venture capital and private equity*. In the fourth chapter, the authors conduct a literature review of Venture Capital (VC). The key research on the relationships between VC fund managers and institutional investors – including fundraising, fund size, and scale diseconomies, and limited partnership contracts – is compiled in this section. The fifth chapter is about Private Equity Investment Activity: Operating Model and Risk-Mitigation Strategies. This chapter's goal is to provide an overview of the complete decision-making process and risk management techniques used by venture capitalists, also known as private equity (PE) investors, to fund high-risk and high-growth-potential companies. The following chapter covers the Importance of Governance in Private Equity Financing. This chapter covers the governance problems that entrepreneurs will face at different stages of their company's growth and tackles the crucial question of how they can establish an efficient, scalable governance structure. It also goes over how a smart investor's due diligence process includes a review of a company's governance structure and how institutional investors require the creation of a particular governance structure before making a financial commitment. The following chapter covers Mapping Venture Capital: Exploring Regional Differences Among Independent and Corporate Venture Capital Investors in Europe. In this chapter, the authors analyse the geographic concentration of investments made by corporate venture capitalists (CVCs) and independent venture capitalists (IVCs) using regional-level data on European venture capital investments. In the European venture capital investment environment, CVCs are becoming more and more prominent. The eighth chapter deals with Navigating the Interplays Between Different Investor Types: A Map of the Entrepreneurial Finance Literature for Future Research. This chapter explores the literature on how various investor types interact, offering a thorough synopsis of the current body of work. In closing, it points out existing gaps and suggests future lines of inquiry. This chapter serves as a starting point for further research and provides an in-depth understanding of the complex dynamics of modern entrepreneurial finance by illuminating new trends.

The third part of the book covers *modern finance*. The ninth chapter covers The Geography of Cryptocurrencies: Drivers of the Adoption of Cryptocurrencies Around the World. It is possible to better characterise the motives for consumer purchases and cryptocurrency exchanges as well as gain a better understanding of a phenomenon that is still relatively unknown by analysing how institutional features affect the use of cryptocurrencies in various nations. The chapter's findings are noteworthy in light of potential future cryptocurrency usage regulations. The following chapter covers Exploring the Impact of Gender Dynamics in Equity Crowdfunding: A Social Role Theory Perspective. Although preliminary research has indicated that gender-related variables may affect the success of crowdfunding, little is known regarding the influence of female team members and all-female teams in VC through crowdfunding. This study uses a quantitative regression analysis of equity crowdfunding initiatives to investigate this subject using the prism of social role theory. The eleventh chapter covers the topic Digitalisation to Artificial Intelligence: The New Frontiers of Entrepreneurial Finance. Artificial intelligence (AI) and digitalisation are pushing the boundaries of entrepreneurial finance. This chapter outlines important developments that have the potential to revolutionise funding access. To shed light on the financing of AI-based firms, the chapter concentrates on the rise of financial technology, or fintech, with a particular emphasis on cutting-edge financing avenues, such as equity crowdfunding and initial coin offerings. The following chapter addresses Innovative Banking and Systemic Risks: The Silicon Valley Bank Case and Entrepreneurial Finance Dynamics. In order to show the interplay between innovation-driven risk-taking and regulatory control within the entrepreneurial banking industry, this chapter examines the rise and fall of Silicon Valley Bank (SVB). It describes how SVB started as a financial leader in the start-up and technology sectors, highlighting the company's deliberate shift to venture debt and other specialised financing options.

The thirteenth chapter covers corporate Green Bonds: A Governance Perspective. The purpose of this chapter is to improve our understanding of green bonds by exploring the market's past, summarising the variables affecting its growth, and integrating research findings regarding the effects of various green bond governance mechanisms on greenium. The final chapter covers Financing Choices and Transition Risk: Economic and Social Implications. This chapter examines how firms' financing choices influence their exposure to transition risk – the economic and social challenges arising from the global shift toward low-carbon economies.

Part 1
Traditional Finance

https://doi.org/10.1142/9781800617032_0001

Chapter 1

What Drives a Firm's Debt Choice?

Han Wang and Elaine Laing
Trinity Business School, Trinity College Dublin,
The University of Dublin, Dublin, Ireland

1.1. Introduction

While early capital structure studies primarily focused on optimal leverage decisions, recent research in corporate financing has highlighted the importance of debt financing. This shift is attributed to the recognition of debt financing as a disciplinary governance mechanism, particularly with the advent of creditor governance. A substantial body of theoretical and empirical work underscores the importance of understanding why firms choose to raise funds from different debt sources, specifically, a firm's debt choice (e.g. Chen *et al.*, 2020; Colla *et al.*, 2013; Denis and Mihov, 2003; Lin *et al.*, 2013).

Within the category of various debt instruments, firms frequently confront a choice between private debt and public debt, each characterised by distinct information disclosure requirements and ownership structures. Due to these fundamental differences, the financial literature has elucidated the advantages of private debt over public debt, particularly in terms of its superior monitoring capabilities as well as its greater efficiency in liquidations and renegotiations during periods of financial distress.

The objective of this chapter is to survey studies examining a firm's choice between private debt and public debt. Our aim is to deepen the understanding of existing literature by presenting a coherent synthesis of theoretical arguments alongside substantial empirical evidence in a concise manner. Drawing from the established advantages of private debt (relative to public debt) in information collection, processing, and monitoring, we classify three categories of theoretical arguments regarding the borrower-specific determinants of the decision between private and public debt: (i) *ex ante* information-related costs associated with addressing adverse selection problems, highlighting the superiority of private debt in terms of lower financing costs and information protection, and in serving firms facing problems related to information collection; (ii) *ex post* monitoring efficiency associated with agency costs in mitigating moral hazard problems, presenting two competing predictions – the need for monitoring versus the avoidance of monitoring – in the context of two classic types of agency conflicts: shareholder–creditor and management–shareholder conflicts; (iii) the trade-offs among information hold-ups, inefficient liquidations, and costly monitoring, where borrowers must balance the benefits of private debt in terms of the flexibility of renegotiations and liquidations against the costs of information monopolies and suboptimal liquidation outcomes. Furthermore, we highlight the role of supply-side factors and institutional environment, which exogenously influence a firm's incentive in choosing a tailored debt policy by affecting the relative availability of different debt varieties.

Drawing from the three categories of theoretical propositions, we then present a survey of empirical work on the determinants of a firm's choice. Among private debt types, banks and non-bank private lenders are frequently discussed in empirical research. While recent empirical evidence includes more types of private debt, such as syndicated loans and privately placed debt, to explain firm-level determinants of private versus public financing, their predictions are still grounded in earlier financial intermediary theories developed from bank lending (Kale and Meneghetti, 2011). Banks are considered superior due to their comparative advantages over other types of private lenders, and contemporary cross-sectional studies examining the determinants of a debt choice often select bank debt as a representative example of private debt for comparison with public debt (e.g. Hasan *et al.*, 2017; Li *et al.*, 2022; Liao, 2015). Therefore, our primary analysis of empirical evidence in this chapter focuses on the comparison between bank debt and public debt.

The remainder of this chapter is structured as follows. The introduction is provided in Section 1.1 Beginning with a brief discussion of the disciplinary role of the debt mechanism, Section 1.2 then discusses the key differences between private and public debt, which underpin the theoretical arguments alongside substantial empirical evidence regarding the cross-sectional determinants of a firm's choice. Section 1.3 explores empirical drivers related to a firm's debt policy. Section 1.4 concludes by outlining future research directions.

1.2. Debt Placement Decisions

1.2.1. *The role of the debt mechanism*

Traditional corporate governance mechanisms are primarily designed to alleviate agency conflicts between managers and shareholders – the principal–agent conflicts stemming from the separation of control from ownership (Jensen and Meckling, 1976). These mechanisms encompass incentive compensation packages aimed at aligning managers' interests with shareholders', the appointment of independent directors, and the presence of large blockholders for effective monitoring to curtail managerial opportunistic behaviour, such as diverting free cash flows for personal gain at the expense of shareholders.

External governance mechanisms also play a role in aligning the interests of shareholders and managers. These mechanisms include the market for corporate control – the takeover market (Shleifer and Vishny, 1997) and, notably, the disciplinary role of debt within the capital structure. Debt, as a governance tool, helps discipline poorly performing managers. In this section, we shed light on specific mechanisms through which debt can fulfil its governance role, while also considering the potential differences between various debt instruments, such as private and public debt.

First, debt can mitigate the inclination of insiders to divert cash flows for self-serving purposes, such as excessive consumption and empire-building, by imposing a fixed obligation to repay these cash flows (Jensen, 1986). Second, debtholders can actively monitor for malfeasance, thereby mitigating conflicts between shareholders and managers (Stulz, 1990). Hoshi *et al.* (1993) argue that monitored debt serves as a mechanism to counteract managerial opportunism. Third, debt can function as an alternative control mechanism. In times of financial distress, debtholders have the ability to liquidate the firm when its economic performance is poor (Dewatripont and Tirole, 1994), and they may also seize control and influence major decision-making processes, such as replacing underperforming management. The prospect of losing control incentivises the management team to contribute to maximising firm value. Therefore, the disciplinary role of debt in mitigating managerial opportunism ultimately benefits shareholders.

However, the introduction of debt mechanisms is not always welcome; it results in another type of agency cost arising from the conflicting interests between shareholders and debtholders. Shareholders may be tempted to prioritise their own wealth maximisation at the expense of debtholders.[1] Unlike shareholders, who are the residual claimants, debtholders typically receive fixed interest income but face substantial downside risk, thus harbouring preferences and return expectations different from those of shareholders.

When we shift our focus from managerial discretion to shareholder decision-making, we observe such divergence manifesting as moral hazards in two forms. First, shareholders may underinvest in low-risk, positive net present value (NPV) projects when leveraged firms have more attractive growth opportunities available in their investment opportunity sets (Myers, 1977). Second, when facing bankruptcy, shareholders may be inclined to substitute high-quality assets with their preferred lower-quality or riskier assets, exacerbating the financial situation (Jensen and Meckling, 1976). These moral hazard problems, in the form of underinvestment and asset substitution, ultimately benefit shareholders but to the detriment of creditors.

To *ex ante* curb shareholders' detrimental decisions, debtholders may design debt contracts in various ways to safeguard their claims.

[1]Throughout this chapter, we interchangeably use 'agency costs of debt' and 'debt–equity conflicts' to refer to the agency conflicts of interests between shareholders and creditors. Analogously, we use 'management–shareholder conflicts' and 'agency costs of equity' to refer to the agency conflicts between opportunistic managers and shareholders.

These measures include granting debtholders the ability to veto internal decisions (e.g. director elections), imposing requirements to maintain economic performance, and exerting control over capital structure and investment decisions (Nini *et al.*, 2009). Contractual restrictions enable debtholders to renegotiate and amend credit agreements *ex post*. Breaching debt covenants can result in the transfer of certain control rights from the borrower to the lender. In the event of default, creditors have the right to seize their assets before the borrower can dissipate them. Such protection embedded in debt contracts empowers lenders to influence governance structures (Ferreira *et al.*, 2018), capital structure (Roberts and Sufi, 2009), dividend payout, and investment policies (Nini *et al.*, 2012), as well as firms' economic performances and prospects (Denis and Wang, 2014). However, these restrictions imposed by debt contracts can also constrain managerial flexibility in maximising firm value (Berlin and Mester, 1992).

Following a brief discussion of debt mechanisms, we summarise the differences between public and private debt in their basic characteristics in Section 1.2.2. Here, we focus on how these two debt types diverge in fulfilling the governance role of resolving the conflict between shareholders and managers (agency costs of equity) and in dealing with shareholder–creditor conflicts (agency costs of debt). Subsequently, we delve into the rationales behind the debt choice decisions in the following sections.

1.2.2. *Private debt versus public debt*

Evidence on the debt choice between public and private debt mainly focuses on two critical distinctions between these two types of claims. First, private debt is usually concentrated among a few lenders, whereas public debt is generally diffusely held, resulting in weaker incentives for public debtholders to engage in costly information collection and monitoring. Second, private debtholders have superior access to private proprietary information and are better positioned to produce information. Earlier financial intermediation theories, which emphasise the role of private debtholders in information production, classify bank debt as 'inside debt' and public debt as 'arm's length debt'. As inside debtholders, private lenders have access to firm-specific information that is not available to outside lenders, who primarily rely on public disclosure. The finance literature widely agrees on the notion that banks possess superior informational advantages compared to public debtholders.

Under different theoretical frameworks and contexts, the two distinctions can lead to contrasting predictions on the preferences of debt sources. On the one hand, due to information advantages, private borrowings tend to result in lower agency costs compared to public borrowings. This is because of more active monitoring facilitated by concentrated ownership and greater flexibility in renegotiations (Houston and James, 1996; Park, 2000). Such information advantages and enhanced creditor control may help alleviate moral hazard problems and adverse selection issues arising from external financing. However, the provision of more private information and the associated intense monitoring can lead to higher intermediation costs (Cantillo and Wright, 2000), costly monitoring (Berlin and Loeys, 1988), information monopolies (Rajan, 1992), and suboptimal liquidation outcomes (Diamond, 1993). Therefore, a firm must carefully consider the potential benefits of private debt against its associated costs when selecting an optimal debt composition.

Prior theoretical literature emphasises three broad categories for the determinants of a firm's debt choice: (i) the *ex ante* cost- and information-related theories, (ii) the information asymmetries and monitoring models associated with agency costs, and (iii) the efficiency of renegotiations and liquidations. Furthermore, these three sets of theories concentrate on the demand-side borrowers' incentives, which may be influenced by supply-side factors and the institutional environment, as we highlight in Section 1.2.6. In Sections 1.2.3–1.2.5, we discuss each theoretical theory alongside the main empirical research supporting it.

1.2.3. *Ex ante cost- and information-related concerns*

From an *ex ante* viewpoint, cost- and information-related concerns are taken into consideration to address adverse selection problems. Banks can offer several advantages over bondholders due to their possession of superior private information at lower registration costs (Blackwell and Kidwell, 1988), a lower probability of private information leakage under competitive pressures (Yosha, 1995), and price benefits (Hadlock and James, 2002).

The transaction cost, also known as the issuance cost, is a starting factor influencing a firm's debt choice. Public offerings are associated with significant issuance costs, including fees for the SEC registration, listing, trustees, investment bankers, and printing (Blackwell and Kidwell, 1988; Easterwood and Kadapakkam, 1991). According to the flotation cost hypothesis, larger firms issuing debt in larger quantities are more inclined towards public debt financing due to economies of scale. The spread of the fixed component of issuance costs over the larger volumes and lower underwriting costs increases the relative attractiveness of public debt (Easterwood and Kadapakkam, 1991). Two well-established proxies utilised for flotation costs are the issue size and the firm size (see Blackwell and Kidwell, 1988; Johnson, 1997).

Another *ex ante* concern relates to the costs of information disclosure. Fama (1985) indicates that public financings require complex information production for public disclosure, which is costlier than the information provided for private lenders. Public disclosure is also associated with 'information leakage' risks under competitive pressures, where the disclosure of information in a public market can divulge company 'secrets' to a firm's competitors for exploitation (e.g. patent and research development information), thus threatening the firm's competitive position and potentially adversely affecting its future growth prospects (Bhattacharya and Chiesa, 1995; Yosha, 1995).

To safeguard private information, it is cheaper and more prudent for borrowers to limit access to proprietary information to fewer lenders than making the information available to a large scale of diffuse public bondholders, i.e. public dissemination (Yosha, 1995). Therefore, from the perspective of information protection, private debt holds an advantageous position over public debt. In this line of research, Dhaliwal *et al.* (2011) provide empirical evidence that firms with low public disclosure policies are more likely to rely on private debt markets for external financing to preserve their proprietary information.

The information advantage also enables private debtholders to better access firm quality and address adverse selection problems. Ramakrishnan and Thakor (1984) state that information-opaque borrowers are more likely to opt for the private market because private lenders, utilising private information, possess a comparative advantage in the pricing of securities that are difficult to value. Hadlock and James (2002) provide further empirical evidence supporting this adverse selection argument by demonstrating that firms experiencing significant security mispricing tend to issue bank debt due to their limited access to public markets at favourable terms. Such firms often exhibit positive stock responses to bank loan announcements. According to Bharath *et al.* (2008), firms with poor information quality are inclined to issue bank debt to mitigate adverse selection costs.

Evidence suggests that banks with private access to information can impose stringent non-price terms (e.g. collateral and maturity) with renegotiation flexibility, thereby reducing borrowers' costs of bank financings (price terms) with less sensitivity to accounting quality compared to public financings (Bharath *et al.*, 2008; Hasan *et al.*, 2014). In contrast, high accounting quality resulting from stringent standards benefits firms' public bond financings by reducing costs. (Florou and Kosi, 2015). Huang *et al.* (2023) also demonstrate that firms facing high political risk prefer to issue private debt rather than public debt due to unfavourable treatment received from the public market (e.g. lower ratings and bond underpricing).

However, bank debt is not always cheaper. While it reduces registration and bankruptcy costs in financial distress, it may also entail higher costs of capital and intermediation (see, for example, Cantillo and Wright, 2000). Banks are subject to stringent regulatory supervision, enabling them to charge higher fees from subsequent borrowers. Additionally, it is also related to information hold-ups that we discuss further in Section 1.2.5.

1.2.4. *Information asymmetry and monitoring models associated with agency costs*

There is a trade-off between costly bank monitoring and the benefits of monitoring certification and credit access. Private and public debt structures differ in the degree of asymmetric information and associated costs of producing information and monitoring. From an *ex post* perspective, private debt can be more effective in addressing moral hazard problems, with private debtholders often perceived as better monitors than arm's length investors (Berlin and Loeys, 1988; Diamond, 1984). As aforementioned, debt issues can exacerbate the agency conflicts of interest between shareholders and debtholders because shareholders may be incentivised to take actions that benefit themselves but at the expense of debtholders. These activities include moral hazard behaviour in the form of asset substitution (Jensen and Meckling, 1976) and underinvestment (Myers, 1977).

Compared with public lenders, private lenders are perceived to have stronger incentives to monitor and superior borrower monitoring abilities due to their access to private proprietary information and information processing capabilities. First, private lenders benefit from economies of scale in pre-screening information-problematic firms (Ramakrishnan and Thakor, 1984), and they are better equipped to access private proprietary information for monitoring purposes (Fama, 1985). Second, public debt is typically diffusely held, whereas private debt claims are concentrated among a few lenders. Diamond (1984) characterises financial intermediaries as 'delegated monitors' capable of overcoming free-rider problems that may hinder information collection and monitoring. Third, private debt, in particular bank debt, is more likely to be secured by collateral (Rajan and Winton, 1995). In combination, private debt exhibits a significant advantage over public debt regarding monitoring effectiveness and alleviation of information asymmetry.

However, in private debt, enhanced private monitoring is typically achieved through the incorporation of more restrictive covenants (Smith and Warner, 1979), which may lead to higher monitoring costs for private debt borrowers. Financial theories claim that the costly monitoring by outsiders can affect the decision-maker's choice (Stiglitz and Weiss, 1981). Berlin and Loeys (1988) propose a model indicating that monitoring costs can steer a firm's debt policy towards the direction of avoiding private debt. Taking bank debt as an example, from a borrower's perspective, dealing with additional requirements in debt contracts and providing collateral for loans makes borrowing from banks more costly (Berger *et al.*, 2011). The enhanced monitoring by banks is often accompanied by an anticipation of potential default risks, which may prompt banks to impose more stringent covenants and conditions on borrowers (Bushman and Williams, 2012). Li *et al.* (2022) find that the intensive monitoring by banks, such as the adoption of IFRS 9, reduces the likelihood of bank debt financings in firms' debt structures. The shift from bank debt to public debt is further reinforced when the regulatory bank supervision becomes more stringent.

Expensive private monitoring is not the only factor that alters a firm's debt preference towards public securities. The opportunistic decision-making of large shareholders or managers can also influence this preference. Because banks are effective monitors at detecting tunnelling activities and deterring self-serving behaviour, company insiders, such as controlling shareholders and opportunistic managers, may avoid bank debt to avoid scrutiny and insulate themselves from intense monitoring (see for example: Cline *et al.*, 2020; Denis and Mihov, 2003; Lin *et al.*, 2013).

Nevertheless, borrowers might also recognise the need for private monitoring, which could lower their financing costs and enhance wealth generation.[2] The value of monitoring primarily comes from two dimensions. First, borrowings from private lenders can signal to other potential lenders that the firm has reduced moral hazard problems, thereby cultivating a favourable reputation in the borrowing market by mitigating the effects of information asymmetries (Diamond, 1991). This established reputation can facilitate firms' access to credit, not only in private borrowings but also for future public borrowings, offering borrowers pricing benefits. The cross-monitoring mechanism provided by private debtholders is favourably priced in the bond market (Booth, 1992). For instance, Datta *et al.* (1999) demonstrate that bank monitoring reduces the at-issue yield spreads for debt initial public offerings (IPOs).[3] Similarly, Ma *et al.* (2019) report that if a firm has recently obtained a private loan, the yield spreads of its public bonds are more likely to be lower and bond issuance amounts tend to be larger. Second, private monitoring is positively associated with market valuations. Datta *et al.* (2000)

---

[2]As discussed earlier, the *ex ante* information advantages of private debt in dealing with adverse selection costs are reflected in the lower issuance costs of private financing and more significantly positive abnormal stock returns to the announcement relative to public financing. Nevertheless, a firm's motivation towards issuing private debt in view of monitoring value is not isolated from these ex ante information considerations (Johnson, 1997). We discuss this again by emphasising the reputation effects in dealing with ex post moral hazard problems associated with the need for private monitoring.

[3]The debt IPOs are the first public debt offers (Datta *et al.*, 1999).

find that, in contrast to negative stock price responses to debt IPOs arising from greater information asymmetries and agency costs, the degree of bank monitoring is positively related to stock reactions.[4]

The pricing benefits and wealth effects empirically explain a firm's need for private monitoring, which theoretically arises from severe incentive conflicts between shareholders and managers and between insiders and outsiders (creditors). The first stream, in view of monitoring value, postulates that managers act in the interest of the shareholders and emphasises the agency conflicts between creditors and shareholders. Firms exposed to more severe insider–outsider conflicts, such as asset substitution (Jensen and Meckling, 1976) and underinvestment (Myers, 1977), are more willing to receive monitoring from private debt markets and thus rely on private debt (Diamond, 1984, 1989). As Smith and Warner (1979) point out, controlling shareholders are likely to voluntarily accept creditor monitoring (though limit their expropriation behaviour) in order to be able to issue bonds at a lower cost. Liao (2015) provides evidence that debt–equity conflicting mechanisms, such as large blockholdings, drive firms to borrow from banks rather than the public market to subject themselves to bank monitoring. As agency conflicts of debt intensify, public debtholders demand stronger price protection than banks, who can price more appropriately by exploiting private information advantages. This remains true even when banks impose stringent covenant restrictions.

Another stream of literature emphasises the significance of private debt in overseeing managerial misconduct, where managers might exploit their authority to enrich themselves, disregarding the interests of both shareholders and creditors – characterised as agency costs of equity. Hoshi *et al.* (1993) posit that monitored debt functions as a strong governance mechanism to mitigate such agency costs. While mounting evidence supports that self-serving managers tend to insulate themselves from intense private monitoring (e.g. Cline *et al.*, 2020; Lin *et al.*, 2013), they can be incentivised to voluntarily subject themselves to additional monitoring through compensation channels (e.g. Albring *et al.*, 2011; Almazan and Suarez,

[4]The findings of positive stock reactions are contingent on model designs and sample selections (discussed in greater detail in Section 1.3.7).

2003; Meneghetti, 2012). Within the framework of managerial discretion concerning debt selection in light of managerial compensation, Almazan and Suarez (2003) and Meneghetti (2012) contend that an optimal compensation level can induce managers to restrain excessive consumption by voluntarily accepting the scrutiny by private lenders. Albring *et al.* (2011) also document a positive relation between the issuance of syndicated loans and CEO equity incentives, which is more pronounced in profitable firms. This demonstrates that CEOs can be incentivised to subject themselves to private monitoring via the nexus between their compensation and firm performance (Meneghetti, 2012).

The firm's reputation can also play a role in the choice of debt financing. Diamond's (1989) model introduces the dynamics of reputation effects in alleviating the conflicts between borrowers and lenders. A concerted effort towards building up a good reputation is related to the higher cost of a default. As the value of reputation rises over time, borrowers have strong incentives to protect this asset through maintaining a good relationship with creditors. From this view, the reputation can substitute for the role that monitoring plays in addressing moral hazard problems (Diamond, 1991). Firms with low and medium credit ratings borrow from banks since their reputation is not sufficiently high to allow them to borrow directly from the public debt market. High-quality firms are strongly motivated to maintain integrity and can access public markets for borrowing without being exposed to monitoring.

In summary, borrowers need to strike a balance between the costs and benefits of the heightened monitoring associated with private debt in the decision-making of debt choices.

1.2.5. *Financial flexibility – The likelihood and costs of inefficient liquidations*

Another stream of *ex post* research discusses the trade-offs among the likelihood of bankruptcy, the liquidation value in the event of possible defaults, and costly monitoring (see, for example, Bolton and Freixas, 2000; Johnson, 1997). A firm's debt placement decision may depend on the ease and efficacy of negotiations with their creditors, reflecting the strength of borrower–lender relationship. In the event of financial distress or liquidity challenges, private lenders hold a superior position compared to public lenders in terms of flexibly adjusting contract terms, exercising control rights, and providing more efficient liquidations (Berlin and Loeys, 1988; Berlin and Mester, 1992; Chemmanur and Fulghieri, 1994; Detragiache, 1994). This adaptability and efficacy stem from the concentrated ownership structure inherent in private debt and the enhanced access to information concerning the borrower's ongoing value. Conversely, the renegotiation process with public lenders proves significantly more complicated due to potential coordination problems arising from conflicts of interest among dispersed public creditors with divergent claim requirements.

As previously discussed, covenants in public debt contracts may be less stringent and acquired at lower costs. However, lower monitoring costs are associated with inefficient monitoring with imperfect information. Berlin and Loeys (1988) highlight that this information often relies on accounting numbers disclosed in public markets, which can be incomplete. Consequently, public lenders may struggle to discern the optimal timing for project liquidation versus continuation. Therefore, the covenants on public debt contracts may either be too stringent (prematurely liquidating profitable projects) or too lenient (allowing unprofitable projects to persist), resulting in an inefficient liquidation policy.

In contrast, private debtholders have access to private proprietary information for more robust monitoring, enabling the design of covenants that incorporate detailed and accurate information on the timing of the liquidation decision. Berlin and Loeys (1988) suggest that this leads to a more efficient liquidation policy by salvaging the liquidation value of unprofitable projects. As the liquidation value decreases, the benefits of efficiently liquidating unprofitable projects diminish, prompting firms to opt for public debt, which avoids costly monitoring.

Take bank debt as an example; some firms prefer bank debt over public debt, hoping that in financial distress, banks are more likely to provide funds for investment and renegotiate existing debts. This suggests that firms may anticipate the likelihood of their bankruptcy to access the liquidation value of private debt in their debt structures. As proposed by Chemmanur and Fulghieri (1994), firms with a low likelihood of financial distress (high credit quality) may find renegotiation less valuable, thus favouring public debt. Conversely, firms with a low credit quality value benefit from renegotiation and therefore prefer private debt even if the costs are high. Denis and Mihov (2003) document a positive relation between the likelihood of bankruptcy (captured by an Altman's Z-score of less than 1.81) and the preference towards private debt, concluding that credit quality is the primary driver of debt choice decisions. By investigating the choices among bank debt, non-bank private debt, and public debt, the authors consider the dimension of credit supply and show that firms choose their debt sources based on the spectrum of credit quality: those with the lowest (highest) credit quality and the highest (lowest) likelihood of distress are more likely to choose non-bank private (public) debt, and those with medium credit quality borrow from banks. This is because low-quality firms have limited access to both bank and public markets. The findings of Morellec *et al.* (2015) also suggest that firms with lower bargaining powers, as measured in terms of ownership by institutional investors, find bank loans in renegotiation valuable, thereby exhibiting a preference towards negotiable private debt.

Although banks are motivated to execute timely renegotiation and liquidation strategies to bolster their reputation (Chemmanur and Fulghieri, 1994), they may experience diminished monitoring incentives due to the seniority hierarchy (Diamond, 1993), particularly as they hold a senior position compared to public debt in bankruptcy proceedings. Consequently, firms with a combination of private and public debt may experience a reduction in renegotiation flexibility due to declining bank incentives, potentially leading to suboptimal liquidation outcomes.

Another drawback of bank debt is the presence of information hold-ups. Sharpe (1990) presents a model illustrating the issues of information hold-ups, wherein private lenders leverage the private information acquired through screening and monitoring to exert control over borrowers. According to Rajan (1992), bank debt may foster information monopolies, imposing switching costs on borrowers and making public debt a more appealing alternative. The bank's excessive control over the continuation of a firm's project represents a major drawback of bank debt, enabling banks to extract monopoly rents from firms in exchange for ongoing project funding. This dynamic has the potential to distort corporate incentives, leading to suboptimal effort exertion and consequently reducing project returns. Since firms with attractive investment opportunities secure funds at favourable rates from both public and private sources, their heightened incentive to mitigate this moral hazard concern is reflected in their reduced reliance on private debt. To empirically test this proposition, where bank debt and growth prospects are expected to exhibit an inverse relation, Houston and James (1996) measure firms' growth using market-to-book ratios and research and development (R&D) expenses and find that firms with a single bank relationship and greater growth opportunities are inclined to utilise less bank debt. Datta *et al.* (2000) further note that firms with greater growth opportunities (proxied by the market-to-book ratio and the proportion of intangible assets) experience less negative stock price responses to the debt IPO announcements. Through a comparison with public bond borrowers, Santos and Winton (2008) reveal that firms reliant on banks are more likely to experience an increase in loan spreads due to information hold-ups.

1.2.6. *Supply of credit and institutional environment*

The framework assessing the trade-offs among three theoretical propositions centres on borrowers' incentives – demand-side drivers, which may also be influenced by the relative availability of private debt versus public debt. Leary (2009) sheds light on the impact of credit supply, particularly bank funding constraints, on the segmentation of the debt market. Access to capital stands as another important factor shaping a firm's debt decision. Macroeconomic conditions can significantly affect the supply of credit by determining the availability and accessibility of different capital markets, which influence a firm's operating environment and financing decisions (Massa and Zhang, 2013). Morellec *et al.* (2015) observe that the likelihood of bank financing increases with the supply of bank loans. Increased bank competition renders it easier for firms to find informed private lenders and obtain bank debt at a lower cost. By comparing public and private placement bonds in 26 non-US countries, Zhang (2016) documents that firms with restricted access to bank loans and public markets often resort to private placement bonds, while a well-established equity market can serve as a substitute for public debt issuances.

However, as highlighted by John *et al.* (2021), supply-side conditions serve as exogenous experiments and do not reveal the underlying motivations that drive firms to alter their debt structures or switch from one type of debt to another. Existing studies commonly employ supply-side variables as controls when examining internal determinants of cross-sectional variance in debt choices. For example, Denis and Mihov (2003) argue that credit quality is positively associated with access to public markets; firms facing higher default risks (even if they intend to issue public debt) may find themselves compelled to seek funding from private sources due to their restricted access to public markets.

A country's institutional environment is an important determinant of firms' debt policy (Hambrick *et al.*, 1996). La Porta *et al.* (1998) demonstrate that a country's legal origin is related to the level of legal protection and enforcement provided to external creditors, with greater investor protection under common law compared to civil law countries. Firms operating in a well-developed financial market characterised by robust credit protection and financial transparency often engage in international markets and issuing public international debt (Zhang, 2016). More recently, Chui *et al.* (2021) document the role of national cultural norms in driving corporate debt preferences.

1.3. Empirical Evidence on a Firm's Debt Policy

Table 1.1 provides an overview of several notable empirical studies, outlining their theoretical underpinnings, empirical drivers, and their primary findings. According to this table, it is evident that firms frequently opt for bank loans owing to attributes such as financial flexibility, operational cost effectiveness, favourable bank–borrower relationships, and the protection of confidential information. When borrowers face greater information risks, such as limited disclosure under stringent regulations, adverse selection tends to induce firms to borrow from banks. However, in matters of corporate governance, firms may opt for either bank debt or public debt, contingent upon the governance framework in place. If a firm's governance is designed to alleviate agency conflicts, bank debt may be their preference to seek monitoring (in the need of monitoring); otherwise, they might favour public debt financing if decision-makers desire to evade intense private monitoring in the pursuit of personal gains (monitoring avoidance) or other monitoring mechanisms can be a better alternative for bank monitoring (governance substitution).

Table 1.1. Representative studies on the determinants of a firm's choice between private debt and public debt.

Theoretical arguments	Empirical drivers	Specific drivers	Conclusions	Source
Information-related (cost efficiency)	Costs of registration	Flotation costs, agency costs and costs of search	It is expensive to comply with the security exchange commission (SEC) requirements upon public debt issuance.	Blackwell and Kidwell (1988)
		Costs of information production	Since the cost of information production required for public debt financing is high, small firms have a greater reliance on bank loans.	Fama (1985)
	Bank–borrower relationship	Close relationships with main banks	Firms with closer relationships with their banks are more likely to borrow from the public market than from banks.	Arikawa and Miyajima (2005)
	Costs of information disclosure	Confidential information protection	Revealing information to public lenders may weaken their competitive position in relation to their rivals, referred to as information leakage risks. High-quality firms turn away public debt because of higher costs of information disclosure and information leakage.	Boot (2000) and Yosha (1995)
		Disclosure policy	A low-disclosure policy is positively related to the percentage of private debt, suggesting that such firms do not want to reveal proprietary information publicly.	Dhaliwal *et al.* (2011)

(*Continued*)

Table 1.1. (*Continued*)

Theoretical arguments	Empirical drivers	Specific drivers	Conclusions	Source
Information-related (adverse selection)	Information risk, firm quality, and security mispricing	Undervaluation	The banks' superior information can better price the firms' claims and thus reduce the adverse selection costs the firm incurs when undervalued. Under this framework, undervalued firms (measured by stock volatility) may rely more on bank debt.	Hadlock and James (2002)
		Accounting quality	Superior access to propriety information by banks reduces the adverse selection costs faced by borrowers, especially those with low-quality accounting information, which indicate that the likelihood of bank debt usage is negatively associated with accounting quality.	Bharath *et al.* (2008)
		Accounting quality	For firms that adopt high-quality accounting standards, i.e. International Financial Reporting Standards (IFRS), the public bond market charges lower yield spreads, relative to the loan market. Thus, such adopters are more inclined to issue public bonds.	Florou and Kosi (2015)
		Pension-related mandatory disclosure	The enhanced pension-related disclosure is positively associated with a firm's preference towards public debt over private debt because public disclosure can significantly lower information risk (i.e. uncertainty and asymmetry) and thus issue costs related to public debt while the same reduction of costs is not identified in private debt.	Almaghrabi *et al.* (2021)

Corporate social responsibility (CSR) disclosure	There is a positive association between CSR disclosure and the proportion of public debt, which is stronger when borrowers have superior CSR performances and reports assured by a third party.	Tan *et al.* (2020)
Corporate social responsibility (CSR) performance	Firms across 40 nations with better CSR performance (measured as ESG global rating) are more likely to issue bonds because CSR enhances corporate transparency and acts as a substitute to bank monitoring in managerial self-interested behaviour.	Abbassi *et al.* (2022)
Tax avoidance	Firms with aggressive tax avoidance policies are more inclined to issue bank loans. In the presence of information asymmetry, such firms tend to have higher costs of financing and banks could offer lower incremental costs than public lenders.	Hasan *et al.* (2014)
Political risk	Firms suffering from political risks are more likely to borrow from private debtholders than public debtholders who tend to underprice the bonds and assign lower ratings. This benefits from the advantages of private borrowings, including the efficient reorganisation capabilities, monitoring superiorities, and potential long-term relationship with firms.	Huang *et al.* (2023)

(*Continued*)

Table 1.1. (*Continued*)

Theoretical arguments	Empirical drivers	Specific drivers	Conclusions	Source
Information-related, monitoring-based and flexibility	Financial characteristics	Information asymmetry, contracting cost, growth options, size	Firms with higher contracting costs (i.e. more growth options) and a higher level of information asymmetry tend to issue more private debt because of its lower information production costs, but larger firms issue lower percentages of private debt.	Krishnaswami *et al.* (1999)
Monitoring-related (the need for monitoring)	Managerial compensation	Incentive compensation	Manager's preference for bank debt over public debt is positively related to the pay–performance sensitivity (PPS).	Meneghetti (2012)
		Managerial compensation tied to firm performance	The issuance of syndicated loans and chief executive officer (CEO) equity incentives have a positive relation, which is stronger for profitable firms, providing evidence that when managers' compensation is linked with corporate profitability, they can be incentivised to submit themselves to private monitoring.	Albring *et al.* (2011)
Monitoring-related (monitoring avoidance)		Equity risk-taking incentives	The executives whose pay is more sensitive to firms' stock volatility (vega-induced) are more likely to issue public debt rather than bank debt to avoid more stringent covenants and tight bank monitoring.	Chen *et al.* (2021)

Ownership structure	Control–ownership wedge (divergences between controlling shareholders' voting rights and cash-flow rights)	Utilising a multinational panel data set in 20 countries, the authors find that wider divergences are positively related with firms' reliance on public debt financing, and this relation is stronger for family-controlled firms, firms without multiple large shareholders, and countries with weak shareholder rights. This is consistent with the monitoring avoidance hypothesis, in contrast to the need for the monitoring hypothesis.	Lin *et al.* (2013)
	Multiple large shareholders (MLS)	The positive relation between the presence and voting power of MLS and firms' reliance on bank borrowings supports that MLS can serve as a monitoring vehicle rather than expropriate private benefits at the expense of minority shareholders.	Boubaker *et al.* (2017)
	Shareholder investment horizons	Institutional investors with short-term horizons, having less incentive to monitor, tend to act in their own interests at the expense of debtholders, inducing stronger monitoring by banks. In line with this monitoring avoidance notion, short-term investors reduce the reliance on bank debt. The reduction can be attenuated by managerial ownership and motivated investors but exacerbated by information opacity.	Cline *et al.* (2020)

(*Continued*)

Table 1.1. (*Continued*)

Theoretical arguments	Empirical drivers	Specific drivers	Conclusions	Source
Monitoring-based (the need for monitoring)		Intensified agency conflicts of debt (large block-holder ownership)	Firms with large block-holdings aggravating shareholder–creditor conflicts are more inclined to borrow from banks than from the public debt market, to be subject to banks' monitoring to lower the cost of financing. Public debtholders demand stronger price protection than banks, who can price more appropriately exploiting private information advantages.	Liao (2015)
Monitoring-related (monitoring avoidance)	Risk	Labor unemployment risk	The US unemployment insurance (UI) benefits contribute to a heavier reliance on bank debt, under the monitoring avoidance channel that UI benefits help mitigate unemployment risk to reduce the need to avoid bank monitoring.	Ben-Nasr (2019)
Monitoring-based vs information-related	Monitoring avoidance (substitute the need for bank monitoring)	Confidential information protection, liquidations, and monitoring	Two competing views are proposed regarding the relation between competition and reliance on bank debt financing. To protect private information from being leaked and mitigate liquidation risks arising from intense competition, bank debt can be positively related to competitive pressure. A negative link, however, supports the opposing view that firms facing greater pressure tend to have a lower monitoring need from banks (bank monitoring substitution).	Boubaker *et al.* (2018)

Monitoring-based (governance substitution)	External governance	Product market competition and takeover market	Under the 'substitution of governance mechanisms' hypothesis, they find that intensified pressure from the product market and takeover market (as external governance mechanisms) reduces the need for bank debt when compared with public debt.	Bharath and Hertzel (2018)
	Social capital (CSR)	Social networks in US counties	Social capital, captured by the density of social networks in US counties, is positivity associated with the use of public bond financing because strong cooperative norms can reduce the need for bank monitoring.	Hasan *et al.* (2017)
	Board monitoring	Board reforms, information opacity and institutions	Firms involved in major board reforms substitute away from private to public debt, which is stronger for firms with higher information opacity and those in countries with strong institutional environments.	Ben-Nasr *et al.* (2021)
Monitoring-related (costly monitoring)	Bank monitoring intensity	Bank monitoring, ease of switching between debt sources	After IFRS 9 adoption, firms reduce their proportion of bank debt and increase the relative issuance of public debt, especially senior bonds and notes. The adverse effect of accounting-driven intensified bank monitoring on bank debt reliance tends to be stronger when firms can flexibly switch to public debt and regulatory bank supervision is more severe. This supports that borrowers trade-off costs and benefits of bank monitoring, and if monitoring costs outweigh certification benefits, they will shy away from private monitoring.	Li *et al.* (2022)

(*Continued*)

Table 1.1. (*Continued*)

Theoretical arguments	Empirical drivers	Specific drivers	Conclusions	Source
Reputation and monitoring substitution	Firm-level characteristics	Monitoring costs, reputation, firm age	As older firms with high reputation capital give them sufficient incentives to avoid risky behaviour without being monitored (costs of default or being caught in risky behaviour are high), younger firms with less established reputations tend to borrow from banks, while more successful firms tend to issue bonds.	Diamond (1991)
Information-related, monitoring-based and financial flexibility	Credit quality, access to debt sources, financial flexibility in distress	Flotation costs, adverse selection, managerial discretion, tangibility	Relative to private borrowers, public borrowers tend to be larger, more profitable, and have high asset tangibility and credit quality. Managers with high equity ownership tend to avoid stringent private monitoring, exhibiting a higher propensity towards public debt. Firms with highest (lowest) ratings rely on public debt (non-bank private debt), while those with a medium level of quality rely on bank debt.	Denis and Mihov (2003)
		The likelihood of financial probability, flotation costs, and information asymmetry	Firms facing lower information and monitoring costs and a lower probability of filing for bankruptcy are more likely to issue public debt than private debt.	Johnson (1997)
	Flotation costs, financial flexibility in distress		Utilising large amounts of foreign bonds, Eurobonds and syndicated bank loans from ten Asian countries, they find that the preference for public bonds is consistent with scale economies and negatively linked with the likelihood of distress.	Esho *et al.* (2001)

Financial flexibility	Financial flexibility	The likelihood of financial distress	Re-contracting flexibility makes bank lenders more effective in helping firms through financial distress periods.	Bolton and Freixas (2000)
	Collateral and renegotiation flexibility	Tangibility	The likelihood of a firm issuing public debt increases with the percentage of its tangible assets because a greater amount of tangible assets as collateral lowers the importance of outside lender monitoring.	Hoshi *et al.* (1993)
	Collateral	Tangibility	An increase in the proportion of bank debt can be seen with the increase in firms' collateral value.	Lin (2015)
	Collateral	Asset redeployability	The redeployability of a firm's assets affects its preference for public debt positively because such firms tend to sell assets rather than use them for alternative purposes in the case of default and thus are unlikely to renegotiate bank contracts.	Chen *et al.* (2020)
	Information hold-up	Project quality, information hold-up, and bargaining power	Owing to information hold-up problems, bank control over continuation decisions is more valuable for firms with low-quality projects, so they are more likely to prefer bank debt. The bargaining power is also related to the firm's debt choice.	Rajan (1992)

(*Continued*)

Table 1.1. (*Continued*)

Theoretical arguments	Empirical drivers	Specific drivers	Conclusions	Source
	Financial characteristics	Growth opportunities, size, and leverage	Firm size and leverage are negatively associated with bank debt usage, which is positively related to growth opportunities, whereby firms can diversify their borrowings with multiple lenders, mitigating information asymmetries and bank monopolies.	Houston and James (1996)
		Growth opportunities, leverage, profitability, and size	Utilising syndicated loans and corporate bonds in the euro area, the authors find that large, profitable, and high-leveraged firms with higher liquidation values (asset tangibility) are more likely to reply on syndicated loans than corporate bonds.	Altunbaş *et al.* (2010)
	Corporate governance	Bank renegotiation, default costs, and outside block-holder ownership	The enforcement of more restrictive covenants and easier renegotiation protects banks from potential takeover threats, so firms with higher exposure to takeovers, associated with lower credit quality, are more likely to issue private debt than public bonds; the likelihood of private debt issues increases with outside block-holder ownership.	Arena and Howe (2009)

Financial flexibility and supply of credit	Financial characteristics	Firm bargaining power, growth options, competition, and credit supply	Firms with more growth options (proxied by sales growth), stronger bargaining power in default (proxied by % institutional ownership), more intense product competition (Hoberg *et al.*, 2014), and lower credit supply are more likely to issue bonds.	Morellec *et al.* (2015)
Environment	Access to debt sources	Bank credit crisis during 2007–2009	The bank credit shock causes the substitution of bank debt with private non-bank debt and public debt, but the substitutions may vary across 34 countries with different creditor rights and information sharing systems.	Fernández *et al.* (2018)
		A natural hazard – Hurricane Katrina	A negative shock on bonds induces firms to shift from bond financing to bank-based borrowing.	Massa and Zhang (2021)
	Risk	Political uncertainty	Political uncertainty resulting from national elections has a positive effect on the ratio of bank debt for 35 countries, strengthened by higher opacity, more financial constraints, and weaker national governance.	Ben-Nasr *et al.* (2020)

(*Continued*)

Table 1.1. (*Continued*)

Theoretical arguments	Empirical drivers	Specific drivers	Conclusions	Source
	Institutional environment	Financial market, legal protection and enforcement and financial transparency	A comparative analysis of the determinants of private placement and public bonds shows that stronger creditor protection, legal enforcement, and level of financial market development can not only drive a firm's preference towards the issuance of public bonds but also promote the issuances in the international public market.	Zhang (2016)
		Top executive education and national culture	The examination of 11 Sub-Saharan African countries shows that firms operated by more educated managers in more developed capital markets are associated with a higher likelihood of bank debt usage. An efficient court system and a non-corrupted political and macro-stable environment can foster the use of non-bank debt.	Gwatidzo and Ojah (2014)
		National culture	Different dimensions of Schwartz's cultural index exhibit different relations with bank debt preferences; egalitarianism is adversely related to bank debt usage, while embeddedness exhibits a positive association.	Chui *et al.* (2021)

In the realm of a firm's debt choice, the three theoretical models outlined above offer diverging forecasts. However, the distinction between these broad theoretical categories is frequently obscured in empirical analyses, as the measures employed often represent multiple theoretical concepts. The following section investigates how these empirical proxies are related to various contexts, offering evidence to assess the validity of different theoretical predictions.

1.3.1. *Firm size and issue size*

Large firms with substantial issuance volumes are expected to demonstrate a greater propensity towards public debt financings, attributable to economies of scale, as conveyed in the flotation cost hypothesis. The spread of the fixed issuance costs across larger volumes and the resultant reduction in lower underwriting costs increase the relative attractiveness of public debt (Easterwood and Kadapakkam, 1991). Datta *et al.* (2000) show that larger firms with significant financing requirements are inclined towards the public debt market. Furthermore, reputation effects suggest that large-scale firms, benefiting from established reputations and lower asymmetric information, find it easier to issue public debt (Diamond, 1991). In addition, since large firms suffer from fewer information hold-up issues, they enjoy pricing benefits during the crisis periods (Santos and Winton, 2008), and it is more likely for these firms to issue public debt.

1.3.2. *Information risk and adverse selection*

Leland and Pyle (1977) suggest that adverse selection problems can be mitigated by borrowing from private sources. Bharath *et al.* (2008) find that compared to public debt, bank debt is preferred by borrowers with higher information asymmetries, as banks can offer them lower incremental interest spreads when compared with public lenders. More recent empirical studies support this finding. Since aggressive tax avoidance policies are viewed as risk-engendering activities due to the higher unexpected risk exposure, Hasan *et al.* (2014) find that, in the presence of information asymmetries, firms tend to have higher costs of financing and thus choose to borrow from banks that can offer lower incremental costs than public lenders.

Richardson *et al.* (2020) find that the US multinational corporations (MNCs) may prefer bank financing over bond financing because their tax haven subsidiaries impose smaller incremental effects on the public bond spreads. Huang *et al.* (2023) highlight the comparative advantages of the private debt market in the pricing and renegotiation terms by emphasising that firms with higher political risks value banks' support during financially difficult times and hence rely more on private debt than public debt.

In contrast to firms facing information problems who prefer private borrowings over public financings, information-transparent firms value less the private financing advantages in information processing and monitoring and hence are more likely to rely on public debt. As the costs of public financing are more asymmetrically sensitive to an increase in the quality of information, any improvement in the accounting quality (e.g. stringent standards) may benefit public financing (Florou and Kosi, 2015). Extant research also documents that firms with better corporate social responsibility (CSR) disclosure and/or performances exhibit a preference for public debt because transparent CSR activities may diminish the information value of private debtholders. Since public investors can be better informed about the firm's operations, performances, and prospects, firms with extensive coverage of CSR disclosure and better performances are more likely to issue public debt than private debt because they can enjoy more favourable price terms associated with public issuances (Abbassi *et al.*, 2022; Tan *et al.*, 2020). Moreover, more transparent pension-related mandatory disclosures are positively associated with a firm's tendency towards public debt issuances, whereby it can receive a lower issue spread (Almaghrabi *et al.*, 2021).

1.3.3. *Information asymmetry, growth opportunities, and reputation*

Extant research has emphasised the role of information asymmetries in tilting a firm's debt policy. Common measures of information problems are firm size, R&D expenses, market-to-book ratios, asset tangibility (the proportion of tangible assets), and earning volatility, which capture the uncertainty of future benefits associated with complex financial operations and rapidly growing projects.

The literature offers mixed predictions regarding the relation between information asymmetry (or, to be specific, growth opportunities) and the reliance on private debt financing.[5] First, the demand for monitoring and thus private debt is positively related to the level of information asymmetry. In the presence of a higher level of asymmetric information, private debt can be preferable over public debt because private lenders are better informed about borrowers' prospects and act as active and effective monitors (Johnson, 1997; Ovtchinnikov, 2016). Consistent with this notion, high-growth firms tend to value the benefits of private monitoring in alleviating agency costs of debt and equity and hence are more likely to use private financing (Krishnaswami *et al.*, 1999). However, the monitoring-avoidance channel implies the opposite from the perspective of the discretion of a firm's decision-makers, who may avoid the monitoring and turn to borrow from the public market. In addition, the information hold-up argument further documents a negative relation between debt types and growth opportunities, in which the bank's control over the continuation of a firm's investment project is a major cost of bank debt (Rajan, 1992), driving a firm's reliance towards public debt financing. Hadlock and James (2002) and Denis and Mihov (2003) do not identify a clear relation between a firm's growth options (market-to-book ratios or R&D expenses) and the inclination towards private debt financing.

Firm age and size are used as proxies for information asymmetries but also reflect a firm's reputation. Firms with longer public histories have fewer information asymmetries in the public market (Johnson, 1997). Datta *et al.* (2000) demonstrate that older and high-reputation firms are more likely to issue public debt because their well-established reputations over time can help them avoid opportunistic behaviour even in the absence of monitoring.

1.3.4. *Asset structure, the likelihood of bankruptcy, and liquidation value*

Another important determinant of a firm's debt placement choice is the firm's asset composition, especially the proportions of tangible

[5]Growth options typically represent the degree of information asymmetry, as firms with significant future growth opportunities are viewed to be relatively hard to monitor and control. Similar to information asymmetry, R&D expenditures, market-to-book ratios, and asset tangibility are common proxies for growth opportunities.

assets and reusable assets. Empirical evidence on the renegotiation and liquidation hypothesis shows that having more physical assets indicates a higher collateral value and residual value in the event of financial distress (Rajan and Winton, 1995). As private lenders are superior in information processing, asset evaluation, and appraisal, they can make optimal liquidation decisions to the benefit of borrowers in liquidations (Berlin and Loeys, 1988). Consistent with this notion, the fixed-to-total asset ratio (asset tangibility), commonly used to proxy for a project's liquidation value, is evidenced to be positively related to the propensity of private debt financing (see e.g. Esho *et al.*, 2001; Johnson, 1997; Marshall *et al.*, 2016).

In contrast, Denis and Mihov (2003) contend that an opposite relation may also exist. According to Cantillo and Wright (2000), firms with fewer tangible assets might encounter challenges in reselling these assets, thus placing greater emphasis on the relative flexibility of the renegotiation terms of their private lenders. Supporting this notion, Chen *et al.* (2020) affirm that firms with a lower resale value of their tangible assets tend to rely on bank debt over public debt, prioritising the ability to renegotiate debt contracts over liquidation value in bankruptcy scenarios. In terms of public financing, Hoshi *et al.* (1993) state that firms with higher asset tangibility tend to experience lower distress costs, thereby enhancing their access to the public market.

The empirical evidence regarding the underlying asset structure is anchored in the renegotiation and liquidation hypothesis, with an emphasis on the relative advantages of private lenders. Borrowers weigh up the value of liquidations and renegotiations in light of their perceived likelihood of financial distress against the costs of monitoring and information hold-ups (Chemmanur and Fulghieri, 1994). Firms facing a lower likelihood of bankruptcy tend to find the renegotiation capabilities less valuable and rely on public financing instead. Huang *et al.* (2023) highlight the comparative information advantages present in the private debt market by demonstrating that firms with higher political risks value the support of banks during periods of financial turmoil, consequently relying more on private debt. Financial distress incurs significant costs during the complex renegotiation process involving various groups of claimants. Measures such as leverage ratios, Altman's Z-scores, speculative credit ratings, and earning or stock volatilities are commonly utilised to gauge the likelihood of financial distress (e.g. Albring *et al.*, 2011; Denis and Mihov, 2003; Johnson, 1997).

1.3.5. *Corporate governance and monitoring mechanisms*

To evaluate the competing predictions of monitoring-based models, Lin *et al.* (2013) formulate two contrasting views regarding the relation between agency conflicts of equity and debt preferences across bank and public debt: the need for monitoring hypothesis versus monitoring avoidance hypothesis. Given the superior monitoring capabilities afforded by private debtholders through their concentrated ownership and information advantages, the need for monitoring hypothesis postulates that firms exposed to acute agency conflicts need monitoring and thus rely on bank debt. Conversely, the monitoring avoidance hypothesis contends that self-interested insiders may seek to avoid stringent bank monitoring by raising funds from the public market.

Utilising a cross-country dataset in the East Asian and West European contexts, Lin *et al.* (2013) provide support for the latter hypothesis – monitoring avoidance, wherein a wider divergence between controlling shareholders' voting rights and cash-flow rights (control-ownership wedge) is inversely related to the proportionate utilisation of bank debt. This inverse relation tends to be accentuated in firms facing higher bankruptcy risks and heightened degrees of information asymmetry, indicative of insiders' strong incentives to circumvent bank monitoring. The choice of debt, at times, fails to resolve agency problems but rather exacerbates the agency conflict between controlling and minority shareholders.

Other studies focusing on ownership-related dynamics also yield similar conclusions. For example, Boubaker *et al.* (2017) show that multiple large shareholders (MLS) can utilise their voting power to monitor controlling shareholders instead of colluding with them. This indicates that the presence of MLS in a firm facilitates the utilisation of bank debt financings as a mechanism for monitoring devices. Consistent with the monitoring avoidance channel, Cline *et al.* (2020) find that short-term institutional owners tend to employ less bank debt, potentially dissuading them from diverting corporate resources for private purposes.

Ben-Nasr (2019) investigate whether the reduction of labour unemployment risks through unemployment insurances (UIs) increases the proportion of bank debt in the capital structure. Lending support to the monitoring avoidance channel, the author demonstrates that the UI mitigates the need to alter employees' perceptions of unemployment risks, thereby reducing the likelihood of opportunistic managers or large shareholders evading bank monitoring.

Aligned with the monitoring avoidance channel, substitution effects of two effective governance mechanisms can elucidate why firms with a strong internal or external mechanism may eschew private monitoring and opt for public bond financings (Ben-Nasr *et al.*, 2021; Bharath and Hertzel, 2018). Bharath and Hertzel (2018) examine the interplay between external governance mechanisms (proxied by the pressure from product market competitions and takeover markets) and the choice between bank and public debt. Under a proposed 'substitution of governance mechanisms' hypothesis, the study posits that firms can endogenously substitute high governance mechanisms with creditor governance.[6] Consistent with this conjecture, the authors document a negative relation between external pressures and a firm's preference towards bank debt over public debt. Their findings resonate with the essence of the monitoring avoidance channel.

Such substitution effects are also examined between other governance mechanisms and debt choices. Ben-Nasr *et al.* (2021) suggest that board reforms can drive firms towards public bond financings, as board quality and bank debt can work as substitutes in monitoring managerial opportunistic behaviour. Hasan *et al.* (2017) show that US firms with higher social capital are more likely to issue public bonds because their strong social networks reduce the need for private monitoring. Similarly, a superior corporate culture can curb managerial malfeasance, thus reducing the need for external monitoring and, subsequently, the reliance on bank debt (Hasan, 2022).

[6]Notably, theoretical arguments provide contrasting views on the relation between competitive market pressure and a firm's choice between private and public debt based on information leakage risks and monitoring models (see Boubaker *et al.*, 2018). However, prevalent empirical evidence tends to support the negative relation between market competition and the propensity of bank debt financing based on the monitoring avoidance argument.

Hu *et al.* (2019) also find that firms with higher foreign institutional ownerships are more inclined to borrow from public sources, shedding light on the substitutive role of monitoring by foreign institutional investors in lieu of bank monitoring.

1.3.6. *Specialisation in private market lending*

As highlighted by Boot and Thakor (2000), the finance literature typically distinguishes between relationship lending in private finance, encompassing bank loans and private placements, and transaction lending in public finance, namely, capital market debt. Earlier studies on relationship-oriented financing focus on bilateral loans and emphasise the lender–borrower relationship. A firm's choice between a single bank relationship and multiple bank relationships emerged as a notable empirical question.

Detragiache *et al.* (2000) assert that, in contrast to a single bank relationship, multiple bank relationships may diminish the likelihood of premature project liquidation. They develop a model demonstrating that, due to the adverse selection in instances of financial distress, firms relying solely on a single bank relationship may encounter difficulties renegotiating their loans, consequently facing rejection when seeking refinancing from non-relationship banks. In contrast, firms with multiple banking relationships are better positioned to secure refinancing, thereby reducing the likelihood of inefficient liquidations.

Although banks are not the sole choice of private lending, they often possess a comparative advantage in screening and monitoring borrowers than other non-bank financial intermediaries, primarily due to deposit relationships providing access to more private information (Fama, 1985). Carey *et al.* (1998) conclude that observable risk plays a pivotal role in private lending preferences, noting that financial companies are more inclined than banks to serve riskier borrowers, particularly those with a higher leverage. This inclination is attributed to bank-side dimensions such as bank conservatism and reputation considerations. As evidenced by Denis and Mihov (2003), banks limit lending resources to relatively low-quality borrowers who may turn to rely on non-bank private debt. However, Carey *et al.* (1998) do not observe differences between finance companies and banks in financing firms with a higher level of information asymmetry.

Relationship lending via loans is limited in the size of supply. Nonetheless, loans have gradually evolved to encompass not only relationship-oriented lending but also transaction-oriented lending. With the growing popularity of syndicated loans – loans originated by multiple arrangers responsible for screening and monitoring – firms can harness the benefits of both bank loans and bond financing to meet substantial financing needs (Altunbaş *et al.*, 2010). In this regard, the syndicated loan market can serve as a viable substitute for the public market, as both markets enable firms to raise significant funds with comparable maturity terms.[7] However, since banks participating in the syndication delegate most of the screening and monitoring to an agent bank (Holmstrom and Tirole, 1997), this potentially introduces another information asymmetry problem between the arranger and the other subscribers of the loan. Sufi (2007) suggests that arrangers can hold a larger percentage of shares in syndicated loans to mitigate the information asymmetry, thereby signalling their commitments towards proper monitoring and due diligence.

Another type of private debt is the private placements, particularly Rule 144A private placements. According to Berlin and Mester (1992), privately placed debt tends to incur higher costs compared to other types of private debt, often due to the absence of stringent covenants. However, Fenn (2000) finds that the higher costs are observed primarily among first-time issuers under Rule 144A, with no evidence of such costs for subsequent issuers. Recent studies delve into the determinants of a firm's choice among private placements, syndicated loans, bilateral loans, and public bonds, as well as their unique implications (e.g. Arena and Dewally, 2012; Arena and Howe, 2009; Marshall *et al.*, 2019).

[7] It is important to note that syndicated loans can assume various forms: they can be private, public, or a hybrid of private and public loans. However, earlier studies do not clearly state their private debt sample composition, which can be either syndicated or bilateral loans (e.g. Denis and Mihov, 2003). Only in the recent decade, more studies (e.g. Marshall *et al.*, 2016) have begun to incorporate the distinction between bilateral and syndicate loans into the analysis of the determinants of a firm's choice. Syndicate loans discussed in this study are a type of private bank debt.

1.3.7. *Comparative analysis of the wealth effects of debt types*

As discussed in Section 1.2.3, the market valuation of debt instruments serves as an indicator of the magnitude of adverse selection costs, thereby influencing a firm's debt decision. In this section, we review select studies on the comparative analysis of abnormal stock returns associated with the announcements of private debt versus public debt, with the objective of identifying any differences in the announcement effects between these two debt types, as well as the underlying drivers of these effects. While much of the research focuses primarily on one single type of debt, only a handful of studies compare the two types (e.g. Fungáčová *et al.*, 2020).

Before delving into the comparison of these two debt types, we first shed light on the divergent conclusions drawn in the existing research regarding whether debt financing contributes to corporate wealth creation. Considering the disciplinary role in curbing managerial opportunism, the issuance of debt can be interpreted as a positive signal in the stock market, reducing information asymmetry between insiders and outsiders (Leland and Pyle, 1977). Managers face pressure from debtholders to refrain from self-serving behaviour. However, other studies (e.g. Eckbo, 1986; James, 1987) argue that, compared to monitoring benefits, the issuance of debt tends to incur greater costs in terms of its agency conflicts between shareholders and debtholders. Additionally, since debt increases bankruptcy costs, particularly for highly leveraged firms that are more susceptible to leverage increases, debt issuance is often perceived as a value-diminishing activity.

Second, in terms of the impact of different debt types on firm market valuations, existing literature documents the wealth effects associated with various debt sources. Earlier evidence on private debt announcements, such as James (1987) and Lummer and McConnell (1989), highlights the unique role of private debt, particularly bank debt, in alleviating informational asymmetries. James (1987) reports that US firms' stock markets respond more favourably to the announcements of bank loans compared to private placements or public bonds, suggesting the value of enhanced monitoring in demonstrating the borrower's creditworthiness, especially when the loan renewals result in more significant positive reactions

(Lummer and McConnell, 1989). The informational advantage of private debt serves as a certification of creditworthiness perceived by stock market investors. This positive stock price response to the bank loan announcements is also corroborated by Hadlock and James (2002), who emphasise that bank debt can aid issuers with significant security mispricing in addressing adverse selection concerns. A recent study by Fungáčová *et al.* (2020) compares the announcement effects of loan and bond issuances in the Western European context and finds that bank loan announcements can evoke higher positive stock responses than bond issuances, which are positively related to the strength of financial development and negatively impacted by the European crisis.

While a substantial body of research highlights the positive abnormal return associated with loans, Chemmanur and Fulghieri (1994) develop a theoretical model arguing that firms seeking assistance from banks during financial distress may withhold private information as trade secrets in an attempt to attract bank loans. This implies that the announcement of bank loans could potentially send unfavourable signals to the stock market. Billett *et al.* (2006) challenge the 'uniqueness' of banks in monitoring and the associated favourable market valuations, arguing that borrowers announcing bank loans experience negative stock returns over a longer horizon. Although Chandra and Nayar (2008) report positive stock market reactions to the private placements of non-bank debt in the short term, they contend that over a longer three-year horizon, operating performances and market valuations underperform. This suggests that the certification benefits of private financing are only evidenced at the announcement and are not substantiated in the long run.

Maskara and Mullineaux (2011) raise an important concern regarding the potential selection bias inherent in prior studies that utilise small loan samples, particularly those with a higher proportion of smaller firms. They argue that this bias may not accurately represent the entire loan population. By employing a comprehensive sample of loan announcements, they report non-significant positive stock responses and attribute the previous positive bias to the fact that small firms, which are more likely to heavily rely on loans, tend to announce them more frequently. Additionally, the sample period can influence the findings. Utilising a sample of large UK firms, Marshall *et al.* (2019) highlight the significant impact of the 2008 global financial crisis (GFC) on the wealth effects of bank debt. In their comparative analysis of stock reactions to the announcement of public syndicated bank loans and privately placed debt, the authors find that, prior to the GFC, bank debt was the only type of debt associated with positive abnormal returns. However, these positive returns diminished after the GFC. Nevertheless, bank debt remains the most informative indicator of borrowers' creditworthiness when compared to private placements and public debt.

Market reactions to debt announcements also depend on firm- and debt-specific characteristics. For example, Billett *et al.* (1995) find that, while there isn't a significant difference in the market's reaction to bank and non-bank loans, lenders with strong creditworthiness tend to generate more positive market reactions. Similarly, Focarelli *et al.* (2008) suggest that a positive stock reaction to syndicated loans is positively correlated with the shares retained by the syndication arranger.

1.3.8. *Incremental approach and proportionate analysis of debt choices*

Prior research on the determinants of debt choices has adopted various empirical methodologies, which can be broadly categorised into two main streams. The first stream focuses on a firm's marginal financing choice using logit or probit models (e.g. Denis and Mihov, 2003; Esho *et al.*, 2001; Hadlock and James, 2002). The incremental approach relates the likelihood of having a particular debt source to an issuer's firm-level characteristics existing immediately before the time of the debt choice decision. By investigating a firm's incremental financing decisions via multinomial logit models, Denis and Mihov (2003) derive simultaneous comparisons among the determinants of bank, non-bank private, and public sources. Furthermore, Albring *et al.* (2011) estimate this discrete choice approach for straight public bonds and syndicated loans issued by US public non-financial corporations throughout the period from 1980 to 2010. Using 1,377 public non-financial corporations with a multinomial logistic approach, Altunbaş *et al.* (2010) link the firm's choice between syndicated loans and corporate bonds to firm-specific attributes measured prior to the financing decision. The instrumental approach is also employed to deal with endogeneity and reverse causal issues in studies that investigate the implications of a particular debt structure (Liu, 2006).

Since a firm might have multiple debt issues of the same type within a stipulated period, using each debt issue as an individual observation may overfit the data where standard errors are either over- or underestimated (Petersen, 2009). To address this, scholars have aggregated debt issues of the same type by a firm within each calendar year (Albring *et al.*, 2011; Denis and Mihov, 2003), within each quarter (Arena and Dewally, 2012; Arena and Howe, 2009), or within each month (Gomes and Phillips, 2007). In the cases where a firm issues both debt types in a certain period, resulting in a measurement issue, some related studies delete such observations (e.g. Arena and Dewally, 2012; Hasan *et al.*, 2014; Richardson *et al.*, 2020) or select the debt type with the highest aggregated issuance amount for corresponding firm-year observations (Liao, 2015).

However, the incremental approach is not without its limitations, as it overlooks the possibility that marginal financing decisions might represent temporary deviations from the issuer's optimal debt composition rather than persistent changes (Denis and Mihov, 2003). An alternative approach involves examining the determinants of the proportions of different debt instruments in the debt structure. This entails analysing metrics such as the ratio of bank debt to total debt, which provides insights into the extents of borrowers' reliance on bank financing (e.g. Boubakri and Saffar, 2019; Chen *et al.*, 2021; Li *et al.*, 2022).

Esho *et al.* (2001) highlight the merits and drawbacks inherent in both incremental and proportional approaches. The proportional analysis, such as examining the ratios of private or public debt relative to total debt, typically relies on balance sheet figures, potentially smoothing out financing decisions over time through averaging. This averaging process may yield misleading insights into a firm's debt choice. In contrast, incremental analyses do not involve such temporal averaging of financing decisions.

To comprehensively capture a firm's reliance on specific debt instruments, incorporating both incremental and proportional methods is advocated. This dual approach allows for a nuanced understanding of both the appropriate utilisation of debt instruments and the impact of marginal debt decisions.

1.3.9. *Evidence on the determinants of debt concentration*

In prior sections, we discuss the determinants of a firm's debt choice, particularly between bank debt and public debt. Yet, in practice, firms often strive to attain an optimal debt structure that incorporates multiple debt types. This optimal structure typically encompasses a blend of bank debt, which may offer higher monitoring efficiencies and lower bankruptcy costs, and public bonds, which are characterised by lower monitoring and hold-up costs (Park, 2000).[8]

Table 1.2 provides a comprehensive overview of key studies investigating the determinants of employing multiple debt types simultaneously. While various papers explore different debt classifications, such as Rauh and Sufi (2010) who classify debt into bank debt, straight bond debt, convertible bond debt, program debt, mortgage debt, and others, it's noteworthy that Colla *et al.* (2013) hold a prominent position in the field examining the extent and determinants of firm-level debt heterogeneity. Colla *et al.* (2013) introduce the concentration ratio to measure the level of concentration in a firm's debt structure, referred to as the debt specification, which is extensively applied in recent empirical studies (e.g. Castro *et al.*, 2020; Li *et al.*, 2021; Lou and Otto, 2020). In this section, our focus lies on exploring the theoretical underpinnings, empirical drivers, and the approach proposed by Colla *et al.* (2013) concerning the degree of debt concentration.

1.3.9.1. *Theoretical evidence on the degree of debt concentration*

Since distinct types of debt instruments have different cash flow claims and contractual features, the choice between private and public debt sometimes cannot reflect the overall distribution of debt structure. Scholars have recently recognised the heterogeneity in the sources of debt financing. Rauh and Sufi (2010) demonstrate that

[8]It is worth noting that our primary focus in this section remains centred on a firm's choice of debt instruments rather than delving into broader aspects of debt structure pertaining to priority or maturity.

Table 1.2. Selected studies on the determinants of a firm's debt concentration.

Drivers	Debt categories (database)	Conclusions	Source
Credit quality	Bank debt, straight bond debt, convertible bond debt, program debt, mortgage debt, and all other debt (manual collection)	Investment-grade firms primarily borrow from senior unsecured debt, while speculative-grade firms use multiple tiers of debt, including secured, senior unsecured, and subordinated issues.	Rauh and Sufi (2010)
	Public debt, bank loans, traditional private debt placements, and 144A debt issues (I&Q database)	Firms follow a pecking order to make their debt choices: traditional private placements, bank loans, 144A debt, and public debt, which is conditional on credit quality. And traditional private placements are the favourite private debt source for firms with good credit quality.	Arena (2011)
Bankruptcy costs, information-related costs, and access to capital	Commercial paper, lines of credit, capital leases, subordinated bonds and notes, senior bonds and notes, term loans, and other debts (I&Q database)	Firms in debt specialisation have higher bankruptcy costs, are exposed to greater information risk, and have limited access to some segments of debt markets.	Colla *et al.* (2013)
Bankruptcy costs and information-related costs		In countries with strong creditor protections, firms prefer a more concentrated debt structure that reduces *ex post* renegotiation inefficiencies in distress.	John *et al.* (2021)

Coordination problems related to bankruptcy costs	After credit default swaps (CDS) initiation on already issued debt, firms are exposed to intensified creditor conflicts and bankruptcy costs and tend to employ fewer types of debt.	Clark *et al.* (2023)
	Firms with stronger chief executive officer (CEO) risk-taking incentives are prone to specialise in debt types.	Castro *et al.* (2020)
	Firms with high-quality accounting information are more likely to diversify their debt types because the bankruptcy costs would be reduced due to lower coordination costs pertaining to transparent information.	Li *et al.* (2021)
	Firms are more inclined to adopt fewer debt types when they face high political risk.	Gyimah *et al.* (2022)
Bankruptcy cost and access to finance	Firms facing greater physical and regulatory risks are more likely to increase their debt specialisation, while transition risk shows limited impact.	Francis *et al.* (2022)

credit quality is a crucial driver of a firm's debt choice, corroborating previous theoretical arguments, such as in Denis and Mihov (2003) and Park (2000). Specifically, investment-grade firms primarily borrow from senior unsecured debt, while speculative-grade firms use multiple tiers of debt, including secured, senior unsecured, and subordinated issues (Rauh and Sufi, 2010).

A simultaneous use of varying debt types in the capital structure potentially generates another conflict of interest among different groups of debtholders (Bris and Welch, 2005; Welch, 1997), and this additional conflict can shape debt policies. Intuitively, it is difficult for multiple groups of lenders to coordinate and reach an agreement on liquidation decisions. Often, in the event of bankruptcy, coordination is required not only for shareholder–creditor relationships but also for different groups of debt claimants, who may vary in terms of priority and seniority, control rights, and cash flow claims. Consequently, a dispersion of debt structures significantly increases coordination costs and hence financial distress costs (Lou and Otto, 2020). Besides, the coexistence of multiple debt types often includes cross-acceleration or cross-default provisions (Beatty *et al.*, 2012). In addition, free-rider problems are likely to arise, which undermines the monitoring efficiencies from debtholders, resulting in a higher likelihood of inefficient liquidations in financial distress. Therefore, in the presence of agency conflicts between shareholders and creditors, a concentrated debt structure empowers creditors to an advantageous position in the event of financial distress through fewer coordination failures.

However, it can be costly to form a concentrated debt structure. Whilst a concentrated debt structure lowers the probability of coordination failures, it is likely that borrowers are incentivised to engage in strategic defaults to maximise the firm's liquidation value in times of financial distress (Bolton and Scharfstein, 1996).

From a theoretical perspective, Colla *et al.* (2013) establish three channels to explain why some firms tend to specialise, as follows: (i) the bankruptcy-costs channel associated with bargaining power (Bolton and Scharfstein, 1996) states that firms with higher bankruptcy costs, measured in terms of asset tangibility and cash flow volatility, are prone to specialise in fewer debt types; (ii) the information channel claims that opaque firms with higher information collection and monitoring costs are in greater need of monitoring and thereby more likely to have concentrated debt structures; (iii) the access-to-capital channel posits that firms with limited access to some debt sources due to debt rationing in credit supplies exhibit a higher degree of debt specialisation. Colla *et al.* (2013) also find that the degree of debt specification is related to firm-specific financial characteristics (e.g. size, age, and growth options) and credit quality, where high-quality, large, older, and profitable firms with high leverages are more likely to diversify their debt sources, while low-quality and small firms with more growth opportunities are inclined to engage in debt specification.

Viewed collectively, a more specialised debt structure fosters heightened monitoring and facilitates efficient liquidations, albeit potentially elevating the risk of strategic defaults. In practical terms, when determining the degree of debt specification, borrowers must carefully assess the trade-offs between the benefits of shareholder–creditor conflict mitigation against the costs of strategic defaults.

1.3.9.2. *Empirical drivers of debt concentration*

Colla *et al.* (2013) propose that firms facing higher costs of bankruptcy are more inclined to adopt a concentrated debt structure to mitigate potential coordination costs. Clark *et al.* (2023) find that after credit default swap (CDS) initiations on issued debt, firms are exposed to increased creditor conflicts and bankruptcy costs and hence choose to specialise in fewer debt instruments.

Risk-taking incentives as a type of shareholder–creditor conflict mechanism not only affect the debt choice between private and public debt but also influence the debt specification. Castro *et al.* (2020) find that firms with stronger CEO risk-taking incentives, captured by the sensitivity of CEO compensation to stock return volatility (vega), are more likely to adopt specialised debt policies. This is because the reduction of coordination problems in the concentrated debt structure can accrue more benefits (i.e. efficient liquidations and lower distress costs) to these firms with intensified shareholder–creditor conflicts via risk-taking incentives. Apart from internal governance mechanisms, country-level governance can also exert an influence on debt specialisation. John *et al.* (2021) find that in countries with strong creditor protections, firms prefer a more concentrated debt structure that reduces *ex post* renegotiation inefficiencies in distress.

Analogous to the analysis of *ex ante* information advantages in the decision-making of private versus public financings, the extant literature explaining a firm's debt specification also finds that exposures to information asymmetry can positively influence a firm's debt specification because of higher bankruptcy costs associated with greater information risks. For example, Li *et al.* (2021) postulate that high-quality accounting information lowers the costs of debt diversification because increased transparency in public disclosure can coordinate different groups of creditors more efficiently, which potentially lowers distress costs and leads to an effective liquidation process. A positive relation between accounting disclosure quality and a dispersed debt structure in their findings is consistent with the trade-off between coordination failures and efficient liquidations. Similarly, Gyimah *et al.* (2022) show that firms exposed to a higher level of political risks tend to engage in debt specialisation. Furthermore, Francis *et al.* (2022) document that a firm's climate risk exposure is positively associated with its debt specification.

1.3.9.3. *Data collection methods for debt specification*

The S&P Capital I&Q database, which categorises corporate debt claims of global public and private companies into seven distinct categories, namely, commercial paper, lines of credit, capital leases, subordinated bonds and notes, senior bonds and notes, term loans, and other debts, is used as a primary source of data in the literature (e.g. Ben-Nasr, 2019; Boubaker *et al.*, 2018; Colla *et al.*, 2013; Lin *et al.*, 2013). Bank debt, as the proxy for the choice between bank and public debt, is measured as the ratio of the sum of revolving credit and term loans over total debt. Total debt is the sum of revolving credit, term loans, senior bonds, and notes, subordinated bonds and notes, commercial paper, capital leases, and other debt.

To measure the debt concentration, studies mainly follow Colla *et al.* (2013) to compute the normalised Herfindahl–Hirschman Index (HHI) for the variety of specific debt instruments used by the firm. For each firm i in year t,

$$\mathrm{SS}_{i,t} = \left(\frac{\mathrm{CP}_{i,t}}{\mathrm{TD}_{i,t}}\right)^2 + \left(\frac{\mathrm{LC}_{i,t}}{\mathrm{TD}_{i,t}}\right)^2 + \left(\frac{\mathrm{CL}_{i,t}}{\mathrm{TD}_{i,t}}\right)^2 + \left(\frac{\mathrm{SUB}_{i,t}}{\mathrm{TD}_{i,t}}\right)^2 + \left(\frac{\mathrm{SEB}_{i,t}}{\mathrm{TD}_{i,t}}\right)^2 + \left(\frac{\mathrm{TL}_{i,t}}{\mathrm{TD}_{i,t}}\right)^2 + \left(\frac{\mathrm{Other}_{i,t}}{\mathrm{TD}_{i,t}}\right)^2,$$

where $CP_{i,t}$, $LC_{i,t}$, $CL_{i,t}$, $SUB_{i,t}$, $SEB_{i,t}$, $TL_{i,t}$, and $Other_{i,t}$, respectively, denote the seven groups of debt types: commercial paper, lines of credit, capital leases, subordinated bonds and notes, senior bonds and notes, term loans, and other debts. HHI is the normalised concentration ratio, given as follows:

$$\mathrm{HHI}_{i,t} = (\mathrm{SS}_{i,t} - 1/7)/(1 - 1/7).$$

The HHI ranges between zero and one, and the closer its value to one, the greater the debt concentration a firm has, indicating that it is exclusively reliant on one single type of debt. The closer to zero its value, the greater a firm's debt diversification is, suggesting the simultaneous use of multiple debt types.

Colla *et al.* (2013) additionally construct another measure of debt specialisation, referred to as *Excl90*. This indicator variable is assigned the value of one if a single type of debt comprises at least 90% of a firm's debt financing sources, and zero otherwise.

A growing stream of research examining the drivers of debt concentration employs Colla's *et al.* (2013) measures (see John *et al.*, 2021; Clark *et al.*, 2023; Castro *et al.*, 2020), highlighting the need for further studies on new classifications of debt concentration.

1.4. Conclusion

The objective of this chapter is to provide a comprehensive survey of significant studies examining a firm's decision between private debt and public debt. Drawing from the established advantages of private debt over public debt, particularly in information collection, processing, and monitoring (Section 1.2.2), we have classified and summarised three categories of theoretical arguments concerning the borrower-specific determinants influencing the choice between private debt and public debt. The first stream (Section 1.2.3) focuses on *ex ante* information-related costs in relation to adverse selection cost reductions. Here, we delve into the perceived superiority of private debt in terms of lower financing costs, enhanced information protection, and reduced information asymmetry.

The second strand (Section 1.2.4) emphasises the distinction between private and public debt in the effectiveness of monitoring associated with agency costs related to addressing moral hazard problems. In light of two typical types of agency conflicts – shareholder–creditor and management–shareholder conflicts – extant theories posit two competing predictions: the need for monitoring versus monitoring avoidance (substitution effects).

The third set of theories (Section 1.2.5) emphasises the trade-off among the likelihood of bankruptcy, efficient liquidations in the event of financial distress, and costly monitoring, where borrowers weigh the benefits of private debt in the flexibility of renegotiations and liquidations against the costs of information monopoly and suboptimal liquidation outcomes. Furthermore, we highlight supply-side factors and institutional environment (Section 1.2.6), which tend to exogenously influence a firm's debt policy through the relative availability of the supply of debt varieties.

Section 1.3 explores the empirical drivers of a firm's debt policy by investigating how different proxies are related to various contexts, which offers evidence to assess the validity of different theoretical predictions. We also note a recently growing stream of literature on the firm's choice of the degree of debt specialisation (Section 1.3.9). Available theories provide conflicting views on firms' preferences towards a concentrated debt structure, particularly in the trade-off between the benefits of coordination efficiencies and the possibility of strategic default. Moreover, access to different debt markets, the need for monitoring, and bankruptcy costs are all viewed as potential channels to influence a firm's degree of debt specialisation.

Our research contribution to this field becomes evident through our efforts to enhance the comprehension of existing literature by providing a cohesive amalgamation of theoretical predictions and substantial empirical analysis in a concise manner. We conclude this study by providing suggestions for future research avenues:

(i) To date, none of the existing theories have been able to fully elucidate the decision-making process regarding debt choices. To address potential conflicts among disparate theoretical frameworks, further theoretical frameworks in this area are anticipated.
(ii) Empirical evidence tends to rely on one or two theoretical arguments to explicate a specific determinant of a firm's borrowing sources. Yet, there is a dynamic interplay among three outlined channels: *ex ante* information-related costs, *ex post* monitoring-based channel, and *ex post* efficiency of

renegotiations and liquidations. Future studies could potentially involve an investigation of a multitude of these factors as well as their interactive effects.

(iii) Most studies in this field conduct OLS regressions or incremental approaches for a firm's debt choice between private and public debt or tobit regressions for a firm's choice of debt specialisation (e.g. Ben-Nasr *et al.*, 2021; Clark *et al.*, 2023; Lin *et al.*, 2013). Although these methodologies can capture a firm's marginal debt decision and cross-sectional variance in a debt structure spanning a certain period, it is unclear how the established determinants of borrowing sources interact with each other in a dynamic structure and thus influence a firm's debt policy. Hence, there is an anticipation for a significant advancement in the application of methodologies within this domain.

(iv) There is a dearth of studies in developing economies and in cross-country contexts, which can be attributed the limited coverage of firms and the difficulty in accessing data in developing countries. While an increasing number of debt choice studies have been conducted in developing countries (e.g. Abbassi *et al.*, 2022; Gwatidzo and Ojah, 2014), the overall coverage is still very limited, especially for a comparative analysis of the determinants of a firm's debt choice in developed versus developing markets, as well as the associated wealth effects. Consequently, we recommend additional cross-country studies conducted in developing countries' contexts.

(v) The similarities between the determinants of private debt versus public debt and those of a concentrated debt structure prompt intriguing questions that can deepen our understanding of the rationales driving a firm's choice of debt specialisation. Drawing from the literature on the former, several questions may emerge in this direction. From the perspective of agency costs of equity, one may enquire about the forms in which opportunistic managers voluntarily subject themselves to increased monitoring by adopting a specialised debt structure. Furthermore, recent research sheds light on the implications of debt specification (diversification) in various areas, such as innovation investment (Guo *et al.*, 2022) and the design of debt contracts (Lou and Otto, 2020). Exploring how firms that opt for a concentrated debt policy fare in terms of financial performances compared to those that do not could offer valuable insights. If superior financial performance is observed among firms with a concentrated debt policy, what are the specific factors driving these superior performances?

References

Abbassi, W., Boubaker, S., and Louhichi, W. (2022). Why do corporate social responsibility-oriented companies opt for bond debt? Evidence from crisis periods. *International Journal of Finance and Economics*, forthcoming.

Albring, S. M., Khurana, I. K., Nejadmalayeri, A., and Pereira, R. (2011). Managerial compensation and the debt placement decision. *Journal of Corporate Finance*, 17(4), 1023–1039.

Almaghrabi, K. S., Opong, K., and Tsalavoutas, I. (2021). Compliance with pension-related mandatory disclosures and debt financing. *Journal of Business Finance and Accounting*, 48(1), 148–184.

Almazan, A. and Suarez, J. (2003). Managerial compensation and the market reaction to bank loans. *The Review of Financial Studies*, 16(1), 237–261.

Altunbaş, Y., Kara, A., and Marques-Ibanez, D. (2010). Large debt financing: Syndicated loans versus corporate bonds. *The European Journal of Finance*, 16(5), 437–458.

Arena, M. P. (2011). The corporate choice between public debt, bank loans, traditional private debt placements, and 144A debt issues. *Review of Quantitative Finance and Accounting*, 36(3), 391–416.

Arena, M. P., and Dewally, M. (2012). Firm location and corporate debt. *Journal of Banking and Finance*, 36(4), 1079–1092.

Arena, M. P. and Howe, J. S. (2009). Takeover exposure, agency, and the choice between private and public debt. *Journal of Financial Research*, 32(2), 199–230.

Arikawa, Y. and Miyajima, H. (2005). Relationship banking and debt choice: Evidence from Japan. *Corporate Governance: An International Review*, 13(3), 408–418.

Beatty, A., Liao, S., and Weber, J. (2012). Evidence on the determinants and economic consequences of delegated monitoring. *Journal of Accounting and Economics*, 53(3), 555–576.

Ben-Nasr, H. (2019). Do unemployment benefits affect the choice of debt source? *Journal of Corporate Finance*, 56, 88–107.

Ben-Nasr, H., Boubaker, S., and Sassi, S. (2021). Board reforms and debt choice. *Journal of Corporate Finance*, 69, 102009.

Ben-Nasr, H., Bouslimi, L., Ebrahim, M. S., and Zhong, R. (2020). Political uncertainty and the choice of debt sources. *Journal of International Financial Markets, Institutions and Money*, 64, 101142.

Berger, A. N., Espinosa-Vega, M. A., Frame, W. S., and Miller, N. H. (2011). Why do borrowers pledge collateral? New empirical evidence on the role of asymmetric information. *Journal of Financial Intermediation*, 20(1), 55–70.

Berlin, M., and Loeys, J. (1988). Bond covenants and delegated monitoring. *The Journal of Finance*, 43(2), 397–412.

Berlin, M., and Mester, L. J. (1992). Debt covenants and renegotiation. *Journal of Financial Intermediation*, 2(2), 95–133.

Bharath, S. T., and Hertzel, M. (2018). External governance and debt structure. *The Review of Financial Studies*, 31(9), 3344–3383.

Bharath, S. T., Sunder, J., and Sunder, S. V. (2008). Accounting quality and debt contracting. *The Accounting Review*, 83(1), 1–28.

Bhattacharya, S., and Chiesa, G. (1995). Proprietary information, financial intermediation, and research incentives. *Journal of Financial Intermediation*, 4(4), 328–357.

Billett, M. T., Flannery, M. J., and Garfinkel, J. A. (1995). The effect of lender identity on a borrowing firm's equity return. *The Journal of Finance*, 50(2), 699–718.

Billett, M. T., Flannery, M. J., and Garfinkel, J. A. (2006). Are bank loans special? Evidence on the post-announcement performance of bank borrowers. *Journal of Financial and Quantitative Analysis*, 41(4), 733–751.

Blackwell, D. W., and Kidwell, D. S. (1988). An investigation of cost differences between public sales and private placements of debt. *Journal of Financial Economics*, 22(2), 253–278.

Bolton, P., and Freixas, X. (2000). Equity, bonds, and bank debt: Capital structure and financial market equilibrium under asymmetric information. *Journal of Political Economy*, 108(2), 324–351.

Bolton, P., and Scharfstein, D. S. (1996). Optimal debt structure and the number of creditors. *Journal of Political Economy*, 104(1), 1–25.

Boot, A. W. A. (2000). Relationship banking: What do we know? *Journal of Financial Intermediation*, 9(1), 7–25.

Boot, A. W. A., and Thakor, A. V. (2000). Can relationship banking survive competition? *The Journal of Finance*, 55(2), 679–713.

Booth, J. R. (1992). Contract costs, bank loans, and the cross-monitoring hypothesis. *Journal of Financial Economics*, 31(1), 25–41.

Boubaker, S., Rouatbi, W., and Saffar, W. (2017). The role of multiple large shareholders in the choice of debt source. *Financial Management*, 46(1), 241–274.

Boubaker, S., Saffar, W., and Sassi, S. (2018). Product market competition and debt choice. *Journal of Corporate Finance*, 49, 204–224.

Boubakri, N., and Saffar, W. (2019). State ownership and debt choice: Evidence from privatization. *Journal of Financial and Quantitative Analysis*, 54(3), 1313–1346.

Bris, A., and Welch, I. (2005). The optimal concentration of creditors. *The Journal of Finance*, 60(5), 2193–2212.

Bushman, R. M., and Williams, C. D. (2012). Accounting discretion, loan loss provisioning, and discipline of banks' risk-taking. *Journal of Accounting and Economics*, 54(1), 1–18.

Cantillo, M., and Wright, J. (2000). How do firms choose their lenders? An empirical investigation. *The Review of Financial Studies*, 13(1), 155–189.

Carey, M., Post, M., and Sharpe, S. A. (1998). Does corporate lending by banks and finance companies differ? Evidence on specialization in private debt contracting. *The Journal of Finance*, 53(3), 845–878.

Castro, P., Keasey, K., Amor-Tapia, B., Tascon, M. T., and Vallascas, F. (2020). Does debt concentration depend on the risk-taking incentives in CEO compensation? *Journal of Corporate Finance*, 64, 101684.

Chandra, U., and Nayar, N. (2008). The information content of private debt placements. *Journal of Business Finance and Accounting*, 35(9), 1164–1195.

Chemmanur, T., and Fulghieri, P. (1994). Reputation, renegotiation, and the choice between bank loans and publicly traded debt. *The Review of Financial Studies*, 7(3), 475–506.

Chen, Y., Hasan, I., Saffar, W., and Zolotoy, L. (2021). Executive equity risk-taking incentives and firms' choice of debt structure. *Journal of Banking and Finance*, 133, 106274.

Chen, H., Maslar, D. A., and Serfling, M. (2020). Asset redeployability and the choice between bank debt and public debt. *Journal of Corporate Finance*, 64, 101678.

Chui, A. C. W., Li, X., and Saffar, W. (2021). National culture and the choice between bank debt and public debt. *Pacific-Basin Finance Journal*, 70, 101655.

Clark, B., Donato, J., and Francis, B. B. (2023). Credit default swaps and debt specialization. *Journal of Financial Intermediation*, 54, 101029.

Cline, B. N., Fu, X., and Tang, T. (2020). Shareholder investment horizons and bank debt financing. *Journal of Banking and Finance*, 110, 105656.

Colla, P., Ippolito, F., and Li, K. (2013). Debt specialization. *The Journal of Finance*, 68(5), 2117–2141.

Datta, S., Iskandar-Datta, M., and Patel, A. (1999). Bank monitoring and the pricing of corporate public debt. *Journal of Financial Economics*, 51(3), 435–449.

Datta, S., Iskandar-Datta, M., and Patel, A. (2000). Some evidence on the uniqueness of initial public debt offerings. *The Journal of Finance*, 55(2), 715–743.

Denis, D. J., and Mihov, V. T. (2003). The choice among bank debt, non-bank private debt, and public debt: Evidence from new corporate borrowings. *Journal of Financial Economics*, 70(1), 3–28.

Denis, D. J., and Wang, J. (2014). Debt covenant renegotiations and creditor control rights. *Journal of Financial Economics*, 113(3), 348–367.

Detragiache, E. (1994). Public versus private borrowing: A theory with implications for bankruptcy reform. *Journal of Financial Intermediation*, 3(4), 327–354.

Detragiache, E., Garella, P., and Guiso, L. (2000). Multiple versus single banking relationships: Theory and evidence. *The Journal of Finance*, 55(3), 1133–1161.

Dewatripont, M., and Tirole, J. (1994). A theory of debt and equity: Diversity of securities and manager-shareholder congruence. *The Quarterly Journal of Economics*, 109(4), 1027–1054.

Dhaliwal, D. S., Khurana, I. K., and Pereira, R. (2011). Firm disclosure policy and the choice between private and public debt. *Contemporary Accounting Research*, 28(1), 293–330.

Diamond, D. W. (1984). Financial intermediation and delegated monitoring. *The Review of Economic Studies*, 51(3), 393–414.

Diamond, D. W. (1989). Reputation acquisition in debt markets. *Journal of Political Economy*, 97(4), 828–862.

Diamond, D. W. (1991). Monitoring and reputation: The choice between bank loans and directly placed debt. *Journal of Political Economy*, 99(4), 689–721.

Diamond, D. W. (1993). Seniority and maturity of debt contracts. *Journal of Financial Economics*, 33(3), 341–368.

Easterwood, J. C., and Kadapakkam, P. R. (1991). The role of private and public debt in corporate capital structures. *Financial Management*, 20(3), 49–59.

Eckbo, B. E. (1986). Valuation effects of corporate debt offerings. *Journal of Financial Economics*, 15(1), 119–151.

Esho, N., Lam, Y., and Sharpe, I. G. (2001). Choice of financing source in international debt markets. *Journal of Financial Intermediation*, 10(3), 276–305.

Fama, E. F. (1985). What's different about banks? *Journal of Monetary Economics*, 15(1), 29–39.

Fenn, G. W. (2000). Speed of issuance and the adequacy of disclosure in the 144A high-yield debt market. *Journal of Financial Economics*, 56(2), 383–405.

Fernández, A. I., González, F., and Suárez, N. (2018). Bank supply shocks and the substitution between bank and nonbank debt. *Journal of Corporate Finance*, 48, 122–147.

Ferreira, D., Ferreira, M. A., and Mariano, B. (2018). Creditor control rights and board independence. *The Journal of Finance*, 73(5), 2385–2423.

Florou, A., and Kosi, U. (2015). Does mandatory IFRS adoption facilitate debt financing? *Review of Accounting Studies*, 20(4), 1407–1456.

Focarelli, D., Pozzolo, A. F., and Casolaro, L. (2008). The pricing effect of certification on syndicated loans. *Journal of Monetary Economics*, 55(2), 335–349.

Francis, B., Hasan, I., Jiang, C., Sharma, Z., and Zhu, Y. (2022). Climate risks and debt specialization. *Journal of Financial Economics*, forthcoming.

Fungáčová, Z., Godlewski, C. J., and Weill, L. (2020). Does the type of debt matter? Stock market perception in Europe. *The Quarterly Review of Economics and Finance*, 75, 247–256.

Gomes, A., and Phillips, G. (2007). Why do public firms issue private and public securities? *Journal of Financial Intermediation*, 21(4), 619–658.

Guo, C., Su, W., Song, X., and Hu, X. (2022). Heterogeneous debt financing and environmental research and development: Evidence from China. *International Review of Economics and Finance*, 82, 65–81.

Gwatidzo, T., and Ojah, K. (2014). Firms' debt choice in Africa: Are institutional infrastructure and non-traditional determinants important? *International Review of Financial Analysis*, 31, 152–166.

Gyimah, D., Danso, A., Adu-Ameyaw, E., and Boateng, A. (2022). Firm-level political risk and corporate leverage decisions. *International Review of Financial Analysis*, 84, 102354.

Hadlock, C. J., and James, C. M. (2002). Do banks provide financial slack? *The Journal of Finance*, 57(3), 1383–1419.

Hasan, I., Hoi, C. K., Wu, Q., and Zhang, H. (2014). Beauty is in the eye of the beholder: The effect of corporate tax avoidance on the cost of bank loans. *Journal of Financial Economics*, 113(1), 109–130.

Hasan, I., Hoi, C. K., Wu, Q., and Zhang, H. (2017). Social capital and debt contracting: Evidence from bank loans and public bonds. *Journal of Financial and Quantitative Analysis*, 52(3), 1017–1047.

Hasan, M. M. (2022). Corporate culture and bank debt. *Finance Research Letters*, 49, 103152.

Hoberg, G., Phillips, G., and Prabhala, N. (2014). Product market threats, payouts, and financial flexibility. *The Journal of Finance*, 69(1), 293–324.

Holmstrom, B., and Tirole, J. (1997). Financial intermediation, loanable funds, and the real sector. *The Quarterly Journal of Economics*, 112(3), 663–691.

Hoshi, T., Kashyap, A., and Scharfstein, D. (1993). The choice between public and private debt: An analysis of post-deregulation corporate financing in Japan. *Journal of Financial Economics*, 33(2), 219–244.

Houston, J., and James, C. (1996). Bank information monopolies and the mix of private and public debt claims. *The Journal of Finance*, 51(5), 1863–1889.

Hu, J., Mensah, A. K., and Tsang, A. (2019). Foreign institutional ownership and the choice between public and private debt. *Journal of International Accounting Research*, 18(2), 31–64.

Huang, G.-Y., Shen, C. H., and Wu, Z.-X. (2023). Firm-level political risk and debt choice. *Journal of Corporate Finance*, 78, 102332.

James, C. (1987). Some evidence on the uniqueness of bank loans. *Journal of Financial Economics*, 19(2), 217–235.

Jensen, M. C. (1986). Agency costs of free cash flow, corporate finance, and takeovers. *American Economic Review*, 76(2), 323–329.

Jensen, M. C., and Meckling, W. H. (1976). Theory of the firm: Managerial behavior, agency costs and ownership structure. *Journal of Financial Economics*, 3(4), 305–360.

John, K., Kaviani, M. S., Kryzanowski, L., and Maleki, H. (2021). Do country-level creditor protections affect firm-level debt structure concentration? *Review of Finance*, 25(6), 1677–1725.

Johnson, S. A. (1997). An empirical analysis of the determinants of corporate debt ownership structure. *Journal of Financial and Quantitative Analysis*, 32(1), 47–64.

Kale, J. R., and Meneghetti, C. (2011). The choice between public and private debt: A survey. *IIMB Management Review*, 23(1), 5–14.

Krishnaswami, S., Spindt, P. A., and Subramaniam, V. (1999). Information asymmetry, monitoring, and the placement structure of corporate debt. *Journal of Financial Economics*, 51(3), 407–434.

La Porta, R., Lopez-de-Silanes, F., Shleifer, A., and Vishny, R. W. (1998). Law and finance. *Journal of Political Economy*, 106(6), 1113–1155.

Leary, M. T. (2009). Bank loan supply, lender choice, and corporate capital structure. *The Journal of Finance*, 64(3), 1143–1185.

Leland, H. E., and Pyle, D. H. (1977). Informational asymmetries, financial structure, and financial intermediation. *The Journal of Finance*, 32(2), 371–387.

Li, N., Lou, Y., Otto, C. A., and Wittenberg-Moerman, R. (2021). Accounting quality and debt concentration. *The Accounting Review*, 96(1), 377–400.

Li, X., Ng, J., and Saffar, W. (2022). Accounting-driven bank monitoring and firms' debt structure: Evidence from IFRS 9 adoption. *Management Science*, forthcoming.

Liao, S. (2015). Outside blockholders' monitoring of management and debt financing. *Contemporary Accounting Research*, 32(4), 1373–1404.

Lin, C., Ma, Y., Malatesta, P., and Xuan, Y. (2013). Corporate ownership structure and the choice between bank debt and public debt. *Journal of Financial Economics*, 109(2), 517–534.

Lin, L. (2015). Collateral and the choice between bank debt and public debt. *Management Science*, 61(8), 1892–1915.

Liu, Y. (2006). The sources of debt matter too. *Journal of Financial and Quantitative Analysis*, 41(2), 295–316.

Lou, Y., and Otto, C. A. (2020). Debt heterogeneity and covenants. *Management Science*, 66(1), 70–92.

Lummer, S. L., and McConnell, J. J. (1989). Further evidence on the bank lending process and the capital-market response to bank loan agreements. *Journal of Financial Economics*, 25(1), 99–122.

Ma, Z., Stice, D., and Williams, C. (2019). The effect of bank monitoring on public bond terms. *Journal of Financial Economics*, 133(2), 379–396.

Marshall, A., McCann, L., and McColgan, P. (2016). The choice of debt source by UK firms. *Journal of Business Finance and Accounting*, 43(5), 729–764.

Marshall, A., McCann, L., and McColgan, P. (2019). The market reaction to debt announcements: UK evidence surrounding the global financial crisis. *The British Accounting Review*, 51(1), 92–109.

Maskara, P. K., and Mullineaux, D. J. (2011). Information asymmetry and self-selection bias in bank loan announcement studies. *Journal of Financial Economics*, 101(3), 684–694.

Massa, M., and Zhang, L. (2013). Monetary policy and regional availability of debt financing. *Journal of Monetary Economics*, 60(4), 439–458.

Massa, M., and Zhang, L. (2021). The spillover effects of Hurricane Katrina on corporate bonds and the choice between bank and bond financing. *Journal of Financial and Quantitative Analysis*, 56(3), 885–913.

Meneghetti, C. (2012). Managerial incentives and the choice between public and bank debt. *Journal of Corporate Finance*, 18(1), 65–91.

Morellec, E., Valta, P., and Zhdanov, A. (2015). Financing investment: The choice between bonds and bank loans. *Management Science*, 61(11), 2580–2602.

Myers, S. C. (1977). Determinants of corporate borrowing. *Journal of Financial Economics*, 5(2), 147–175.

Nini, G., Smith, D. C., and Sufi, A. (2009). Creditor control rights and firm investment policy. *Journal of Financial Economics*, 92(3), 400–420.

Nini, G., Smith, D. C., and Sufi, A. (2012). Creditor control rights, corporate governance, and firm value. *Review of Financial Studies*, 25(6), 1713–1761.

Ovtchinnikov, A. V. (2016). Debt decisions in deregulated industries. *Journal of Corporate Finance*, 37, 216–234.

Park, C. (2000). Monitoring and structure of debt contracts. *The Journal of Finance*, 55(5), 2157–2195.

Petersen, M. A. (2009). Estimating standard errors in finance panel data sets: Comparing approaches. *Review of Financial Studies*, 22(1), 435–480.

Rajan, R. G. (1992). Insiders and outsiders: The choice between informed and arm's-length debt. *The Journal of Finance*, 47(4), 1367–1400.

Rajan, R., and Winton, A. (1995). Covenants and collateral as incentives to monitor. *The Journal of Finance*, 50(4), 1113–1146.

Ramakrishnan, R. T. S., and Thakor, A. V. (1984). Information reliability and a theory of financial intermediation. *The Review of Economic Studies*, 51(3), 415–432.

Rauh, J. D., and Sufi, A. (2010). Capital structure and debt structure. *Review of Financial Studies*, 23(12), 4242–4280.

Richardson, G., Taylor, G., and Obaydin, I. (2020). Does the use of tax haven subsidiaries by U.S. multinational corporations affect the cost of bank loans? *Journal of Corporate Finance*, 64, 101663.

Roberts, M. R., and Sufi, A. (2009). Control rights and capital structure: An empirical investigation. *The Journal of Finance*, 64(4), 1657–1695.

Santos, J. A. C., and Winton, A. (2008). Bank loans, bonds, and information monopolies across the business cycle. *The Journal of Finance*, 63(3), 1315–1359.

Sharpe, S. A. (1990). Asymmetric information, bank lending, and implicit contracts: A stylized model of customer relationships. *The Journal of Finance*, 45(4), 1069–1087.

Shleifer, A., and Vishny, R. W. (1997). A survey of corporate governance. *The Journal of Finance*, 52(2), 737–783.

Smith, C. W., and Warner, J. B. (1979). On financial contracting. *Journal of Financial Economics*, 7(2), 117–161.

Stiglitz, J. E., and Weiss, A. (1981). Credit rationing in markets with imperfect information. *The American Economic Review*, 71(3), 393–410.

Stulz, R. M. (1990). Managerial discretion and optimal financing policies. *Journal of Financial Economics*, 26(1), 3–27.

Sufi, A. (2007). Information asymmetry and financing arrangements: Evidence from syndicated loans. *The Journal of Finance*, 62(2), 629–668.

Tan, W., Tsang, A., Wang, W., and Zhang, W. (2020). Corporate social responsibility (CSR) disclosure and the choice between bank debt and public debt. *Accounting Horizons*, 34(1), 151–173.

Welch, I. (1997). Why is bank debt senior? A theory of asymmetry and claim priority based on influence costs. *Review of Financial Studies*, 10(4), 1203–1236.

Yosha, O. (1995). Information disclosure costs and the choice of financing source. *Journal of Financial Intermediation*, 4(1), 3–20.

Zhang, S. (2016). Institutional arrangements and debt financing. *Research in International Business and Finance*, 36, 362–372.

https://doi.org/10.1142/9781800617032_0002

Chapter 2

Is Firm Leverage Target Adjustment Mechanically Determined by Other Financial Behaviours?

Hafiz Hoque* **and Shengfeng Li**†

**Swansea University, Swansea, UK*

†*University of Sheffield, Sheffield, UK*

2.1. Introduction

This chapter discusses how other financial behaviours (i.e. investment, cash, equity issuance, and profitability) influence firms' leverage decisions. Recent studies debate whether the leverage target adjustment observed by using the classical partial adjustment model (Flannery and Rangan, 2006) is mechanically determined. The trade-off theory of capital structure (Kraus and Litzenberger, 1973) suggests that firms target an optimal leverage ratio at which firm value is maximised. Numerous empirical studies[1] demonstrate the existence of a leverage target by measuring the speed of adjustment (SOA). However, several studies (such as Chang and Dasgupta, 2009; Hovakimian and Li, 2011, 2012) question the validity of the measurement of SOA. The other financial behaviours lead to variations

[1]For example, Jalilvand and Harris (1984), Hovakimian *et al.* (2001), Flannery and Rangan (2006), Antoniou *et al.* (2008), Cook and Tang (2010), Faulkender *et al.* (2012), and DeAngelo and Roll (2015).

in the leverage ratio through cash flows in the firm; are they also the sources of leverage target adjustment? If yes, to what extent do these factors drive leverage target adjustment? The observed target adjustment being purely mechanically determined could invalidate the trade-off theory. Is there any active target adjustment beyond the reversion driven by the mechanical effects? This chapter aims to differentiate the mechanical effects from the active target adjustment. We contribute to the literature by discussing how the other financial behaviours result in a mechanical target adjustment and whether there remains a discretionary fraction of the SOA that can be used to support the trade-off theory.

The trade-off theory suggests there is an optimal leverage ratio at which firm value is maximised. On the one hand, firms need a certain amount of debt to shield tax (Modigliani and Miller, 1963), to defend against takeovers (Berger *et al.*, 1997), and to discipline managers (Jensen, 1986). On the other hand, overleverage leads to high bankruptcy costs and a heavy interest burden (Kraus and Litzenberger, 1973). The trade-off theory indicates that firm value is maximised when the marginal revenue of debt financing equals the marginal cost. Hovakimian *et al.* (2001) enrich the trade-off theory by suggesting that firms target an optimal leverage ratio, although the target can change over time. The partial adjustment model is widely used to test the trade-off theory and to estimate the SOA.[2] Using this model, Flannery and Rangan (2006) document an SOA of approximately 30% per year. Other empirical studies (such as Antoniou *et al.*, 2008; DeAngelo and Roll, 2015) find qualitatively similar results, although the estimated SOA varies. Recent studies investigate the heterogeneous features of the SOA estimated using partial adjustment models, such as Oztekin and Flannery (2012), Cook and Tang (2010), and Drobetz *et al.* (2015). The existence of a leverage target is robust across all of their partitioned samples.

A few studies question the validity of the estimated SOA. Shyam-Sunder and Myers (1999) argue that the motivation of external

[2]As an alternative to the partial adjustment model, Hovakimian and Li (2011) find that debt-equity choice models generate similar results. Specifically, whether the current leverage ratio is above or below the leverage target influences firms' financing decisions on whether to raise debt or equity.

financing is the demand for funds rather than targeting a leverage ratio. They find that the pecking order theory (Myers and Majluf, 1984) predicts firm capital structure better than the trade-off theory does. Moreover, cyclical fluctuations in firm investment and profitability could lead to a mechanical mean reversion in leverage. Hence, Shyam-Sunder and Myers argue that the mean reversion does not prove targeting of a specific ratio. Simulation results by Chang and Dasgupta (2009) show that the estimated SOA of firms financing randomly (0.31) is very close to that of firms with leverage targets (0.37). Hovakimian and Li (2011, 2012) and Elsas and Florysiak (2015) criticise the validity of partial adjustment models and question whether the small value of estimated SOAs is economically meaningful.[3] As Hovakimian and Li (2011) state, many overleveraged firms reduce leverage because of financial transactions rather than targeting a specific ratio. In a theoretical study, Lambrecht and Myers (2012) find that firms must issue or repurchase debt to smooth investment and distributions. DeAngelo and Roll (2015) further note that firms cannot complete all of the financial tasks (i.e. dividend target, leverage target, investment, and market timing) at the same time and that debt decisions can be residually determined. According to these studies, the estimated SOA can fail to capture the real adjustment speed because the former cannot differentiate active target adjustment from mechanical reversions driven by other financial motives. Although potential mechanical effects have been observed in these studies, the impact and importance of the mechanical effects have not been examined.

This chapter proposes a method of capturing the mechanical effects. Classical partial adjustment models tend to use a vector of firm-level and institutional-level characteristics to model the target leverage ratio and examine an identical SOA. Although some studies (such as Oztekin and Flannery, 2012; Cook and Tang, 2010; Drobetz *et al.*, 2015) shed light on the heterogeneous features, to our knowledge, there are no studies explaining how other financial behaviours are involved. We extend the classical partial adjustment

[3] According to Hovakimian and Li (2011), the 'real SOA' is between 5% and 8%, which is much lower than the results generated by the partial adjustment model (approximately 30%) by Flannery and Rangan (2006).

model by using interaction terms to capture the mechanical effects, which control the proportion of the SOA that can be explained by other financial motives. We also test whether there remains a fraction of the SOA that indicates discretionary target adjustment.

We find that nearly one-half of the leverage target adjustment is driven by the mechanical effects due to variations in firm investment, cash holdings, equity issuance, and profitability. Equity issuance and variation in net income lead to mechanical target adjustment from above the leverage target, whereas investment and variation in cash holdings lead to mechanical target adjustment from below. Controlling for these effects decreases the estimated SOA by 45%. These results align with the concerns raised by Shyam-Sunder and Myers (1999), Chang and Dasgupta (2009), and Hovakimian and Li (2011) that leverage mean reversion is not entirely discretionary. Our results suggest that other financial decisions lead to nearly one-half of leverage target adjustments. The classical partial adjustment model, without controlling for the mechanical effects, overestimates the active target adjustment speed.

Although the estimated SOA decreases substantially after controlling for the mechanical effects, there remains evidence implying an active target adjustment. First, firms' financing behaviours show a tendency to revert. Descriptive evidence shows that firms with a higher leverage ratio are more reluctant to issue debt in the subsequent period. Instead, these firms are more willing to fund the capital demand with equity, suggesting that leverage mean reversion is at least partly driven by firms' financing behaviours rather than by a purely mechanical reversion in the leverage ratio.[4] Second, controlling for the mechanical effects does not wipe out active target adjustment. In addition to the mechanical reversion driven by other financial behaviours, there remains a substantial fraction of the SOA (approximately 55%), which indicates active adjustments. Our results, after controlling for the mechanical effects, suggest a slow SOA that closely resembles the results of Fama and French (2002)

[4]Chang and Dasgupta (2009) note that the mean reversion observed in previous studies can be driven by the autoregression of the leverage ratio. Hence, Chang and Dasgupta suggest relying on firms' financing behaviours rather than on changes in the leverage ratio for evidence to support the existence of a leverage target.

and DeAngelo and Roll (2015).[5] The active adjustment holds for both overleveraged and underleveraged firms, and the active SOA is faster in the group of unconstrained firms. The active target adjustment is robust to other definitions of leverage and the leverage target as well as to alternative estimation methods. Overall, our evidence supports the trade-off theory, countering the criticism of mechanical reversion.

Previous studies have not agreed on the difference between SOAs from above and from below the leverage target. A few studies (such as Faulkender *et al.*, 2012) find that the adjustment is faster from above the leverage target. A possible reason is that firms benefit more from reducing risk when leverage is high than from shielding the tax when leverage is low. However, the leverage ratchet effect (Admati *et al.*, 2018) predicts that that adjustment is faster from below the target because overleveraged firms are unwilling to reduce leverage and then refinance. By examining the active SOA, our results reconcile these conflicts. We find that although the classical partial adjustment model reports a faster SOA of overleveraged firms, after controlling for the mechanical effects, underleveraged firms show a faster active SOA. It appears that the active SOA estimated by using the extended partial adjustment model reflects the leverage ratchet effects (Admati *et al.*, 2018) better than the classical partial adjustment model does.

We contribute to the literature in the following ways. First, we explain why and how other financial behaviours can lead to mechanical leverage target adjustments. Second, we extend the classical partial adjustment model by using interaction terms to capture the mechanical effects. The extended model is able to accommodate both the mechanical effects and the active target adjustment. Third, the active SOA reconciles the opposite predictions in the literature on SOAs from above and below the leverage target. We find that overleveraged firms mechanically adjust the leverage ratio more often and that underleveraged firms actively adjust leverage more often. Fourth, our empirical results point to a unified theory of capital structure. The trade-off theory suggests that firms benefit from targeting

---

[5]Fama and French (2002) use simultaneous equations and find an SOA of 7–17%. DeAngelo and Roll (2015) use simulations and find an SOA of 15%.

an optimal leverage ratio. We show that issuing (or retiring) debt to balance the budget constraint motivates part of the variation in leverage. These mechanical variations in leverage coexist with discretionary leverage target adjustments. It appears that firms consider both the optimal leverage ratio and the need to balance the budget constraints when making financing decisions.

The remainder of the chapter is organised as follows. Section 2.2 presents the theoretical background on why other financial behaviours lead to leverage target adjustment and explains our methodology to capture these mechanical effects. Section 2.3 describes the data. Section 2.4 presents empirical evidence and discusses the robustness of our findings. Section 2.5 concludes the chapter.

2.2. Theoretical Background and Methodology

2.2.1. *Mechanical effects*

We refer to the mechanical effects as variations in the leverage ratio driven by other financial behaviours through firms' cash flows. The mechanical effects are also revealed in the estimated SOA. Lambrecht and Myers (2012) use a budget constraint equation to link firms' debt decisions to other financial behaviours.[6] If decisions on investment, dividend, and equity are more important than leverage decisions, as stated by DeAngelo and Roll (2015), debt decisions should play the role of balancing the budget constraints.[7] Considering that

---

[6]Lambrecht and Myers (2012) use the following budget constraint equation:

$$\Delta\text{Debt} + \text{Net income} = \text{CAPEX} + \text{Payout}.$$

The left-hand side of the budget constraint equation shows that funds are generated through debt financing (ΔDebt) and operating profit (Net income). The right-hand side of the budget constraint equation shows that the funds are used in investment activities (CAPEX) and distributions to shareholders.

[7]The empirical setting in this chapter is based on the condition that other financial decisions are more important than leverage decisions. Otherwise, there will be endogeneity problems. In a recent empirical study, Li *et al.* (2018) decompose the forecast errors of firms' financial behaviours and find that their investment, equity issuance (or repurchase), and profitability are more exogenous (independent) than their leverage decisions.

investment activities are driven by investment opportunities and that equity decisions are driven by market timing opportunities (Fama and French, 2005), it is reasonable to accept that firms' investment and equity issuance are more important than the leverage target because firms tend to take advantage of these opportunities. Considering that firms must maintain stable and attractive dividends in the interest of shareholders (Fama and French, 2002; DeAngelo and Roll, 2015), it is reasonable to accept that firms prioritise targeting a dividend payout ratio over targeting a leverage ratio. Therefore, if issuing or retiring debt is costless, firms are likely to adjust their debt decisions to absorb shocks from other factors. Thus, other financial behaviours drive debt decisions and lead to mechanical variations in the leverage ratio.

Now, we consider the leverage adjustment cost. Flannery and Rangan (2006) suggest that adjustment costs are the reason for a slow SOA. If there are no adjustment costs, such as the debt issuance cost, firms would immediately revert to the optimal leverage ratio. If the adjustment costs outweigh the benefits from reversion, firms would remain deviated from the optimal leverage ratio. Cross-sectionally, the firms with higher adjustment costs show a slow SOA (Cook and Tang, 2010; Oztekin and Flannery, 2012; Drobetz *et al.*, 2015). If firms must accommodate other financial tasks that fortuitously bring extra benefits by moving the leverage ratio closer to the target, they are more likely to incorporate these changes.

In Modigliani and Miller's framework, the benefit of debt financing is equal to the difference between the value of leveraged firms (V^L) and the value of unleveraged firms (V^U). $B(L) = V^L - V^U$ denotes the net benefit of debt. Now, we use $B(L^*)$ to represent the net benefit of debt at the optimal leverage ratio L^*. Then, $B(L^*) - B(L)$ measures the benefit of moving the leverage ratio from L to the optimal leverage ratio L^*, which equals the adjustment costs. Using debt to balance the budget constraint brings extra benefits to firms, for example, by pursuing a profitable investment project. We denote the extra benefit by $B(T)$. If balancing the budget constraint leads to a full leverage target adjustment, the benefit of adjustment becomes $B(L^*) - B(L) + B(T)$, which exceeds the adjustment cost $B(L^*) - B(L)$; hence, firms would revert. Conversely, balancing the budget constraint can result in a further deviation from leverage to L'. In this situation, if $B(T)$ is larger than the lost value due to the further deviation $B(L) - B(L')$, firms would allow the mechanical deviation.

Figure 2.1 illustrates the routes that firm leverage ratio could be driven by other financial behaviours, followed by reversions. The Y-axis shows the leverage ratio, and the X-axis shows the time. The horizontal line indicates the optimal leverage ratio (the leverage target).[8] Position A stands for the situation when the current leverage ratio is above the leverage target, whereas position B stands for

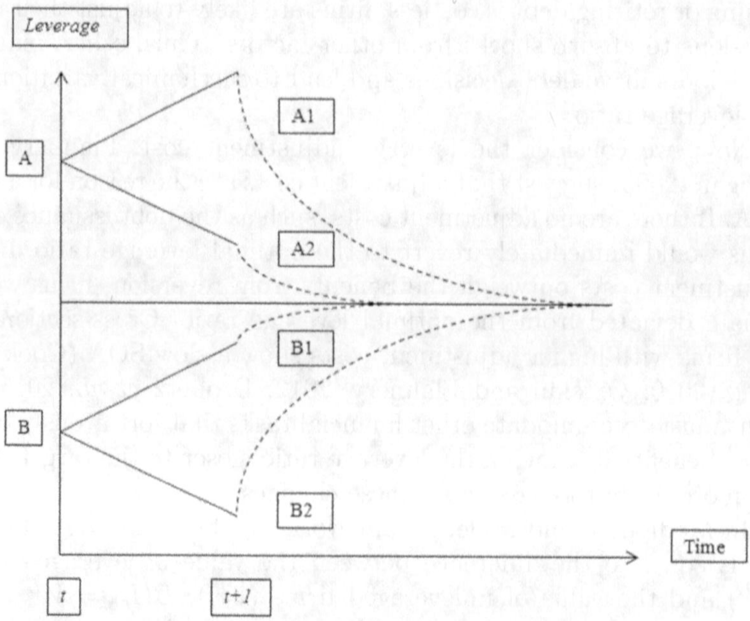

Figure 2.1. The routes of the mechanical effects on firm leverage ratio. The Y-axis shows the leverage ratio, and the X-axis shows the time. The horizontal line in the middle is the leverage target. Status A and status B are the situations when firms are above and below the target leverage ratio at t, respectively. A1, A2, B1, and B2 are the four routes that the leverage ratio could follow. The solid line from t to $t+1$ shows the influence of the mechanical effects on the leverage ratio, and the dashed line after $t+1$ shows adjustments towards the target.

[8]To simplify, we assume that the optimal (target) leverage ratio is constant during the process, and the movement of the leverage ratio from t to $t+1$ is driven by the motivation to balance the budget constraint (the mechanical effects).

the situation when the current leverage ratio is below the leverage target. The four routes (A1/A2/B1/B2) show the routes that firm leverage ratio could follow. The solid line, from t to $t+1$, shows the variation in leverage that is driven by other financial behaviours. The dashed line after $t+1$ shows target adjustments in subsequent periods.

Issuing debt to balance the budget constraint leads to a mechanical increase in the leverage ratio. Let L_t denote the leverage ratio at year t:

$$L_t = \frac{D_t}{D_t + E_t} = 1 - \frac{E_t}{D_t + E_t}, \tag{2.1}$$

where D_t is the book value of total debt and E_t is the book value of total equity. Suppose firms issue new debt d_{t+1} to fund new investment projects or increased cash holdings[9] and there is no equity issuance or new net income at the same time, the leverage ratio at $t+1$ becomes the following:

$$L_{t+1} = \frac{D_t + d_{t+1}}{D_t + E_t + d_{t+1}} = 1 - \frac{E_t}{D_t + E_t + d_{t+1}}. \tag{2.2}$$

Note that L_{t+1} is greater than L_t. Depending on whether the initial leverage ratio is at A or B, to balance the budget constraint, the leverage ratio follows route A1 or B1 in Figure 2.1 to fund investment and the increased cash holdings. Conversely, reducing investment or cash holdings leads to a reduction in debt capital. The leverage ratio follows route A2 or B2. An additional case is that, if firms consider the debt capacity (Lemmon and Zender, 2010) and issue equity to fund investment projects from above the leverage target, the leverage ratio will follow A2.

Holding capital demand constant, an increase in profitability leads to a decrease in the leverage ratio. To balance the budget constraint, firms use the increased net income to reduce debt. When the net income at year $t+1$ increases by p_{t+1}, the leverage ratio becomes

[9]The budget constraint equation by Lambrecht and Myers (2012) uses the net debt ratio. However, if cash is considered separately from debt, the former should be on the right-hand side of the budget constraint equation. Debt capital should react in the same direction as the variation in cash, according to firms' cash flow identity.

the following:

$$L_{t+1} = \frac{D_t - p_{t+1}}{D_t + E_t - p_{t+1}} = 1 - \frac{E_t}{D_t + E_t - p_{t+1}}. \tag{2.3}$$

Note that L_{t+1} is less than L_t. Therefore, the leverage ratio follows route A2 or B2 if more funds are generated internally. Conversely, a negative profitability shock is absorbed by the newly issued debt to balance the budget constraint; hence, the leverage ratio follows route A1 or B1 in Figure 2.1.

Equity issuance or repurchase activities also influence firms' debt decisions in the short term. Several studies (such as Baker and Wurgler, 2002; Fama and French, 2005) indicate that equity financing is conducted following market timing opportunities rather than as the last resort after debt financing.[10] Fama and French (2005) provide three pieces of evidence. First, the fact that the net issuance of equity often succeeds the net issuance of debt violates the trade-off theory. Second, the fact that equity repurchases also occur among those firms with huge capital demand violates the pecking order theory. Third, equity issuance and repurchase activities often occur in the same year, indicating that firms are timing the market rather than using equity financing as the last resort after debt financing. According to the market timing theory (Baker and Wurgler, 2002), firms' equity issuances and repurchases are highly based on stock price fluctuations rather than the need to rebalance the leverage ratio or maintain the debt capacity. As one of the financing sources, equity capital is a substitution for debt capital. An equity issuance mechanically decreases the demand for debt capital, which drives the leverage ratio to follow route A2 or B2 in Figure 2.1. In contrast, an equity repurchase increases the leverage ratio (following route A1 or B1) in the short term,[11] *ceteris paribus*.

[10] According to the trade-off theory, equity financing is used as a tool to rebalance debt ratios. With respect to the pecking order theory, equity financing is used only if retained earnings and the raised debt are insufficient to meet the demand for capital. Both the trade-off theory and the pecking order theory indicate that equity financing is considered only after debt financing.

[11] Although researchers debate whether there is a long-term effect of market timing on the firm leverage ratio, its short-term effect has been widely recognised in the literature (such as in Baker and Wurgler, 2002; Flannery and Rangan, 2006; Faulkender *et al.*, 2012).

The passive variation in leverage can result in a mechanical target adjustment. As shown in Figure 2.1, routes A1 and B2 drive the leverage ratio further away from the target; thus, the leverage target reversion takes a longer time. In contrast, routes A2 and B1 drive the firm leverage ratio closer to the target; thus, the leverage ratio takes a shorter time to fully revert. In A2 and B1, the mechanical effects even constitute part of the target adjustment, consequently exaggerating the estimated SOA, which is supposed to be self-motivated. In summary, this study anticipates that other financial behaviours would lead to a mechanical mean reversion (or deviation). For the mechanical effects, we develop three hypotheses:

Hypothesis One: *If leverage target adjustment is mechanically determined, other financial behaviours should contribute to explaining the SOA* because these financial behaviours either drive leverage target adjustments and accelerate the SOA or delay leverage target adjustments and reduce the SOA. The effect differs when firms are above or below the leverage target, as illustrated in Figure 2.1.

Hypothesis Two: *If leverage target adjustment is discretionary, there should be a proportion of the SOA that cannot be explained by the mechanical effects*, indicating that firms actively rebalance the leverage ratio rather than leave it purely mechanically determined.

Hypothesis Three: Active adjustments should be connected to the financial constraint. *Unconstrained firms have more discretion, and they are more likely to actively rebalance the leverage ratio towards the target. Hence, a faster active SOA is expected. In contrast, constrained firms have less discretion and, in turn, a lower active SOA.*

2.2.2. *Methodology*

Partial adjustment models have been widely used to model leverage target adjustment and to estimate the SOA, such as by Flannery and Rangan (2006), Antoniou *et al.* (2008), and DeAngelo and Roll (2015). Due to adjustment costs, firms do not immediately and completely rebalance after the deviation from an optimal leverage ratio. Instead, they gradually adjust towards the optimal leverage ratio. Every year, firms offset a proportion of the deviation from the leverage target.

Equation (2.4) gives the partial adjustment function (the second step), in which the change in leverage ratio at year t is a proportion of the leverage deviation from the target. $\text{Lev}_{i,t}$ denotes the book leverage ratio of firm i at year t. $\text{Lev}^*_{i,t}$ is the target leverage ratio of firm i at year t. λ captures the SOA. $\varepsilon_{i,t}$ is the error term. According to Flannery and Rangan (2006) and Antoniou *et al.* (2008), λ falling within $(0, 1)$ is interpreted as evidence for partial adjustment towards the target:

$$\text{Lev}_{i,t} - \text{Lev}_{i,t-1} = \lambda(\text{Lev}^*_{i,t} - \text{Lev}_{i,t-1}) + \varepsilon_{i,t}. \quad (2.4)$$

The time-varying leverage target $\text{Lev}^*_{i,t}$ is captured by a list of firm-level characteristics X in the first-step equation:

$$\text{Lev}^*_{i,t} = \beta^* X_{i,t-1} + \nu_{i,t}, \nu_{i,t} \sim \text{i.i.d. } N(0, \sigma^2_\nu). \quad (2.5)$$

This chapter proposes to capture the mechanical effects by using interaction terms in the two-step partial adjustment framework. Motivated by Hypothesis One, we set the adjustment speed λ as a function of other financial behaviours at year t:

$$\lambda = \gamma_0 + \gamma^*_1 Z_{i,t} + \epsilon_{i,t}, \epsilon_{i,t} \sim \text{ i.i.d. } N(0, \sigma^2_\nu), \quad (2.6)$$

where Z captures the mechanical effects. Z contains the changes in *Investment, Cash holdings, Net income*, and *Equity*. A positive value of γ_1 indicates an increase in the SOA (route A2 or B1 in Figure 2.1), whereas a negative value indicates a reduction in the SOA (route A1 or B2 in Figure 2.1). γ_0 captures the proportion of SOA which cannot be explained by the mechanical effects. $\epsilon_{i,t}$ is the error term.

Our model shares the same first step as the classical partial adjustment model. Specifically, we estimate and predict the leverage target $\text{Lev}^*_{i,t}$. Following Rajan and Zingales (1995) and Leary and Roberts (2010), we use the conventional set of firm characteristics to proxy the target leverage ratio, namely, tangibility, market-to-book ratio (M/B), firm size, and profitability. According to Rajan and Zingales (1995), tangible assets serve as the collateral that reduces the risk of debt holders. Increased collateral reduces the cost of borrowing and raises the leverage ratio. The market-to-book ratio captures growth opportunities. The firm with a higher M/B ratio tends to have a lower cost of equity financing. Hence, debt capital is less attractive to fast-growing firms. Firm size is expected to be positively associated with the leverage ratio because larger firms are more diversified and have lower bankruptcy costs. Firms with a higher profitability tend to use lower leverage because of the lower demand for external funding. We regress leverage on the leverage determinants and use the predicted leverage ratio as the target leverage ratio of each firm at each period.

We substitute equation (2.6) into equation (2.4). Then, we re-parameterise and derive a testable equation as follows:

$$\begin{aligned}\text{Lev}_{i,t} = \alpha_0 &+ \beta_0^* \text{Lev}_{i,t-1} + \beta_1^* Z_{i,t}^* \text{Lev}_{i,t-1} + \beta_2^* X_{i,t-1} \\ &+ \beta_3^* Z_{i,t}^* \text{Lev}_{i,t}^* + \varepsilon_{i,t}, \end{aligned} \tag{2.7}$$

where α_0 is a constant and $\varepsilon_{i,t}$ is an error term with a mean of zero and clustered by firms. Equation (2.7) differs from the classical partial adjustment model specification by including the two interaction terms $Z_{i,t}^*\text{Lev}_{i,t-1}$ and $Z_{i,t}^*\text{Lev}_{i,t}^*$. $Z_{i,t}^*\text{Lev}_{i,t-1}$, which capture the mechanical effects of the other financial behaviours on leverage target adjustments. In this chapter, we evaluate the mechanical effects by testing whether β_1 is different from zero. $\text{Lev}_{i,t-1}$ tests the remaining proportion of the SOA which is not explained by the mechanical effects. We take this remaining proportion as discretionary target adjustments. The active SOA is calculated by $1 - \beta_0$. In equation (2.7), we accommodate both the mechanical and non-mechanical components in the SOA.

The variables $(Z_{i,t})$ capturing the mechanical effects, along with the predicted relationship with the SOA and the predicted signs of interaction terms in model (2.7), are summarised in Table 2.1. As discussed in Section 2.2, investment by issuing debt when leverage is above the target decreases the SOA (A1 in Figure 2.1). Hence, we anticipate a positive sign on $\Delta\text{Inv}_{i,t}^*\text{Lev}_{i,t-1}$. There is also the possibility of a negative sign because firms can choose equity financing due to the constraint of debt capacity. When firms are underleveraged, investment will increase the SOA (B1 in Figure 2.1). We anticipate a negative sign on $\Delta\text{Inv}_{i,t}^*\text{Lev}_{i,t-1}$. Similarly, we anticipate a positive sign on $\Delta\text{Cash}_{i,t}^*\text{Lev}_{i,t-1}$ when leverage is above the target and a negative sign when leverage is below the target. Issuing equity when leverage is above the target mechanically increases the SOA (A2 in Figure 2.1). We anticipate a negative sign on $\text{Equ}_{i,t}^*\text{Lev}_{i,t-1}$. Issuing equity when leverage is below the target decreases the SOA (B2 in Figure 2.1). We anticipate a positive sign on $\text{Equ}_{i,t}^*\text{Lev}_{i,t-1}$.

Table 2.1. Predicted signs of the mechanical effects.

	(1)	(2)	(3)	(4)
	Above target		Below target	
Interactions	On SOA	On Lev	On SOA	On Lev
ΔInv	−/+	+/−	+	−
ΔCash	−	+	+	−
Equ	+	−	−	+
ΔNI	+	−	−	+

Note: This table shows the predicted signs of the mechanical effects. 'Above Target' and 'Below Target' indicate whether sample firms are overleveraged or underleveraged in the previous year. Columns (1) and (3) show the predicted signs of $Z_{i,t}$ in equation (2.8). Columns (2) and (4) show the predicted signs of $Z^*_{i,t}\text{Lev}_{i,t-1}$ in equation (2.9):

$$\lambda = \gamma_0 + \gamma_1^* Z_{i,t} + \epsilon_{i,t}, \epsilon_{i,t} \sim \text{i.i.d. } N(0, \sigma_v^2), \tag{2.8}$$

$$\begin{aligned}\text{Lev}_{i,t} = \alpha_0 + \beta_0^*\text{Lev}_{i,t-1} + \beta_1^* Z^*_{i,t}\text{Lev}_{i,t-1} \\ + \beta_2^* X_{i,t-1} + \beta_3^* Z^*_{i,t}\text{Lev}^*_{i,t} + \varepsilon_{i,t},.\end{aligned} \tag{2.9}$$

Similarly, we anticipate a negative sign on $\Delta\text{NI}^*_{i,t}\text{Lev}_{i,t-1}$ when leverage is above the target and a positive sign on $\Delta\text{NI}^*_{i,t}\text{Lev}_{i,t-1}$ when leverage is below the target. We do not have a prediction for the signs in the whole sample because they depend on the trade-off between the mechanical effects from above and below. One should not rely on the signs of the coefficients in the whole sample to interpret the impact of mechanical effects because these effects should have opposite impacts when firms are above or below the leverage target. In the regression of the whole sample, we are more interested in whether the estimated SOA decreases after controlling for the mechanical effects and whether the active SOA is robust.

2.3. Data

2.3.1. *Data and descriptive statistics*

This study uses data collected from the CRSP/Compustat merged database, and the sample period is from 1970 to 2016. Consistent with previous capital structure studies (such as Graham *et al.*, 2014;

DeAngelo and Roll, 2015), we collect annual report data on all of the firms, with financials (SIC Codes 6000–6999), utilities (4900–4949), railroads (4000–4100), and telecommunications (4800–4900) excluded.[12] We exclude regulated firms for two reasons. First, these firms tend to maintain extraordinarily high leverage, and the leverage ratio is constrained by financial regulations (Graham *et al.*, 2014). Second, this study uses sample criteria consistent with the capital structure literature; thus, our results are comparable with previous studies. Sample firms are requested to maintain records for at least five years in the sample period to perform regression analysis. Definitions of variables are shown in Appendix 2A.

Table 2.2 presents the descriptive statistics of the sample firms. All of the variables are winsorised at the 1% level on both tails to remove the effect of outliers. *Leverage* measures the proportion of total debt to the book value of total assets and has a mean of 0.271. We use book leverage ratio as the dependent variable, rather than market leverage ratio, because firms tend to make financial decisions based on the book value of assets (Graham *et al.*, 2014). Specifically, book leverage ratio reflects the 'active rebalancing' of firms, whereas market leverage ratio contains shocks to the stock price, which are not controlled by firms. We leave the alternative definitions of leverage in the robustness check section. Table 2.2 also presents the descriptive statistics of the estimated leverage target. We use three different estimation methods and find that all of the predicted leverage targets have a mean value of 0.263.

2.3.2. *Mean reversion revealed in financing behaviours*

Previous studies suggest that firms' financing behaviours are more valid evidence than the reversion in leverage ratio to support the existence of a leverage target. Shyam-Sunder and Myers (1999) argue that the mean reversion in leverage could be driven by cyclical fluctuations in firms' investment and profitability. If the observed

---

[12]Slightly earlier studies tend to exclude only financials and utilities. We also exclude telecommunications and railroads because these firms are labelled as regulated firms by Graham *et al.* (2014) and DeAngelo and Roll (2015).

Table 2.2. Descriptive statistics.

Variable	N	Mean	Median	Std. dev	$p1$	$p99$
Leverage	248,558	0.271	0.216	0.291	0	1.77
Market leverage ratio	219,310	0.259	0.184	0.257	0	0.940
Debt issuance ratio	233,923	0.012	0	0.159	−0.717	0.584
Total assets	249,761	1,860.48	82.25	12,754.25	0.276	33,055.45
Tangibility	248,912	0.295	0.235	0.235	0	0.912
Market-to-book ratio	219,127	2.129	1.349	2.541	0.513	18.742
Net income to assets	248,568	−0.094	0.031	0.451	−2.983	0.324
Return on assets	248,483	−0.034	0.065	0.388	−2.441	0.376
Investment/ assets	245,606	0.069	0.044	0.079	0	0.447
Cash dividend/ assets	241,155	0.009	0	0.021	0	0.138
Equity issuance ratio	230,752	0.108	0.005	0.307	−0.219	1.953
Cash/assets	231,990	0.119	0.049	0.169	0	0.861
Deficit	231,415	0.138	0.054	0.386	−0.997	2.144
Targetols	212,174	0.263	0.243	0.089	0.135	0.663
Targetfe	212,174	0.263	0.250	0.079	0.143	0.659
Targetfed	212,174	0.263	0.249	0.082	0.142	0.666
KZ index	206,894	−1.817	0.902	907.29	−143.57	139.56

Note: This table presents the descriptive statistics of sample firms. The data are collected from the CRSP/Compustat database. The sample includes all of the unregulated firms. Financials (SIC codes 6000–6999), utilities (4900–4949), railroads (4000–4100), and telecommunications (4800–4900) are not included. The sample period is from 1970 to 2016. We report the number of observations (N), the mean, the median, the standard deviation, and the values at the 1st and 99th percentiles. The definitions of variables are summarised in Appendix 2A. We also report the descriptive statistics of the estimated leverage target, using equation (2.5). Targetols is predicted using OLS estimation. Targetfe is predicted using the fixed effects method to control unobservable firm features. Targetfed controls fixed effects at the firm level and includes dummy variables to control industry and year features.

reversion is driven by cyclical fluctuations rather than discretionary target adjustments, regression models using the change in leverage ratio as the dependent variable may fail to reject the mechanical reversion. A mechanical mean reversion is passively determined; thus, it does not indicate that firms target an optimal leverage ratio.

Chang and Dasgupta (2009) also note the mechanical effects and suggest examining firms' financing behaviours rather than only the change in leverage ratio. Therefore, before presenting regression results, we calculate the probability of net debt issuance and net equity issuance to show evidence of active reversion.

More specifically, we examine the financing behaviour of sample firms at year t, given the range of *Leverage ratio* at year $t-1$. Sample firms are divided into 10 groups based on the leverage ratio at year $t-1$. For each leverage interval, the number of observations is reported. *Leverage reduction* shows the percentage of observations with a decrease in the leverage ratio at year t ($\text{Lev}_t < \text{Lev}_{t-1}$). *Net debt issuance* reports the percentage of firms with *Total debt*$_t$ greater than *Total debt*$_{t-1}$. Similarly, *Net equity issuance* reports the percentage of firms with an *Equity issuance ratio* greater than zero at year t. We also report the percentage of firms with a positive value of financing deficit at year t for comparison.

The results in Table 2.3 show a tendency to reduce reliance on debt capital as the leverage ratio increases. From the 0.1–0.2 interval to the 0.8–0.9 interval,[13] the percentage of firms with net debt issuance is decreasing. Fifty-five percent of firms with Lev_{t-1} in the 0.1–0.2 interval have net debt issuance in the following year. The ratio decreases to 44% for firms in the 0.8–0.9 interval. At the same time, the percentage of firms with net equity issuance is increasing. Among firms with Lev_{t-1} in the 0.1–0.2 interval, 71% of the observations have net equity issuance in the subsequent year. The ratio increases to 77–78% for firms with the previous leverage ratio above 0.6. Table 2.3 shows that firms become reluctant to issue debt when the leverage ratio increases. We can observe a clear and consistent tendency in *Net debt issuance*, although the trend in *Leverage reduction* is not persistent when the previous leverage ratio is above 0.5. These results suggest that firms actively adjust the leverage ratio. The mean reversion and target adjustment observed in

[13]Strebulaev and Yang (2013) find that zero-leverage policy and almost-zero-leverage policy are persistent. In Table 2.3, fewer firms in the 0–0.1 interval (51%) have net debt issuance at year t than do those firms in the 0.1–0.2 interval (55%). The persistence of leverage policy is also found in firms employing a high-leverage policy (over 0.9), possibly because firms in the 0–0.1 and 0.9–1.0 intervals do not exhibit target adjustment behaviours. Therefore, we do not interpret results based on the firms falling into these two intervals.

Table 2.3. Mean reversion revealed by financing behaviours.

Leverage intervals	Observations	Leverage reduction (%)	Net debt issuance (%)	Net equity issuance (%)	Positive deficit (%)
0.9–1.0	1,355	47	45	81	66
0.8–0.9	2,545	46	44	77	65
0.7–0.8	4,657	45	45	78	64
0.6–0.7	8,058	45	47	77	64
0.5–0.6	13,604	45	50	76	66
0.4–0.5	22,113	46	51	74	65
0.3–0.4	32,450	47	53	73	67
0.2–0.3	39,485	49	55	72	70
0.1–0.2	37,911	51	55	71	72
0.0–0.1	47,446	50	51	75	77
Overall	209,624	48	52	73	70

Note: This table reports the percentage of firms having net debt (equity) issuance at year t, conditional on the percentage of observations falling in each leverage interval. *Leverage intervals* list the intervals of leverage ratio at year $t-1$, and the number of observations is reported. *Leverage reduction* indicates reducing the leverage ratio at year t. *Net debt issuance* indicates a positive value of *Debt issuance ratio*, and *Net equity issuance* indicates a positive value of *Equity issuance ratio*. The percentages of firms with net debt (equity) issuance at year t are reported. *Positive deficit* refers to the percentage of firms with a $Deficit_t$ greater than zero.

previous studies (such as Marsh, 1982; Jalilvand and Harris, 1984; Fama and French, 2002) are at least partly discretionarily determined and not completely driven by a mechanical mean reversion. We test this prediction in the following section.

2.4. Empirical Results

In this section, we first estimate the classical partial adjustment model. Then, we test the mechanical effects by estimating model (2.7) and compare our results with those generated by the classical partial adjustment model. Third, we test the effects of financial constraints on active adjustment activities. Finally, we discuss the robustness of the mechanical effects and the active adjustments.

2.4.1. *Classical partial adjustment model and the estimated SOA*

Table 2.4 presents the regression results of the classical partial adjustment model. The baseline model in column (1) reports a coefficient of $leverage_{i,t-1}$ of 0.83, indicating that leverage adjusts at a speed of 0.17 per year towards the time-varying leverage target. In column (2), we use an interaction term to capture the effects of being above the leverage target. The results show that overleveraged firms adjust

Table 2.4. Classical partial adjustment model.

	OLS, cluster	
Estimation methods	(1)	(2)
Leverage $i, t-1$	0.830***	0.830***
	(214.74)	(125.03)
Leverage $i, t-1$ * Overleveraged		−0.023**
		(−2.42)
Leverage* i, t	0.172***	0.163***
	(18.71)	(17.07)
Leverage* i, t * Overleveraged		0.061***
		(4.99)
Constant	0.008***	0.008***
	(3.57)	(3.67)
R^2	65.2%	65.3%
Observation	201,430	201,430

Note: This table reports regression results of the classical partial adjustment model. The sample includes all of the unregulated Compustat firms, and the sample period is from 1970 to 2016. Column (2) uses interaction terms to capture the difference in adjustment speed between overleveraged and underleveraged firms. Firm-clustered standard errors are used in the OLS estimation. The dependent variable is firm book leverage ratio, and a one-year lagged dependent variable is used as one of the independent variables. *Leverage*$^*i, t$ is the target leverage ratio. Coefficients and t-statistics are reported. R^2 and the number of observations are reported. *** indicates significant difference at the 1% level; ** indicates significant difference at the 5% level; and * indicates significant difference at the 10% level.

at a faster SOA (0.193). The difference is statistically significant at the 5% level. This result is consistent with that reported by Faulkender *et al.* (2012), i.e. the target adjustment is faster from above than from below. This result favours the risk explanation that firms benefit more from cutting debt when the leverage is high than from raising debt to shield from taxes when the leverage ratio is low; however, this is contrary to the prediction of the leverage ratchet effect (Admati *et al.*, 2018) that overleveraged firms are reluctant to cut debt.

2.4.2. *Mechanical effects*

Table 2.5 presents regression results of model (2.7), using which we find that other financial behaviours are related to leverage target adjustments. Consistent with our prediction, the coefficients of $\text{Equ}^*_{i,t}\text{Lev}_{i,t-1}$ and $\Delta\text{NI}^*_{i,t}\text{Lev}_{i,t-1}$ are negative in column (2), suggesting that equity market timing and variation in net income result in mechanical target adjustment of overleveraged firms. The coefficients of $\Delta\text{Inv}^*_{i,t}\text{Lev}_{i,t-1}$ and $\Delta\text{Cash}^*_{i,t}\text{Lev}_{i,t-1}$ are negative in column (4), as predicted, suggesting that investment and adjusting cash holdings result in mechanical target adjustment of underleveraged firms. An interesting point is that $\Delta\text{NI}^*_{i,t}\text{Lev}_{i,t-1}$ has a negative sign in column (4), which appears to suggest that underleveraged firms facing an increase in earnings raise leverage to shield from taxes. In column (5), in which we pooled both overleveraged and underleveraged firms, we find that all of the coefficients of interaction terms are significantly different from zero. These results are consistent with *Hypothesis One* that other financial behaviours lead to mechanical target adjustment.

The estimated SOA decreases after controlling for the mechanical effects. Once we control for these effects, we observe an SOA of 0.075 for overleveraged firms (column 2 of Table 2.5), whereas it is 0.194 when the mechanical effects are not controlled for (column 1 of Table 2.5). The estimated SOA is 0.162 for underleveraged firms (column 4 of Table 2.5), compared with 0.174 when the mechanical effects are not controlled for (column 3 of Table 2.5). In the regression of the whole sample, after controlling for the mechanical effects, the estimated SOA decreases by 45% from 0.17 (column 1 of Table 2.4) to 0.094 (column 5 of Table 2.5). These results suggest that the mechanical effects play an important role in formulating leverage

Table 2.5. Mechanical effects on leverage target adjustment.

	(1)	(2)	(3)	(4)	(5)	(6)
Estimation methods	OLS, cluster					
	Overleveraged		Underleveraged		Whole	
Leverage $i, t-1$	0.806***	0.925***	0.826***	0.838***	0.906***	0.856***
	(109.25)	(136.85)	(123.31)	(113.52)	(268.67)	(110.58)
ΔInv i,t * Leverage $i, t-1$		−0.164		−0.386***	−0.135**	−0.138***
		(−1.53)		(−2.89)	(−2.52)	(−2.57)
ΔCash i,t * Leverage $i, t-1$		0.001		−0.260**	−0.065**	−0.068**
		(0.02)		(−2.27)	(−2.03)	(−2.11)
Equ i,t * Leverage $i, t-1$		−0.207***		0.005	−0.152***	−0.151***
		(−9.67)		(0.14)	(−15.79)	(−15.68)
ΔNI i,t * Leverage $i, t-1$		−0.033**		−0.374***	−0.115***	−0.115***
		(−2.10)		(−11.32)	(−12.76)	(−12.71)
Leverage $i, t-1$* Overleveraged						0.060***
						(5.88)
Leverage* $i, t-1$	0.057***	0.357***	0.278***	0.350***	0.339***	0.367***
	(2.87)	(18.67)	(21.99)	(21.77)	(29.31)	(27.94)
Constant	0.058***	−0.065***	−0.025***	−0.047***	−0.051***	−0.053***
	(11.89)	(−13.97)	(−8.75)	(−13.88)	(−19.45)	(−19.59)
Interactions with moving target		Yes		Yes	Yes	Yes
R^2	55.5%	63.9%	33.0%	37.8%	70.1%	70.1%
Observation	82,603	73,708	118,827	107,126	180,834	180,834

Note: This table reports regression results of model (2.7). The sample includes all the unregulated Compustat firms, and the sample period is from 1970 to 2016. Columns (1) and (2) report results for overleveraged firms. Columns (3) and (4) report results for underleveraged firms. Columns (5) and (6) shows the results of the whole sample.

$$\text{Lev}_{i,t} = \alpha_0 + \beta_0^*\text{Lev}_{i,t-1} + \beta_1^* Z_{i,t}^*\text{Lev}_{i,t-1} + \beta_2^* X_{i,t-1} + \beta_3^* Z_{i,t}^*\text{Lev}_{i,t}^* + \varepsilon_{i,t}. \tag{2.10}$$

The dependent variable is firm book leverage ratio, and a one-year lagged dependent variable is used as one of the independent variables. *Leverage*i,t* is the target leverage ratio. Z denotes the variables to capture the mechanical effects. We also control $Z_{i,t}^*\text{Lev}_{i,t}^*$, but to save space, these terms are not reported. We use $\lambda = 1 - \beta_0$ to calculate the active SOA if $\lambda\epsilon(0,1)$. All variables are defined and explained in Appendix 2A. Firm-clustered standard errors are used in the OLS estimation. Coefficients and t-statistics are reported. R^2 and the number of observations are reported. *** indicates significant difference at the 1% level; ** indicates significant difference at the 5% level; and * indicates significant difference at the 10% level.

mean reversion. The classical partial adjustment model, without controlling for the mechanical effects, overestimates the active adjustment speed.

We find that the active adjustment is faster when leverage is below the target than when it is above. In column (6) of Table 2.5, *Leverage*$^*_{i,t-1}$ *Overleveraged* has a coefficient of $0.06(t = 5.88)$, indicating that overleveraged firms adjust slower. This finding is opposite to the result obtained when not controlling for the mechanical effects (column 2 of Table 2.4). This result reconciles the conflict between the risk explanation and the leverage ratchet effects explanation. After controlling for the mechanical effects, the SOA of overleveraged firms decreases by 61.3%, whereas the SOA of underleveraged firms decreases by 6.9%, suggesting that mechanical target adjustment stands for a larger proportion of the target adjustment for overleveraged firms than for underleveraged firms. Overleveraged firms are reluctant to actively cut debt but are more likely to take advantage of market timing opportunities and use the positive profitability shock to reduce leverage, which ultimately results in a low actual SOA. In contrast, the active SOA is faster when firms are below the target leverage ratio, indicating that underleveraged firms are eager to raise the leverage ratio to take better advantage of the tax shield.

Although other financial behaviours drive nearly one-half of leverage target adjustments, capturing the mechanical effects does not reduce the estimated SOA to zero. In Table 2.5, all of the reported SOAs are higher than zero. Overleveraged firms revert at an active speed of 0.075, while underleveraged firms revert at an active speed of 0.162, indicating that a substantial fraction of target adjustment activities is not explained by the mechanical effects. This is consistent with our *Hypothesis Two* that at least some of the target adjustment is discretionary, indicating that firms actively adjust the leverage ratio towards the target. Our evidence argues against the assertion that leverage target adjustments are purely mechanically determined by other financial behaviours.

2.4.3. *Financial constraints and active SOA*

Previous studies (such as Cook and Tang, 2010; Faulkender *et al.*, 2012) suggest that financial constraint has an influence on the SOA because accessibility to the financial market influences the leverage target adjustment. In this section, we investigate the influence of financial constraints on the active target adjustment. We use three popular measures of financial constraints in the literature: firm size (Antoniou *et al.*, 2008; Faulkender *et al.*, 2012), dividend payment (Cook and Tang, 2010; Faulkender *et al.*, 2012),[14] and the KZ index (Kaplan and Zingales, 1997). Specifically, we label the firms below the median size, without paying cash dividend and below the median KZ index value as financially constrained firms, respectively. Regression results are reported in Table 2.6.

The results are consistent with our *Hypothesis Three* that unconstrained firms have a higher active SOA. Although columns (1) and (3) of Table 2.6 report positive coefficients of $Unconstraint^*_{i,t}Leverage_{i,t}$, the coefficients become negative once the mechanical effects are controlled for in columns (2) and (4). These results suggest that classical partial adjustment models might fail to show the relationship between financial constraints and leverage target adjustments. We find that $Unconstraint^*_{i,t}Leverage_{i,t}$ has negative signs in the partitions based on firm size ($-0.045, t = -10.99$), dividend payment ($-0.027, t = -6.81$), and KZ index value ($-0.348, t = -48.25$). These results suggest that unconstrained firms have more discretion with respect to capital and are more willing to adjust their leverage ratios towards the target. In contrast, it is more costly for financially constrained firms to raise external funds. Therefore, these firms are less willing to actively adjust their leverage ratios towards the target. These results are consistent with the previous studies (such as Cook and Tang, 2010; Faulkender *et al.*, 2012), which show that firms with better access to capital markets exhibit a higher adjustment speed, although previous studies do not differentiate between active adjustments and mechanical adjustments.

[14] Antoniou *et al.* (2008) suggest that large firms tend to have a better reputation and more-diversified operation activities and that it is easier (less costly) for them to raise external capital. Faulkender *et al.* (2012) use dividend payment as one measure of the financial constraints and find that dividend-paying firms adjust the leverage ratio substantially faster than non-payers do.

Table 2.6. Financial constraint and the active speed of adjustment.

	(1)	(2)	(3)	(4)	(5)	(6)
Estimation methods	OLS, cluster					
Differentiated by	Size		Dividend payment		KZ Index	
Leverage $i, t-1$	0.816***	0.928***	0.827***	0.912***	0.841***	0.909***
	(164.76)	(205.73)	(123.31)	(113.52)	(228.85)	(277.40)
Unconstraint i,t * Leverage $i, t-1$	0.036*** (8.68)	−0.045*** (−10.99)	0.016*** (4.44)	−0.027*** (−6.81)	−0.359*** (−42.38)	−0.348*** (−48.25)
ΔInv i,t * Leverage $i, t-1$		−0.139*** (−2.58)		−0.138*** (−2.57)		−0.129*** (−2.54)
ΔCash i,t * Leverage $i, t-1$		−0.066** (−2.05)		−0.066** (−2.05)		−0.016 (−0.53)
Equ i,t * Leverage $i, t-1$		−0.164*** (−16.54)		−0.155*** (−15.93)		−0.142*** (−15.22)
ΔNI i,t * Leverage $i, t-1$		−0.118*** (−12.83)		−0.116*** (−12.80)		−0.110*** (−12.59)
Leverage* $i, t-1$	0.175***	0.348***	0.173***	0.342***	0.187***	0.368***
	(18.9)	(29.80)	(18.78)	(29.52)	(20.97)	(32.59)
Constant	0.006***	−0.052***	0.007***	−0.051***	0.023***	−0.039***
	(2.56)	(−19.82)	(3.14)	(−19.46)	(10.37)	(−15.54)
Interactions with moving target		Yes		Yes		Yes
R^2	65.29%	70.2%	65.25%	70.1%	67.5%	72.1%
Observation	201,430	180,834	201,430	180,834	201,430	180,834

Note: This table tests the effect of financial constraint on the active speed of adjustment. The sample includes all of the unregulated Compustat firms, and the sample period is from 1970 to 2016. Columns (2), (4), and (6) use interaction terms to control the mechanical effects. The dependent variable is firm book leverage ratio, and a one-year lagged dependent variable is used as one of the independent variables. $Leverage^*_{i,t}$ is the target leverage ratio. *Unconstraint i,t* is the dummy variable indicating that the firm is not financially constrained. We also control $Z^*_{i,t}\text{Lev}^*_{i,t}$, but to save space, these terms are not reported. All variables are defined and explained in Appendix 2A. Firm-clustered standard errors are used in the OLS estimation. Coefficients and t-statistics are reported. R^2 and the number of observations are reported. *** indicates significant difference at the 1% level; ** indicates significant difference at the 5% level; and * indicates significant difference at the 10% level.

2.4.4. *Robustness*

We perform several tests to check the robustness of our results. We find that our results are robust to alternative measures of the leverage target, alternative definitions of leverage, alternative estimation methods, and when controlling for fractional effects.

First, we use three alternative measures to calculate the leverage target. The first measure extends the baseline measure by using the fixed effects method to capture firm-specific effects because unobservable firm-specific effects are important determinants of firm capital structure (Graham and Leary, 2011). The second measure extends by using the fixed effects method to capture firm-specific effects and by using dummy variables to control heterogeneous features at industry and year levels. The third measure uses a firm-specific median leverage ratio as the leverage target. Compared with the other methods, the third method partitions sample firms into two equally weighted subsamples. The results from using the three alternative measures of the leverage target, as shown in Table 2.7, are qualitatively the same as the baseline results. We find that other financial behaviours generate mechanical leverage target adjustments. The estimated SOA decreases after controlling for the mechanical effects (in columns 2, 4, and 6), but not towards zero.

Second, we use two alternative definitions of leverage to allow our results to be linked to the broader capital structure literature. The first definition scales total debt with the sum of the market value of equity (compared with the book value used in the baseline model) and the book value of total liabilities. Although we agree with Graham *et al.* (2014) that the book leverage ratio is a precise measure of firms' financing decisions, many studies (such as Flannery and Rangan, 2006) use the market leverage ratio. The second definition uses the net leverage ratio (Lambrecht and Myers, 2012), in which we treat firms' cash holdings as negative debt. ΔCash is not used as one of the interaction terms in this specification because cash holdings are already captured by the net leverage ratio. Table 2.8 reports the results. We find that controlling for other financial behaviours decreases the estimated SOA by a smaller extent in the case of the market leverage ratio, possibly because a large amount of variation in the market leverage ratio is accounted for by the stock price. The net leverage ratio shows a faster SOA, possibly indicating that net debt, compared to the general level of debt, is more important to firms.

Table 2.7. Alternative measures of the leverage target.

	(1)	(2)	(3)	(4)	(5)	(6)
Estimation methods	OLS, cluster					
Leverage target	Targetfe		Targetfed		Targetmedian	
Leverage $i, t-1$	0.833***	0.907***	0.832***	0.907***	0.627***	0.790***
	(219.13)	(271.55)	(219.51)	(273.96)	(106.34)	(151.06)
ΔInv i,t * Leverage $i, t-1$		−0.134**		−0.137***		−0.131**
		(−2.52)		(−2.56)		(−2.47)
ΔCash i,t * Leverage $i, t-1$		−0.074**		−0.075**		−0.181**
		(−2.31)		(−2.32)		(−6.60)
Equ i,t * Leverage $i, t-1$		−0.152***		−0.152***		−0.153***
		(−15.88)		(−15.88)		(−15.05)
ΔNI i,t * Leverage $i, t-1$		−0.115**		−0.115***		−0.126***
		(−12.69)		(−12.61)		(−17.47)
Leverage* $i, t-1$	0.172***	0.404***	0.185***	0.408***	0.352***	0.221***
	(16.18)	(28.49)	(18.19)	(30.36)	(58.02)	(39.76)
Constant	0.007***	−0.068***	0.004*	−0.069***	−0.051***	0.011***
	(2.70)	(−20.46)	(1.70)	(−21.82)	(−19.45)	(19.33)
Interactions with moving target		Yes		Yes		Yes
R^2	65.2%	70.1%	65.2%	70.2%	63.8%	68.7%
Observation	201,430	180,834	201,430	180,834	231,038	204,589

Note: This table reports the results of using alternative measures of the leverage target. The sample includes all of the unregulated Compustat firms, and the sample period is from 1970 to 2016. Columns (2), (4), and (6) use interaction terms to control the mechanical effects. The dependent variable is firm book leverage ratio, and a one-year lagged dependent variable is used as one of the independent variables. *Leverage**i,t is the target leverage ratio. *Targetfe* extends by using fixed effects method to capture firm-specific effects. *Targetfed* extends by using fixed effects method to capture firm-specific effects, and using dummy variables to control heterogeneous features at industry and year levels. *Targetmedian* uses firm-specific median leverage ratio as the leverage target. We also control $Z^*_{i,t}\text{Lev}^*_{i,t}$, but to save space, these terms are not reported. All variables are defined and explained in Appendix 2A. Firm-clustered standard errors are used in the OLS estimation. Coefficients and t-statistics are reported. R^2 and the number of observations are reported. *** indicates significant difference at the 1% level; ** indicates significant difference at the 5% level; and * indicates significant difference at the 10% level.

Table 2.8. Alternative definitions of leverage.

	(1)	(2)	(3)	(4)
	OLS, cluster			
Estimation methods	Market leverage		Net leverage	
Leverage $i, t-1$	0.859***	0.878***	0.649***	0.695***
	(487.50)	(491.38)	(96.00)	(98.60)
ΔInv i,t * Leverage $i, t-1$		−0.170***		−1.274***
		(−4.89)		(−15.90)
ΔCash i,t * Leverage $i, t-1$		−0.616***		
		(−16.38)		
Equ i,t * Leverage $i, t-1$		−0.199***		−0.057***
		(−14.59)		(−4.61)
ΔROA i,t * Leverage $i, t-1$		−0.099***		0.010
		(−13.18)		(0.237)
Leverage* $i, t-1$	0.088***	0.408***	0.264***	0.165***
	(22.54)	(30.36)	(19.64)	(16.13)
Constant	0.023***	−0.069***	0.023***	0.028***
	(25.42)	(−21.82)	(10.66)	(15.15)
Interactions with moving target		Yes		Yes
R^2	72.6%	74.9%	49.07%	51.19%
Observation	199,880	179,517	185,038	180,575

Note: This table reports the results of using alternative definitions of leverage. Market leverage is defined by total debt over the sum of market value of equity and the book value of total liabilities. Net leverage treats cash holdings as negative debt. The sample includes all of the unregulated Compustat firms, and the sample period is from 1970 to 2016. Columns (2) and (4) use interaction terms to control the mechanical effects. The dependent variable is the leverage ratio, and a one-year lagged dependent variable is used as one of the independent variables. *Leverage*i,t* is the target leverage ratio re-estimated using the new definitions of debt. We also control $Z_{i,t}$*$\text{Lev}^*_{i,t}$, but to save space, these terms are not reported. All variables are defined and explained in Appendix 2A. Firm-clustered standard errors are used in the OLS estimation. Coefficients and t-statistics are reported. R^2 and the number of observations are reported. *** indicates significant difference at the 1% level; ** indicates significant difference at the 5% level; and * indicates significant difference at the 10% level.

Our main findings of the mechanical effects and the active target adjustment are robust to different definitions of the leverage ratio.

Third, we use alternative estimation methods to test the mechanical effects and estimate the active adjustment speed. In the first test, we use OLS estimation and introduce dummy variables to capture industry and year effects in the second-step regression. In the second test, we use the fixed effects method in the second-step regression.

Firm-specific effects explain over 32.4% of the variance in leverage, according to column (4) of Table 2.9. In the third test, we use system GMM (SYS-GMM) to address the potential endogeneity problem. Antoniou *et al.* (2008) and Wintoki *et al.* (2012) highlight the endogeneity problem in corporate finance studies; they propose using SYS-GMM to estimate the dynamic model and control the endogeneity problem. Flannery and Hankins (2013) compare a few methods and suggest that SYS-GMM is the most robust method to estimate the dynamic capital structure model with the endogeneity problem. We find that the three methods report qualitatively similar results according to Table 2.9.[15] The estimated active SOA using OLS (0.1 in column 2) is economically very close to that estimated using SYS-GMM (0.088 in column 6), indicating that our results are robust to different estimation methods.

Fourth, we remove the observations close to the boundary 0 or 1 of the leverage ratio to reduce the fractional effects. A few studies (such as Chang and Dasgupta, 2009; Elsas and Florysiak, 2015) question the classical partial adjustment model because leverage is technically bounded between 0 and 1. The boundary has the potential to lead to a mechanical reversion. To reduce this effect, we use the common practice of dropping extreme leverage values (as done by, e.g. Hovakimian and Li, 2011; Oztekin and Flannery, 2012) and remove the observations with a leverage ratio greater than 95% or less than 5%.[16] We find that the results in Table 2.10 are very close to the baseline results in Table 2.5, suggesting that the extended partial adjustment model is immune to the fractional effects and that the observed active adjustment is not driven by the boundaries of the leverage ratio.

---

[15] Although we used collapsed instrumental variables (IVs) to reduce the number of IVs and our IVs appear to be exogenous according to the results of the AR(2) test, because we use a very long time period, the SYS-GMM estimation might not avoid the potential over-identification problem, as shown by the results of the Hansen test (P-value = 0.00). Please refer to Wintoki *et al.* (2012) for explanations of these tests.

[16] We also tried to remove the observations with a leverage ratio less than 0.1 or greater than 0.9, which generate similar results. To save space, we do not report these results.

Table 2.9. Alternative estimation methods.

	(1)	(2)	(3)	(4)	(5)	(6)
Estimation methods	OLS, dummy		FE		SYS-GMM	
Leverage $i, t-1$	0.823***	0.900***	0.646***	0.748***	0.749***	0.912***
	(203.15)	(248.97)	(102.96)	(127.3)	(89.97)	(28.89)
ΔInv i,t * Leverage $i, t-1$		−0.146**		−0.136**		−0.120
		(−2.73)		(−2.54)		(−0.20)
ΔCash i,t * Leverage $i, t-1$		−0.066**		−0.071**		−0.062
		(−2.06)		(−2.20)		(−0.23)
Equ i,t * Leverage $i, t-1$		−0.148***		−0.139***		−0.230***
		(−15.30)		(−12.56)		(−3.55)
ΔROA i,t * Leverage $i, t-1$		−0.115**		−0.103***		−0.218***
		(−12.66)		(−11.45)		(−4.84)
Leverage* $i, t-1$	0.189***	0.446***	0.206***	0.670***	0.359***	0.577***
	(16.79)	(29.13)	(11.77)	(28.17)	(13.41)	(10.69)
Constant	−0.032***	−0.128***	0.045***	−0.094***	−0.021***	−0.116***
	(−7.14)	(−22.59)	(9.98)	(−15.72)	(−3.17)	(−8.92)
Number of IVs					93	93
AR(2)					0.637	0.691
Hansen test p-value					0.000	0.000
Interactions with moving target		Yes		Yes		Yes
Variance due to firm fixed effects			33.6%	32.4%		
R^2	65.6%	70.5%	65.2%	79.0%		
Observation	201,430	180,834	201,430	180,834	201,430	180,834

Note: This table reports the results of using alternative estimation methods. The sample includes all of the unregulated Compustat firms, and the sample period is from 1970 to 2016. Columns (2), (4), and (6) use interaction terms to control the mechanical effects. The dependent variable is firm book leverage ratio, and a one-year lagged dependent variable is used as one of the independent variables. *Leverage*i,t* is the target leverage ratio. We also control $Z_{i,t}$*$\text{Lev}^*_{i,t}$, but to save space, these terms are not reported. All variables are defined and explained in Appendix 2A. The first method uses OLS estimation and dummy variables to capture industry effects and year effects. The second test uses fixed effects method. We also report the percentage of variance due to firm fixed effects. The third test uses system GMM to address the potential endogeneity issue. We report the number of instrumental variables (IVs) and the results of the AR(2) and Hansen tests. Coefficients and t-statistics (z-stats in SYS-GMM estimation) are reported. R^2 and the number of observations are reported. *** indicates significant difference at the 1% level; ** indicates significant difference at the 5% level; and * indicates significant difference at the 10% level.

Table 2.10. Control the fractional nature.

	(1)	(2)	(3)	(4)	(5)	(6)
Estimation methods	OLS, cluster					
	Overleveraged		Underleveraged		Pooled	
Leverage $i, t-1$	0.847***	0.916***	0.713***	0.766***	0.832***	0.883***
	(212.48)	(235.44)	(88.61)	(94.46)	(344.66)	(380.76)
ΔInv i,t * Leverage $i, t-1$		−0.137		−0.344***		−0.222***
		(−1.57)		(−2.97)		(−5.19)
ΔCash i,t * Leverage $i, t-1$		−0.151*		−0.194		−0.111***
		(−1.92)		(−1.40)		(−2.68)
Equ i,t * Leverage $i, t-1$		−0.675***		−0.266***		−0.480***
		(−19.82)		(−7.61)		(−30.14)
ΔROA i,t * Leverage $i, t-1$		−0.243***		−0.326***		−0.257***
		(−7.05)		(−8.43)		(−17.34)
Leverage* $i, t-1$	0.067***	0.149***	0.168***	0.215***	0.094***	0.170***
	(7.30)	(17.86)	(17.68)	(19.51)	(16.40)	(27.14)
Constant	0.035***	−0.007***	0.033***	0.011***	0.034***	0.002
	(15.33)	(−3.44)	(14.72)	(4.41)	(21.95)	(1.42)
Interactions with moving target		Yes		Yes		Yes
R^2	57.16%	64.2%	28.63%	33.59%	65.64%	70.0%
Observation	75,789	67,456	60,526	53,334	136,315	120,790

Note: This table reports the results of controlling the fractional nature. The sample includes all of the unregulated Compustat firms, and the sample period is from 1970 to 2016. Columns (2), (4), and (6) use interaction terms to control the mechanical effects. We exclude those observations when the leverage ratio is below 5% or above 95%. The dependent variable is firm book leverage ratio, and a one-year lagged dependent variable is used as one of the independent variables. $Leverage^*_{i,t}$ is the target leverage ratio. We also control $Z^*_{i,t}\text{Lev}^*_{i,t}$, but to save space, these terms are not reported. All variables are defined and explained in Appendix 2A. Firm-clustered standard errors are used in the OLS estimation. Coefficients and t-statistics are reported. R^2 and the number of observations are reported. *** indicates significant difference at the 1% level; ** indicates significant difference at the 5% level; and * indicates significant difference at the 10% level.

2.5. Conclusion

Recent studies question whether firms' leverage target adjustments are mechanically determined (Shyam-Sunder and Myers, 1999; Chang and Dasgupta, 2009) and whether the classical partial adjustment model (Flannery and Rangan, 2006) provides a valid estimation of the true adjustment speed (Hovakimian and Li, 2011, 2012). This chapter explains why and how other financial behaviours lead to mechanical target adjustments. Methodologically, we extend the classical partial adjustment model by using interaction terms to capture the mechanical effects of other financial behaviours (i.e. investment, cash holdings, equity issuance, and profitability) on leverage target adjustments.

We provide an explanation for the mean reversion in leverage by investigating the extent to which other financing behaviours mechanically drive leverage target adjustments and whether there are discretionary target adjustments. We find that other financial behaviours have a mechanical effect on the leverage target adjustment. Specifically, equity issuance and variation in net income are associated with the target adjustment of overleveraged firms, whereas investment and cash holdings are associated with the target adjustment of underleveraged firms. These results suggest that overleveraged firms are more likely to use equity market timing opportunities and positive income shocks to adjust leverage and that underleveraged firms are more likely to use investment opportunities and the variation in the demand for cash holdings to adjust leverage. On average, the mechanical effects constitute 45% of the observed leverage target adjustments using the classical partial adjustment model.

In addition to mechanical reversion, firms also actively adjust their leverage ratios. We find that controlling for the mechanical effects does not reduce the estimated SOA to zero, indicating that leverage target adjustments are not completely driven by other financial behaviours. Approximately 55% of leverage target adjustments are discretionarily determined. Overleveraged firms are relatively reluctant to actively cut debt and hence more likely to take advantage of the opportunities to mechanically adjust their leverage ratios. In contrast, underleveraged firms show a stronger willingness to actively adjust their leverage ratios, as predicted by the leverage ratchet effect theory (Admati *et al.*, 2018). Compared with financially constrained firms, unconstrained firms with more access to capital show a faster active SOA.

Our empirical evidence points to a unified theory of capital structure in which firms consider both targeting an optimal leverage ratio and balancing the budget constraint. This study observes both mechanical adjustments and active target adjustments. This finding is also robust to alternative measures of the leverage target, alternative definitions of leverage, alternative estimation methods, and when controlling for the fractional effects. These results suggest that mechanical adjustments and discretionary adjustments coexist. The classical partial adjustment model overestimates the SOA. Hence, we suggest that further studies should consider the benefits of balancing the budget constraint, together with the classical factors in the trade-off theory (such as tax shield, bankruptcy costs, and adjustment costs) when analysing firms' financing decisions.

Appendix 2A

Definitions of Variables

Briefs	Variables	Definitions	Sources and reasons for inclusion
Lev	Leverage	Total debt/Total assets (book value)	To measure firm leverage (Graham *et al.*, 2014), in which total debt is measured by the sum of long-term and short-term debts
	Debt issuance (repurchase) ratio	(Total debt_t − Total debt_{t-1})/Total assets_t	To measure annual debt net issuance (or repurchase if < 0), used in Fama and French (2002) and Graham *et al.* (2014)
Levm	Market leverage	Total debt/(Total debt + Market value of equity)	We use the market leverage ratio (defined following Graham *et al.*, 2014) to test the robustness of our results
Tan	Tangibility	Tangible assets/ Total assets	To measure firm tangibility, following Rajan and Zingales (1995), we use property, plant, and equipment divided by total assets to measure tangibility
M/B	Market-to-book ratio	(Market value of equity + Book value of total liability)/Book value of total assets	To measure firm growth rate, following Rajan and Zingales (1995), we use M/B to capture potential investment opportunities
ROA	Return on assets	Earnings before interest and tax/Total assets	To measure firm profitability, we follow Rajan and Zingales (1995)

(*Continued*)

Briefs	Variables	Definitions	Sources and reasons for inclusion
NI	Net income	Net income/Total assets	To capture firm net income, following Lambrecht and Myers (2012), who use net income in the budget constraint equation
Inv	Investment to assets	Capital expenditure/ Total assets	To measure firm investment, we follow
Cash	Cash holdings to assets ratio	Cash/Total assets	To measure firm cash holdings, we follow
Equ	Equity issuance (repur-chase) ratio	(ΔShareholders' equity$_t$ − ΔRetained earnings t)/ Total assets	Being consistent with the measurement for debt issuance (Graham *et al.*, 2014), we use the increase (decrease) in equity scaled by total assets to measure equity issuance (repurchase) speed
Deficit	Financing deficit	(ΔTotal assets − ΔRetained earnings)/Total assets	To capture the demand for external capital (Fama and French, 2005)

References

Admati, A. R., Demarzo, P. M., Hellwig, M. F., and Pfleiderer, P. (2018). The leverage ratchet effect. *Journal of Finance*, 73(1), 145–198.

Antoniou, A., Guney, Y., and Paudyal, K. (2008). The determinants of capital structure: Capital market-oriented versus bank-oriented institutions. *Journal of Financial and Quantitative Analysis*, 43(1), 59–92.

Baker, M. and Wurgler, J. (2002). Market timing and capital structure. *Journal of Finance*, 57(1), 1–32.

Berger, P. G., Ofek, E., and Yermack, D. L. (1997). Managerial entrenchment and capital structure decisions. *Journal of Finance*, 52(4), 1411–1438.

Chang, X. and Dasgupta, S. (2009). Target behaviour and financing: how conclusive is the evidence, *Journal of Finance*, 64(4), 1767–1796.

Cook, D. O. and Tang, T. (2010). Macroeconomic conditions and capital structure adjustment speed. *Journal of Corporate Finance*, 16(1), 73–87.

DeAngelo, H. and Roll, R. (2015). How stable are corporate capital structures? *Journal of Finance*, 70(1), 373–418.

Drobetz, W., Schilling, D. C., and Schroder, H. (2015). Heterogeneity in the speed of capital structure adjustment across countries and over the business cycle. *European Financial Management*, 21(5), 936–973.

Elsas, R. and Florysiak, D. (2015). Dynamic capital structure adjustment and the impact of fractional dependent variables. *Journal of Financial and Quantitative Analysis*, 50(5), 1105–1133.

Fama, E. F. and French, K, R, (2002). Testing trade-off and pecking order predictions about dividends and debt. *The Review of Financial Studies*, 15 (1), 1–33.

Fama, E. F. and French, K. R. (2005). Financial decisions: who issues stock. *Journal of Financial Economics*, 76(3), 549–582.

Faulkender, M., Flannery, M. J., Hankins, K. W., and Smith, J. M. (2012). Cash flows and leverage adjustments. *Journal of Financial Economics*, 103(3), 632–646.

Flannery, M. J. and Hankins, K. W. (2013). Estimating dynamic panel models in corporate finance. *Journal of Corporate Finance*, 19, 1–19.

Flannery, M. J. and Rangan., K. P. (2006). Partial adjustment toward target capital structures. *Journal of Financial Economics*, 79(3), 469–506.

Graham, J. R. and Leary, M. T. (2011). A review of empirical capital structure research and directions for the future. *Annual Review of Financial Economics*, 3, 309–345.

Graham, J. R., Leary, M. T., and Roberts, M. R. (2014). A century of capital structure: The leveraging of corporate America. *Journal of Financial Economics*, 118(3), 658–683.

Hovakimian, A. and Li, G. (2011). In search of conclusive evidence: How to test for adjustment to target capital structure. *Journal of corporate Finance*, 17(1), 33–44.

Hovakimian, A. and Li, G. (2012). Is the partial adjustment model a useful tool for capital structure research? *Review of Finance*, 16(3), 733–754.

Hovakimian, A., Opler, T., and Titman, S. (2001). The debt-equity choice. *Journal of Financial and Quantitative Analysis*, 36(1), 1–24.

Jalilvand, A. and Harris, R. S. (1984). Corporate behaviour in adjusting to capital structure and dividend targets: An econometric study. *Journal of Finance*, 39(1), 127–145.

Jensen, M. C. (1986). Agency costs of free cash flow, corporate finance, and takeovers. *American Economic Review*, 76(2), 323–329.

Kaplan, S. N. and Zingales, L. (1997). Do investment-cash flow sensitivities provide useful measures of financing constraints? *Quarterly Journal of Economics*, 112(1), 169–215.

Kraus, A. and Litzenberger, R. H. (1973). A state-preference model of optimal financial leverage. *Journal of Finance*, 28(4), 911–922.

Lambrecht, B. M. and Myers, S. C. (2012). A Lintner model of payout and managerial rents. *Journal of Finance*, 67(5), 1761–1810.

Leary, M. T. and Roberts, M. R. (2010). Do peer firms affect corporate financial policy? *Journal of Financial Economics*, 95(3), 332–355.

Lemmon, M. L. and Zender, J. F. (2010). Debt capacity and test of capital structure theories. *Journal of Financial and Quantitative Analysis*, 49(5), 1161–1187.

Li, S., Hoque, H., and Thijssen, J. (2018). Firm financial behaviour dynamics and interactions: A Structural Vector Autoregression approach. *University of York*, Working Paper.

Myers, S. C. and Majluf, N. S. (1984). Corporate financing and investment decisions when firms have information that investors do not have. *Journal of Financial Economics*, 13(2), 187–221.

Modigliani, F. and Miller, M. H. (1963). Corporate income taxes and the cost of capital: A correction. *American Economic Review*, 53(3), 433–443.

Oztekin, O. and Flannery, M. J. (2012). Institutional determinants of capital structure adjustment speeds. *Journal of Financial Economics*, 103(1), 88–112.

Rajan, R. G. and Zingales, L. (1995). What do we know about capital structure? Some evidence from international data. *Journal of Finance*, 50(5), 1421–1460.

Shyam-Sunder, L. and Myers, S. C. (1999). Testing static tradeoff against pecking order models of capital structure. *Journal of Financial Economics*, 51(2), 219–244.

Strebulaev, I. and Yang, B. (2013). The mystery of zero-leverage firms. *Journal of Financial Economics*, 109(1), 1–23.

Wintoki, M. B., Linck, J., and Netter, J. M. (2012). Endogeneity and the dynamics of internal corporate governance. *Journal of Financial Economics*, 105(3), 581–606.

https://doi.org/10.1142/9781800617032_0003

Chapter 3

Corporate Innovation and IPO Survival: Evidence from the UK Alternative Investment Market

Tariq Qaysi*, Wasim Ahmad†, and Eilnaz Kashefi-Pour‡

**Prince Sattam Bin Abdulaziz University, Al-Kharj, Saudi Arabia*

†Heriot-Watt University, Dubai

‡University of Birmingham, Birmingham, UK

3.1. Introduction

Corporate innovation and its effect on a firm's productivity, profitability, competitive advantage, and long-term performance have been well researched and acknowledged in prior studies (Porter and Wayland, 1992; Baer, 2012; Atalay *et al.*, 2013; Tuan *et al.*, 2016). As documented in the literature, innovation activities not only play a critical role in driving the long-term performance of corporations but also contribute to promoting the economic growth and development of countries (Solow, 1956). Over the past 40 years, the technological companies in the US market have accounted for almost 40% of all listed companies, as shown by Bernstein (2015). While some studies in the existing literature have investigated the determinants of the failure risk and survival of large, mature companies using various innovation proxies, such as patents and R&D (e.g. Wagner and Cockburn, 2010; Useche, 2015; Guo and Zhou, 2016), the influential power of pre-listing innovation profiles on the aftermarket survival likelihood of small, young, and fast-growing initial public offering

(IPO) and highlight initial public offering companies is, to the best of our knowledge, limited and inconclusive.

For example, focusing on the high-tech companies listed on Germany's Neuer stock exchange over the period 1997–2002, Audretsch and Lehmann (2005) find a negative and significant relationship between firms' innovation activity prior to going public and the time-to-failure of high-tech IPOs after going public. Cao *et al.* (2015) document that newly listed firms backed by venture capitalists and with at least one patent application at the time of going public significantly outperform those without patent applications. In addition to Audretsch and Lehmann (2005), Wagner and Cockburn (2010) also examine the impact of patenting activities prior to going public on the post-IPO survival profile of a sample of 356 internet-based companies that went public on the US NASDAQ during the dot-com bubble. They find that IPO firms that filed a good number of patents during the dot-com period experienced lower risks of collapse and were more likely to survive longer in the stock market after the bubble compared to those without any patent applications. Similarly, Useche (2015) reaffirms previous studies by reporting that the number of patents held by newly listed software firms is negatively correlated with post-IPO failure risk and acquisition; however, higher patent quality can increase a firm's attractiveness as an acquisition target.

Considering the evidence from the previous studies, we believe that this study stands apart due to the following reasons. First of all, unlike previous studies, which explored the link between corporate innovation and long-term performance, focusing predominantly on large, well-established listed companies in highly regulated markets, particularly those in the US market, this study focuses on the small, young, and fast-growing companies that are either unable or have difficulty going public on upper-regulated markets, known as primarily stock markets (e.g. the London Stock Exchange, LSE, and the New York Stock Exchange, NYSE), due to their characteristics and listing requirements. In the literature, small and young listed companies are often viewed as risky corporates with a lower survival probability, as argued by Carpentier and Suret (2011) and Vismara *et al.* (2012). Moreover, Gerakos *et al.* (2013) and Nielsson (2013) claim that Alternative Investment Market (AIM) IPO firms are quite different from those listed on the Main Market of the LSE and other highly regulated US stock exchanges in terms of their characteristics. In addition, Mendoza (2008) states that the US NASDAQ stock exchange is no longer a junior stock market for small and high-growth companies; it has shifted its attention and listing standards to attract primarily large and mature private companies. Second, in contrast to the existing literature, our study assesses the effect of pre-listing corporate innovation activities on the survival profiles of both high-tech IPOs and non-high-tech companies. Finally, the AIM is the leading and most popular secondary market in the EU and the world. Since the opening of the AIM in mid-1995, it has attracted more domestic and foreign businesses to the market compared to other markets in the world, even during periods of economic crash such as the dot-com bubble and the global financial crisis, when most stock markets around the world saw a significant drop in the number of IPOs and market admissions.[1]

In this study, we aim to answer the following questions: (1) Does pre-listing innovation activities improve the survivability of small and young IPO firms after going public? If so, (2) to what extent, and (3) does the effect of pre-listing innovation differ across various market industries? (4) How do survival rates compare between newly listed firms engaging in such activities and those not doing so? The answers to these questions are important not only for the firm's shareholders and directors planning to take their private companies public market to expand and increase the firm's future growth but also for market regulators, policymakers, and the other market participants (e.g. investors, creditors, venture capitalists, and private equity companies) for the success and sustainability of the

[1]According to issues and IPO data from the LSE website, during the period from 1995 to the end of December 2012, more than 3,901 companies have joined the AIM, accounting for approximately 67% of the total LSE admissions. The remaining 33% of companies went public on the Main Market of the LSE. In addition, looking at the IPO activity data from the US and UK markets, we find that from 2001 to the end of 2007, the US stock market crash of 2001 had an adverse impact on the IPO listings in the US markets, shifting the attention of the private companies to the UK stock markets, specifically to the AIM. For example, over the period from 2004 to 2006, AIM attracted over 856 companies compared to only 223 and 489 companies which joined the LSE Main Market and the US markets, respectively. The number of IPOs in the AIM segment peaked in 2005, when 335 private companies were admitted.

stock market. Unlike highly standardised and regulated stock markets (e.g. the primary market of the LSE, NYSE, and NASDAQ capital markets), the extant empirical evidence from the second-tier markets (including the AIM) has documented that, over the past two decades, firms listed on these stock exchanges have shown a higher risk of failure within their first five years after market listing.[2] For example, Espenlaub *et al.* (2012), Vismara *et al.* (2012), and Amini and Keasey (2013) find that almost half of the newly listed firms admitted into the AIM segment of the LSE have delisted from the market within five years after going public due to negative reasons or mergers and acquisitions (M&As).[3] Therefore, based on the above evidence and empirical findings from the existing innovation studies (e.g. Atalay *et al.*, 2013; Audretsch and Lehmann, 2005; Tuan *et al.*, 2016; Wagner and Cockburn, 2010; Useche, 2015; Guo and Zhou, 2016), we expect that pre-listing innovation and its competitive advantage and capabilities will lead to a lower risk of failure for newly listed firms and increase their survival times after going public.

Using unique hand-collected data resulting in a sample of 463 non-financial UK and non-UK incorporated IPO firms that went public on the London's AIM between 2005 and 2012, our study provides new insights about the existing innovation and corporate finance literature. It confirms that a pre-listing firm's innovation is not only an important determining factor for the survival of large, high-tech companies, but it can also improve the survival rate and period of small, young newly listed companies. Following the works of Galasso and Simcoe (2011), Wagner and Cockburn (2010),

[2]In the US market, Schultz (1993) finds that the three-year failure rate for unit IPOs is 42%. Hensler *et al.* (1997) report that, by the end of the fifth year, the failure rate for IPOs is 28%. This value is 28% in the study by Jain and Kini (2000), 58.5 % in Fama and French's (2004) study, 45% in Kooli and Meknassi's (2007) study, 35% in Jain and Kini's (2008) investigation, and 7.5% in Gounopoulos and Pham's (2018) analysis. In the Main Market of the LSE, Ahmad and Jelic (2014) report that the five-year survival rate for UK IPOs is 69%. For more empirical evidence on IPO survival, please see Section 3.3.

[3]For example, Bradley *et al.* (2006) examine the survival profiles of penny stock versus non-penny stocks listed on the US market and report that the three-year (five-year) failure rate of non-penny stock is almost 32% (51%) compared to 6% (14%) for penny stocks.

Cefis and Marsili (2006), Hirshleifer *et al.* (2018), and Cumming *et al.* (2020), a pre-listing innovation in this study is measured based on (3.1) the number of successful patent applications that the IPO firm had filed prior to the date of going public and (3.2) the total number of pre-listing patent applications divided by the total assets at the time of IPO. For the purpose of comparison, in line with many innovation studies, we use patent citation data and an innovation dummy as additional proxies to capture an IPO firm's innovation profile. Although patenting information is not the most appropriate proxy for capturing a firm's innovation, as it only considers the outputs of the firm's innovation, scholars in the existing literature argue that patenting-related data remain the best and direct proxy for measuring the quantity and economic value of innovation (e.g. Bernstein, 2015; Aghion *et al.*, 2013). While R&D spending is a good measure to capture the inputs of innovation, this information is not available in the IPO prospectus and annual reports of small and young companies, particularly for AIM IPOs (Cao *et al.*, 2013; Hirshleifer *et al.*, 2013). Moreover, with respect to empirical analyses in the corporate finance literature, consistent with most recent studies, we find that patenting data are commonly and widely used over R&D spending information to measure a firm's innovation at the time of its IPO. Lerner *et al.* (2011) and Baranchuk *et al.* (2014) argue that, in recent years, patenting-related data have emerged as the best and most acceptable innovation data for investigating the impact of innovations.

Using various survival methods, specifically the Kaplan–Meier (KM) survival method and the accelerated failure time (AFT) model, we find a positive and significant effect of pre-listing patenting activities on the aftermarket survival periods of small and young IPO firms, in line with the conclusions of Audretsch (1995), Wagner and Cockburn (2010), Useche (2015), and Zhang *et al.* (2018). This suggests that IPO firms with higher innovation profiles and more patent applications prior to going public are more likely to experience lower failure risks and tend to survive longer in the subsequent years following the IPO. More specifically, the results show that a one-unit increase in the number of pre-listing patents leads to an approximate 16% increase in the survival time of small and young firms in the subsequent period. In addition to that, with all else held equal, sensitivity tests also show that an increase of one standard deviation in the number of pre-listing patents correlates with an increase of nearly 24 months in the average predicted survival time of the new issuers. Finally, inspired by the studies of Chemmanur and Tian (2018) and Mazouz and Zhao (2019), this study further explores if the survival time is affected by whether or not the IPO firm operates in a highly competitive environment. We find that a higher degree of market competition amplifies the effect of pre-listing innovation profiles on the survival time of IPO firms. This influence is more pronounced in highly competitive industries compared to less competitive ones (24.3% vs. 12.5%, respectively). The results are robust to a series of additional tests, including alternative estimation models, different definitions of failure and survival, alternative measurements of corporate innovation, different tracking periods, and endogeneity.

The study makes several valuable contributions to the existing innovation and IPO literature. First, while prior literature (e.g. Hsu, 2014; Porter and Wayland, 1992; Maksimovic and Pichler, 2015; Cao *et al.*, 2015; Guo and Zhou, 2016; Bedford *et al.*, 2021) well acknowledges the impact of corporate innovation on a firm's profitability and future performance, focusing mainly on large companies in highly regulated markets, the role of pre-listing innovation on smaller and newly established firms is not well investigated due to data limitations on these firms. Given the data availability in this study and the impressive growth in the number of firms on the AIM, it is important to examine the role of pre-listing corporate innovation on post-market long-term performance and survivability. Furthermore, in contrast to previous studies, the depth of data in EPO's Worldwide Patent Statistical Database (PATSTAT) allows us to obtain information not only about innovation activities of firms that filed patents in one country but also about all patent applications filed globally (Cumming *et al.*, 2020). To the best of our knowledge, this analysis is the first to explore the direct relationship between corporate innovation and post-market survival of small and high-risk issuers. Given the importance of innovation activities for creating and maintaining long-term competitive advantage, these data allow us to consider the effects of corporate innovation on the survival probability of the high-tech IPOs across various market sectors.

Second, our extended investigation also contributes to the literature on the determinants of IPO survival and failure by adding new insights into the important role of pre-listing innovation activities as a vital determinant for the success and survival of small and young issuers. Audretsch (1995) and Agarwal (1998) argue that innovation is the key driver behind rapid growth and profitability of small companies. Earlier studies have documented various positive and negative effects of numerous firm-level and IPO-level characteristics on the survivability of new issues after listing. Some of these characteristics are as follows: firm age and size (e.g. Hensler *et al.*, 1997; Demers and Joos, 2007); venture capital (VC) participation (Jain and Kini, 2000); the quality of audit backing (Jain and Martin Jr., 2005); insider ownerships (Audretsch and Lehmann, 2005); board structure and effectiveness (Goktan *et al.*, 2018; Chancharat *et al.*, 2012); nominated advisors (Espenlaub *et al.*, 2012); lockup agreement (Ahmad and Jelic, 2014); earning management (e.g. Alhadab *et al.*, 2015; Anagnostopoulou *et al.*, 2021); CEO's work experience and power (Gounopoulos and Pham, 2018; Kashefi Pour, 2015); geographic dispersion (Gounopoulos and Huang, 2018); and, most recently, CEO compensation (Colak *et al.*, 2021). Our study further provides additional evidence that a strong patenting profile in the period before going public can enhance the survival profile of an IPO after its offering.

The remaining sections of this chapter are structured as follows. In Section 3.2, we review the most relevant theories and literature on IPO survival and the determinants of corporate innovation, followed by hypothesis development. In Section 3.3, we discuss our sample selection procedure, data sources, and the measurement of corporate innovation. Section 3.4 discusses the empirical methods we used to test our main hypothesis. Section 3.5 provides various descriptive statistics, estimated empirical results, and robustness tests. In Section 3.6, we conclude this study.

3.2. Related Literature and Hypothesis Development

3.2.1. *Theoretical framework*

The first theoretical perspective that may explain the relationship between pre-listing corporate innovation and post-IPO survival is the agency theory. In the literature, scholars argue that IPO markets are characterised by high information asymmetry because the investors in these markets are less informed in comparison to the firm's insiders about the firm's financial and operational performance. The theory assumes that the agency problem arises when the firm's agents (e.g. managers and executives) make decisions based on their personal interests rather than the interests of the firm's principals (e.g. shareholders). Brav and Gompers (1997), Chan *et al.* (2008), and Field and Lowry (2009) argue that most of the newly listed firms in the IPO markets are young, high-growth companies, which are susceptible to information asymmetry and agency problems. Moreover, Holmstrom (1989) claims that the agency costs associated with innovation projects are very high because these projects are high-risk investments with a high possibility of failure while offering lower returns. In addition, they are unpredictable, involve long-term and multi-stage investments, and require more human capital and resources. Therefore, based on this theory and given the high risk linked with innovation investments, we therefore expect that disclosing innovation information in the IPO prospectus at the time of going public reduces the firm's information asymmetry and the agency costs between the managers and the firm's shareholders as well as the firm's potential investors. This would lead to lower agency conflict and uncertainty and, consequently, improve the performance and survival time of the IPO firm after going public.

The second theory that we also believe can provide another theoretical framework for the relationship between corporate innovation and post-IPO performance and survival is the upper echelons theory, proposed by Hambrick and Mason (1984). The theory suggests that the decisions made by the firm's managers and directors, including investment and strategic decisions, such as innovation projects, can be influenced by the directors' past work background, experiences, personalities, cultures, and values. In the literature, a number of studies have attempted to explain the direct and indirect effects of various managerial characteristics on firm performance and overall firm-level decisions, such as investment projects. Some studies report that corporate innovation and its impact on future performance and survival are mainly explained by managerial attributes (e.g. past experience and confidence), as documented by Custodio *et al.* (2017), Balsmeier *et al.* (2014), and Yuan and Wen (2018). For example, Cho *et al.* (2016) examine the variation in firms' innovation productivity by focusing on the effect of various firm and manager characteristics. They find that, relative to the firms' characteristics, managers' attributes have less impact on firm innovation. Lin *et al.* (2011) find a positive impact of the CEO's education level and professional experience on the firm's innovation outcomes. Balsmeier *et al.* (2017) claim that the presence of independent directors on the firm's board not only improves governance and reduces agency costs but also improves the firm's innovation.

Third, according to the pecking-order theory, innovation projects involve high costs, and firms, in particular, small and high-growth companies, can only access a limited and relatively small amount of capital from external financing entities. In this case, the financial constraints may impact the firm's innovative activities, leading to fewer innovation projects or stopping them altogether, which could harm the firm's position in the market as well as its growth and survivability. This is especially true for firms operating in highly competitive markets (Audretsch, 1995; Chemmanur and Tian, 2018; Hottenrott *et al.*, 2016; Giannetti, 2012; Cefis and Marsili, 2006). Therefore, due to the above reasons and arguments, innovation projects are risky investments and associated with higher uncertainty; thus, a higher information asymmetry in the market may lead to greater financial constraints and therefore an increased risk of failure. As a result, external lenders may refuse to finance a firm's innovation projects if the firm's resources are concentrated mostly on intangible investments.

3.2.2. *IPO survival*

Evidence from the existing IPO literature has documented that, even though going public provides newly listed firms with numerous advantages over being a private company, such as capital raising and enhancing public image and visibility (e.g. Ritter, 1991; Bancel and Mittoo, 2009), during the transition from private to public ownership, most new issuers often face a number of business and governance challenges. These include increased market competition, new governance mechanisms, investor scrutiny, inspection by analysts, and more institutional investors, as discussed by Jain and Kini (2008), Ritter (1987), and Chemmanur and Fulghieri (1999), which may negatively and significantly affect the firm's operation, decisions, future performance, and survivability in the stock market (Welbourne and Andrews, 1996; Agarwal and Gort, 1996).

Examining the survival of all IPOs listed in the US market over the period from 1975 to 1984, Hensler *et al.* (1997) find that a higher level of debt at the time of issuing adversely and significantly reduces the survival time of newly listed firms and increases the risk of failure after going public. Schultz (1993) finds that larger and older issuers at the time of the IPO are more likely to survive longer after the IPO. Jain and Kini (2000) investigate the role of venture capital (VC) participation in the IPO process and board decisions; they find that the survival time of new issuers is positively and significantly increased if the IPO firm was backed by a VC at the time of listing. In addition, Jain and Martin Jr. (2005) report that IPO firms that are supported by a reputable and high-quality auditor, such as one of the big four auditors, at the time of listing tend to have a lower risk of delisting in the period after the IPO compared to those with lesser quality auditors. Alhadab *et al.* (2015) document a positive and significant relationship between real and accrual earnings management and the probability of post-IPO failure. Furthermore, Demers and Joos (2007) find that the presence of auditors in the period before the IPO can reduce failure risk for high-tech IPOs in the subsequent period after the IPO.

Moreover, using a sample of 7,957 IPOs that went public in the US market over the period from 1985 to 2005, Kooli and Meknassi (2007) find that IPO underpricing is negatively and significantly associated with post-IPO survival, while backing from a prestigious underwriter or VC can increase the survival time of new issuers after the IPO. Focusing on Canadian issuers, Carpentier and Suret (2011) observe that the failure risk for small and unprofitable Canadian IPOs is much lower than that of IPOs listed on the US market. Kashefi Pour (2015) documents that IPO firms with a CEO who is also the chairman of the board or the founder tend to have a lower risk of failure and survive longer in the periods following the IPO. Recently, Gounopoulos and Pham (2018) report that IPO firms which hired a CEO with special industry experience have a relatively lower five-year failure risk and survive longer after the IPO, in comparison to those with a CEO director with only general experience. Colak *et al.* (2021) observe that a larger pay gap between the CEO and executive directors is positively associated with the chance of firms' post-offering survival.

While a large number of studies in the corporate finance literature have investigated various firm and offering factors on the post-IPO survival of large and mature firms, to the best of our knowledge, only limited studies have paid attention to the impact of pre-IPO firm innovation activities on the post-survival profiles of the newly listed firms, in particular small, young, and fast-growing firms. Studies conducted an initial public offering in less regulated stock markets, such as the AIM, are even fewer in number. The existing literature on the relationship between corporate innovation and a firm's long-term performance, so far, remains mixed and unclear. In our study, we argue that due to variations in firm size, ability, knowledge, and financial constraints, together with market competition, the effect of the pre-listing innovation activity on aftermarket performance and survival could vary significantly (Audretsch, 1995; Ritter, 1991; Pérez *et al.*, 2004). Undoubtedly, IPO firms with better innovation capabilities and innovation outcomes tend to be more profitable, grow faster, and show better future performance (Atalay *et al.*, 2013; Guo and Zhou, 2016; Santa *et al.*, 2014). Murphy *et al.* (1996) argue that a firm's future performance is a multidimensional concept relating the firm's growth and its profit.

Furthermore, innovative outcomes are defined as the firm's overall accumulated achievements due to enhancement efforts that were applied, taking into consideration the different aspects of the firm's innovation capabilities, e.g. its structure, culture, processes, products, and marketing (Wang *et al.*, 2021; Ombaka *et al.*, 2015; Tuan *et al.*, 2016). Additionally, Cefis and Marsili (2012) state that delisting or exit strategies are fully bound to the nature and synergies of the firm's innovative efforts. Nevertheless, Audretsch (1995) claims that the survival probability of newly listed firms is not only dependent on their specific levels of knowledge but also dependent on their size and the presence of economic scales. Therefore, larger and mature firms at the time of listing are more likely to survive longer in the market compared to small ones (Agarwal, 1998; Useche, 2015; Audretsch and Lehmann, 2005). Moreover, large firms are usually more diversified than smaller ones, which may reduce their risk of failure since adverse conditions in one sector can be offset by better conditions in others (Robson *et al.*, 1993; Gounopoulos and Huang, 2018). Similarly, Schultz (1993), Ritter (1991), Agarwal and Gort (2002), and Audretsch and Lehmann (2005) state that the firm's size can be used as a proxy for capturing its accumulated learning, capabilities, and experience.

Furthermore, previous studies, such as those by Cefis and Marsili (2006) and Cefis and Marsili (2012), also look at the effect of other factors on the relationship between innovation and survival, arguing that the knowledge and capabilities of firms are the strategic assets for innovation, which may help them build a competitive advantage and lower their risk of failure. Therefore, investing in innovation projects can enable firms, in particular, small and young firms, to deal with new and emerging technologies and continuously expand their existing innovation capabilities, as argued by Banbury and Mitchell (1995), Taneja *et al.* (2016), and Christensen *et al.* (1998). Likewise, Cefis and Marsili (2006) state that innovation is a successful niche strategy for any firm, especially newly listed ones. There are several reasons why having more innovation activities, in particular patents prior to the date of offering, may improve a firm's long-term performance and increase its survival time after going public. First, patents provide a competitive advantage for the firm through their value and the legal protection they grant (Hall and Ziedonis, 2001; Audretsch and Lehmann, 2005; Mazzoleni and Nelson, 1998). Second, through the patents, firms, in particular, small and young issuers, may use their patent portfolios to send a positive signal to market investors that the firm is worth the investment (Useche, 2014; Zhou and Sadeghi, 2019). Third, firms with more successful patents prior to going public can use their patent profiles to convince financial providers and decrease financial restrictions (Chava *et al.*, 2017; Muller and Pénin, 2007; Hottenrott *et al.*, 2016), which may lead to a better performance and, therefore, a longer survival time. Therefore, having more patents should increase the probability of surviving after going public, specifically for small and young firms. Analysing the signalling effect of innovation data in the IPO prospectuses, Signori (2016) finds that investors are more likely to participate in the IPO firms with greater innovation potential, measured in terms of R&D spending. Based on the above discussions, arguments, and evidence from prior studies, we believe that pre-listing innovation may improve the survival profile of small and young newly listed companies through its powerful influence on the firm's growth, profitability, and competitive advantage. Hence, we expect that having more innovation outcomes in the period before going public will significantly enhance the survivability of the newly listed firms after the IPO. The following hypothesis is therefore proposed:

Hypothesis: IPO firms with better pre-listing innovation profiles are more likely to have lower risks of failure and tend to survive longer in the market in the subsequent periods after the IPO.

3.3. Sample Construction and Variable Measurements

3.3.1. *Sample construction*

Our data have been collected mainly from eight reliable databases: (1) the LSE website, (2) IPO prospectuses, (3) the Perfect Information database (PI Filings Expert), (4) the London Share Price Database (LSPD), (5) DataStream, (6) the Thomson One database, (7) the BoardEx database, and (8) the EPO's Worldwide Patent Statistical Database (PATSTAT). We began our selection procedure with the New Issues and IPOs database from the LSE website to identify companies that were listed on the AIM over the period ranging from 1 January 2005 to 31 December 2012.[4] Our decision to choose the year 2012 as the cut-off year and not include those companies that were listed on the AIM after 2012 is mainly due to the five-year tracking window. In line with the prior survival and failure studies (e.g. Espenlaub *et al.*, 2012; Gounopoulos and Pham, 2018), to determine whether a newly listed firm is a failure or a survivor, each firm in our sample is tracked for at least five years from its date of going public. For example, firms that were admitted to the AIM in 2012 are tracked until the end of December 2017, while those listed in 2005 are tracked from the date of listing up to the end of December 2017.

[4]Our decision to consider only IPOs listed on the AIM and not include those from the Main Market of the LSE is due to the differences in the characteristics between the firms listed on the AIM and the Main Market, as well as the differences in the regulatory environments between the two markets. For example, firms seeking a public admission into the AIM are not required to have a minimum of three years' operating record or a minimum market capitalisation at the time of offer, while these are required for listing on the LSE Main Market. For details on the differences in the listing requirements between the AIM and the Main Market of the LSE, please see Section 3.2 above.

Using the LSE database, we find that there were 1,680 companies admitted to the AIM between 2005 and 2012, out of which 699 companies classify as non-IPOs (e.g. direct listing, re-admission, reverse takeovers, and transferred companies). Consistent with most IPO survival studies, financial companies are excluded from our sample because they have different structures, environments, and regulatory systems. Moreover, in order to avoid the effects of irregular IPOs in our analysis, spin-offs, privatisations, and cash-sell companies are also eliminated from our sample. Finally, we further excluded 91 IPO firms due to missing data and IPO prospectus. After applying all the above restrictions, we are left with a final sample of 463 IPOs.

IPO prospectuses are downloaded manually from the Perfect Information Navigation (Filling Experts) database. The company name, offering date, the country of incorporation, issue price, the firm's market capitalisation at the time of offering, the total money raised at the time of offering (IPO), industry sector, and the firm's nominated advisor (known as NOMAD) are obtained from the LSE database. The stock price for each firm is obtained from DataStream. The board data are obtained from IPO prospectuses and the BoardEx database.

In addition, to determine the dates and the reasons for delisting, we use the AIM monthly reports from the LSE website, alongside the LSPD and Perfect Filings database. Each IPO firm is tracked from the first day of being public until the end of the tracking window (31 December 2017) or the date of delisting, whichever is earlier. Finally, following the leading UK and European research on corporate innovation (e.g. Balsmeier *et al.*, 2014; Cumming *et al.*, 2020), we use the Worldwide Patent Statistical Database (PATSTAT) from the European Patent Office (EPO) to collect firms' innovation activities. PATSTAT provides us with comprehensive patenting bibliographic information for more than 100 million patent applications that have been filed to more than 100 EPO's offices around the world over the period from 1850 to 2018.

3.3.2. *Measurement of corporate innovation*

To date, and to the best of our knowledge, in the literature, there is still ongoing debate about the best and most appropriate measurement methods for measuring corporate innovation. The question of how to capture the level of corporate innovation has been one of the key questions that scholars often ask before conducting empirical research. Different from other operation activities of firms, innovation often requires a long-term investment with very high risk and high uncertainty (Holmstrom, 1989). For example, in the early 1990s, most researchers in the related corporate innovation field relied largely on firms' research and development (R&D) spending as an innovation proxy (Barker and Mueller, 2002; Greve, 2003; Wu and Tu, 2007; Shen and Zhang, 2013). However, due to limitations in the R&D data and the availability of patenting information, in recent studies, R&D spending is no longer the primary source for measuring firms' innovations.

There are several reasons why scholars in academic research prefer to use the patenting-related data over R&D expenditure. The first reason is that a higher level of R&D spending in a firm's balance sheet does not necessarily mean successful innovation outputs, as argued by Aghion *et al.* (2013), Fang *et al.* (2014), and He and Tian (2013). Second, the R&D spending is more likely to be sensitive to accounting norms and errors (Acharya and Subramanian, 2009). Third, Atanassov (2013) argues that high R&D spending is less likely to result in successful innovation when other inputs (e.g. human capital, managerial and employee effort, and creativity) are not effectively utilised. Fourth, managers and directors may substitute R&D spending with other inputs by spending an excessive amount, which, rather than helping, may hurt the firm's innovation. Finally, unlike the patenting-related data, R&D spending cannot capture the quality and economic value of innovation (He and Tian, 2013).

Therefore, in line with recent studies, in our analysis, we use the patenting-related data to measure and proxy pre-listing innovation activities. Following Wagner and Cockburn (2010), Chemmanur *et al.* (2014), Vismara (2014), Zhou and Sadeghi (2019), and Atanassov (2013), our first proxy for innovation is *Ln(1+Patents)*, which is the natural logarithm of one plus the total number of successful patents that an IPO firm filed prior to the date of IPO. We add one to the number of pre-listing patents because almost 50% of the IPO firms in our dataset do not have any patent applications before going public. Second, following the work of Hirshleifer *et al.* (2017), we use *Patents/Assets* (PTA) as the second innovation proxy, which is the total number of successful pre-listing patent applications scaled by the firm's total assets at the time of the IPO. For comparison and the purpose of robustness checking, we further use the patent's citation-related data.[5] More specifically, following the research of Cho *et al.* (2016), Cumming *et al.* (2020), and Wang *et al.* (2021), we use *ln(1+Citations)*, which is the natural logarithm of one plus the total number of patent citations. Moreover, in line with Hall *et al.* (2005) and He and Tian (2013), we also measure the firm's innovation using *Citations-per-patent,* which is the number of a firm's patent citations divided by the number of patents. Additionally, following the studies of Adhikari and Agrawal (2016) and Zhang *et al.* (2018), the firm's innovation is measured by one plus the natural logarithm of the citations adjusted per patent *ln(1+CitesPat)*. Unlike the number of patents, citations per patent measurement allows us to capture the economic significance of a firm's innovation output. The importance of patent citation data in measuring innovation is motivated by the argument that patent count cannot differentiate the breakthrough innovations from less important, or incremental, and advanced technological ones. For example, Pakes and Schankerman (1984) find that the distribution of the value of patents is exceptionally skewed, with most of the value focused on a small number of very significant and highly cited ones. Finally, in addition to all the above proxies, corporate innovation is also measured by using the natural logarithm of one plus patent citations divided by the firm's total assets around the date of the IPO, *ln(1+Citations)/Assets*, as well as *the Innovation Dummy,* which is an indicator variable that equals one if the IPO firm had at least one successful patent application prior to the IPO, and zero otherwise.

3.4. Methodology

To examine the relationship between pre-listing innovation and the probability of post-IPO survival, we apply survival analysis, consistent with most IPO survival studies. Survival analysis is a statistical parametric and non-parametric estimation method widely used in the literature for predicting the determinates of firm survival and the risk

[5]For more information on patent's citation-related proxies, please contact the corresponding author.

of failure after going public (see Hensler *et al.*, 1997; Jenkins, 2005; Espenlaub *et al.*, 2012).

In line with Demers and Joos (2007), Kooli and Meknassi (2007), Espenlaub *et al.* (2012), Alhadab *et al.* (2015), Jain and Kini (2008), and Anagnostopoulou *et al.* (2021), in our analysis, survivors are defined as firms that either continued to trade on the AIM at the end of our tracking period (31 December 2017) or transferred to the Main Market of the LSE. Conversely, failures are firms that were delisted or removed from the AIM due to voluntary or involuntary (negative) reasons, including company request, administration, liquidation, receivership, insufficient capital, insufficient float, and failing to meet market standards and rules. IPOs are classified as 'right-censored observations' if they had not been delisted from the stock exchange at the end of our study tracking period (31 December 2017). For the purpose of robustness check, following the study of Espenlaub *et al.* (2012), we further distinguish in our regression between M&As delisted from the AIM due to financial distress and those delisted due to other non-negative reasons because the impact of delisting on the shareholders is typically more negative and harmful in the case of the former compared to the latter (e.g. a good exit deal).

3.4.1. *Kaplan–Meier survival method*

The survival rates after going public of the two sub-samples (IPO firms with pre-listing patents and IPO firms without pre-listing patents) over the period of one to five years are estimated using the non-parametric survival method, known as the Kaplan–Meier (KM) method. To assess the significance differences in the survival curves and determine whether the IPOs in different year and industry cohorts share the same KM survival curves, we use the log-rank test, following Ahmad and Jelic (2014) and Espenlaub *et al.* (2016). The KM survival method is estimated as follows:

$$S(t_j) = \left(\frac{n_j - d_j}{n_j}\right) S(t_{j-1}), \tag{3.1}$$

where $S(t_j)$ is the KM survival function at time t_j in months (also known as the estimated survival probability), n_j is the number of survival IPOs prior to time t_j, d_j is the number of delisted (failed) IPOs at time t_j, and $S(t_{j-1})$ is the probability of IPO survival at time t_{j-1}. In the case of this study, if innovation positively impacts the survival function of IPO firms, then we would expect the survival function curve of those IPO firms with pre-listing patents to be above that of non-innovative IPO firms.

3.4.2. *Accelerated failure time model*

Next, in the second stage of our empirical analysis, we examine the determents of post-IPO survival with respect to pre-listing innovation outcomes using the AFT model, following Hensler *et al.* (1997) and Espenlaub *et al.* (2012). The AFT model is a parametric survival method typically defined in the terms of a log-linear model with respect to the survival time as a function of various explanatory variables (Bradburn *et al.*, 2003). The AFT model is widely used in the literature to measure the direct impact of each covariate on survival time after an IPO. The key advantage of using the AFT model over the Cox proportional hazards (CPH) model is that it allows us to assess the effect of each independent variable (covariate) on the survival time throughout the post-IPO period depending on the time horizon since the date of going public or the IPO. The AFT model is normally expressed in the following form:

$$\mathrm{Ln}(T_j) = \beta_0 + \beta_1 X_1 + \beta_2 X_2 + \beta_3 X_3 + \cdots + \beta_p X_p + \varepsilon j, \qquad (3.2)$$

where $\mathrm{Ln}(T_j)$ is the natural logarithm of the survival time (or the time to delist) at time i, $B_0, B_1, \ldots, B_p$ are the estimated parameters in the model, $X_1, X_2, \ldots, X_p$ are the independent variables (covariates), and ε_j is the error term. The underlying distribution for our AFT model is the 'log-normal distribution', which is determined by the lowest value the Akaike information criterion (AIC) tests. The baseline AFT model is estimated as follows:

$$\begin{aligned}\mathrm{Ln}(T_i) = [\beta_0 &+ \beta_1 \mathrm{Ln}\ (\text{Innovation} - \text{Related proxies} \\ &+ \beta_2 \mathrm{Ln}\ (\text{Firm age}) + \beta_3 \mathrm{Ln}\ (\text{Firm size}) \\ &+ \beta_4 \mathrm{Ln}\ (\text{Proceeds}) + \beta_5\ \text{Insider ownership} \\ &+ \beta_6\ \text{Initial return} + \beta_7\ \text{PEVC} - \text{Backed} \\ &+ \beta_8\ \text{Big4 Auditor} + \beta_9\ \text{Sponsor reputation}\end{aligned}$$

$$
\begin{aligned}
&+\beta_{10}\text{ Leverage } +\beta_{11}\text{ Profitability}\\
&+\beta_{12}\text{ UK-IPO } + \text{ Year dummies}\\
&+\text{ Industry dummies}]. \qquad (3.3)
\end{aligned}
$$

The main variable of interest is innovation-related proxies $Ln(1+Number\ of\ Patents)$ and $Patents/Assets$ (PTA). Based on evidence from prior studies (e.g. Schultz, 1993; Hensler *et al.*, 1997; Jain and Martin Jr., 2005; Demers and Joos, 2007; Espenlaub *et al.*, 2012; Gounopoulos and Pham, 2018), we control for various firm-, offering-, and board-level characteristics, including firm age, size, offering proceeds, insider ownership, initial return, PEVC backing, Big4 auditor, sponsor reputation, and firm's financial performance, specifically leverage and profitability. Since firms operate in different industries and are listed in different years, the year and industry dummies are also added to our regressions to control for the environment and time-varying heterogeneity. For more information on the definitions of variables we used in our analysis, please see Table 3A.1.

3.5. Empirical Results and Discussion

3.5.1. *Descriptive analysis*

Table 3.1 reports the number of delisted IPOs based on various delisting reasons and over two different tracking periods: a five-year fixed window and a full tracking period (up to the end of December 2017). By tracking IPO firms for five years after the IPO, we find that 40.72% of total new issuers in our sample were delisted from the AIM due to the voluntary reason 'company request' and 27.32% due to M&As. The involuntary reasons 'breaking market regulations' and 'administration & liquidation' accounted for 26.29% and 2.58%, respectively, of total IPOs. By tracking our sample of IPOs from the date of offering to the end of December 2017, we find that, consistent with prior survival literature on UK firms, such as Alhadab *et al.* (2015) and Espenlaub *et al.* (2012), nearly 30% of the total IPO firms in our sample were delisted from the market due to involuntary (negative) reasons, 31.39% due to the M&As, and only nine firms over moved from the AIM to the upper-tier market of the LSE, namely the Main (Official) Market of the LSE.

Table 3.1. Distribution of IPO failures.

	From date of IPO to five years post-offering		From date of IPO to end of December 2017	
Reason for delisting	No	(%)	No	(%)
Administration & liquidation	5	2.58	7	2.27
Mergers & acquisitions	53	27.32	97	31.39
Breaking market regulation	51	26.29	84	27.18
Company request	79	40.72	112	36.25
Market transferred	6	3.09	9	2.91
Total	**194**	**100**	**309**	**100**

Note: This table displays the total number and percentage of the delisted IPO firms across different reasons for delisting and over two different tracking periods: a five-year tracking window and a full tracking window, where firms are tracked from the date of IPO to the end of December 2017. *Failed IPOs* are defined as firms that were voluntarily (e.g. company request) or involuntarily (e.g. administration, liquidation, receivership, and failure to meet market standards and rules) delisted from AIM before the end of 31 December 2017. The definitions of all variables are reported and discussed in Table 3A.1.

Table 3.2 displays the distributional statistics for the full sample of IPOs and the two sub-samples by the listing year, industry sector based on the two-digit Standard Industrial Classification Codes (two-digit SIC), innovation status, and PEVC-backing status. Our sample consists of 463 AIM IPOs listed on the AIM between January 2005 and December 2012. In Panel A of Table 3.2, we report the number and percentage of IPO firms by the year of listing. Focusing on the first two columns, we find that the crash of the equity markets in 2008 due to the global financial crisis (2007–2008) had a significant adverse impact on the AIM IPO activity until the end of 2012. The number of new issuers dropped substantially from 160 in 2005 to 33 in 2012. Only three firms went public in the year 2009, which is the lowest number among our time-series, while the highest number was in the year 2005, when 160 newly listed firms were admitted into the market. More than 60% of the AIM IPOs in our sample took place in the market between 2005–2006. Additionally, by focusing on the innovation status, we observe that over our sample period, the percentage of non-innovative IPOs exceeds those with

Table 3.2. IPO distribution by issue year, industry, innovation, and PEVC-backing status.

Panel A: IPO distribution by year of listing

			Innovation				PEVC-backing			
	All IPOs		Firms with pre-IPO innovation		Firms without pre-IPO innovation		PEVC-backed		Non-PEVC-backing	
Year of listing	*N*	(%)	*N*	(%)	*N*	(%)	*N*	(%)	*N*	(%)
2005	160	34.56	68	42.50	92	57.50	56	35.00	104	65.00
2006	122	26.35	55	45.08	67	54.92	53	43.44	69	56.56
2007	72	15.55	32	44.44	40	55.56	32	44.44	40	55.56
2008	17	3.67	7	41.18	10	58.82	4	23.53	13	76.47
2009	3	0.65	0	0.00	3	100	0	0	3	100
2010	28	6.05	5	17.86	23	82.14	14	50	14	50
2011	28	6.05	12	42.86	16	57.14	19	67.86	9	32.14
2012	33	7.13	9	27.27	24	72.73	11	33.33	22	66.67
2005–2012	**463**	**100**	**188**	**40.60**	**275**	**59.40**	**189**	**40.82**	**274**	**59.18**

(*Continued*)

Table 3.2. (*Continued*)

Panel B: IPO distribution by industry

			Innovation				PEVC-backing			
	All IPOs		Firms with pre-IPO innovation		Firms without pre-IPO innovation		PEVC-backed		Non-PEVC-backing	
Industry sector (two-digit SIC classification)	*N*	(%)	*N*	(%)	*N*	(%)	*N*	(%)	*N*	(%)
Mining (10, 12)	53	11.45	2	3.77	51	96.23	19	35.85	34	64.15
Oil and gas extraction (13)	43	9.29	3	6.98	40	93.02	12	27.91	31	72.09
Food products (20)	16	3.46	5	31.25	11	68.75	7	43.75	9	56.25
Chemical & allied products (28)	39	8.42	33	84.62	6	15.38	30	76.92	9	23.08
Industrial machinery and computer equipment (35)	35	7.56	22	62.86	13	37.14	20	57.14	15	42.86
Electronic equipment (36)	31	6.70	28	90.32	3	9.68	19	61.29	12	38.71
Scientific instruments and related products (38)	17	3.67	15	88.24	2	11.76	10	58.82	7	41.18
Communications (48)	11	2.38	2	18.18	9	81.82	4	36.36	7	63.64
Wholesale and retail trade (50–59)	23	4.97	2	8.70	21	91.30	9	39.13	14	60.87
Hotels and leisure (70)	23	4.97	2	8.70	21	91.30	1	4.35	22	95.65
Business services (73)	100	21.60	51	51	49	49	34	34.00	66	66.00
Auto repair and services (75)	3	0.65	3	100	0	0	3	100	0	0.00
Media and entertainment services (78)	29	6.26	5	17.24	24	82.76	11	37.93	18	62.07
Engineering & management services (87)	9	1.94	5	55.56	4	44.44	3	33.33	6	66.67
All others	31	6.70	10	32.26	21	67.74	7	22.58	24	77.42

Note: This table displays the distribution of the overall sample by the year of listing (Panel A), industry sector based on two-digit SIC classification (Panel B) as well as innovation status and PEVC-backing status. Our final sample comprises 463 IPO firms that listed on the Alternative Investment Market (AIM) between January 2005 and December 2012. *Failed IPOs* are defined as those firms that were voluntarily (e.g. company request) or involuntarily (e.g. administration, liquidation, receivership, and failure to meet market standards and rules) delisted from AIM before the end of 31 December 2017. The definitions of all variables are reported and discussed in Table 3A.1.

pre-listing innovation. Out of the 463 IPO, around 41% had at least one patent application before going public. The highest number of IPOs with pre-listing innovation is observed in 2005, with 68 IPOs. In the last two columns of the table, we report the number and percentage of IPO activity based on the PEVC-backing status. In general, we observe that the number of non-PEVC-backed IPOs is more than the number of PEVC-backed IPOs in most issue years. The number of PEVC-backed IPOs hit its peak in 2005, when 56 got listed on the AIM.

In Panel B of Table 3.2, we present the IPO distribution across different industry sectors based on the two-digit SIC classification. We find that IPO firms that are operating in the business services and mining sector together occupy around 21.6% of the total IPO activities in our sample, followed by IPOs in the mining sector at 11.45%. The lowest percentage of the IPOs was in the auto repair sector at 1.94 %. Moreover, comparing the IPO distribution under the pre-innovation status and the PEVC-backing status, we find that most innovative IPO firms are clustered in the high-technology industries, such as chemical & allied products, industrial machinery and computer equipment, electronic equipment, and scientific instruments & related products. The percentage of innovative IPOs ranges from 3.77% in the mining sector to 100% in the auto repair and services. Specifically, the proportion of innovative IPOs was the highest in the chemical & allied products and business service sectors, with 33 IPOs and 51 IPOs, respectively. Moreover, the highest numbers and percentages of PEVC-backed IPOs are found among the high-technological products, for example, chemical & allied products (code 28), computer equipment (code 35), electronic equipment (code 36), and business service (code 73).

Table 3.3 reports the summary statistics for all the variables we used in our empirical analysis for the full IPOs sample and the subsamples of IPOs: IPOs with pre-listing innovation and IPOs without pre-listing innovation over the period 2005–2012. We find that the full IPOs sample has a mean pre-listing patent applications of 9.70 (std. dev. of 23.84), and an average patents/assets (PTA) of 3.63 (std. dev. of 8.07), suggesting that, on average, each IPO firm in our study has 10 patents at the time of IPO. With regard to the control variables, the average IPO age is 8.5 years, with a mean market capitalisation (IPO proceeds) of £46.90 million (£14.22 million). In addition to

Table 3.3. Descriptive statistics.

	All IPOs						Firms with pre-IPO innovation				Firms without pre-IPO innovation				Difference	
Variable	Obs.	Mean	Median	Std dev.	Min	Max	Obs.	Mean	Median	Std dev.	Obs.	Mean	Median	Std dev.	t	p-value
Innovation																
No. of patents	463	9.70	0.00	23.84	0.00	141.00	188	23.89	13.00	32.60	275	0.00	0.00	0.00	−10.05	0.00
Ln(1+patents)	463	1.02	0.00	1.47	0.00	5.69	188	2.51	2.64	1.25	275	0.00	0.00	0.00	−27.53	0.00
Patents/Assets (PTA)	463	3.63	0.00	8.07	0.00	29.23	188	8.94	3.11	10.65	275	0.00	0.00	0.00	−11.50	0.00
Citations	463	85.43	0.00	198.47	0.00	781.00	188	211.75	79.00	266.56	275	0.00	0.00	0.00	−10.83	0.00
Ln(1+Citations)	463	1.72	0.00	2.46	0.00	9.21	188	4.27	4.38	2.03	275	0.00	0.00	0.00	−28.73	0.00
Firm and IPO characteristics																
Firm age (years)	463	8.52	6.07	7.97	1.16	43.96	188	10.02	7.22	9.06	275	7.50	5.31	6.97	−3.22	0.00
Firm size (million £)	463	46.90	26.92	56.49	2.02	320.56	188	45.35	28.26	50.42	275	47.96	25.65	60.35	0.50	0.61
Proceeds (million £)	463	14.22	7.75	18.80	0.30	108.00	188	13.88	8.73	18.01	275	14.46	6.90	19.36	0.33	0.74
Insider ownership (%)	463	30.68	25.90	24.67	0.00	93.10	188	27.74	23.69	24.22	275	32.69	29.20	24.81	2.14	0.03
Initial returns (%)	463	10.15	7.78	13.28	−27.78	51.85	188	10.05	6.42	13.14	275	10.21	8.40	13.40	0.13	0.90
PEVC-backed	463	0.41	0.00	0.49	0.00	1.00	188	0.59	1.00	0.49	275	0.29	0.00	0.45	−6.59	0.00
Sponsor reputation	463	0.43	0.00	0.49	0.00	1.00	188	0.49	0.00	0.50	275	0.38	0.00	0.49	−2.49	0.01

Big4 auditor	463	0.31	0.00	0.46	0.00	1.00	188	0.38	0.00	0.49	275	0.27	0.00	0.44	−2.53	0.01
Leverage	463	0.46	0.15	1.03	0.00	7.80	188	0.39	0.19	0.48	275	0.28	0.12	0.37	−2.60	0.01
Profitability	463	−0.38	−0.03	1.20	−8.10	0.79	188	−0.44	−0.13	0.76	275	−0.16	−0.01	0.52	4.24	0.00
Cash holding	463	0.24	0.16	0.25	0.00	0.97	188	0.26	0.19	0.23	275	0.22	0.14	0.23	−1.64	0.10
Capital expenditure	463	0.08	0.02	0.14	0.00	0.84	188	0.06	0.03	0.08	275	0.07	0.02	0.10	1.13	0.26
Market-to-book	463	3.23	2.53	2.17	0.69	9.26	188	5.06	2.49	5.80	275	3.82	1.85	4.90	−2.41	0.02
UK-IPO	463	0.75	1.00	0.43	0.00	1.00	188	0.65	1.00	0.48	275	0.82	1.00	0.38	4.01	0.00
Survival time (months)	463	77.56	67.40	42.10	8.98	154.72	188	79.68	70.72	42.16	275	76.11	66.08	42.07	−0.90	0.37
Board characteristics																
Board size	463	5.67	6.00	1.35	3.00	9.00	188	5.83	6.00	1.25	275	5.55	5.00	1.40	−2.23	0.03
Board ind (%)	463	52.44	50.00	14.38	20.00	85.71	188	0.54	0.50	0.15	275	0.52	0.50	0.14	−1.65	0.10
CEO-duality	463	0.13	0.00	0.34	0.00	1.00	188	0.11	0.00	0.31	275	0.15	0.00	0.35	1.26	0.21

Note: This table displays the descriptive statistics for the overall sample and the two sub-samples: IPO firms with pre-listing innovation and IPO firms without pre-listing innovation. Our final sample comprises 463 IPO companies that listed on the AIM between January 2005 and December 2012. *Failed IPOs* are defined as those firms that were voluntarily (e.g. company request) or involuntarily (e.g. administration, liquidation, receivership, and failure to meet market standards and rules) delisted from AIM before the end of 31 December 2017. The definitions of all variables are reported and discussed in Table 3A.1.

that, insiders, on average, own 30.68 of the firm's shares at the time of the IPO. Around 41% of the IPO firms in our sample are backed by either private equity or venture capital companies at the time of offering, 43% are sponsored by a prestigious nominated advisor (NOMAD), and 31% are sponsored by a big four auditing company. Moreover, 75% of the total IPO firms are incorporated in the UK. The average leverage ratio, profitability, cash holding, capital expenditure, and market-to-book ratio are 0.46, −0.38, 0.24, 0.08, and 3.23, respectively. On average, our sample of IPOs has six directors on the firm's board, 52% of the directors are independent directors, and 13% of the IPO firms have a CEO who is also the chairman of the board. The mean survival time in our sample is 77.56 months, suggesting that, on average, AIM IPOs survive for about 77 months after going public, which is consistent with the findings of Espenlaub *et al.* (2012).[6]

Further, we divide our full IPOs sample into sub-samples. In general, IPO firms with pre-listing innovation (patents) are significantly different from those without pre-listing innovation in terms of most control variables, such as *Firm age, Insider ownership, PEVC-backing, Sponsor reputation, Big4 auditor, Leverage, Profitability, Market-to-book, Board size,* and *UK-IPO*. In particular, on average, IPO firms with pre-listing patents are older than those without pre-IPO patents, and they have a mean insider ownership of 27.74% compared to 32.69% for those without pre-listing patents. The finding aligns with that reported by Sørensen and Stuart (2000), who find that innovation is significantly and positively related to the firm's age and experience. Furthermore, the data also show that almost 59% (49%) of the innovative IPOs are backed by PEVC (prestigious sponsor), compared to only 29% (38%) for IPO firms without pre-IPO innovation. On average, 38% of the innovative IPOs are backed by a high-quality accounting company (big four) compared to only 27% for those without pre-listing innovation. In terms of the financial ratios, consistent with previous innovation studies (e.g. Cao *et al.*, 2020; Wagner and Cockburn, 2010), IPO firms with pre-listing innovation are less profitable, highly leveraged, and have higher growths

[6]Examining the survival profile of AIM IPOs listed between 1995 and 2004, Espenlaub *et al.* (2012) find that the median survival time is 76 months.

compared to those without innovation (*Profitability ratio* of −0.44 vs. −0.16, *Leverage ratio* of 0.39 vs. 0.28, and *Market-to-book ratio* of 5.06 vs. 3.82). Finally, in order to mitigate the effect of extreme observations in our dataset, most continuous variables are winsorised at 1 and 99 percentile levels, except profitability, leverage, cash holding, capital expenditure, and market-to-book ratio, which are winsorised at the levels of 5th and 95th percentiles. This procedure is consistent with the existing literature (e.g. Huyghebaert and Van Hulle, 2006; Srivastava, 2014; Kashefi Pour and Lasfer, 2013).

Finally, in Table 3.4, we report the Pearson and Spearman correlation matrix for all variables we employed in our empirical analysis, with a 5% significance level. Looking at the significant levels, we note that, even though there are some significant coefficients between some variables, there is no multicollinearity detected because the significant levels are not high enough to cause a multicollinearity issue.

3.5.2. *Kaplan-Meier survival analysis*

In Table 3.5, we compare the cumulated survival rates between IPO firms with pre-listing innovation (patents) and those without pre-listing innovation by the issue year (Panel A) and across various industry sectors (Panel B). The survival rates are estimated for one, three, and five years after the offering using the KM estimation method, a non-parametric method of survival analysis. In line with our expectations and the findings from previous studies (e.g. Audretsch and Lehmann, 2005; Wagner and Cockburn, 2010), we find that pre-listing innovation has a significant impact on the survival rates of small and young IPOs. In particular, we find that, at the end of the first year after the IPO, almost all the year cohorts of innovative IPOs have 100% survival rates compared to only four-year cohorts for the non-innovative IPO firms. By the end of the third year after issuing (midterm), the survival rates for the innovative IPO firms range from 71.43% for firms that went public in 2008 to 100% for those listed on the AIM in 2012. On the other hand, the highest (lowest) three-year survival rate among the non-innovative IPO firms is 94.86% (66.67%). Similar to Panel A of Table 3.5, in Panel B, we find that, in general, the three- and five-year survival rates among the innovative IPO firms are higher than those without pre-listing innovation in most industry sectors.

Table 3.4. Correlation matrix.

	1	2	3	4	5	6	7	8	9	10
1 Survival times	1									
2 Ln(1+Patents)	0.01	1								
3 Patents/Asset	0.03	0.42*	1							
4 Ln(Firm age)	0.04	0.16*	−0.12*	1						
5 Ln(Firm size)	−0.01	0.84*	−0.09*	0.11*	1					
6 Ln(Proceed)	0.01	0.99*	−0.11*	0.16*	0.83*	1				
7 Insider ownership	0.03	−0.20*	0.01	0.06	−0.07	−0.22*	1			
8 Initial return	0.00	−0.24*	0.05	−0.02	−0.22*	−0.23*	0.05	1		
9 PEVC-backing	0.14*	−0.01	0.12*	0.03	−0.05	0.00	−0.20*	−0.06	1	
10 Sponsor reputation	0.08	0.13*	0.02	0.10*	0.06	0.13*	−0.07	−0.03	−0.06	1
11 Big4 auditor	0.01	0.35*	−0.04	0.14*	0.32*	0.34*	−0.12*	−0.09	0.06	0.15*
12 Leverage	−0.09	−0.06	0.41*	−0.07	−0.01	−0.05	0.05	0.01	0.00	−0.05
13 Profitability	0.08	0.12*	−0.58*	0.17*	0.13*	0.11*	0.09	−0.03	−0.07	0.00
14 Cash holding	0.06	0.00	0.05	−0.11*	0.00	0.00	−0.16*	−0.06	0.12*	0.11*
15 Capital expenditure	−0.03	0.05	0.06	−0.07	0.01	0.04	−0.04	−0.01	−0.11*	0.03
16 Market-to-book	0.09	−0.13*	0.09	−0.06	0.00	−0.14*	0.19*	0.05	−0.07	−0.07
17 UK-IPO	0.08	−0.15*	−0.02	−0.14*	−0.17*	−0.16*	0.06	0.03	0.08	−0.06
18 Board size	−0.07	0.25*	0.01	0.15*	0.28*	0.25*	0.03	−0.12*	0.07	0.14*
19 Board ind	0.02	0.20*	0.01	0.06	0.21*	0.21*	−0.13*	−0.14*	0.17*	0.06
20 CEO-duality	−0.03	−0.04	−0.04	−0.05	−0.02	−0.04	0.04	0.04	−0.03	−0.11*

Table 3.4. (*Continued*)

	11	12	13	14	15	16	17	18	19	20
1 Survival times										
2 Ln(1+Patents)										
3 Patents/Asset										
4 Ln(Firm age)										
5 Ln(Firm size)										
6 Ln(Proceed)										
7 Insider ownership										
8 Initial return										
9 PEVC-backing										
10 Sponsor reputation										
11 Big4 auditor	1									
12 Leverage	0.00	1								
13 Profitability	0.03	−0.56*	1							
14 Cash holding	0.04	−0.11*	−0.06	1						
15 Capital expenditure	0.01	0.09	−0.14*	−0.12*	1					
16 Market-to-book	−0.10*	−0.08	−0.04	0.02	−0.06	1				
17 UK-IPO	−0.15*	−0.05	0.03	−0.04	0.01	−0.03	1			
18 Board size	0.14*	−0.02	−0.03	0.00	0.01	0.00	−0.22*	1		
19 Board ind	0.09	−0.03	−0.02	0.07	0.00	−0.03	−0.26*	0.21*	1	
20 CEO-duality	−0.08	0.01	0.02	0.01	−0.02	0.08	0.01	−0.10*	−0.15*	1

Note: This table displays the Pearson and Spearman correlation coefficients across all the variables used in the empirical analysis. The * asterisk denotes the statistical significance level at 5%. The definitions of all variables are reported and discussed in Table 3A.1.

Table 3.5. Kaplan–Meier survival rates.

	Cumulative survival rates							
		Firms with pre-IPO innovation				Firms without pre-IPO innovation		
Panel A: Issue years	Log-rank	1 yr	3 yrs	5 yrs	Log-rank	1 yr	3 yrs	5 yrs
2005	12.03	100	93.98	78.08	11.82	98.91	84.62	61.75
2006	0.061	100	94.31	84.82	0.107	98.51	78.38	69.52
2007		100	95.65	81.23		97.5	94.86	78.19
2008		100	71.43	71.43		100	90	90
2009		—	—	—		100	66.67	33.33
2010		100	100	100		95.65	95.65	78.26
2011		100	91.67	83.33		100	75	61.88
2012		100	100	100		100	85.91	65.7
Panel B: By industry (two-digit SIC classification)	**Log-rank**	**1 yr**	**3 yrs**	**5 yrs**	**Log-rank**	**1 yr**	**3 yrs**	**5 yrs**
Mining (10, 12)	18.3	100	100	50	37.54	100	100	91.19
Oil and gas extraction (13)	0.193	100	100	100	0.000	100	92.43	76.03
Food products (20)		100	100	100		100	81.82	71.59
Chemical & allied products (28)		100	96.88	89.82		100	80	80
Industrial machinery and computer equipment (35)		100	95.45	89.84		84.62	69.23	53.85
Electronic equipment (36)		100	92.11	78.67		100	66.67	33.33
Scientific instruments and related products (38)		100	92.86	83.57		100	50	0
Communications (48)		100	100	100		100	77.78	77.78
Wholesale and retail trade (50–59)		100	100	50		100	74.12	62.2
Hotels and leisure (70)		100	100	100		95.24	65.55	30.25
Business services (73)		100	89.95	76.14		97.96	79.2	64.47
Auto repair and services (75)		100	66.67	33.33		0	0	0
Media and entertainment services (78)		100	100	50		100	91.67	60.97
Engineering & management services (87)		100	100	100		100	66.67	33.33
All others		100	100	100		100	90	73.23

Panel C: Full sample			100	93.78	82.67	98.54	85.05	68.32
Panel D: By number of patents	Obs	Log-rank	1 yr	3 yrs	5 yrs			
0–1 patent	297	5.08	98.65	86.12	69.75			
2–25 patents	127	0.078	100	94.12	81.64			
>25 patents	39		100	89.37	83.21			

Note: This table displays the cumulative survival rates for the overall sample of IPO firms and the two sub-samples: firms with pre-listing innovation and firms without pre-listing innovation. The cumulative survival rates are computed using the Kaplan–Meier (KM) survival method. Our final sample comprises 463 IPO firms listed on the AIM between January 2005 and December 2012. Panel A shows the cumulative survival rates at the end of the first, third, and fifth years after the date of offering (IPO) across different issuing years. Panel B shows the cumulative survival rates at the end of the first, third, and fifth years after the date of offering (IPO) across different industry sectors based on two-digit Standard Industrial Classification Codes (two-digit SIC). Panel C shows the overall cumulative survival rates for the overall sample of IPOs and the two sub-samples: firms with pre-listing innovation and firms without pre-listing innovations at the end of the first, third, and fifth years after the date of offering (IPO). Panel D reports the cumulative survival rates by the number of pre-listing patents. *Failed IPOs* are defined as those firms that were voluntarily (e.g. company request) or involuntarily (e.g. administration, liquidation, receivership, and failure to meet market standards and rules) delisted from the AIM before the end of 31 December 2017. The significance differences between the survival curves across issuing years and industry sectors are assessed using the log-rank tests. The definitions of all variables are reported and discussed in Table 3A.1.

Panel C of Table 3.5 reports the overall survival rates for the two sub-samples at the end of the first, third, and fifth years after the IPO. Clearly, the three- and five-year survival rates for the innovative IPOs are much higher than the survival rates for the non-innovative IPOs (93.78% vs. 85.05% and 82.67% vs. 68.32%). Finally, in Panel D of Table 3.5, we report the cumulative survival rates by breaking down the level of pre-listing patents into sub-groups: 0 or 1 patent, 2–25 patents, and more than 25 patents. We find that IPO firms with 2–25 pre-listing patents exhibit higher survival rates compared to those with only one patent at the time of offering (81.64% vs. 69.75%). Moreover, the five-year survival rate for the IPO firms with more than 25 pre-IPO patents is 83.21%. Overall, the results of the KM method support and are consistent with our main hypothesis that IPO firms with pre-listing innovation activities are more likely to experience a lower failure risk and survive longer in the subsequent periods after issuing compared to those without pre-listing patents.

Moreover, Figure 3.1 displays graphically the KM survival estimation and the Nelson–Aalen cumulative hazard estimation for IPO firms with the pre-listing innovation and non-pre-listing innovation sub-samples across various survival time-series. As expected and consistent with our hypothesis, in Panel A of Figure 3.1, the survival curve for the innovative IPO firms is above that of IPO firms without pre-listing innovation, and the difference between the two curves becomes wider with time, clearly suggesting that firms with pre-IPO

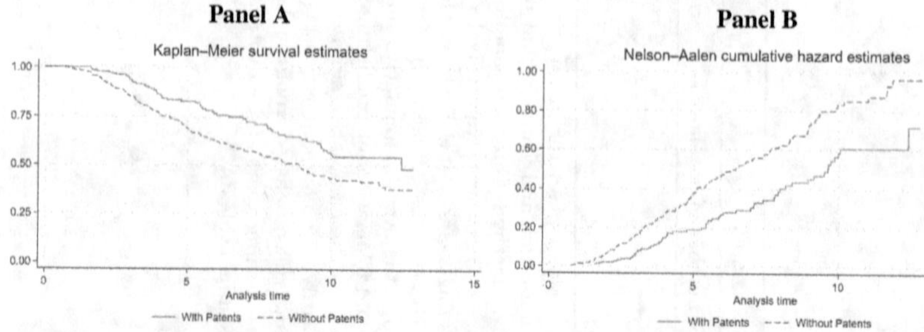

Figure 3.1. Kaplan–Meier survival and Nelson–Aalen hazard estimations.
Note: This figure displays graphically the estimated survival and failure curves of the two sub-samples: firms with pre-listing innovation and firms without pre-listing innovation using the Kaplan–Meier survival estimation method (Panel A) and the Nelson–Aalen hazard estimation method (Panel B).

innovation are less likely to fail and more likely to survive longer after going public. On the other hand, looking at the Nelson–Aalen cumulative hazard estimation, displayed in Panel B of Figure 3.1, the hazard curve for the IPO firms with pre-IPO innovation is below the hazard curve for those without pre-listing innovation, with the gap increasing over the time-series. This indicates that the failure risk of innovative IPO firms is lower than that of non-innovative IPO firms.

3.5.3. *Multivariate analysis*

After controlling for several characteristics at the offering, firm, and board levels, the AFT regression results (Table 3.6) indicate that, overall, the key variables of interest *Ln(1+Patents)* and *Patents/Assets* (PTA) exhibit a positive and statistically significant (at the 1% level) association with post-IPO survival across all our regressions, except in specification (4), in which the second proxy of innovation (*PTA*) is significant at the 5% level. The results are consistent with the findings of Wagner and Cockburn (2010), Cao *et al.* (2013), and Useche (2015), who found that high-tech firms with a better profile of innovation are more likely to survive in the following period after going public. Our findings are also in line with those of Useche (2014) and Zhou and Sadeghi (2019), who argued that the number of patents reported in the IPO prospectus around the date of going public can serve as a 'certification' for the quality and innovation ability of the newly listed firm, leading to lower underpricing and reduced uncertainty between the IPO firm and its investors and therefore a better long-term performance and profitability (Guo and Zhou, 2016; Cao *et al.*, 2015). More specifically, in specifications (1) and (2), after controlling only for the firm- and IPO-level characteristics, in line with the literature, in particular the study by Audretsch and Lehmann (2005), we find that IPO firms with a higher profile of innovation activities in the period prior to going public are more likely to survive longer in the period after the IPO compared to those with less or no innovation. Moreover, after including the board characteristics, mainly *Board size, Board ind (%), and CEO-duality,* our results continue the trend of showing that the effect of pre-listing related-innovation proxies (displayed in specifications 2 and 4) is quantitatively and significantly similar to that reported in the specifications 1 and 3. The time ratios of 1.159

Table 3.6. Innovation and survival times: accelerated failure time regressions.

Variable	(1) Coeff.	(1) TR	(2) Coeff.	(2) TR	(3) Coeff.	(3) TR	(4) Coeff.	(4) TR
Innovation								
Ln(1+Patents)	0.150***	1.162	0.148***	1.159				
	(3.15)		(3.12)					
Patents/Assets (PTA)					0.083***	1.087	0.079**	1.082
					(2.67)		(2.54)	
Firm and IPO characteristics								
Ln(Firm age)	0.131*	1.140	0.143*	1.154	0.156**	1.169	0.167**	1.181
	(1.68)		(1.83)		(2.01)		(2.14)	
Ln(Firm size)	0.048	1.050	0.083	1.087	0.040	1.041	0.072	1.075
	(0.56)		(0.94)		(0.46)		(0.82)	
Ln(Proceed)	−0.064	0.938	−0.072	0.930	−0.037	0.964	−0.046	0.955
	(−0.82)		(−0.93)		(−0.47)		(−0.58)	
Insider ownership	0.010***	1.010	0.010***	1.010	0.010***	1.009	0.009***	1.009
	(4.34)		(4.32)		(3.89)		(3.90)	
Initial return	−0.003	0.997	−0.004	0.996	−0.004	0.996	−0.004	0.996
	(−0.94)		(−1.08)		(−0.97)		(−1.06)	
PEVC-backing	0.492***	1.636	0.525***	1.690	0.563***	1.756	0.591***	1.806
	(4.29)		(4.51)		(5.09)		(5.22)	
Sponsor reputation	0.255**	1.290	0.257**	1.293	0.253**	1.288	0.254**	1.289
	(2.50)		(2.52)		(2.49)		(2.50)	
Big4 auditor	−0.132	0.876	−0.143	0.867	−0.092	0.912	−0.099	0.905
	(−1.15)		(−1.24)		(−0.82)		(−0.88)	
Leverage	−0.347***	0.707	−0.360***	0.698	−0.380***	0.684	−0.389***	0.678
	(−2.73)		(−2.84)		(−2.99)		(−3.07)	
Profitability	0.140	1.150	0.127	1.135	0.136	1.146	0.123	1.131
	(1.40)		(1.27)		(1.36)		(1.23)	
Cash holding	0.186	1.205	0.181	1.199	0.306	1.358	0.297	1.346
	(0.79)		(0.77)		(1.30)		(1.27)	

Capital expenditure	−0.092	0.912	−0.069	0.933	−0.222	0.801	−0.193	0.824
	(−0.19)		(−0.14)		(−0.44)		(−0.39)	
Market-to-book	0.018	1.018	0.019	1.019	0.006	1.006	0.008	1.008
	(1.49)		(1.58)		(0.49)		(0.62)	
UK-IPO	0.010	1.009	−0.041	0.959	−0.023	0.977	−0.066	0.937
	(0.08)		(−0.33)		(−0.19)		(−0.53)	
Board characteristics								
Board size			−0.058	0.943			−0.057	0.945
			(−1.50)				(−1.46)	
Board ind			−0.229	0.795			−0.129	0.879
			(−0.61)				(−0.34)	
CEO-duality			−0.179	0.836			−0.164	0.849
			(−1.26)				(−1.16)	
Constant	4.265***		4.658***		4.277***		4.604***	
	(13.12)		(11.38)		(13.17)		(11.35)	
Year control	Yes		Yes		Yes		Yes	
Industry control	Yes		Yes		Yes		Yes	
Log–likelihood	−352.91		−350.95		−353.91		−352.23	
LR(Prob.>chi)^2	107.35***		111.28***		105.36***		108.72***	
Time at risk	35, 911.87		35, 911.87		35, 911.87		35, 911.87	
Obs	463		463		463		463	

Note: This table displays the estimated results of the accelerated failure time (ATF) model. *Failure* is a dummy variable that takes a value of one if the IPO firm was delisted from the AIM before the end of December 2017 due to voluntary (e.g. company request) or involuntary reasons (e.g. administration, liquidation, receivership, and failure to meet market standards and rules). *Ln(1+Patents)* is the natural logarithm of one plus the total number of pre-listing successful patent applications. *Patents/Assets* (PTA) is the total number of pre-listing successful patent applications divided by the firm's total assets at the date of offering. The time ratio (TR) for each independent variable is measured as the exponentiated coefficients, exp (β), which compute the changes in covariates by increasing or decreasing the occurrence of the delisting. The time ratio above (below) one implies an increase (a decrease) in the post-IPO survival time. The Z-statistics are shown in the parentheses below each coefficient estimate. The *, **, and *** asterisks denote the statistical significance at the 10%, 5%, and 1% levels, respectively. The definitions of all variables are reported and discussed in Table 3A.1.

(in specification 2 using *Ln(1+Patents)* and 1.082 (in specification 4 using *Patents/Assets*) provide regression coefficients of economic significance, suggesting that for one-unit increase in the innovation-related proxies *Ln(1+Patents)* and *Patents/Assets* (PTA), the survival time for small and young IPO firms in the period following the IPO rises by approximately 15.9% and 8.2%, respectively. Overall, the above-mentioned results support our earlier findings from the non-parametric approach (the KM method) and our main hypothesis that having a strong pre-listing innovation profile can positively improve the survival profile of newly listed firms after going public.

3.5.3.1. *Control variables*

Consistent with most previous studies, our results show that the coefficients of most control variables across all regressions are generally in line and have an expected sign and influence on the probability of post-IPO survival. For example, consistent with Ahmad and Jelic (2014) and Colak *et al.* (2021), we find that older IPO firms with a higher proportion of insider ownership at the time of IPO are more likely to survive longer after the issuing at a higher statistically significant level (1%). Also, in line with the findings of Jain and Kini (2000) and Chou *et al.* (2013), we find that the involvement of VCs and PEs in the IPO process and board monitoring can positively and significantly (at the 1% level) influence the survival probability of new issuers after the IPO. Moreover, the variable sponsor reputation shows a positive and significant effect (at the 5% significance level) across all specifications, suggesting that IPO firms that are backed by one of the top-ranked AIM-nominated advisors (NOMIDs) are nearly 29% more likely to survive longer in the stock market after the IPO than those backed by a less reputable nominated advisor, which is consistent with the conclusions of Espenlaub *et al.* (2012). In addition to that, our AFT results also show that IPO firms with a higher level of debt (heavily leveraged firms) at the time of IPO tend to have a higher ecumenically significant failure risk and a shorter survival time in the following years after the IPO, which is consistent with the results of Demers and Joos (2007). In terms of other control variables, we observe that, consistent with the IPO literature (e.g. Fama and French, 2004; Cressy and Farag, 2014; Gounopoulos and Pham, 2018), our AFT estimations show positive effects of *Firm age, Profitability*, and *Market-to-book* on the aftermarket IPO survival time; however, they are insignificant across all specifications. Notably, different from previous studies (e.g. Alhadab *et al.*, 2015; Gounopoulos and Pham, 2018), the sign of all board control variables, *Board size, Board ind* (%), and *CEO-duality*, is negative in relation to survival time but insignificant. However, even though the coefficients of *Board size and CEO-duality* are economically insignificant, they are in line with the findings of Chancharat *et al.* (2012) and Kashefi Pour (2015), suggesting that new issuers with a higher number of directors on the firm's board and run by a CEO who also acts as the chairman of the board experience a higher risk of failure and delisting risk in the subsequent periods after the IPO.

3.5.3.2. *Sensitivity analysis*

Inspired by the works of Hensler *et al.* (1997) and Espenlaub *et al.* (2012), we also perform a sensitivity analysis in order to estimate the predicted survival time in response to changes in both related innovation proxies. Our sensitivity estimations are based on the coefficients from the baseline AFT regressions that are reported in Table 3.6, specifically those under specifications 2 and 4. Bearing this in mind, the estimated results in Table 3.8 are displayed in the form of expected survival times, absolute changes in the survival time (in months), and the percentage changes across different standard deviations. The changes in the predicted survival times are measured relative to the base value of the survival time estimated at the mean values of all the independent variables in the baseline model, in line with Espenlaub *et al.* (2012). Based on that, the base value of our predicted survival time is 89 months. Using the number of pre-listing patents, in the first half of Table 3.7, we find that a one (or two)-standard deviation increase in the number of pre-listing patents increases the expected survival time of the IPO firms substantially and significantly by 24 (or 27%) and 55 months (or 62%).[7] Similar to the number of pre-listing patents proxy, using *Patents/Assets*, we also find that the expected survival time of small and young issuers

[7]For the purposes of robustness checking and comparison, we also re-run our sensitivity tests using one plus the number of pre-listing patents rather than the number of pre-listing patents and the median of the patents instead of the mean of patents, following the work of Espenlaub *et al.* (2012). We find that the results are almost in line with our previous results presented in Table 3.6.

Table 3.7. Sensitivity of AFT survival times to the changes in innovation.

Variable	$+2\delta$	$+\delta$	$+\delta/2$	$+\delta/4$	$-\delta/4$	$-\delta/2$	$-\delta$	-2δ
Patents								
Expected survival time (months)	144	113	100	94	83	78	69	53
Absolute change (months)	55	24	11	5	−6	−11	−20	−36
Percentage change	62%	27%	12%	6%	−7%	−12%	−22%	−40%
Patents/Assets (PTA)								
Expected survival time (months)	149	119	106	100	89	84	75	59
Absolute change (months)	60	30	17	11	0	−5	−14	−30
Percentage change	67%	34%	19%	12%	0%	−6%	−16%	−34%

Note: This table displays the sensitivity analysis of AFT survival times to the changes in the pre-listing innovation. Based on the estimated coefficient in AFT regressions (specifications 2 and 4) of Table 3.7, this table shows the estimated actual, absolute, and percentage changes in the predicted median of survival times as the independent variables change by the multiples of their standard deviations σ, holding all other parameters constant, in line with the analysis of Hensler *et al.* (1997) and Espenlaub *et al.* (2012). The changes are calculated relative to the base of the predicted survival time estimated at the means of all independent variables in the main AFT models. The predicted survival time at the base is 89 months. The variable patents are expressed in the number of patents rather than the natural logarithms of one plus the number of patents. *Failure* is a dummy variable takes a value of one if the IPO firm was delisted from AIM before the end December 2017 due to voluntary (e.g. company request) or involuntary reasons (e.g. administration, liquidation, receivership, and failure to meet market standards and rules). *Patents/Assets* (PTA) is the total number of pre-listing successful patent applications divided by the firm's total assets at the date of offering. The definitions of all variables are reported and discussed in Table 3A.1.

on the AIM can be improved by approximately 30 months (34%) for a one-standard deviation increase in the Patents/Assets (PTA) proxy. The above results clearly continue to support our hypothesis and previous results of KM and baseline AFT regressions on the positive effect of pre-listing innovation outcomes in relation to the probability of post-IPO survival. Overall, the above sensitivity tests strongly support our expectation and hypothesis that pre-listing innovation activities are positively associated with the aftermarket survival time of IPO firms.

3.5.4. *Robustness test*

We further test our hypothesis using an alternative survival model, the CPH model, as a robustness test and for further comparison with other prior studies (e.g. Jain and Kini, 2008; Carpentier and Suret, 2011; Gounopoulos and Pham, 2018). The dependent variable in the CPH model measures the failure risk of IPO firms in the following period after the IPO, unlike the AFT regression model, which focuses on survival time. The marginal effect of each independent variable in the CPH model is estimated by what is called the 'hazard ratio', which is computed as the exponentiated coefficient for each independent variable. Furthermore, the CPH model differs from the AFT model in that the survival time in the AFT model captures the increase or decrease in the survival time after the offering for one unit change in each independent variable, whereas the hazard ratio in the CPH model estimates changes in the risk of delisting or failure for each unit increase in the value of each independent variable.[8] Therefore, a negative coefficient of the independent variable in the CPH model indicates a hazard ratio of less than one, which suggests that an increase in the covariate/independent variable leads to a decrease in the risk of failure after the offering. Consistent with this, a positive coefficient indicates a hazard ratio greater than one, suggesting that a unit increase in the covariate/independent variable leads to an increase in the aftermarket failure risk of the IPO firm (or, in other words, a decrease in the survival rate). For continuous independent variables, the estimated changes in the hazard ratio for one-unit increase is expressed in the form of $100 \times (hazard\ ratio\ - 1)$ (Alhadab *et al.*, 2015). Considering the differences in the sign of the coefficients between the CPH and AFT models, the results from the CPH regressions (reported in Table 3.8) on innovation-related proxies are qualitatively and significantly similar to those presented in the AFT regressions: pre-listing innovation is positively and significantly related to post-IPO survival.

[8]For more detail on the CPH model, please see Klein (1996) and Jain and Kini (2008).

Table 3.8. The results of Cox proportional hazard (CPH) regression estimation.

Variable	(1) Coeff.	(1) HR	(2) Coeff.	(2) HR	(3) Coeff.	(3) HR	(4) Coeff.	(4) HR
Innovation								
Ln(1+Patents)	−0.223***	0.800	−0.219***	0.803				
	(−2.70)		(−2.65)					
Patents/Assets (PTA)					−0.014*	0.986	−0.013*	0.987
					(−1.87)		(−1.74)	
Firm and IPO characteristics								
Ln(Firm age)	−0.208*	0.812	−0.230*	0.795	−0.237*	0.789	−0.262**	0.770
	(−1.68)		(−1.82)		(−1.91)		(−2.07)	
Ln(Firm size)	−0.001	0.999	−0.058	0.943	−0.016	0.984	−0.079	0.924
	(−0.01)		(−0.38)		(−0.11)		(−0.52)	
Ln(Proceed)	0.035	1.036	0.052	1.053	0.011	1.011	0.035	1.036
	(0.27)		(0.39)		(0.087)		(0.26)	
Insider ownership	−0.017***	0.983	−0.017***	0.983	−0.016***	0.984	−0.016***	0.984
	(−4.39)		(−4.36)		(−4.15)		(−4.14)	
Initial return	0.008	1.008	0.009	1.009	0.007	1.007	0.008	1.008
	(1.51)		(1.618)		(1.29)		(1.42)	
PEVC-backing	−0.747***	0.474	−0.840***	0.432	−0.863***	0.422	−0.957***	0.384
	(−3.85)		(−4.20)		(−4.66)		(−4.96)	
Sponsor reputation	−0.438***	0.646	−0.470***	0.625	−0.426***	0.653	−0.452***	0.637
	(−2.71)		(−2.87)		(−2.63)		(−2.76)	
Big4 auditor	0.186	1.204	0.200	1.221	0.168	1.182	0.165	1.179
	(1.01)		(1.10)		(0.91)		(0.91)	
Leverage	0.416**	1.516	0.406**	1.501	0.467**	1.595	0.462**	1.587
	(2.13)		(2.05)		(2.42)		(2.37)	
Profitability	−0.312*	0.732	−0.319*	0.727	−0.273*	0.761	−0.272	0.762
	(−1.85)		(−1.87)		(−1.65)		(−1.64)	
Cash holding	−0.338	0.713	−0.375	0.687	−0.380	0.684	−0.406	0.666
	(−0.84)		(−0.93)		(−0.95)		(−1.01)	

Capital expenditure	0.449	1.566	0.389	1.476	0.510	1.665	0.459	1.582
	(0.58)		(0.50)		(0.66)		(0.58)	
Market-to-book	−0.026	0.975	−0.029	0.972	−0.019	0.981	−0.023	0.977
	(−1.16)		(−1.30)		(−0.84)		(−1.02)	
UK-IPO	0.028	1.028	0.110	1.117	0.083	1.086	0.157	1.170
	(0.14)		(0.53)		(0.42)		(0.75)	
Board characteristics								
Board size			0.077	1.080			0.083	1.087
			(1.23)				(1.33)	
Board ind			0.641	1.899			0.574	1.775
			(1.06)				(0.95)	
CEO-duality			0.402*	1.495			0.380*	1.462
			(1.85)				(1.74)	
Year control	Yes		Yes		Yes		Yes	
Industry control	Yes		Yes		Yes		Yes	
Log-likelihood	−992.69		−989.81		−994.40		−991.67	
LR(Prob.>chi)^2	100.79***		106.55***		97.36***		102.82***	
Time at risk	35,911.87		35,911.87		35,911.87		35,911.87	
Obs	463		463		463		463	

Note: This table displays the estimated results of the CPH model for testing whether and to what extent the pre-listing innovation affects the likelihood of IPO survival in the subsequent periods after the offering. *Failure* is a dummy variable that equals one if the IPO firm was delisted from AIM before the end of December 2017 due to voluntary (e.g. company request) or involuntary reasons (e.g. administration, liquidation, receivership, and failure to meet market standards and rules). *Ln(1+Patents)* is the natural logarithm of one plus the total number of pre-listing successful patent applications. *Patents/Assets* (PTA) is the total number of pre-listing successful patent applications divided by the firm's total assets at the date of offering. The hazard ratio (HR) for each independent variable is estimated as the exponential of the estimated coefficient, exp (β), which measures the failure risk of IPO firm post-offering for one point increase in the independent variables. The hazard ratio above (below) one implies an increase (a decrease) in the failure risk. The Z-statistics are shown in the parentheses below each coefficient estimate. The *, **, and ***asterisks denote the statistical significance at the 10%, 5%, and 1% levels, respectively. The definitions of all variables are reported and discussed in Table 3A.1.

3.6. Conclusion

Using various survival methods and a unique hand-collected dataset encompassing 463 non-financial IPO firms that went public on the UK AIM between 2005 and 2012, in this study, we examine the direct and indirect impacts of a firm's innovation outcomes filed in the period before going public on its post-IPO survival profile and failure. Following previous innovation studies (e.g. Cumming *et al.*, 2020; Cao *et al.*, 2015; Hirshleifer *et al.*, 2012), a firm's innovation is measured based on patent-based metrics derived from the EPO database. Adding to the studies of Wagner and Cockburn (2010), Zhang *et al.* (2018), and Useche (2015), we find a strong and significant indication between pre-listing innovation outcomes and post-IPO performance and survival. Moreover, we also find that the positive effect of pre-listing innovation outputs is stronger and more pronounced among new issuers that are backed by VC and PE companies.

In particular, first, using the non-parametric approach of the survival method (known as the KM method), our results show that the five-year survival rates for IPO firms with pre-listing innovation outcomes is higher (82.67%) than those with no pre-listing innovation (68.32%). Second, controlling for a large number of board-, IPO-, and firm-level characteristics, we further test the association between corporate innovation and post-IPO survival using the parametric approach (called the AFT method), finding that IPO firms with a higher level of pre-listing innovation profile, mainly patents, tend to have a lower probability of failure risk and survive longer in the subsequent years following the IPO compared to their counterparts with less or no innovation. More specifically, we find that, on average, with one unit increase in the number of pre-IPO patents, the aftermarket survival time is more likely to increase by approximately 16%. In addition to that, with all else held equal, sensitivity tests also show that an increase of one standard deviation in the number of pre-listing patents results in an increase of nearly 24 months in the average predicted survival time of new issuers. Finally, by carrying out different types of robustness checks, such as alternative estimation models (e.g. CPH), we find that our results and conclusion are robust and qualitatively similar to those reported in the main analysis.

This study makes significant contributions to the fast-growing literature on the link between innovation and IPO performance by providing fresh evidence that innovation is not only an important factor for the survivability of large and high-tech companies but also a critical and key determinant for the long-term competitiveness, performance, sustainability, and survivability of small and fast-growing companies, regardless of their market environments. We believe that our findings in this chapter can provide some important implications not only for IPO firms regarding the positive and influential power of having patents before going public on their long-term performance and subsequent survivability, but they also provide strong evidence for the firm's managers, boards, shareholders, and other market participants that pre-listing innovation is another significant determinant to consider in decision-making. Furthermore, given that innovation is a key factor in the sustainable economic growth and development of a country, as argued by Solow (1956), our findings also provide clear evidence to market regulators and policymakers that governments need to continue providing innovation support and funds, promoting new innovations, and removing barriers to encourage firms to innovate in order to increase firms' survival profiles and sustainability. Last but not least, although in this study we have conducted a battery of robustness tests and endogeneity checks, as in other studies, our analysis does suffer from a number of limitations. For example, while patenting data have been widely used in recent innovation studies for measuring a firm's innovation over its R&D spending, it is still an imperfect proxy for capturing the whole firm's innovation activities (Karolyi, 2016) or innovations that are still not patented. Further research may consider the impact of pre-listing innovation outcomes on the risk of failure in other European second-tier markets and the LSE.

Appendix 3A

Table 3A.1. Definitions of variables and data sources.

Variable	Definition	Data source
Innovation		
Ln(1+Patents)	The natural logarithm of one plus the total number of successful patent applications that the IPO firm filed prior the date of going public (IPO)	EPO's PATSTAT database
Patents/Assets (PTA)	Total number of successful pre-listing patent applications that IPO firm filed prior to the date of going public (IPO) divided by the firm's total assets, following the work of Hirshleifer *et al.* (2017)	EPO's PATSTAT database, IPO prospectus
Ln(1+ Citations)	The natural logarithm of one plus the total number of forward family citations that firm's patents received prior the date of going public	EPO's PATSTAT database
Ln CitePerPat	The natural logarithm of one plus the adjusted forward family citations per firm's patent, following the work of Adhikari and Agrawal (2016)	EPO's PATSTAT database
Ln(1+ Citations)/ Assets	The natural logarithm of one plus the total number of forward family citations received by the firm's patents scaled by the total assets	EPO's PATSTAT database, IPO prospectus
Innovation dummy	A dummy variable that coded for one if the IPO firm had at least one successful patent application prior to the date of going public (IPO), and zero otherwise, following the work of Cao *et al.* (2015) and Zhang *et al.* (2018)	EPO's PATSTAT database
Board characteristics		
Board size	The total number of directors sitting on the firm board at the time of IPO, including the independent directors	IPO prospectus
Board ind	The proportion of the independent directors sitting on the firm board at the time of IPO, in (percentage),	IPO prospectus

Table 3A.1. (*Continued*)

Variable	Definition	Data source
CEO-duality	A dummy variable that takes a value of one if the CEO of the IPO firm was also the chairman of the firm's board at the time of IPO, and zero otherwise	IPO prospectus
Firm and IPO characteristics		
Ln(Firm age)	The nature logarithm of one plus the firm age in (years). The firm age is measured as the difference between the date of offering (IPO) and the date when the company was incorporated	LSE, IPO prospectus
Ln(Firm size)	The nature logarithm of the market value of the firm's outstanding equities at the time of offering, in (£ million)	LSE
Ln(Proceeds)	The nature logarithm of the total new capital that the newly listed firm was raised at the time of IPO, in (£ million)	LSE
Insider ownership	The proportion of shares that were held by the firm's directors and managers at the time of offering (IPO) in (percentage)	IPO prospectus
Initial returns	The return of the firm's stock on the first trading day. The return is computed as the first closing price minus the offering price divided by the offering price, in (percentage)	LSE and Datastream
PEVC-backing	A dummy variable that takes a value of one if the IPO firm was backed by either venture capital (VC) or private equity (PE) company at the time of offering (IPO), and zero otherwise	IPO prospectus
Sponsor reputation	A dummy variable that takes a value of one if the IPO firm was sponsored by one of the top 20% AIM-nominated advisors (known as NOMADs) at the time of offering (IPO), and zero otherwise. The nominated advisors are ranked based on the number of IPO firms that the nomad was backed prior to the date of the firm offering divided by the total number of the market IPOs, following the work of Espenlaub *et al.* (2012) and Ahmad and Jelic (2014)	LSE, IPO prospectus

(*Continued*)

Table 3A.1. (*Continued*)

Variable	Definition	Data source
Big4 auditor	A dummy variable that takes a value of one if the IPO firm was backed by one of the big four auditing companies (the KPMG, Ernst & Young, Deloitte, and PricewaterhouseCoopers) at the time of offering (IPO), and zero otherwise, following most survival studies (e.g. Gounopoulos and Pham, 2018)	IPO prospectus
Leverage	The book value of debt divided by the book value of firm's assets around the date of offering (IPO)	IPO prospectus
Profitability	The total value of earnings before interests and taxes (EBIT) at the time of offering (IPO) divided by the firm's total assets, following the work of Espenlaub *et al.* (2016)	IPO prospectus
Cash holding	The total value of cash and cash equivalents at the time of offering divided by the firm's total assets	IPO prospectus
Capital expenditure	The total value of capital expenditure at the time of offering (IPO) divided by the firm's total assets	IPO prospectus,
Market-to-book	The market value of the IPO firm at the time of offering divided by its book value of equities	IPO prospectus, datastream
UK-IPO	A dummy variable that takes a value of one if the IPO firm was incorporated in the UK, and zero otherwise	LSE
Other characteristics		
Survival time	The natural logarithm of the survival time, in (months). The survival time is computed as the number of months between the date of offering and the date when the firm was delisted or the end of our tracking period (31 December 2017), whichever was earlier	LSE, AIM monthly reports, LSPD

Table 3A.1. (*Continued*)

Variable	Definition	Data Source
Failure (delist)	A dummy variable that takes a value of one if the IPO firm was delisted from the stock market (AIM) before the end of my tracking period (31st December 2017) due to the voluntary and involuntary (negative) reasons (including administration, liquidation, receivership, and breaking market regulations, bankruptcy, winding up, and company request), and zero otherwise, following the works of Alhadab *et al.* (2015) and Gounopoulos and Pham (2018)	LSE, AIM monthly report, LSPD
HHI	The Herfindahl–Hirschman index, which is the sum of squared market shares of the firms in the same industry at the time of IPO. The market shares are calculated as the ratio of a firm's sales divided by the entire industry sales. A lower HHI suggests a lower concentrated industry and, therefore, a higher product market competition, and vice versa	LSE, IPO prospectus
High-tech	IPO firm is classified as a high-tech IPO if the firm were operating in one of the high-tech market industries, including computer equipment, data processing, technology information, electronic equipment, medical equipment, and scientific equipment, following the work of Kashefi Pour and Lasfer (2013)	LSE

Note: This table displays the data sources and the definitions of all the variables that we used in our empirical analysis.

References

Acharya, V. V. and Subramanian, K. V. (2009). Bankruptcy codes and innovation. *The Review of Financial Studies*, 22(12), 4949–4988.

Adhikari, B. K. and Agrawal, A. (2016). Religion, gambling attitudes and corporate innovation. *Journal of Corporate Finance*, 37, 229–248.

Agarwal, R. (1998). Small firm survival and technological activity. *Small Business Economics*, 11(3), 215–224.

Agarwal, R. and Gort, M. (1996). The evolution of markets and entry, exit and survival of firms. *The Review of Economics and Statistics*, 78(3), 489–498.

Agarwal, R. and Gort, M. (2002). Firm and product life cycles and firm survival. *American Economic Review*, 92(2), 184–190.

Aghion, P., Van Reenen, J., and Zingales, L. (2013). Innovation and institutional ownership. *American Economic Review*, 103(1), 277–304.

Ahmad, W. and Jelic, R. (2014). Lockup agreements and survival of UK IPOs. *Journal of Business Finance and Accounting*, 41(5), 717–742.

Alhadab, M., Clacher, I., and Keasey, K. (2015). Real and accrual earnings management and IPO failure risk. *Accounting and Business Research*, 45(1), 55–92.

Amini, S. and Keasey, K. (2013). The failure of small British Initial Public Offerings on the UK Alternative Investment Market: A research note on spatial and industry effects. *International Small Business Journal*, 31(6), 722–733.

Anagnostopoulou, S. C., Gounopoulos, D., Malikov, K., and Pham, H. (2021). Earnings management by classification shifting and IPO survival. *Journal of Corporate Finance*, 66, 101796.

Atalay, M., Anafarta, N., and Sarvan, F. (2013). The relationship between innovation and firm performance: An empirical evidence from Turkish automotive supplier industry. *Procedia — Social and Behavioral Sciences*, 75, 226–235.

Atanassov, J. (2013). Do hostile takeovers stifle innovation? Evidence from antitakeover legislation and corporate patenting. *The Journal of Finance*, 68(3), 1097–1131.

Audretsch, D. B. (1995). Innovation, growth and survival. *International Journal of Industrial Organization*, 13(4), 441–457.

Audretsch, D. B. and Lehmann, E. E. (2005). The effects of experience, ownership, and knowledge on IPO survival: Empirical evidence from Germany. *Review of Accounting and Finance*, 4(4), 13–33.

Baer, M. (2012). Putting creativity to work: The implementation of creative ideas in organizations. *Academy of Management Journal*, 55(5), 1102–1119.

Balsmeier, B., Buchwald, A., and Stiebale, J. (2014). Outside directors on the board and innovative firm performance. *Research Policy*, 43(10), 1800–1815.

Balsmeier, B., Fleming, L., and Manso, G. (2017). Independent boards and innovation. *Journal of Financial Economics*, 123(3), 536–557.

Banbury, C. M. and Mitchell, W. (1995). The effect of introducing important incremental innovations on market share and business survival. *Strategic Management Journal*, 16(S1), 161–182.

Bancel, F. and Mittoo, U. R. (2009). Why do European firms go public? *European Financial Management*, 15(4), 844–884.

Baranchuk, N., Kieschnick, R., and Moussawi, R. (2014). Motivating innovation in newly public firms. *Journal of Financial Economics*, 111(3), 578–588.

Barker, V. L. and Mueller, G. C. (2002). CEO characteristics and firm R&D spending. *Management Science*, 48(6), 782–801.

Bedford, A., Ma, L., Ma, N., and Vojvoda, K. (2021). Future profitability and stock returns of innovative firms in Australia. *Pacific-Basin Finance Journal*, 66, 101508.

Bernstein, S. (2015). Does going public affect innovation? *The Journal of Finance*, 70(4), 1365–1403.

Bradburn, M. J., Clark, T. G., Love, S. B., and Altman, D. G. (2003). Survival analysis part II: Multivariate data analysis–an introduction to concepts and methods. *British Journal of Cancer*, 89(3), 431–436.

Brav, A. and Gompers, P. A. (1997). Myth or reality? The long-run underperformance of initial public offerings: Evidence from venture and nonventure capital-backed companies. *The Journal of Finance*, 52(5), 1791–1821.

Cao, J., Jiang, F., and Ritter, J. R. (2013). Patent and innovation-driven performance in venture capital-backed IPOs. Working Paper.

Cao, J., Jiang, F., and Ritter, J. R. (2015). Patents, innovation, and performance of venture capital-backed IPOs. Working Paper.

Cao, X., Cumming, D., and Zhou, S. (2020). State ownership and corporate innovative efficiency. *Emerging Markets Review*, 44, 100699.

Carpentier, C. and Suret, J.-M. (2011). The survival and success of Canadian penny stock IPOs. *Small Business Economics*, 36(1), 101–121.

Cefis, E. and Marsili, O. (2006). Survivor: The role of innovation in firms' survival. *Research Policy*, 35(5), 626–641.

Cefis, E. and Marsili, O. (2012). Going, going, gone. Exit forms and the innovative capabilities of firms. *Research Policy*, 41(5), 795–807.

Chan, K., Cooney Jr, J. W., Kim, J., and Singh, A. K. (2008). The IPO derby: Are there consistent losers and winners on this track? *Financial Management*, 37(1), 45–79.

Chancharat, N., Krishnamurti, C., and Tian, G. (2012). Board structure and survival of new economy IPO firms. *Corporate Governance: An International Review*, 20(2), 144–163.

Chava, S., Nanda, V., and Xiao, S. C. (2017). Lending to innovative firms. *The Review of Corporate Finance Studies*, 6(2), 234–289.

Chemmanur, T. J. and Fulghieri, P. (1999). A theory of the going-public decision. *The Review of Financial Studies*, 12(2), 249–279.

Chemmanur, T. J., Loutskina, E., and Tian, X. (2014). Corporate venture capital, value creation, and innovation. *The Review of Financial Studies*, 27(8), 2434–2473.

Chemmanur, T. J. and Tian, X. (2018). Do antitakeover provisions spur corporate innovation? A regression discontinuity analysis. *Journal of Financial and Quantitative Analysis*, 53(3), 1163–1194.

Cho, C., Halford, J. T., Hsu, S., and Ng, L. (2016). Do managers matter for corporate innovation? *Journal of Corporate Finance*, 36, 206–229.

Chou, T.-K., Cheng, J.-C., and Chien, C.-C. (2013). How useful is venture capital prestige? Evidence from IPO survivability. *Small Business Economics*, 40(4), 843–863.

Christensen, C. M., Suarez, F. F., and Utterback, J. M. (1998). Strategies for survival in fast-changing industries. *Management Science*, 44(12), 207–220.

Colak, G., Gounopoulos, D., Loukopoulos, P., and Loukopoulos, G. (2021). Tournament incentives and IPO failure risk. *Journal of Banking and Finance*, 130, 106193.

Cressy, R. and Farag, H. (2014). Stairway to heaven or gateway to hell? A competing risks analysis of delistings from Hong Kong's Growth Enterprise Market. *International Review of Financial Analysis*, 36, 195–205.

Cumming, D., Peter, R., and Tarsalewska, M. (2020). Public-to-private buyouts and innovation. *British Journal of Management*, 31(4), 811–829.

Custodio, C., Ferreira, M. A., and Matos, P. P. (2017). Do general managerial skills spur innovation? Working Paper.

Demers, E. and Joos, P. (2007). IPO failure risk. *Journal of Accounting Research*, 45(2), 333–371.

Espenlaub, S., Goyal, A., and Mohamed, A. (2016). Impact of legal institutions on IPO survival: A global perspective. *Journal of Financial Stability*, 25, 98–112.

Espenlaub, S., Khurshed, A., and Mohamed, A. (2012). IPO survival in a reputational market. *Journal of Business Finance and Accounting*, 39(3), 427–463.

Espenlaub, S., Khurshed, A., Mohamed, A., and Saadouni, B. (2016). Committed anchor investment and IPO survival – The roles of cornerstone and strategic investors. *Journal of Corporate Finance*, 41, 139–155.

Fama, E. F. and French, K. R. (2004). New lists: Fundamentals and survival rates. *Journal of Financial Economics*, 73(2), 229–269.

Fang, V. W., Tian, X., and Tice, S. (2014). Does stock liquidity enhance or impede firm innovation? *The Journal of Finance*, 69(5), 2085–2125.

Field, L. C. and Lowry, M. (2009). Institutional versus individual investment in IPOs: The importance of firm fundamentals. *Journal of Financial and Quantitative Analysis*, 44(3), 489–516.

Galasso, A. and Simcoe, T. S. (2011). CEO overconfidence and innovation. *Management Science*, 57(8), 1469–1484.

Gerakos, J., Lang, M., and Maffett, M. (2013). Post-listing performance and private sector regulation: The experience of London's Alternative Investment Market. *Journal of Accounting and Economics*, 56(2), 189–215.

Giannetti, C. (2012). Relationship lending and firm innovativeness. *Journal of Empirical Finance*, 19(5), 762–781.

Goktan, M. S., Kieschnick, R., and Moussawi, R. (2018). Corporate governance and firm survival. *Financial Review*, 53(2), 209–253.

Gounopoulos, D. and Huang, C. (2018). Geographic dispersion and IPO survival. Working Paper.

Gounopoulos, D. and Pham, H. (2018). Specialist CEOs and IPO survival. *Journal of Corporate Finance*, 48, 217–243.

Greve, H. R. (2003). A behavioral theory of R&D expenditures and innovations: Evidence from shipbuilding. *Academy of Management Journal*, 46(6), 685–702.

Guo, R.-J. and Zhou, N. (2016). Innovation capability and post-IPO performance. *Review of Quantitative Finance and Accounting*, 46(2), 335–357.

Hall, B. H., Jaffe, A., and Trajtenberg, M. (2005). Market value and patent citations. *The RAND Journal of Economics*, 36(1), 16–38.

Hall, B. H. and Ziedonis, R. H. (2001). The patent paradox revisited: An empirical study of patenting in the U.S. semiconductor industry, 1979–1995. *The RAND Journal of Economics*, 32(1), 101–128.

Hambrick, D. C. and Mason, P. A. (1984). Upper echelons: The organization as a reflection of its top managers. *Academy of Management Review*, 9(2), 193–206.

He, J. and Tian, X. (2013). The dark side of analyst coverage: The case of innovation. *Journal of Financial Economics*, 109(3), 856–878.

Hensler, D. A., Rutherford, R. C., and Springer, T. M. (1997). The survival of initial public offerings in the aftermarket. *Journal of Financial Research*, 20(1), 93–110.

Hirshleifer, D., Hsu, P.-H., and Li, D. (2013). Innovative efficiency and stock returns. *Journal of Financial Economics*, 107(3), 632–654.

Hirshleifer, D., Hsu, P.-H., and Li, D. (2017). Innovative originality, profitability, and stock returns. *The Review of Financial Studies*, 31(7), 2553–2605.

Hirshleifer, D., Hsu, P.-H., and Li, D. (2018). Innovative originality, profitability, and stock returns. *The Review of Financial Studies*, 31(7), 2553–2605.

Hirshleifer, D., Low, A., and Teoh, S. H. (2012). Are overconfident CEOs better innovators? *The Journal of Finance*, 67(4), 1457–1498.

Holmstrom, B. (1989). Agency costs and innovation. *Journal of Economic Behavior and Organization*, 12(3), 305–327.

Hottenrott, H., Hall, B. H., and Czarnitzki, D. (2016). Patents as quality signals? The implications for financing constraints on R&D. *Economics of Innovation and New Technology*, 25(3), 197–217.

Hsu, H.-C. (2014). Industry technological innovations and initial public offerings: An empirical analysis. *Journal of Accounting and Finance*, 14(1), 38–61.

Huyghebaert, N. and Van Hulle, C. (2006). Structuring the IPO: Empirical evidence on the portions of primary and secondary shares. *Journal of Corporate Finance*, 12(2), 296–320.

Jain, B. A. and Kini, O. (2000). Does the presence of venture capitalists improve the survival profile of IPO firms? *Journal of Business Finance and Accounting*, 27(9), 1139–1183.

Jain, B. A. and Kini, O. (2008). The impact of strategic investment choices on post-issue operating performance and survival of US IPO firms. *Journal of Business Finance and Accounting*, 35(3), 459–490.

Jain, B. A. and Martin Jr, C. L. (2005). The association between audit quality and post-IPO performance: A survival analysis approach. *Review of Accounting and Finance*, 4(4), 50–75.

Jenkins, S. P. (2005). Survival analysis. Working Paper, Institute for Social and Economic Research.

Karolyi, G. A. (2016). The gravity of culture for finance. *Journal of Corporate Finance*, 41, 610–625.

Kashefi Pour, E. (2015). IPO survival and CEOs' decision-making power: The evidence of China. *Research in International Business and Finance*, 33, 247–267.

Kashefi Pour, E. and Lasfer, M. (2013). Why do companies delist voluntarily from the stock market? *Journal of Banking and Finance*, 37(12), 4850–4860.

Kooli, M. and Meknassi, S. (2007). The survival profile of US IPO issuers: 1985-2005. *The Journal of Wealth Management*, 10(2), 105–119.

Lerner, J., Sorensen, M., and Strömberg, P. (2011). Private equity and long-run investment: The case of innovation. *The Journal of Finance*, 66(2), 445–477.

Lin, C., Lin, P., Song, F. M., and Li, C. (2011). Managerial incentives, CEO characteristics and corporate innovation in China's private sector. *Journal of Comparative Economics*, 39(2), 176–190.

Maksimovic, V. and Pichler, P. (2015). Technological innovation and initial public offerings. *The Review of Financial Studies*, 14(2), 459–494.

Mazouz, K. and Zhao, Y. (2019). CEO incentives, takeover protection and corporate innovation. *British Journal of Management*, 30(2), 494–515.

Mazzoleni, R. and Nelson, R. R. (1998). The benefits and costs of strong patent protection: A contribution to the current debate. *Research Policy*, 27(3), 273–284.

Mendoza, J. M. (2008). Securities regulation in low-tier listing venues: The rise of the alternative investment market. *Fordham Journal of Corporate and Financial Law*, 13(2), 257–328.

Muller, P. and Pénin, J. (2007). Why do firms disclose knowledge and how does it matter? In *Innovation, Industrial Dynamics and Structural Transformation*, 149–172.

Murphy, G. B., Trailer, J. W., and Hill, R. C. (1996). Measuring performance in entrepreneurship research. *Journal of Business Research*, 36(1), 15–23.

Nielsson, U. (2013). Do less regulated markets attract lower quality firms? Evidence from the London AIM market. *Journal of Financial Intermediation*, 22(3), 335–352.

Ombaka, B., Machuki, V., and Mahasi, J. (2015). Organizational resources, external environment, innovation and firm performance: A critical review of literature. *DBA Africa Management Review*, 5(1), 41–57.

Pakes, A. and Schankerman, M. (1984). The rate of obsolescence of patents, research gestation lags, and the private rate of return to research resources. In *R&D, Patents, and Productivity*, 73–88.

Pérez, S. E., Llopis, A. S., and Llopis, J. A. S. (2004). The determinants of survival of Spanish manufacturing firms. *Review of Industrial Organization*, 25(3), 251–273.

Porter, M. E. and Wayland, R. (1992). Capital disadvantage: America's failing capital investment system. *Harvard Business Review*, 70(5), 65–82.

Ritter, J. R. (1987). The costs of going public. *Journal of Financial Economics*, 19(2), 269–281.

Ritter, J. R. (1991). The long-run performance of initial public offerings. *The Journal of Finance*, 46(1), 3–27.

Robson, G., Gallagher, C., and Daly, M. (1993). Diversification strategy and practice in small firms. *International Small Business Journal*, 11(2), 37–53.

Santa, R., Hyland, P., and Ferrer, M. (2014). Technological innovation and operational effectiveness: Their role in achieving performance improvements. *Production Planning and Control*, 25(12), 969–979.

Schultz, P. (1993). Unit initial public offerings: A form of staged financing. *Journal of Financial Economics*, 34(2), 199–229.

Shen, C. H. and Zhang, H. (2013). CEO risk incentives and firm performance following R&D increases. *Journal of Banking and Finance*, 37(4), 1176–1194.

Signori, A. (2016). Signaling through innovation in IPOs. In *University Evolution, Entrepreneurial Activity and Regional Competitiveness*, 427–439.

Solow, R. M. (1956). A contribution to the theory of economic growth. *The Quarterly Journal of Economics*, 70(1), 65–94.

Sørensen, J. B. and Stuart, T. E. (2000). Aging, obsolescence, and organizational innovation. *Administrative Science Quarterly*, 45(1), 81–112.

Srivastava, A. (2014). Selling-price estimates in revenue recognition and the usefulness of financial statements. *Review of Accounting Studies*, 19(2), 661–697.

Taneja, S., Pryor, M. G., and Hayek, M. (2016). Leaping innovation barriers to small business longevity. *Journal of Business Strategy*, 37(3), 44–51.

Tuan, N., Nhan, N., Giang, P., and Ngoc, N. (2016). The effects of innovation on firm performance of supporting industries in Hanoi, Vietnam. *Journal of Industrial Engineering and Management*, 9(2), 413–431.

Useche, D. (2014). Are patents signals for the IPO market? An EU–US comparison for the software industry. *Research Policy*, 43(8), 1299–1311.

Useche, D. (2015). Patenting behaviour and the survival of newly listed European software firms. *Industry and Innovation*, 22(1), 37–58.

Vismara, S. (2014). Patents, R&D investments and post-IPO strategies. *Review of Managerial Science*, 8(3), 419–435.

Vismara, S., Paleari, S., and Ritter, J. R. (2012). Europe's second markets for small companies. *European Financial Management*, 18(3), 352–388.

Wagner, S. and Cockburn, I. (2010). Patents and the survival of Internet-related IPOs. *Research Policy*, 39(2), 214–228.

Wang, Y., Farag, H., and Ahmad, W. (2021). Corporate culture and innovation: A tale from an emerging market. *British Journal of Management*, forthcoming.

Welbourne, T. M. and Andrews, A. O. (1996). Predicting the performance of initial public offerings: Should human resource management be in the equation? *Academy of Management Journal*, 39(4), 891–919.

Wu, J. and Tu, R. (2007). CEO stock option pay and R&D spending: A behavioral agency explanation. *Journal of Business Research*, 60(5), 482–492.

Yuan, R. and Wen, W. (2018). Managerial foreign experience and corporate innovation. *Journal of Corporate Finance*, 48, 752–770.

Zhang, D., Zheng, W., and Ning, L. (2018). Does innovation facilitate firm survival? Evidence from Chinese high-tech firms. *Economic Modelling*, 75, 458–468.

Zhou, L. and Sadeghi, M. (2019). The impact of innovation on IPO short-term performance — Evidence from the Chinese markets. *Pacific-Basin Finance Journal*, 53, 208–235.

Part 2
Venture Capital and Private Equity

https://doi.org/10.1142/9781800617032_0004

Chapter 4

Venture Capital

Murad Zeynalov and Yelin Zhang
Gonzaga University, Spokane, USA

4.1. Introduction

To many businesses, raising money from external resources is critically important to their survival and development because the cash generated from sales can be insufficient. Large and mature businesses, especially publicly traded companies, have relatively easy access to capital markets: they receive more attention from investors and media, maintain more detailed business records, and enjoy lower information asymmetry with external investors. Small and young businesses, on the other hand, face more difficulties in external financing: they usually lack stable cash inflows and extensive business tracking records; moreover, quality signalling to external investors is no easy task for small business entrepreneurs. Further, many small and young businesses cannot provide sufficient collateral to borrow money from traditional banking systems. However, great businesses can have humble starts. Without financing support for small and young businesses, fewer companies would grow large and strong. More directly, small businesses are critically important in economic development: they account for the majority of businesses and contribute to more than 50% of employment worldwide.[1]

[1]https://www.worldbank.org/en/topic/smefinance.

Venture capital (VC) offers an important alternative financing channel for small businesses. Compared with traditional banking systems, VC funds are willing to take much higher risks when financing small and young businesses. While traditional banks emphasise the tracking records and current profitability of a business, VC funds focus on its future growth potential: a young venture without significant business transaction records and losing money in the concurrent period may be favoured by VC funds due to its large market size, strong product traction, and an efficient management team. VC funds' risk-taking is supported by their active involvement in the venture's business operations and strategic developments. Most VC funds specialise in one industry sector, bring valuable experience and insights into the investee companies, and guide entrepreneurs in important strategic decision-making. In exchange for capital investment, VC funds usually receive equity or convertible debt issued by the investee companies and often have board seats in investee companies. VC funds' active engagement with investee companies is very different from the passive lending from traditional banks, credit unions, or savings and loan associations, which rarely get involved in investee companies' business activities and receive only principal and interest payments for their investments.

VC funds' active investment calls for significant devotion of time, effort, and capital into every investee company. Consequently, they cannot diversify their investment portfolios. It is rarely heard that a VC fund invests in more than 100 companies, although the Canadian labour-sponsored venture capital corporation (LSVCC) is an exception. Most VC funds only invest in a small group of companies in the same industry sector. As expected, VC funds are highly selective when making investment decisions and are very effective at turning down business proposals. Ironically, despite the highly selective investment screening process and VC funds' active engagement with entrepreneurs and the underlying businesses, most VC investments end up losing money. The risks embedded in small business investment can never be exaggerated, even for professionally managed VC funds.

While a VC fund can guide its investee companies towards great success, it can also result in unexpected consequences for the companies, such as a forced merger & acquisition (M&A) or even CEO replacement. The main reason pertains to the nature of VC funds – they must cash out and return profit to their own investors within a predetermined investment horizon, usually 6–8 years, with a possible short-term extension. Although entrepreneurs may have non-pecuniary interest in running a business, for example, self-fulfilment or making social contributions, VC funds, however, focus exclusively on monetary returns. When an IPO is not feasible on the horizon, VC funds will seek alternative exit channels, such as M&A or buyouts from other investors. If entrepreneurs have plans different from VC funds on business development, they could be removed from executive positions by the VC funds. The complex interactions between entrepreneurs and VC funds imply a mutual principal–agent relationship: on the one hand, VC acts as the principal, and entrepreneurs owe fiduciary duties to VC funds and need to generate returns on VC investments; on the other hand, the entrepreneur acts as the principal, and VC funds need to provide resources and proper guidance to entrepreneurs in exchange for the entrepreneurs' trust in forming the strategic cooperation.

The dynamics in VC investments and small business development have long attracted attention from scholars worldwide. Over the years, VC investments have been an important topic in academic research. Because VC funds invest in private businesses, it is often not straightforward to obtain their investment information or the investee companies' conditions. Traditionally, analyses on VC investments rely on surveys, questionnaires, and interviews; more recently, formalised data venders have become available. In the following, we review and summarise influential studies on VC investments in each decade since the 1980s.

4.2. Literature on the Relation Between Institutional Investors and VC Fund Managers

In this section, we summarise important literature examining the interactions between institutional investors and VC fund managers, including fundraising, fund size and scale diseconomies, and contractual agreements for limited partnerships.

Wetzel (1987) found that the informal VC market is twice the size of the professional VC market. The number of ventures financed by informal investors appears to be at least 10 times the number of ventures financed by professional VC firms. Florida and Kenney (1988) found that VC is concentrated in distinct types of areas: those with high concentrations of financial resources, those with high concentrations of technology-intensive small businesses, and those featuring both. Further, VC complexes based in financial centres, such as New York or Chicago, contain relatively large proportions of VC subsidiaries of financial institutions and export their funds. Poterba (1989) argued that reductions in the capital gains tax rate raise the attractiveness of VC projects for some investors and potential entrepreneurs, and such reductions exert a positive effect on the level of venture activity.

Harrison and Mason (1992) found that informal investors play an important role in financing new and small ventures in the UK. Entrepreneurs are more likely to raise small investments under 50,000 pounds from informal investors than from formal VCs. Berglöf (1994) found that VC agreements typically allow for the possibility of the firm becoming widely held in the future. This possibility should also affect the design of financial instruments in the closely held entrepreneurial firm. Fiet (1995) found that the more an investor is concerned about a particular type of risk, the less likely he or she will be to use informal network informants, even if the information is market related. Gompers and Lerner (1999) found that VC entrants may not possess superior information about their investment abilities and may be more concerned about establishing a reputation.

Zacharakis and Meyer (2000) showed that more information appears to hinder the VC's decision process, even though most people prefer more information when making complex decisions. Wong *et al.* (2002) found that angels have a complementary role to VC in the financing of new ventures. Wright and Lockett (2003) found that a high proportion of VC firms act as both leads and non-leads in different syndicates over time. Informational asymmetries are dealt with through contracting arrangements between the lead and non-lead syndicate members. Jones and Rhodes-Kropf (2003) argued that unavoidable principal–agent problems in the private equity and VC markets, combined with the need for investment oversight, result in idiosyncratic risk that must be priced. Kanniainen and Keuschnigg (2004) found that VC investment can expand only if the existing funds finance more start-ups each. However, when the total cost of managerial effort increases progressively, a larger number of portfolio companies tend to dilute the managerial support available to each individual firm, making start-ups riskier. Hsu (2004) found that VC funds' reputation may be more distinctive than their functionally equivalent financial capital. Smith (2005) found that venture capitalists and entrepreneurs may have different interests regarding the timing and form of exit. Hellmann *et al.* (2008) noted that banks build relationships in the VC market that can be mutually advantageous in the loan market. Winton and Yerramilli (2008) suggested that VC differs from bank finance by greater use of equity features and by more active monitoring, particularly when the firm is choosing continuation strategies.

Hochberg (2011) found that pre-IPO VC backing influences the governance and monitoring of the entrepreneurial firm during transition to the public markets. Other types of pre-IPO large shareholders, such as corporate and angel investors, do not appear to have similar effects on the governance of the entrepreneurial firm. Hopp and Rieder (2011) found that more risks and higher capital requirements affect the incentives of VCs to involve partners positively. Puri and Zarutskie (2012) found that VC-financed firms make up an extremely small percentage of all new firms created. Further, venture capitalists disproportionately invest in firms that have no commercial sales but exhibit high levels of initial investment. They also reported that VC-financed firms grew larger than non-VC-financed firms, as measured by employment and sales, suggesting that VC backs firms capable of achieving large scale. Hellmann and Thiele (2015) found that venture capitalists' bargaining power depends on how competitive venture markets are and how well angels are legally protected. Robinson (2022) found that mentors in accelerator programmes prioritise entrepreneurial signalling over initial venture characteristics.

4.3. Literature on the Relation Between VC Fund Managers and Entrepreneurs

In this section, we summarise important literature investigating the relation between VC fund managers and entrepreneurs, including contract choices, portfolio size, portfolio managers, valuation, board seats, staging, and syndication.

Ruhnka and Young (1987) found that VC firms exhibited a high degree of consensus on strategic benchmarks. Khan (1987) argues that the venture capitalists must exercise scrutiny on the entrepreneurs' potential for creativity and ingenuity. Bygrave (1987) revealed that entrepreneurs looking for VC should seek firms that are known to invest in the type of product that they make or plan to make. It is more important to pick the VC firm that will give the most support after it invests its money rather than the one that offers the cheapest financing. Maier and Walker (1987) revealed that most of the VC investments are in small firms and that most venture capitalists receive fewer than 700 requests per year. Rosenstein (1988) discussed the elements that are conducive to active involvement of the board in strategy formulation and in the monitoring of its implementation.

Hisrich and Jankowicz (1990) found that there was a predominant management component in the investment decision with relatively few constructs dealing with the issue of an adequate return on investment. Barry *et al.* (1990) found that venture capitalists participate actively in and monitor the progress of their portfolio companies. Further, the venture capitalists specialise in a narrow set of industries for which they can develop expertise. Ruhnka and Young (1991) reported that a high proportion of the anticipated risks for early-stage ventures consisted of internally determined venture-specific factors, such as difficulties in product development and the capabilities and weaknesses of specific management teams. Norton and Tenenbaum (1993) found that investors in seed deals are less diversified across different industries and firms. Further, venture capitalists appear to specialise in certain financing stages rather than stagger their investments over different financing stages. Elango *et al.* (1995) found that earlier-stage investors are interested in unique, proprietary products with high growth potential, whereas late-stage investors demand a market-proven product. Zider (1998) argued that an entrepreneur needs to show the venture capitalist that their team and idea fit into the VC's current focus and that their equity participation and management skills will make the VC's job easier and the returns higher. When the entrepreneur understands the needs of the funding source and sets expectations properly, both the VC and the entrepreneur can profit handsomely. Fried *et al.* (1998) demonstrated that boards of VC-backed firms are much more active than traditional boards. Hellmann (1998) found that when venture capitalists have control, they put greater effort into finding professional managers who increase the value of the company. Furthermore, wealth-constrained entrepreneurs may relinquish control, even if the replacement decision hurts the entrepreneur more than it benefits the venture capitalists. Smith (1998) showed that the market for venture capitalist reputation is the glue that holds the VC process together. Entrepreneurs face substantial agency costs in 'hiring' venture capitalists to perform value-added services, and the explicit terms of VC contracts do not adequately protect entrepreneurs from opportunism and incompetence. Trester (1998) contributed to the VC literature by analysing the role of asymmetric information conditions. He showed that the choice of preferred equity over debt has been explored and shown to be potentially motivated by intertemporal incentive inconsistencies due to the possibility of information asymmetries in certain states of intermediate return. Bergemann and Hege (1998) provided a rationale for long-term contracting that these contracts achieve best the goal of distributing the entrepreneur's return over time in a way which maximises the research horizon. Amit *et al.* (1998) argued that moral hazard and adverse selection create a market failure in entrepreneurial financing, which might lead many worthwhile projects to remain unfunded or underfunded. The more skilled the venture capitalist is in reducing these sources of market failure, the more effectively this sector will function.

Hellmann and Puri (2000) argued that firms pursuing an innovator rather than an imitator strategy are more likely to obtain VC financing. Keuschnigg and Nielsen (2001) found that, to preserve incentives and simultaneously provide insurance to risk-averse entrepreneurs, venture capitalists typically arrange for a combination of an equity share and a modest base salary. Engel (2002) found that the impact of VC on new firms' growth does not differ between high-tech and low-tech industries. Hellmann and Puri (2002) provided evidence for the role of VC in the professionalisation of start-up companies. Obtaining VC is related to a variety of organisational milestones, such as the formulation of human resource policies, the adoption of stock option plans, or the hiring of a VP of sales. Schmidt (2003) found that convertible securities endogenously allocate cash flow rights based on the realisation of the state of the world and the effort provided by the entrepreneur. By choosing the conversion rate appropriately, the venture capitalist can invest efficiently if and only if the entrepreneur invested at least the efficient amount. Keuschnigg and Nielsen (2003) found that even though financiers may, in principle, diversify project risk, some risk-bearing on the part of entrepreneurs is nevertheless required to contain moral hazard in the relation between VCs and entrepreneurs. Apart from financing, VCs also help with valuable business advice to enhance the survival chances of their portfolio companies. Ueda (2004) found that low collateral value, high growth, high return, and high risk of the project all raise the cost of the asymmetric information and thereby drive the entrepreneur to finance through the venture capitalist. Stronger protection of intellectual property rights weakens the potential threat of the venture capitalist expropriating the entrepreneur's project, thereby encouraging the entrepreneur to finance through the venture capitalist. Romain and Pottelsberghe (2004) suggested that VC contributes to growth through two main channels. The first one is the introduction of new products and processes on the market. The second one is the development of an improved absorptive capacity of the knowledge generated by private and public research institutions. Bettignies and Brander (2007) argued that the desirability of VC finance depends largely on the venture capitalist's ability to provide managerial contributions to the venture. Engel and Keilbach (2007) found that firms with higher innovative output and higher educated management have a larger probability of getting venture capital.

Colombo and Grilli (2010) noted that firms founded by individuals with specific human capital characteristics can leverage the distinctive capabilities associated with the knowledge and skills of their founders to grow larger than other firms. Ferrary (2010) found that the funding of a seed stage is a formal contract that allows a learning-by-collaborating relationship between investors and entrepreneurs to transform uncertainty into risk. The formal contract sustains the construction of the strong social ties needed to create and transfer tacit knowledge. Xuan (2011) reported that a VC investor who is located farther away from an entrepreneurial firm tends to finance the firm with a larger number of financing rounds, a shorter duration between successive rounds, and with a smaller amount in each round. Tian (2012) found that VC syndication creates value for their entrepreneurial firms in two dimensions. First, VC syndication creates product market value by investing significant amounts in younger firms, in earlier financing rounds, and in early-stage firms. Furthermore, VC syndicates nurture innovation in their portfolio firms and help them achieve better post-IPO operating performance. Popov and Roosenboom (2012) reported that venture capitalists force firms to professionalise and become more business-oriented but not more innovative after they have invested. Bottazzi *et al.* (2016) found that generalised trust is a force that cannot be ignored in the analysis of VC investment. Ewens *et al.* (2022) found that contracts materially affect the value of the firm, as well as its split between entrepreneur and investor. There is an internally optimal split between investor and entrepreneur that maximises the probability of success. However, VCs receive more equity than is value-maximising for the start-up.

4.4. Literature on Venture Exits

In this section, we summarise important studies addressing venture exits, including IPOs, acquisitions, secondary sales, buybacks, and write-offs.

Gompers (1996) argued that the tremendous entry of new VC firms and the incentives to grandstand explain some of the declining returns on VC in the 1980s. Black and Gilson (1998) showed that economies of scope among financial and nonfinancial contributions by VC providers, plus VC investors' need for a quantitative measure of VC funds' skill, can explain the importance of an exit strategy. Moreover, the potential for exit through an IPO, possible in a stock-market-centred capital market, allows the venture capitalist and the entrepreneur to contract implicitly over control in a manner that is not easily duplicable in a bank-centred capital market.

Jeng and Wells (2000) showed that over time, IPOs become the main force behind the cyclical swings in VC. Liang (2001) showed that the geometric average annual return for VC from 1987 to 1999 is 55.18%, with an upper bound of 60.93% and a lower bound of 28.28%. In addition, the VC returns are volatile. There is a strong correlation between the VC index returns and the returns of NASDAQ on a yearly scale. Brander *et al.* (2002) found that syndicated projects should have higher rates of return than standalone projects. Hochberg *et al.* (2007) observed that VC funds whose parent firms enjoy more influential network positions realise significantly better performance, as measured by the proportion of portfolio investments that are successfully exited through an IPO or a sale to another company. Cumming (2008) found that the probability of an acquisition is approximately 30% higher when VCs have effective contractual control rights, such as drag-along rights, board control, and the ability to replace the founding entrepreneur as CEO. Further, weak VC control rights are associated with a greater probability of IPO write-off exits. Schwienbacher (2008) found that more innovative and profitable ventures are more likely to go public than ventures with more imitative or derivative projects. Nahata (2008) noted that companies led by more reputable VCs based on the cumulative market capitalisation of IPOs backed by the VC firm are more likely to exit successfully, access public markets faster, and have higher asset productivity at IPOs.

Chen *et al.* (2010) concluded that the success rate of VC investments in a region is an important determinant of VC firms' decisions to open new branches. Nanda *et al.* (2020) found that the initial level of success of VC predicts future success for as many as 50 subsequent investments. Fuchs *et al.* (2022) found that the higher the average university ranking of the management team, the higher its fund performance. Investors can use the educational profiles of the team members in their evaluation of fund managers and that success in private equity is conditional on team resources.

4.5. Literature on Other VC Topics

In this section, we summarise important studies on other interesting topics, including corporate VC, government VC, and international differences in VC.

Rind (1981) summarised the role of VC in corporate development. Winters and Murfin (1988) found that the success of a corporate venture investing programme depends on a clear definition of financial and/or strategic goals. The main determinants of success are organisational structure, creation of a large, quality deal stream, and the involvement of high-quality people at the VC/corporate interface.

Sahlman (1990) argued that the VC organisational form may be applicable in other settings, particularly corporate and project governance. Florida and Smith (1990) proposed that there are serious reasons to question the efficacy of government involvement in VC. Ooghe *et al.* (1991) found that the United Kingdom, the Netherlands, and France account for 80% of all European VC. Gompers and Lerner (1999) demonstrated that higher GDP growth and increases in R&D spending led to greater VC activity. They further revealed that capital gains tax rates matter, with lower rates leading to a greater quantity of VC raised.

Hamao *et al.* (2000) found that in Japan, most of the major VC firms are subsidiaries of securities firms and banks. They documented that VC-backed IPOs in Japan do not perform better in the long run than other IPOs relative to size- or industry-matched firms, except for those backed by foreign-owned or independent venture capitalists. Harrison and Mason (2000) showed that significant complementarities exist in the UK between business angels and VC funds focused on relatively small-scale start-up and early-stage investments. Kortum and Lerner (2001) argued that VC has had a substantial impact on innovation in the US economy. Further, the jump in venture disbursements since 1995 may trigger an additional wave of innovative activity. Schwienbacher (2002) found that young venture capitalists in Europe tend to monitor less but invest proportionally more in early stages than their more established colleagues. Gilson (2002) proposed that the government should address the simultaneity problem by providing seed capital and help create the necessary financial intermediaries that, together, will encourage the supply of entrepreneurs while, at the same time, maintaining the pattern of intense incentives coupled with intense monitoring that characterises US VC contracting. Bruton *et al.* (2002) found that the Singapore VC industry has developed some characteristics that are rather unique in Asia. The industry was largely created by incentives and other regulatory efforts and by the direct participation of the government. Powell *et al.* (2002) found a strong pattern of spatial concentration in biotech and VC. Manigart *et al.* (2002c) found that European VC managers are well aware of the financial benefits that syndication may yield, but they seem to underestimate the importance of additional benefits, such as getting access to additional resources, building strong and trustworthy networks, and increasing deal flow. Randjelovic *et al.* (2003) found that the development of green VC depends on the implementation of some specific types of regulation. Cumming and MacIntosh (2004) reported significant differences between the US and Canadian VC investments, both in the frequency with which types of exits were used and in their profitability. Brush *et al.* (2004) found that women constitute a very small percentage of VC decision-makers. Wright *et al.* (2005) identified major research gaps in relation to work dealing with the international development of VC industries and crossing of country borders by VC firms. Cumming (2006) found that Canadian VC investors appear to face the greatest uncertainty among firms with high expected variability in returns in financing start-up stages and high-tech firms. Furthermore, syndication mitigates problems of adverse selection. VC syndicates facilitate an important role in screening potential investees and mitigating the risk of financing low-quality firms. Rin *et al.* (2006) found that policies aimed at increasing the expected return of projects are more successful in altering the composition of VC markets towards projects with less collateral, namely early-stage projects and projects in high-tech industries. Cumming (2006) found that there is a trade-off between VC assistance to entrepreneurial firms in the VC's portfolio and the size of the portfolio. Fund-raising and the number of funds operated by the VC firm have a significantly positive impact on VC portfolio size. Ahlstrom and Bruton (2006) found that VC practice in emerging economies diverges from Anglo-American models in several specific areas. In emerging economies with weak formal institutions, less formal institutions sometimes act as substitutes for the lack of formal institutions. Dushnitsky and Lenox (2006) found that corporate venture capitalists experience increased value creation, as measured by levels of Tobin's q. Hsu (2007) found that human capital accumulation can help build ventures' social capital. Furthermore, measures of human capital and social capital are positively related to venture valuation. Mollica and Zingales (2007) found that VC has a positive impact on innovation and the creation of new companies. Guler and Guillén (2009) highlighted the importance of national systems of innovation in attracting foreign VC investment. Hege *et al.* (2009) found that the US VC industry strongly outperforms its European counterpart.

Samila and Sorenson (2010) concluded that public research funding generates more patents and start-ups in regions rich in VC. Ghosh and Nanda (2010) argued that longer-term innovation in this space by venture-backed start-ups in the US will depend critically on the ability of the innovation ecosystem to adapt to the different structural characteristics of the clean energy sector. Further, one of the most important bottlenecks threatening the innovation pipeline in energy production is the inability of VCs to exit their investments at the appropriate time. Chemmanur *et al.* (2011) found that the overall efficiency of VC-backed firms is higher than that of non-VC-backed firms at every point in time. This efficiency advantage of VC-backed firms arises from both screening and monitoring. The efficiency of VC-backed firms prior to receiving financing is higher than that of non-VC-backed firms, and further, the growth in efficiency subsequent to VC financing is greater for such firms. Schertler and Tykvová (2011) found that domestically experienced venture capitalists seem to be able to exploit the advantages of internationalisation more effectively than their less experienced counterparts. Foreign venture capitalists are more likely to participate in larger deals, especially when the portfolio company is in a small country. Hargadon and Kenney (2012) argued that VC is an ill-suited investment vehicle – let alone policy framework – for fostering a clean technology revolution. Lerner and Tåg (2013) argued that the legal environment and financial market development matter for the development of active VC markets. Block *et al.* (2013) found that trademarks are associated with not only the market valuations of large firms but also VC funds' financial valuations of start-ups. Popov and Roosenboom (2013) found that VC investment has a sizeable effect on new business creation. Faria and Barbosa (2014) found that only the later-stage VC capital is promoting innovation. Bertoni *et al.* (2015) found that in Europe, VC investor types exhibit different investment patterns in terms of industry, age, size, stage of development, and localisation of their investee companies. Cumming *et al.* (2016) reported that oil prices have a curvilinear effect on cleantech VC investments. Increases in oil prices increase cleantech VC deals but with a slowing rate of increase. Uncertainty avoidance has a negative and statistically significant impact on cleantech VC deals. Maula and Murray (2017) indicated that the association of new enterprises with industry-leading corporations via the agency of corporate venture capitalists may lead to higher IPO valuations. Ewens *et al.* (2018) showed how technological shocks to the cost of experimentation can play a central role in shaping both the rate and trajectory of start-up innovation by allowing more long-shot bets to receive initial funding and thereby also reducing the chance of 'false negatives' in the economy. Cumming and Schweinbacher (2018) found that fintech start-ups have been able to raise significant amounts of capital in the most recent years. They provided evidence that this change is more pronounced among smaller, private, independent, limited-partnership VCs and in countries without a major financial centre. Metrick and Yasuda (2021) found that a high-reputation VC is more likely to have its term sheets accepted and can pay lower prices for shares than a low-reputation one. More recently, Dai (2022) showed that the total volume of angel investment has long surpassed VC investment in the US and is increasingly doing so in some other countries as well. Some accelerators enhance venture development. Bianchini and Croce (2022) found that environmental taxes evidence a U-shaped relationship with the number of IVC investments and the amount invested in the cleantech sector, with an initial positive effect of these instruments in fostering VC investment in cleantech and a subsequent negative effect in the presence of extremely high taxation levels. A moderate level of environmental taxes fosters innovation and provides an incentive for private VC funds to invest in clean technologies. Koenig and Burghof (2022) found that style drifts represent shifts in the risk profile of a fund. When drifts are deliberate risk-taking decisions motivated by potential compensation benefits for general partners, they constitute an agency conflict. Further, VCs have a higher risk-taking attitude regarding all investment-style drifts when public markets are rising. Smith *et al.* (2022) documented that the probability of limited partner (LP) reporting is strongly related to LP FOIA eligibility.

Table 4.1 summarises the dataset used in recent studies on VC.

Table 4.1. Empirical dataset used in recent studies on venture capital.

Panel A. Studies on the relation between institutional investors and VC fund managers							
Authors	Title of the paper	Journal	Publication year	Data source	Data country	Data time span	Key finding
Wetzel	The informal venture capital market: Aspects of scale and market efficiency	*Journal of Business Venturing*	1987	SEC reports, Applied Economics Group, Inc. (AEG)	US data	1984–1986	Informal VC market is twice the size of the professional VC market. The number of ventures financed by informal investors appears to be at least 10 times the number of ventures financed by professional VC firms.
Florida and Kenney	Venture capital, high technology and regional development	*Regional Studies*	1988a	Venture Capital Journal	US data	1978–1986	There are significant differences among the major VC complexes. Not surprisingly, VC is concentrated in distinct types of areas: those with high concentrations of financial resources, those with high concentrations of technology-intensive small businesses, and those with both.

(*Continued*)

Table 4.1. (*Continued*)

Panel A. Studies on the relation between institutional investors and VC fund managers							
Authors' names	Title of the paper	Journal name	Publication year	Data source	Data country	Data time span	Key finding
Florida and Kenney	Venture capital-financed innovation and technological change in the USA	*Research Policy*	1988b	Venture Economics (*Venture Capital Yearbook*)	US data	1972–1983	VC-financed innovation accelerates the processes of technology innovation and business formation by combining resources and personnel drawn from a variety of organisations. In addition, VC-financed innovation occupies a particular niche in the technology cycle.
Poterba	Venture capital and capital gains taxation	*Tax Policy and The Economy*	1989	*Venture Capital Yearbook* (Venture Economics), *An Analysis of Venture Capital Market Imperfections* (Charles River Associates)	US data (British and Canadian comparison)	1969–1987	Reductions in the capital gains tax rate are likely to exert some positive effect on the level of venture activity.
Harrison and Mason	International perspectives on the supply of informal venture capital	*Journal of Business Venturing*	1992	Postal survey, snowball sample	US, UK, Canadian data	1990s	Informal investors play an important role in financing new and small ventures in UK; entrepreneurs are more likely to raise small investments under 50000 pounds from informal investors than from formal VCs

Florida and Smith	Venture capital formation, investment, and regional industrialization	*Annals of the Association of American Geographers*	1993	Venture Economics, Pratt and Morris, *Venture Capital Journal*	US data	1983–1987	The findings indicate that supply clusters around concentrations of financial institutions and assets, concentrations of high-technology industry, and the presence of VC co-investment networks.
Berglöf	A control theory of venture capital finance	*Journal of Law, Economics, and Organization*	1994	N/A	N/A	N/A	VC agreements typically allow for the possibility that the firm will be widely held in the future.
Fried and Hisrich	Toward a model of venture capital investment decision making	*Financial Management*	1994	Interviews (18 VCs)	US data	Early 1990s	VCs provide benefits to both the supply and demand sides of the market. VCs negotiate basic contract terms fairly early in the process.
Mason and Harrison	Closing the regional equity capital gap: The role of informal venture capital	*Small Business Economics*	1995	N/A (other research)	UK, US, Swedish, Canadian data	Late 1980s and early 1990s	An equity gap exists for companies seeking small amounts of risk capital which constrains the development of the SME sector.
Fiet	Reliance upon informants in the venture capital industry	*Journal of Business Venturing*	1995a	National Venture Capital Association (NVCA), Houston	US data	1992–1994	The more an investor is concerned about a particular type of risk, the less likely he or she will be to use informal network informants, even if the information is market related.

(*Continued*)

Table 4.1. (*Continued*)

Panel A. Studies on the relation between institutional investors and VC fund managers

Authors	Title of the paper	Journal	Publication year	Data source	Data country	Data time span	Key finding
Fiet	Risk avoidance strategies in venture capital markets	*Journal of Management Studies*	1995b	National Venture Capital Association (NVCA), Houston	US data	1982–1987	Angels attach more importance to agency risk because they believe that if they can find the right entrepreneur, they can rely upon him or her to limit their losses due to adverse market conditions.
Gompers	Venture capital growing pains: Should the market diet?	*Journal of Banking & Finance*	1998	Venture Economics, Asset Alternatives, Gompers and Lerner	US data	1969–1997	Institutions are already responding to current market conditions by looking for alternatives to the American private equity market.
Gompers and Lerner	An analysis of compensation in the U.S. venture capital partnership	*Journal of Financial Economics*	1999	Aeneas Group, Kemper Financial Services, Venture Economics	US data	1978–1992	VC entrants may not have superior information about their investment abilities and may be concerned about establishing a reputation.
Zacharakis and Meyer	The potential of actuarial decision models: Can they improve the venture capital investment decision?	*Journal of Business Venturing*	2000	Anonymous scenarios provided by VCs	US data	1981–1986	More information appears to hinder the VC's decision process, even though most people prefer more information when making complex decisions.

Mason and Harrison	The size of the informal venture capital market in the United Kingdom	*Small Business Economics*	2000	BANs, Private Investor Forum (London 1996), British Venture Capital Association (BVCA, 1999b)	UK data	1992–1996	For entrepreneurs seeking start-up and early-stage finance in UK, unless they are seeking amounts more than £250,000, they should direct their efforts towards the informal VC market rather than institutional VC funds.
Wong, Bhatia, Freeman	Angel finance: The other venture capital	*Strategic Change*	2002	Newswires, periodicals, content and design firms, and business-to-business/consumer companies	US data	1994–2001	Analysis of the data indicates that angels have a complementary role to VC in the financing of new ventures. Angels take on more risks and invest smaller amounts in younger firms than venture capitalists. Angel investors appear to nurture younger firms until the company is established enough for venture consideration

(*Continued*)

Table 4.1. (*Continued*)

Panel A. Studies on the relation between institutional investors and VC fund managers							
Authors	Title of the paper	Journal	Publication year	Data source	Data country	Data time span	Key finding
Wright and Lockett	The structure and management of alliances: Syndication in the venture capital industry	*Journal of Management Studies*	2003	Questionnaire sent to VCs, interviews	UK data	1989–2001	Many VC firms alternate between lead and non-lead roles in syndicates. Lead investors typically hold larger equity stakes, and syndicated investment agreements primarily outline participant rights rather than behaviour. Contracting arrangements between lead and non-lead members address informational asymmetries.
Jones and Rhodes-Kropf	The price of diversifiable risk in venture capital and private equity	*Columbia University*	2003	Venture Economics	US data	1987–2000	In private equity and VC markets, inherent principal-agent issues and the necessity for investment oversight led to idiosyncratic risk that must be accounted for in pricing.
De Clercq and Dimov	Explaining venture capital firms' syndication behavior: A longitudinal study	*Venture Capital: An International Journal of Entrepreneurial Finance*	2004	VentureXpert	US data	1990 to 2001	Reducing financial risk, and possibly window dressing, is a significant driver for syndication.

Kanniainen and Keuschnigg	Start-up investment with scarce venture capital support	*Journal of Banking & Finance*	2004	N/A	N/A	N/A	In the short run, VC expansion relies on existing funds financing more start-ups. However, increasing the number of portfolio companies dilutes managerial support, heightening start-up risk.
Hsu	What do entrepreneurs pay for venture capital affiliation?	*The Journal of Finance*	2004	Survey, Venture Economics database	US data	1995–2000	Venture capitalists' reputation, built on experience, information networks, and direct assistance to portfolio firms, may be more distinctive than their financial capital.
Smith	The exit structure of venture capital	*UCLA Law Review*	2005	VentureOne, Electronic Data Gathering, Analysis, and Retrieval (EDGAR)	US data	1984–1994	Venture capitalists and entrepreneurs may have different interests regarding the timing and form of exit. Venture capitalists view exits from their portfolio companies in relatively simple terms. Often lacking either board control or contractual rights to initiate exit, venture capitalists allow entrepreneurs time to prove the business concept.

(Continued)

Table 4.1. *(Continued)*

Panel A. Studies on the relation between institutional investors and VC fund managers							
Authors	Title of the paper	Journal	Publication year	Data source	Data country	Data time span	Key finding
Murray	Venture capital and government policy	*Handbook of Research on Venture Capital*	2007	Small Business Service etc.	UK data, EU data	1986–2006	There are trade-offs between VC or business angel programme outcomes. Institutional or informal VC programmes should harness private investors' interests and experience as agents of government programme goals.
Hellmann, Lindsey, and Puri	Building relationships early: Banks in venture capital	*The Review of Financial Studies*	2008	Venture Economics, Loan Pricing Corporation, Compustat, and FDIC, augmented by hand-collected data from *Moody's Manuals*. Venture Economics (henceforth VE), a division of Thomson Financial	US data	1980–2000	The evidence suggests that banks build relationships in the VC market that can be mutually advantageous in the loan market. Banks avoid early-stage investments.

Winton and Yerramilli	Entrepreneurial finance: Banks versus venture capital	*Journal of Financial Economics*	2008	N/A	N/A	N/A	VC distinguishes itself from bank finance through increased use of equity features and more active monitoring, especially during continuation strategies. From the manager's perspective, monitoring is sometimes viewed as a necessary inconvenience.
Gompers, Kovner, Lerner, and Scharferstein	Venture capital investment cycles: The impact of public markets	*Journal of Financial Economics*	2008	Venture Economics	US data	1975–1998	Experienced specialised organisations, rather than new or inexperienced groups, exhibit the greatest response to shifts in public markets. Their investments are generally more successful, with no notable decline in performance amidst changing conditions.

(Continued)

Table 4.1. (*Continued*)

Panel A. Studies on the relation between institutional investors and VC fund managers							
Authors	Title of the paper	Journal	Publication year	Data source	Data country	Data time span	Key finding
Bruton, Ahlstrom, and Puky	Institutional differences and the development of entrepreneurial ventures: A comparison of the venture capital industries in Latin America and Asia	*Journal of International Business Studies*	2009	Interviews, but in addition gathered company archival material and published stories	Latin America data, US data, Asia data	1996–2005	This evidence underscores the significance of institutions in influencing organisational decision-makers. Future VC research should expand beyond traditional models focusing on industry conditions and firm resources to gain deeper insights into this global industry.
Gompers, Kovner, and Lerner	Specialization and success: Evidence from venture capital	*Journal of Economics & Management Strategy*	2009	Dow Jones Venture Source	US data	1975–2003	Specialised firms generally perform better, possibly due to the industry-specific expertise of their investors. When individual partners are highly specialised, the incremental benefit of increased VC firm concentration seems limited.

Ibrahim	Debt as venture capital	*University of Illinois Law Review*	2010	Interviews	US data	2006	VC presence substitutes traditional loan repayment criteria, making venture debt appealing to specific lenders.
Hochberg	Venture capital and corporate governance in the newly public firm	*Review of Finance*	2011	Securities Data Corporation (SDC) Global New Issues database, Thomson Financial Global Access database, *Pratt's Guide to Venture Capital Sources*, Venture Economics	US data	1975–1998	Pre-IPO VC backing influences the governance and monitoring of the entrepreneurial firm during its transition to public markets. However, other pre-IPO large shareholders like corporate and angel investors do not yield similar effects on the firm's governance.
Hopp and Rieder	What drives venture capital syndication?	*Applied Economics*	2011	Thomson Venture Economics (TVE) database	German data	1980–2003	Increased risks and potentially higher capital requirements positively influence VCs' incentives to engage partners. Results suggest that, all else being equal, more syndication leads to greater focus on specific industries.

(*Continued*)

Table 4.1. (*Continued*)

Panel A. Studies on the relation between institutional investors and VC fund managers							
Authors	Title of the paper	Journal	Publication year	Data source	Data country	Data time span	Key finding
Puri and Zarutskie	On the life cycle dynamics of venture-capital-and non-venture-capital-financed firms	*The Journal of Finance*	2012	Longitudinal Business Database (LBD), Economic Censuses, the Longitudinal Research Database, and the Standard Statistical Establishment List	US data	1981–2005	VC-financed firms represent a small fraction of new firm formations. Venture capitalists tend to invest disproportionately in firms without commercial sales but with high initial investment levels. Moreover, VC-backed firms demonstrate greater growth in employment and sales compared to non-VC-backed firms, indicating a focus on scalable ventures.
Grilli and Murtinu	Government, venture capital and the growth of European high-tech entrepreneurial firms	*Research Policy*	2014	VICO dataset	Belgium, Finland, France, Germany, Italy, Spain and the United Kingdom data	1993–2010	Our analyses consistently demonstrate a significant positive impact of IVC investors on the real sales growth of high-tech entrepreneurial firms. GVC investors can positively influence firm growth when serving as non-leading partners in a VC syndicate.

Hellmann and Thiele	Friends or foes? The interrelationship between angel and venture capital markets	*Journal of Financial Economics*	2015	N/A	N/A	N/A	On the one hand, the two investor types are 'friends' in the sense that they rely upon each other's investments. On the other hand, they are 'foes' because venture capitalists no longer need the angels when they make their follow-up investments. The venture capitalists' bargaining power depends on how competitive venture markets are and how well angels are legally protected.
Gornall and Strebulayev	The economic impact of venture capital: Evidence from public companies	*Sauder School of Business, University of British Columbia*	2015	CRSP/ Compustat Merged Database, Thomson ONE database	US data	1974–2014	VC was not even the sole source of financing for many of these companies. However, large and growing fractions of entrepreneurs are choosing VC financing.
Robinson	Factors impacting entrepreneurial success in accelerators: Revealed preferences of sophisticated mentors.	*Review of Corporate Finance*	2022	CDL Rockies	Canadian data	2017–2020	Mentors in accelerator programmes prioritise entrepreneurial signalling over initial venture characteristics. Success depends on balancing development needs. Entrepreneurs who address product/market fit and corporate strategies are more likely to advance in CDL Rockies Sessions.

(*Continued*)

Table 4.1. (*Continued*)

Panel B. Studies on the relation between VC fund managers and entrepreneurs							
Authors	Title of the paper	Journal	Publication year	Data source	Data country	Data time span	Key finding
Ruhnka and Young	A venture capital model of the development process for new ventures	*Journal of Business Venturing*	1987	Questionnaires sent to 73 US venture capital firms	US data	1987–1999	VC firms exhibited a high degree of consensus on strategic benchmarks and key risks for 'third stage' and 'exist stage'.
Khan	Assessing venture capital investments with noncom-pensatory behavioral decision models	*Journal of Business Venturing*	1987	*A Guide to Venture Capital Sources* published by Venture Economics	US data	1980s	Venture capitalist must exercise particular scrutiny on the entrepreneur's potential for creativity and ingenuity.
Bygrave	Syndicated investments by venture capital firms: A networking perspective	*Journal of Business Venturing*	1987	Venture Economics database	US data	1966–1982	It is more important for entrepreneurs to pick the VC firm that will give the most support after it invests its money, rather than the one that offers the cheapest financing.
Maier and Walker	The role of venture capital in financing small business	*Journal of Business Venturing*	1987	Survey (NVCA)	US data	1981–1984	Most of the VC investments are in small firms; most venture capitalists receive fewer than 700 requests per year.

Rosenstein	The board and strategy: Venture capital and high technology	*Journal of Business Venturing*	1988	Dallas informants etc.	N/A	N/A	For the small high-technology companies studied, many elements are conducive to an active involvement of the board in strategy formulation and in the monitoring of its implementation. These include: the size and composition of the board, the frequency of its meetings, the expertise and involvement of many of the board members from the VC side, the existence of an explicit strategy (periodically revised), and the urgency of staying on plan in order to meet investment goals.
Bygrave	The structure of the investment networks of venture capital firms	*Journal of Business Venturing*	1988	Venture Economics	US data (mostly)	1966–1982	This study reveals how VC firms are interconnected by their joint investments. In general, the findings are consistent with the predictions of the resource exchange mode.

(*Continued*)

Table 4.1. (*Continued*)

Panel B. Studies on the relation between VC fund managers and entrepreneurs							
Authors	Title of the paper	Journal	Publication year	Data source	Data country	Data time span	Key finding
Fried and Hisrich	Venture capital research: past, present and future	*Entrepreneurship Theory and Practice*	1988	N/A	N/A	N/A	VC plays an active role in the strategy, marketing, management, and legal structure of the entrepreneurial firm.
Hisrich and Jankowicz	Intuition in venture capital decisions: An exploratory study using a new technique	*Journal of Business Venturing*	1990	Interviews	US data	1980s	Venture capitalists were led to take adequate returns for granted and volunteered relatively few constructs on this issue.
Chan, Siegel, and Thakor	Learning, corporate control and performance requirements in venture capital contracts	*International Economic Review*	1990	N/A	N/A	N/A	Optimal financial claim for the VC is to have a risky position in the firm.
Barry, Muscarella, Peavy III, and Vetsuypens	The role of venture capital in the creation of public companies: Evidence from the going-public process	*Journal of Financial Economics*	1990	*Venture Capital Journal, Pratt's Guide to Venture Capital Sources, Dow Jones Newswires, Wall Street Journal* etc.	US data	1978–1987	Venture capitalists participate actively in and monitor the progress of their portfolio companies. The venture capitalists specialise in a narrow set of industries for which they can develop expertise.

Ruhnka and Young	Some hypotheses about risk in venture capital investing	*Journal of Business Venturing*	1991	Surveys	US data	1986	The authors found that a high proportion of the anticipated risks for early-stage ventures consisted of internally determined venture-specific factors, such as difficulties in product development and the capabilities and weaknesses of specific management teams.
Gupta and Sapienza	Determinants of venture capital firms' preferences regarding the industry diversity and geographic scope of their investments	*Journal of Business Venturing*	1992	*Pratt's Guide to Venture Capital Sources* (Pratt and Morris, 1987)	US data	1987	VCFs who specialise in early-stage ventures attempt to bring both specialised knowledge and greater involvement and assistance to the investee ventures.
Norton and Tenenbaum	Specialization versus diversification as a venture capital investment strategy	*Journal of Business Venturing*	1993	Survey	US data	1969–1985	Investors in seed deals are less diversified across different industries and firms. Venture capitalists appear to specialise in certain financing stages rather than stagger their investments over different financing stages.

(*Continued*)

Table 4.1. (*Continued*)

Panel B. Studies on the relation between VC fund managers and entrepreneurs							
Authors	Title of the paper	Journal	Publication year	Data source	Data country	Data time span	Key finding
Barry	New directions in research on venture capital finance	*Financial Management*	1994	N/A	N/A	N/A	Although recent work explains what venture capitalists do, it does not show whether those activities in fact create value.
Elango, Fried, Hisrich, and Polonchek	How venture capital firms differ	*Journal of Business Venturing*	1995	Questionnaire sent to VCs	US data	1984–1992	Earlier stage investors are interested in unique, proprietary products with high growth potential, whereas late-stage investors demand a market-proven product.
Zider	How venture capital works	*Harvard Business Review*	1998	N/A	N/A	N/A	The entrepreneur needs to show the venture capitalist that his team and idea fit into the VC's current focus and that his equity participation and management skills will make the VC's job easier and the returns higher.
Fried, Bruton, and Hisrich	Strategy and the board of directors in venture capital-backed firms	*Journal of Business Venturing*	1998	Survey by mail	US data	1985–1991	Boards of VC-backed firms are much more active than traditional boards.

Hellmann	The allocation of control rights in venture capital contracts	*The Rand Journal of Economics*	1998	N/A	N/A	N/A	When venture capitalists have control, they provide greater effort in finding professional managers who increase the value of the company.
Smith	Venture capital contracting in the information age	*Journal of Small and Emerging Business Law*	1998	N/A	N/A	N/A	The market for venture capitalist reputation is the glue that holds the VC process together.
Trester	Venture capital contracting under asymmetric information	*Journal of Banking & Finance*	1998	Surveys	US data	1990s	Asymmetric information may arise after the time of contracting can play in the choice of contract type.
Bergemann and Hege	Venture capital financing, moral hazard, and learning	*Journal of Banking & Finance*	1998	N/A	N/A	N/A	Compensation of the entrepreneur is like an option contract, and as such depends on the length of the contract and the volatility of the information induced through her actions.

(*Continued*)

Table 4.1. (*Continued*)

Panel B. Studies on the relation between VC fund managers and entrepreneurs							
Authors	Title of the paper	Journal	Publication year	Data source	Data country	Data time span	Key finding
Amit, Brander, and Zott	Why do venture capital firms exist? Theory and Canadian evidence	*Journal of Business Venturing*	1998	Macdonald & Associates Ltd., survey	Canadian data	1991–1996	Moral hazard and adverse selection create a market failure in entrepreneurial financing, which might lead many worthwhile projects to be unfunded or underfunded. The more skilled the venture capitalist is in reducing these sources of market failure, the more effectively this sector will function.
Hellmann and Puri	The interaction between product market and financing strategy: The role of venture capital	*The Review of Financial Studies*	2000	Surveys, *Rich's Everyday Sales Prospecting Guide, Technology Resource Guide to Greater Silicon Valley,* The Silicon Valley business press, Venture Economics, VentureOne	US data	1994–1997	Firms pursuing an innovator rather than an imitator strategy are more likely to obtain VC financing. Obtaining VC is associated with faster time to market, especially for innovators.

Lockett and Wright	The syndication of venture capital investments	*The International Journal of Management Science*	2001	EVCA yearbook, CMBOR database	UK data	1980–1989	Syndicating deals seems motivated by financial factors rather than resource exchange. This study emphasises differing approaches between VC firms focusing on MBO/MBI stage investments and those in early-stage investments.
Engel	The impact of venture capital on firm growth: An empirical investigation	*ZEW – Centre for European Economic Research Discussion*	2002	ZEW Foundation Panels	German data	1991–1998	Surviving venture-backed firms achieve significantly higher growth rates due to financial involvement and services provided by venture capitalists. Contrary to the expectations, the impact of VC on new firms' growth does not differ between high-tech and low-tech industries.

(*Continued*)

Table 4.1. (*Continued*)

Panel B. Studies on the relation between VC fund managers and entrepreneurs							
Authors	Title of the paper	Journal	Publication year	Data source	Data country	Data time span	Key finding
Hellmann and Puri	Venture capital and the professionalization of start-up firms: Empirical evidence	*The Journal of Finance*	2002	Survey data, interviews, and commercial databases, *Rich's Everyday Sales Prospecting Guide* (Rich's Guide), *Technology Resource Guide to Greater Silicon Valley* (Corptech)	US data	1994–1997	Obtaining VC is related to a variety of organisational milestones, such as the formulation of human resource policies, the adoption of stock option plans, or the hiring of a VP of sales.
Schmidt	Convertible securities and venture capital finance	*The Journal of Finance*	2003	N/A	N/A	N/A	Convertible securities allocate cash flow rights based on the state of the world and the entrepreneur's effort. By selecting the conversion rate correctly, venture capitalists can invest efficiently only if the entrepreneur also invests efficiently.

Keuschnigg and Nielsen	Tax policy, venture capital, and entrepreneurship	*Journal of Public Economics*	2003	N/A	N/A	N/A	Even though financiers may, in principle, diversify project risk, some risk-bearing on the part of entrepreneurs is nevertheless required to contain moral hazard in the relation between VCs and entrepreneurs.
Ueda	Banks versus venture capital: Project evaluation, screening, and expropriation	*The Journal of Finance*	2004	N/A	N/A	N/A	Low collateral value, high growth, high return, and high project risk increase asymmetric information costs, prompting entrepreneurs to seek financing from venture capitalists.

(*Continued*)

Table 4.1. (*Continued*)

Panel B. Studies on the relation between VC fund managers and entrepreneurs

Authors	Title of the paper	Journal	Publication year	Data source	Data country	Data time span	Key finding
Romain and Van Pottelsberghe	The economic impact of venture capital	*Centre Emile Bernheim*	2004	OECD National Accounts	Australia, Belgium, Canada, Denmark, Finland, France, Germany, Ireland, Italy, Japan, the Netherlands, Norway, Spain, Śweden, United Kingdom and United States data	1990–2001	VC contributes to growth through two main channels: introducing new products and processes to the market and enhancing absorptive capacity for knowledge generated by research institutions.
Keuschnigg	Venture capital backed growth	*Journal of Economic Growth*	2004	N/A	N/A	N/A	Entrepreneurs provide key technological ideas, while venture capitalists offer managerial advice based on their business experience and industry knowledge. Organisational structure influences growth rate.

Engel and Keilbach	Firm-level implications of early stage venture capital investment – An empirical investigation	*Journal of Empirical Finance*	2007	ZEW (Creditreform), German Patent Office (DPA)	German data	1995–1998	Firms with higher innovative output (measured by the number of patent applications, corrected for size) and with higher-educated management have a larger probability of getting VC. Venture-funded firms display significantly higher growth rates compared to their non-venture-funded counterparts and apply more patents.
Häussler, Harhoff, and Müller	To be financed or not... – The role of patents for venture capital-financing	*ZEW – Centre for European Economic Research Discussion*	2009	OECD survey, European Patent Office	German, UK data	1990–2005	Our empirical analysis demonstrates that companies' patenting activities have consistent and cogent effects on the timing of VC financing. Having at least one patent application reduces the time to the first VC investment by 76%. Ventures with higher patent quality receive VC faster.

(*Continued*)

Table 4.1. (*Continued*)

Panel B. Studies on the relation between VC fund managers and entrepreneurs							
Authors	Title of the paper	Journal	Publication year	Data source	Data country	Data time span	Key finding
Colombo and Grilli	On growth drivers of high-tech start-ups: Exploring the role of founders' human capital and venture capital	*Journal of Business Venturing*	2010	eResearch on Entrepreneurship in Advanced Technologies (RITA) database (Politecnico di Milano)	Italian data	1994–2003	The findings demonstrate that firms led by founders with specific human capital traits (such as higher education in management and economics and prior technical work experience in the sector) tend to grow larger than others.
Ferrary	Syndication of venture capital investment: The art of resource pooling	*Entrepreneurship Theory and Practice*	2010	PriceWaterhouseCoopers, *Galante's Venture Capital & Private Equity Directory*	US data	2000–2005	In the VC industry, formal contracts can establish social ties. Funding at the seed stage enables a learning-by-collaborating dynamic between investors and entrepreneurs, mitigating uncertainty.

Dimov and Milanov	The interplay of need and opportunity in venture capital investment syndication	*Journal of Business Venturing*	2010	VentureXpert	US data	1980–2004	This study reinforces the notion that firms seek and establish alliances when they undertake novel, uncertain projects. However, it also shows that these very projects can also reduce the firm's desirability as a partner and make it differentially positioned to carry out such projects.
Xuan	The causes and consequences of venture capital stage financing	*Journal of Financial Economics*	2011	VentureXpert, CorpTech	US data	1980–2006	A VC investor located farther away from an entrepreneurial firm tends to finance more rounds, with shorter durations between rounds and smaller amounts per round. However, the investor's propensity to stage is independent of the firm's location in a close-knit community. firm is located far away from the VC investor.

(*Continued*)

Table 4.1. (*Continued*)

Panel B. Studies on the relation between VC fund managers and entrepreneurs							
Authors	Title of the paper	Journal	Publication year	Data source	Data country	Data time span	Key finding
Tian	The Role of venture capital syndication in value creation for entrepreneurial firms	*Review of Finance*	2012	Venture Economics database, Securities Data Company (SDC) Global New Issues database, Factiva, LexisNexis, Dun and Bradstreet Explore, and CorpTech databases	US data	1980–2005	VC syndication adds value in two ways: first, it creates product market value by investing heavily in younger, early-stage firms. Second, VC syndicates foster innovation and enhance post-IPO operating performance for their portfolio firms.
Popov and Roosenboom	Venture capital and patented innovation: evidence from Europe	*Economic Policy*	2012	Thomson VentureXpert, United States Patent and Trademark Office (USPTO), ANBERD-OECD, STAN Database	Austria, Belgium, Czech Republic, Denmark, Finland, France, Germany, Greece, Hungary, Iceland, Ireland, Italy, the Netherlands, Norway, Poland, Portugal, Slovakia, Spain, Switzerland, Sweden and UK data	1991–2005	While venture capitalists push firms to professionalise and focus on business aspects, there's limited evidence of increased innovation post-investment.

Bottazzi, Da Rin, and Hellmann	The importance of trust for investment: Evidence from venture capital	*The Review of Financial Studies*	2016	Surveys (685 VC firms), Thomson ONE	EU, Norway, Switzerland, US data	1990–2015	The findings indicate that lack of trust presents a barrier to investments, as evidenced by the negative correlation between trust and exits. This underscores the importance of generalised trust in the analysis of VC investment.
Ewens, Gorbenko, and Korteweg	Venture capital contracts	*Journal of Financial Economics*	2022	VentureSource, Pitchbook	US data	2002–2015	This study shows contracts significantly affect firm value and the entrepreneur-investor split. Despite an optimal split for success, VCs typically receive more equity than optimal for start-ups.

(*Continued*)

Table 4.1. (*Continued*)

Panel C. Studies on venture exits							
Authors	Title of the paper	Journal	Publication year	Data source	Data country	Data time span	Key finding
Gompers	Grandstanding in the venture capital industry	*Journal of Financial Economics*	1996	N/A	N/A	1978–1987	The tremendous entry of new VC firms and the incentives to grandstand potentially explain some of the declining returns on VC in the 1980s.
Black and Gilson	Venture capital and the structure of capital markets: banks versus stock markets	*Journal of Financial Economics*	1998	*Venture Capital Journal,* European Venture Capital Association	US, France, Italy, Germany, Netherlands, Spain, Sweden, Ireland, Portugal, Belgium, Denmark, Switzerland, Norway, Finland, Iceland, Austria, Japanese data	1962–1992	Economies of scope among financial and nonfinancial contributions by VC providers, plus VC investors 'need for a quantitative measure of VC funds' skill, can explain the importance of an exit strategy.
Black and Gilson	Does venture capital require an active stock market?	*Journal of Applied Corporate Finance*	1999	*Venture Capital Journal, Venture Capital Yearbook, European Venture Capital Association Yearbook, German Venture Capital Association Yearbook*	US and German data	1961–1996	Economies of scope among financial and nonfinancial contributions by VC providers, plus VC investors' need for a quantitative measure of VC funds' skill, can explain the importance of an exit strategy.

Jeng and Wells	The determinants of venture capital funding: evidence across countries	*Journal of Corporate Finance*	2000	*European Venture Capital Journal, Asian Venture Capital Journal*, Macdonald's & Associates for Canadian data and Venture Economics for US data	US, Canadian, Asian data	1986–1995	IPOs are the main force behind the cyclical swings in VC. Early and later stage VC investments are affected quite differently by the determinants of VC.
Peng	Building a venture capital index	*Yale International Center for Finance*	2001	OffRoad Capital, compiled from several sources, including VentureOne database, SDC platinum service, MarketGuide, and other online resources	US data	1987–1999	The geometric average annual return for VC from 1987 to 1999 is 55.18%, with the upper bound 60.93% and the lower bound 28.28%. In addition, the VC returns are volatile. There is a strong correlation between the VC index returns and the returns of NASDAQ on a yearly scale.
Seppä and Laamanen	Valuation of venture capital investments: Empirical evidence	*R&D Management*	2001	Venture Economics, US Federal Reserve bank of Chicago files	US data	1991–1995	The risk-neutral valuation estimates seem to be fairly unbiased, since the mean and median estimation errors are found to be small. Nevertheless, the variance of the estimation error is still large, which is consistent with the 'common sense' observations that VC investments often result in extreme outcomes.

(*Continued*)

Table 4.1. (*Continued*)

Panel C. Studies on venture exits							
Authors	Title of the paper	Journal	Publication year	Data source	Data country	Data time span	Key finding
Brander, Amit, and Antweiler	Venture-capital syndication: Improved venture selection vs. the value-added hypothesis	*Journal of Economics & Management Strategy*	2002	Macdonald & Associates	Canadian data	1992–1998	The value-added hypothesis suggests syndication enhances project value, leading to higher returns. Our analysis supports this, showing syndicated projects generally yield higher returns than standalone ones.
Schwienbacher	An empirical analysis of venture capital exits in Europe and the United States	*EFA 2002 Berlin Meetings Discussion Paper*	2002	European Venture Capital Association (EVCA), National Venture Capital Association, (NVCA) *Pratt's Guide to Venture Capital Sources* (2001 Edition)	EU data US data	1990s–2001	Young venture capitalists in Europe tend to monitor less but invest proportionally more in early stages than their more established colleagues. The likelihood of going public is affected by the number of financing rounds, the investment duration and reporting requirements of the investee to the venture capitalist.

Kaplan, Sensoy, and Strömberg	How well do venture capital databases reflect actual investments?	*University of Chicago Graduate School of Business*	2002	Venture Economics, VentureOne	US data	1986–1999	The Venture Economics database over-represents larger rounds and California companies, while VentureOne shows no significant bias. Both databases offer unbiased but noisy measures of financing amounts and valuations.
Kerins, JK Smith, and R Smith	Opportunity cost of capital for venture capital investors and entrepreneurs	*Journal of Financial and Quantitative Analysis*	2004	IPO filings (1995–2000)	US data	1987–2000	Evidence from data on newly public firms in eight high-tech industries shows that total risk is on average five times higher than market risk, with correlations to market returns around 0.2, and equity betas comparable to the overall market.

(*Continued*)

Table 4.1. (*Continued*)

Panel C. Studies on venture exits							
Authors	Title of the paper	Journal	Publication year	Data source	Data country	Data time span	Key finding
Florin	Is venture capital worth it? Effects on firm performance and founder returns	*Journal of Business Venturing*	2005	IPO prospectuses	US data	1980–2000	Non-VC-backed ventures are significantly older than low-VC-backed ventures but similar to high-VC-backed firms.
Cumming, Fleming, and Schwein-bacher	Liquidity Risk and Venture Capital Finance	*Financial management*	2005	VentureXpert	US data	1985–2004	There is a strong negative relationship between the liquidity of exit markets and the likelihood of investing in new early-stage projects.
Jelic, Saadouni, and Wright	Performance of private to public MBOs: The role of venture capital	*Journal of Business Finance & Accounting*	2005	Centre for Management Buy-out Research (CMBOR) database (compiled from text line searches, stock exchange circulars, EXTEL, financial press, etc.), DataStream database	UK data	1993–2000	Significant initial premiums are evident across different measurement matrices, but there is no notable long-term underperformance. Long-term performance remains robust after using alternative benchmarks and robust statistical tests.

Cochrane	The risk and return of venture capital	*Journal of Financial Economics*	2005	VentureOne database, SDC Platinum Corporate New Issues and Mergers and Acquisitions (M&A) databases, MarketGuide etc.	US data	1987–2000	Something unusual occurs with the smallest Nasdaq stocks in this period. These stocks are small, thinly traded, and illiquid, with some experiencing months of no trading, as indicated by CRSP data.
Cumming, Fleming, and Schwein-bacher	Legality and venture capital exits	*Journal of Corporate Finance*	2006	Hand collected from Information memorandum sent to Wilshire Associates	Australia, China, Hong Kong, India, Indonesia, Malaysia, New Zealand, Philippines, Singapore, South Korea, Taiwan and Thailand	1980–2012	The summary statistics and models did not show a direct link between the probability of an IPO and the size of a country's stock market. This finding is significant because it challenges the conventional wisdom that larger stock markets automatically facilitate VC markets.

(*Continued*)

Table 4.1. (*Continued*)

Panel C. Studies on venture exits							
Authors	Title of the paper	Journal	Publication year	Data source	Data country	Data time span	Key finding
Hochberg, Ljungqvist, and Lu	Whom you know matters: Venture capital networks and investment performance	*The Journal of Finance*	2007	Thomson Financials' Venture Economics database,	US data	1980–1999	VC funds linked to parent firms with influential networks achieve superior performance, with higher success rates in IPOs or sales. Additionally, portfolio companies of well-connected VC firms have better survival and financing prospects, with consistent effects across various specifications.
Cumming	Contracts and exits in venture capital finance	*The Review of Financial Studies*	2008	Surveys sent to European Venture Capital Association (EVCA) and interviews after	European data: Austria, Belgium, Czech, Denmark, France, Germany, Italy, The Netherlands, Poland, Portugal, and Switzerland	1996–2005	Data suggests a 30% higher likelihood of acquisition when VCs possess effective contractual control rights like drag-along provisions and board control. Weak control rights correlate with higher probabilities of IPO or write-off exits, supporting theories linking VC control rights to exit outcomes.

Schwienbacher	Innovation and venture capital exits	*The Economic Journal*	2008	N/A	N/A	N/A	Innovative and profitable ventures are more inclined to go public than imitative ones. The choice of exit route can create an agency problem when entrepreneurs gain private benefits from staying independent post-VC exit.
Nahata	Venture capital reputation and investment performance	*Journal of Financial Economics*	2008	VentureXpert database	US data	1991–2001	Companies backed by reputable VCs, measured by cumulative IPO market capitalisation, are more likely to achieve successful exits, quicker access to public markets, and higher asset productivity at IPOs.

(Continued)

Table 4.1. (*Continued*)

Panel C. Studies on venture exits

Authors	Title of the paper	Journal	Publication year	Data source	Data country	Data time span	Key finding
Chen, Gompers, Kovner, and Lerner	Buy local? The geography of venture capital	*Journal of Urban Economics*	2010	*Pratt's Guide*, VentureXpert	US data	1975–2005	The success rate of VC investments in a region influences firms' decisions to open new branches. Reduced monitoring costs may lead to a lower expected success rate for investments in distant geographies.
Brander, Egan, and Hellmann	Government sponsored versus private venture capital: Canadian evidence	*International Differences in Entrepreneurship*	2010	Canadian Venture Capital Association (CVCA), Réseau Capital, System for Electronic Document Analysis and Retrieval (SEDAR), *Pratt's guide* etc.	Canadian data	1996–2004	Enterprises backed by private VC consistently demonstrate superior performance. They are more likely to achieve successful exits (IPOs or acquisitions), generate higher value upon exit, have lower rates of business closure, and attract US investment.

Kaplan and Lerner	It ain't broke: The past, present, and future of venture capital	*Journal of Applied Corporate Finance*	2010	Private Equity Analyst	US data	1980–2009	The authors find no evidence suggesting that the VC model is broken or has fundamentally changed. Currently, we're transitioning from a period with slightly above-average capital and average to slightly below-average returns to a phase with well below-average capital.
Korteweg and Nagel	Risk-adjusting the returns to venture capital	*The Journal of Finance*	2016	Sand Hill Econometrics (SHE)	US data	1979–2012	The authors introduce an SDF approach for valuing private equity payoffs, demonstrating significant differences between the PME and our generalised PME (GPME) in abnormal performance estimates.
Kaplan and Lerner	Venture capital data: Opportunities and challenges	*Measuring Entre-preneurial Businesses: Current Knowledge and Challenges*	2016	Burgiss, Venture Economics, Cambridge Associates, Preqin	US data	1961–2011	Due to limited disclosure and significant information asymmetries in VC, accurately assessing investment activity and fund performance is challenging.

(*Continued*)

Table 4.1. (*Continued*)

Panel C. Studies on venture exits							
Authors	Title of the paper	Journal	Publication year	Data source	Data country	Data time span	Key finding
Cumming, Grilli, and Murtinu	Governmental and independent venture capital investments in Europe: A firm-level performance analysis	*Journal of Corporate Finance*	2017	VICO database	Belgium, Finland, France, Germany, Italy, Spain and the United Kingdom data	1991–2010	The econometric results show that IVC-backed companies have a higher likelihood of reaching a positive exit (IPO or trade-sale) than GVC-backed ones. More interestingly, mixed IVC-GVC syndicated investments lead to a higher likelihood of a positive exit than that of IVC-backing.
Nanda, Samila, and Sorenson	The persistent effect of initial success: Evidence from venture capital	*Journal of Financial Economics*	2020	VentureXpert	US data	1961–2008	VC firm performance improves with more investments, but initial success predicts future success for up to 50 subsequent investments. Success depends on timing and location, but VC firms don't seem to consistently excel in selecting attractive segments.

Fuchs, Füss, Jenkinson, and Morkoetter	Should investors care where private equity managers went to school?	*Review of Corporate Finance*	2022	Pitchbook database, Preqin, Times Higher Education (THE) Ranking, Academic Ranking of World Universities (ARWU), Financial Times (FT) MBA Ranking, Finance Research Rankings from the Arizona State University (ASU), Business School Research Rankings from UT Dallas (UTD)	US data	1990–2010	The higher the average university ranking of the management team, the higher its fund performance. The evidence suggests that investors can use the educational profile of the team in their evaluation of fund managers and that success in private equity is conditional on team resources.

(Continued)

Table 4.1. (*Continued*)

Panel D. Studies on other topics							
Authors	Title of the paper	Journal	Publication year	Data source	Data country	Data time span	Key finding
Rind	The role of venture capital in corporate development	*Strategic Management Journal*	1981	*The Venture Capital Journal* (Capital Publishing)	US data	1968–1979	Outside partnership investment can provide enhanced investment opportunities.
Winters and Murfin	Venture capital investing for corporate development objectives	*Journal of Business Venturing*	1988	Venture Economics	US data	1979–1986	The success of a corporate venture investing programme depends on a clear definition of financial and/or strategic goals. The main determinants of success are organisational structure, creation of a large, quality deal stream, and the involvement of high-quality people at the VC/corporate interface.
Sahlman	The structure and governance of venture-capital organizations	*Journal of Financial Economics*	1990	Venture Economics, Securities Data Corporation	US data	1980–1988	The venture capital organisational form may be applicable in other settings, particularly corporate and project governance.

Florida and Smith	Venture capital, innovation, and economic development	*Economic Development Quarterly*	1990	*Venture Capital Journal*, Venture Economics	US data	1984–1987	The research findings suggest that there are serious reasons to question the efficacy of government involvement in VC.
Ooghe, Manigart, and Fassin	Growth patterns of the European venture capital industry	*Journal of Business Venturing*	1991	EVCA	EU data	1984–1989	In Europe, the VC industry is concentrated in three countries: the United Kingdom, the Netherlands, and France. Together, they account for 80% of all European VC.
Smart	Management assessment methods in venture capital: An empirical analysis of human capital valuation	*An International Journal of Entrepreneurial Finance*	1999	Questionnaire	US data	1990s	Human capital is far from the 'intangible' factor that it is portrayed to be by accountants and economists.

(Continued)

Table 4.1. (*Continued*)

Panel D. Studies on other topics							
Authors	Title of the paper	Journal	Publication year	Data source	Data country	Data time span	Key finding
Gompers and Lerner	What drives venture capital fundraising?	*National Bureau of Economic Research*	1999	Venture Economics, *Venture Capital Journal*, Private Equity Analyst	US data	1972–1994	Higher GDP growth and increases in R&D spending led to greater VC activity. Capital gains tax rates matter, with lower rates leading to a greater quantity of VC raised.
Hamao, Packer, and Ritter	Institutional affiliation and the role of venture capital: Evidence from initial public offerings in Japan	*Pacific-Basin Finance Journal*	2000	Nikkei NEEDS electronic database (OTC market), *Kaisha Shiki Ho (Japan Company Handbook)*	Japanese data	1989–1995	In Japan, most of the major VC firms are subsidiaries of securities firms and banks. VC-backed IPOs in Japan do not perform better in the long run than other IPOs relative to size/industry matched firms, except for firms backed by foreign owned or independent venture capitalists.
Lemley	Reconceiving patents in the age of venture capital	*Journal of Small and Emerging Business Law*	2000	U.S. Patent and Trademark Office	US data	1983–1998	Patent incentive story as classically told has some serious problems. Patents serve a lot of useful purposes outside that classic incentive story.

Upton and Petty	Venture capital investment and US family business	*Venture Capital: An International Journal of Entrepreneurial Finance*	2000	Surveys (Baylor University's Institute of Family Business)	US data	1990s	Seventy percent of the family-owned companies sampled have undergone a transition of ownership within the past ten years or are planning to so within the next 10 years.
Harrison and Mason	Venture capital market complementarities: The links between business angels and venture capital funds in the United Kingdom	*An International Journal of Entrepreneurial Finance*	2000	Survey, BVCA Directory, *VCR Guide to Sources of Venture Capital in the UK*	UK data	1996–1997	Both business angels and VC funds have participated quite extensively in various forms of complementary relationships, notably deal referral and to a lesser extent co-investing and sequential investing, although in most cases these relationships account for a relatively small proportion of the investment portfolios of either VC funds or business angels.

(*Continued*)

Table 4.1. (*Continued*)

Panel D. Studies on other topics							
Authors	Title of the paper	Journal	Publication year	Data source	Data country	Data time span	Key finding
Kortum and Lerner	Does venture capital spur innovation?	*Entrepreneurial Inputs and Outcomes: New Studies of Entrepreneurship in the United States*	2001	Compustat, Center for Research into Security Prices (CRSP), U.S. National Science Foundation (NSF), Venture Economics, U.S. Patent and Trademark Office (USPTO)	US data	1965–1994	VC has had a substantial impact on innovation in the US economy. The jump in venture disbursements since 1995 may trigger an additional wave of innovative activity.
Gompers and Lerner	The venture capital revolution	*Journal of Economic Perspectives*	2001	Venture Economics data, VentureOne, *Venture Capital Journal*	US data	1978–1999	The manners in which VC funds are raised are now much better understood.
Sorenson and Stuart	Syndication networks and the spatial distribution of venture capital investments	*American Journal of Sociology*	2001	Venture Economics database (Securities Data Corporation (SDC))	US data	1986–1998	People converge in space and time more frequently when they live near one another and have occasion to meet in the course of work and play.

Lerner	Boom and bust in the venture capital industry and the impact on innovation	*Harvard Business School – Finance Unit; Harvard University – Entrepreneurial Management Unit; National Bureau of Economic Research (NBER)*	2002	U.S. National Science Foundation (NSF)	US data	1965–2000	The greatest assistance to VC may be provided by government programmes that seek to enhance the demand for these funds rather than the supply of capital.
Dossani and Kenney	Creating an environment for venture capital in india	*World Development*	2002	Statistical Outline of India, GVFL, Indian Venture Capital Association, Nasscom	Indian data	1993–2000	India remains in a difficult environment for VC.
Manigart, De Waele, Wright, Robbie, Desbrières, Sapienza, and Beekman	Determinants of required return in venture capital investments: A five-country study	*Journal of Business Venturing*	2002b	Questionnaires sent to Venture Associations, *Pratt's Guide to Venture Capital Sources*	US, the UK, the Netherlands, Belgium and France data	1994–1997	Entrepreneurs may face less stringent return requirements but must deliver other valuable outcomes for backers, such as innovation or job creation. Policymakers and researchers should consider these diverse goals when assessing the impact of VC investments.

(*Continued*)

Table 4.1. (*Continued*)

Panel D. Studies on other topics							
Authors	Title of the paper	Journal	Publication year	Data source	Data country	Data time span	Key finding
Gilson	Engineering a venture capital market: Lessons from the American experience	*Stanford Law Review*	2002	N/A	N/A	N/A	The government should tackle the simultaneity issue by offering seed capital and fostering financial intermediaries. This approach should encourage entrepreneur supply while maintaining the intense incentives and monitoring typical of US VC contracts.
Bruton, Ahlstrom, and Singh	The impact of the institutional environment on the venture capital industry in Singapore	*Venture Capital: An International Journal of Entrepreneurial Finance*	2002	Interviews, *Guide to Venture Capital in Asia* (1998)	Singaporean data	1985–2001	Singapore's VC industry, unique in Asia, was primarily shaped by incentives, regulations, and government involvement. It emphasises high technology and early-stage ventures, distinguishing it from most other Asian VC industries.

Powell, Koput, Bowie, and Smith-Doers	The spatial clustering of science and capital: Accounting for biotech firm-venture capital relationships	*Regional Studies*	2002	BioScan, *Pratt's Guide to Venture Capital Sources*	US data, EU data	1988–1999	Biotech and VC exhibit strong spatial concentration, particularly in the Bay Area and Boston. It's unsurprising that a significant portion of VC support is locally based, with over half of biotech firms in the sample receiving local VC disbursements, rising to 58% within key geographic clusters.
Manigart, Baeyens, and Van Hyfte	The survival of venture capital backed companies	*Venture Capital: An International Journal of Entrepreneurial Finance*	2002a	Yearly accounts of the companies	Belgium data	1987–1997	GIMV and SRIW (two large government VC companies) backed investee companies have higher chances of surviving as independent entities. For GIMV backed companies, the results are even stronger: they survive longer than companies backed by independent or captive VC companies.

(*Continued*)

Table 4.1. (*Continued*)

Panel D. Studies on other topics							
Authors	Title of the paper	Journal	Publication year	Data source	Data country	Data time span	Key finding
Mason and Harrison	The geography of venture capital investments in the UK	*Transactions of the Institute of British Geographers*	2002	BVCA	UK data	1984–2000	Growth in VC activity in regions like the East and West Midlands is mainly of the merchant VC type. This involves providing replacement equity for management buyouts, often leading to job losses due to restructuring.
Bottazzi and Da Rin	Venture capital in Europe and the financing of innovative companies	*Economic Policy*	2002	Euro.nm, prospectuses	EU data	1991–2000	The industry is rapidly expanding, yet investment sums are growing less than in the US.
Manigart, Lockett, Meuleman, Wright, Landström, Bruining, Desbrières, and Hommel	Why do european venture capital companies syndicate?	*ERIM Report Series Research in Management*	2002c	Questionnaire	UK and 5 other European countries data	2001	European VC managers recognise the financial benefits of syndication but underestimate the importance of additional benefits like accessing resources, building networks, and increasing deal flow. In contrast, their North American counterparts seem to value these benefits.

Randjelovic, O'Rourke, and Orsato	The emergence of green venture capital	*Business Strategy and Environment*	2003	Websites, company material and interviews	US, EU data	1997–2001	Green VC's growth hinges on specific regulatory implementations, such as rules facilitating funding for eco-entrepreneurs, like those guiding pension funds.
Cumming and MacIntosh	Venture-capital exits in Canada and the United States	*University of Toronto Law Journal*	2003	Survey (sent to Canadian and US VCs)	US, Canadian data	1992–1995	Unlike the US findings, Canadian results confirmed the anticipated low profitability of buyback exits. Additionally, significant disparities were noted between the US and Canadian results, both in exit type frequency and profitability.
Brush, Carter, Gatewood, Greene, and Hart	Gatekeepers of venture growth: A Diana Project report on the role and participation of women in the venture capital industry	*Kauffman Foundation*	2004	*Pratt's Guide to Venture Capital Sources*, interviews	US data	1995–2000	Women make up a small portion of VC decision-makers. Women professionals tend to have more women in their networks compared to men.

(*Continued*)

Table 4.1. (*Continued*)

Panel D. Studies on other topics							
Authors	Title of the paper	Journal	Publication year	Data source	Data country	Data time span	Key finding
Wright, Vohora, and Lockett	The formation of high-tech university spinouts: The role of joint ventures and venture capital investors	*The Journal of Technology Transfer*	2004	Interviews, observations	UK data	2001–2002	A joint venture spin-off (JVSO) may outperform a unique spin-off (USO) in IP commercialisation. This advantage could stem from leveraging the resource strengths of both parents and addressing distinctive inadequacies through coordinated integration across the organisation.
Megginson	Toward a global model of venture capital?	*Journal of Applied Corporate Finance*	2004	Pricewaterhouse-Coopers, Venture Economics, National Venture Capital Association	US data, EU data	1970–2000	Legal system disparities among countries, especially in the US and Europe, pose a significant barrier to convergence, as VC and private equity rely heavily on nation-specific legal regimes that are not easily transferable.
Bruton, Ahlstrom, and Yeh	Understanding venture capital in East Asia: The impact of institutions on the industry today and tomorrow	*Journal of World Business*	2004	Interviews (fund managers)	Chinese, Taiwanese, Singaporean data	1998–2000	Various institutional factors in East Asia significantly shape the actions of local venture capitalists, despite similar training and norms as their Western counterparts.

Wright, Pruthi, and Lockett	International venture capital research: From cross-country comparisons to crossing borders	*International Journal of Management Reviews*	2005	N/A	US, EU, Asia data	1988–2003	Most literature on VC focuses on cross-country comparisons at macro and micro levels. However, significant research gaps exist regarding the international development of VC industries and the expansion of VC firms across borders.
Becker and Hellmann	The genesis of venture capital: Lessons from the German experience	*Venture Capital, Entrepreneurship, and Public Policy*	2005	WFG information (documents, filings etc.), interviews	German data	1976–1991	German norms on contracting and corporate governance lacked adequate investor protection, particularly for financing early-stage, high-risk ventures.
Cumming	Adverse selection and capital structure: Evidence from venture capital	*Entrepreneurship Theory and Practice*	2006	Macdonald and Associates, Ltd, http://www.canadavc.com	Canadian data	1991–2003	Canadian VC investors appear to face the greatest uncertainty among firms with high expected variability in returns (nuts) in financing start-up stages and high-tech firms. Syndication plays a crucial role in mitigating adverse selection problems.

(*Continued*)

Table 4.1. (*Continued*)

Panel D. Studies on other topics							
Authors	Title of the paper	Journal	Publication year	Data source	Data country	Data time span	Key finding
Da Rin, Nicodano, and Sembenelli	Public policy and the creation of active venture capital markets	*Journal of Public Economics*	2006	European Venture Capital Association (EVCA) yearbooks	Austria, Belgium, Denmark, Finland, France, Germany, Greece, Ireland, Italy, the Netherlands, Portugal, Spain, Sweden, and the UK data	1988–2001	Policies focusing on enhancing expected project returns are more effective in shifting VC market composition towards projects with less collateral, like early-stage and high-tech projects. Stock markets catering to entrepreneurial firms and reduced capital gains taxation increase the proportion of early-stage and high-tech investments.
Cumming	The determinants of venture capital portfolio size: Empirical evidence	*The Journal of Business*	2006	Macdonald & Associates, CVCA	Canadian data	1991–2000	There is a trade-off between VC assistance to entrepreneurial firms in the VC's portfolio and the size of the portfolio. Fund-raising and the number of funds operated by the VC firm have a significantly positive impact on VC portfolio size.

Ahlstrom and Bruton	Venture capital in emerging economies: Networks and institutional change	*Entrepreneurship Theory and Practice*	2006	*Guide to Venture Capital in Asia* (2003), questionnaire	Asian data	1999–2003	VC practice in emerging economies diverges from Anglo-American models in several specific areas. With the weak formal institutions in emerging economies, less formal institutions sometimes provide some substitute for the lack of formal institutions. Venture capitalists monitor firms through informal ties to entrepreneurs and their families.
Dushnitsky and Lenox	When does corporate venture capital investment create firm value?	*Journal of Business Venturing*	2006	Venture Economics, VentureXpert database, Standard and Poor's Compustat database	US data	1990–1999	Based on a large sample of all CVC investing firms and their industry peers, we find that corporate venture capitalists experience increased value creation, as measured by levels of Tobin's q. Our analyses suggest that CVC is likely to create firm value only when pursued for strategic reasons.
Kogut, Urso, and Walker	Emergent properties of a new financial market: American venture capital syndication	*Management Science*	2007	Securities Data Corporation (SDC)	US data	1960–2004	Analysis of VC firms' micro behaviour reveals substantial diversification among firms pivotal in establishing national markets.

(*Continued*)

Table 4.1. *(Continued)*

Panel D. Studies on other topics							
Authors	Title of the paper	Journal	Publication year	Data source	Data country	Data time span	Key finding
Hsu	Experienced entrepreneurial founders, organizational capital, and venture capital funding	*Research Policy*	2007	MIT E-Lab	US data	1995–2000	Human capital accumulation can help build ventures' social capital. Measures of human capital and social capital are positively related to venture valuation.
Mann and Sager	Patents, venture capital, and software start-ups	*Research Policy*	2007	VentureXpert, *The Venture Capital Yearbook*	US data	1997–1999	Patenting is not a top investment criterion for most venture-backed start-ups. Correlations between patenting and performance proxies indicate variations in firms' ability to utilise patents to appropriate innovation value, differing even within the industry.
Mollica and Zingales	The impact of venture capital on innovation and the creation of new businesses	*University of Chicago, NBER & CEPR*	2007	Thomson scientific, BEA, Venture Economics, NBER patent dataset, Census Bureau	US data	1992–1999	The results support the idea that VC has a positive impact on innovation and the creation of new companies. These results seem to provide prima facie evidence of the local benefit of the presence of a VC industry.

Ahlstrom, Bruton, and Yeh	Venture capital in China: Past, present, and future	*Asia Pacific Journal of Management*	2007	Interviews	Chinese data	1980s–2000s	China's market research data are becoming more reliable, benefiting private equity investors. Due diligence now extends beyond knowing the promoter, particularly in high-tech investments, a trend expected to persist.
Pintado, De Lema, and Van Auken	Venture capital in Spain by stage of development	*Journal of Small Business Management*	2007	Questionnaire/ survey sent to Spanish Association of VC Firms	Spanish data	2001	Around two-thirds of Spanish VC firms secure capital from private sources. Over half assess more than 100 proposals annually. Most respond promptly to proposals and invest in late-stage companies. Firms receiving fewer than 100 proposals tend to focus on early-stage companies, while those receiving more than 100 tend to favour late-stage ones.

(Continued)

Table 4.1. (*Continued*)

Panel D. Studies on other topics							
Authors	Title of the paper	Journal	Publication year	Data source	Data country	Data time span	Key finding
Mason	Venture capital: A geographical perspective	*Handbook of Research on Venture Capital*	2007	Report on Investment Activity (British Venture Capital Association), Thomson Macdonald, PriceWater-houseCoopers/ National Venture Capital Association Money Tree™ Report	UK, US, Canadian data	1980s–2000s	VC firms often raise funds globally but tend to invest locally to minimise uncertainty and risk, leveraging hands-on involvement. Despite this, a substantial portion of VC is also invested across long distances.
Mäkelä and Maula	Attracting cross-border venture capital: The role of a local investor	*Entrepreneurship and Regional Development*	2008	Interviews, observations and archival data	Finnish data	2000s	Local VC investors play a crucial role in attracting cross-border investors and enhancing the investment readiness of ventures. They leverage their contacts, knowledge, and proximity to manage certain responsibilities effectively.

Sorenson and Stuart	Bringing the context back in: Settings and the search for syndicate partners in venture capital investment networks	*Administrative Science Quarterly*	2008	VentureXpert database	US data	1985–2007	The likelihood of geographically and industrially distant ties forming between VC firms increases with factors such as the industry's recent popularity, the target company's maturity, the syndicate size, and the density of relationships among syndicate members.
Dimov and Murray	Determinants of the incidence and scale of seed capital investments by venture capital firms	*Small Business Economics*	2008	VentureXpert, NASDAQ	30 countries worldwide, America, Europe and Asia (US, UK, South Korea etc.)	1962–2002	The impact of fund age and experience on seed investing varies. Older funds, particularly those raised before 1995, show a positive overall effect. However, for European funds, there's evidence of a negative association between VC firm age and seed investments.

(*Continued*)

Table 4.1. (*Continued*)

Panel D. Studies on other topics							
Authors	Title of the paper	Journal	Publication year	Data source	Data country	Data time span	Key finding
Bottazzi, Da Rin, and Hellmann	Who are the active investors?: Evidence from venture capital	*Journal of Financial Economics*	2008	Survey, Amadeus, Worldscope, and VentureXpert, SDC's M&A database, and SDC's Global New Issues database	Austria, Belgium, Denmark, Finland, France,Germany, Greece, Ireland, Italy, Luxembourg, the Netherlands, Norway, Portugal, Spain, Sweden, Switzerland, and the UK data	2002–2003	Prior business experience strongly predicts an active investment style in VC. Organisational structure, particularly being structured as an independent entity, also significantly influences investment behaviour.
Kirsch, Goldfarb, and Gera	Form or substance: The role of business plans in venture capital decision making	*Strategic Management Journal*	2009	Requests submitted to FVC	US data	1999–2002	Neither the presence of business planning documents nor their content serves a communicative role for venture capitalists. Business planning documents may serve a limited ceremonial role.

Guler and Guillén	Institutions and the internationalization of US venture capital firms	*Journal of International Business Studies*	2009	VentureXpert database (Venture Economics)	US data	1990–2002	The findings underscore the significance of national innovation systems in attracting foreign VC. They align with recent international business research, emphasising firms' overseas expansion to enhance and complement existing capabilities with new knowledge.
Chen	Technology commercialization, incubator and venture capital, and new venture performance	*Journal of Business Research*	2009	Questionnaire, Industrial Technology Research Institute (ITRI) of Taiwan	Taiwanese data	2000s	Abundant human and intangible resources in new ventures positively influence technological competence (TC) and performance. Organisational resources improve performance primarily through their mediation of TC competence.
Hege, Palomino, and Schweinbacher	Venture capital performance: The disparity between Europe and the United States	*Finance*	2009	Venture Economics database	US data, EU data	1997–2003	The US VC industry strongly outperforms its European counterpart. When trying to identify determinants of this performance gap, we find that contracting-related determinants play a crucial role.

(Continued)

Table 4.1. *(Continued)*

Panel D. Studies on other topics

Authors	Title of the paper	Journal	Publication year	Data source	Data country	Data time span	Key finding
Lerner	The future of public efforts to boost entrepreneurship and venture capital	*Small Business Economics*	2010	Central Intelligence Agency (2008), Council of Economic Advisors, Executive Office of the President (2008), and the World Bank's World Development Indicators database	Jamaican, Singaporean data	1973–2007	Key success factors include leveraging local academic and research resources, adhering to global standards, acknowledging long lead times in public venture initiatives, avoiding excessively large or small initiatives, and recognising the significance of global interconnections.
Mason	Venture Capital: Rationale, aims and scope	*An International Journal of Entrepreneurial Finance*	2010	European Venture Capital Association, Fineberg	US, EU data, Israel, Asia data	1988–1997	VC investment is growing globally, driven by government involvement to spur economic development and job creation. This trend is mirrored in increased academic research across various disciplines, emphasising technology and regional economic growth.

Samila and Sorenson	Venture capital as a catalyst to commercialization	*Research Policy*	2010	Patent Network Dataverse, Small Business Administration, VentureXpert database, WebCASPAR database, *The Chronicle of Higher Education*	US data	1993–2002	The authors observe complementarity between public research funding and private VC, with regions abundant in VC experiencing increased patenting and establishment starts over time. VC likely acts as a catalyst for commercialisation by nurturing entrepreneurial talent within a region.
Ghosh and Nanda	Venture capital investment in the clean energy sector	*Harvard Business School Entrepreneurial Management Working Paper*	2010	New Energy Finance reports, Venturexpert, National Venture Capital Association press releases	US data	2000s	Sustained innovation in the US clean energy sector by venture-backed start-ups hinges on the ecosystem's capacity to adapt to sector-specific structural features. A key bottleneck in the energy production innovation pipeline is the challenge VCs face in exiting investments at the right juncture.

(*Continued*)

Table 4.1. (*Continued*)

Panel D. Studies on other topics							
Authors	Title of the paper	Journal	Publication year	Data source	Data country	Data time span	Key finding
Chemmanur, Krishnan, and Nandy	How does venture capital financing improve efficiency in private firms? A look beneath the surface	*The Review of Financial Studies*	2011	Longitudinal Research Database (LRD) (Center of Economic Studies at US Census Bureau)	US data	1972–2000	VC-backed firms consistently exhibit higher overall efficiency compared to non-VC-backed firms. This efficiency advantage stems from both screening and monitoring processes: VC-backed firms demonstrate higher efficiency even before receiving financing, and their efficiency growth post-VC financing surpasses that of non-VC-backed firms.
Basu, Phelps, and Kotha	Towards understanding who makes corporate venture capital investments and why	*Journal of Business Venturing*	2011	VentureXpert, *Fortune* 500 list	US data	1990–2000	Incumbents are motivated to pursue corporate venture capital (CVC) investments in dynamic environments. Industries with rapid technological change, highly competitive intensity, and weak appropriability show greater CVC activity.

Hirukawa and Ueda	Venture capital and innovation: Which is first?	*Pacific Economic Review*	2011	VentureXpert; Bartelsman, Becker and Gray's NBER-CES Manufacturing Industry Database ('the NBER productivity database'); the NBER U.S. Patent Citations Data File ('the NBER patent database'); and Funds for Industrial R&D Performance, by Industry and by Size of Company: 1953–1998 from the National Science Foundation ('the R&D database').	US data	1968–2001	The authors find evidence supporting the innovation-first hypothesis when using TFP growth as the innovation measure. TFP growth causally influences both first and follow-on round VC investments. However, weak support is found for the VC-first hypothesis when using TFP growth as the innovation measure.

(Continued)

Table 4.1. (*Continued*)

Panel D. Studies on other topics

Authors	Title of the paper	Journal	Publication year	Data source	Data country	Data time span	Key finding
Schertler, Tykvová	Venture capital and internationalization	*International Business Review*	2011	Bureau van Dijk's Zephyr database	Australia, Austria, Belgium, Brazil, Bulgaria, Canada, Chile, China, Czech Republic, Denmark, Egypt, Estonia, Finland, France, Germany, Greece, Hong Kong, Hungary, India, Ireland, Israel, Italy, Japan, Jordan	2000–2008	Experienced domestic venture capitalists leverage internationalisation advantages more effectively than their less experienced counterparts. Foreign venture capitalists are inclined to participate in larger deals, particularly with portfolio companies in small countries.
Metrick and Yasuda	Venture capital and other private equity: A survey	*European Financial Management*	2011	N/A	N/A	N/A	Evidence regarding the existence and persistence of excess performance in private equity is mixed, partly due to significant data limitations and methodological challenges arising from them. Naive applications of standard asset pricing approaches often result in overestimates of alphas and underestimates of market beta.

Li and Zahra	Formal institutions, culture, and venture capital activity: A cross-country analysis	*Journal of Business Venturing*	2012	VentureXpert	68 different countries	1996–2006	Economic freedom acquired through entrepreneurship requires a strong institutional framework. The effects of institutional framework are contingent on national culture.
Hargadon, Kenney	Misguided policy? Following venture capital into clean technology	*California Management Review*	2012	VentureXpert etc.	US data	1999–2009	These causes suggest VC is an ill-suited investment vehicle – let alone policy framework – for fostering a clean technology revolution.
Félix, Pires, and Gulamhussen	The determinants of venture capital in europe – evidence across countries	*Journal of Financial Services Research*	2012	European Private Equity and Venture Capital Association (EVCA) yearbooks, AMECO Database from EuroStat, Zephyr Database from Bureau van Dijk, Global Entrepreneurship Monitor (GEM) etc.	EU data	1998–2003	The evidence indicates that explanatory variables are uncorrelated with country-fixed unobserved factors, primarily relying on random effect estimators. Results suggest that in Europe, the size of the M&A market plays a significant role in explaining VC investment.

(Continued)

Table 4.1. *(Continued)*

Panel D. Studies on other topics

Authors	Title of the paper	Journal	Publication year	Data source	Data country	Data time span	Key finding
Aizenman and Kendall	The internationalization of venture capital	*Journal of Economic Studies*	2012	VentureXpert	US data (mostly)	1992–2007	The authors find that the countries which have more often been the sources of international deals have better institutional environments, more developed financial markets, high computer penetration, and more university graduates than countries which have lagged in generating deals. These features likely create a conducive environment for financial companies to form and raise capital, thus facilitating the supply side of this market.

Park and Steensma	When does corporate venture capital add value for new ventures?	*Strategic Management Journal*	2012	VentureXpert, LinkSV (www.linksv.com), archive.org, Factiva, Lexis-Nexis etc.	US data	1990–2003	For ventures needing generic complementary assets, the benefits of CVC funding were limited, potentially leading to loss of access to diverse resources. However, in uncertain environments, CVC funding proved more advantageous in averting failure for new ventures compared to stable environments.
Lerner and Tåg	Institutions and venture capital	*Industrial and Corporate Change*	2013	OECD Factbook, Capital IQ database, VentureXpert etc.	US data, Swedish data	1971–2010	The literature suggests that institutional frameworks, including the legal environment and financial market development, significantly influence active VC markets.
Block, De Vries, Schumann, and Sandner	Trademarks and venture capital valuation	*Journal of Business Venturing*	2013	VentureXpert, United States Patent and Trademark Office (USPTO), PATSTAT	US data	1998–2007	Trademarks impact both the market valuations of large firms and the financial valuations of start-ups by venture capitalists.

(Continued)

Table 4.1. *(Continued)*

Panel D. Studies on other topics

Authors	Title of the paper	Journal	Publication year	Data source	Data country	Data time span	Key finding
Popov and Roosenboom	Venture capital and new business creation	*Journal of Banking & Finance*	2013	VentureXpert, Amadeus database (Bureau van Dijk)	Austria, Belgium, Czech Republic, Denmark, Finland, France, Germany, Greece, Hungary, Iceland, Ireland, Italy, Netherlands, Norway, Poland, Portugal, Slovakia, Spain, Switzerland, Sweden, and UK data	1998–2008	VC investment significantly stimulates new business creation. VC fosters the emergence of innovative ideas through young companies entering the marketplace.
Chemmanur, Loutskina, and Tian	Corporate venture capital, value creation, and innovation	*The Review of Financial Studies*	2014	Thomson VentureXpert, Securities Data Company (SDC) Global New Issues Database	US data	1980–2004	The authors find that CVC-backed firms achieve a higher degree of innovation output, as measured by their patenting, although these firms are younger, riskier, and less profitable.

Faria and Barbosa	Does venture capital really foster innovation?	*Economics Letters*	2014	EUROSTAT	Belgium, Czech Republic, Denmark, Finland, France, Germany, Greece, Hungary, Ireland, Italy, Netherlands, Norway, Poland, Portugal, Spain, Sweden and United Kingdom data	2000–2009	Patents applications are in fact influenced by VC venturing. However, only the later-stage VC capital is promoting innovation. The VC role is more to help the commercialisation of innovation rather than to foster its creation.
Bengtsson and Hsu	Ethnic matching in the US venture capital market	*Journal of Business Venturing*	2015	Venture economics (VE)	US data	1984–2009	The results show that person-based matching based on shared ethnicity is a strong predictor of the likelihood of an investment.
Bocken	Sustainable venture capital – catalyst for sustainable start-up success?	*Journal of Cleaner Production*	2015	Interviews	UK data	2013	Sustainable start-ups can leverage sustainable business model innovation, new technology, and funding platforms to expand beyond the 'green customer base' and develop diverse business cases for success.

(*Continued*)

Table 4.1. (*Continued*)

Panel D. Studies on other topics							
Authors	Title of the paper	Journal	Publication year	Data source	Data country	Data time span	Key finding
Brander, Du, and Hellmann	The effects of government-sponsored venture capital: International evidence	*Review of Finance*	2015	Thomson ONE (T1) (Venturexpert), *Asian Venture Capital Journal* (AVCJ)	US, Canadian, UK, EU, Asian data	2000–2008	GVC activity increases the overall amount of VC funding available. Enterprises receiving mixed funding from both PVCs and GVCs tend to receive more total funding compared to those financed solely by PVCs.
Bertoni, Colombo, and Quas	The patterns of venture capital investment in Europe	*Small Business Economics*	2015	VICO database	EU data	1994–2004	In Europe, various VC investor types display distinct investment patterns based on industry, company age, size, stage of development, and localisation. These patterns remain largely stable over time, except for CVC investors, which shifted notably after the Internet bubble burst.

Cumming, Henriques, and Sadorsky	Cleantech' venture capital around the world	*International Review of Financial Analysis*	2016	The Cleantech group, VentureXpert	Australia, Austria, Belgium, Brazil, Canada, Switzerland, Germany, Denmark, Spain, Finland, France, Great Britain, Greece, Hong Kong, Indonesia, Ireland, Israel, Italy, Japan, Korea, Mexico, Malaysia, Netherlands, Norway, New Zealand, Portugal, Singapore, Sweden, Thailand, United States, South African data	1996–2010	Oil prices have a curvilinear effect on cleantech VC investing. Increases in oil prices increase cleantech VC deals but with a slowing rate of increase. Uncertainty avoidance has a negative and statistically significant impact on cleantech VC deals.

(*Continued*)

Table 4.1. (*Continued*)

Panel D. Studies on other topics							
Authors	Title of the paper	Journal	Publication year	Data source	Data country	Data time span	Key finding
Colombo, Cumming, and Vismara	Governmental venture capital for innovative young firms	*The Journal of Technology Transfer*	2016	N/A	N/A	N/A	The rationale for supporting GVC programs includes addressing the equity gap for innovative young firms, fostering private VC industry development, and anticipating positive economic externalities. However, concerns persist about potential distortions, inadequate skills in firm selection and nurturing, and the risk of crowding out private VCs.
Guerini and Quas	Governmental venture capital in Europe: Screening and certification	*Journal of Business Venturing*	2016	VICO dataset	Belgium, Finland, France, Germany, Italy, Spain and the United Kingdom data	1994–2010	Receiving GVC increases an entrepreneurial company's chance of obtaining PVC by threefold, indicating GVC's screening ability and certification effect in Europe. This reduces information asymmetries for high-tech entrepreneurial firms and enhances their access to the PVC market.

Maula and Murray	Corporate venture capital and the creation of US public companies: The impact of sources of venture capital on the performance of portfolio companies	*Creating Value: Winners In the New Business Environment*	2017	Venture economics database, Thomson financial securities data	US data	1998–1999	New enterprises partnering with industry-leading corporations through corporate venture capitalists may result in higher IPO valuations.
Ewens, Nanda, and Rhodes-Kropf	Cost of experimentation and the evolution of venture capital.	*Journal of Financial Economics*	2018	VentureSource database, Correlation Ventures, Thomson's Venture Economics	US data	2002–2010	The authors illustrate how technological shocks in experimentation costs shape start-up innovation, leading to a 'spray and pray' investment strategy that favours quick and inexpensive information revelation.
Cumming and Schweinbacher	Fintech venture capital	*Corporate Governance an International Review*	2018	VentureXpert, World Bank database, Z/Yen Group Limited	United Kingdom, United States China Singapore Japan South Korea Switzerland Canada Germany and Australia data	1990–2015	Fintech start-ups are raising substantial capital, particularly among smaller, private independent limited partnership VCs and in countries lacking major financial centres. These trends may indicate inefficient VC investments in certain regions.

(*Continued*)

Table 4.1. (*Continued*)

Panel D. Studies on other topics							
Authors	Title of the paper	Journal	Publication year	Data source	Data country	Data time span	Key finding
Metrick and Yasuda	Venture capital and the finance of innovation	(Wiley)	2021	Private Equity Analyst, The Private Equity Performance Monitor	US data	1983–2000s	A high-reputation VC is more likely to have its term sheets accepted and can pay lower prices for shares than do low-reputation VCs. Top-tier VCs earn their reputations with superior investment performance, and many of these top-tier firms raise their carried interest to 25 or even 30 percent. Nevertheless, there is excess demand by potential LPs to invest in such top-tier VCs, even at these higher prices.
Dai	Empirical research on private equity funds: A review of the past decade and future research opportunities	*Review of Corporate Finance*	2022	N/A	N/A	N/A	It is estimated that the total volume of angel investment has long surpassed VC investment in the US and increasingly in some other countries as well. Some (not all) accelerators accelerate venture development.

Bianchini and Croce	The role of environmental policies in promoting venture capital investments in cleantech companies	*Review of Corporate Finance*	2022	VICO database, OECD policy database	European data	1998–2014	Environmental taxes evidence a U-shaped relationship with the number of IVC investments and the amount invested in the cleantech sector, with an initial positive effect of these instruments in fostering VC investment in cleantech and a subsequent negative effect in the presence of extremely high taxation levels: a moderate level of environmental taxes fosters innovation and provides an incentive for private VC funds to invest in clean technologies.

(*Continued*)

Table 4.1. (*Continued*)

Panel D. Studies on other topics							
Authors	Title of the paper	Journal	Publication year	Data source	Data country	Data time span	Key finding
Koenig and Burghof	The investment style drift puzzle and risk-taking in venture capital	*Review of Corporate Finance*	2022	Refinitiv Eikon (formerly known as Thomson Reuters Eikon and Thomson Reuters VentureXpert), Thomson Reuters Datastream, country-level cultural dimensions from Hofstede, country-level legal system quality index from La Porta *et al.* and Berkowitz *et al.*	US and European data	1980–2014	Style drifts represent shifts in the risk profile of a fund. When drifts are deliberate risk-taking decisions motivated by potential compensation benefits for general partners (GPs), they constitute an agency conflict. VCs have a higher risk-taking attitude regarding all investment style drifts when public markets are rising.

Erin E. Smith, Janet Kiholm Smith, and Richard L. Smith	Bias in the reporting of venture capital performance: The disciplinary role of FOIA	*Review of Corporate Finance*	2022	Pitchbook (PB)	US data	2013–2017	The probability of LP reporting is strongly related to LP FOIA eligibility: FOIA-eligible limited partners (LPs) are about 8.5 times more likely to report performance metrics than are other LPs. GPs report better performance mainly because they selectively choose when to report. GPs report better fund performance than do either FOIA eligible or other LPs.
Cappellari and Gucciardi	Equity investments and environmental pressure: The role of venture capital	*Sustainability*	2023	Zephyr (Bureau van Dijk), Eurostat, World Bank	131 countries	2011–2021	There is a negative correlation between VC investments and environmental intensity (measured by CO_2 emissions over GDP).
Heuvel and Popp	The role of venture capital and governments in clean energy: Lessons from the first cleantech bubble	*Energy Economics*	2023	Crunchbase data	US data	2000–2021	Weak demand for clean energy technology hampers returns and VC activity. Governments should implement policies like carbon pricing to stimulate private demand for clean energy products and support early-stage investments.

4.6. Suggested Directions for Future Research on VC

Among the recent studies on VC investment, it is worth noting that a subset of literature analyses the involvement of VC in sustainable cleantech investments. In a groundbreaking work, Cumming *et al.* (2016) examined the cleantech VC around the world. They provided a cross-country analysis of the determinants of cleantech VC investments with a unique worldwide dataset of 31 countries spanning 1996–2010. More recently, Cappellari and Gucciardi (2023) documented a negative correlation between VC investments and environmental intensity. Heuvel and Popp (2023) recorded that weak demand for clean energy technology hampers returns and VC activity. They propose that governments should implement policies such as carbon pricing to stimulate private demand for clean energy products and support early-stage investments. In light of the escalating significance of environmental protection in recent years, there is a growing imperative for academic research to investigate deeper into the role of VC in catalysing the advancement of cleantech businesses on a global scale.

References

Ahlstrom, D. and Bruton, G. D. (2006). Venture capital in emerging economies: Networks and institutional change. *Entrepreneurship Theory and Practice*, 30(2), 299–320.

Ahlstrom, D., Bruton, G. D., and Yeh, K. S. (2007). Venture capital in China: Past, present, and future. *Asia Pacific Journal of Management*, 24(3), 247–268.

Aizenman, J. and Kendall, J. (2012). The internationalization of venture capital. *Journal of Economic Studies*, 39(5), 488–511.

Amit, R., Brander, J., and Zott, C. (1998). Why do venture capital firms exist? Theory and Canadian evidence. *Journal of Business Venturing*, 13(6), 441–466.

Barry, C. B. (1994). New directions in research on venture capital finan. *Financial Management*, 23(3), 3–15.

Barry, C. B., Muscarella, C. J., Peavy, J. W., and Vetsuypens, M. R. (1990). The role of venture capital in the creation of public companies. *Journal of Financial Economics*, 27(2), 447–471.

Basu, S., Phelps, C., and Kotha, S. (2011). Towards understanding who makes corporate venture capital investments and why. *Journal of Business Venturing*, 26(2), 153–171.

Becker, R. and Hellmann, T. (2005). The genesis of venture capital: Lessons from the German experience. *Venture Capital, Entrepreneurship, and Public Policy*, 33–67.

Bengtsson, O. and Hsu, D. H. (2015). Ethnic matching in the US venture capital market. *Journal of Business Venturing*, 30(2), 338–354.

Bertoni, F., Colombo, M. G., and Quas, A. (2015). The patterns of venture capital investment in Europe. *Small Business Economics*, 45(3), 543–560.

Bianchini R. and Croce, A. (2022). The role of environmental policies in promoting venture capital investments in cleantech companies. *Review of Corporate Finance*, 2(3), 587–616.

Black, B. S. and Gilson, R. J. (1998). Venture capital and the structure of capital markets: Banks versus stock markets. *Journal of Financial Economics*, 47(3), 243–277.

Black, B. S. and Gilson, R. J. (1999). Does venture capital require an active stock market? *Journal of Applied Corporate Finance*, 11(4), 36–48.

Bocken, N. M. P. (2015). Sustainable venture capital – catalyst for sustainable start-up success? *Journal of Cleaner Production*, 108(A), 647–658.

Bottazzi, L. and Da Rin, M. (2002). Venture capital in Europe and the financing of innovative companies. *Economic Policy*, 17(34), 229–270.

Bottazzi, L., Da Rin, M., and Hellmann, T. (2008). Who are the active investors? Evidence from venture capital. *Journal of Financial Economics*, 89(3), 488–512.

Bottazzi, L., Da Rin, M., and Hellmann, T. (2016). The importance of trust for investment: Evidence from venture capital. *The Review of Financial Studies*, 29(9), 2283–2318.

Brander, J. A., Amit, R., and Antweiler, W. (2002). Venture-capital syndication: Improved venture selection vs. the value-added hypothesis. *Journal of Economics & Management Strategy*, 11(3), 423–452.

Brander, J. A., Du, Q., and Hellmann, T. (2015). The effects of government-sponsored venture capital: International evidence. *Review of Finance*, 19(2), 571–618.

Brander, J. A., Egan, E., and Hellmann, T. F. (2010). Government sponsored versus private venture capital: Canadian evidence. In *International Differences in Entrepreneurship*, University of Chicago Press, 275–320.

Brush, C. G., Carter, N. M., Gatewood, E. J., Greene, P. G., and Hart, M. (2004). Gatekeepers of venture growth: A Diana Project report on the role and participation of women in the venture capital industry.

Bruton, G., Ahlstrom, D., and Puky, T. (2009). Institutional differences and the development of entrepreneurial ventures: A comparison of the venture capital industries in Latin America and Asia. *Journal of International Business Studies*, 40(5), 762–778.

Bruton, G. D., Ahlstrom, D., and Singh, K. (2002). The impact of the institutional environment on the venture capital industry in Singapore. *Venture Capital: An International Journal of Entrepreneurial Finance*, 4(3), 197–218.

Bruton, G., Ahlstrom, D., and Yeh, K. S. (2004). Understanding venture capital in East Asia: The impact of institutions on the industry today and tomorrow. *Journal of World Business*, 39(1), 72–88.

Bygrave, W. D. (1987). Syndicated investments by venture capital firms: A networking perspective. *Journal of Business Venturing*, 2(2), 139–154.

Bygrave, W. D. (1988). The structure of the investment networks of venture capital firms. *Journal of Business Venturing*, 3(2), 137–157.

Chemmanur, T. J., Krishnan, K., and Nandy, D. K. (2011). How does venture capital financing improve efficiency in private firms? A look beneath the surface. *Review of Financial Studies*, 24(12), 4037–4090.

Chemmanur, T. J., Loutskina, E., and Tian, X. (2014). Corporate venture capital, value creation, and innovation. *The Review of Financial Studies*, 27(8), 2434–2473.

Chen, C.-J. (2009). Technology commercialization, incubator and venture capital, and new venture performance. *Journal of Business Research*, 62(1), 93–103.

Chen, H., Gompers, P., Kovner, A., and Lerner, J. (2010). Buy local? The geography of venture capital. *Journal of Urban Economics*, 67(1), 90–102.

Cochrane, J. H. (2005). The risk and return of venture capital. *Journal of Financial Economics*, 75(1), 3–52.

Colombo, M. G., Cumming, D., and Vismara, S. (2016). Governmental venture capital for innovative young firms. *The Journal of Technology Transfer*, 41, 10–24.

Colombo, M. G. and Grilli, L. (2010). On growth drivers of high-tech startups: Exploring the role of founders' human capital and venture capital. *Journal of Business Venturing*, 25(6), 610–626.

Cumming, D. (2006a). Adverse selection and capital structure: Evidence from venture capital. *Entrepreneurship Theory and Practice*, 30(2), 155–183.

Cumming, D. (2006b). The determinants of venture capital portfolio size: Empirical evidence. *The Journal of Business*, 79(3), 1083–1126.

Cumming, D. (2008). Contracts and exits in venture capital finance. *The Review of Financial Studies*, 21(5), 1947–1982.

Cumming, D., Fleming, G., and Schwienbacher, A. (2005). Liquidity risk and venture capital finance. *Financial Management*, 34(4), 77–105.

Cumming, D., Fleming, G., and Schwienbacher, A. (2006). Legality and venture capital exits. *Journal of Corporate Finance*, 12(2), 214–245.

Cumming, D., Grilli, L., and Murtinu, S. (2017). Governmental and independent venture capital investments in Europe: A firm-level performance analysis. *Journal of Corporate Finance*, 42, 439–459.

Cumming, D., Henriques, I., and Sadorsky, P. (2016). 'Cleantech' venture capital around the world. *International Review of Financial Analysis*, 44, 86–97.

Cumming, D. and MacIntosh, J. G. (2003). Venture-capital exits in Canada and the United States. *The University of Toronto Law Journal*, 53(2), 101.

Cumming, D. and Schwienbacher, A. (2018). Fintech venture capital. *Corporate Governance: An International Review*, 26(5), 374–389.

Da Rin, M., Nicodano, G., and Sembenelli, A. (2006). Public policy and the creation of active venture capital markets. *Journal of Public Economics*, 90(8-9), 1699–1723.

Dai, N. (2022). Empirical research on private equity funds: A review of the past decade and future research opportunities. *Review of Corporate Finance*, 2, 427–450.

De Clercq, D. and Dimov, D. (2004). Explaining venture capital firms' syndication behaviour: A longitudinal study. *Venture Capital: An International Journal of Entrepreneurial Finance*, 6(4), 243–256.

Dimov, D. and Milanov, H. (2010). The interplay of need and opportunity in venture capital investment syndication. *Journal of Business Venturing*, 25(4), 331–348.

Dimov, D. and Murray, G. (2008). Determinants of the incidence and scale of seed capital investments by venture capital firms. *Small Business Economics*, 30(2), 127–152.

Dossani, R. and Kenney, M. (2002). Creating an environment for venture capital in India. *World Development*, 30(2), 227–253.

Dushnitsky, G. and Lenox, M. J. (2006). When does corporate venture capital investment create firm value? *Journal of Business Venturing*, 21(6), 753–772.

Elango, B., Fried, V. H., Hisrich, R. D., and Polonchek, A. (1995). How venture capital firms differ. *Journal of Business Venturing*, 10(2), 157–179.

Engel, D. (2002). The impact of venture capital on firm growth: An empirical investigation. ZEW Discussion Paper No. 02-02.

Engel, D. and Keilbach, M. (2007). Firm-level implications of early stage venture capital investment — An empirical investigation. *Journal of Empirical Finance*, 14(2), 150–167.

Ewens, M., Gorbenko, A., and Korteweg, A. (2022). Venture capital contracts. *Journal of Financial Economics*, 143(1), 131–158.

Ewens, M., Nanda, R., and Rhodes-Kropf, M. (2018). Cost of experimentation and the evolution of venture capital. *Journal of Financial Economics*, 128(3), 422–442.

Faria, A. P. and Barbosa, N. (2014). Does venture capital really foster innovation? *Economics Letters*, 122(2), 129–131.

Félix, E. G. S., Pires, C. P., and Gulamhussen, M. A. (2012). The determinants of venture capital in Europe — Evidence across countries. *Journal of Financial Services Research*, 44(3), 259–279.

Ferrary, M. (2010). Syndication of venture capital investment: The art of resource pooling. *Entrepreneurship Theory and Practice*, 34(5), 885–907.

Fiet, J. O. (1995a). Reliance upon informants in the venture capital industry. *Journal of Business Venturing*, 10(3), 195–223.

Fiet, J. O. (1995b). Risk avoidance strategies in venture capital markets. *Journal of Management Studies*, 32(4), 551–574.

Florida, R. and Kenney, M. (1988a). Venture capital, high technology and regional development. *Regional Studies*, 22(1), 33–48.

Florida, R. and Kenney, M. (1988b). Venture capital-financed innovation and technological change in the USA. *Research Policy*, 17(3), 119–137.

Florida, R. and Smith, D. F. (1990). Venture capital, innovation, and economic development. *Economic Development Quarterly*, 4(4), 345–360.

Florida, R. and Smith, D. F. (1993). Venture capital formation, investment, and regional industrialization. *Annals of the Association of American Geographers*, 83(3), 434–451.

Florin, J. (2005). Is venture capital worth it? Effects on firm performance and founder returns. *Journal of Business Venturing*, 20(1), 113–135.

Fried, V. H., Bruton, G. D., and Hisrich, R. D. (1998). Strategy and the board of directors in venture capital-backed firms. *Journal of Business Venturing*, 13(6), 493–503.

Fried, V. H. and Hisrich, R. D. (1988). Venture capital research: Past, present and future. *Entrepreneurship Theory and Practice*, 13(1), 15–28.

Fried, V. H. and Hisrich, R. D. (1994). Toward a model of venture capital investment decision making. *Financial Management*, 23(3), 28.

Fuchs F., Füss R., Jenkinson T., and Morkoetter, S. (2022). Should investors care where private equity managers went to school? *Review of Corporate Finance*, 2(3), 451–492.

Ghosh, S. and Nanda, R. (2010). Venture capital investment in the clean energy sector. Harvard Business School Entrepreneurial Management Working Paper No. 11-020.

Gompers, P. (1998). Venture capital growing pains: Should the market diet? *Journal of Banking & Finance*, 22(6-8), 1089–1104.

Gompers, P., Kovner, A., Lerner, J., and Scharfstein, D. (2008). Venture capital investment cycles: The impact of public markets. *Journal of Financial Economics*, 87(1), 1–23.

Gompers, P., Kovner, A., Lerner, J., and Scharfstein, D. (2009). Specialization and success: Evidence from venture capital. *Journal of Economics & Management Strategy*, 18(3), 817–844.

Gompers, P. and Lerner, J. (1999a). An analysis of compensation in the U.S. venture capital partnership. *Journal of Financial Economics*, 51(1), 3–44.

Gompers, P. and Lerner, J. (1999b). What drives venture capital fundraising? National Bureau of Economic Research, Working Paper No. 6906.

Gompers, P. and Lerner, J. (2001). The venture capital revolution. *Journal of Economic Perspectives*, 15(2), 145–168.

Gornall, W. and Strebulaev, I. A. (2015). The economic impact of venture capital: Evidence from public companies (June 2021). Available at SSRN: https://ssrn.com/abstract=2681841 or http://dx.doi.org/10.2139/ssrn.2681841.

Grilli, L. and Murtinu, S. (2014). Government, venture capital and the growth of European high-tech entrepreneurial firms. *Research Policy*, 43(9), 1523–1543.

Guerini, M. and Quas, A. (2016). Governmental venture capital in Europe: Screening and certification. *Journal of Business Venturing*, 31(2), 175–195.

Guler, I. and Guillén, M. F. (2009). Institutions and the internationalization of US venture capital firms. *Journal of International Business Studies*, 41(2), 185–205.

Gupta, A. K. and Sapienza, H. J. (1992). Determinants of venture capital firms' preferences regarding the industry diversity and geographic scope of their investments. *Journal of Business Venturing*, 7(5), 347–362.

Häussler, C., Harhoff, D., and Mueller, E. (2009). To be financed or not... The role of patents for venture capital financing. ZEW Discussion Papers, No. 09-003.

Harrison, R. T. and Mason, C. (2000). Venture capital market complementarities: The links between business angels and venture capital funds in the United Kingdom. *Venture Capital*, 2(3), 223–242.

Hamao, Y., Packer, F., and Ritter, J. R. (2000). Institutional affiliation and the role of venture capital: Evidence from initial public offerings in Japan. *Pacific-Basin Finance Journal*, 8(5), 529–558.

Hargadon, A. B. and Kenney, M. (2012). Misguided policy? Following venture capital into clean technology. *California Management Review*, 54(2), 118–139.

Harrison, R. T. and Mason, C. M. (1992). International perspectives on the supply of informal venture capital. *Journal of Business Venturing*, 7(6), 459–475.

Hege, U., Palomino, F., and Schwienbacher, A. (2009). Venture capital performance: The disparity between Europe and the United States. *Finance*, 30(1), 7.

Hellmann, T., Lindsey, L., and Puri, M. (2008). Building relationships early: Banks in venture capital. *The Review of Financial Studies*, 21(2), 513–541.

Hellmann, T. and Puri, M. (2000). The interaction between product market and financing strategy: The role of venture capital. *Review of Financial Studies*, 13(4), 959–984.

Hellmann, T. and Puri, M. (2002). Venture capital and the professionalization of start-up firms: Empirical evidence. *The Journal of Finance*, 57(1), 169–197.

Heuvel, M. V. D. and Popp, D. (2023). The role of venture capital and governments in clean energy: Lessons from the first cleantech bubble. *Energy Economics*, 124, 106877.

Hirukawa, M. and Ueda, M. (2011). Venture capital and innovation: Which is first? *Pacific Economic Review*, 16(4), 421–465.

Hisrich, R. D. and Jankowicz, A. D. (1990). Intuition in venture capital decisions: An exploratory study using a new technique. *Journal of Business Venturing*, 5(1), 49–62.

Hochberg, Y. V. (2011). Venture capital and corporate governance in the newly public firm. *Review of Finance*, 16(2), 429–480.

Hochberg, Y. V., Ljungqvist, A., and Lu, Y. (2007). Whom you know matters: Venture capital networks and investment performance. *The Journal of Finance*, 62(1), 251–301.

Hopp, C. and Rieder, F. (2011). What drives venture capital syndication? *Applied Economics*, 43(23), 3089–3102.

Hsu, D. H. (2004). What do entrepreneurs pay for venture capital affiliation? *The Journal of Finance*, 59(4), 1805–1844.

Hsu, D. H. (2007). Experienced entrepreneurial founders, organizational capital, and venture capital funding. *Research Policy*, 36(5), 722–741.

Ibrahim, D. M. (2010). Debt as venture capital. *University of Illinois Law Review*, 2010(4), 1169–1210.

Jelic, R., Saadouni, B., and Wright, M. (2005). Performance of private to public MBOs: The role of venture capital. *Journal of Business Finance & Accounting*, 32(3-4), 643–682.

Jeng, L. A. and Wells, P. C. (2000). The determinants of venture capital funding: Evidence across countries. *Journal of Corporate Finance*, 6(3), 241–289.

Jones, C. M. and Rhodes-Kropf, M. (2003). The price of diversifiable risk in venture capital and private equity. Working Paper, Columbia University.

Kaplan, S. N. and Lerner, J. (2010). It ain't broke: The past, present, and future of venture capital. *Journal of Applied Corporate Finance*, 22(2), 36–47.

Kaplan, S. N. and Lerner, J. (2016). Venture capital data: Opportunities and challenges. In *Measuring Entrepreneurial Businesses: Current Knowledge and Challenges*, 413–431.

Kaplan, S. N., Strömberg, P., and Sensoy, B. A. (2002). How well do venture capital databases reflect actual investments? Available at SSRN 939073.

Kerins, F., Smith, J. K., and Smith, R. (2004). Opportunity cost of capital for venture capital investors and entrepreneurs. *Journal of Financial and Quantitative Analysis*, 39(2), 385–405.

Khan, A. M. (1987). Assessing venture capital investments with noncompensatory behavioral decision models. *Journal of Business Venturing*, 2(3), 193–205.

Kirsch, D., Goldfarb, B., and Gera, A. (2009). Form or substance: The role of business plans in venture capital decision making. *Strategic Management Journal*, 30(5), 487–515.

Koenig, L. and Burghof, H. P. (2022). The investment style drift puzzle and risk-taking in venture capital. *Review of Corporate Finance*, 2(3), 527–585.

Kogut, B., Urso, P., and Walker, G. (2007). Emergent properties of a new financial market: American venture capital syndication, 1960–2005. *Management Science*, 53(7), 1181–1198.

Korteweg, A. and Nagel, S. (2016). Risk-adjusting the returns to venture capital. *The Journal of Finance*, 71(3), 1437–1470.

Kortum, S. and Lerner, J. (2001). Does venture capital spur innovation? In *Entrepreneurial Inputs and Outcomes: New Studies of Entrepreneurship in the United States*, 1–44. Emerald Group Publishing Limited.

Lemley, M. A. (2000). Reconceiving patents in the age of venture capital. *Journal of Small and Emerging Business Law*, 4(1), 137–148.

Lerner, J. (2002). Boom and bust in the venture capital industry and the impact on innovation. Available at SSRN: https://ssrn.com/abstract=366041 or http://dx.doi.org/10.2139/ssrn.366041.

Lerner, J. (2010). The future of public efforts to boost entrepreneurship and venture capital. *Small Business Economics*, 35(3), 255–264.

Lerner, J. and Tåg, J. (2013). Institutions and venture capital. *Industrial and Corporate Change*, 22(1), 153–182.

Li, Y. and Zahra, S. A. (2012). Formal institutions, culture, and venture capital activity: A cross-country analysis. *Journal of Business Venturing*, 27(1), 95–111.

Lockett, A. and Wright, M. (2001). The syndication of venture capital investments. *Omega*, 29(5), 375–390.

Maier, J. B. and Walker, D. A. (1987). The role of venture capital in financing small business. *Journal of Business Venturing*, 2(3), 207–214.

Mäkelä, M. M. and Maula, M. V. (2008). Attracting cross-border venture capital: The role of a local investor. *Entrepreneurship and Regional Development*, 20(3), 237–257.

Manigart, S., Baeyens, K., and Van Hyfte, W. (2002a). The survival of venture capital backed companies. *Venture Capital: An International Journal of Entrepreneurial Finance*, 4(2), 103–124.

Manigart, S., De Waele, K., Wright, M., Robbie, K., Desbrières, P., Sapienza, H. J., and Beekman, A. (2002b). Determinants of required return in venture capital investments: A five-country study. *Journal of Business Venturing*, 17(4), 291–312.

Manigart, S., Lockett, A., Meuleman, M., Wright, M., Landström, H., Bruining, H., Desbrieres, P., and Hommel, U. (2002c). Why do European venture capital companies syndicate? ERIM Report Series Reference No. ERS-2002-98-ORG.

Mann, R. J. and Sager, T. W. (2007). Patents, venture capital, and software start-ups. *Research Policy*, 36(2), 193–208.

Mason, C. (2007). Venture capital: A geographical perspective. In *Handbook of Research on Venture Capital*, Edward Elgar, Cheltenham, 86–112.

Mason, C. (2010). Venture capital: Rationale, aims and scope. *Venture Capital: An International Journal of Entrepreneurial Finance*, 1(1), 1–46.

Mason, C. and Harrison, R. T. (1995). Closing the regional equity capital gap: The role of informal venture capital. *Small Business Economics*, 7, 153–172.

Mason, C. and Harrison, R. T. (2000). The size of the informal venture capital market in the United Kingdom. *Small Business Economics*, 15, 137–148.

Mason, C. and Harrison, R. T. (2002). The geography of venture capital investments in the UK. *Transactions of the Institute of British Geographers*, 27(4), 427–451.

Maula, M. and Murray, G. (2017). Corporate venture capital and the creation of US public companies: The impact of sources of venture capital on the performance of portfolio companies. In *Creating Value: Winners in the New Business Environment*, 161–183.

Megginson, W. L. (2004). Toward a global model of venture capital? *Journal of Applied Corporate Finance*, 16(1), 89–107.

Metrick, A. and Yasuda, A. (2021). *Venture Capital and the Finance of Innovation.* John Wiley & Sons.

Mollica, M. and Zingales, L. (2007). The impact of venture capital on innovation and the creation of new businesses. Unpublished Working Paper, University of Chicago.

Murray, G. C. (2007). Venture capital and government policy. In *Handbook of Research on Venture Capital*, Cheltenham: Edward Elgar, 113–151.

Nahata, R. (2008). Venture capital reputation and investment performance. *Journal of Financial Economics*, 90(2), 127–151.

Nanda, R., Samila, S., and Sorenson, O. (2020). The persistent effect of initial success: Evidence from venture capital. *Journal of Financial Economics*, 137(1).

Norton, E. and Tenenbaum, B. H. (1993). Specialization versus diversification as a venture capital investment strategy. *Journal of Business Venturing*, 8(5), 431–442.

Ooghe, H., Manigart, S., and Fassin, Y. (1991). Growth patterns of the European venture capital industry. *Journal of Business Venturing*, 6(6), 381–404.

Park, H. D. and Steensma, H. K. (2012). When does corporate venture capital add value for new ventures? *Strategic Management Journal*, 33(1), 1–22.

Peng, L. (2001). Building a venture capital index. Available at SSRN 281804.

Pintado, T. R., De Lema, D. G. P., and Van Auken, H. (2007). Venture capital in Spain by stage of development. *Journal of Small Business Management*, 45(1), 68–88.

Popov, A. and Roosenboom, P. (2012). Venture capital and patented innovation: Evidence from Europe. *Economic Policy*, 27(71), 447–482.

Popov, A. and Roosenboom, P. (2013). Venture capital and new business creation. *Journal of* Banking & *Finance*, 37(12), 4695–4710.

Poterba, J. M. (1989). Venture capital and capital gains taxation. *Tax Policy and the Economy*, 3, 47–67.

Powell, W. W., Koput, K. W., Bowie, J. I., and Smith-Doerr, L. (2002). The spatial clustering of science and capital: Accounting for biotech firm-venture capital relationships. *Regional Studies*, 36(3), 291–305.

Puri, M. and Zarutskie, R. (2012). On the life cycle dynamics of venture-capital-and non-venture-capital-financed firms. *The Journal of Finance*, 67(6), 2247–2293.

Randjelovic, J., O'Rourke, A. R., and Orsato, R. J. (2003). The emergence of green venture capital. *Business Strategy and the Environment*, 12(4), 240–253.

Rind, K. W. (1981). The role of venture capital in corporate development. *Strategic Management Journal*, 2(2), 169–180.

Robinson, M. J. (2022). Factors impacting entrepreneurial success in accelerators: Revealed preferences of sophisticated mentors. *Review of Corporate Finance*, 2(3), 617–661.

Romain, A. and Van Pottelsberghe de la Potterie, B. (2004). The economic impact of venture capital. Working Paper: WP-CEB 04/014. Université Libre de Bruxelles — Solvay Business School — Centre Emile Bernheim.

Ruhnka, J. C. and Young, J. E. (1987). A venture capital model of the development process for new ventures. *Journal of Business Venturing*, 2(2), 167–184.

Ruhnka, J. C. and Young, J. E. (1991). Some hypotheses about risk in venture capital investing. *Journal of Business Venturing*, 6(2), 115–133.

Sahlman, W. A. (1990). The structure and governance of venture-capital organizations. *Journal of Financial Economics*, 27(2), 473–521.

Samila, S. and Sorenson, O. (2010). Venture capital as a catalyst to commercialization. *Research Policy*, 39(10), 1348–1360.

Schertler, A. and Tykvová, T. (2011). Venture capital and internationalization. *International Business Review*, 20(4), 423–439.

Schwienbacher, A. (2002). An empirical analysis of venture capital exits in Europe and the United States. In EFA 2002 Berlin Meetings Discussion Paper.

Seppä, T. J. and Laamanen, T. (2001). Valuation of venture capital investments: Empirical evidence. *R&D Management*, 31(2), 215–230.

Smart, G. H. (1999). Management assessment methods in venture capital: An empirical analysis of human capital valuation. *Venture Capital*, 1(1), 59–82.

Smith, D. G. (2005). The exit structure of venture capital. *UCLA Law Review*, 53(2), 315–356.

Smith, E. E., Smith, J. K., and Smith, R. L. (2022). Bias in the reporting of venture capital performance: The disciplinary role of FOIA. *Review of Corporate Finance*, 2(3), 493–525.

Sorenson, O. and Stuart, T. E. (2001). Syndication networks and the spatial distribution of venture capital investments. *American Journal of Sociology*, 106(6), 1546–1588.

Sorenson, O. and Stuart, T. E. (2008). Bringing the context back in: Settings and the search for syndicate partners in venture capital investment networks. *Administrative Science Quarterly*, 53(2), 266–294.

Tian, X. (2012). The role of venture capital syndication in value creation for entrepreneurial firms. *Review of Finance*, 16(1), 245–283.

Trester, J. J. (1998). Venture capital contracting under asymmetric information. *Journal of Banking & Finance*, 22(6-8), 675–699.

Upton, N. and Petty, W. (2000). Venture capital investment and US family business. *Venture Capital*, 2(1), 27–39.

Wetzel, W. E. (1987). The informal venture capital market: Aspects of scale and market efficiency. *Journal of Business Venturing*, 2(4), 299–313.

Winters, T. E. and Murfin, D. L. (1988). Venture capital investing for corporate development objectives. *Journal of Business Venturing*, 3(3), 207–222.

Wong, A. Y. (2002). Angel finance: The other venture capital. Available at SSRN 941228.

Wright, M. and Lockett, A. (2003). The structure and management of alliances: Syndication in the venture capital industry. *Journal of Management Studies*, 40(8), 2073–2102.

Zacharakis, A. L. and Meyer, G. D. (2000). The potential of actuarial decision models. *Journal of Business Venturing*, 15(4), 323–346.

https://doi.org/10.1142/9781800617032_0005

Chapter 5

Private Equity Investment Activity: Operating Model and Risk-Mitigation Strategies

Simona Zambelli

University of Florence, Florence, Italy

5.1. Introduction

Extensive research has emphasised the crucial role of venture finance in fostering small business development and innovation, positively impacting the industrial and economic landscape of countries (see, e.g. Lerner and Nanda, 2020; Li *et al.*, 2020a, 2020b; Quas *et al.*, 2021; Cohn *et al.*, 2022; Cumming *et al.*, 2023; Burström *et al.*, 2023; Rawal and Kapil, 2023; McGrath and Nerkar, 2023).[1]

The purpose of this chapter is to review the entire decision-making process and the risk management strategies employed by private equity (PE) investors (hereafter venture capitalists, or VCs) when financing high-risk and high-growth potential firms.[2] To this end,

[1]See also: Devigne *et al.* (2018), Cumming and Johan (2014, 2017), Lerner (2012), Bertoni *et al.* (2010), Suchard (2009), Cumming *et al.* (2004), Hellmann and Puri (2002a, 2002b), and Kortum and Lerner (2000).

[2]The table reported in the Appendix highlights the most recent systematic reviews of PE investment activity, according to specific topics discussed in this chapter. For recent overviews on the distinctive characteristics of PE and VC, see: Cumming *et al.* (2023), McGrath and Nerkar (2023), Burström *et al.* (2023),

we first review the PE investment activity, or VC cycle (Gompers and Lerner, 2006; Torres, 2020; Dai, 2022), emphasising the proactive role of PE investors in promoting the growth of innovative businesses and enhancing the value of their portfolio companies (Cohn *et al.*, 2022). Second, we focus on the selection and evaluation process of the prospective investments, highlighting the 'frog-kissing' role of PE investors in selecting their target firms (Bertoni *et al.*, 2016), as well as the critical importance of implementing a rigorous due diligence to enjoy higher investee performance (Cumming and Zambelli, 2017; Zambelli, 2024).

The remainder of this chapter is organised as follows. Section 5.2 describes the PE investment activity and its business model in light of the recent academic literature and PE industry trends in Europe. Section 5.3 discusses the main risk-mitigation mechanisms employed by PE investors to reduce the risk of adverse selection and moral hazard problems, setting the foundation for a deeper discussion in Section 5.4 of the entire evaluation process performed by investors (i.e. preliminary screening and due diligence). The last section provides concluding remarks.

5.2. PE Investment Activity: Business Model and Industry Trends

In economic literature and industry practice, there is no unique and universally accepted definition for the terms PE and VC. Definitions vary across geographic areas and industry reports. Sometimes these terms are used interchangeably, and other times they are kept distinct. For the purposes of this study, we adopt the original broad definition generally accepted within the EU and US contexts, where

---

Dai (2022), Levasseur *et al.* (2022), Wilson *et al.* (2022), Gerhardt *et al.* (2022), Hammer *et al.* (2022), Dai (2022), Lerner and Nanda (2020), Gornall and Strebulaev (2020), Harrison and Mason (2019), Grilli *et al.* (2019), Cancino *et al.* (2018), Tykvova (2018), Devigne *et al.* (2018), and Drover *et al.* (2017). For comprehensive analyses of PE and VC activities, see also: Cumming (2010, 2012), Cumming and Johan (2014, 2017), Chemmanur and Fulghieri (2014), Wood and Wright (2009), Gompers and Lerner (2001, 2006), Metrick and Yasuda (2010, 2011, 2021), Da Rin *et al.* (2011), Tykvova (2007), De Clercq *et al.* (2005, 2006), Cumming and Walz (2010), Wright and Robbie (1998), and Sahlman (1990).

PE refers to any equity investments in innovative private companies with high growth potential, aimed at boosting their expansion process by providing both financial support and managerial assistance (see, e.g. Metrick and Yasuda, 2011, 2021; Cumming and Walz, 2010; Suchard, 2009).[3] Typically, the financing involves either acquiring equity stakes in the target firms or investing in their hybrid securities, such as convertible debt or convertible preferred shares (Schmidt, 2003; Cumming, 2005a, 2005b, 2006a, 2007, 2008, 2010; Hellmann, 2002, 2006; Cumming and Johan, 2014; Lerner and Nanda, 2020; Zambelli, 2024).[4]

PE is typically divided into two main categories (see Figure 5.1): VC and merchant banking (MB). While VC and MB share similarities regarding equity financing and governance mechanisms, the primary difference between them lies in the development stage of the target companies. From this perspective, VC is a subset of PE and represents the provision of equity financing to new firms or recently established companies with the purpose of supporting their growth and boosting their early- or mid-development stage (Metrick and Yasuda, 2010, 2011, 2021; Suchard, 2009; Gompers and Lerner, 2006; Sahlman, 1990). Conversely, MB deals with the equity financing of more mature companies to support their further growth (late-expansion stage financing) and their eventual public listing (see Figure 5.1). This latter category includes buyouts, which dominate the PE industry in Europe both in terms of raised capital and amount

[3]It is important to note that in specific geographical contexts (such as Italy) or within certain industry practices, the terms PE and VC may be adopted with different definitions. For example, in some cases, the term PE is used to represent the equity investments in developed and mature companies, while VC is used specifically for equity financing in new or recently established firms. This latter definition of PE excludes VC investments and includes buyouts (see, e.g. Stowell and Stowell, 2023; Cumming and Zambelli, 2019; Kaplan and Strömberg, 2009). Other times, the term VC is confused with business angel investing. However, an important difference exists, as venture capitalists are financial intermediaries and, as such, provide equity financing by using external investors' money, while business angels make equity investments by using their own money (for reviews of business angel investments, see, e.g. Drover *et al.*, 2017; Metrick, 2010, 2011, 2021).

[4]For overviews of the securities adopted in PE settings see, e.g. Zambelli (2014) and Tykvova (2018).

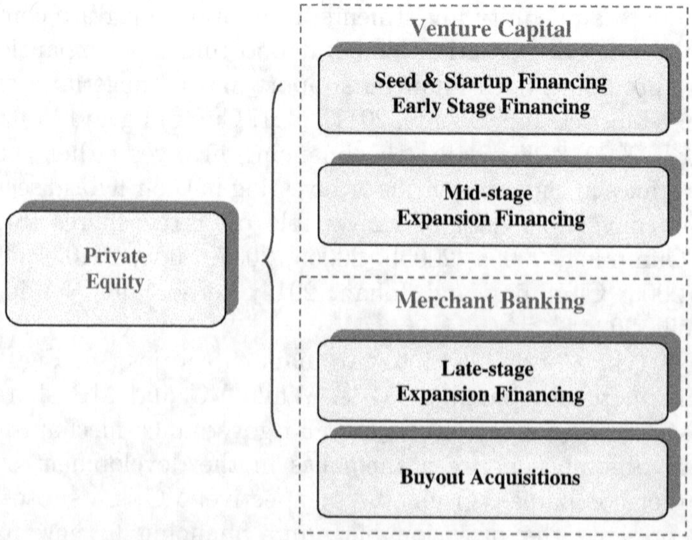

Figure 5.1. Private equity: traditional definition.
Sources: Elaboration from Metrick and Yasuda (2011, 2021), Talmor and Vasvari (2011), Suchard (2009), Gompers and Lerner (2006), and Sahlman (1990).

invested. Buyouts can be defined as acquisitions where an investor acquires control of a certain target company, either by purchasing a majority or a significant portion of its equity capital to gain control rights, relevant to the decision-making process (see, e.g. Jelic and Wright, 2011; Jelic *et al.*, 2019; Wright, 2019; Cumming and Zambelli, 2010, 2013, 2019; Axelson *et al.*, 2009a, 2009b; Kaplan and Strömberg, 2009; Wright *et al.*, 2009).[5] In the context of PE, buyouts are usually structured in the form of leveraged buyout (LBO) transactions. LBOs involve the acquisition of a company (known as target) by another company usually established for the sole purpose of accomplishing such acquisition (named 'newco'), with the recourse of a significant level of debt (leverage) compared with the asset value of the target (Cumming and Zambelli, 2010, 2013; Wright, 2019; Gruener and Marburger, 2022; Sannajust and Groh, 2023). Usually, the debt financing accounts for 60–70% of the asset value of the target company (see e.g. Wright, 2019; Axelson *et al.*, 2009a,

[5]For a recent review on PE financing, see Dai (2022).

2009b; Wright *et al.*, 2009).[6] In an LBO transaction, the assets of the target firm are often used as collateral for the debt, along with the assets of the acquiring company (see also, Cumming and Zambelli, 2019).

5.2.1. *LBO debate*

Over the past two decades, especially after the 2007 financial crisis, LBOs have faced global scrutiny and strong criticism in Europe (especially in Italy) and the US. The major concerns focus on the lack of transparency and disclosure associated with PE funds, as well as the economic and financial implications underlying the particular structure of LBOs (see Cumming and Zambelli, 2019, for a detailed overview of the major critical aspects associated with LBOs).

The core of the criticism raised against LBOs is focused on the potential perils of LBOs for the target companies and their survival potential, as their assets often serve as collaterals for the debt contracted by the newco (Jelic and Wright, 2011; Ferran, 2011). More specifically, in an LBO, the debt is obtained by the newco under the assumption that it will be repaid by the target firm with its future post-acquisition cash flows, hopefully generated by the new governing team or with the sale of its non-essential assets (Cumming and Zambelli, 2010).

From a financial perspective, the rationale behind an LBO is the belief that, following the acquisition, the new governance of the target will boost the company's cash flows, which in turn will help repay the debt originally obtained for its acquisition. The LBO model is based on the assumption that the future cash flows of the target company will grow and be ample enough to fully repay the initial loan incurred to complete the buyout. Prior research has shown that the debt financing underlying an LBO transaction helps companies promote tangible investments (Bernstein *et al.*, 2019).

Despite the positive expectations motivating LBO transactions, legal scholars and courts in Europe have raised severe concerns against such types of transactions, questioning their sustainability due to the potential negative impact of high levels of debt transferred

[6]For a recent review of the literature on buyouts, see Sannajust and Groh (2023).

to target companies (see Cumming and Zambelli, 2019, for details on such international debate). In the US, critics have even asserted that LBOs should be prohibited, given their potential detrimental effects on targets' survival due to the high amount of debt involved in LBO transactions (Stein, 2006). Such global criticism against LBOs even led to defining PE investors promoting LBOs as 'locusts' or 'asset strippers', accusing them of contributing to the weakening of their acquired firms (see, e.g. Petitt, 2014; Wall Street Journal, 2005; The Guardian, 2007, 2008; The Economist, 2005, 2009, 2016).[7]

The 2007 financial crisis further intensified the global demand for LBO restrictions and tighter regulations of PE funds, although PE investors were not directly responsible for the crisis (Cumming and Zambelli, 2019).[8] This worldwide criticism against LBOs led

[7]Italy anticipated such global criticism against LBOs by declaring the LBO model illegal and prohibiting its adoption within the domestic market, as stated by the Supreme Court Decision 5503/2000 (see Cumming and Zambelli, 2010 for more details). Subsequently, LBOs were legalised with a new reform (effective from 2004), which represented an important turning point for the Italian PE industry as well as a unique example of conditional legalisation of LBOs that could inspire other policymakers or regulators around the world. The impact of such reform was empirically investigated by Cumming and Zambelli (2010, 2013, 2017), who highlight various beneficial effects associated with the legalisation of LBOs. The authors show that the assets and interests of the target company are better protected when LBOs are deemed legal under certain disclosure conditions, rather than restricted or outright prohibited. More specifically, they show that a prohibiting LBO regulation is ineffective, as it does not eliminate LBOs but, instead, reduces the incentives for PE investors to be actively involved in the governance of their target firms, compromising their value-adding potentials (Cumming and Zambelli, 2010) and investor performance (Cumming and Zambelli, 2013), as well as distorts the selection of target firms and the due diligence process, with a detrimental impact on firm performance (Cumming and Zambelli, 2017). Overall, their studies show that regulations aimed at legalising LBOs and increasing transparency and disclosures produce beneficial effects on target firms and investors, while repressive LBO regulations only inhibit the efficient structure of LBOs and the governance of investee firms to the detriment of the targets, obtaining the exact opposite of what policymakers intended to reach with a prohibiting regulation of LBOs.

[8]In Europe, a major criticism against private equity funds and the subsequent demand for tighter regulation of their activities was ironically well captured by *The Economist* (2009): 'When a fight breaks out in a bar, you don't hit the man who started it. You clobber the person you don't like instead'.

Europe to introduce new tighter regulatory propositions for PE investors (and hedge funds) to properly protect the interests of the acquired firms and their stakeholders (see the Directive 2011/61/EU on Alternative Investment Fund managers, known as AIFM regulation; for more details, also see Ferran, 2011; Financial Services Authority, 2006).[9]

5.2.2. *PE value creation*

PE investors are more than just providers of long-term equity capital. They provide both financial support and managerial guidance, playing an active role in the management and development of their investee companies (see, e.g. Cumming *et al.*, 2023; McGrath and Nerkar, 2023; Wilson *et al.*, 2022; Lerner and Nanda, 2020; Cumming and Johan, 2014). PE investors offer important supporting services to their target companies, as well as managerial assistance, which is especially crucial during their early stages of development (Quas *et al.*, 2021; Ed-dafali *et al.*, 2016; Bonini *et al.*, 2012; Bottazzi *et al.*, 2008). From this perspective, PE investors play a critical role in supporting their investee companies in various strategic areas, including finance, marketing, sales, business and financial planning, recruitment, and even replacing management teams and CEOs, when necessary. This active involvement of PE investors helps increase the value added of their investments, both in terms of investor returns and investee performance (e.g. Granz *et al.*, 2021; Acharya *et al.*, 2013; Bonini *et al.*, 2012; Jelic and Wright, 2011). Such guidance is particularly important for nascent firms that require direction to foster their sustainable growth. The degree of involvement tends to diminish with the company's developmental stage, as the need for assistance decreases over time (see, e.g. Lerner, 1995; Gompers, 1995; Gompers and Lerner, 2001, 2006; Kaplan and Strömberg, 2003; Cumming, 2012; Cumming and Johan, 2014; Cumming *et al.*, 2023).

PE and, especially, VC investors also play a crucial role in spurring innovation within small and medium enterprises (SMEs) by promoting greater levels of intangible investments and patents

---

[9] A recent overview of AIFM regulation and its amendments is available at the following website: https://eur-lex.europa.eu/EN/legal-content/summary/hedge-funds-and-private-equity-funds-rules-for-managers.html.

(Bernstein *et al.*, 2016). Furthermore, by selecting and supporting rapidly growing innovative companies, venture finance also contributes to the overall technological advancement of a country (Asuamah Yeboah, 2023; Lerner and Nanda, 2020; Devigne *et al.*, 2018; Drover *et al.*, 2017; Bertoni *et al.*, 2010; Kortum and Lerner, 2000).

Echoing this crucial role, the PE industry in Europe has significantly grown over the past decade, both in terms of funds raised and investments made (Invest Europe, 2023). This trend is especially evident after 2020, despite the recent global pandemic.

As reported in Figure 5.2, data from Invest Europe (2023) highlight an impressive expansion of the European PE industry. For example, the total amount raised by PE investors increased from €29 billion in 2012 to a substantial €170 billion in 2022, reaching the highest level ever realised and 30% above the amount collected in 2021. In parallel, the amount invested in PE projects expanded from €41 billion in 2012 to €130 billion in 2022, despite experiencing a modest decline compared to 2021 (for details, see Invest Europe, 2023).[10]

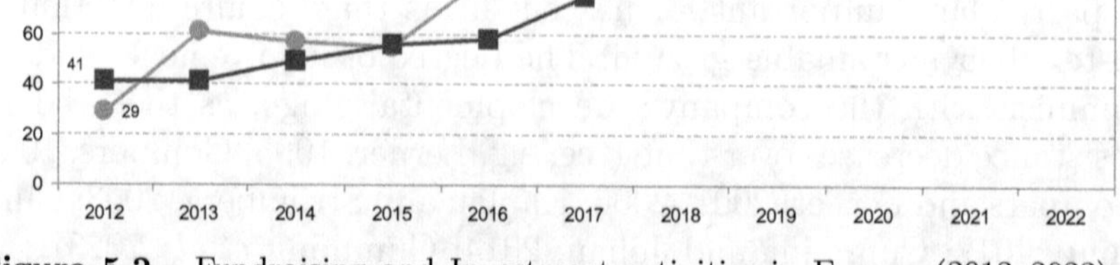

Figure 5.2. Fundraising and Investment activities in Europe (2012–2022) in terms of € billions.
Source: Elaboration from Invest Europe (2023), PE Activity Report 2022, p. 9. Available online at https://www.investeurope.eu/media/6809/invest-europe_pe-activity-2022.pdf.

[10]The report by Invest Europe (2023) is available online at the following website: https://www.investeurope.eu; https:/www.investeurope.eu/media/6809/invest-europe_pe-activity-2022.pdf. For details on the impact of COVID-19 on the PE industry, see, e.g. Brown *et al.* (2020).

5.2.3. *PE operating model and industry patterns*

The PE investing process, also known as the VC cycle (Gompers and Lerner, 2006), starts with the fundraising activity, proceeds with the investment in selected target companies, and ends with the exit from such targets after an involvement period of three to seven years (Cumming and Johan, 2014). The fundraising activity involves the creation and management of closed-end funds (PE funds), through which VCs raise money from external investors, including institutional investors, corporations, and private individuals (fundraising phase). PE funds have a long expiration date, typically 10 years (Metrick and Yasuda, 2021). During the first five years, VCs are in charge of managing the pooled fund by selecting investment proposals and acquiring equity participations in target companies with high growth expectations (entrance phase or investment period), providing them with financial resources and managerial support until the exit stage.[11] Figure 5.3 summarises the entire PE operating model described above.

As summarised in Figure 5.3, closed-end funds represent the central mechanism adopted by VCs to raise money. During the fundraising process, PE investors gather resources from various external investors (who act as limited partners, LPs), such as pension funds, insurance companies, banks, and other investors, who subscribe a share of the closed-end fund. Unlike 'open-end' funds, closed-end funds are characterised by a fixed target size and a fixed lifespan, generally 10 years (Ewens and Farre-Mensa, 2020; Cumming and Johan, 2014).

Once the planned fixed capital is fully subscribed by external investors, the fund is closed; no further subscriptions are admitted, and subscribers are not allowed to redeem their shares before the expiration date is reached (Metrick and Yasuda, 2021; Phalippou and Gottschalg, 2009). Once the fund is closed, PE investors (acting as general partners, GPs) start managing the raised funds by selecting a number of target firms to finance. The discretion power of VCs in managing the fund and choosing the target firms may

[11]The PE operating model described above is well documented in the literature (see, e.g. Torres, 2020; Cumming and Johan, 2014; Axelson, 2009a, 2009b; De Clercq *et al.*, 2006; Metrick and Yasuda, 2021; Phalippou and Gottschalg, 2009; Gompers and Lerner, 2001, 2006; Sahlman, 1990).

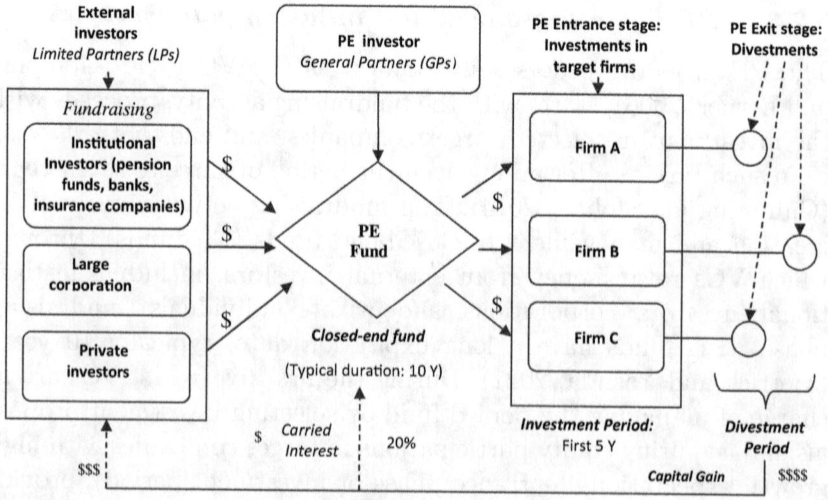

Figure 5.3. Fundraising and divestment process.
Sources: Own elaboration from the finance literature (e.g. Sahlman, 1990; Gompers and Lerner, 2001, 2006; De Clercq *et al.*, 2006; Axelson, 2009a, 2009b; Phalippou and Gottschalg, 2009; Cumming and Johan, 2014; Ewens and Farre-Mensa, 2020; Torres, 2020; Metrick and Yasuda, 2021).

be restricted by a set of binding contractual provisions (*covenants*) to better protect external investors' interests. Covenants help align the interests of the external investors (LPs) with those of the PE investors, ensuring that the PE fund managers act in a way that maximises fund value while minimising the risks (for more details on covenants in the context of PE, see, e.g. Gompers and Lerner, 1996, 2006; Liu and Nguyen, 2021). Also, GPs must periodically report to their LPs the fund-level performance, disclosing information on the returns of realised investments and the estimated value of the ongoing investments (Smith *et al.*, 2022).

When the investee companies have reached their expected growth potential and maturity stage, VCs usually divest their equity stakes (exit phase), and the related capital gains are split between VCs and external investors (see, e.g. Metrick and Yasuda, 2021; Torres, 2020; Cumming *et al.*, 2004). The share of capital gains kept by VCs is known as '*carried interest*' and serves as a compensation mechanism for their realised investments. Typically, VCs receive, on average, 20% of carried interest (Gompers and Lerner, 2006; Metrick and

Yasuda, 2021). Sometimes a minimum return rate (known as the 'hurdle rate') is set, and VCs can retain part of the capital gains only after this specific return rate is reached (see, e.g. Gompers and Lerner, 2006; Cumming and Johan, 2014; Metrick and Yasuda, 2021).[12] Additionally, for their fund management activity, PE investors (GPs) charge their external investors (LPs) an annual management fee, which is usually around 2–3% of the committed capital depending on the VCs' reputation (Metrick and Yasuda, 2021; Smith *et al.*, 2022).

5.2.3.1. *Agency conflicts between external investors and PE fund managers*

The relationship between LPs (who provide capital) and GPs (who manage this committed capital) can be complicated by asymmetric information and agency conflicts (Cumming and Walz, 2010). This occurs because GPs have more detailed knowledge about their ongoing investments' risk–return profile and the real performance of their portfolio companies. Even though GPs are requested to inform and update their LPs about the fund performance, LPs may receive less frequent and less detailed information about the performance of their investments. The literature highlights the following two main sources of agency conflicts:

(a) GPs might delay reporting underperforming investments, present information in a more favourable light, or even misrepresent and inflate the performance of the non-realised investment (*report biases*) in order to maintain LP investor satisfaction and attract higher funds in further fundraising processes. Recent evidence by Brown *et al.* (2019) shows that PE investors (especially those managing underperforming funds) may be tempted to inflate information on their portfolio returns to their external investors

[12]Once the hurdle rate is surpassed, the VCs can participate in the realised profits, usually receiving a percentage that ranges from 15% to 20% of the excess returns, depending on the fund's contractual terms. The hurdle rate mechanism is considered a form of protection for the LPs, ensuring that the VCs are properly motivated to generate returns that exceed a certain minimum level before they can receive a share of the realised returns (known as carried interest). For more details, see Metrick and Yasuda (2011, 2021).

during the fundraising process in order to increase the probability of raising more funds. However, Brown *et al.* (2019) demonstrate that external investors can easily detect such types of return manipulation, and as a consequence, dishonest fund managers are less likely to raise other funds in the future. As shown by Cumming and Walz (2010), such report biases can lead to relevant irreversible reputational costs. The authors also show that such report biases are more frequent in legal settings with weaker disclosure and accounting rules. From this perspective, Smith *et al.* (2022) investigate the disciplinary role of the *Freedom of Information Act* (FOIA) in reducing the probability of incurring in report distortions in relation to fund performance. According to their evidence, FOIA-eligible LPs are more likely to invest in more reputable funds, and the propensity of fund managers to inflate reported performance is significantly reduced in the cases involving FOIA-eligible LPs (for more details, see the study by Smith *et al.*, 2022). This evidence supports the disciplinary role of FOIA in facilitating more accurate reporting, further reinforcing the results of Cumming and Walz (2010).

(b) Another source of potential agency conflict between LPs and PE fund managers is driven by the limited control power exercised by LPs over GPs and by the specific PE compensation mechanism, which includes management fees and carried interest. Although both GPs and LPs benefit from the success of the investments, the PE compensation structure can lead to potential agency conflicts. As PE fund managers receive performance incentives based on a share of realised returns, in some circumstances they may be tempted to change their preferred investment style (in terms of development stage, industry, or the location of target firms), undertaking riskier investments in order to benefit from higher potential returns. This phenomenon, known as '*style drift*' (Cumming *et al.*, 2009), represents a significant source of concern for LPs, as recent evidence has shown that riskier investment style drifts have a detrimental impact on the realised fund's performance and exit rate potentials (for more details, see Koenig and Burghof, 2022).

The risk of incurring in a riskier style drift is also increased by the fact that LPs have no means to influence individual investment decisions taken by PE fund managers, and as such, LPs must trust that the latter will act in their best interests (Koenig and Burghof, 2022). Moreover, the investment style of a PE fund is not contractually set. This increases the opportunity for VCs to engage in subsequent riskier style drifts, changing the preferred development stages and locations of targets, to enhance their compensation potential in case of venture success (e.g. later-stage funds investing in early-stage targets or domestic funds investing in international deals).[13]

5.2.3.2. *Industry trends*

Figure 5.4 shows a 'snapshot' of the fundraising activity in Europe in 2022, categorised by PE stage (VC, expansion, and buyouts). According to Invest Europe (2023), out of the €170 billion raised for the entire PE industry in 2022, a significant 65% was collected for buyout investments (accounting for a total amount of €111 billion). In contrast, the VC sector attracted a smaller portion, accounting for only 13% of the total funds raised.[14] By looking at the fundraising

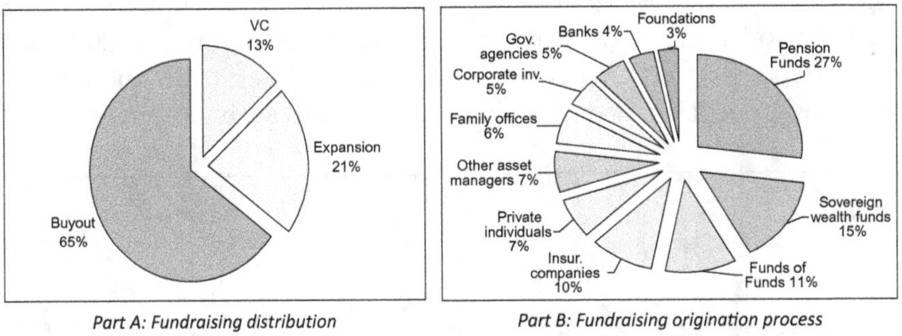

Figure 5.4. Summary of fundraising activity in Europe (2022).
Source: Elaboration from Invest Europe (2023), Invest Europe PE Activity Report 2022, p. 12, 20. https://www.investeurope.eu/media/6809/invest-europe_pe-activity-2022.pdf.

[13]Koenig and Burghof (2022) also distinguish the impact of different types of style drift. Their evidence shows that only some types of investment drifts can lead to agency conflicts between LPs and GPs (specifically the development-stage and location drifts), while industry-style drifts are mainly implemented out of necessity in order to better protect the interests of LPs. In the latter case, there is no agency conflict (for more details, see Koenig and Burghof, 2022).
[14]See Invest Europe (2023), pp. 12–20.

origination process (Figure 5.4, Part B), in 2022, the majority of capital raised for PE investments was collected from pension funds, who contributed the largest share (27%), followed by sovereign funds (15%), funds of funds (11%), and insurance companies (10%). Private individuals and corporate investors supplied 7% and 5%, respectively, while foundations and academic institutions accounted for 3% of the total. Notably, banks provided only a minor fraction (4%) of the capital raised for PE activities (for more details, see Figure 5.4 and Invest Europe, 2023).[15]

Figure 5.5 illustrates the distribution of PE investments in Europe, classified by PE stage: VC, expansion, and buyouts. Consistent with the fundraising distribution reported in Figure 5.4 (Part A), the evidence highlighted in Figure 5.5 shows the pronounced dominance of buyout transactions, at least in terms of the amount invested (Part A). According to Invest Europe (2023), this segment has experienced significant growth over the past decade, climbing from €29.3 billion in 2012 to an impressive €80.7 billion in 2022. In contrast, when we look at the number of companies backed by PE investors, the VC segment dominates the European scene, accounting for 60% of the total number of firms that received PE funding in 2022 (see Figure 5.5, Part B). According to Invest Europe (2023), the number of firms benefiting from VC financing significantly rose from 3,526

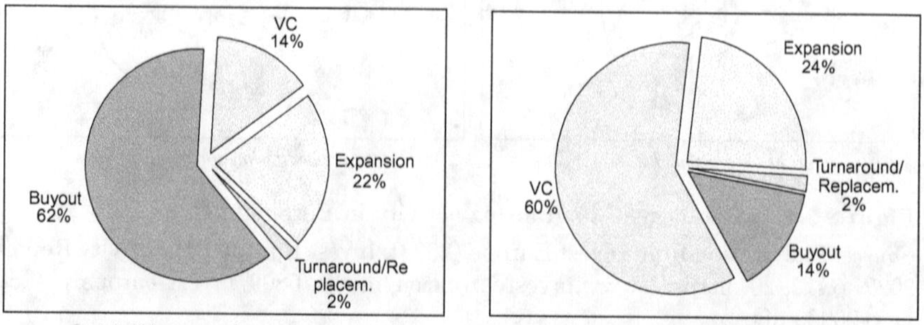

Part A: % in terms of amount invested *Part B: % in terms of no. of investee companies*

Figure 5.5. Summary of investment activity in Europe (2022).
Source: Elaboration from Invest Europe (2023), PE Activity Report 2022, p. 48, 37, 38, 60. http://www.investeurope.eu/research, https://www.investeurope.eu/media/6809/invest-europe_pe-activity-2022.pdf.

[15] See the Invest Europe database, available at http://www.investeurope.eu.

in 2012 to 5,435 in 2022. Such an increased trend is particularly relevant for European economic advancement, as VC plays a key role in supporting the development and innovation processes of both start-up firms and SMEs (see, e.g. Silva Júnior *et al.*, 2023; Gerhardt *et al.*, 2022; Bongini *et al.*, 2021; Li *et al.*, 2020a, 2020b; Motoyama *et al.*, 2020a, 2020b; Cumming and Johan, 2017; Bertoni *et al.*, 2010; Gompers and Lerner, 2001, 2006; Kortum and Lerner, 2000).[16] As expected, of the 5,435 firms backed by VC in 2022, 98% are represented by SMEs (Invest Europe, 2023).

Table 5.1 (Panel A) shows the allocation of PE investments in Europe across numerous industries, underscoring the prominent appeal of certain sectors. PE investors primarily target companies with high growth potential, often characterised by a high degree of innovation and operating in high-tech sectors (Gompers and Lerner, 2006; Lerner, 2012). In line with this type of target, the ICT sector leads the European scene, with 37% of financed companies belonging to this technology-driven industry. The biotech and healthcare sector as well as consumer goods and services also show a considerable investment appeal for PE investors in 2022. The ICT sector, in combination with the biotech and healthcare industries, accounts for more than half of the financed companies (see Table 5.1 and Invest Europe, 2023, for more details). Panel B of Table 5.1 highlights the recent dramatic growth experienced by an emerging PE sector involving 'clean technologies' (known as the cleantech industry), spurred by the recent issuance of more stringent environmental policies to manage climate change (Bianchini and Croce, 2022; Cumming *et al.*, 2016a). This sector is attracting an increasing amount of PE investments worldwide. As shown in Panel B, the EU lies behind Asia Pacific and North America (which is leading the scene). The EU seems to have reached a plateau of €11 billion invested in the cleantech sector as a whole. This amount is also confirmed for 2023 (for details, see the Report by Cleantech for Europe, 2024).[17]

[16]For a recent overview of financing resources available to SMEs, see Bongini *et al.* (2021).

[17]The cleantech industry involves a variety of companies (across various sectors), specialised in developing technologies with the purpose of cleaning the environment and increasing environmental sustainability. Cleantech includes various

Table 5.1. Industry distribution of PE investments.

Panel A: Industry distribution of PE investments in Europe in 2022 (percentages are expressed in terms of amount invested and number of target firms, within each sector)

2022	Amount invested (%)	Number of companies (%)
ICT sector	33	37
Consumer goods/services	18	16
Biotech & healthcare sector	13	15
Business products/services	18	14
Financial & insurance sector	8	4
Energy & environment & chemicals	6	7
Construction & transportations	4	4
Other (real estate & agriculture)	1	3
	100	100

Panel B: Yearly distribution of PE investments in Cleantech sector in EU, compared to Asia Pacific and North America (amount invested is expressed in € millions)

	EU 27	Asia Pacific	North America
2019	€3.9	€5.1	€19.8
2020	€4.5	€6.9	€23.8
2021	€11.1	€12.0	€37
2022	€11.2	€13.7	€38

Source: Panel A: Elaboration from the PE Activity Report written by Invest Europe (2023), p. 57. http://www.investeurope.eu/research; https://www.investeurope.eu/media/6809/invest-europe_pe-activity-2022.pdf.
Panel B: Cleantech for Europe Report (2024), A Cleantech Investment Plan for European Competitiveness, by Cleantech Group, various year, p. 16. Available at https://www.cleantechforeurope.com/cleantech-investment-plan; https://bit.ly/EUCleantechInvestmentPlan.

The last phase of the PE business model involves the exit of VCs. As anticipated in previous sections, PE investors do not seek permanent control in their target companies. Instead, they typically

areas, from renewable energies, energy efficiency, water management, and environmental friendly chemicals to sustainable agriculture material and practices (for details, see, e.g. Cumming *et al.*, 2016a; Bianchini and Croce, 2022).

hold a portion of the equity for a medium-term period, between two and seven years (Cumming and Johan, 2014). Early-stage investments may take a longer period to reach the maturity stage, while later-stage investments may take only a few years. The primary goal of PE investors is to enhance the value of their portfolio firms in order to maximise the potential capital gain (CG) that can be realised when VCs sell their equity stakes (divestment or exit stage). Recent empirical evidence shows that exit performance and related returns are negatively affected by geographic distance, as well as institutional and cultural differences (see, e.g. Cumming and Dai, 2011; Nahata *et al.*, 2014; Dai and Nahata, 2016). Due to these factors, cross-border investments tend to yield lower returns relative to similar PE domestic deals (as shown in Buchner *et al.*, 2018; Wright *et al.*, 2005).

VCs can exit their investments through various routes, listed as follows (Espenlaub *et al.*, 2015; Cumming, 2008):

- Public Offering (or IPO): The company is quoted on the stock market by issuing shares publicly for the first time, becoming a publicly traded firm.
- Private Sale (or Trade Sale): The company is either merged with or acquired by a larger entity.
- Secondary Sale: The PE stake is sold to another PE investor.
- Share Repurchase (also known as Buyback): The entrepreneur repurchases the equity stake originally acquired by the VCs in order to regain majority control or ownership.
- Write-off: The formal acknowledgement that an investment has failed to realise its expected potential, resulting in a total or partial loss for the VCs involved. This has various implications for financial reporting, tax, and investor relations. Following a write-off, the PE investor may engage in various actions regarding the portfolio company, ranging from discontinuing any further support to such company to proceeding with investment liquidation or asset sales.

Among the exit routes described above, IPOs are considered the most successful ones (Sahlman, 1990), as they enhance the reputation of the investors involved (Cumming and MacIntosh, 2003), providing the highest returns to VC investors (Gompers and Lerner, 2006) and the fastest exit time (Espenlaub *et al.*, 2015). VC investors' reputation also plays a significant role in facilitating successful exits via IPOs (Nahata, 2008; Ewelt-Knauer *et al.*, 2014; Chahine *et al.*, 2021). The positive impact on the public image of the involved VCs increases the chances of raising more funds in the future (Cumming and MacIntosh, 2003). Moreover, legal and institutional differences affect the type and timing of exit route chosen by venture investors (Cumming and MacIntosh, 2003; Cumming, 2008; Cumming and Johan, 2014).

Cumming *et al.* (2006) show that IPO exits are more likely to occur in more advanced legal systems (in terms of higher legality index), probably because such legal settings are better equipped to alleviate agency problems between shareholders and entrepreneurs and provide better protection for shareholders. This, in turn, helps spur the simultaneous development of IPOs and VC markets. IPO exits are more frequent in North America, characterised by more liquid markets, as well as in the cases of coinvestment or syndication (see, e.g. Cumming and MacIntosh, 2003; Cumming *et al.*, 2006; Cumming, 2008; Cumming and Johan, 2008; Jelic and Wright, 2011; Ewelt-Knauer *et al.*, 2014). However, the process of going public has various drawbacks, including high costs associated with listing requirements, the potential for underpricing, and the relatively long underlying transaction period (Ritter, 1987). Additionally, IPO potentials may be limited by contractual restrictions, which can impede a sale within a certain lock-up period (Cumming and MacIntosh, 2003), as well as by weak legal environments and illiquid markets (Cumming, 2008; Coming and Johan, 2014). Given the difficulties underlying the IPO exit process, PE investors commonly opt to exit via a trade sale or secondary sale, especially in Europe (see Figure 5.6 and Table 5.2).[18]

[18]Furthermore, Espenlaub *et al.* (2015) show that the time employed to exit an investment is influenced by the experience of the investors, market conditions, and location of the investment, as well as syndication and industry type. Specifically, more experienced VC firms (in terms of age at the time of investment) tend to delay the exit stage compared to what less experienced firms generally do. For a comprehensive overview of VC exits, see, e.g. Ewelt-Knauer *et al.* (2014). See also Jelic and Wright (2011), Cumming *et al.* (2006), Cumming (2008), Cumming and Johan (2008), and Cumming and MacIntosh (2003). For recent reviews of PE performance, see, e.g. Gohil and Vyas (2016) and Kaplan and Sensoy (2015). See also Korteweg (2019) and Korteweg and Sorensen (2017).

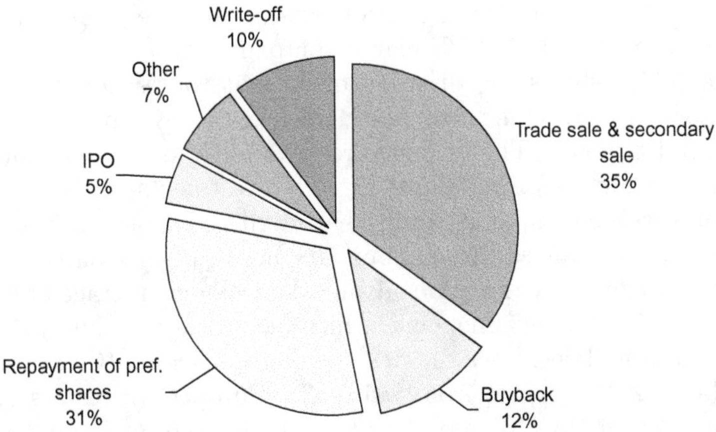

Figure 5.6. Total PE divestments in 2022 (percentages reflect the number of exited firms).
Source: Elaboration from Invest Europe (2023), Invest Europe PE Activity Report 2022, p. 64. https://www.investeurope.eu/media/6809/invest-europe_pe-activity-2022.pdf.

Table 5.2. PE exit routes in Europe in 2022 by type (in terms of exited companies).

2022	VC	Expansion	Buyout
Number of companies exited	1352	1354	750
Percentages (by type of exit)	%	%	%
Trade sale & secondary sale	33	25	54
Buyback	10	14	16
Repayment of preference shares, or loans, or mezzanine	28	40	19
IPO	5	6	3
Other	6	9	5
Write-off	18	6	3
	100	100	100

Source: Elaboration from Invest Europe (2023), Invest Europe PE Activity Report 2022, pp. 63, 66. https://www.investeurope.eu/media/6809/invest-europe_pe-activity-2022.pdf.

As reported in Figure 5.6, IPO exits are less frequent in Europe, representing only 5% of PE exited companies.

Table 5.2 shows the distribution of exit routes adopted by PE investors in Europe in 2022, distinguished by PE type: VC, expansion, and buyouts. The evidence reported in the first column highlights the high risk of failure of VC investments, as 18% of the venture-backed companies resulted in a write-off. Conversely, only 3% of companies financed through buyouts faced the same outcome. This can be explained by the more advanced development stage of companies receiving buyout financing, which facilitates due diligence (DD) procedures and decreases the risk of adverse selection (Cumming and Zambelli, 2017). Apart from write-offs, European investors exhibit consistency in their preferred exit strategies across VC, expansion, and buyouts, with a net preference for trade sales and secondary sales as well as repayments of preferred shares, loans, or mezzanine financing (see Table 5.2).

5.3. PE Investments and Risk-Mitigation Strategies

PE investments are characterised by a high level of uncertainty and risk, mainly due to the unpredictable nature of outcomes, especially if referred to innovative expansion projects, and the limited interim liquidity of such investments (Hellmann and Puri, 2002a, 2002b; Cumming, 2005a; Kut *et al.*, 2007; Matusik and Fitza, 2012; Cumming and Walz, 2010). Additionally, the success of the venture largely depends on the ability and commitment of the entrepreneur to complete the financed project. The risk associated with PE investments varies depending on the company's developmental phase. The risks are even more pronounced when financing new businesses in highly technological and innovative sectors, offering potentially higher returns (see, e.g. Silva Júnior *et al.*, 2023). In the early stages, the probability of failure within the first year may even reach 40% of the financed companies (Dimov and De Clercq, 2006). Over the first development years, internal risks connected to the company tend to prevail (e.g. start-up challenges, production issues, lack of control, and limited managerial skills), while as companies progress to later development stages, the risk of failure decreases and external risks become more significant, especially regarding market conditions, economic trends, and competitive pressures (Knill, 2009). As well known, higher risks offer higher expected returns, but in a typical VC portfolio, only a small fraction (10–15%) of investments yield excellent returns, while 50% yield mediocre returns, and the remaining investments result in losses (see Knill, 2009; also see Gompers and Lerner, 2006; Cumming and Dai, 2011; Nahata *et al.*, 2014; Dai and Nahata, 2016; Korteweg, 2019; Korteweg and Sorensen, 2017; Buchner *et al.*, 2018).[19]

The risks of PE investments are also amplified by *asymmetric information* and various agency conflicts that can occur between PE fund managers and investee companies (e.g. conflict of interests, free riding, effort problems, and information issues). Agency problems negatively affect the relationship between the VC, acting as the principal, and the entrepreneur, acting as the agent (see, e.g. Sahlman, 1990; Kaplan and Strömberg, 2003, 2004; Cumming, 2005a, 2005b, 2006a, 2006b; Gompers and Lerner, 2006; Kut *et al.*, 2007; Tykvová, 2007; Meuleman *et al.*, 2009; Baldwin, 2012). Agency conflicts may derive from insufficient information about the real performance of the target firms or from the lack of agent ability, which increases the risk of the entire venture, as well as from the possibility of the agent engaging in opportunistic actions that are in conflict with the interests of the principal (Johan and Zhang, 2021; Cumming and Zambelli, 2019). Without appropriate screening and control mechanisms, the existence of asymmetric information may lead to the following:

(1) *Adverse selection* problems (also known as *hidden information*), which arise before making the investment or providing the financing. They refer to the cases in which an entrepreneur misrepresents the reality or hides information regarding the quality of a proposed project to induce the VCs to finance the company (Cumming and Zambelli, 2019).
(2) *Moral hazard* problems (also known as *hidden actions*), which arise once the investment is made and financing is provided (see Bellavitis *et al.*, 2019; Bergemann and Hege, 1998). This problem refers to the possibility of the entrepreneur employing harmful actions or opportunistic behaviours in conflict with the interests of the investor. The moral hazard problem is typically driven by a misalignment of interests between principals and

[19]For overviews of PE returns, see, e.g. Cumming (2010), Cumming and Walz (2010), Gohil and Vyas (2016), and Kaplan and Sensoy (2015).

agents (conflict-alignment problem) or by the difficulty of monitoring the actions of the entrepreneur (goal-verification problem), which opens up space for detrimental opportunistic behaviour (Zambelli, 2014). Additionally, in the context of PE, interactions between VCs and portfolio companies are further complicated by a double-sided moral hazard problem, as the venture outcome depends on both the quality and effort of the managerial team, as well as on the efforts of the VCs, who should provide valuable support, time, and attention to their portfolio companies (see e.g. Schmidt, 2003; Casamatta, 2003; Bernile *et al.*, 2007).

To address the above agency issues, VCs need to properly motivate the entrepreneur to provide realistic information about the venture and act in such a way that maximises the interests of the company, minimising the risks of hidden information and opportunistic actions. To mitigate such agency problems, VCs can employ several strategies, including screening and rigorous DD, monitoring, syndication, stage financing, contracting, different financing tools, and contingent control rights (Cestone, 2014; Kaplan and Strömberg, 2003, 2004; Cumming, 2005a, 2005b, 2006a, 2006b, 2007, 2008; Cumming and Johan, 2014; Johan and Zhang, 2021). These mechanisms are specifically designed to motivate the entrepreneur and the VCs to act in the best interests of the venture, minimising the potential for double-sided moral hazard (see, e.g. Sahlman, 1990; Lerner, 1994a, 1994b, 1995; Gompers, 1995; Hellmann, 1998, 2002, 2006; Casamatta, 2003; Cestone and White, 2003; Kaplan and Strömberg, 2004; Cumming, 2005a, 2007; Tykvová, 2007; Jääskeläinen, 2012; Cumming and Johan, 2014; Bellavitis *et al.*, 2019; Bernstein *et al.*, 2019).

Figure 5.7 provides a schematic overview of the agency conflicts affecting the relationship between VCs and investee firms, along with various risk-mitigation strategies that can be employed by VCs before and after the financing to minimise the risks of adverse selection, moral hazard, and misrepresentation of reality (or 'window dressing', as labelled by Cornelli and Yosha, 2003). Additionally, Figure 5.7 reports the main literature addressing the various specific risk-mitigation mechanisms, which are briefly discussed in the following sections.[20]

[20]For a systematic review of the literature on the risk-mitigation mechanisms, control rights, and security design employed in venture finance and PE, see Zambelli (2012, 2014).

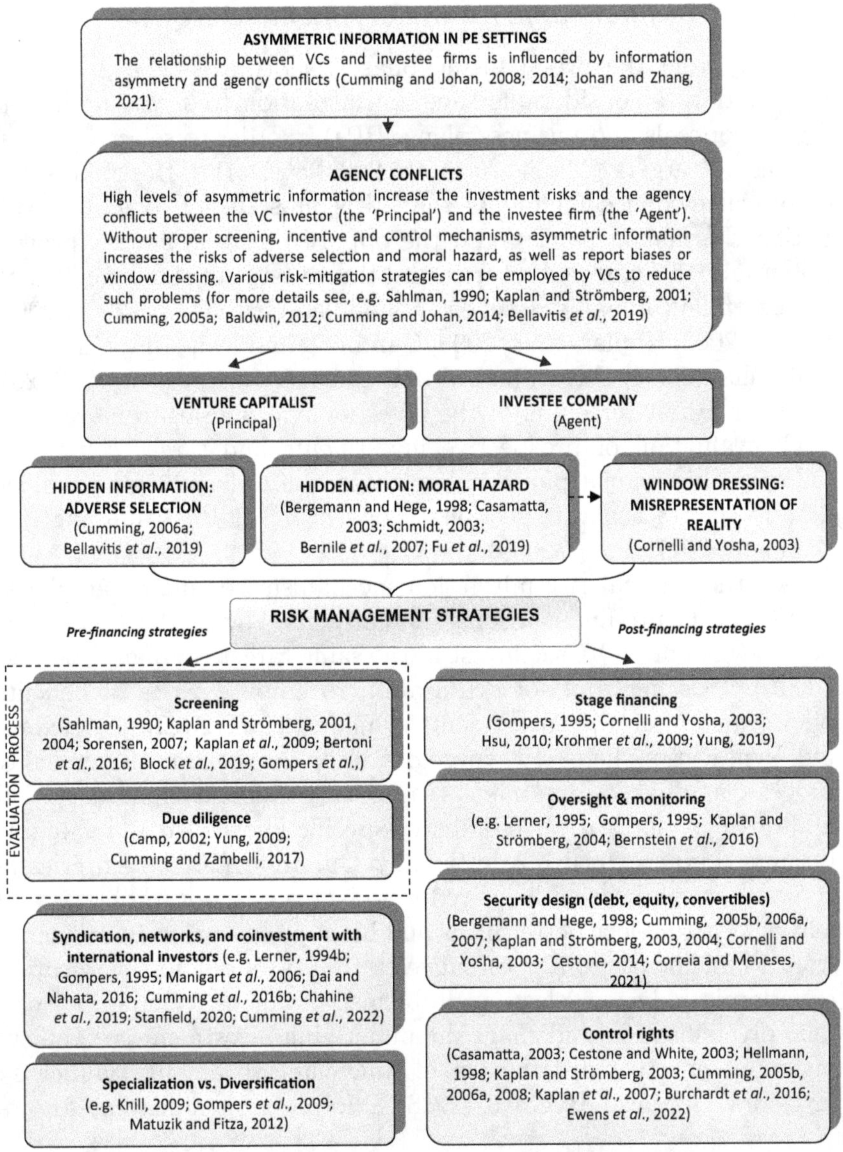

Figure 5.7. Risk-management strategies in PE settings.
Source: Own elaboration adapted and updated from Zambelli (2012), p. 159.

5.3.1. *Pre-financing risk management strategies*

Starting from the pre-financing phase, before closing a deal, VCs usually devote considerable time and attention to *screening* investment proposals and business plans (BPs) in order to select the most promising targets (Manigart *et al.*, 2006).[21] During this phase, the empirical evidence highlights that VCs most likely focus on evaluating the management team, the opportunity, the market growth potentials, the expected returns, and the investment strategic fit with the portfolio companies (see, e.g. Kaplan and Strömberg, 2000, 2001; Lerner, 2002; Kaplan *et al.*, 2009; Cumming and Dai, 2011; Cumming and Johan, 2014; Ferrati and Muffatto, 2019; Gompers *et al.*, 2020).

After a first screening of the investment proposals, a more thorough evaluation of prospective investments and target companies follows. This crucial phase is known as 'due diligence' and will be described in a separate section (Block *et al.*, 2019; Cumming and Zambelli, 2017; Yung, 2009).[22]

Another crucial risk-mitigation mechanism commonly employed by VCs in the pre-financing stage is represented by *syndication*, which occurs when more VCs coinvest in the same target company (Lerner, 1994b). VCs may opt for syndication to enjoy a series of benefits before and after the investment is made (Tian, 2012). For example, syndication helps PE investors improve the overall screening process, as diverse investment teams with different experience and abilities may share diverse industry-specific knowledge and valuable insights (Lerner, 1994b). Additionally, Cumming (2006a) empirically shows that syndication helps reduce adverse selection problems and allows VCs to select better firms and high-quality projects. Evidence from Manigart *et al.* (2006) suggests that VCs opt for syndication to minimise adverse selection problems, as well as to enhance portfolio diversification and share the underlying investment risk, allowing more effective distribution of financial risk among syndicated investors (see also Bygrave, 1988). Moreover, syndication fosters

[21]For a recent overview of the selection process implemented by VCs, see Gompers *et al.* (2020).

[22]The pre-financing evaluation carried out by VCs to select promising targets is one of the most crucial phases in the PE investment cycle (see Cumming and Zambelli, 2017; Gompers *et al.*, 2020).

collaboration and cooperation among VCs, reducing competition (Gu and Lu, 2014). In cross-border investments, syndication can help VCs overcome information disadvantages (or '*liability of foreignness*', as labelled by Nahata *et al.*, 2014) associated with different environments due to differences in language, institutional, legal, and cultural settings (Cumming *et al.*, 2022; see also Wang *et al.*, 2017, 2018; Dai and Nahata, 2016). The presence of international investors also appears to enhance the success of the venture, in terms of IPO exits and IPO proceeds (Cumming *et al.*, 2006).[23]

Also, the *specialisation* and industrial *experience* of VCs can play a crucial role in enhancing the probabilities of investment success. Gompers *et al.* (2009) show that investments carried out by generalist (or non-specialised) VCs are associated with lower investee performance, possibly due to inefficient allocation of funds across too many industries and suboptimal selection of different types of target companies.[24]

5.3.2. *Post-financing risk management strategies*

Once the screening and evaluation process is completed, the VCs select the target firms, close the deal, and proceed to the financing phase (see Figure 5.7). In this stage, the VCs negotiate the specific *security design* and *contractual provisions* regarding cash flow rights, control rights, exit rights, monitoring rights, and governance mechanisms. This deal structure phase is essential to mitigate the occurrence of agency conflicts between PE investors and entrepreneurs (Ewens *et al.*, 2022; Burchardt *et al.*, 2016). Proper security design mechanisms that separate control rights from cash flow rights have proven to help reduce the risk of facing moral hazard problems in PE settings (Cumming, 2005b, 2006a, 2007, 2008; Cumming *et al.*, 2016b; Burchardt *et al.*, 2016; Yung, 2019; Correia and Meneses, 2021).

---

[23]For recent overviews on syndication in venture finance, see Chahine *et al.* (2019) and Jääskeläinen (2012).

[24]The empirical evidence on the optimal portfolio strategies employed by VCs to reduce the underlying investment risk is mixed (see, e.g. Knill, 2009; Matusik and Fitza 2012, for overviews on the mixed results regarding the VC strategies of specialisation versus diversification).

As highlighted by Kaplan and Strömberg (2003) and Cumming (2008), VCs have the option to employ a wide set of control rights, including the power to hire or dismiss the CEO, the right to have board representation or board control, and veto rights over strategic decisions such as the issuance of further securities, mergers and acquisitions, or significant capital expenditures. Kaplan and Strömberg (2003, 2004) show that VCs usually allocate control and cash flow rights separately, often making them contingent on the performance levels of their investee firms. In this way, VCs gain increased control if target firms do not perform well or if specific milestones are not met. Conversely, if the firm performs well and meets the planned milestones, VCs progressively reduce their control rights over the target company and receive more cash flow rights in return. Overall, these contingent control rights help minimise the risk of moral hazard by better motivating entrepreneurs to act in the best interests of both the VCs and the venture (Sahlman, 1990; Hellmann, 1998, Kaplan and Strömberg, 2001). Cumming (2008) expands the previous literature by analysing the connection between control rights and exit routes, showing that strong VC control rights, such as board control and veto rights, are associated with a higher likelihood of exiting through acquisitions rather than IPOs.

Regarding the *types of securities* chosen by VCs, the theoretical and empirical literature presents contrasting results (Zambelli, 2014). In particular, according to the economic theory, convertible securities represent the optimal choice to minimise agency conflicts between VCs and financed firms (see, e.g. Cornelli and Yosha, 2003; Casamatta, 2003; Cestone and White, 2003; Schmidt, 2003; Hellmann, 2006; Cestone, 2014). However, the empirical evidence shows contrasting and mixed results, which seem to be associated with different geographical contexts. For example, in the US, convertible securities are confirmed as the most commonly used form of VC financing, as shown by Sahlman (1990) and further supported by Kaplan and Strömberg (2001, 2003, 2004) and Kaplan *et al.* (2007). However, empirical analyses on VC security design in Canada (Cumming, 2005a, 2005b, 2006a, 2007), Europe (Cumming, 2008), and developing countries (Lerner and Schoar, 2005) show that convertible securities are not the most frequent financing tool employed in VC investments. In these countries, a wider set of security types is adopted, especially common stocks. Cumming (2005b) challenges the notion of a universally accepted optimal security design in VC investments by highlighting the significant influence of other factors driving such choices, such as legal and regulatory differences.[25]

A further risk management mechanism employed by VCs is represented by their proactive role in governing and *monitoring* their investee companies. VCs provide managerial guidance and often hold significant positions in their targets' boards (Sahlman, 1990; Lerner, 1995; Gompers, 1995; Hellmann and Puri, 2002a, 2002b; Kaplan and Strömberg, 2004; Cumming *et al.*, 2010; Cohn *et al.*, 2022).[26] Recent research demonstrates that VCs contribute to enhancing the governance of their target firms by influencing board composition, fostering more independent boards, and providing stronger oversight (see, e.g. Suchard, 2009; Wright *et al.*, 2009; Cumming *et al.*, 2010; Cumming and Johan, 2014). The positive influence of VCs on the governance of target firms is also associated with improved firm performance (Suchard, 2009).

Another incentive mechanism typically employed by VC investors is represented by *stage financing*, according to which the total amount of capital requested by the target firm is not provided all at once but, instead, divided into various rounds (or stages) in association with specific economic, financial, or organisational milestones (e.g. Sahlman, 1990; Gompers, 1995; Kaplan and Strömberg, 2004; Gompers and Lerner, 2006; Tian, 2011). This strategy enables VCs to closely monitor the progress of the financed project as well as the development of the firm. By connecting capital injections with specific milestones, VCs retain the option of abandoning the firm before the completion of the planned project, minimising potential losses (Hsu, 2010). This threat serves as an incentive mechanism for the target firms by encouraging their entrepreneurial and managerial teams to maximise their efforts and act in the best interests of the venture (Gompers, 1995). However, stage financing can also lead to unintended outcomes and 'side effects' by potentially encouraging entrepreneurs to manipulate signals opportunistically

[25]For a systematic overview of contractual provisions, security design, and control rights chosen by VCs to mitigate agency conflicts and mitigate moral hazard problems, see Zambelli (2014). See also Burchardt *et al.* (2016).

[26]For recent reviews of the literature on PE governance and successful exits, see Gogineni and Upadhyay (2023).

(Cornelli and Yosha, 2003). For example, stage financing can push target firms to misrepresent or manipulate the interim results for the sole purpose of inducing VCs to provide further rounds of financing. (This problem is known as '*window dressing*', as explained by Cornelli and Yosha 2003; see also Krohmer *et al.*, 2009.)

5.3.3. *The influence of legal, cultural, and educational factors*

Recent research has shown that investor behaviour, deal structuring, security design, and the evolution of the PE industry are influenced by formal institutions, such as political and legal regulations, as well as by informal institutions, including behavioural norms and cultural practices (see, e.g. Tykvová, 2018; Li and Zahra, 2012; Nahata *et al.*, 2014; Wang *et al.*, 2018; Lichtenthaler, 2021). This perspective has challenged the results of previous comparative studies focused on comparing formal institutions across different countries (e.g. La Porta *et al.*, 2006; Beck *et al.*, 2003). These studies have been criticised for ignoring the impact of diverse cultural backgrounds on investor behaviour. Specifically, the main critique against these comparative law studies is that they analyse the impact of law without considering the '*law in context*', i.e. the specific cultural contexts that shape each regulatory environment (see, e.g. Siems, 2005; Cumming *et al.*, 2022). Legal systems are strongly linked with societies, and as such, when making international comparisons, it is crucial to consider the underlying social and cultural contexts to gain a comprehensive picture of their impact. Echoing this criticism, an emerging consensus in the international business literature emphasises the importance of integrating formal and informal institutions to better assess the moderating influence of culture on governance and investment decisions (see Wang *et al.*, 2017, 2018). In the context of a VC setting, a few new studies have begun exploring in this direction: Li and Zahra (2012) show how culture moderates the impact of law on the VC activity, while Fuentelsaz *et al.* (2019) demonstrate how culture moderates the impact of law on new business developments. More recently, Cumming *et al.* (2022) have advanced the understanding of the combined impact of formal and informal institutions by analysing how legal enforcement and cultural differences can shape the investment behaviour of

VCs, particularly in their propensity to syndicate and form denser networks.[27]

Figure 5.8 provides a summary of studies investigating the moderating impact of legal and cultural differences on investor behaviour (for more details, also see Guler and Guillén, 2010).

Another important factor affecting investing behaviour is represented by the PE investor abilities to add value to their investee firms. Before undertaking an investment, PE fund managers have to properly collect, analyse, and assess a great amount of data on the prospective target firms and their expected growth potential. After the investment decision is made, PE fund managers are required to undertake a complex negotiation phase with the entrepreneurial team in order to properly anticipate, monitor, and manage the high underlying risk involved. As highlighted by Fuchs *et al.* (2022), the VCs ability to add value to their target firms also depends on their educational background. The evidence by Fuchs *et al.* (2022) shows that the educational diversity of PE fund managers (in terms of interdisciplinary skills) and their academic background positively influence fund performance (Fuchs *et al.*, 2022). Furthermore, they find

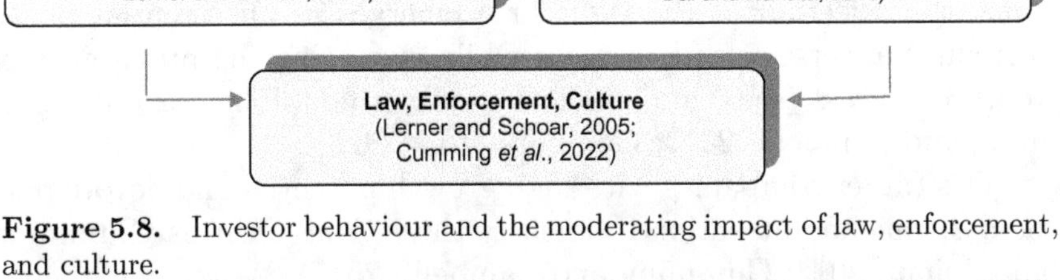

Figure 5.8. Investor behaviour and the moderating impact of law, enforcement, and culture.
Sources: Own elaboration from Nahata *et al.* (2014), Want *et al.* (2017, 2018), and Lerner and Schoar (2005, 2010).

[27]See Cumming *et al.* (2022) for a literature review regarding the impact of formal and informal institutions on VC behaviour. See also: Lichtenthaler (2021), Wang *et al.* (2017), Nahata *et al.* (2014), and Lerner and Schoar (2005, 2010).

that the highest value-added contribution comes from fund managers who graduated from top-quality universities (e.g. Times Higher Education).

Among the various risk-mitigation tools previously discussed and summarised in Figure 5.7, the selection of the right target firms is crucial to reduce the negative consequences of asymmetric information. Moreover, a rigorous DD has been proven to play a fundamental role in selecting the right firms, thereby enhancing the overall chances of success of the entire venture (Cumming and Zambelli, 2017).

The following two sections dig deeper into the pre-financing evaluation process carried out by PE investors, which involves two important selection phases: screening and DD, as highlighted within the dashed box of Figure 5.7. In these sections, we focus on addressing the following questions:

- How do VCs choose their target firms?
- What is DD and how do VCs implement it?
- How beneficial is the time invested in performing DD?

5.4. Evaluation Process of Target Firms

The evaluation process can be defined as a sequence of steps undertaken by VCs to choose and finance the right target firms (e.g. Sahlman, 1990; Gompers and Lerner, 2006; Gompers *et al.*, 2020). As anticipated in the previous section, among the various risk-mitigation mechanisms used by VCs to minimise asymmetric information problems, the selection of the right firm emerges as an essential phase to reduce adverse selection issues while increasing the probability of venture success (see Yung, 2009; Cumming and Johan, 2014; Cumming and Zambelli, 2017; Gompers *et al.*, 2020).

VCs target companies with high growth potential and devote particular time and attention to identify these types of firms (Cumming and Johan, 2014; Cumming and Zambelli, 2017). With a wide number of investment proposals at their disposal (deal origination or deal flow), the real challenge for VCs lies in how they choose their right target firms. According to Bertoni *et al.* (2016), the selection activity implemented by VCs resembles more a 'frog-kissing' process rather than cherry-picking the best (i.e. 'princess'). More specifically, VCs are not necessarily attracted by the most performing companies at the time of selection (i.e. 'princess'), but instead, they actively pursue the most promising firms ('frogs') to be transformed into winning ventures. More specifically, instead of cherry-picking the already best-performing firms, VCs select promising firms with the highest expectation of growth (for additional information, refer to Bertoni *et al.*, 2016).

Various studies have analysed the complex PE decision-making process by primarily relying on survey data and examining the selection criteria adopted by VCs (for a recent overview, see Esen *et al.*, 2023; see also Block *et al.*, 2019; Gompers *et al.*, 2020). The entire evaluation process carried out by VCs can be simplified through various steps (for details, see, e.g. Tyebjee and Bruno, 1984; Kaplan *et al.*, 2009; Block *et al.*, 2019; Gompers *et al.*, 2016, 2020)[28]:

1. collection of investment proposals (i.e. *deal origination and flow of proposals*);
2. preliminary selection of investment proposals through a double screening procedure of the BPs collected by VCs (*screening*);
3. rigorous assessment of prospective investments and target companies (*DD*), followed by the evaluation of the related expected risk and return;
4. valuation, negotiation, and final decision (*deal structure and closure*), which is crucial to assess the proper value of the selected investee firms and their acquisition price, the potential equity participation, as well as the optimal control rights and security set that can better motivate the entrepreneurial and managerial team to act in the best interests of the venture, reducing the risk of moral hazard.[29]

[28]For other empirical studies on the evaluation process, see MacMillan *et al.* (1985, 1987), Gorman and Sahlman (1989), Zacharakis and Meyer (1995, 1998), Fried and Hisrich (1994), Wright and Robbie (1996), Kaplan and Strömberg (2004, 2000), Cumming (2006a), Khanin *et al.* (2008), Kaplan *et al.* (2009), Block *et al.* (2019), Gompers *et al.* (2020), and Esen *et al.* (2023). For details on formal DD in PE, see Scharfman (2012).

[29]For additional details, see the study by Tyebjee and Bruno (1984). See also the model proposed by Fried and Hisrich (1994), who consider a slightly different VC evaluation process, divided into six stages: deal origination, firm-specific and generic screening, first-phase and second-phase evaluations, and deal closure.

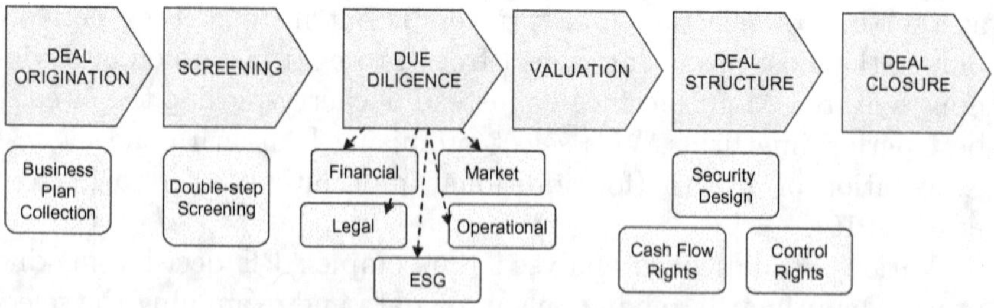

Figure 5.9. VC evaluation process.
Sources: Elaboration from Tyebjee and Bruno (1984), Fried and Hisrich (1994), Kaplan *et al.* (2003, 2004, 2009), Cumming (2006a), Block *et al.* (2019), Gompers *et al.* (2020), and Esen *et al.* (2023).

Figure 5.9 summarises the entire evaluation process carried out by PE investors, from deal origination (also known as deal flow) to the final deal closure. This VC evaluation process aims not only to select the most promising companies to invest in but also to choose the most appropriate methods to implement the proposed projects as well as the optimal security design or combination of financial instruments (i.e. equity, debt, or hybrid securities) to minimise moral hazard problems and future complications (Cornelli and Yosha, 2003; Kaplan and Strömberg, 2003, 2004; Cumming, 2005b, 2006a, 2007; Cestone, 2014; Correia and Meneses, 2021).

In the following sections, we briefly discuss the steps involved within the VC evaluation process, as highlighted in Figure 5.9.

5.4.1. *Preliminary screening*

In the PE setting, the selection process heavily relies on subjective evaluations of various characteristics of target companies. Empirical evidence has highlighted the significant subjectivity and variability in the criteria VCs use, which can differ greatly from one case to another. Despite these challenges, this section aims at providing a basic framework to understand how VCs handle the 'evaluation dilemma' in assessing risky projects within non-publicly traded firms. This dilemma is particularly pronounced for early-stage innovative companies lacking a trading history and sufficient accounting data for traditional valuation based on financial theory. The evaluation complexity increases when VCs have to assess start-ups, whose main asset is often characterised by the intangible business idea itself.

The entire screening and evaluation process is highly selective. VCs usually receive a large number of investment proposals, which may come from a variety of channels, including companies they have previously funded, other VCs looking for coinvestment opportunities, and their own proactive deal searches. Gompers *et al.* (2016) show that out of 100 initial investment proposals collected by VCs, only eight semifinalist companies are considered valuable enough to enter the negotiation phase (deal structure). Ultimately, only four target companies pass the entire evaluation process and receive the financing (for additional details, see Block *et al.*, 2019, and Figure 5.10).

The various investment proposals received by VCs are subjected to a first-step screening based on a qualitative overview of the submitted BPs.[30] Afterwards, the proposals that pass this first stage are subjected to a second-step screening based on the investment size (Cumming, 2006b), as well as the industry, location, and development stage of the target company (Zambelli, 2024).[31]

The *geographic proximity* of a prospective company represents a crucial factor in the preliminary screening phase, as VCs usually expect to be actively involved in the governance and management of their investee firms (Cumming and Johan, 2014). Cumming and Dai (2012) found that VCs prefer to invest in companies that are located nearby or in the same country ('local bias') in order to facilitate monitoring, reduce travel expenses, and enable more cost-effective interactions with their targets. Cumming and Dai (2012) also show that the enhanced monitoring increases the value-added potential and the success rates of the venture. Additionally, they observed that VC experience can reduce local biases. In fact, VCs with higher experience and a stronger reputation are less affected by local biases,

---

[30]In the context of PE, a well-structured business plan is crucial for securing financing. Essential for attracting VC interest, the BP serves as a quality signal and a roadmap. It must include various key elements: business mission, management, product or service specifics, market analysis, competition, and financial projections. It should clearly articulate the company's goals, including growth prospects, and outline the strategies for production, commercialisation, and finance. For further details, see De Clercq *et al.* (2006) and Sahlman (1999).

[31]For further information, please refer to Tyebjee and Bruno (1984).

probably because of their greater ability to deal with asymmetric information issues underlying longer-distance investments. Similarly, coinvesting with international investors helps reduce this local bias (Cumming and Dai, 2012; see also Cumming *et al.*, 2022, who reinforce this view by showing that this local bias is less pronounced in cases of dense syndicated networks).[32]

Another important 'evaluation dilemma' in the preliminary screening is related to the investment *size*. On the one hand, VCs may be tempted to allocate a small amount of capital in each financing round to reduce their exposure to company-specific risk. However, an insufficient amount of capital can increase the likelihood of the venture's default. On the other hand, providing an excessively large amount of capital may raise the venture's chances of success but can increase the risk of opportunistic behaviour, misuse of capital, or excessive capital expenditures.[33]

5.4.2. *Due diligence*

The proposals that successfully pass the preliminary screening are subject to a deeper investigation process known as 'due diligence'. DD represents a comprehensive analysis of a variety of factors involving various *key areas* regarding the target company, its management team, financial projections, product uniqueness, technology used, and market growth potential, as well as the target's industry, competitors, and regulatory context (Camp, 2002; Brown *et al.*, 2008; Scharfman, 2012; Afyonoğlu, 2013; Metrick and Yasuda, 2021).

Different types of DD exist. Financial DD involves the analysis of the target's financial statements, profit margins, and expected cash flows (Afyonoğlu, 2013). Legal DD involves the assessment of the term sheet, intellectual property rights, regulatory compliance, and potential legal risks, such as litigation risks. This type of DD is fundamental in cross-border investments, which require full alignment with different legal environments. Operational DD assesses the company's activities, with a particular focus on its operating and business model, its management group, and its IT infrastructure (Porsgaard

[32]For details on the relevance of geographic proximity in the VC selection process, see Cumming and Dai (2012).

[33]For further information on this subject, please refer to Bernile *et al.* (2007) and Cumming (2006b).

et al., 2018). Market DD involves the analysis of the target industry, its market position relative to its competitors, and growth potential (Scharfman, 2012; Metrick and Yasuda, 2021). The DD can also involve non-financial factors, such as Environment, Social, and Governance (ESG) considerations, in order to assess the overall company's sustainability (Duke, 2015).

Cumming and Zambelli (2017) show the existence of two additional types of DD: internal and external. Specifically, VCs can choose to implement the majority of the DD either internally ('*internal* DD') or externally by delegating it to external agents specialised in specific areas, such as lawyers, accountants, or strategic consultants ('*external* DD'). Internal and external DD are not mutually exclusive, and VCs can choose to implement both in a complementary manner.

DD represents a fundamental phase in PE financing for two main reasons. First, VCs usually expect to play an active role in the governance and management of their target companies, and such active involvement increases the risk exposure (Yung, 2009; Scharfman, 2012). Second, PE investors tend to have less diversified portfolios, and as such, they need to pay extra diligence in evaluating their investment proposals to minimise the specific idiosyncratic risk associated with their target companies (Knill, 2009; Cumming and Zambelli, 2017; Zambelli, 2024).[34]

The ultimate goal of DD is to assist VCs in their decision-making process by helping them choose the most promising investee companies with the greatest potential in the hope of achieving higher future portfolio returns. The following sections focus on how VCs ultimately select the target firm to invest in.

5.4.2.1. *Ultimate selection criteria*

A large number of studies have analysed the decision-making process carried out by VCs by investigating their ultimate selection criteria (e.g. Tyebjee and Bruno, 1984; MacMillan *et al.*, 1985, 1987; Gorman and Sahlman, 1989; Hall and Hofer, 1993; Wright and Robbie, 1996; Zacharakis and Meyer, 1995, 1998; Kaplan and Strömberg, 2000, 2004; Cumming, 2006a; Khanin *et al.*, 2008; Kaplan *et al.*,

[34]Additional studies demonstrate the importance of DD in other contexts: Brown *et al.* (2008), in relation to hedge funds; Cumming *et al.* (2019), for crowdfunding; Wangerin (2019), in relation to mergers and acquisitions (M&As).

2009; Scharfman, 2012; Block *et al.*, 2019; Gompers *et al.*, 2020; Esen *et al.*, 2023). A comprehensive review of these studies highlights the challenge in identifying a universal selection model used by VCs. The various selection criteria differ across various studies. However, despite these differences, there exists a consensus on certain fundamental selection factors that VCs prioritise, such as the qualities of the entrepreneurial and management teams as well as the characteristics of the business and the market growth potential (Zambelli, 2024).

The study of Tyebjee and Bruno (1984) stands as one of the first empirical studies investigating the selection criteria in VC settings. Through a survey methodology, the authors identified 23 specific criteria, further grouped into five distinct categories, as follows[35]:

(1) Market attractiveness (*context*): This involves the assessment of the market's growth potential and eventual entry barriers influencing the market's accessibility.
(2) Product-uniqueness (*opportunity*): This criterion involves the evaluation of the product differentiation, in terms of its novelty, patentability, and technical characteristics, in comparison with the products offered by competitors. The more innovative and unique a product is perceived to be, the greater its ability to establish barriers to entry. This, in turn, decreases the risk of competitors' entrance and enhances the expected returns for VCs.
(3) Entrepreneurial and managerial team (*people*): This category is fundamental for VCs and involves the assessment of the founders' and managers' skills in terms of their past experience, track record, reputation, and leadership capacity. VCs invest in people, along with the product. As such, selecting the right team to implement the proposed business idea and develop the project is crucial.

[35]Sahlman (1999) further reinforces the study of Tyebjee and Bruno (1984) by highlighting the pillars of business plans (i.e. people, opportunity, context, and risk-reward potential). For more recent overviews on the VC decision-making process and selection criteria, see Kaplan *et al.* (2009), Gompers *et al.* (2016), Gompers *et al.* (2020), and Esen *et al.* (2023). See also: Chemmanur and Fulghieri (2014), Köhn (2018), Ferrati and Muffatto (2019), Röhm (2018), and Rawal and Kapil (2023).

(4) Resilience against environmental threats, such as unfavourable economic trends, obsolescence due to technological changes, and increased market competition (*risks*): This category involves a further assessment of the barriers to entry; the lower the entry barriers, the greater the environmental threats for the target company and its VC investors.
(5) Expected liquidity of the investment at the exit stage, via IPOs, trade sale, or secondary sale (*cash-out potential*).[36]

Figure 5.10 summarises the steps and criteria involved in the complex evaluation process implemented by VCs. First, it highlights the high selectivity underlying the entire evaluation process, showing that over an initial pool of 100 prospective investments, only 15 of them manage to pass the initial screening phase to undergo a more thorough investigation, at the end of which, only four target companies are ultimately chosen and reach the final closure stage (as highlighted by Gompers *et al.*, 2016 and reported by Block *et al.*, 2019). Second, Figure 5.10 shows the main selection criteria and areas involved in the DD, which can be condensed into the 'jockey' and the 'horse', as described by Kaplan *et al.* (2009).

Among the various selection criteria highlighted above, which are considered the most important ones for VC investors? To address

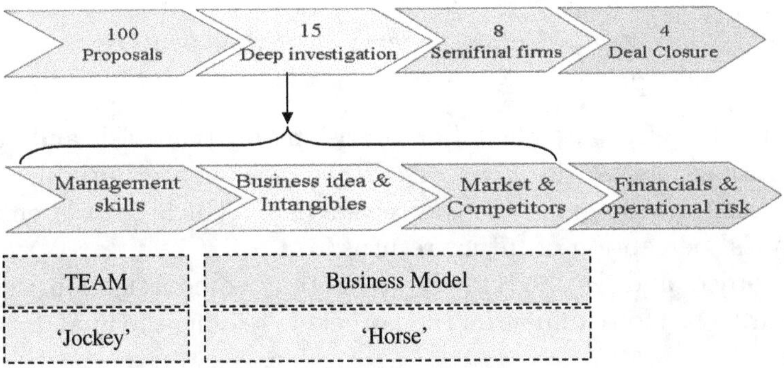

Figure 5.10. Private equity evaluation process.
Sources: Own elaboration from: Gompers *et al.* (2016), Block *et al.* (2019), Kaplan *et al.* (2009), Cumming and Zambelli (2017), Gompers *et al.* (2020), Metrick and Yasuda (2021), and Esen *et al.* (2023).

[36]For more details, see Tyebjee and Bruno (1984).

this question, Kaplan *et al.* (2009) further grouped the various VC selection criteria into two main categories, metaphorically labelled as:

- the '*jockey*', which refers to the human capital of the investee company (i.e. founders and the management team);
- the '*horse*', which refers to the business activity and various business-related elements (for example, the business idea, the market potential, and the business model).[37]

Among the above two categories, Kaplan *et al.* (2009) identified the quality of human capital (the jockey) as the most significant selection criterion for VCs. Their results provide support for the '*people matters*' view: VCs first invest in people and then in the opportunities provided by the business idea. Further empirical research (Gompers *et al.*, 2020; Esen *et al.*, 2023) has strengthened this conclusion, underlining the essential role of human capital in PE and VC settings.[38]

More recently, Block *et al.* (2019) conducted a conjoint experiment and confirmed the relevance of the management team as a selection criterion used by VCs. However, Block *et al.* (2019) highlight two additional selection criteria that seem to be more relevant: revenue growth and value-added potential of the product or service proposed by the target company.[39]

5.4.2.2. *Impact of selection criteria on risk and return perceptions*

Ultimately, VCs base their final decisions on their risk and return perceptions, as do any investors. Which selection criteria are most influential in changing VCs' perceived risk? Which criteria enhance the VCs' perception of future returns?

Tyebjee and Bruno (1984) show that some selection criteria appear to be more influential than others in driving the final decisions

[37] See also Block *et al.* (2019) and Gompers *et al.* (2020).

[38] In the literature, additional empirical studies have investigated the VC selection process (see, e.g. MacMillan *et al.*, 1985; Hall and Hofer, 1993; Kaplan and Strömberg, 2000, 2004; Hudson and Evans, 2005; Kaplan *et al.*, 2009; Hsu *et al.*, 2014; Gompers *et al.* 2016, 2020; Röhm, 2018; Esen *et al.*, 2023).

[39] For recent overviews of the VC decision-making process, also see Gompers *et al.* (2020) and Esen *et al.* (2023).

of VCs, either by increasing their expectations of future returns or by decreasing their risk perception, as summarised in Figure 5.11.

In line with the 'people matters' view discussed in the previous sections, the analyses by Tyebjee and Bruno (1984) identify the quality of the management team as the most influential factor in affecting the risk perception of VCs. A highly skilled management team significantly decreases the perceived risk of the investment, increasing its acceptance rate, and vice versa. Another relevant factor in reducing the risk perception of VCs is represented by the high resilience against changes or threats from the external environment (e.g. obsolescence, economic downturns, and increased competition from new entrants).

Conversely, the study by Tyebjee and Bruno (1984) shows that the attractiveness of the market plays the most influential role in enhancing the perception of future returns, followed by the uniqueness of the proposed product. Surprisingly, according to their findings, the cash-out potentials do not seem to have any influence on the risk and return perceptions. This evidence calls for new international

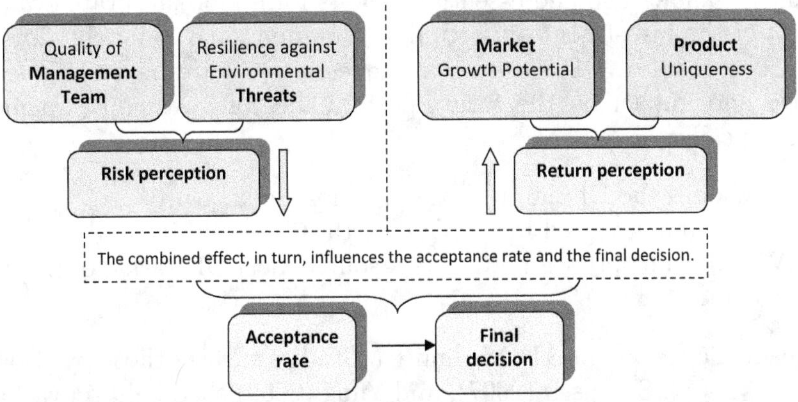

Figure 5.11. Impact of risk and return perceptions.
Source: Elaboration from the findings of Tyebjee and Bruno (1984).
Note: This figure highlights the impact of selection criteria on investors' risk and return perceptions, based on the study of Tyebjee and Bruno (1984). The authors isolated the criteria that have the strongest impact on the VCs' final decisions, highlighting the way in which each criterion influences the acceptance rate. Specifically, they showed that the management team and the resilience against environmental threats diminish the investor risk perception, while the market and product characteristics affect the final decision by increasing the return perception.

research on the impact of PE selection criteria on the risk and return perceptions of VCs.

5.4.2.3. *Is due diligence worth the time?*

This section reviews the economic value of DD in PE financing based on the findings by Cumming and Zambelli (2017). A thorough investigation process of prospective investments is crucial but very expensive and highly challenging for VCs due to the high direct and indirect costs underlying the DD (Yung, 2009). Direct costs emerge from the extensive time required to properly review economic, financial, and legal documents, as well as from the money spent to acquire additional data and information about potential investments. The indirect expenses are instead associated with the opportunity cost of time not invested in adding value to the existing portfolio companies (Cumming and Zambelli, 2017). Faced with these high costs, VCs may be tempted to either expedite the DD process or outsource it entirely or in part to external consultants, such as financial and legal experts. These experts are theoretically expected to provide specialised knowledge and essential insights for a more accurate evaluation of the investment opportunity (Cumming and Zambelli, 2017).

The costs of DD raise critical questions regarding its effectiveness and impact on the future performance of investee companies. Specifically:

- How does the DD improve the decision-making process?
- Is the time invested in the DD worth it?
- Would it be better for VCs to outsource most DD tasks to external agents?

Academic research on DD is limited. Studies such as those by Brown *et al.* (2008), Sorensen (2007), and Yung (2009) shed light on various aspects of DD, from its role in increasing investment alpha (Brown *et al.*, 2008) to its effectiveness in finding the right match (Sorensen, 2007), as well as in mitigating adverse selection issues under high asymmetric information (Yung, 2009). In particular, Brown *et al.* (2008) focus on hedge funds and find that DD is a significant source of alpha. Sorensen (2007) focuses on VC and highlights the strategic value of DD in enhancing investment outcomes by ensuring a better fit between VCs and investee companies. Yung (2009) presents a theoretical model examining the interplay between asymmetric information and the costs associated with DD and signalling in venture finance. His study suggests that in environments characterised by high information asymmetry, the DD conducted by VCs is more effective in reducing the risk of adverse selection than costly quality signals incurred by target firms (Zambelli, 2024). This is explainable by the fact that target firms often face cash constraints that limit their ability to signal their quality effectively, while investors generally have greater capacity to cover the costs underlying a rigorous DD process. As a result, costly DD is more successful at identifying high-quality target companies than depending on the quality signals these companies can send.

Cumming and Zambelli (2017) take a step forward by investigating the economic value and effectiveness of DD in PE, analysing how the duration of DD efforts relates to investee company performance. Their research not only emphasises the significance of DD in the investment decision-making process but also examines the implications of outsourcing DD to external agents, offering insights into the strategic considerations and trade-offs involved in the DD. Specifically, Cumming and Zambelli (2017) examine the relationship between the length of time spent on DD and the performance outcomes for investee companies, considering the various agents implementing it. Their findings suggest that the time invested in DD has a crucial economic value and serves as an indirect indicator (or proxy) of its perceived importance and thoroughness. This is based on the idea that the time invested in executing an activity indicates its importance to the investor and the degree of focus the investor commits to it.[40] DD is particularly relevant in the PE industry, where the opportunity cost of time is quite high (Cumming and Zambelli, 2017). The considerable variation in the time PE investors spend on implementing the DD, both across different investors and within the same PE fund, suggests that the allocation of time can represent a relevant key variable in measuring the different levels of effort and

[40]The study of Wangerin (2019) has further reinforced this view. Specifically, Wangerin (2019) investigates the value of time spent on DD in the context of mergers and acquisitions (M&As), by focusing on the time spent on negotiating and closing M&A transactions. He finds that competitive pressures and agency issues often lead to reduced DD, and this, in turn, is associated with lower post-acquisition profitability, reinforcing the main findings of Cumming and Zambelli (2017).

priority devoted to implementing such specific activity. The more time a PE investor spends investigating a particular target firm, the higher the importance and effort allocated to that firm. Additionally, Cumming and Zambelli (2017) investigate the impact of DD delegation by focusing on the agents performing the major part of DD and comparing the post-acquisition performance of the target firms, in connection with different types of agents performing it. Their findings show that the time invested by VCs on DD is crucial for their decision-making process, as a more thorough DD process is associated with improved post-acquisition performance of investee companies (both in terms of ROA and EBITDA/sales ratios). This evidence is significant only when the major part of DD is carried out internally by the investors. Instead, when the majority of the DD is outsourced to legal firms, accountants, and external strategic consultants, surprisingly, their results show no significant impact of DD on the post-acquisition performance of investee firms. These results remain valid after implementing various robustness checks and controlling for potential endogeneity issues. In conclusion, according to the findings highlighted by Cumming and Zambelli (2017), when the majority of DD is conducted internally, there are improvements on the post-acquisition performance of the target firm. Conversely, in the case of external DD, no significant performance improvements emerge. This puzzling evidence emphasises evident agency costs underlying the DD delegation and calls for more empirical investigations of the costs and implications of DD in venture finance (for more empirical details, see the study by Cumming and Zambelli, 2017).

5.5. Conclusion

PE investors are active financial intermediaries investing in high-risk growth potential firms with the intention of exiting their target firms within two to seven years. VCs seek target companies with strong growth potential and a drive to accelerate their development. The relationship between VCs and target firms is affected by high asymmetric information and agency costs, which can exacerbate investment risks, especially in young and innovative firms (e.g. Johan and Zhang, 2021). Without proper screening and control mechanisms, high information asymmetry may lead to adverse selection, moral hazard issues, and window dressing (see, e.g. Cornelli and Yosha,

2003; Cumming, 2005a, 2005b, 2006a). VCs can employ various risk-mitigation strategies to reduce such problems, including screening, DD (DD), syndication, stage financing, contractual arrangements, and monitoring (for details, see, e.g. Gompers and Lerner, 2006; Cumming and Johan, 2014; Buchner *et al.*, 2018).

One of the most important strategies for reducing risk and avoiding post-investment complications is DD, which helps in enhancing the likelihood of the venture's overall success. A rigorous DD helps minimise investment risks by improving the quality of the VC decision-making process and minimising the risk of adverse selection. DD helps better assess the potential value of the investment and its growth potential. DD can be performed mainly internally by the VCs or externally by hiring external specialists. Cumming and Zambelli (2017) show that a rigorous DD is associated with significant improvements in post-acquisition investee performance and helps improve the success of the entire venture, as long as it is performed internally (Cumming and Zambelli, 2017). No significant improvements are associated with DD delegation. Their results highlight the existence of evident agency costs associated with external DD and call for further research investigating its impact and implications in PE and venture finance settings.

Appendix 5A

Bibliography Regarding Recent Systematic Reviews of PE Investment Activity, Classified by Key Areas: Synthesis and Future Research Perspectives

VC & innovation	Lerner, J., Nanda, R. (2020). Venture capital's role in financing innovation: What we know and how much we still need to learn. *Journal of Economic Perspectives*, 34(3): 237–261. Li, M., Chen, H., Chen, R., Pan, Z. (2020a). Venture capital and firm innovation: A comprehensive review and future research agenda. *Journal of Business Research*, 108: 106–116. Cumming, D., Johan, S. (2017). The problems with and promise of entrepreneurial finance. *Strategic Entrepreneurship Journal*, 11(3): 357–370.

(*Continued*)

(*Continued*)

PE and VC financing	Cumming, D., Kumar, S., Lim, W. M., Pandey, N. (2023). Mapping the venture capital and private equity research: A bibliometric review and future research agenda. *Small Business Economics*, 61(1): 173–221.
	McGrath, P. J., Nerkar, A. (2023). Private equity: antecedents, outcomes, mediators, and moderators. *Journal of Management*, 49(1).
	Burström, T., Lahti, T., Parida, V., Wartiovaara, M., Wincent, J. (2023). A definition, review, and extension of global ecosystems theory: Trends, architecture and orchestration of global VCs and mechanisms behind unicorns. *Journal of Business Research*, 157. forthcoming, doi.org/10.1016/ j.jbusres.2022.113605
	Dai, N. (2022). Empirical research on private equity funds: A review of the past decade and future research opportunities. *Review of Corporate Finance*, 2: 427–450.
	Levasseur, L., Johan, S., Eckhardt, J. (2022). Mixed methods in venture capital research: An illustrative study and directions for future work. *British Journal of Management*, 33(1): 26–45.
	Gerhardt, V., Siluk, J., Neuenfeldt Júnior, Á. L., Júnior, C. R. S., Michelin, C. (2022). Evolution of start-up investments: An overview and future research directions. *International Journal of Business Innovation and Research*, 1(1).
	Grilli, L., Latifi, G., Mrkajic, B. (2019). Institutional determinants of venture capital activity: An empirically driven literature review and a research agenda. *Journal of Economic Surveys*, 33(4): 1094–1122.
	Tykvová, T. (2018). Venture capital and private equity financing: An overview of recent literature and an agenda for future research. *Journal of Business Economics*, 88(3–4): 325–362.
	Harrison, R. T., Mason, C. M. (2019). Venture capital 20 years on: Reflections on the evolution of a field. *Venture Capital*, 21(1): 1–34.
	Cancino, C. A., Merigo, J. M., Torres, J. P., Diaz, D. (2018). A bibliometric analysis of venture capital research. *Journal of Economics, Finance and Administrative Science*, 23(45): 182–195.
	Devigne, D., Manigart, S., Vanacker, T., Mulier, K. (2018). Venture capital internationalization: Synthesis and future research directions. *Journal of Economic Surveys*, 32(5): 1414–1445.

(*Continued*)

	Drover, W., Busenitz, L., Matusik, S., Townsend, D., Anglin, A., Dushnitsky, G. (2017). A review and road map of entrepreneurial equity financing research: Venture capital, corporate venture capital, angel investment, crowdfunding, and accelerators. *Journal of Management*, 43(6): 1820–1853.
Buyout financing	Sannajust, A., Groh, A. (2023). Pioneering management buy–out and entrepreneurial finance research: Mike Wright's research legacy. *Small Business Economics*, 60(1): 1–35.
	Wright, M. (2019). Entrepreneurship, context, and buyouts. In: Wright, M., Amess, K., Bacon, N., Siegel, D. (2019), *The Routledge Companion to Management Buyouts*. London: Routledge (Ch. 21, 406–417).
VC cycle	Torres, J. P. (2020). The venture capital feedback cycle: A critical review and future directions. *Entrepreneurship Research Journal*, doi:10.1515/erj–2017–0205
Agency costs & asymetric information	Johan, S., Zhang, M. (2021). Information asymmetries in private equity: Reporting frequency, endowments, and governance. *Journal of Business Ethics*, 174(1), 199–220.
	Baldwin, A. (2012). Private equity and agency costs: An economic analysis. *Economic Affairs*, 32(3): 107–109.
Selection & evaluation process	Rawal, V., Kapil, S. (2023). Selection determinants and value creation in private equity investment: A systematic literature review. *Journal of Indian Business Research*. Forthcoming.
	Ferrati, F., Muffatto, M. (2019). A systematic literature review of the assessment criteria applied by equity investors. Paper presented at the Proceedings of the European Conference on Innovation and Entrepreneurship, *ECIE*, 1 304–312.
	Chemmanur, T. J., Fulghieri, P. (2014). Entrepreneurial finance and innovation: An introduction and agenda for future research! *The Review of Financial Studies* 27 (1): 1–19
	Köhn, A. (2018). The determinants of startup valuation in the venture capital context: A systematic review and avenues for future research. *Management Review Quarterly*, 68(1): 3–36.
	Röhm, P. (2018). Exploring the landscape of corporate venture capital: A systematic review of the entrepreneurial and finance literature. *Management Review Quarterly*, 68(3), 279–319.
Deal structure & security design	Zambelli, S. (2014). 'If the facts don't fit the theory ... ': The security design puzzle in venture finance. *International Journal of Management Reviews*, 16(4), 500–520. doi:10.1111/ijmr.12032
	Burchardt, J., Hommel, U., Kamuriwo, D. S., Billitteri, C. (2016). Venture capital contracting in theory and practice: Implications for entrepreneurship research. *Entrepreneurship: Theory and Practice*, 40(1): 25–48.

(*Continued*)

(*Continued*)

Syndication	Jääskeläinen, M. (2012). Venture capital syndication: Synthesis and future directions. *International Journal of Management Reviews*, 14(4): 444–463.
Risks & performance	Silva Júnior, C.R., Mairesse Siluk, J.C., Neuenfeldt–Júnior, A.L., Binotto Francescatto, M., de Freitas Michelin, C. (2023). Mapping Risks Faced by Startup Investors: An Approach Based on the Apriori Algorithm. *Risks* 11(10): 1–19.
	Gohil, R. K., Vyas, V. (2016). Private equity performance: A literature review. *Journal of Private Equity*, 19(3): 76–88.
	Kaplan, S. N., Sensoy, B. A. (2015). Private equity performance: A survey. *Annual Review of Financial Economics*, 7: 597–614.

References

Acharya, V., Gottschalg, O., Hahn, M., and Kehoe, C. (2013). Corporate governance and value creation: Evidence from private equity. *Review of Financial Studies*, 26, 368–402.

Afyonoğlu, G. (2013). Alternative investments and due diligence. In H. K. Baker and G. Filbeck (Eds.), *Alternative Investments: Instruments, Performance, Benchmarks, and Strategies* (pp. 53–75). Wiley.

Asuamah, S. Y. (2023). Catalysing entrepreneurial growth: Unleashing the potential of venture capital and private equity in developing nations. MPRA Paper No. 117977.

Axelson, U., Strömberg, P., and Weisbach, M. (2009a). Why are buyouts levered? The financial structure of private equity firms. *Journal of Finance*, 64, 1549–1582.

Axelson, U., Weisbach, M., and Strömberg, P. (2009b). The financial structure of private equity funds. *Journal of Finance*, 64, 1549–1582.

Baldwin, A. (2012). Private equity and agency costs: An economic analysis. *Economic Affairs*, 32(3), 107–109.

Beck, T., Demirgüç-Kunt, A., and Levine, R. (2003). Law and finance: Why does legal origin matter? *Journal of Comparative Economics*, 31(4), 653–675.

Bellavitis, C., Kamuriwo, D. S., and Hommel, U. (2019). Mitigation of moral hazard and adverse selection in venture capital financing: The influence of the country's institutional setting. *Journal of Small Business Management*, 57(4), 1328–1349.

Bergemann, D. and Hege, U. (1998). Venture capital financing, moral hazard, and learning. *Journal of Banking and Finance*, 22(6-8), 703–735.

Bernile, G., Cumming, D., and Lyandres, E. (2007). The size of venture capital and private equity fund portfolios. *Journal of Corporate Finance*, 13(4), 564–590.

Bernstein, S., Giroud, X., and Townsend, R. R. (2016). The impact of venture capital monitoring. *Journal of Finance*, 71(4), 1591–1622.

Bernstein, S., Lerner, J., and Mezzanotti, F. (2019). Private equity and financial fragility during the crisis. *Review of Financial Studies*, 32(4), 1309–1373.

Bertoni, F., Colombo, M., D'Adda, D., and Grilli, L. (2010). Venture capital financing and the growth of new technology-based firms: Correcting for sample self-selection. In D. Audretsch, G. Dagnino, R. Faraci, and R. Hoskisson (Eds.), *New Frontiers in Entrepreneurship. International Studies in Entrepreneurship* (pp. 125–144). Springer.

Bertoni, F., D'Adda, D., and Grilli, L. (2016). Cherry-picking or frog-kissing? A theoretical analysis of how investors select entrepreneurial ventures in thin venture capital markets. *Small Business Economics*, 46(3), 391–405.

Bianchini, R. and Croce, A. (2022). The role of environmental policies in promoting venture capital investments in cleantech companies. *Review of Corporate Finance*, 2, 587–616.

Block, J., Fisch, C., Vismara, S., and Andres, R. (2019). Private equity investment criteria: An experimental conjoint analysis of venture capital, business angels, and family offices. *Journal of Corporate Finance*, 58, 329–352.

Bongini, P., Ferrando, A., Rossi, E., and Rossolini, M. (2021). SME access to market-based finance across Eurozone countries. *Small Business Economics*, 56(4), 1667–1697.

Bonini, S., Alkan, S., and Salvi, A. (2012). The effects of venture capitalists on the governance of firms. *Corporate Governance: An International Review*, 20, 21–45.

Bottazzi, L., Da Rin, M., and Hellmann, T. (2008). Who are the active investors? Evidence from venture capital. *Journal of Financial Economics*, 89(3), 488–512.

Brown, G. W., Gredil, O. R., and Kaplan, S. N. (2019). Do private equity funds manipulate reported returns? *Journal of Financial Economics*, 132(2), 267–297.

Brown, S., Fraser, T., and Liang, B. (2008). Hedge fund due diligence: A source of alpha in a hedge fund portfolio strategy. *Journal of Investment Management*, 6, 23–33.

Brown, R., Rocha, A., and Cowling, M. (2020). Financing entrepreneurship in times of crisis: Exploring the impact of COVID-19 on the market for entrepreneurial finance in the United Kingdom. *International Small Business Journal: Researching Entrepreneurship*, 38(5), 380–390.

Buchner, A., Espenlaub, S., Khurshed, A., and Mohamed, A. (2018). Cross-border venture capital investments: The impact of foreignness on returns. *Journal of International Business Studies*, 49(5), 575–604.

Burchardt, J., Hommel, U., Kamuriwo, D. S., and Billitteri, C. (2016). Venture capital contracting in theory and practice: Implications for entrepreneurship research. *Entrepreneurship: Theory and Practice*, 40(1), 25–48.

Burström, T., Lahti, T., Parida, V., Wartiovaara, M., and Wincent, J. (2023). A definition, review, and extension of global ecosystems theory: Trends, architecture and orchestration of global VCs and mechanisms behind unicorns. *Journal of Business Research*, 157, 113605.

Bygrave, W. D. (1988). The structure of the investment networks of venture capital firms. *Journal of Business Venturing*, 3, 137–157.

Camp, J. J. (2002). *Venture Capital Due Diligence*. Wiley.

Cancino, C. A., Merigo, J. M., Torres, J. P., and Diaz, D. (2018). A bibliometric analysis of venture capital research. *Journal of Economics, Finance and Administrative Science*, 23(45), 182–195.

Casamatta, C. (2003). Financing and advising: Optimal financial contracts with venture capitalists. *Journal of Finance*, 58(5), 2059–2086.

Cestone, G. (2014). Venture capital meets contract theory: Risky claims or formal control? *Review of Finance*, 18(3), 1097–1137.

Cestone, G. and White, L. (2003). Anticompetitive financial contracting: The design of financial claims. *Journal of Finance*, 58(5), 2109–2142.

Chahine, S., Filatotchev, I., Bruton, G. D., and Wright, M. (2021). Success by association: The impact of venture capital firm reputation trend on initial public offering valuations. *Journal of Management*, 47(2), 368–398.

Chahine, S., Saade, S., and Goergen, M. (2019). Foreign business activities, foreignness of the VC syndicate, and IPO value. *Entrepreneurship: Theory and Practice*, 43(5), 947–973.

Chemmanur, T. J. and Fulghieri, P. (2014). Entrepreneurial finance and innovation: An introduction and agenda for future research. *The Review of Financial Studies*, 27(1), 1–19.

Cleantech for Europe (2024). A cleantech investment plan for European competitiveness. Cleantech Group Investment Report.

Cohn, J. B., Hotchkiss, E. S., and Towery, E. M. (2022). Sources of value creation in private equity buyouts of private firms. *Review of Finance*, 26(2), 257–285.

Cornelli, F. and Yosha, O. (2003). Stage financing and the role of convertible debt. *Review of Economics Studies*, 70, 1–32.

Correia, M. D. R. and Meneses, R. F. C. (2021). Venture capital and the use of convertible securities and control rights covenants: A fuzzy set approach. *European Journal of Business Science and Technology*, 5(1), 5–20.

Cumming, D. (2005a). Agency costs, institutions, learning, and taxation in venture capital contracting. *Journal of Business Venturing*, 20(5), 573–622.

Cumming, D. (2005b). Capital structure in venture finance. *Journal of Corporate Finance*, 11(3), 550–585.

Cumming, D. (2006a). Adverse selection and capital structure: Evidence from venture capital. *Entrepreneurship Theory and Practice*, 30(2), 155–183.

Cumming, D. (2006b). The determinants of venture capital portfolio size: Empirical evidence. *Journal of Business*, 79, 1083–1126.

Cumming, D. (2007). United States venture capital financial contracting: Foreign securities. *Advances in Financial Economics*, 12(2), 405–444.

Cumming, D. (2008). Contracts and exits in venture capital finance. *Review of Financial Studies*, 21(5), 1947–1982.

Cumming, D. (2010). *Private Equity: Fund Types, Risks and Returns, and Regulation.* Wiley.

Cumming, D. (2012). *The Oxford Handbook of Private Equity.* Oxford University Press.

Cumming, D. and Dai, N. (2011). Limited attention, fund size and the valuation of venture capital backed companies. *Journal of Empirical Finance*, 18, 2–15.

Cumming, D. and Dai, N. (2012). The role of geographic proximity in venture capital. In D. Cumming (Ed.), *The Oxford Handbook of Venture Capital* (pp. 897–937). Oxford University Press.

Cumming, D., Fleming, G., and Schwienbacher, A. (2004). Venture capitalist value-added activities, fundraising and drawdowns. *Journal of Banking and Finance*, 29(2), 295–331.

Cumming, D., Fleming, G., and Schwienbacher, A. (2006). Legality and venture capital exits. *Journal of Corporate Finance*, 12(2), 214–245.

Cumming, D., Fleming, G., and Schwienbacher, A. (2009). Style drift in private equity. *Journal of Business Finance and Accounting*, 36(5–6), 645–678.

Cumming, D., Henriques, I., and Sadorsky, P. (2016a). Cleantech venture capital around the world. *International Review of Financial Analysis*, 44, 86–97.

Cumming, D. and Johan, S. (2008). Information asymmetries, agency costs and venture capital exit outcomes. *Venture Capital*, 10(3), 197–231.

Cumming, D. and Johan, S. (2014). *Venture Capital and Private Equity Contracting.* Elsevier Academic Press.

Cumming, D. and Johan, S. (2017). The problems with and promise of entrepreneurial finance. *Strategic Entrepreneurship Journal*, 11(3), 357–370.

Cumming, D., Johan, S., and Zhang, Y. (2019). The role of due diligence in crowdfunding platforms. *Journal of Banking and Finance*, 108, 1–17.

Cumming, D., Knill, A., and Syvrud, K. (2016b). Do international investors enhance private firm value? Evidence from venture capital. *Journal of International Business Studies*, 47(3), 347–373.

Cumming, D., Kumar, S., Lim, W. M., and Pandey, N. (2023). Mapping the venture capital and private equity research: A bibliometric review and future research agenda. *Small Business Economics*, 61(1), forthcoming.

Cumming, D. and MacIntosh, J. (2003). A cross-country comparison of full and partial venture capital exit. *Journal of Banking and Finance*, 27, 511–548.

Cumming, D. J., Mohammadi, A., and Zambelli, S. (2022). Misconduct risks, legal enforcement and venture capital networks. *European Financial Management*, 28(3), 607–650.

Cumming, D., Schmidt, D., and Walz, U. (2010). Legality and venture capital governance around the world. *Journal of Business Venturing*, 25(1), 54–72.

Cumming, D. and Walz, U. (2010). Private equity returns and disclosure around the world. *Journal of International Business Studies*, 41(4), 727–754.

Cumming, D. and Zambelli, S. (2010). Illegal buyouts. *Journal of Banking and Finance*, 34, 441–456.

Cumming, D. and Zambelli, S. (2013). Private equity performance under extreme regulation. *Journal of Banking and Finance*, 37, 1508–1523.

Cumming, D. and Zambelli, S. (2017). Due diligence and investee performance. *European Financial Management*, 23, 211–253.

Cumming, D. and Zambelli, S. (2019). Interpreting the M&A black box by thinking outside the box. In M. Wright, K. Amess, N. Bacon, and D. Siegel (Eds.), *The Routledge Companion to Management Buyouts* (pp. 51–73). Routledge Taylor and Francis.

Da Rin, M., Hellmann, T., and Puri, M. (2011). A survey of venture capital research. In G. Constantinides, M. Harris, and R. Stulz (Eds.), *Handbook of the Economics of Finance, Vol. 2.* North Holland.

Dai, N. (2022). Empirical research on private equity funds: A review of the past decade and future research opportunities. *Review of Corporate Finance*, 2, 427–450.

Dai, N. and Nahata, R. (2016). Cultural differences and cross-border venture capital syndication. *Journal of International Business Studies*, 47, 140–169.

De Clercq, D., Fried, V. H., Lehtonen, O., and Sapienza, H. J. (2006). An entrepreneur's guide to the venture capital galaxy. *Academy of Management Perspectives*, 20(3), 90–112.

De Clercq, D., Sapienza, H. J., and Crijns, H. (2005). The internationalization of venture capital firms: A research agenda. *Venture Capital*, 7(2-3), 127–152.

Devigne, D., Manigart, S., Vanacker, T., and Mulier, K. (2018). Venture capital internationalization: Synthesis and future research directions. *Journal of Economic Surveys*, 32(5), 1414–1445.

Dimov, D. and De Clercq, D. (2006). Venture capital investments strategy and portfolio failure rate: A longitudinal study. *Entrepreneurship Theory and Practice*, 30, 207–223.

Drover, W., Busenitz, L., Matusik, S., Townsend, D., Anglin, A., and Dushnitsky, G. (2017). A review and road map of entrepreneurial equity financing research: Venture capital, corporate venture capital, angel investment, crowdfunding, and accelerators. *Journal of Management*, 43, 1820–1853.

Duke, G. (2015). Sustainable private equity investments and ESG due diligence frameworks. In K. Wendt (Ed.), *Responsible Investment Banking. CSR, Sustainability, Ethics and Governance* (pp. 349–358). Springer.

The Economist (2005). Locust versus locust. May 26. Available at: http://www.economist.com/node/4010780.

The Economist (2009). Payback time. November 19. Available at: http://www.economist.com/node/14921335.

The Economist (2016). Private equity: The barbarian establishment. October 22. Available at: http://www.economist.com/news/briefing/21709007-private-equity-has-prospered-while-almost-every-other-approach-business-has-stumbled.

Ed-dafali, S., Chakir, A., and Bouzahir, B. (2016). Value-adding and monitoring activities of venture capital: A synthesis literature review. *Research Journal of Finance and Accounting*, 7(22), 66–75.

Esen, T., Dahl, M. S., and Sorenson, O. (2023). Jockeys, horses or teams? The selection of startups by venture capitalists. *Journal of Business Venturing Insights*, 19, e00383.

Espenlaub, S., Khurshed, A., and Mohamed, A. (2015). Venture capital exits in domestic and cross-border investments. *Journal of Banking and Finance*, 53, 215–232.

Ewelt-Knauer, C., Knauer, T., and Thielemann, M. (2014). Exit behaviour of investment companies: The choice of exit channel. *Journal of Business Economics*, 84(4), 571–607.

Ewens, M. and Farre-Mensa, J. (2020). The deregulation of the private equity markets and the decline in IPOs. *Review of Financial Studies*, 33(12), 5463–5509.

Ewens, M., Gorbenko, A., and Korteweg, A. (2022). Venture capital contracts. *Journal of Financial Economics*, 143(1), 131–158.

Ferran, E. (2011). The regulation of hedge funds and private equity in the EU. *European Business Organization Law Review*, 12, 379–414.

Ferrati, F. and Muffatto, M. (2019). A systematic literature review of the assessment criteria applied by equity investors. *Proceedings of the European Conference on Innovation and Entrepreneurship*, 1, 304–312.

Financial Services Authority [FSA] (2006). Private equity: A discussion of risk and regulatory engagement. November.

Fried, V. H. and Hisrich, R. (1994). Toward a model of venture capital decision making. *Financial Management*, 23(3), 28–37.

Fu, H., Yang, J., and An, Y. (2019). Contracts for venture capital financing with double-sided moral hazard. *Small Business Economics*, 53, 129–144.

Fuchs, F., Füss, R., Jenkinson, T., and Morkoetter, S. (2022). Should investors care where private equity managers went to school? *Review of Corporate Finance*, 2, 451–492.

Fuentelsaz, L., González, C., and Maicas, J. P. (2019). Formal institutions and opportunity entrepreneurship. The contingent role of informal institutions. *BRQ Business Research Quarterly*, 22(1), 5–24.

The Guardian (2007). Saviors or asset-strippers: The private equity debate. February 11. Available at: https://www.theguardian.com/business/2007/feb/11/workandcareers.politics.

The Guardian (2008). Taming the private equity 'locusts'. April 10. Available at: https://www.theguardian.com/commentisfree/2008/apr/10/tamingtheprivateequity.

Gerhardt, V., Siluk, J., Neuenfeldt Júnior, Á. L., Júnior, C. R. S., and Michelin, C. (2022). Evolution of start-up investments: An overview and future research directions. *International Journal of Business Innovation and Research*, 1(1), 1.

Gogineni, S. and Upadhyay, A. (2023). Venture capital and private equity investors, governance, and success of IPOs: Evidence from India. *Journal of Financial Research*, 46(2), 437–468.

Gohil, R. K. and Vyas, V. (2016). Private equity performance: A literature review. *Journal of Private Equity*, 19(3), 76–88.

Gompers, P. A. (1995). Optimal investment, monitoring, and the staging of venture capital. *The Journal of Finance*, 50(5), 1461–1489.

Gompers, P. A., Gornall, W., Kaplan, S. N., and Strebulaev, I. A. (2020). How do venture capitalists make decisions? *Journal of Financial Economics*, 135(1), 169–190.

Gompers, P. A., Kaplan, S. N., and Mukharlyamov, V. (2016). What do private equity firms say they do? *Journal of Financial Economics*, 121(3), 449–476.

Gompers, P. A., Kovner, A., and Lerner, J. (2009). Specialization and success: Evidence from venture capital. *Journal of Economics and Management Strategy*, 18(3), 817–844.

Gompers, P. A. and Lerner, J. (1996). The use of covenants: An empirical analysis of venture partnership agreements. *Journal of Law and Economics*, 39(2), 463–498.

Gompers, P. A. and Lerner, J. (2001). The venture capital revolution. *Journal of Economic Perspectives*, 15(2), 145–168.

Gompers, P. A. and Lerner, J. (2006). *The Venture Capital Cycle*. MIT Press.

Gorman, M. and Sahlman, W. A. (1989). What do venture capitalists do? *Journal of Business Venturing*, 4(4), 231–248.

Gornall, W. and Strebulaev, I. A. (2020). Squaring venture capital valuations with reality. *Journal of Financial Economics*, 135(1), 120–143.

Granz, C., Lutz, E., and Henn, M. (2021). Scout or coach? Value-added services as selection criteria in entrepreneurs' venture capitalist selection. *Venture Capital*, 23(1), 5–40.

Grilli, L., Latifi, G., and Mrkajic, B. (2019). Institutional determinants of venture capital activity: An empirically driven literature review and a research agenda. *Journal of Economic Surveys*, 33(4), 1094–1122.

Gruener, A. and Marburger, L. (2022). New insights into private equity: Empirical evidence from more than 500 buyouts. *Journal of Portfolio Management*, 48(9), 103–116.

Gu, Q. and Lu, X. (2014). Unraveling the mechanisms of reputation and alliance formation: A study of venture capital syndication in China. *Strategic Management Journal*, 35, 739–750.

Guler, I. and Guillén, M. (2010). Institutions and the internationalization of US venture capital firms. *Journal of International Business Studies*, 41, 185–205.

Hall, J. and Hofer, C. W. (1993). Venture capitalists' decision criteria in new venture evaluation. *Journal of Business Venturing*, 8(1), 25–42.

Hammer, B., Marcotty-Dehm, N., Schweizer, D., and Schwetzler, B. (2022). Pricing and value creation in private equity-backed buy-and-build strategies. *Journal of Corporate Finance*, 77, 102285.

Harrison, R. T. and Mason, C. M. (2019). Venture capital 20 years on: Reflections on the evolution of a field. *Venture Capital*, 21(1), 1–34.

Hellmann, T. (1998). The allocation of control rights in venture capital contracts. *RAND Journal of Economics*, 29(1), 57–76.

Hellmann, T. (2002). A theory of strategic venture investing. *Journal of Financial Economics*, 64, 285–314.

Hellmann, T. (2006). IPOs, acquisitions and the use of convertible securities in venture capital. *Journal of Financial Economics*, 81, 649–679.

Hellmann, T. and Puri, M. (2002a). On the fundamental role of venture capital. *Economic Review*, Q4, 19–23.

Hellmann, T. and Puri, M. (2002b). Venture capital and the professionalization of start-up firms: Empirical evidence. *Journal of Finance*, 57(1), 169–197.

Hsu, D. K., Haynie, J. M., Simmons, S. A., and McKelvie, A. (2014). What matters, matters differently: A conjoint analysis of the decision policies of angel and venture capital investors. *Venture Capital*, 16(1), 1–25.

Hsu, Y. W. (2010). Staging of venture capital investment: A real options analysis. *Small Business Economics*, 35(3), 265–281.

Hudson, E. and Evans, M. (2005). A review of research into venture capitalists' decision making: Implications for entrepreneurs, venture capitalists and researchers. *Journal of Economic and Social Policy*, 10, 45–63.

Invest Europe (2020). Investing in Europe: Private equity activity 2019. Online verfügbar unter: https://www.investeurope.eu/research/publications.

Jääskeläinen, M. (2012). Venture capital syndication: Synthesis and future directions. *International Journal of Management Reviews*, 14(4), 444–463.

Jelic, R. and Wright, M. (2011). Exits, performance, and late stage private equity: The case of UK management buy-outs. *European Financial Management*, 17, 560–593.

Jelic, R., Zhou, D., and Wright, M. (2019). Sustaining the buyout governance model: Inside secondary management buyout boards. *British Journal of Management*, 30(1), 30–52.

Johan, S. and Zhang, M. (2021). Information asymmetries in private equity: Reporting frequency, endowments, and governance. *Journal of Business Ethics*, 174(1), 199–220.

Kaplan, S. N., Martel, F., and Strömberg, P. (2007). How do legal differences and learning affect financial contracts? *Journal of Financial Intermediation*, 16(3), 273–311.

Kaplan, S. N. and Sensoy, B. A. (2015). Private equity performance: A survey. *Annual Review of Financial Economics*, 7, 597–614.

Kaplan, S. N., Sensoy, B. A., and Strömberg, P. (2009). Should investors bet on the jockey or the horse? Evidence from the evolution of firms from early business plans to public companies. *Journal of Finance*, 64(1), 75–115.

Kaplan, S. N. and Strömberg, P. (2000). How do venture capitalists choose investments? Discussion Paper, Department of Economics, University of Chicago.

Kaplan, S. N. and Strömberg, P. (2001). Venture capitalists as principals: Contracting, screening, and monitoring. *The American Economic Review*, 91(2), 426–430.

Kaplan, S. N. and Strömberg, P. (2003). Financial contracting theory meets the real world: An empirical analysis of venture capital contracts. *The Review of Economic Studies*, 70(2), 281–315.

Kaplan, S. N. and Strömberg, P. (2004). Characteristics, contracts, and actions: Evidence from venture capitalist analyses. *The Journal of Finance*, 59, 2177–2210.

Kaplan, S. N. and Strömberg, P. (2009). Leveraged buyouts and private equity. *Journal of Economic Perspectives*, 23(1), 121–146.

Khanin, D., Baum, J. R., Mahto, R. V., and Heller, C. (2008). Venture capitalists' investment criteria: 40 years of research. *Small Business Institute Research Review*, 35(1), 187–192.

Knill, A. M. (2009). Should venture capitalists put all their eggs in one basket? Diversification versus pure play strategies in venture capital. *Financial Management*, 38, 441–486.

Köhn, A. (2018). The determinants of startup valuation in the venture capital context: A systematic review and avenues for future research. *Management Review Quarterly*, 68(1), 3–36.

Koenig, L. and Burghof, H. P. (2022). The investment style drift puzzle and risk-taking in venture capital. *Review of Corporate Finance*, 2, 527–585.

Korteweg, A. (2019). Risk adjustment in private equity returns. *Annual Review of Financial Economics*, 11, 131–152.

Korteweg, A. and Sorensen, M. (2017). Skill and luck in private equity performance. *Journal of Financial Economics*, 124(3), 535–562.

Kortum, S. and Lerner, J. (2000). Assessing the contribution of venture capital to innovation. *RAND Journal of Economics*, 31(4), 674–692.

Krohmer, P., Lauterbach, R., and Calanog, V. F. M. (2009). The bright and dark side of staging: Investment performance and the varying motivations of private equity firms. *Journal of Banking and Finance*, 33(9), 1597–1609.

Kut, C., Pramborg, B., and Smolarski, J. (2007). Managing financial risk and uncertainty: The case of venture capital and buy-out funds. *Global Business and Organizational Excellence*, 26(2), 53–64.

La Porta, R., Lopez-de-Silanes, F., and Shleifer, A. (2006). What works in securities laws? *Journal of Finance*, 61, 1–32.

Lerner, J. (1994a). Venture capitalists and the decision to go public. *Journal of Financial Economics*, 35, 317–348.

Lerner, J. (1994b). The syndication of venture capital investments. *Financial Management*, 23, 16–27.

Lerner, J. (1995). Venture capitalists and the oversight of private firms. *Journal of Finance*, 50, 301–319.

Lerner, J. (2002). When bureaucrats meet entrepreneurs: The design of effective 'public venture capital' programmes. *The Economic Journal*, 112, 73–84.

Lerner, J. (2012). *The Architecture of Innovation: The Economics of Creative Organizations*. Harvard Business Review Press.

Lerner, J. and Nanda, R. (2020). Venture capital's role in financing innovation: What we know and how much we still need to learn. *Journal of Economic Perspectives*, 34(3), 237–261.

Lerner, J. and Schoar, A. (2005). Does legal enforcement affect financial transactions? The contractual channel in private equity. *Quarterly Journal of Economics*, 120, 223–246.

Lerner, J. and Schoar, A. (2010). International differences in entrepreneurial finance. *Journal of Financial Economics*, 96(3), 487–508.

Levasseur, L., Johan, S., and Eckhardt, J. (2022). Mixed methods in venture capital research: An illustrative study and directions for future work. *British Journal of Management*, 33(1), 26–45.

Li, M., Chen, H., Chen, R., and Pan, Z. (2020a). Venture capital and firm innovation: A comprehensive review and future research agenda. *Journal of Business Research*, 108, 106–116.

Li, X., Ding, S., Li, J., and Xie, E. (2020b). The role of venture capital in the innovation performance of high-tech firms: A meta-analysis. *Research Policy*, 49(5), 103976.

Li, Y. and Zahra, S. (2012). Formal institutions, culture, and venture capital activity: A cross-country analysis. *Journal of Business Venturing*, 27, 95–111.

Lichtenthaler, U. (2021). Navigating regulatory and legal challenges in international entrepreneurship. *Journal of International Business Studies*, 52(4), 615–639.

Liu, Y. and Nguyen, C. (2021). The role of financial covenants in pricing private investments in public equity. *Journal of Corporate Finance*, 82, 102466.

MacMillan, I. C., Siegel, R., and Narasimha, P. N. (1985). Criteria used by venture capitalists to evaluate new venture proposals. *Journal of Business Venturing*, 1(1), 119–128.

MacMillan, I. C., Zemann, L., and Subbanarasimha, P. N. (1987). Criteria distinguishing successful from unsuccessful ventures in the venture screening process. *Journal of Business Venturing*, 2(2), 123–137.

Manigart, S., Lockett, A., Meuleman, M., Wright, M., Landström, H., Bruining, H., Desbrières, P., and Hommel, U. (2006). Venture capitalists' decision to syndicate. *Entrepreneurship: Theory and Practice*, 30(2), 131–153.

Matusik, S. F. and Fitza, M. A. (2012). Diversification in the venture capital industry: Leveraging knowledge under uncertainty. *Strategic Management Journal*, 33(4), 407–426.

McGrath, P. J. and Nerkar, A. (2023). Private equity: Antecedents, outcomes, mediators, and moderators. *Journal of Management*, 49(1), 158–195.

Metrick, A. and Yasuda, A. (2010). The economics of private equity funds. *Review of Financial Studies*, 23(6), 2303–2341.

Metrick, A. and Yasuda, A. (2011). Venture capital and other private equity: A survey. *European Financial Management*, 17(4), 619–654.

Metrick, A. and Yasuda, A. (2021). *Venture Capital and the Finance of Innovation*. Wiley.

Meuleman, M., Wright, M., Manigart, S., and Lockett, A. (2009). Private equity syndication: Agency costs, reputation and collaboration. *Journal of Business Finance and Accounting*, 36(5-6), 616–644.

Motoyama, Y., Cao, C., and Appelbaum, R. (2020a). Navigating the innovation ecosystem: Policy and research challenges. *Research Policy*, 49(1), 103868.

Motoyama, Y., Cao, J., Fryer, K., and Hardré, P. (2020b). Globalization and innovation in developing countries: A systematization and review of research. *World Development*, 125, 104678.

Nahata, R. (2008). Venture capital reputation and investment performance. *Journal of Financial Economics*, 90(2), 127–151.

Nahata, R., Hazarika, S., and Tandon, K. (2014). Success in global venture capital investing: Do institutional and cultural differences matter? *Journal of Financial and Quantitative Analysis*, 49, 1039–1070.

Petitt, B. (2014). The return of the leveraged buyout 'locusts'. *Financial Times*.

Phalippou, L. and Gottschalg, O. (2009). The performance of private equity funds. *The Review of Financial Studies*, 22(4), 1747–1776.

Porsgaard, C. B., Haubjerg, M., and Hansen, Z. N. L. (2018). A framework for operational due diligence. *Production Engineering*, 12(5), 633–645.

Quas, A., Martí, J., and Reverte, C. (2021). What money cannot buy: A new approach to measure venture capital ability to add non-financial resources. *Small Business Economics*, 57(3), 1361–1382.

Rawal, V. and Kapil, S. (2023). Selection determinants and value creation in private equity investment: A systematic literature review. *Journal of Indian Business Research*, forthcoming.

Ritter, J. (1987). The costs of going public. *Journal of Financial Economics*, 19, 269–281.

Röhm, P. (2018). Exploring the landscape of corporate venture capital: A systematic review of the entrepreneurial and finance literature. *Management Review Quarterly*, 68(3), 279–319.

Sahlman, W. A. (1990). The structure and governance of venture capital organizations. *Journal of Financial Economics*, 27, 473–521.

Sahlman, W. A. (1999). Some thoughts on business plans. In W. A. Sahlman, H. H. Stevenson, M. J. Roberts, and A. Bhide (Eds.), *The Entrepreneurial Venture* (pp. 138–176). Harvard Business School Press.

Sannajust, A. and Groh, A. (2023). Pioneering management buy-out and entrepreneurial finance research: Mike Wright's research legacy. *Small Business Economics*, 60(1), 1–35.

Scharfman, J. A. (2012). *Private Equity Operational Due Diligence: Tools to Evaluate Liquidity, Valuation, and Documentation.* Wiley.

Schmidt, K. M. (2003). Convertible securities and venture capital finance. *Journal of Finance*, 58(3), 1139–1166.

Siems, M. (2005). What does not work in comparing securities laws: A critique on La Porta et al.'s methodology. *International Company and Commercial Law Review*, 16, 300–305.

Silva Júnior, C. R., Mairesse Siluk, J. C., Neuenfeldt-Júnior, A. L., Binotto Francescatto, M., and de Freitas Michelin, C. (2023). Mapping risks faced by startup investors: An approach based on the Apriori algorithm. *Risks*, 11(10), 1–19.

Smith, E. E., Smith, J. K., and Smith, R. L. (2022). Bias in the reporting of venture capital performance: The disciplinary role of FOIA. *Review of Corporate Finance*, 3, 493–525.

Sorensen, M. (2007). How smart is smart money? A two-sided matching model of venture capital. *Journal of Finance*, 62(6), 2725–2762.

Stanfield, J. (2020). Skill, syndication, and performance: Evidence from leveraged buyouts. *Journal of Corporate Finance*, 65, 1–22.

Stein, B. (2006). On buyouts, there ought to be a law. *The New York Times*, September 3. Available at: http://www.nytimes.com/2006/09/03/business/yourmoney/03every.html.

Stowell, D. P. and Stowell, P. (2023). Overview of private equity. In D. P. Stowell and P. Stowell (Eds.), *Investment Banks, Hedge Funds, and Private Equity* (pp. 357–390), forthcoming.

Suchard, J. A. (2009). The impact of venture capital backing on the corporate governance of Australian initial public offerings. *Journal of Banking and Finance*, 33(4), 765–774.

Talmor, E. and Vasvari, F. (2011). *International Private Equity.* Wiley.

Tian, X. (2011). The causes and consequences of venture capital stage financing. *Journal of Financial Economics*, 101(1), 132–159.

Tian, X. (2012). The role of venture capital syndication in value creation for entrepreneurial firms. *Review of Finance*, 16(1), 245–283.

Torres, J. P. (2020). The venture capital feedback cycle: A critical review and future directions. *Entrepreneurship Research Journal.* doi:10.1515/erj-2017-0205

Tyebjee, T. and Bruno, A. V. (1984). A model of venture capitalist investment activity. *Management Science*, 30, 1051–1066.

Tykvova, T. (2007). What do economists tell us about venture capital contracts? *Journal of Economic Surveys*, 21(1), 65–89.

Tykvova, T. (2018). Venture capital and private equity financing: An overview of recent literature and an agenda for future research. *Journal of Business Economics*, 88(3-4), 325–362.

Wall Street Journal (2005). German party calls investors 'locusts'. Available at: https://www.wsj.com/articles/SB111498371843621593.

Wang, M., Rieger, M. O., and Hens, T. (2017). The impact of culture on loss aversion. *Journal of Behavioral Decision Making*, 30, 270–281.

Wang, H., Weisheng, L., Soderlund, J., and Chen, K. (2018). The interplay between formal and informal institutions in projects: A social network analysis. *Project Management Journal*, 49, 20–35.

Wangerin, D. (2019). M&A due diligence, post-acquisition performance, and financial reporting for business combinations. *Contemporary Accounting Research*, 36(4), 2344–2378.

Wilson, N., Amini, S., and Wright, M. (2022). Determining the characteristics of the private equity targets: UK evidence. *British Journal of Management*, 33(1), 138–159.

Wood, G. and Wright, M. (2009). Private equity: A review and synthesis. *International Journal of Management Reviews*, 11(4), 361–380.

Wright, M. (2019). Entrepreneurship, context, and buyouts. In M. Wright, K. Amess, N. Bacon, and D. Siegel (Eds.), *The Routledge Companion to Management Buyouts* (pp. 406–417). Routledge Taylor and Francis.

Wright, M., Amess, K., Weir, C., and Girma, S. (2009). Private equity and corporate governance: Retrospect and prospect. *Corporate Governance: An International Review*, 17(3), 353–375.

Wright, M. and Robbie, K. (1996). Venture capitalists, unquoted equity investment appraisal and the role of accounting information. *Accounting and Business Research*, 26(2), 153–168.

Wright, M. and Robbie, K. (1998). Venture capital and private equity: A review and synthesis. *Journal of Business Finance and Accounting*, 25(5-6), 521–570.

Wright, M., Pruthi, S., and Lockett, A. (2005). International venture capital research: From cross-country comparisons to crossing borders. *International Journal of Management Reviews*, 7(3), 135–165.

Yung, C. (2009). Entrepreneurial financing and costly due diligence. *Financial Review*, 44(1), 137–149.

Yung, C. (2019). Entrepreneurial manipulation with staged financing. *Journal of Banking and Finance*, 100, 273–282.

Zacharakis, A. L. and Meyer, G. D. (1995). The venture capitalist decision: Understanding process versus outcome. *Frontiers of Entrepreneurship Research*, 465–478.

Zacharakis, A. L. and Meyer, G. D. (1998). A lack of insight: Do venture capitalists really understand their own decision process? *Journal of Business Venturing*, 13(1), 57–76.

Zambelli, S. (2012). Private equity governance and financing decisions. In D. Cumming (Ed.), *The Oxford Handbook of Private Equity* (pp. 156–196). Oxford University Press.

Zambelli, S. (2014). 'If the facts don't fit the theory...': The security design puzzle in venture finance. *International Journal of Management Reviews*, 16(4), 500–520.

Zambelli, S. (2024). Due diligence in private equity. In D. Cumming and B. Hammer (Eds.), *The Palgrave Encyclopedia of Private Equity*. Palgrave Macmillan, forthcoming.

https://doi.org/10.1142/9781800617032_0006

Chapter 6

The Importance of Governance in Private Equity Financing

Michael Robinson
Haskayne School of Business, The University of Calgary, Calgary, Canada

6.1. Introduction

While many individuals have dreams of becoming an entrepreneur, only one in ten will ever take the first step to actually create a business to exploit a perceived opportunity. Of those who do pursue their dream, only 40% will create defendable IP or develop a distinct product or service, which allows their venture to enter the development stage. Across all ventures, only 7.2% will exit this stage as an independent entity. Even those entrepreneurs who are able to attract at least one round of venture capital financing will have difficulties finding success, as 30–40% will fail completely, while 95% will fail to achieve their pre-investment objectives (Gage, 2012).

Part of the problem is that most entrepreneurs, especially first-time ones, have an extremely limited understanding of what it takes to build an effective venture. Many of a successful entrepreneur's required activities are interpersonal in nature, e.g. persuading, negotiating, and selling, and most first-time entrepreneurs have limited capacity in these critical areas. More importantly, they have no idea that they even need these skills and are subject to the well-known psychological phenomenon called the Dunning–Kruger effect, in which individuals with low ability in a certain area mistakenly overestimate their own abilities. Due to this effect, '...people who are unskilled in these domains suffer a dual burden. Not only do these people reach erroneous conclusions and make unfortunate choices, but their incompetence robs them of the metacognitive ability to realize it' (Kruger and Dunning, 1999, p. 1121).

Entrepreneurs also have an unrealistic understanding of their chances of success. As noted by Cooper *et al.* (1988), a survey of entrepreneurs founds that 81% of respondents set their odds of success at seven out of ten, while 33% believed that they had a 100% chances of success. These statistics are significantly different from actual success rates, and the authors note that '...the assessment by entrepreneurs of their own likelihood of success was dramatically detached from past macro statistics, from perceived prospects for peer firms, and from characteristics typically associated with higher performing new firms' (Cooper *et al.*, 1988, p. 97).

Practical guidance for entrepreneurs to increase their chance of success was provided by Blank (2003), and those ideas evolved into the lean start-up model (Ries, 2011; Blank, 2013). According to Blank, the reason that most start-ups fail is that they do not develop a sustainable business model (Zimmerman, 2015). The lean start-up model recommends that an entrepreneur focus on customer development, agile engineering, and building minimum viable products to test with potential customers. Although developed by practitioners, the model has been adopted and extended by entrepreneurship scholars. The entrepreneurship academic literature recommends that entrepreneurs should focus their attention on product development, determining market orientation, and pivoting their venture's business model as required.

Missing from the lean start-up model are important questions such as how an entrepreneur can attract the required resources, notably human and financial capital, needed to operate the business while it is searching for the scalable business model. According to an analysis of 473 start-ups conducted in 2017 by CB Insights, the number one reason (40%) for failure was a lack of a business model (Skynova, 2023). By 2022, this reason accounted for only 16% of failures, and the number one cited reason for failures in that year was a lack of financing and investors (47%), which led to the venture running out of cash (40%). The importance of being able to access financing is reinforced by the finding that 40% of founders reported a need to pivot their business model to achieve success.

While startup financing is becoming an increasingly important issue, Cumming and Vismara (2017) identify that segmentation between the entrepreneurship strategy and the finance literature has limited the ability of researchers to identify the factors that affect the availability and timing of start-up financing. The entrepreneurial finance literature does note, however, that firm growth is accelerated and the probability of venture survival is increased if a venture if able to attract financing from angel groups or VCs (Cooper *et al.*, 1994; Davila *et al.*, 2003; Audretsch and Lehmann, 2004; Bertoni *et al.*, 2011; Clarysse *et al.*, 2013; Cavallo *et al.*, 2019). Such financing will also increase a venture's innovation (Cumming and Groh, 2018; Parpaleix *et al.*, 2019).

Although the data show that attracting financing is becoming increasingly important for venture survival, Cumming *et al.* (2019) identify that many ventures have difficulty attracting capital due to the high degree of information asymmetry associated with a startup (Cumming and Groh, 2018). This issue is even more difficult to overcome for first-time entrepreneurs (Cumming *et al.*, 2019), who are also limited by their low level of personal wealth (Andersen and Nielsen, 2012).

There is also a gap between the issues of interest to academics and practitioners. As Achtenhagen *et al.* (2010) note, academics measure success based on sales and accounting measures, while practitioners are most concerned with organisational development measures. Another interesting finding from the CB Insights data was that disharmony among the founding team and with investors was the fourth most common reason (21%) for startup failure in 2022.

Burton *et al.* (2019) note that although building an effective organisation is critical to future success, there is a lack of guidance for entrepreneurs about how to accomplish this task. Organisational development requires hiring quality employees at the correct stages of growth, creating a compensation system to align employee incentives with corporate objectives, and developing a robust governance structure. Governance entails several issues, including the creation of a corporate structure and decision-making processes that serve to attract employees, effective mentors, qualified directors, and investors willing to support the corporation's development. Effective governance is an important element of building a successful venture and should be a key consideration for an entrepreneur even during the very early stages of their corporation. This perspective is reinforced by an interview with a leading early-stage legal practitioner who started: 'I think the primary reason that many entrepreneurs fail, or their corporations just fizzles out is that they do not develop the structures or the networks that are key for their success ... I mean that too often the focus is on the product and the customer without regard to proper governance and corporate structures' (Robinson, 2023, p. 4).

The remainder of this chapter addresses the critical issue of how an entrepreneur can establish an effective, scalable governance structure and highlights the governance challenges that will be faced at various stages of corporate growth. It also discusses how an examination of a corporation's governance structure is a key aspect of a sophisticated investor's due diligence process and how institutional investors will make the establishment of a specific governance structure a requirement before committing financial capital. The chapter also identifies the way in which effective governance can be of value to a corporation developing sustainable cleantech solutions. Table 6.1 provides an overview of the key governance agreements that should be developed during the different stages of a corporation's development. In addition, it discusses the purpose of each type of agreement and provides a listing of key references. Further details about these agreements are as follows.

Table 6.1. Recommended governance mechanisms by stage of corporate development.

Governance agreement	Importance of this agreement	References
Pre-Seed Stage		
Founders' Agreement	To establish the expected future relationship among cofounders and between each cofounder and the corporation. This will identify expectations with respect to work assignment, the requirement to provide investment capital, and the allocation of shares between cofounders.	Wasserman (2012), Thiel (2014), Barron and Green (2020), and Kagan *et al.* (2020)
Share Vesting Agreement	To provide an incentive for founders and other key employees to remain fully engaged with the corporation as it develops.	Hodak (2014, 2019) and Core and Packard (2022)
IP Assignment Agreement	To ensure that all intellectual property (IP) brought to the corporation by a cofounder or that is developed within the corporation remains the property of the corporation.	Ganor (2019) and Barron and Green (2020)
Confidentiality Agreement	To ensure that critical IP, including formal IP such as patents, as well as business practices and related information are protected from potential competitors.	McBratney and Downie (2011), Anonymous (2018), and Hrdy and Seaman (2024)
Seed Stage		
Advisor Agreement	A first step in developing external-oriented governance is to attract a set of advisors who will provide valuable guidance to the cofounders while accepting the personal liability of a director.	Fanimokun *et al.* (2012), Kurato *et al.* (2021), and Penaskovic (2023)
Employment Agreement	To clearly identify the responsibilities of critical first and ongoing employee hires.	Burton *et al.* (2019), Meyerowitz and Spears (2021), and Knuppel (2022)

(*Continued*)

The value of a thoughtful founders' agreement is highlighted by the following quote from a seasoned VC investor: 'Founders' agreements are very important and shouldn't be overlooked, especially as it relates to founder vesting. The reality is that many founding teams are going to have some sort of issue come up at some point. If you're going to have a team of three or four people in the company, one or two of those people may eventually realize that it's not the right fit for them anymore or they want to go off and work somewhere else. You have to have some sort of mechanism in place that allows for a smooth transition that doesn't destroy the company' (Robinson, 2023, p. 79).

Additional problems can arise as a corporation starts operations. The founding team members are likely the sole shareholders, who then appoint themselves as directors, and serving as directors hire themselves as officers (managers). At this stage of development, the significant overlap in the corporate roles means that the corporation has a founder-controlled governance model. The founding team members may not realise that each role has certain responsibilities and that a failure to make an explicit distinction as to what role they are serving when they make corporate decisions can lead to future issues.

As directors and officers, the founders have a fiduciary duty to act in the best interest of all shareholders (US) or the best interest of the corporation (Canada and many other countries). In the US, this entails having a consideration of the interests of other shareholders when making corporate decisions, while in Canada and many other countries, this duty requires considering the interests of a diverse group of external stakeholders. A violation of their fiduciary duty will expose the directors and officers to potential litigation if their decisions are questioned in the future. Establishing an effective decision-making process and maintaining appropriate records are two of the best ways for a fiduciary to mitigate this risk.

6.2.2. *Seed stage*

As the corporation grows, the founders will need to begin accessing outside resources, including people, technology, and financing. A significant problem with the founder-controlled governance structure is that corporate decisions will be made solely from an insider perspective, without the benefit of external insights. Outside perspectives are valuable in that they challenge the founding teams' assumptions and bring a different set of perspectives to the decision-making process (Hill *et al.*, 2021). While the founders may not be willing, or able, to attract high-quality individuals to serve as corporate directors during the development stage, they should seek to add high-quality informal mentors or formal advisors. Mentors or advisors are chosen for their ability to provide guidance to the founders with respect to a specific issue, as opposed to having to have a complete understanding of the corporation's business as is required for a corporate director. A best practice when adding formal advisors to a corporation is to develop an advisory agreement for each such individual that clearly outlines their expected contributions in terms of time and skills, as well as how they will be compensated (Fanimokun *et al.*, 2012; Kurato *et al.*, 2021; Penaskovic, 2023).

The importance of mentors has been well established in previous studies, and such support is often found in an accelerator programme. To benefit from such a programme, founders must be willing to listen to and consider guidance, as Kuratoko *et al.* (2021) report that more coachable entrepreneurs receive greater benefits from engagement with an accelerator. In a study of the Creative Destruction Lab Rockies (CDL-Rockies) programme, a member of one of the world's leading accelerator programmes. Robinson (2022) finds that a founder's ability to attract mentors is significantly enhanced if they can demonstrate an understanding of the importance of governance and are committed to developing a governance structure that can attract financing. The CDL-Rockies programme requires founders to participate in a series of five meetings spaced two months apart. During each meeting, a founder is required to develop a set of two to four key deliverables, which will dramatically accelerate their venture's development that they will accomplish before the next meeting. Continuation in the programme requires that at least one mentor in each meeting agrees to provide guidance until the next meeting. The study found that founders who focused solely on product/market fit issues were able to attract a mentor 72.8% of the time, but a founder who also focused on building a governance structure and attracting financing significantly increased their odds to 90.7%. The findings illustrate the importance that sophisticated mentors place on founders understanding the importance of having a balanced perspective of their corporation's development needs and being committed to developing effective governance.

The mentors in the CDL-Rockies programme are predominately angel investors (wealthy individuals), with there being a limited number of VC investors willing to serve in that role. There is a programme expectation that these mentors will also choose to invest in some of the programme's ventures. In most cases, angel investors will not require explicit governance mechanisms before making their investment and will invest in a simple agreement for future equity (SAFE) security to minimise the administrative burden associated with the financing. Robinson and Cottrell (2007) find evidence that angel investors use a staged financing approach to minimise their investment risk. Under this approach, an angel investor will provide the founder with a limited amount of capital to observe how their venture develops and how they behave and, if satisfied with both criteria, will invest increasing amounts of capital over time.

As the founders' corporation continues to grow, it will continue to hire employees, and effective governance requires the development of employment agreements (Burton *et al.*, 2019; Meyerowitz and Spears, 2021; Knuppel, 2022) and non-compete agreements to protect corporate value (Starr *et al.*, 2018; Marx, 2022). Also, an employee stock ownership plan (ESOP) is helpful both to attract and retain talented employees (Sullivan, 1977; Buxton and Gilbert, 2004; Gilmore, 2022). The corporation will also likely attract financing from external individual investors, including employees, relationship investors (family, friends, and business associates), and angel investors.

6.2.3. *Series A stage and beyond*

As the corporation continues to grow, the financing needs may begin to exceed the capital available from individual investors, and institutional capital may be sought from venture capitalists (VCs) or other private equity (PE) investors. To help minimise future disputes and create a framework that will allow the corporation to attract institutional financing in a later financing round, good governance requires the development of a unanimous shareholders' agreement

(USA) (Kaplan and Stromberg, 2001; Denis, 2004; Anonymous, 2010; Cumming and Groh, 2018; Pollman, 2019; Braut Filipović, 2022).

Certain investors may be able to serve as mentors, formal advisors, or even corporate directors depending on their background and skill level. Even in the case where an investor joins the board of directors, the majority of the board will still be made up of founders, and the corporation will continue to have a founder-controlled governance structure. If founders do decide to add non-founder directors to their board, then it is important that they choose highly qualified individuals who will challenge management assumptions, ask tough questions about proposed alternatives, and provide expert advice. Unfortunately, this is not always the case, as some founders are not willing to be challenged. As one highly experienced VC investor noted, 'Some founders are looking to add friends to their board who will agree with them. This is not helpful for the founder, nor is it a good use of time for a board member. ... All too frequently, board meetings become sales updates by a CEO to ensure continued support. That simply becomes a reporting board, which is a tax on time and energy and does not increase the likelihood of success' (Robinson, 2023, p. 76).

VC and PE investors have a fiduciary duty to their limited partner (LP) investors who have provided them with their capital and, as such, engage in an extensive due diligence process before making an investment. A major part of the due diligence process is examining the governance structure of the corporation. As noted by a seasoned angel and VC investor, 'The current model of venture and institutional investing is that we get way more demand than we have supply. And we're looking for a reason to say no. Governance is absolutely the easiest one to say no to, and I've seen it time and time again' (Robinson, 2023, p. 60).

A successful US-based tech entrepreneur who wrote a best-selling book about how to build a successful start-up also identifies the critical importance of evaluating a start-up's team as part of the due diligence process. They state, 'Now when I consider investing in a startup, I study the founding teams. Technical abilities and complimentary skill sets matter, but how well the founders know each other and how well they work together matter just as much' (Thiel, 2014, p. 109).

If a founder's corporation passes an institutional investor's due diligence process, that investor will then negotiate extensive contracts to establish governance, control mechanisms, and other protections to manage their investment risk (Kaplan and Stromberg, 2001; Denis, 2004; Cumming and Groh, 2018). In discussing the relationship between governance and financing, it is worthwhile making a distinction between corporate governance and PE governance. Corporate governance entails the mechanisms that are in place to provide oversight and guidance to the corporation's senior managers as they work to create value on a daily basis. A key element of an effective corporate governance system is a well-structured board of directors. Such a board provides three key functions to the corporation: oversight of the managers who operate the corporation on a day-to-day basis, providing foresight to those managers as they develop strategy, and offering insights and mentorship to help those managers become more effective when discharging their roles (Colombo and Grilli, 2010). Key board responsibilities include overseeing the strategic planning process, ensuring that key corporate risks have been identified and are being managed, that there are effective human performance systems in place to ensure an orderly succession of key management roles, the development of an appropriate compensation policy, and that the internal controls and financing reporting systems are robust (Canadian Securities Administrators, 2005; Columbo and Grilli, 2010; Canadian Coalition for Good Governance, 2014; Robinson, 2023).

The usual structure for the board of a VC-backed corporation includes five directors: two nominated by the founders, two nominees of the VC investor(s), and one independent director mutually agreeable to the founders and investors. This is called a shared-control governance structure and requires that founder nominees work collaboratively with the other directors to create long-term corporate value. It is important for all directors to realise that no matter who appointed them to the board, their fiduciary duty when serving as a director is to all shareholders (US) or to the corporation (Canada and other countries).

An employee of a VC fund who also serves as a director on a corporation in which that fund has invested is a dual fiduciary. That individual owes a fiduciary duty to the LP investors who invested in their fund but, when serving as a director of an investee corporation, also has a fiduciary duty to that corporation. It is important for this individual to realise that their duty to the corporation has priority so that a VC nominee to the board of an investee corporation must take off their investor hat before entering the board room and put on their director hat.

Unfortunately, not all institutional investors have a strong understanding of how to separate their investor role from their director role. One founder described a situation where they were being asked by investor-nominated directors during a board meeting to agree to vote their shares a certain way in an upcoming shareholder meeting and to have that agreement noted in the board meeting minutes. This pressure being exerted on the founder was inappropriate for two key reasons. First, a board meeting is not the appropriate place to discuss how shareholders should, or should not, vote on a certain issue. The board meeting is where corporate, not individual shareholder, decisions are made. Second, the decision that these investor-nominated directors favoured would benefit their position as investors but would disadvantage other investors. These investor-nominated directors were in a conflict-of-interest position when pushing for a certain decision that would benefit their investment and thus were violating their fiduciary duty in that board meeting. The best practice when a board member is in a conflict-of-interest position with respect to a corporate decision is for that director to declare their conflict and avoid voting on the specific decision.

Another way for a VC investor to avoid being in a conflict-of-interest position while serving as a corporate director of an investee corporation is to seek the ability to influence corporate decisions as an investor instead of as a director. This will allow those individuals to discharge their fiduciary duty to their LP investors without violating their director duties. PE governance provides these investors with the ability to mitigate their investment risk by developing certain mechanisms. These mechanisms result from negotiations between the external investors, typically institutional VC and PE investors, and the corporation that lead to the development of a series of contracts. For example, many agreements allow the VC to influence corporate decisions by having the ability to veto certain decisions of the corporate board and senior managers. Second, the mechanisms include the corporation allowing the investor to purchase a specific type of security with superior rights to those of other investors. Such a security is designed to limit the downside risk of the institutional investor's investment while maximising its upside potential (Feld and Mendelson, 2019; Pollman, 2019; Grantmyre and Unruch, 2024; Wilson Sonsini ECP, 2024). Securities regulations preclude the use of these mechanisms in publicly traded corporations as they place certain investors in an advantageous position compared with other investors.

During the development stage, VC and PE investors typically purchase preferred shares that are convertible into common shares. Such a security provides those investors with some downside protection, in that they have a priority claim over common shareholders in a liquidation situation. Data with respect to the characteristics of the securities purchased by development-stage institutional investors in 2023 are available from sources in the US and Canada (see Table 6.2). The data show that all these investors purchased preferred shares, which have superior liquidation rights to those of common shareholders. In the US and Canada, 90% of these financings have a 1× liquidation preference, which allows the investor to either receive all their investments back before the common shareholders or convert their preferred shares into common shares and receive their pro-rata share of the liquidation proceeds. There are additional data that show how many of the US and Canadian financings entailed preferred shares with participation rights. These rights allow the investor to receive one or more times their investment back and then receive

Table 6.2. Early-stage investor preferred share characteristics in the US and Canada, 2023 (percentage of financings with a given characteristic).

Preferred share characteristics	US (%)	Canada (%)
Liquidation preference	100	100
• 1× liquidation	90	90
• Participating preference	8 (No Cap) 2 (Capped)	9
• Senior preferred with preference	26	26
Anti-dilution protection (weighted average anti-dilution)	99	99
Cumulative 8% dividend	3	14
Redemption right	5	3

Sources: For US: Wilson Sonsini ECP (2024); for Canada: Grantmyre and Unruch (2024).

their pro-rata percentage (on a fully converted basis) of the remaining proceeds. In Canada, 9% of the financings included this participation feature, while in the US the value was 10%, with 8% having no upside cap (limit) on the liquidation proceeds and 2% having a cap on liquidation proceeds. If there is no cap on the liquidation proceeds, then regardless of the corporation's liquidation value, the security holder will have no incentive to convert their preferred shares into common shares, as they will first receive one or two times their investment back and then receive their pro-rata percentage of any amount remaining. The purpose of the cap is to force the security holder to convert their preferred shares into common shares if the liquidation proceeds exceed some value.

When there is more than one round of VC or PE financing, it is possible for the earlier rounds to become disadvantaged compared to the later rounds. The data show that for a Series B or beyond financing, 26% of the US and Canadian investments were structured so that the later financing rounds had a liquidation preference over the preceding rounds. In such cases, the corporation will have multiple classes of preferred shares with differential rights. Another way that an earlier investor can be disadvantaged is if the later financing round is completed at a lower price. To protect against this possibility, 99% of both US and Canadian financing required weighted-average anti-dilution protection. A limited number of investors (3% in the US and 14% in Canada) wanted to receive an annual return for their investment by requiring that the preferred shares pay a dividend. The most common required return was 8%, with this typically being an in-kind, cumulative dividend that would increase the investor's ownership percentage across time. Finally, 5% of financings in the US and 3% of those in Canada required the ability to redeem their preferred share investment at a future point in time if the corporation did not develop as expected.

As previously discussed, another form of PE governance mechanism required by an institutional investor is the development of a USA. This agreement is highly customised but typically follows a well-developed template. Shareholders who sign this agreement are agreeing to forego some of the protections afforded to them by securities law, including the right to elect directors. This explains the earlier discussion about how a typical shared-control board will include two founder nominees, two investors' nominees, and one independent.

A USA provides many benefits to the investors, including the ability to control the way other shareholders can sell their shares or participate in future financings. In addition, it can provide certain investors with the ability to override decisions that are typically under the purview of the corporate board, such as the future strategic direction or even the appointment of the corporate CEO. A standardised VC USA, along with other standardised agreements, is available at the National Venture Capital Association website (National Venture Capital Association, 2024).

While these investor-friendly agreements may seem punitive to entrepreneurs, VC and PE investors have learned over several decades of PE investing that they need these protections to allow them to discharge their fiduciary duty to their LP investors. When serving on a corporate board as their fund's nominee, a VC will be subject to lawsuits if they make decisions that benefit their investment to the detriment of other investors or other stakeholders. An investor nominee board member can avoid this risk by having the ability to influence corporate decision-making using the investor agreements outside of board meetings. These agreements are necessary to help convince LP investors to provide financial capital to the VC and PE funds, so that these funds are then able to invest in private corporations. Thus, these mechanisms are an important element of ensuring that there is financing available for high-potential private corporations.

Ultimately, the ability of a corporation that is not yet profitable to be able to operate and grow is contingent on its continued ability to raise capital. As the discussion earlier in this chapter noted, the CB Insights data indicated that after COVID-19, there has been a significant increase in the number of ventures failing because they were not able to maintain access to financial capital. In such an environment, the negotiations between a corporation and the VC and PE investors would favour the investors, and the negotiated terms would be more investor-friendly than observed in earlier time periods.

Cleantech venture capital is different from traditional VC investing, as the projects are highly capital intensive, have a higher degree of technology risk, and have a different exit profile (Cumming *et al.*, 2016). Another consideration is that this type of VC investment generates societal benefits, such as a positive impact on the environment, that are difficult for the VC to capture. For those VC investors who accept these challenges, Shakeel and Juszcyk (2019) find that they can add great value at the board level through assisting with strategy development, by helping build an effective management team, and by helping with international marketing efforts. Enhanced corporate governance has also been found to increase the likelihood that a corporation will report sustainability development goals (Martinez-Ferrero and Garcia-Meca, 2020) and will enhance a corporation's environmental innovation (Shui *et al.*, 2022). Zavarko (2023) finds that a corporation's governance has a positive impact on its ability to help with the development of the hydrogen economy.

Another governance outcome associated with increased investment by VC and PE investors is a significant turnover in the CEO. Being the CEO of an early-stage start-up entails having the ability to deal with the uncertainty associated with that stage of development, but as a corporation grows and accesses increasing amounts of external equity capital, the challenge becomes how to manage the complexities of a scale-up. It is rare to find an individual who has the capability to adapt to the changing responsibilities of the CEO as the corporation matures. Table 6.3 presents data that show the average percentage of CEOs of institutional investor-backed corporations who were either founders or non-founders after each of a series of US financing rounds.

The data show that there is a significant turnover in the CEO role as a corporation grows so that, by the time of the third institutional financing round (Series C), less than half of founders are still

Table 6.3. Percentage of start-ups with founder and non-founder CEOs.

	Founder still the CEO (%)	On second CEO (%)	On third or higher CEO (%)
At Founding	100	0	0
After Series A	75	19	6
After Series B	62	29	9
After Series C	48	35	17
After Series D	39	38	23

Source: Wasserman (2012), p. 299.

serving as the CEO. This reinforces how difficult it is for a founder to have both the skill and the motivation to continue to lead their corporation through the different stages of development. It would be ideal if founders had the self-awareness to realise that they were reaching the limit of their capabilities and seek an orderly transition in the CEO role. Unfortunately, that does not appear to be the case as the data also found that only 27% of the CEO transitions were an orderly succession, and 73% were initiated by the board (62%) or by investors or other outsiders (11%) (Wasserman, 2012, p. 301). The data do, however, provide some evidence that the corporate governance and PE governance mechanisms are working as expected, as it indicates that the board and investors are actively monitoring CEO performance and making changes as warranted.

Unfortunately, there have been several situations where the boards of VC-backed corporations did not seem to be doing an effective job of overseeing the CEO and actively assessing corporate performance. One famous case involves the life science corporation called Theranos Inc., which was able to raise more than $700 million and was valued at $10 billion before its collapse in 2018. While its former CEO and president were each sentenced to a lengthy prison term for fraud, Wasley (2016) raises several issues with the board, including a lack of medical expertise among its members as well as an apparent reluctance to effectively challenge management. While creating a strong board charter and term of reference for the board and its committees and developing a robust code of ethics (Brooks, 1989; Loughran *et al.*, 2023) may have helped mitigate the problems that occurred at Theranos, having a vigilant, engaged board of directors would have also been useful.

6.2.4. *Maturity and decline stages*

Following multiple rounds of VC financing or one large PE investment, the ownership percentage of the corporation changes so that the institutional investors are the majority owners. Wasserman (2012, p. 279) notes that institutional investors, on average, own over 50% of the corporation's equity after a Series C financing round. After these multiple financing rounds, the corporation will have multiple classes of preferred shares outstanding, and the majority of the directors will be investor nominees.

Gompers *et al.* (2016) report that PE investors purchase an average of 80% (median 85%) of a corporation's equity in a change of control transaction. Since the PE investors are purchasing majority ownership of the corporation, they choose to purchase common shares to maintain a relatively simple capital structure. The PE investors will typically replace the existing management team and hire a new smaller, focused management team of executives who are incentivised with a significant ownership percentage. These executives are typically not founders but professional managers with a proven ability to make significant changes in a short period of time.

During this stage, a corporation will transition to an investor-controlled governance structure that is significantly different from the boards of other types of corporations. For one thing, the strategy of the corporation is being set by the investors as opposed to by the management team. The strategy is based on a specific investment thesis, and the corporation is operated to position it for an exit opportunity within a period of four to five years. Senior managers are hired for their ability to execute against this strategy and are given a strong incentive to achieve investor-established objectives.

The typical PE board includes between five and seven members with three PE investor nominees, one or two board seats for the senior executives, and one or two independent outsiders. In some cases, if the executives do not have a significant ownership percentage, there may be no management personnel on the board. The directors closely monitor the performance of the CEO, and the rest of the senior executives and independent directors are chosen for their ability to provide strong guidance and mentorship to the management team.

If there are multiple VC or PE investors who own a percentage of the corporation, then they will likely negotiate a shareholders' agreement between themselves that may also include any management shareholders. The purpose of this agreement is to clarify roles, rights, and responsibilities between various parties. The agreement is designed to help minimise potential future disputes, provide a framework for future growth, help manage corporate risk, or accommodate a certain investor's demands. The agreement may be a general shareholders' agreement (GSA) between only certain shareholders or a USA between all shareholders. A GSA is a commercial contract between the shareholders and does not limit the decision-making powers of the board of directors, whereas, as discussed earlier, a USA may allow certain investors to veto specific director decisions.

6.3. Summary and Conclusions

An international study (World Economic Forum, 2015) identified the founder characteristics that help increase a venture's chances of success. These characteristics include an ability to identify business opportunities and then having the skills and capabilities to effectively build an organisation to exploit the opportunities. A key aspect of skills is the understanding of the need to develop an effective governance structure that will be able to attract the support from employees, mentors, advisors, directors, and investors that the corporation needs to operate until it has identified a scalable business model.

Governance is important at all stages of a corporation's development, and it needs to evolve as the corporation grows. During the development stage, governance helps to create alignment between founders, develop methods of overcoming founder disputes, and establish the systems that will protect the corporation's IP. External investors during this stage are likely either individuals who already know the founders (relationship investors) or angel investors. None of these types of investors usually require extensive governance mechanisms before committing capital, but a founder who has begun to create an effective governance structure will increase their chances of attracting financing. The corporation will likely have adopted a founder-controlled governance structure, as it will be difficult and expensive for a founder to attract strong independent directors to their board. Nonetheless, informal mentors and formal advisors can help provide a valuable outside perspective when key corporate decisions are to be made.

As the corporation grows and is considering raising money from institutional VC or PE investors, these investors will conduct extensive due diligence before making an investment. A key element of that process will be examining the governance and other corporate documents to identify any potential shareholder issues or other major risks. If issues are found, the investor will likely decline to pursue the investment, as experience has shown that cleaning up past mistakes requires a great deal of time and takes management focus away from the creation of corporate value. If the VC or PE investor does make an investment, it will require the development of governance mechanisms designed to mitigate that investor's risk. These mechanisms include the purchase of a security with characteristics that favour the institutional investor and the development of a shareholders' agreement that provides significant benefits to the investor. These benefits include the ability to appoint a certain number of directors to the corporate board (which then becomes a shared-control governance board), and that may include the ability to veto certain corporate decisions even if they have been approved by the board. Any entrepreneur negotiating with a VC or PE investor is strongly encouraged to seek guidance from experienced advisors or legal experts to avoid establishing a governance structure that will constrain the ability of the corporation to make critical decisions or that will serve to limit the willingness of other investors to provide financing.

As a PE corporation enters the maturity or decline phases, it will likely have the majority of its directors being nominated by investors. This investor-controlled board will hire professional management to operate the corporation and incentivise those managers to create value by providing them with a large ownership percentage. As the key strategic decisions are being made by the investors, in some cases the managers are not invited to join the board.

Overall, the purpose of this chapter was to highlight the fact that corporate development is dependent on the founders realising that they need to establish an effective governance structure during the earliest stages of their corporation's development. Having such a structure will lower the corporation's risk and increase its chances of attracting external capital. In addition, founders must monitor the effectiveness of this structure and be willing to adjust it as the corporation grows. Such adjustments will be imposed by institutional investors who use standard control mechanisms to mitigate their investment risk so that they can effectively discharge their fiduciary duty to the LP investors. Learning how to negotiate these mechanisms and work collaboratively with institutional VC and PE investors will significantly increase the chances of success for a start-up.

References

Achtenhagen, L., Naldi, L., and Melin, L. (2010). Business growth: Do practitioners and scholars really talk about the same thing? *Entrepreneurship Theory and Practice*, 34(2), 289–316.

Andersen, S. and Nielsen, K. M. (2012). Ability or finances as constraints on entrepreneurship? Evidence from survival rates in a natural experiment. *Review of Financial Studies*, 25(12), 3684–3720.

Anonymous (2010). The enforceability and effectiveness of typical shareholders agreement provisions. *Business Lawyer*, 65(4), 1153–1203.

Anonymous (2018). How to protect trade secrets. *Director*, 71(3), 48–48.

Audretsch, D. B. and Lehmann, E. E. (2004). Financing high-tech growth: The role of banks and venture capitalists. *Schmalenbach Business Review*, 56(4), 340–357.

Barron, E. and Green, D. (2020). Accidental founders: The race from class project to start-up. *Stanford Journal of Law, Business and Finance*, 25(1), 86–130.

Bertoni, F., Colombo, M. G., and Grilli, L. (2011). Venture capital financing and the growth of high-tech start-ups: Disentangling treatment from selection effects. *Research Policy*, 40(7), 1028–1043.

Blank, S. G. (2003). *The Four Steps to the Epiphany: The Road Map for Successful Start-ups*. Steven Blank.

Blank, S. G. (2013). Why the lean start-up changes everything. *Harvard Business Review*, 91(5), 63–72.

Braut Filipović, M. (2022). How can shareholders' agreements shape corporate governance and directors' liability? *InterEULawEast: Journal for International and European Law, Economics and Market Integrations*, 9(2), 193–222.

Brooks, L. J. (1989). Corporate code of ethics. *Journal of Business Ethics*, 8(2-3), 117–129.

Burton, M. D., Colombo, M. G., Rossi-Lamastra, C., and Wasserman, N. (2019). The organizational design of entrepreneurial ventures. *Strategic Entrepreneurship Journal*, 13(3), 243–255.

Buxton, D. C. and Gilbert, R. J. (2004). ESOP: A four-letter word? Liquidity and perpetuation pros and cons. *Journal of Financial Service Professionals*, 58(6), 84–92.

Canadian Coalition for Good Governance (2014). Building high performance boards. Available at: https://ccgg.ca/policies/.

Canadian Securities Administrators (2005). National Policy 58-201 (NP 58-201): Corporate governance guidelines.

Cavallo, A., Ghezzi, A., Dell'Era, C., and Pellizzoni, E. (2019). Fostering digital entrepreneurship from start-up to scaleup: The role of venture capital funds and angel groups. *Technological Forecasting and Social Change*, 145, 24–35.

Clarysse, B., Bobelyn, A., and Palacio Aguirre, I. (2013). Learning from own and others' previous experience: The contribution of the venture capital firm to the likelihood of a portfolio company's trade sale. *Small Business Economics*, 40(3), 575–590.

Colombo, M. G. and Grilli, L. (2010). On growth drivers of high-tech start-ups: Exploring the role of founders' human capital and venture capital. *Journal of Business Venturing*, 25(6), 610–626.

Cooper, A. C., Dunkelberg, W. C., and Woo, C. Y. (1988). Entrepreneurs' perceived chances of success. *Journal of Business Venturing*, 3(2), 97–108.

Cooper, A. C., Gimeno-Gascon, F. J., and Woo, C. Y. (1994). Initial human and financial capital as predictors of new venture performance. *Journal of Business Venturing*, 9(5), 372–395.

Core, J. E. and Packard, H. A. (2022). Non-price and price performance vesting provisions and CEO incentives. *Accounting Review*, 97(7), 109–134.

Cumming, D., Deloof, M., Manigart, S., and Wright, M. (2019). New directions in entrepreneurial finance. *Journal of Banking and Finance*, 100, 252–260.

Cumming, D. and Groh, A. P. (2018). Entrepreneurial finance: Unifying themes and future directions. *Journal of Corporate Finance*, 50, 538–555.

Cumming, D., Henriques, I., and Sadorsky, P. (2016). 'Cleantech' venture capital around the world. *International Review of Financial Analysis*, 44, 86–97.

Cumming, D. and Vismara, S. (2017). De-segmenting research in entrepreneurial finance. *Venture Capital*, 19(1–2), 17–27.

Davila, A., Foster, G., and Gupta, M. (2003). Venture capital financing and the growth of start-up firms. *Journal of Business Venturing*, 18(6), 689–708.

Denis, D. J. (2004). Entrepreneurial finance: An overview of the issues and evidence. *Journal of Corporate Finance*, 10(2), 301–326.

Fanimokun, A. O., Castrogiovanni, G., and Peterson, M. F. (2012). Developing high-tech ventures: Entrepreneurs, advisors, and the use of non-disclosure agreements (NDAs). *Journal of Small Business and Entrepreneurship*, 25(1), 103–119.

Feld, B. and Mendelson, J. (2019). *Venture Deals: Be Smarter Than Your Lawyer and Venture Capitalist* (4th ed.). Wiley.

Gage, D. (2012). The venture capital secret: 3 out of 4 start-ups fail. *The Wall Street Journal*, September 20. Available at: https://www.wsj.com/articles/SB10000872396390443720204578004980476429190

Ganor, I. (2019). Recoupling founders with their IP–improving innovation by rationalizing IRC Section 351: (Licensing vs. assignment of founders' IP in VC-backed startups). *Journal of Corporate Law*, 44(3), 494–513.

Gilmore, T. J. (2022). Employee incentive ESOPs: An equity tool to promote engagement and performance. *Compensation and Benefits Review*, 54(1), 100–102.

Gompers, P., Kaplan, S. N., and Mukharlyamov, V. (2016). What do private equity firms say they do? *Journal of Financial Economics*, 121(3), 449–476.

Grantmyre, M. and Unruch, R. (2024). 2023 deal points report: Venture capital financings. Osler, Hoskin & Harcourt LLP.

Hill, L. A., Tedards, E., Swan, T., and Balsamini, M. (2021). Drive innovation with better decision-making. *Harvard Business Review*, 99(6), 70–79.

Hodak, M. (2014). The growing executive compensation advantage of private versus public companies. *Journal of Applied Corporate Finance*, 26(1), 20–28.

Hodak, M. (2019). Are performance shares shareholder friendly? *Journal of Applied Corporate Finance*, 31(3), 126–130.

Hrdy, C. A. and Seaman, C. B. (2024). Beyond trade secrecy: Confidentiality agreements that act like noncompetes. *Yale Law Journal*, 133(3), 669–754.

Kagan, E., Leider, S., and Lovejoy, W. (2020). Equity contracts and incentive design in start-up teams. *Management Science*, 66(10), 4879–4898.

Kaplan, S. N. and Strömberg, P. (2001). Venture capitalists as principals: Contracting, screening, and monitoring. *American Economic Review*, 91(2), 426–430.

Knuppel, E. (2022). A mortgage on a man's brain: The unconscionability of overly broad intellectual property assignment clauses in employment contracts. *Texas Law Review*, 100(5), 971–997.

Kruger, J. and Dunning, D. (1999). Unskilled and unaware of it: How difficulties in recognizing one's own incompetence lead to inflated self-assessments. *Journal of Personality and Social Psychology*, 77(6), 1121–1134.

Kurato, D. F., Neubert, E., and Marvel, M. R. (2021). Insights on the mentorship and coachability of entrepreneurs. *Business Horizons*, 64(2), 199–209.

Loughran, T., McDonald, B., and Otteson, J. R. (2023). How have corporate codes of ethics responded to an era of increased scrutiny? *Journal of Business Ethics*, 183(4), 1029–1044.

Martinez-Ferrero, J. and Garcia-Meca, E. (2020). Internal corporate governance strength as a mechanism for achieving sustainable development goals. *Sustainable Development*, 28(5), 1189–1198.

Marx, M. (2022). Employee non-compete agreements, gender, and entrepreneurship. *Organization Science*, 33(5), 1756–1772.

McBratney, M. and Downie, D. (2011). The top ten confidentiality agreement mistakes. *Keeping Good Companies*, 63(6), 365–367.

Meyerowitz, S. A. and Spears, V. P. (2021). Employment agreements. *Employee Relations Law Journal*, 47(3), 1–2.

National Venture Capital Association (2024). Model legal documents. Available at: https://nvca.org/model-legal-documents/.

Parpaleix, L. A., Levillain, K., and Segrestin, B. (2019). Financing the next generations of innovation: New dimensions in the private equity model. *Journal of Innovation Economics*, 29(1), 7–27.

Penaskovic, E. (2023). Five tips for avoiding common startup pitfalls. *Business NH Magazine*, 40(7), 46–47.

Pollman, E. (2019). Startup governance. *University of Pennsylvania Law Review*, 168(1), 155–221.

Ries, E. (2011). *The Lean Startup: How Today's Entrepreneurs Use Continuous Innovation to Create Radically Successful Businesses.* Penguin Random House.

Robinson, M. J. (2022). Factors impacting entrepreneurial success in accelerators: Revealed preferences of sophisticated mentors. *Review of Corporate Finance*, 2(3), 617–661.

Robinson, M. J. (2023). *Founder's Guide to Governance: Beyond a Good Idea.* FriesenPress.

Robinson, M. J. and Cottrell, T. C. (2007). Investment patterns of informal investors in the Alberta private equity market. *Journal of Small Business Management*, 45(1), 47–67.

Shakeel, S. R. and Juszcyk, O. (2019). The role of venture capital in the commercialization of cleantech companies. *Management*, 14(4), 325–339.

Shui, X., Zhang, M., Smart, P., and Ye, F. (2022). Sustainable corporate governance for environmental innovation: A configurational analysis on board capital, CEO power and ownership structure. *Journal of Business Research*, 149, 786–794.

Skynova (2023). Why startups failed in 2022. Available at: https://www.skynova.com/blog/top-reasons-startups-fail.

Starr, E., Balasubramanian, N., and Sakakibara, M. (2018). Screening spinouts? How noncompete enforceability affects the creation, growth, and survival of new firms. *Management Science*, 64(2), 552–572.

Sullivan, D. E. (1977). ESOPs: Panacea or placebo? *California Management Review*, 20(1), 55–61.

Thiel, P. (2014). *Zero to One*. Penguin Random House.

Wasley, P. (2016). The Theranos crisis: Where was the board? *Forbes*, April 27.

Wasserman, M. (2012). *The Founder's Dilemmas*. Princeton University Press.

Wilson Sonsini ECP (2024). The entrepreneurs report: Full year 2023. Available at: https://www.jdsupra.com/legalnews/the-entrepreneurs-report-full-year-2023-3725733/.

World Economic Forum (2015). Leveraging entrepreneurial ambition and innovation: A global perspective on entrepreneurship, competitiveness and development. Available at: https://www3.weforum.org/docs/WEFUSA_EntrepreneurialInnovation_Report.pdf.

Zavarko, M. (2023). The global ESG trend and adaptation opportunities in the emerging hydrogen economy: A corporate governance perspective. *Society and Economy*, 45(4), 372–392.

Zimmerman, E. (2015). Steve Blank on why most startups fail, and it's got nothing to do with technology. *Forbes*, April 20.

https://doi.org/10.1142/9781800617032_0007

Chapter 7

Mapping Venture Capital: Exploring Regional Differences Among Independent and Corporate Venture Capital Investors in Europe

Massimo G. Colombo*, Massimiliano Guerini*, Benedetta Montanaro*, and Francesca Tenca†

**Politecnico di Milano, Milan, Italy*

†*Università del Piemonte Orientale, Vercelli, Italy*

7.1. Introduction

Venture capital (VC) plays a crucial role in funding start-ups and fast-growing companies within high-tech sectors (Florida and Kenney, 1988). The accessibility and abundance of VC funds vary across different regions, exerting significant influence on the technological landscape within those areas. Extensive research has demonstrated that fluctuations in the availability of VC have pronounced effects on regional economic dynamics in terms of, e.g. entrepreneurial activity, job creation, and regional income (Samila and Sorenson, 2011; Chowdhury *et al.*, 2019).

The geographical concentration of VC activity has been studied mainly in the US, with a particular focus on VC hubs and high-tech districts, such as Silicon Valley (e.g. Florida and Smith, 1993; Florida and Mellander, 2016; Kwon and Sorenson, 2023). While numerous studies have explored the factors contributing to the geographical clustering of VC activity, looking both at the supply-side (e.g. Sorenson and Stuart, 2001; Lindgaard Christensen, 2007; Chen *et al.*, 2010; Cumming and Dai, 2010; Guerini and Tenca, 2018) and demand-side (e.g. Mason and Harrison, 2002; Bertoni *et al.*, 2016; Colombo *et al.*, 2019) factors, relatively little attention has been paid to the understanding of variations among different VC types and their VC geographical concentration of investment activity. Furthermore, there remains a gap in research regarding the regional-level factors influencing the geographical concentration of VC activity in Europe.

In this chapter, we employ regional-level data on European VC investments to compare the geographical concentration of investments made by independent venture capital (IVCs) with investments of corporate venture capital (CVCs; Dushnitsky, 2012). CVC is increasingly gaining prominence in the landscape of VC investments in Europe.[1] As established corporations recognise the necessity of innovation to stay competitive in rapidly evolving markets, many are turning to CVC as a strategic tool (Ma, 2020). Moreover, CVCs offer start-ups more than just financial support. It provides access to resources, expertise, and market insights that can significantly accelerate their growth trajectories (Chemmanur *et al.*, 2014; Colombo and Murtinu, 2017).

The main source of data for this study is the VICO dataset, which has been extensively used for European studies on VC (e.g. Colombo and Shafi, 2016; Guerini and Tenca, 2018; Colombo *et al.*, 2023). VICO aggregates information on VC received by start-ups located in 27 European Union (EU) countries, the UK, and Israel in 1998–2021 from three commercial databases (namely, Thomson Eikon, Bureau van Dijk Zephyr, and Crunchbase). In this work, we consider IVC and CVC investments that start-ups located in 285 European metropolitan areas (based on EUROSTAT's classification) received in 1998–2021, corresponding to around 80% of all IVC and CVC investments in the VICO dataset.

We first present descriptive evidence indicating that VC investments are not evenly distributed across different countries and regions, with higher concentrations observed in the UK, Germany, and France and in large metropolitan areas such as London, Paris,

[1]https://pitchbook.com/news/articles/cvc-participation-european-vc-deals.

and Berlin. Quite interestingly, our descriptive analysis shows that CVC investments are less concentrated in large metropolitan areas compared to overall VC investments. We then investigate the regional-level factors influencing the VC geographical concentration activity by using various econometric models that relate the volume of VC investments within metropolitan areas to a set of variables that describe the characteristics of these areas, such as population density, regional income, and presence of prestigious university. Results from econometric estimates confirm that CVC investments are less concentrated in large metropolitan areas compared to IVC investments. Furthermore, higher population density and regional income are associated with a greater number of IVC investments, while the positive effects of these factors are weaker for CVC investments. The presence of a top university in a metropolitan area does not significantly influence VC investments, regardless of the type of VC, except in the medical, health, and life sciences industries and the R&D and engineering industries.

This study contributes to a deeper understanding of the geographical dynamics of VC investments in Europe, thereby enriching the existing literature on VC geography and informing future research in this domain. Understanding the geographical determinants of the distribution of IVC and CVC investments is crucial for policymakers, entrepreneurs, and investors alike, as it provides insights into the dynamics of entrepreneurial ecosystem agglomeration and informs strategies aimed at fostering innovation, entrepreneurship, and economic growth of different regional markets.

The chapter proceeds as follows. In Section 7.2, we review the existing literature concerning the role of geography in VC. In Section 7.3, we describe the data source, sample, and methodology used in this study. In Section 7.4, we present the results of the empirical analysis. Finally, Section 7.5 presents the conclusions and future research directions.

7.2. Literature Background

This study aims to explore the regional factors influencing the geographical distribution of different VC types, contributing to the relatively sparse literature within the domain of the geography of VC. VC investments are not uniformly spread geographically; rather, they tend to concentrate in specific locations, such as Silicon Valley, the metropolitan areas of Boston and New York in the US, and large metropolitan areas, such as London and Paris in Europe (Sorenson and Stuart, 2001; Lindgaard Christensen, 2007; Chen *et al.*, 2010; Cumming and Dai, 2010; Guerini and Tenca, 2018). The existing literature has primarily focused on explaining the supply-side dynamics that account for this uneven distribution. Scholars have shown that VC investors cluster in VC hub situated within financial and high-tech centres and are more inclined to invest in start-ups located in the proximity of their premises (e.g. Florida and Kenney, 1988; Sorenson and Stuart, 2001; Chen *et al.*, 2010).

A group of studies within this research stream has highlighted the significance of institutional differences in influencing the level and distribution of VC investments in different countries. Favourable fiscal and legal environments, as noted by Armour and Cumming (2006), play a crucial role in facilitating VC funding and enhancing the supply of VC. Also, elements pertaining to enhanced legal safeguards for investors and increased transparency in accounting standards have a positive influence on VC investments, facilitating the structuring of VC contracts. These institutional characteristics not only ease the realisation of deals by providing better access to information for investors but also support deal syndication, mitigating the potential risks associated with co-investments (Cumming *et al.*, 2010).

Apart from the importance of institutional characteristics in explaining cross-country differences in VC activity, it is widely recognised that VC investments tend to be highly concentrated in particular regions within countries, called VC hub (Lindgaard Christensen, 2007; Florida and Smith, 1993; Chen *et al.*, 2010; Cumming and Dai, 2010). These regions are often characterised by a high level of innovation and entrepreneurial activity (Gompers and Lerner, 1998; Schertler, 2003; Chen *et al.*, 2010), as well as dense urban centres, which promote frequent and direct engagement between investors and highly skilled individuals (Florida and Mellander, 2016). In the US, more than half of VC offices are clustered in three key regions: Silicon Valley, Massachusetts, and New York (PitchBook-NVCA Venture Monitor, 2023). The agglomeration of VC activity is linked with the development of industrial and technological entrepreneurial ecosystems. Within these ecosystems, there is a notable trend of industry and knowledge providers gravitating towards spatial concentration. This clustering phenomenon also extends to industry-specific service providers, such as venture capitalists, and occurs at a quick pace over time, especially if compared with the slower concentration of start-ups (Li *et al.*, 2023). The VC geographical concentration activity also affects the economy of a region in varying ways across different sectors. Kwon and Sorenson (2023) show that an infusion of VC in a region leads to an expansion in the portion of the tradable sector[2] of interest to VC investment, particularly in terms of aggregate employment, and in the entry rates and employment in the non-tradable sector (i.e. local services). Conversely, VC investments in a region tend to result in a reduction of both the number of businesses and employment opportunities within non-high-tech industries in that same area. Moreover, in non-tradable sectors, income inequality increases as the average income declines for lower-wage workers like bartenders and waiters, while it rises for higher-paid professionals like dentists and doctors. Therefore, according to this study, the concentration of VC investments and high-tech start-ups in a region comes with an increasing economic inequality.

As shown above, most of the research in the field of VC geography is focused on the US, with limited attention given to the European VC market. The study by Guerini and Tenca (2018) is an exception. The authors find that in Europe, VC-backed start-ups and VC deals tend to cluster in VC hub, with large metropolitan cities[3] such as London, Paris, Berlin, and Munich leading the way. Moreover, the study finds that the number of regional VC investments is positively correlated with the degree of regional knowledge intensity (i.e. R &D expenditures and the number of universities ranked among the top 100 world universities), regional human capital (i.e. the percentage of employees in high-tech and knowledge-intensive sectors), and the regional number of active VC investors.

Finally, a subset of studies has proposed that the unequal geographical distribution of VC investments is influenced by factors

---

[2]Tradable sectors are those that produce goods or services that can be traded across regions and international borders.

[3]Cities with more than 1.5 million inhabitants.

depending on the demand side, as firms located in more peripheral regions exhibit a lower propensity to seek VC funding (Mason and Harrison, 2002; Bertoni *et al.*, 2016). Colombo *et al.* (2019) investigate how the location of start-ups influences the demand for VC in Europe. They find that the local availability of VC investments positively affects start-ups' propensity to seek external equity funding. In particular, the stimulating effect of the VC supply on the demand for external equity rapidly decreases with distance from VC headquarters, vanishing at around 250 km and especially upon crossing national borders, except in the cases of countries with similar cultural and institutional distance.

To the best of our knowledge, no research has delved into the VC geographical concentration activities of different VC types and the factors that differently influence it. This study seeks to address this research question, focusing on two distinct VC categories: IVCs and CVCs, and investigating their investment activity in Europe. CVC firms have different investment goals compared to IVC firms. In addition to financial objectives, CVC firms have strategic objectives related to the open innovation strategies of their parent corporations (e.g. Dushnitsky and Lenox, 2005; Maula *et al.*, 2013). Moreover, their parent corporations are typically large multinational companies with geographically dispersed operations.[4] Hence, it is interesting to investigate whether CVC investments concentrate in VC hub as IVC investments do and, more generally, whether their spatial distribution is influenced similarly by the same factors that influence the spatial concentration of IVC investments.

7.3. Data

7.3.1. *Data source and sample of VC investments*

As our primary data source to address our research question, we used the VICO 6.0 dataset, which was created as part of the 'RISIS, Research Infrastructures for the Assessment of Science, Technology,

[4]In 2023, the five most active CVC investors worldwide were GV, Salesforce Ventures, Sony Innovation Fund, Intel Capital, and Samsung Venture Investment (*Source*: Pitchbook). All of them are subsidiaries of large, high-tech, multinational corporations.

and Innovation Policy' project. The benefit of employing the VICO 6.0 dataset stems from its integration of information sourced from three commercial databases widely used in VC research: Thompson One Private Equity, Zephyr, and Crunchbase. The dataset includes geographical, industrial, and financial information on 53,714 companies (corresponding to 81,801 VC investment deals) that (i) received their first VC investment from 1998 to 2021, (ii) were established after 1988, and (iii) are localised in the EU countries, the UK, or Israel.

To perform our analysis, we first exclude companies located in Israel, as detailed geographical information on the Israeli geographical areas (e.g. at the regional and metropolitan level) is not available. Second, we discard all the companies located in rural areas (8.88% of the initial sample), given our focus on metropolitan areas. Third, we discard all the investments performed by bank-affiliated VCs, university-affiliated VCs, and governmental VCs, thus leaving only deals either performed by a single IVC or CVC or syndicated by at least one IVC or CVC. Fourth, we focus on initial ties between a given venture and a given IVC or CVC investor, thus discarding all follow-on investments performed by VCs in companies already in their portfolios. This process results in a final sample of 285 metropolitan areas, where 58,275 VC investments (i.e. initial ties) were performed between 1998 and 2021. 89.9% of these ties are IVC investments, and the remaining 10.1% are CVC investments.

7.3.2. *Descriptive statistics*

Figures 7.1 and 7.2 depict two maps illustrating the VC geographical concentration and the ratio of the number of CVC investments to the total number of VC investments, respectively. Unsurprisingly, VC investments are heavily concentrated in large metropolitan areas. London, Paris, Berlin, Stockholm, and Munich account for a 43% share of the number of VC investments under consideration. Figure 7.2 reports the ratio of CVC investments to total VC investments in each metropolitan area. The minimum value is 0, the maximum is 20.63%, and the mean is equal to 10.31%. The figure shows that CVC investments are less concentrated in large metropolitan areas compared to IVC investments. Indeed, the percentage of CVC investments over the total number of investments is higher than the mean

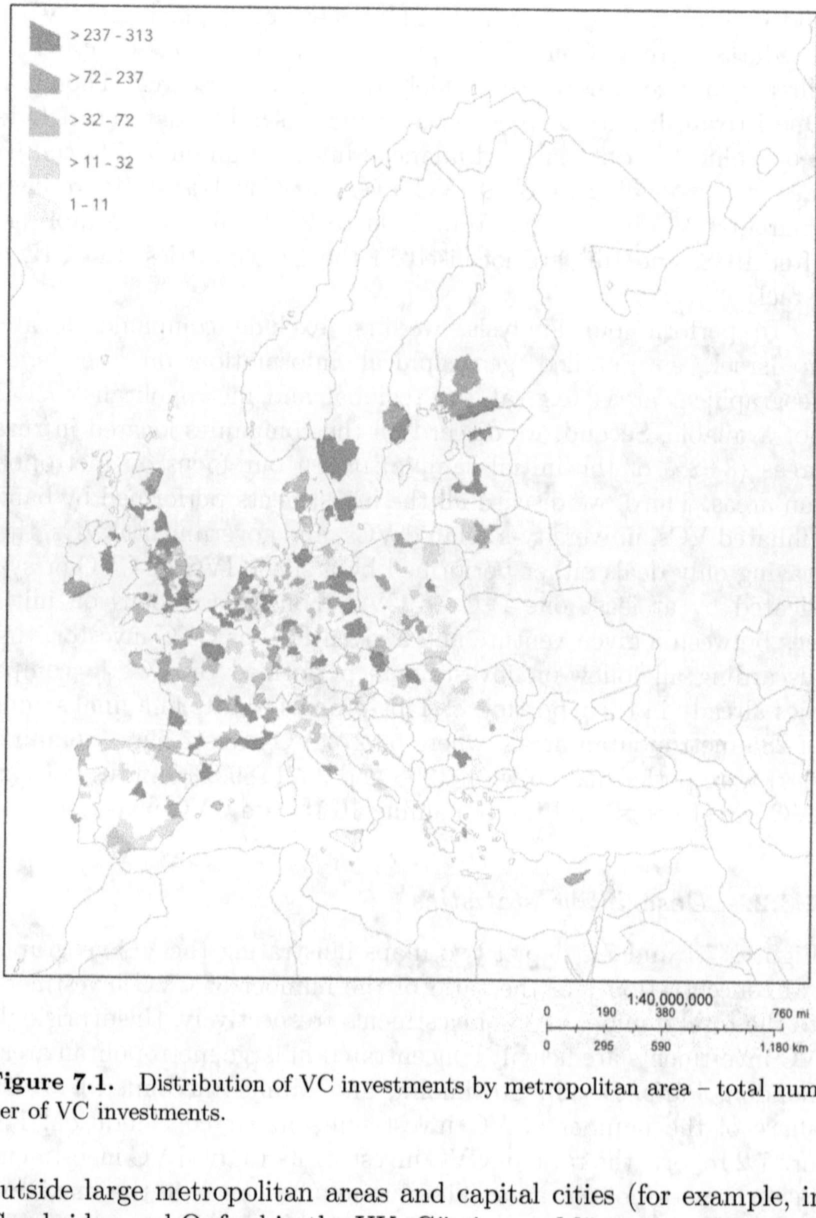

Figure 7.1. Distribution of VC investments by metropolitan area – total number of VC investments.

outside large metropolitan areas and capital cities (for example, in Cambridge and Oxford in the UK; Göttingen, Münster, and Bonn in Germany; Poitiers, Grenoble, and Rouen in France).

Figure 7.3 focuses on the top metropolitan areas by total number of investments. Results are coherent with what Figure 7.1 shows.

Figure 7.2. Distribution of VC investments by metropolitan area – ratio between CVC and total VC investments.

The top 20 metropolitan areas collectively represent approximately 66% of all VC investments. This evidence is further proof that VC investments are indeed concentrated in a few metropolitan areas. It also aligns with findings from prior studies on the US market and emphasises the prominence of major metropolitan hubs such as London, Paris, Berlin, Stockholm, and Munich. More specifically,

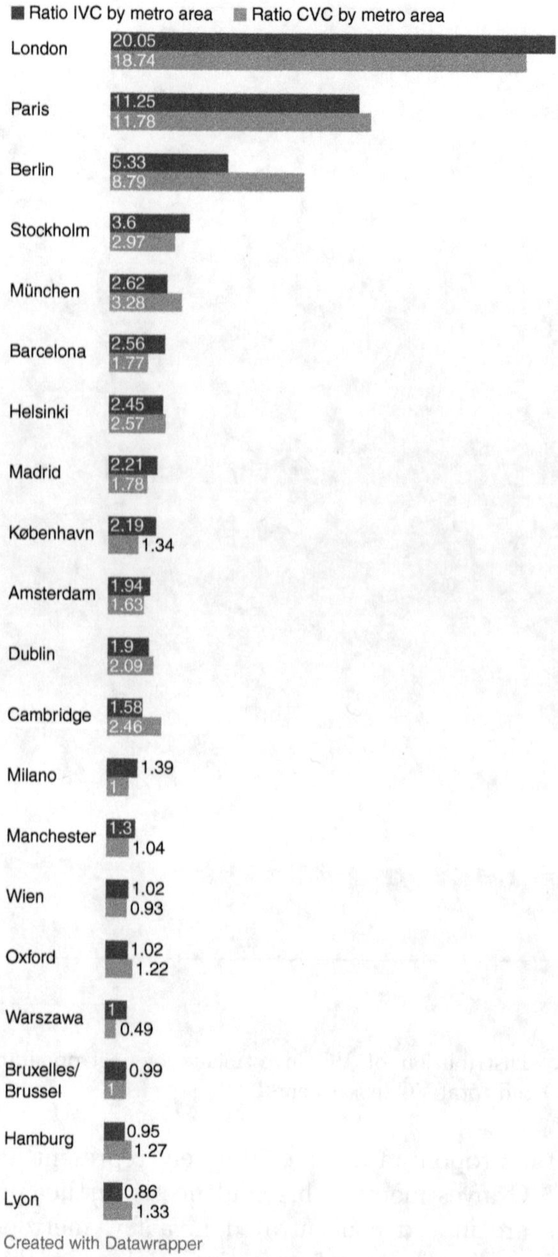

Figure 7.3. Distribution of VC investments by metropolitan areas – top 20 metropolitan areas in Europe.

London accounts for 63% of total VC investments in the UK, while Paris leads in France with 62% of the total. In Germany, Berlin and Munich together account for 58% of the country's VC investments. In Sweden, Stockholm emerges as a key VC hub, capturing 70% of the nation's total VC investments. In Figure 7.3, we also distinguish IVC and CVC investments. The figure shows the contributions of the different metropolitan areas to the total number of IVC and CVC investments, offering valuable insights into the geographical distribution of the investment activity of IVC and CVC investors. The figure clearly highlights London's prominence as the leading VC hub in Europe, capturing 20% of all IVC investments and 18.7% of CVC investments. This underscores London's pivotal role in the European VC landscape, offering a vibrant ecosystem for start-ups and attracting both financial and corporate VC. Similarly, Paris accounts for 11.3% and 11.8% of all investments by IVCs and CVCs, respectively. In contrast, Berlin and Munich exhibit a higher share of CVC investments compared to IVC investments. In particular, Berlin accounts for almost 9% of all investments by CVCs in Europe, while it only accounts for 5.3% of all IVC investments. In addition, Figure 7.3 highlights the notable contributions of smaller metropolitan areas to CVC investments. For instance, Cambridge emerges as a significant attractor of CVC investments; with a 2.5% share of all CVC investments, it is the sixth-largest metropolitan area for CVC investments in Europe. Similarly, Dublin accounts for 2.1% of all CVC investments and is among the top 10 metropolitan areas for CVC investments.

Figures 7.4(a), 7.4(b), and 7.4(c) replicate Figure 7.3, distinguishing investments by industries of operations (software, communication, and media; medical, health, and life sciences; and R&D and engineering, respectively). Respectively 8.2% and 7% of the investments in our sample involved target companies belonging to the medical, health, and life sciences industries and the R&D and engineering industries. Companies belonging to the software, communication, and media industries accounted for 32.8% of the investments. The remaining 27.8% involved companies in other industries (24.3% of companies had missing industry classification;

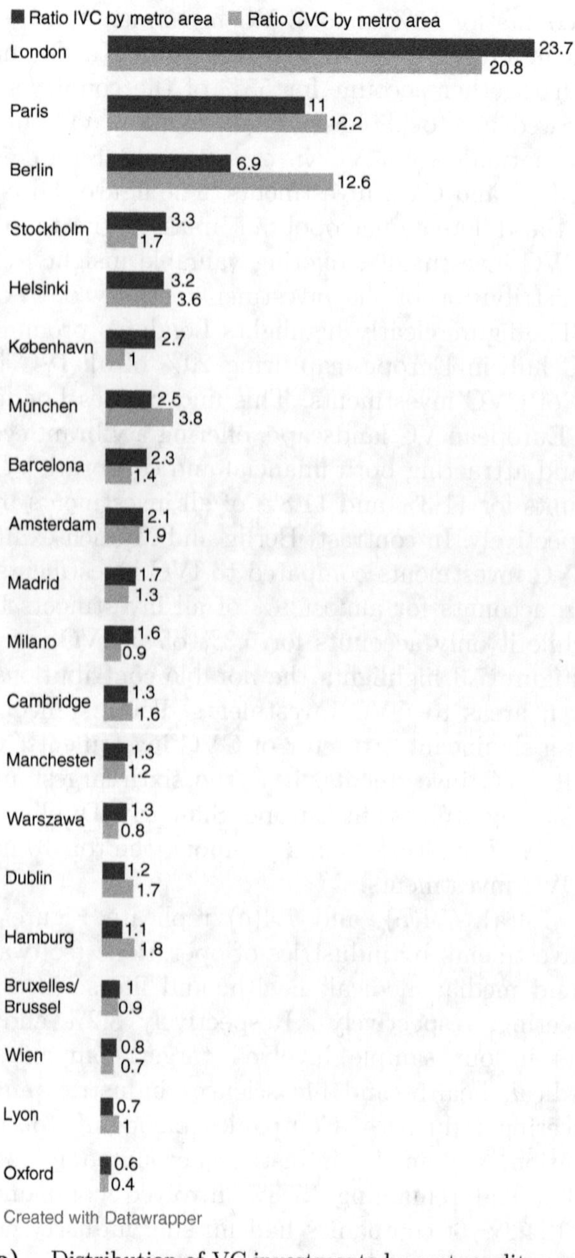

Figure 7.4(a). Distribution of VC investments by metropolitan areas – top 20 metropolitan areas in Europe by industry: software, communication, and media.

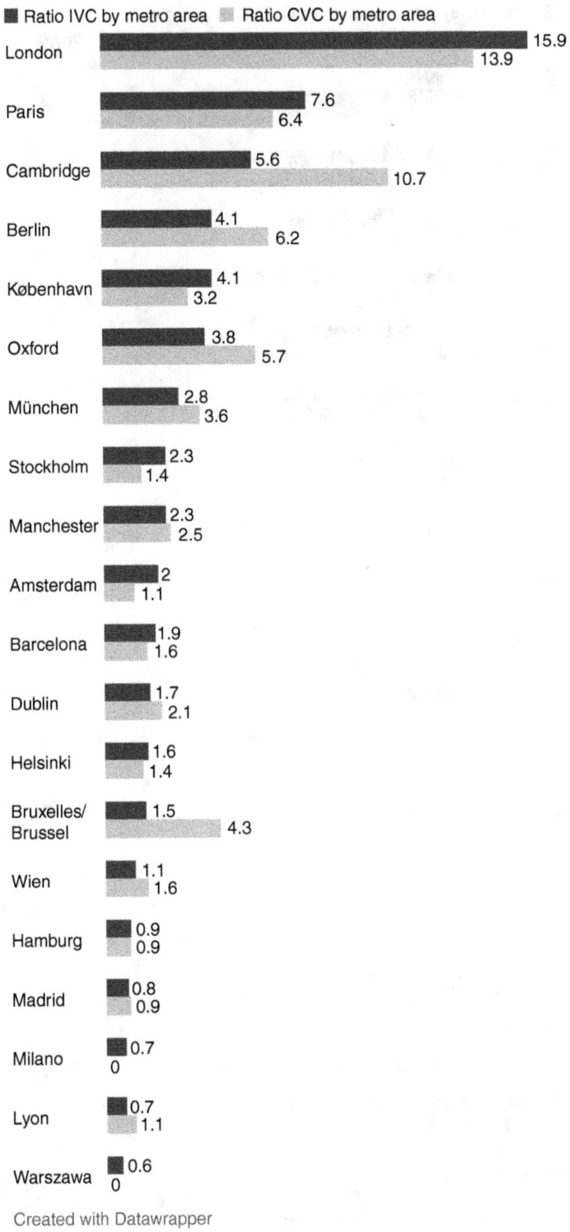

Figure 7.4(b). Distribution of VC investments by metropolitan areas – top 20 metropolitan areas in Europe by industry: medical, health, and life sciences.

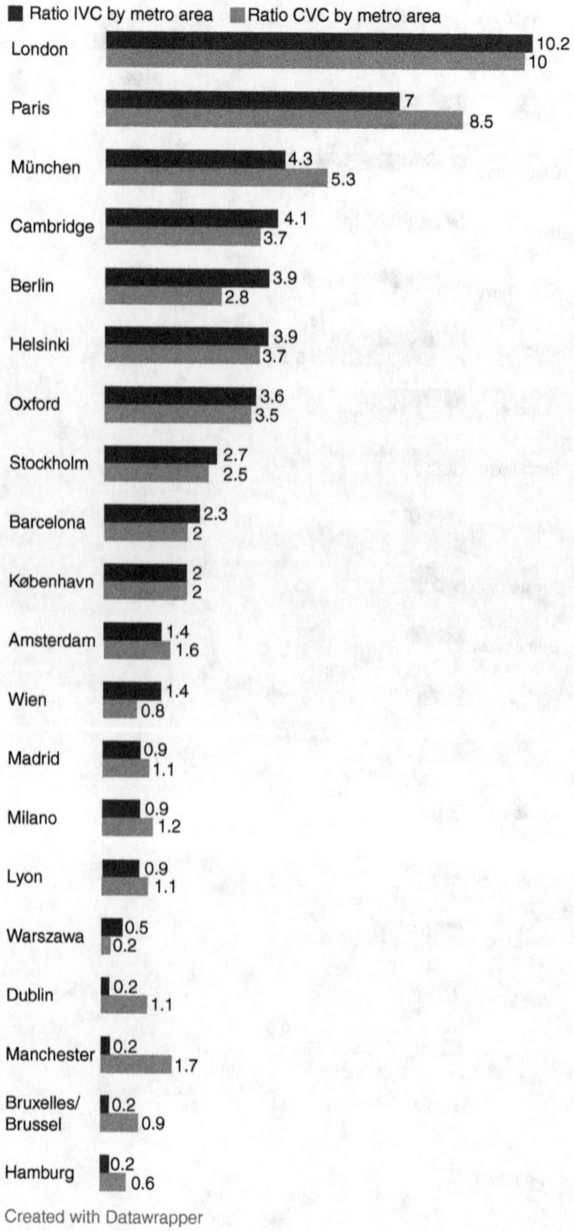

Figure 7.4(c). Distribution of VC investments by metropolitan areas – top 20 metropolitan areas in Europe by industry: R&D and engineering.

Source: Orbis by Moody's).[5] Figures 7.4(a)–(c) reveal that while the ranking of top metropolitan areas remains quite consistent with Figure 7.3 for the software, communication, and media industries, the same cannot be said for the medical, health, and life sciences and the R&D and engineering industries. Regarding life science, Cambridge is at the third place for IVC investments and at the second place for CVC ones. More precisely, Cambridge accounts for more than 10% of all CVC investments in life science, while its share of IVC investments is just above 5%. Similarly, with a 5.7% share, Oxford secures its position as the fifth-largest metropolitan area for CVC investments in life science in Europe, while accounting for 3.8% of all IVC investments. In terms of CVC investments, Brussels climbs to the sixth position in the ranking for CVC investments, representing 4.3% of all CVC investments in Europe in the life science sector, compared to only 1.5% of IVC investments. Last, in the R&D and engineering industries, we observe a notable balance in weights between metropolitan areas for IVC and CVC investments, with the exception of Paris, whose share of CVC investments is larger than the one of IVC investments. Additionally, non-capital cities such as Manchester and Hamburg account for a larger share of CVC investments compared to IVC investments.

7.3.3. *Variables of the econometric models*

To study the determinants of the VC geographical concentration, we employed different econometric models that investigate the relationship between the number of VC investments of type j (respectively, IVC and CVC investments) in metropolitan area k (according to the

[5]We included in the medical, health, and life sciences industries the companies with NACERev2 core codes equal to 2100, 2110, 2120, 2660, 3250, 4646, 4773, 4774, 7500, 8610, 8621, 8622, 8623, 8690, 8710, 8720, 8730, 8790, 9604, and 9609. We included in the R&D and engineering industries the companies with NACERev2 core codes equal to 7110, 7111, 7112, 7120, 7200, 7210, 7219, 7220, and 7490. We included in the software, communication, and media industries the companies with NACERev2 core codes equal to 5820, 5821, 5829, 6200, 6201, 6202, 6203, 6209, 1811, 1812, 1813, 1814, 1820, 4742, 4743, 4763, 4791, 5810, 5811, 5813, 5814, 5819, 5911, 5912, 5913, 5914, 5920, 6000, 6010, 6020, 6100, 6110, 6120, 6130, 6190, 6300, 6310, 6311, 6312, 6390, 6391, 6399, and 9512 (*Source*: Orbis by Moody's).

EUROSTAT classification of metropolitan areas[6]) in time t and a set of independent and control variables that distinguish IVC and CVC investments and reflect the characteristics at the metropolitan area or country (when metropolitan area characteristics were not available) level.

Table 7.1 summarises the variables used in our analysis. More specifically, our dependent variable in this study is *VC investments*$_{jkt}$. This variable is computed as the number of VC investments of type j in metropolitan area k in year t (*Source*: VICO 6.0).

As an independent variable, *CVC Dummy*$_j$ distinguishes CVC investments from IVC investments (*Source*: VICO 6.0). Moreover, we include in our models the *Large Metropolitan Area Dummy* (LMA_k), which equals 1 for metropolitan areas with more than 1,500,000 inhabitants, or 0 otherwise (*Source*: Eurostat). In addition, we use a set of explanatory variables to measure the development of each metropolitan area. Indeed, we consider the gross domestic product per capita (*GDP per capita*$_{kt}$) in each metropolitan area per year (*Source*: Eurostat) as a proxy of economic wealth at the metropolitan area level. We also consider population density by including the number of inhabitants per square km (*Population Density*$_{kt}$) in each metropolitan area per year (*Source*: Eurostat). Last, to capture metropolitan areas' availability of academic knowledge, we include the *Top University Dummy*$_k$, which equals 1 if at least one university based in the focal metropolitan area is ranked among the top 100 universities in the world, or 0 otherwise (*Source*: QS World University Rankings 2010).

Among our control variables, we include *Time to startup*$_{kt}$, measured as the average number of days required to start a new business in each country (*Source*: World Bank, Doing Business project). This variable is a proxy for the ease of starting a business. Then, we control for each country's fiscal pressure through the corporate tax rate (*Corporate Tax Rate*$_{kt}$), measured as the level of taxation on

[6]Metropolitan areas are based on Eurostat's nomenclature of territorial units for statistics (NUTS). They refer to NUTS 3 regions or a combination of NUTS 3 regions that encompass all functional urban areas (FUAs) with a population of at least 250,000 people. For details, see https://ec.europa.eu/eurostat/web/metropolitan-regions/information-data.

Table 7.1. Variables description.

Variable name	Definition
Dependent variable	
VC investments$_{jkt}$	Number of VC investments of type j in metropolitan area k in year t (*Source*: VICO 6.0)
Independent variables	
Large metropolitan area dummy (LMA)$_k$	Dummy that equals 1 if the metropolitan area has more than 1,500,000 inhabitants, 0 otherwise (*Source*: Eurostat)
CVC dummy$_j$	Dummy that equals 1 if the investor type is CVC, 0 otherwise (*Source*: VICO 6.0)
Population density$_{kt}$	Number of inhabitants per square km in metropolitan area k in year t (*Source*: Eurostat)
GDP per capita$_{kt}$	Gross domestic product per number of inhabitants in each metropolitan area k in year t (*Source*: Eurostat)
Top university dummy$_k$	Dummy that equals 1 if, in metropolitan area k, there is at least one university ranked among the top 100 world universities, 0 otherwise (*Source*: QS World University Rankings 2010)
Control variables	
Time to startup$_{kt}$	Average time in days required to start a new business in the country of metropolitan area k in year t (*Source*: World Bank)
Corporate tax rate$_{kt}$	Level of taxation on income and capital gains in the country of metropolitan area k in year t (*Source*: taxfoundation.org).
Number of individuals using the internet$_{kt}$	Number of individuals with internet access in the country of metropolitan area k in year t (*Source*: World Telecommunication/ICT Indicators Database – OECD)
Power distance index$_k$	Degree of inequality that exists – and is accepted – between people with and without power in the country of metropolitan area k. 0–100 scale (*Source*: https://www.hofstede-insights.com)
Individualism vs. collectivism$_k$	Degree of individualism versus collectivism in the country of metropolitan area k. 0–100 scale (*Source*: https://www.hofstede-insights.com)
Masculinity vs. femininity$_k$	Degree of masculinity versus femininity in the country of metropolitan area k. 0–100 scale (*Source*: https://www.hofstede-insights.com)

(*Continued*)

Table 7.1. (*Continued*)

Variable name	Definition
Uncertainty avoidance index$_k$	Degree to which the members of the country of metropolitan area k feel uncomfortable with uncertainty. 0–100 scale (*Source*: https://www.hofstede-insights.com)
Long-term orientation vs. short-term orientation$_k$	Degree of long-term versus short-term normative orientation in the country of metropolitan area k. 0–100 scale (*Source*: https://www.hofstede-insights.com)
Indulgence vs. restraint$_k$	Degree of indulgence versus restraint in each country. 0–100 scale (*Source*: https://www.hofstede-insights.com)

income and capital gains (*Source*: taxfoundation.org). Furthermore, we add to our models the variable *Number of individuals using the internet*$_{kt}$, computed as the total number of people in a given country with access to the internet in their households, to control for the technological development at the country level (*Source*: World Telecommunication/ICT Indicators Database – OECD). Last, we consider the role of national cultural values (Li and Zahra, 2012). Specifically, we include the six cultural dimensions used in the study by Hofstede (2010) to measure cultural distance (i.e. power distance index, individualism vs. collectivism, uncertainty avoidance index, masculinity vs. femininity, long-term orientation vs. short-term orientation, and indulgence vs. restraint) in each country.

7.4. Results

Given the panel structure of the data and our interest in the relationship between certain variables that do not vary over time, we estimate random effects regressions. On top of the control variables presented above, we include in all models year- and country-level fixed effects. To perform our estimates, we base our analysis on a subsample of deals that occurred between 2003 and 2019 due to availability constraints of some of the control variables at the metropolitan area or country level that we include in the models. Due to the data availability of some of the control variables at the metropolitan area, our estimates focus on the 27 countries belonging to the EU. Hence, our estimates are run on a subsample of 237 metropolitan areas, where 26,235 VC investments (i.e. initial ties; 89.3% of these ties involve IVC investors, with the remaining being CVC investors) were performed between 2003 and 2019. In Table 7.2, we provide summary statistics and correlations for the variables included in our models.

Table 7.3 shows the results of panel regression models with – as dependent variable – the (natural logarithm of the) number of VC investments (i.e. initial ties between each venture and each VC) in each metropolitan area per year and categorised by VC types. In Model 1, we include as independent variables both LMA_k and $CVC\ Dummy_j$. In Model 2, we also add to the specification the interaction term between LMA_k and $CVC\ Dummy_j$. In Model 3, we replicate the estimate presented in Model 1 but substitute LMA_k with the other characteristics capturing the development of the metropolitan area, i.e. *GDP per capita*$_{kt}$, *Population Density*$_{kt}$, and *Top University Dummy*$_k$. Finally, in Model 4, we also include the interaction effects between *CVC dummy*$_j$ and *GDP per capita*$_{kt}$, *Population Density*$_{kt}$, and *Top University Dummy*$_k$. We report these two alternative specifications, putting LMA_k and *GDP per capita*$_{kt}$, *Population Density*$_{kt}$ and *Top University Dummy*$_k$ in two separate sets of models for two reasons. First, we want to avoid multicollinearity problems, as LMA_k shows high correlations with the other three variables. Second, with Models 3 and 4, we want to better investigate whether specific characteristics at the metropolitan level have an impact on our dependent variable beyond the more simplistic binary classification of areas based on their size. In all models, to ease the interpretation of coefficients, all continuous explanatory variables have been standardised (zero mean and unit standard deviation). Accordingly, coefficients (β) of continuous variables reported in Table 7.3 can be interpreted as the change in the natural logarithm of VC investments due to one standard deviation increase in these continuous explanatory variables.[7]

[7]The percentage change in the number of VC investments due to one unit increase in the explanatory variable can be obtained by calculating $e^{\beta} - 1$.

Table 7.2. Statistics and correlation matrix.

Variable	Mean	Std. dev.	(1)	(2)	(3)	(4)	(5)	(6)	(7)	(8)
(1) VC investments$_{jkt}$	5.716	21.909	1.000							
(2) CVC dummy$_j$	0.5	0.5	−0.205	1.000						
			(0.000)							
(3) LMA$_k$	0.273	0.445	0.273	0.000	1.000					
			(0.000)	(1.000)						
(4) Population density$_{kt}$	5.881	1.115	0.172	0.000	0.420	1.000				
			(0.000)	(1.000)	(0.000)					
(5) GDP per capita$_{kt}$	0.098	0.105	0.493	0.000	0.490	0.250	1.000			
			(0.000)	(1.000)	(0.000)	(0.000)				
(6) Top university dummy$_k$	0.03	0.17	0.297	0.000	0.187	0.237	0.371	1.000		
			(0.000)	(1.000)	(0.000)	(0.000)	(0.000)			
(7) Time to startup$_{kt}$	17.401	17.945	−0.063	0.000	0.080	0.040	−0.187	−0.034	1.000	
			(0.000)	(1.000)	(0.000)	(0.007)	(0.000)	(0.021)		
(8) Corporate tax rate$_{kt}$	28.947	6.702	0.000	0.000	−0.018	−0.003	0.019	0.122	−0.050	1.000
			(0.987)	(1.000)	(0.210)	(0.823)	(0.194)	(0.000)	(0.001)	
(9) Number of individuals using the internet$_{kt}$	73.189	16.104	0.079	0.000	−0.115	−0.020	0.310	0.023	−0.497	−0.097
			(0.000)	(1.000)	(0.000)	(0.171)	(0.000)	(0.114)	(0.000)	(0.000)
(10) Power distance index$_k$	50.103	17.304	−0.008	0.000	−0.008	−0.136	−0.214	0.007	0.098	0.023
			(0.603)	(1.000)	(0.583)	(0.000)	(0.000)	(0.658)	(0.000)	(0.122)
(11) Individualism vs. collectivism$_k$	65.247	12.017	0.034	0.000	−0.149	0.005	0.181	0.069	−0.350	0.286
			(0.022)	(1.000)	(0.000)	(0.755)	(0.000)	(0.000)	(0.000)	(0.000)
(12) Masculinity vs. femininity$_k$	49.967	20.769	−0.047	0.000	0.014	0.259	−0.125	0.061	0.160	0.068
			(0.002)	(1.000)	(0.334)	(0.000)	(0.000)	(0.000)	(0.000)	(0.000)
(13) Uncertainty avoidance index$_k$	73.779	17.046	−0.033	0.000	0.042	0.018	−0.272	0.038	0.189	0.138
			(0.024)	(1.000)	(0.004)	(0.215)	(0.000)	(0.010)	(0.000)	(0.000)
(14) Long-term orientation vs. short-term or.$_k$	63.569	15.717	−0.009	0.000	−0.089	0.260	0.058	0.158	−0.244	0.396
			(0.540)	(1.000)	(0.000)	(0.000)	(0.000)	(0.000)	(0.000)	(0.000)
(15) Indulgence vs. restraint$_k$	44.533	13.779	0.059	0.000	−0.029	−0.169	0.321	0.023	−0.223	0.191
			(0.000)	(1.000)	(0.050)	(0.000)	(0.000)	(0.125)	(0.000)	(0.000)

Table 7.2. (*Continued*)

Variable	(9)	(10)	(11)	(12)	(13)	(14)	(15)
(1) VC investments$_{jkt}$							
(2) CVC dummy$_j$							
(3) LMA$_k$							
(4) Population density$_{kt}$							
(5) GDP per capita$_{kt}$							
(6) Top university dummy$_k$							
(7) Time to startup$_{kt}$							
(8) Corporate tax rate$_{kt}$							
(9) Number of individuals using the internet$_{kt}$	1.000						
(10) Power distance index$_k$	−0.410*	1.000					
	(0.000)						
(11) Individualism vs. collectivism$_k$	0.268*	−0.298*	1.000				
	(0.000)	(0.000)					
(12) Masculinity vs. femininity$_k$	−0.184*	−0.017	−0.007	1.000			
	(0.000)	(0.260)	(0.653)				
(13) Uncertainty avoidance index$_k$	−0.464*	0.728*	−0.411*	0.256*	1.000		
	(0.000)	(0.000)	(0.000)	(0.000)			
(14) Long-term orientation vs. short-term or.$_k$	0.218*	−0.294*	0.392*	0.308*	−0.240*	1.000	
	(0.000)	(0.000)	(0.000)	(0.000)	(0.000)		
(15) Indulgence vs. restraint$_k$	0.439*	−0.370*	0.358*	−0.535*	−0.476*	−0.082*	1.000
	(0.000)	(0.000)	(0.000)	(0.000)	(0.000)	(0.000)	

Note: This table summarises the descriptive statistics (mean and standard deviation) and correlation coefficients for the variables in the study.

Table 7.3. Results.

	Model 1	Model 2	Model 3	Model 4
Large metropolitan area dummy (LMA)$_k$	1.088***	1.430***		
	(0.054)	(0.070)		
CVC dummy$_j$	−1.072***	−0.941***	−1.088***	−1.148***
	(0.041)	(0.043)	(0.027)	(0.023)
LMA$_k$ × CVC dummy$_j$		−0.684***		
		(0.097)		
Population density$_{kt}$			0.100***	0.136***
			(0.019)	(0.020)
Population density$_{kt}$ × CVC dummy$_j$				−0.064***
				(0.023)
GDP per capita$_{kt}$			0.648***	0.799***
			(0.013)	(0.016)
GDP per capita$_{kt}$ × CVC dummy$_j$				−0.269***
				(0.020)
Top university dummy$_k$			0.042	−0.025
			(0.105)	(0.115)
Top university dummy$_k$ × CVC dummy$_j$				0.043
				(0.159)
Time to startup$_{kt}$	−0.032**	−0.032**	−0.047***	−0.046***
	(0.013)	(0.013)	(0.011)	(0.011)
Corporate tax rate$_{kt}$	−0.115***	−0.115***	−0.094***	−0.092***
	(0.025)	(0.025)	(0.021)	(0.022)
Number of individuals using the internet$_{kt}$	0.076***	0.076***	0.159***	0.160***
	(0.027)	(0.027)	(0.023)	(0.023)
Power distance index$_k$	−0.044	−0.039	−0.467**	−0.459**
	(0.327)	(0.311)	(0.222)	(0.184)
Individualism vs. collectivism$_k$	0.101	0.104	−0.112	−0.102
	(0.139)	(0.132)	(0.093)	(0.077)
Masculinity vs. femininity$_k$	−0.034	−0.034	0.059	0.053
	(0.130)	(0.124)	(0.088)	(0.073)
Uncertainty avoidance index$_k$	−0.013	−0.011	0.011	0.031
	(0.153)	(0.145)	(0.102)	(0.082)
Long-term orientation vs. short-term or$_k$	0.131	0.128	0.240**	0.252***
	(0.159)	(0.151)	(0.108)	(0.089)

Table 7.3. (*Continued*)

	Model 1	Model 2	Model 3	Model 4
Indulgence vs. restraint$_k$	0.081	0.085	-0.340^{*}	-0.334^{**}
	(0.272)	(0.259)	(0.184)	(0.152)
Constant	1.560^{***}	1.491^{***}	1.926^{***}	1.972^{***}
	(0.259)	(0.246)	(0.177)	(0.146)
Year and country FE	YES	YES	YES	YES
N of observations	4,590	4,590	4,590	4,590
N of groups	474	474	474	474
Wald chi2	$2{,}033.49^{***}$	$2{,}220.40^{***}$	$6{,}105.62^{***}$	$8{,}305.40^{***}$

Note: * $p < 0.10$, ** $p < 0.05$, *** $p < 0.01$. Standard errors in parentheses. This table shows the results of random effects panel regression models with – as the dependent variable – the (natural logarithm of the) number of VC investments (i.e. initial ties between each venture and each VC) in each metropolitan area/year and categorised by VC types. To ease the interpretation of coefficients, all continuous explanatory variables have been standardised (zero mean and unit standard deviation).

Results reported in Model 1 show that LMA_k has a positive and statistically significant coefficient $(1.088, p < 0.001)$, indicating that being in a metropolitan area with more than 1,500,000 inhabitants is associated with a $e^{1.088} - 1 = 197\%$ increase in the number of VC investments. The $CVC\ Dummy_j$ has a negative and significant coefficient $(-1.072, p < 0.001)$, suggesting that, in general, CVCs make 66% less investments compared to IVCs. In Model 2, the interaction term $LMA_k \times CVC\ Dummy_j$ has a negative and significant coefficient $(-0.684, p < 0.001)$. This suggests that CVCs invest even less in large metropolitan areas compared to IVCs. Indeed, the marginal effect of being in a large metropolitan area on the number of VC investments is $1.430 (p < 0.001)$ for IVCs (i.e. when $CVC\ Dummy_j$ is equal to 0) and $0.746 (p < 0.001)$ for CVCs (i.e. when $CVC\ Dummy_j$ is equal to 1). In other words, the number of IVC investments in large metropolitan areas is 317% larger than in other metropolitan areas; the corresponding figure for CVC investments is 110%.

Results from Models 3 and 4 support the notion that more developed metropolitan regions are associated with a heightened level of VC activity, particularly notable in the case of IVC investments. Indeed, in Model 3, both $Population\ Density_{kt}$ and $GDP\ per\ Capita_{kt}$

have positive and significant coefficients (respectively, $0.100, p < 0.001$, and $0.648, p < 0.001$), indicating that higher population density and higher wealth at the metropolitan level are associated with a higher number of VC investments. In particular, one standard deviation increase in $Population\ Density_{kt}$ and in $GDP\ per\ Capita_{kt}$ results in a 11% and 91% increase in the number of VC investments, respectively. In Model 4, the interaction term $Population\ Density_{kt} \times CVC\ Dummy_j$ has a negative coefficient $(-0.064, p < 0.001)$, suggesting that the positive effect of one standard deviation increase in population density on the number of VC investments is approximately 6% weaker for CVCs compared to IVCs. Similarly, the interaction term $GDP\ per\ Capita_{kt} \times CVC\ Dummy_j$ has a negative coefficient $(-0.269, p < 0.001)$. This indicates that the effect of a one standard deviation increase in the level of regional wealth is approximately 24% lower for CVCs compared to IVCs. Conversely, neither the $Top\ University\ Dummy_k$ (Model 3) nor its interaction with the $CVC\ Dummy_j$ (Model 4) are significant, suggesting that the presence of a top university in a given metropolitan area is not associated with the number of IVC and CVC investments.

In Tables 7.4–7.6, we replicate the estimates reported in Table 7.3, distinguishing between three different type of industries. In Table 7.4, we only consider VC investments in companies operating in the software, communication, and media industries; in Table 7.5, we only consider VC investments in companies operating in the medical, health, and life sciences industries; in Table 7.6, we only consider VC investments in companies operating in the R&D and engineering industries.

Results for the software, communication, and media industries are very similar to those of our main estimates. Indeed, Table 7.4 shows that being in a large metropolitan area is positively correlated to the number of VC investments, but CVCs make fewer investments in these areas compared to IVCs. Similarly, CVCs invest less in richer and more densely populated areas compared to IVCs. Contrarywise, the presence of a top university in a given metropolitan area does not have any significant effect on the number of VC investments, regardless of the VC types.

Table 7.4. Results – software, communication, and media VC investments.

	Model 1	Model 2	Model 3	Model 4
Large metropolitan area dummy $(\text{LMA})_k$	1.088***	1.430***		
	(0.047)	(0.060)		
CVC dummy_j	−0.461***	−0.328***	−0.476***	−0.556***
	(0.036)	(0.037)	(0.026)	(0.021)
$\text{LMA}_k \times$ CVC dummy_j		−0.686***		
		(0.083)		
Population density_{kt}			0.087***	0.104***
			(0.020)	(0.019)
Population $\text{density}_{kt} \times$ CVC dummy_j				−0.047**
				(0.023)
GDP per capita_{kt}			0.444***	0.672***
			(0.014)	(0.016)
GDP per $\text{capita}_{kt} \times$ CVC dummy_j				−0.395***
				(0.020)
Top university dummy_k			0.153	−0.006
			(0.100)	(0.105)
Top university $\text{dummy}_k \times$ CVC dummy_j				0.193
				(0.145)
Time to startup_{kt}	0.002	0.002	−0.008	−0.006
	(0.013)	(0.013)	(0.013)	(0.012)
Corporate tax rate_{kt}	−0.115***	−0.115***	−0.100***	−0.098***
	(0.026)	(0.026)	(0.025)	(0.025)
Number of individuals using the internet_{kt}	0.033	0.034	0.111***	0.117***
	(0.035)	(0.035)	(0.034)	(0.033)
Power distance index_k	0.278	0.285	−0.049	−0.022
	(0.284)	(0.267)	(0.214)	(0.172)
Individualism vs. collectivism_k	0.226	0.230	0.030	0.047
	(0.150)	(0.140)	(0.111)	(0.088)
Masculinity vs. femininity_k	−0.092	−0.091	−0.028	−0.028
	(0.101)	(0.094)	(0.075)	(0.060)
Uncertainty avoidance index_k	0.138	0.141	0.138	0.170*
	(0.159)	(0.148)	(0.116)	(0.091)
Long-term orientation vs. short-term or._k	0.021	0.016	0.102	0.096
	(0.138)	(0.129)	(0.104)	(0.082)

(*Continued*)

Table 7.4. (*Continued*)

	Model 1	Model 2	Model 3	Model 4
Indulgence vs. restraint$_k$	0.266	0.273	−0.075	−0.053
	(0.269)	(0.252)	(0.201)	(0.161)
Constant	0.513**	0.441**	0.770***	0.787***
	(0.226)	(0.212)	(0.172)	(0.138)
Year and country FE	YES	YES	YES	YES
N of observations	4,590	4,590	4,590	4,590
N of groups	474	474	474	474
Wald chi2	1,154.04***	1,294.40***	2,538.00***	3,996.45***

Note: * $p < 0.10$, ** $p < 0.05$, *** $p < 0.01$. Standard errors in parentheses. This table shows the results of random effects panel regression models with – as dependent variable – the (natural logarithm of the) number of VC investments (i.e. initial ties between each venture and each VC) in software, communication, and media in each metropolitan area/year and categorised by VC types. To ease the interpretation of coefficients, all continuous explanatory variables have been standardised (zero mean and unit standard deviation).

Results for the medical, health, and life sciences industries are somewhat different. Our main result about CVCs investing less than IVCs in large metropolitan areas is confirmed. However, in Model 3 of Table 7.5, the coefficient of *Top University Dummy*$_k$ is positive and significant ($0.174, p < 0.001$). This suggests that in the medical, health, and life sciences industries, the presence of a top university in a given metropolitan area is associated with a 19% increase in the number of VC investments. In Model 4 of Table 7.5, the interaction term *Top University Dummy*$_k$ × *CVC Dummy*$_j$ is negative and significant ($-0.174, p < 0.001$). In other words, the presence of one or more top universities in a metropolitan area is associated with a 19% decrease in the number of CVC investments compared to IVC investments.

Last, results for the R&D and engineering industries are similar to those of the medical, health, and life sciences industries (Table 7.6) in that they show a positive association between the presence in a metropolitan area of one or more top universities and the number of IVC investments, but not CVC investments, in that area.

Table 7.5. Results – medical, health, and life sciences industry VC investments.

	Model 1	Model 2	Model 3	Model 4
Large metropolitan area dummy $(\text{LMA})_k$	1.088***	1.430***		
	(0.024)	(0.031)		
CVC dummy_j	−0.219***	−0.149***	−0.229***	−0.263***
	(0.019)	(0.020)	(0.015)	(0.010)
LMA_k × CVC dummy_j		−0.343***		
		(0.043)		
Population density_{kt}			−0.008	−0.011
			(0.012)	(0.010)
Population density_{kt} × CVC dummy_j				0.001
				(0.011)
GDP per capita_{kt}			0.234***	0.381***
			(0.009)	(0.009)
GDP per capita_{kt} × CVC Dummy_j				−0.271***
				(0.011)
Top university dummy_k			0.174***	0.246***
			(0.055)	(0.045)
Top university dummy_k × CVC dummy_j				−0.174***
				(0.062)
Time to startup_{kt}	−0.002	−0.002	−0.009	−0.007
	(0.009)	(0.009)	(0.009)	(0.009)
Corporate tax rate_{kt}	−0.035*	−0.035*	−0.025	−0.022
	(0.019)	(0.019)	(0.018)	(0.018)
Number of individuals using the internet_{kt}	0.030	0.030	0.066***	0.066***
	(0.025)	(0.025)	(0.024)	(0.024)
Power distance index_k	−0.023	−0.022	−0.098	−0.097
	(0.155)	(0.147)	(0.126)	(0.092)
Individualism vs. collectivism_k	0.016	0.017	−0.035	−0.025
	(0.081)	(0.076)	(0.065)	(0.046)
Masculinity vs. femininity_k	0.011	0.012	0.028	0.019
	(0.055)	(0.052)	(0.044)	(0.032)
Uncertainty avoidance index_k	−0.001	0.001	0.040	0.059
	(0.084)	(0.079)	(0.066)	(0.044)
Long-term orientation vs. short-term or._k	−0.002	−0.001	0.014	0.033
	(0.074)	(0.070)	(0.060)	(0.042)

(*Continued*)

Table 7.5. (*Continued*)

	Model 1	Model 2	Model 3	Model 4
Indulgence vs. restraint$_k$	0.056	0.059	−0.068	−0.073
	(0.146)	(0.138)	(0.117)	(0.083)
Constant	0.235*	0.199*	0.257**	0.292***
	(0.123)	(0.116)	(0.101)	(0.073)
Year and country FE	YES	YES	YES	YES
N of observations	4,590	4,590	4,590	4,590
N of groups	474	474	474	474
Wald chi2	451.88***	574.49***	1371.95***	3914.54***

Note: * $p < 0.10$, ** $p < 0.05$, *** $p < 0.01$. Standard errors in parentheses. This table shows the results of random effects panel regression models with – as dependent variable – the (natural logarithm of the) number of VC investments (i.e. initial ties between each venture and each VC) only in the medical, health, and life sciences industry in each metropolitan area/year and categorised by VC types. To ease the interpretation of coefficients, all continuous explanatory variables have been standardised (zero mean and unit standard deviation).

Table 7.6. Results – R&D and engineering VC investments.

	Model 1	Model 2	Model 3	Model 4
Large metropolitan area dummy (LMA)$_k$	1.088***	1.430***		
	(0.024)	(0.032)		
CVC dummy$_j$	−0.205***	−0.141***	−0.217***	−0.246***
	(0.019)	(0.020)	(0.015)	(0.010)
LMA$_k$ × CVC dummy$_j$		−0.311***		
		(0.044)		
Population density$_{kt}$			0.012	−0.004
			(0.011)	(0.010)
Population density$_{kt}$ × CVC dummy$_j$				0.035***
				(0.011)
GDP per capita$_{kt}$			0.229***	0.373***
			(0.009)	(0.009)
GDP per capita$_{kt}$ × CVC dummy$_j$				−0.280***
				(0.011)
Top university dummy$_k$			0.166***	0.285***
			(0.054)	(0.045)

Table 7.6. (*Continued*)

	Model 1	Model 2	Model 3	Model 4
Top university dummy$_k$ × CVC dummy$_j$				−0.249***
				(0.062)
Time to startup$_{kt}$	−0.007	−0.007	−0.014	−0.014
	(0.010)	(0.010)	(0.009)	(0.009)
Corporate tax rate$_{kt}$	0.031	0.031	0.039**	0.040**
	(0.019)	(0.019)	(0.018)	(0.018)
Number of individuals using the internet$_{kt}$	0.054**	0.054**	0.092***	0.092***
	(0.026)	(0.026)	(0.025)	(0.025)
Power distance index$_k$	0.140	0.142	0.071	0.076
	(0.157)	(0.150)	(0.125)	(0.092)
Individualism vs. collectivism$_k$	0.134*	0.135*	0.086	0.088*
	(0.081)	(0.077)	(0.064)	(0.047)
Masculinity vs. femininity$_k$	−0.084	−0.084	−0.070	−0.071**
	(0.055)	(0.053)	(0.044)	(0.032)
Uncertainty avoidance index$_k$	0.001	0.002	0.050	0.062
	(0.085)	(0.080)	(0.066)	(0.044)
Long-term orientation vs. short-term or.$_k$	−0.014	−0.014	0.016	0.022
	(0.075)	(0.071)	(0.060)	(0.042)
Indulgence vs. restraint$_k$	0.095	0.098	−0.016	−0.005
	(0.147)	(0.140)	(0.116)	(0.083)
Constant	0.256**	0.221*	0.286***	0.303***
	(0.124)	(0.119)	(0.100)	(0.073)
Year and country FE	YES	YES	YES	YES
N of observations	4,590	4,590	4,590	4,590
N of groups	474	474	474	474
Wald chi2	477.94***	574.37***	1,476.35***	4,130.21***

Note: * $p < 0.10$, ** $p < 0.05$, *** $p < 0.01$. Standard errors in parentheses. This table shows the results of random effects panel regression models with – as dependent variable – the (natural logarithm of the) number of VC investments (i.e. initial ties between each venture and each VC) only in R&D and engineering in each metropolitan area/year and categorised by VC types. To ease the interpretation of coefficients, all continuous explanatory variables have been standardised (zero mean and unit standard deviation).

7.5. Conclusions

In this study, we provided descriptive evidence on the VC geographical concentration of IVC and CVC investments across European metropolitan areas and different sectors. Moreover, we analysed the regional-level factors explaining such geographical distribution, giving for the first time an overview of the regional investment patterns of IVCs and CVCs in the European VC market.

Our results suggest that CVC investments are less concentrated in large metropolitan areas compared to IVC investments. Furthermore, higher population density and regional income are associated with a greater number of IVC investments, while the positive effects of these factors are weaker for CVC investments. The presence of a top university in a metropolitan area does not significantly influence VC investments, regardless of the VC types, except for the medical, health, and life sciences and the R&D and engineering industries. In these science-oriented industries, metropolitan areas where there are one or more top universities show a larger number of IVC investments but not of CVC investments. These results show that the geography of VC is deeply influenced by investors' governance and that the characteristics of a metropolitan area that explain its attractiveness for IVC investments do not extend to CVC investments.

These results have relevant implications for policymakers who are interested in designing effective policy initiatives to stimulate regional IVC and CVC investments. First, the concentration of VC investments in large metropolitan areas is known to exacerbate regional inequalities, with peripheral and less developed regions receiving fewer and fewer investments. However, the fact that CVC investment activity concentrates less in large metropolitan areas suggests an untapped potential for less wealthy and less densely populated entrepreneurial ecosystems, which are relatively more attractive to CVCs than to IVCs. Policymakers should consider these disparities between CVC and IVC investment patterns to devise incentives that encourage VC investment and promote entrepreneurship in relatively 'underdeveloped' regions. This could involve directing CVC investments towards these regions or facilitating collaboration and syndication between CVCs and IVCs to spur investment activity in those places. Moreover, our findings provide nuanced evidence about the role of knowledge hubs, represented by metropolitan areas hosting top universities. While CVCs do not demonstrate a higher tendency to invest in areas with top universities, IVCs exhibit a stronger propensity to do so, especially in highly research-intensive sectors, such as the medical, health, and life sciences and the R&D and engineering sectors. The academic reputation of these universities and of the scientists they employ is a strong attractor of IVC investments. The divergence in the geographic pattern of CVC and IVC investments in these industries might indicate that CVC investors are able to spot promising start-ups created in less prominent research centres or that they can compensate for the lack of first-class research infrastructures by leveraging their corporate R&D capabilities. Further investigation into this topic could shed light on the optimal policy measures to foster the development of industry-specific clusters in metropolitan areas, with and without top-tier research institutions, aiming to cater to the investment preferences of either VC types.

The findings of this study suggest various future directions. First, it would be valuable to explore the VC geographical concentration of different types of VCs in diverse institutional settings. Indeed, institutional and legal frameworks may be relevant, especially within specific sectors targeted by VCs, as shown by our findings. An emerging trend involves VC funding of green, sustainable, and cleantech start-ups (see for a review Dhayal *et al.*, 2023). Future work could explore the role of national and EU environmental policies in influencing the allocation of VC (Croce and Bianchini, 2022), particularly IVC and CVC investments, in different regions.

Second, future work could delve into the distinctions among various types of VCs, such as governmental VCs, whose mandate may lead to distinct regional investment patterns compared to IVCs and CVCs. Another promising avenue for exploration involves examining the potential impact of VC general partners' style drifts on investments across various European regions. Style drifts, characterised by the risk-seeking or risk-avoiding behaviour of general partners relative to the VC fund expected risk profile, constitute a significant phenomenon within the VC landscape (Koenig and Burghof, 2022). The presence of style drifts has the potential to shape VC investment behaviour across diverse geographic regions. For instance, these drifts may be more prevalent in smaller markets compared to larger ones, driving investments towards earlier stages, international deals, or a lower degree of industry specialisation, while also being contingent upon the governance of VC funds. For instance, CVCs, whose investment targets are driven by strong strategic objectives aligned with those of the parent company, might exhibit a lower susceptibility to style drifts. Fourth, scholars might analyse the influence of additional regional characteristics on the different VC investment patterns. For example, the presence in a given area of R &D centres and subsidiaries or branches of high-tech multinational corporations may make the area attractive to the CVC activity of these corporations. Additionally, researchers could explore the correlation between VC investments and the presence in a given area of technology transfer organisations, such as business incubators and accelerators, or the quality of the human capital, including entrepreneurial skills.

Finally, the regional distribution of investments by IVCs and CVCs may be correlated with variations in the network structures across different regions. A number of recent studies underscore the significance of networks in influencing both VC investment decisions and subsequent performance outcomes (e.g. Alvarez–Garrido and Guler, 2018; Liu and Maula, 2021; Hu *et al.*, 2022). It is plausible that networks exhibit considerable diversity across various European regions, potentially exerting an impact on VC investment strategies and performance.

References

Alvarez-Garrido, E. and Guler, I. (2018). Status in a strange land? Context-dependent value of status in cross-border venture capital. *Strategic Management Journal*, 39(7), 1887–1911.

Armour, J. and Cumming, D. (2006). The legislative road to Silicon Valley. *Oxford Economic Papers*, 58(4), 596–635.

Bertoni, F., D'Adda, D., and Grilli, L. (2016). Cherry-picking or frog-kissing? A theoretical analysis of how investors select entrepreneurial ventures in thin venture capital markets. *Small Business Economics*, 46, 391–405.

Chemmanur, T. J., Loutskina, E., and Tian, X. (2014). Corporate venture capital, value creation, and innovation. *The Review of Financial Studies*, 27(8), 2434–2473.

Chen, H., Gompers, P., Kovner, A., and Lerner, J. (2010). Buy local? The geography of venture capital. *Journal of Urban Economics*, 67(1), 90–102.

Chowdhury, F., Audretsch, D. B., and Belitski, M. (2019). Institutions and entrepreneurship quality. *Entrepreneurship Theory and Practice*, 43(1), 51–81.

Colombo, M. G., D'Adda, D., and Quas, A. (2019). The geography of venture capital and entrepreneurial ventures' demand for external equity. *Research Policy*, 48(5), 1150–1170.

Colombo, M. G., Guerini, M., Hoisl, K., and Zeiner, N. M. (2023). The dark side of signals: Patents protecting radical inventions and venture capital investments. *Research Policy*, 52(5), 104741.

Colombo, M. G. and Murtinu, S. (2017). Venture capital investments in Europe and portfolio firms' economic performance: Independent versus corporate investors. *Journal of Economics and Management Strategy*, 26(1), 35–66.

Colombo, M. G. and Shafi, K. (2016). Swimming with sharks in Europe: When are they dangerous and what can new ventures do to defend themselves? *Strategic Management Journal*, 37(11), 2307–2322.

Croce, A. and Bianchini, R. (2022). The role of environmental policies in promoting venture capital investments in cleantech companies. *Review of Corporate Finance*, 2(3), 587–616.

Cumming, D. and Dai, N. (2010). Local bias in venture capital investments. *Journal of Empirical Finance*, 17(3), 362–380.

Cumming, D., Schmidt, D., and Walz, U. (2010). Legality and venture capital governance around the world. *Journal of Business Venturing*, 25(1), 54–72.

Dhayal, K. S., Giri, A. K., Esposito, L., and Agrawal, S. (2023). Mapping the significance of green venture capital for sustainable development: A systematic review and future research agenda. *Journal of Cleaner Production*, 396, 136489.

Dushnitsky, G. (2012). Corporate venture capital in the 21st century: An integral part of firms' innovation toolkit. In D. Cumming (Ed.), *The Oxford Handbook of Venture Capital* (pp. 185–219). Oxford University Press.

Dushnitsky, G. and Lenox, M. J. (2005). When do incumbents learn from entrepreneurial ventures? Corporate venture capital and investing firm innovation rates. *Research Policy*, 34(5), 615–639.

Florida, R. L. and Kenney, M. (1988). Venture capital-financed innovation and technological change in the USA. *Research Policy*, 17(3), 119–137.

Florida, R. L. and Mellander, C. (2016). Rise of the startup city: The changing geography of the venture capital financed innovation. *California Management Review*, 59(1), 14–38.

Florida, R. L. and Smith Jr, D. F. (1993). Venture capital formation, investment, and regional industrialization. *Annals of the Association of American Geographers*, 83(3), 434–451.

Gompers, P. and Lerner, J. (1998). What drives venture fundraising? *Brookings Papers on Economic Activity: Microeconomics*, 29, 149–192.

Guerini, M. and Tenca, F. (2018). The geography of technology-intensive start-ups and venture capital: European evidence. *Economia e Politica Industriale*, 45, 361–386.

Hofstede, G. (2010). The GLOBE debate: Back to relevance. *Journal of International Business Studies*, 41(8), 1339–1346.

Hu, S., Gu, Q., and Xia, J. (2022). Problemistic search of the embedded firm: The joint effects of performance feedback and network positions on venture capital firms' risk taking. *Organization Science*, 33(5), 1889–1908.

Koenig, L. and Burghof, H. P. (2022). The investment style drift puzzle and risk-taking in venture capital. *Review of Corporate Finance*, 2(3), 587–616.

Kwon, D. and Sorenson, O. (2023). The Silicon Valley syndrome. *Entrepreneurship Theory and Practice*, 47(2), 344–368.

Li, Y., Kenney, M., Patton, D., and Song, A. (2023). Entrepreneurial ecosystems and industry knowledge: Does the winning region take all? *Small Business Economics*, 61(1), 153–172.

Li, Y. and Zahra, S. A. (2012). Formal institutions, culture, and venture capital activity: A cross-country analysis. *Journal of Business Venturing*, 27(1), 95–111.

Lindgaard Christensen, J. (2007). The development of geographical specialization of venture capital. *European Planning Studies*, 15(6), 817–833.

Liu, Y. and Maula, M. (2021). Contextual status effects: The performance effects of host-country network status and regulatory institutions in cross-border venture capital. *Research Policy*, 50(5), 104216.

Ma, S. (2020). The life cycle of corporate venture capital. *The Review of Financial Studies*, 33(1), 358–394.

Mason, C. M. and Harrison, R. T. (2002). The geography of venture capital investments in the UK. *Transactions of the Institute of British Geographers*, 27(4), 427–451.

Maula, M. V. J., Keil, T., and Zahra, S. A. (2013). Top management's attention to discontinuous technological change: Corporate venture capital as an alert mechanism. *Organization Science*, 24(3), 926–947.

PitchBook-NVCA (2023). Venture Monitor Q4 2023. National Venture Capital Association.

Samila, S. and Sorenson, O. (2011). Venture capital, entrepreneurship, and economic growth. *The Review of Economics and Statistics*, 93(1), 338–349.

Schertler, A. (2003). Driving Forces of Venture Capital Investments in Europe: A Dynamic Panel Data Analysis. Kiel Working Paper No. 1172.

Sorenson, O. and Stuart, T. E. (2001). Syndication networks and the spatial distribution of venture capital investments. *American Journal of Sociology*, 106(6), 1546–1588.

https://doi.org/10.1142/9781800617032_0008

Chapter 8

Navigating the Interplays Between Different Investor Types: A Map of the Entrepreneurial Finance Literature for Future Research

Vincenzo Capizzi[*], **Nicola Carta**[†], **and Elisa Cavezzali**[†]

[*]*Department of Economics and Business Studies, Università del Piemonte Orientale, Via E. Perrone, Novara, Italy*

[†]*Department of Management, Università Ca' Foscari, Fondamenta San Giobbe, Venezia, Italy*

8.1. Introduction

New firms serve as the backbone of economies, setting the course for future progress and societal evolution. The emergence of entrepreneurial initiatives fosters innovation and infuses dynamism into the economic landscape, exerting a disproportionate impact on regional economic development and the creation of new employment opportunities (Chemmanur *et al.*, 2011; Hall and Lerner, 2010; Kerr *et al.*, 2014; Kortum and Lerner, 2000; Lerner *et al.*, 2018;

Samila and Sorenson, 2011). Despite their vital role, these enterprises often encounter the challenge of securing adequate financial capital to sustain their growth, mainly due to the opaque nature of their operations and their inherently high risk (Berger and Udell, 1998, 2002; Dunn and Cheatham, 1993; Ebben and Johnson, 2011; Schmalz *et al.*, 2017).

Over the past two decades, the rise of new players and alternative financing avenues has significantly mitigated the existing financing gap for early-stage ventures (Bellavitis *et al.*, 2017; Bonini and Capizzi, 2019; Bruton *et al.*, 2015; Fraser *et al.*, 2015; Landström and Mason, 2016). Nowadays, entrepreneurs enjoy unprecedented access to myriad funding sources that were unavailable two decades ago. These new sources encompass incubators and accelerators,[1] science and technology parks,[2] proof-of-concept centres,[3]

[1]Incubators and accelerators are organisations that provide specialised programmes to help start-ups and emerging companies grow. These programmes offer participating start-ups a variety of resources, including office spaces, guidance from seasoned entrepreneurs and industry experts, training sessions, networking opportunities, and access to legal and accounting services (Cohen *et al.*, 2019b; Cohen and Hochberg, 2014). Incubators are usually not-for-profit or publicly managed organisations and therefore maintain an open admission policy with flexible programme durations; furthermore, they typically do not provide direct investments. Conversely, accelerators offer shorter and more intense programmes and, notably, provide funding (although limited) to participating start-ups (Cohen, 2013; Woolley and MacGregor, 2022).

[2]Science and technology parks, often referred to as simply research parks or innovation districts, are environments designed to bring together high-technology firms with the promise that knowledge spillovers will make them more innovative and successful (Koçak and Can, 2014; Ribeiro *et al.*, 2016; Zhang, 2005). Science and technology parks often use their own investment funds to support promising start-ups or establish partnerships with financiers such as accelerators, venture capitalists (VCs), business angels (BAs), big corporations, or governments.

[3]Proof-of-concept centres are specialised facilities or programmes established within academic or research institutions that aim at accelerating the commercialisation of innovations out of the university into the marketplace (Bradley *et al.*, 2013; Gulbranson and Audretsch, 2008; Hayter and Link, 2015; Maia and Claro, 2013). These centres serve as collaborative environments where academic researchers converge with industry experts, entrepreneurs, and big corporations to assess the feasibility and potential of novel technologies, products, or ideas in

seed funds affiliated with universities or large corporations, business angel (BA) groups and networks,[4] crowdfunding (CF) platforms,[5]

order to scale them up for commercialisation. Proof-of-concept centres often provide access to resources such as funding, expertise, equipment, and networking opportunities.

[4]Over the past decade, there has been a notable rise in the establishment and progressive growth of BA associations, ranging from exclusive and formalised investment groups to national or international reference networks (Bonini and Capizzi, 2019; Bonnet *et al.*, 2022; Harrison and Mason, 1999; Mason *et al.*, 2016). These associations have differentiated themselves in terms of size, rules, internal structure, and services offered. Membership in a BA group provides several advantages to its members (Bonini *et al.*, 2018; Bonnet *et al.*, 2022; Butticè *et al.*, 2021; Cumming and Zhang, 2019; Lerner *et al.*, 2018; Mason *et al.*, 2016; Wallmeroth *et al.*, 2018). First, BA associations enjoy greater visibility compared to individual BAs, enabling them to benefit from a deal flow of superior size and quality (Croce *et al.*, 2017). Second, BAs have the chance of making larger investments by pooling their financial resources and diversifying their portfolio to optimise risk (Bonini *et al.*, 2018). Furthermore, by sharing the costs of evaluation, negotiation, and monitoring, they can lower the costs associated with each investment, thereby increasing the overall efficiency of the entire investment process. Finally, the sharing of information and knowledge within the community benefits all its members.

[5]CF stands as one of the most recent and pivotal innovations within the contemporary start-up ecosystem. This funding channel allows founders of for-profit, artistic, or cultural ventures to obtain financial resources by leveraging relatively modest contributions from a wide range of individuals (Mollick, 2014). There are several types of CF that differ on the basis of the reward offered to investors in return for their financial support. Notably, start-ups typically opt for either product CF, where investors receive the product being developed with their contributions, or equity CF, where investors acquire shares in the company. At the core of this financing model, there is an online platform that enables the matching between demand (requests for funds) and supply (the crowd of financiers), concurrently providing detailed insights into individual projects (Bonini and Capizzi, 2019). CF facilitates the raising of capital by start-ups and innovators, mitigating the difficulties often encountered in raising the funds needed to start or grow their businesses. At the same time, it democratises the economic process of value creation, opening up the possibility for the general public to access a segment of the capital markets usually dominated by professional investors (Agrawal *et al.*, 2015; Catalini and Hui, 2018; Cumming *et al.*, 2021; Gafni *et al.*, 2021).

token fundraising,[6] and financial instruments backed by intellectual property.[7] The latter developments have gone hand in hand with the growing interest in the start-up ecosystem by banks (Cassar, 2004; Hanssens *et al.*, 2016; Hirsch and Walz, 2019; Robb and Robinson, 2014) and governments (Cumming *et al.*, 2017; Cumming and Johan, 2009; Grilli and Murtinu, 2014). Consequently, start-ups and emerging companies have adeptly navigated this diversification, strategically securing funding from various sources and leveraging them simultaneously and across multiple financing rounds.

Despite these developments, most studies within the entrepreneurial finance domain still consider funding sources in isolation, neglecting their interactions as part of a larger interconnected financial ecosystem (Bellavitis *et al.*, 2017; Cumming *et al.*, 2019a; Drover *et al.*, 2017a). This literature segmentation can also be attributed to the paucity of publicly available data on entrepreneurial finance, compounded by the challenges associated with integrating different data sources (Cumming and Vismara, 2017). Indeed, most empirical papers on financing entrepreneurs are based on data from one source of capital. For instance, research articles on venture capital (VC) commonly rely on data from vendors such as Thomson Economics, which gathers information directly from the venture capitalists. Consequently, these data provide limited insights into alternative sources

[6]Token fundraising refers to the issuance and sale of digital tokens, typically based on blockchain technology, as a means of raising capital for a project or venture. These tokens may represent various forms of value, such as ownership rights, access to services, or utility within a decentralised ecosystem. The domain of token fundraising initially encompassed only initial coin offerings (ICOs) (Adhami *et al.*, 2018; Chen, 2018; Fisch, 2019) but has since undergone a rapid evolution. Nowadays, we are witnessing the emergence of security token offerings (STOs), initial exchange offerings (IEOs), and initial decentralised exchange offerings (IDOs). Each of these fundraising methods carries distinct regulatory and operational considerations.

[7]Within the entrepreneurial context, patents often stand out as the most valuable asset for start-ups. Although these intangible assets are often hard to value for investors, recent studies indicate a significant growth in the number of start-ups using patents as collateral to secure debt financing (Caviggioli *et al.*, 2020; Hochberg *et al.*, 2018; Mann, 2018). This innovative financing option, known as intellectual property-backed lending, or simply IP-backed lending, partially mitigates the funding gap that informationally opaque start-ups face in their earlier stages.

of capital for entrepreneurs beyond VC. Conversely, investigating the interactions among different funding avenues often requires aggregating information from various channels and data providers, including information from investors, entrepreneurs, the internet, groups, or organisations.

Although numerous scholars have emphasised the importance of conducting research on the interplay between different sources of capital (Bellavitis *et al.*, 2017; Block *et al.*, 2017; Capizzi *et al.*, 2024a; Cosh *et al.*, 2009; Cumming *et al.*, 2019a, 2018; Cumming and Groh, 2018; Cumming and Vismara, 2017; Drover *et al.*, 2017a; Masiak *et al.*, 2017; Moritz *et al.*, 2016), these calls have, to date, garnered limited attention. Furthermore, the absence of a comprehensive literature map on the intricate interconnections between diverse investor types further intensifies the challenges for researchers.

This chapter aims to provide a comprehensive overview of the existing research and recent developments in the field, bringing out interesting research gaps and stimulating further scholarly enquiry to integrate research on different sources of finance for entrepreneurial ventures. Indeed, a deeper understanding of the relationships between various investor types is imperative for unravelling the intricacies of the modern entrepreneurial finance ecosystem.

8.2. New Financing Trajectories for Start-Ups

In recent years, the entrepreneurial finance landscape has undergone significant transformations due to technological advancements, regulatory changes, evolving market dynamics, and the emergence of alternative financing channels. These shifts have notably altered the 'traditional' financing path of young entrepreneurial firms.

According to the financing growth cycle paradigm (Berger and Udell, 1998), entrepreneurs seeking seed finance initiated their fundraising efforts within their closest network, comprising family, friends, and 'fools' (the three Fs). Upon achieving crucial milestones, such as developing a prototype or garnering customers' interests, they expanded their pool of investors by engaging with BAs. This strategic choice facilitated their ventures' scaling, rendering them more attractive to institutional investors such as VCs and debt capital providers, including banks. Finally, after receiving VC funding, the entrepreneurs and the investors were driven by the common aim of pursuing an initial public offering (IPO) or selling the business to a prominent corporation.

By contrast, within the current entrepreneurial ecosystem, entrepreneurs can harness an extensive range of funding sources, which can be seamlessly utilised multiple times and interchangeably to meet their financial needs. The globalisation of the start-up segment of capital markets has further enhanced start-ups' capability to attract timely investments from a diverse range of investors worldwide (Chemmanur *et al.*, 2016; Croce *et al.*, 2023; Cumming and Johan, 2017; Dai *et al.*, 2012; Mäkelä and Maula, 2008). Nowadays, entrepreneurs can creatively and strategically time and customise their fundraising in an iterative process involving various funding sources according to the evolving business needs. For instance, a start-up might enrol in an acceleration programme to leverage its powerful network of professionals and increase the chances of securing funds from VCs. Other start-ups might use a CF campaign to cultivate an initial customer base or launch an ICO to avoid diluting the capital share. Yet, some entrepreneurs may combine diverse funding sources to capitalise on their unique advantages.

Furthermore, over the past decades, banks have increased their interest in the entrepreneurial ecosystem. Numerous studies underscore the significance of bank debt as a crucial component of the new ventures' capital structure (Cassar, 2004; Cole and Sokolyk, 2018; Cosh *et al.*, 2009; Deloof and Vanacker, 2018; Hirsch and Walz, 2019; Huyghebaert and Van De Gucht, 2007; Masiak *et al.*, 2017; Robb and Robinson, 2014; Robinson, 2012). Indeed, banks can adopt diverse and flexible lending strategies that align with the respective risk profiles of emerging companies. New companies can, therefore, access bank financing earlier than previously thought.

The adoption rate of new technologies has also been exponentially accelerated by the increasing pervasive power of digital tools. This change in consumer behaviours has led start-ups to shorten their time-to-market, pushing them to follow the new paradigm of 'fail fast and succeed faster'. These days, investors are willing to bear higher risks to support ventures that demonstrate the ability to change course based on market feedback; however, they also expect start-ups to deliver results in shorter time frames. Within this fast-paced environment, entrepreneurs must refine their fundraising strategies, focusing not only on showcasing innovative ideas but also on their ability to execute and adapt swiftly.

Finally, the costs associated with conducting business, transportation, and communication have also experienced a substantial decline. Therefore, many start-ups often employ financial bootstrapping techniques to build and grow their businesses during periods when external financing is not available (Harrison *et al.*, 2004; Jonsson and Lindbergh, 2013; Vanacker *et al.*, 2011; Winborg and Landström, 2001).

All these changes have added further nuances to the initially proposed financing growth cycle paradigm (Bessière *et al.*, 2020; Cohen and Wirtz, 2018), also increasing from a theoretical point of view the complexity of the various relationships between the entrepreneurs and investors and between different investor types. Nowadays, the funding cycle for entrepreneurial ventures is not as straightforward as it used to be, and numerous research questions arise for entrepreneurial finance researchers. The wide range of funding sources offers opportunities for synergies between investor types but also introduces challenges, including heightened agency costs and conflicts of interest.

8.3. Literature on the Interactions Between Different Investor Types

The scholarly discourse pertaining to the interactions among different investor types can be categorised into two overarching streams. The first stream encompasses an extensive body of literature that delves into the domain of sequential interactions. This line of research investigates the intricate dynamics that arise from the indirect interactions among various investor categories during the successive financing rounds of a start-up's funding journey. Conversely, a parallel avenue of scholarly investigation revolves around direct interactions, which occur when different investor types act as co-investors in the same investment round.

Sections 8.3.1 and 8.3.2 offer a comprehensive overview of the literature on sequential and direct interactions. Table 8.1, adopting a matrix form, provides a concise and clear map of the academic discourse.

Table 8.1 Map of the literature on the interplays between different investor types (sequential and direct interactions).

	(2)	(3)	(4)	(5)	(6)
	Accelerators	Reward crowdfunding	Equity crowdfunding	Token offerings	Business angels
(1) Incubators	No evidence	No evidence	No evidence	No evidence	• Incubators exert a positive influence on the start-ups' likelihood of receiving BA support (Cumming and Fischer, 2012).

	(7)	(8)	(9)	(10)
	Venture capital	Private debt	Government grants	Government venture capital
(1) Incubators	• Incubators positively influence the start-ups' likelihood of receiving VC support (Woolley and MacGregor, 2022). The latter relationship is moderated by the characteristics of the support programme (Cao *et al.* 2024) and the start-ups' founders (Clayton, 2024). • When tech parks and VCs invest together, there are negative spillovers on acquisitions (Cumming *et al.* 2019c).	No evidence	• Incubators positively influence the start-ups' likelihood of receiving grants (Colombo and Delmastro, 2002; Woolley and MacGregor, 2022). The latter relationship is moderated by the characteristics of the start-ups' founders (Clayton, 2024).	• Government VC and incubators constitute integral components of the vibrant Israelian ecosystem for successful entrepreneurial and innovation (Avnimelech and Teubal, 2006).

Table 8.1 (*Continued*)

	(2)	(3)	(4)	(5)	(6)
	Accelerators	Reward crowdfunding	Equity crowdfunding	Token offerings	Business angels
(2) Accelerators	–	No evidence	• Within the fintech domain, participation in accelerator programmes exerts a counter-signalling influence on subsequent external equity financing (Browne *et al.*, 2024).	No evidence	• Accelerators attract more capital and investors in the regions where they are located (Fehder and Hochberg, 2019; Goswami *et al.* 2018). • Within the fintech domain, participation in accelerator programmes exerts a counter-signalling influence on subsequent external equity financing (Browne *et al.*, 2024).

(*Continued*)

Table 8.1 (*Continued*)

	(7)	(8)	(9)	(10)
	Venture capital	Private debt	Government grants	Government venture capital
(2) Accelerators	• Accelerators attract more capital and investors in the regions where they are located (Fehder and Hochberg, 2019; Goswami *et al.* 2018). • Accelerators positively influence the start-ups' likelihood of receiving VC support (Woolley and MacGregor, 2022), although this effect may vary significantly (Hallen *et al.*, 2023). • Follow-up funding from VCs occurs more slowly for start-ups participating in an accelerator than non-participating start-ups (Winston Smith and Hannigan, 2014). • Within the fintech domain, participation in accelerator programmes exerts a counter-signalling influence on subsequent external equity financing (Browne *et al.*, 2024). • Specialised accelerators can hinder follow-up VC financing (Seitz *et al.*, 2023).	No evidence	• Accelerators positively influence the start-ups' likelihood of receiving government grants (Woolley and MacGregor, 2022).	No evidence

Table 8.1 (*Continued*)

	(2)	(3)	(4)	(5)	(6)
	Accelerators	Reward crowdfunding	Equity crowdfunding	Token offerings	Business angels
(3) Reward crowd-funding	–	–	• Equity CF does not crowd out rewards CF (Cholakova and Clarysse, 2015).	No evidence	• The success of a reward CF campaign enhances the likelihood of obtaining subsequent funding from BAs (Kaminski *et al.*, 2019).

	(7)	(8)	(9)	(10)
	Venture capital	Private debt	Government grants	Government venture capital
(3) Reward crowd-funding	• The success of a reward CF campaign enhances the likelihood of obtaining subsequent funding from VCs (Kaminski *et al.*, 2019; Sorenson *et al.*, 2016; Thies *et al.*, 2019). The latter effect is contingent upon prior professional investors' support (Colombo and Shafi, 2021), the CF platform's reputation, and its volume of backers (Drover *et al.*, 2017b).	• Development of theoretical models to analyse a start-up's choice between reward CF and bank financing Miglo, 2022; Xu *et al.*, 2018). • Bank failures in a county lead to fewer crowdfunded projects, supporting a complementary relationship between traditional banks and reward CF (Cole *et al.*, 2019).	No evidence	• Government programmes can use reward CF to leverage success (McCahery and Vermeulen, 2014, 2016)

(*Continued*)

Table 8.1 (*Continued*)

	(2)	(3)	(4)	(5)	(6)
	Accelerators	Reward crowdfunding	Equity crowdfunding	Token offerings	Business angels
(4) Equity crowd-funding	–	–	–	No evidence	• The success of an equity CF campaign enhances the likelihood of obtaining subsequent funding from BAs (Hornuf *et al.*, 2018; Signori and Vismara, 2018). • Prior BA support mitigates information asymmetries in follow-on equity CF campaigns (Kleinert *et al.*, 2020; Capizzi *et al.*, 2024b) • There are systematic differences in fundraising outcomes and subsequent financing trajectories between BA-backed and CF-backed companies (Bonini *et al.*, 2023). • Antecedents of professional investors' involvement in an equity CF campaign (Cumming *et al.*, 2019b). • BAs co-investing with the crowd in an equity CF campaign have a positive signalling effect on the crowd (Wang *et al.*, 2019).

Table 8.1 (*Continued*)

	(7)	(8)	(9)	(10)
	Venture capital	Private debt	Government grants	Government venture capital
(4) Equity crowd-funding	• The success of an equity CF campaign enhances the likelihood of obtaining subsequent funding from VCs (Hornuf *et al.*, 2018; Signori and Vismara, 2018). The latter effect is contingent upon the choice of the shareholder structure (Butticè *et al.* 2020), the CF platform's reputation, and its volume of backers (Drover *et al.*, 2017b). • Prior VC support mitigates information asymmetries in follow-on equity CF campaigns (Kleinert *et al.*, 2020). • CF and VCs fund different types of firms (Stevenson *et al.*, 2019). • From a theoretical point of view, there is increasing early-stage market competition between equity CF and VC (Andreu and Groh, 2023). • Antecedents of professional investors' involvement in an equity CF campaign (Cumming *et al.*, 2019b).	• Ventures facing tighter funding constraints from banks are more likely to turn to equity CF, but such ventures are also more prone to failure (Blaseg and Koetter, 2016; Blaseg *et al.*, 2021).	• Start-ups receiving government grants are more likely to successfully raise an equity CF campaign (Kleinert *et al.*, 2020). • Receiving government grants do not affect the likelihood of successfully raising an equity CF campaign (Ahlers *et al.*, 2015).	• Government programmes can use equity CF to leverage success (McCahery and Vermeulen, 2014, 2016)

(*Continued*)

Table 8.1 (*Continued*)

	(2)	(3)	(4)	(5)	(6)
	Accelerators	Reward crowdfunding	Equity crowdfunding	Token offerings	Business angels
(5) Token offerings	–	–	–	–	• Analysis of the factors influencing a start-up's choice between an ICO and traditional forms of finance (Fisch *et al.*, 2022; Schückes and Gutmann, 2021). • Prior BA support positively influences an ICO's success (Belitski and Boreiko, 2022).

	(7)	(8)	(9)	(10)
	Venture capital	Private debt	Government grants	Government venture capital
(5) Token offerings	• Analysis of the factors influencing a start-up's choice between an ICO and traditional forms of finance (Fisch *et al.*, 2022; Schückes and Gutmann, 2021). • Prior VC support positively influences an ICO's success (Belitski and Boreiko, 2022; Hackober and Bock, 2021).	• Development of theoretical models to analyse a start-up's choice between an ICO and bank financing (Choi, 2022; Hu *et al.*, 2023).	No evidence	No evidence

Table 8.1 (*Continued*)

	(2)	(3)	(4)	(5)	(6)
	Accelerators	Reward crowdfunding	Equity crowdfunding	Token offerings	Business angels
(6) Business angels	–	–	–	–	–

	(7)	(8)	(9)	(10)
	Venture capital	Private debt	Government grants	Government venture capital
(6) Business angels	• Performance comparison between VC-backed and BA-backed companies (Bruton *et al.*, 2009; Cavallo *et al.*, 2019; Johnson and Sohl, 2012; Vanacker *et al.*, 2013). • Studies supporting a complementary perspective: BAs take care of seed funding, and VCs provide follow-on funding (Capizzi *et al.*, 2022; Chemmanur and Chen, 2014; Croce *et al.*, 2018; Drover *et al.*, 2017b; Harrison and Mason, 2000; Madill *et al.*, 2005; Sørheim, 2005; Wong *et al.*, 2009).	• BAs positively influence follow-on bank financing (Capizzi *et al.*, 2023; Sørheim, 2005).	No evidence	• Angel capital is unrelated to the removal of tax-subsidised government VC programmes in Canada (Cumming and Johan, 2010).

(*Continued*)

Table 8.1 (*Continued*)

	(7)	(8)	(9)	(10)
	Venture capital	Private debt	Government grants	Government venture capital
(6) Business angels	• Studies supporting a substitutability perspective: BAs and VCs represent distinct financing paths (Hellmann and Thiele, 2015; Hellmann *et al.*, 2021; Ibrahim, 2013; Peters, 2009). • Descriptive statistics on co-investments between BAs and VCs (Cumming and Zhang, 2019; Croce *et al.*, 2018; Goldfarb *et al.*, 2013; Harrison and Mason, 2000; Johnson and Sohl, 2012). • Influence of co-investments between BAs and VCs on start-up performance and cost of capital (Bonnet and Wirtz 2012; Goldfarb *et al.* 2013; Hellmann *et al.*, 2021). • Antecedents of co-investments between BAs and VCs (Maus *et al.*, 2023; Verbouw *et al.*, 2023).			

Table 8.1 (*Continued*)

	(2)	(3)	(4)	(5)	(6)
	Accelerators	Reward crowdfunding	Equity crowdfunding	Token offerings	Business angels
(7) Venture capital	–	–	–	–	–

(7)	(8)	(9)	(10)
Venture capital	Private debt	Government grants	Government venture capital
–	• Start-up's choice between bank and VC financing (Andrieu and Groh, 2012; De Bettignies and Brander, 2007; Robb and Robinson, 2014; Winton and Yerramilli, 2008). • Impact of bank and VC financing on the formation and growth of small firms (Cole *et al.*, 2016; Cosh *et al.*, 2009; Hellmann *et al.*, 2008; Takahashi, 2015). • Banks and VCs as complementary versus substitute funding sources (Barry and Mihov, 2015; Bottazzi *et al.*, 2008; Kolokas *et al.*, 2020; Mason and Stark, 2004; Ueda, 2004)	• Government grants improve firms' chances of obtaining follow-on VC investments (Howell, 2017; Islam *et al.*, 2018; Lerner, 2000; Shinkle and Suchard, 2019). • Grants in the cleantech industry can attract VCs' interest (Bürer and Wüstenhagen, 2009).	• Government VC programmes where government acts as a limited partner attract further investments from private VC into the industry (Cumming and Johan, 2014; Leleux and Surlemont, 2003). • Government VC initiatives organised as tax-subsidised, mutual fund-like entities displace private VC funds (Cumming and MacIntosh, 2006, 2007).

(*Continued*)

Table 8.1 (*Continued*)

	(2)	(3)	(4)	(5)	(6)
	Accelerators	Reward crowdfunding	Equity crowdfunding	Token offerings	Business angels
(8) Private debt	–	–	–	–	–

	(7)	(8)	(9)	(10)
	Venture capital	Private debt	Government grants	Government venture capital
(8) Private debt	–	–	No evidence	• Government VC funds in Canada are more likely to make use of debt finance (Cumming and Johan, 2014)

Note: The table presents a map of the entrepreneurial finance literature on the interplay between different sources of finance. '–' refers to a redundant part of the matrix as the matrix is symmetrical.

8.3.1. *Sequential interactions*

8.3.1.1. *Incubators, accelerators, and other funding sources*

In today's entrepreneurial landscape, start-up incubators and accelerators have emerged as critical players in the economic process of innovation and value creation.

On the one hand, incubators are typically not-for-profit or publicly managed organisations that uphold an open admission policy and offer flexible programme durations (Aernoudt, 2004; Cumming and Johan, 2013; Phan *et al.*, 2005). While they generally do not provide direct investments, they serve as the initial stage for entrepreneurs, often paving the way for subsequent financial opportunities. Few studies have delved into the impact of business incubators on subsequent funding rounds for participating start-ups. Colombo and Delmastro (2002) reveal that incubated start-ups tend to have greater access to public subsidies. Similarly, incubators positively influence a start-up's likelihood of receiving follow-on grants and support from both VCs and BAs (Cumming and Fischer, 2012; Woolley and MacGregor, 2022). However, the latter relationship is moderated by the characteristics of the support programme (Cao *et al.*, 2024) and the start-up's founders (Clayton, 2024).

Furthermore, Cumming *et al.* (2019c) highlight that incubators and technology parks can foster the acquisitions of entrepreneurial start-ups by adopting a supportive and advisory approach, contrasting with VC-led acquisitions that typically follow a control-oriented approach. Drawing insights from the current literature, there seem to be positive synergies between incubators and all financing sources within the entrepreneurial ecosystem (Cumming *et al.*, 2018). However, potential drawbacks may arise when incubators co-invest with other investor types (Cumming *et al.*, 2019c).

On the other hand, accelerators offer shorter and more intense programmes and, notably, provide funding (although limited) to participating start-ups (Cohen, 2013; Cohen *et al.*, 2019a; Woolley and MacGregor, 2022). Practical evidence suggests that accelerators frequently interact with BAs, VCs, and corporate partners (Cohen, 2013; Robinson, 2022). A first set of studies highlights that regions where new start-up accelerators emerge attract more capital and investors than other regions (Fehder and Hochberg, 2019;

Goswami *et al.*, 2018). Another set of studies explores the influence of accelerators on the performance outcomes of new ventures. Most studies find that start-ups benefit from participating in such programmes in terms of exit and follow-on financing opportunities (Hallen *et al.*, 2023; Winston Smith and Hannigan, 2014; Woolley and MacGregor, 2022). However, Browne *et al.* (2024) have recently provided compelling evidence that within the realm of fintech, participation in accelerator programmes exerts a counter-signalling influence on subsequent external equity financing. This phenomenon occurs as top-tier fintech ventures appear inclined to avoid acceleration programmes strategically. Furthermore, according to Seitz *et al.* (2023), specialised accelerators can hinder follow-up VC financing. Thus, conflicting evidence persists regarding the synergistic effects between accelerators and other forms of finance.

8.3.1.2. *CF and other funding sources*

An increasing number of scholars have begun to delve into the sequential interplay between CF campaigns and other investor types.

A first set of studies has examined the certification role of early CF campaigns on successive funding rounds. Specifically, the success of a CF campaign has been shown to enhance the likelihood of obtaining subsequent funding from BAs and VCs. For instance, Signori and Vismara (2018), using a UK-based sample, observe that 34.9% of companies that secured equity CF experienced additional funding, either through private equity injection (9%) or a follow-on offering on a CF platform (25%). Hornuf *et al.* (2018) report analogous findings within the German context and demonstrate that firms receiving equity CF are more likely to secure follow-on financing from both BAs and VCs. Similar results are also found for reward-based CFs (Kaminski *et al.*, 2019; Sorenson *et al.*, 2016; Thies *et al.*, 2019).

Additional in-depth investigations into the factors affecting the association between CF and subsequent financing rounds reveal noteworthy insights. For instance, in the context of equity CF offerings, the choice of shareholder structure plays a significant role in attracting follow-on VC financing (Butticè *et al.*, 2020). Conversely, in reward CF offerings, the likelihood of follow-on VC investments seems contingent upon whether the ventures already have backing from professional investors (Colombo and Shafi, 2021). Adding to the discourse, Drover *et al.* (2017b) also find that the CF platform's reputation and the volume of backers serve as positive indicators for VCs.

Considering the opposite financing sequence, Kleinert *et al.* (2020) have considered the role of prior funding sources, including BAs, VCs, and grants, in mitigating information asymmetries in follow-on equity CF campaigns, highlighting a positive certification effect on CF investors. Deepening this viewpoint, Capizzi *et al.* (2024b) offer empirical evidence into the correlation between certain BAs' attributes and the probability of angel-backed companies using a follow-on equity CF round. Conversely, Ahlers *et al.* (2015) report that government grants are less successful in spurring equity CF.

Finally, a separate set of studies has compared CF with alternative funding sources, yielding noteworthy insights. Bonini *et al.* (2023) highlight systematic differences in fundraising outcomes and subsequent financing trajectories when investigating BA-backed versus CF-backed companies. Despite BAs and CF addressing similar needs, they serve companies with inherently distinct characteristics. Similarly, Stevenson *et al.* (2019) show that CF allocates funding to industries VCs typically do not fund. Lastly, Andrieu and Groh (2023) propose a theoretical model for entrepreneurs choosing between equity CF and VC, predicting increased early-stage market competition.

Building upon insights gleaned from the literature discussed, it becomes evident that reward and equity CF demonstrate positive synergies with both BA and VC investments. However, it is noteworthy that certain scholars posit concerns regarding the potential for angel syndicates to impede the democratisation of capital inherent in equity CF (Agrawal *et al.*, 2016). Additionally, while government grants have exhibited efficacy in fostering the success of CF initiatives, their impact may vary across different contexts (Ahlers *et al.*, 2015; Kleinert *et al.*, 2020).

8.3.1.3. *Token offerings and other funding sources*

Token offerings refer to the issuance and sale of digital tokens, typically based on blockchain technology, as a means of raising capital for a project or venture. These tokens may represent various forms of value, such as ownership rights, access to services, or utility within a decentralised ecosystem. The domain of token fundraising encompasses several types of offerings, i.e. ICOs, STOs, IEOs, and IDOs. Each of these fundraising methods carries distinct regulatory and operational considerations.

ICO is the most widespread form of token offering. Although studies have started to investigate the factors affecting the success and performance of ICO projects and their advantages for ventures, there is a notable gap in understanding their interplay with other investor types.

A first set of studies has explored the determinants guiding the choice between ICOs and traditional financing alternatives. For instance, through in-depth interviews, Schückes and Gutmann (2021) unearth some qualitative dimensions that significantly impact a start-up's decision to undertake an ICO instead of alternative funding methods. Additionally, Fisch *et al.* (2022) discover that ethical minorities are more likely to opt for ICOs over traditional financing and are more likely to succeed. Meanwhile, Hu *et al.* (2023) and Choi (2022) introduce two theoretical models to explore a venture's decision between ICO and traditional bank financing.

A second small set of studies has investigated the sequential interactions between ICOs and other funding sources during the successive financing rounds of a start-up's funding journey. Specifically, Hackober and Bock (2021) and Belitski and Boreiko (2022) focus on start-ups that garnered support from VCs or BAs and subsequently pursued an ICO, revealing a noteworthy positive signalling impact of both previous VC and BA investments on the overall ICOs' success.

The scholarly discourse lacks consensus regarding the synergistic relationship between ICOs and alternative financing mechanisms. While certain scholars suggest that ICOs may compete with traditional sources of finance, others highlight the beneficial spillover effects stemming from prior support by BAs and VCs on the success of ICOs.

The interplay between other forms of token fundraising (STOs, IEOs, and IDOs) and traditional finance mechanisms remains unexplored.

8.3.1.4. *VCs and BAs*

In the ever-evolving entrepreneurial finance landscape, the intricate interplay between BAs and VCs takes centre stage in the scholarly discourse.

Early studies seeking to integrate the realms of these two pivotal investors compared their unique traits (e.g. investment strategies, selection criteria, and exit plans) and their distinctive impact on firm outcomes (e.g. performance). For instance, Johnson and Sohl (2012) juxtapose the post-IPO performance of VC- and BA-backed US companies and report that VCs achieve higher post-IPO performance in their portfolio firms. On the other side of the ocean, Bruton *et al.* (2009) find analogous findings in the UK but not in France, implying a significant influence of institutional factors. VCs also demonstrate a heightened effectiveness in fostering the growth of digital enterprises compared to BAs (Cavallo *et al.*, 2019). These performance differences can be ascribed to the unique selection criteria embraced by BAs and VCs, encompassing diverse geographic, industry, and timing considerations (Cosh *et al.*, 2009; Goldfarb *et al.*, 2013; Hsu *et al.*, 2014; Johnson and Sohl, 2012; Mason and Stark, 2004). Variations in performance between VC- and BA-backed companies can also be attributed to how these two investor types engage with their companies in the post-investment phase (Vanacker *et al.*, 2013).

More recently, the academic discourse has shifted towards investigating the nature of BAs and VCs as complementary or substitute funding sources for start-ups and entrepreneurial companies. On the one hand, BAs and VCs are often regarded as two complementary players within the entrepreneurial finance ecosystem. Their relationship is frequently depicted through a chronological pecking-order model wherein companies initially secure equity capital from BAs and subsequent funding rounds from VCs (Benjamin and Margulis, 2005; Chemmanur and Chen, 2014; Schwienbacher, 2009). This view is consistent with the traditional paradigm of a company's lifecycle and the identification of the different sources of financing associated with each stage (Berger and Udell, 1998). Practical evidence manifests that BAs have limited funding capacity and need VCs to provide additional capital. Empirical studies further demonstrate a positive association between receiving BA financing and follow-on rounds from VCs (Croce *et al.*, 2018; Madill *et al.*, 2005). Survey-based studies indicate that BAs function as a crucial launch pad, actively helping companies to get VC funding (Sørheim, 2005; Wong *et al.*, 2009). Moreover, several studies confirm that VCs leverage BAs' screening capabilities to find viable investment opportunities (Capizzi *et al.*, 2022; Drover *et al.*, 2017b; Harrison and Mason, 2000).

On the other hand, a recent stream of literature has popularised the existence of a substitution-based relationship between BAs and VCs rather than a complementary-based one. According to this perspective, BAs and VCs represent two alternative financing paths: entrepreneurial companies that obtain funding from one investor type are likely to remain loyal to that type (Cumming and Zhang, 2019; Hellmann and Thiele, 2015; Ibrahim, 2013; Peters, 2009). This phenomenon could be justified either by intrinsic characteristics of the firm that are better suited to a particular kind of investor or by pressure from the investors themselves, explicitly or implicitly guiding the firm towards a financing path involving investors of the same type. Recent findings by Hellmann *et al.* (2021) provide compelling evidence in support of the substitution-based perspective. The authors find that Canadian entrepreneurial firms rarely switch between BA and VC financing across successive investment rounds. Furthermore, Mason *et al.* (2016) contend that the emergence of angel networks and angel funds makes it easier for BAs to offer larger follow-on financing rounds, thus reducing their need for VCs.

While the precise nature of the relationship between BAs and VCs remains a topic of ongoing debate, scholars agree that there is a need for further investigations to clarify the role played by institutional factors and the digital environment (Cumming and Zhang, 2019).

8.3.1.5. *Debt and equity investors*

A burgeoning body of entrepreneurial finance research reveals that young entrepreneurial firms strategically orchestrate a blend of debt and equity financing to meet their financial needs (Cassar, 2004; Cole and Sokolyk, 2018; Cosh *et al.*, 2009; Deloof and Vanacker, 2018; Hirsch and Walz, 2019; Huyghebaert and Van De Gucht, 2007; Masiak *et al.*, 2017; Robb and Robinson, 2014). Accordingly, many scholars have delved into the intricate interplays that unfold between banks and equity finance providers throughout the growth process of young entrepreneurial firms.

In particular, many studies have focused on the interplay between VCs and banks (Block *et al.*, 2017). For instance, several theoretical contributions have modelled the choice of bank financing relative to VC financing (De Bettignies and Brander, 2007; Winton and Yerramilli, 2008). These studies demonstrate that entrepreneurs gain advantages from the value-adding activities of VCs, albeit at the cost of shared ownership and reduced incentives for individual effort. As a result, VC financing is preferred over bank financing in situations where the VC investor can substantially amplify value and entrepreneurial productivity is relatively modest. On the other hand, Robb and Robinson (2014) scrutinise actual capital structure decisions made by US-based start-ups in their initial year of operation, offering valuable insights into the real-world capital structure dynamics. In contrast, Andrieu and Groh (2012) theorise that an entrepreneur's choice between bank-affiliated and independent VC firms depends on project characteristics.

A different stream of research has delved into the impact of bank and VC financing on the formation and growth of small firms. Notably, Cole *et al.* (2016) observed a substantial influence of VC financing in stimulating new firms, whereas no supporting evidence for a similar effect from banks was identified. Furthermore, Cosh *et al.* (2009) delve into the determinants influencing rejection rates in applications for outside finance among various investor categories, offering empirical support for the conventional pecking-order theory. Other studies also reveal that banks are strategic investors who capitalise on their connection with small and young firms to facilitate subsequent VC investments (Takahashi, 2015) or vice versa use their affiliated VC funds to build lending relationships (Hellmann *et al.*, 2008).

An additional line of enquiry has addressed whether banks and VCs function as complements or substitutes. Although the distinctive selection criteria (Mason and Stark, 2004; Ueda, 2004) and value-adding capabilities (Bottazzi *et al.*, 2008) of traditional banking and VC suggest they have a complementary relationship, some scholars propose that, in specific contexts, these two actors operate as viable substitutes. This perspective is underscored by findings indicating that VCs and lenders fund different types of firms (Barry and

Mihov, 2015), along with evidence highlighting competition between the credit market and VCs in fintech entrepreneurship (Kolokas *et al.*, 2020).

In stark contrast, the intricate interplay between the banking system and other equity financiers within the entrepreneurial ecosystem remains largely uncharted within the current body of literature. As for the interplay between banks and BAs, Sørheim (2005) represents a pioneering effort. Through their case study analysis, they underscore the pivotal role that regionally focused BAs play in securing bank financing for supported firms, often accompanied by negotiating more favourable contractual terms. These BAs, boasting direct affiliations with key figures in regional banks, leverage their established reputations as potent instruments in negotiation. In a more recent study, Capizzi *et al.* (2023) empirically validate the positive impact of BAs through an analysis of their influence on follow-on bank financing for backed companies. Through their seasoned experience and close monitoring of investments, BAs enhance entrepreneurial firms' strategic capability to set up a profitable business model, effectively mitigating the risk perceived by banks. This perspective suggests that bank and BA financing can be complementary funding sources. However, further research is essential to understand how institutional factors may shape and influence the nature of this relationship.

Finally, there is a notable dearth of empirical studies regarding the relationship between banks and CF. Miglo (2022) and Xu *et al.* (2018) propose two distinct mathematical models to analyse a firm choice between reward CF and bank financing, whereas model a bargaining game. Furthermore, Cole *et al.* (2019) conclude that bank failures in a county lead to fewer crowdfunded projects, supporting the complementary nature of traditional banks and reward-based CF. As for equity CF, Blaseg and Koetter (2016) and Blaseg *et al.* (2021) find that ventures facing tighter funding constraints from banks are more likely to turn to equity CF; however, such ventures are also more prone to failure, implying that CF may attract lower-quality entrepreneurs seeking alternative funding. In sum, the literature suggests a complementary relationship between reward-based CF and bank financing, as opposed to a substitution relationship between equity-based CF and bank financing. Nevertheless, there remains a pressing need for scholars to delve deeper into these intricate interplays.

8.3.1.6. *Public and private funding*

Over the past two decades, governments worldwide have increasingly recognised the paramount importance of fostering a vibrant start-up ecosystem. This heightened interest is a strategic response to the transformative role that new firms play in shaping regional economies. Indeed, a wealth of research has substantiated the notion that innovative start-ups exert a disproportionate impact on economic development and employment opportunities (Chemmanur *et al.*, 2011; Hall and Lerner, 2010; Kerr *et al.*, 2014; Kortum and Lerner, 2000; Lerner *et al.*, 2018; Samila and Sorenson, 2011). Governments can employ diverse instruments to foster the growth of new firms, including grants, tax subsidies, government-affiliated VCs, loan programmes, public–private partnerships, affiliated investment funds for innovation, and microfinance initiatives. However, research on the interplay between public and private funding sources is still underdeveloped.

Most studies within this stream of literature have focused on the relationship between government grants and other sources of finance. Government grants are widely used in countries worldwide to encourage the earliest level of entrepreneurial activity. Several authors have proved that winning a government grant increases a firm's chances of receiving follow-on VC funding (Howell, 2017; Islam *et al.*, 2018; Lerner, 2000; Shinkle and Suchard, 2019). Indeed, government grants can serve as a strong positive signal for follow-on professional investors. Bürer and Wüstenhagen (2009) also show that industry-specific grants, particularly within the cleantech industry, can effectively attract the attention and interest of cleantech VCs.

Similarly, research on incubators and accelerators (see Section 8.3.1.1) has found that incubated and accelerated start-ups have greater access to grants and public subsidies (Colombo and Delmastro, 2002; Woolley and MacGregor, 2022). According to some scholars, government grants must operate alongside other programmes such as incubators (Etzkowitz, 2002) and support for angel networks (Mason and Harrison, 2015) to increase their effectiveness. Conversely, the relationship between government grants and different types of CF remains ambiguous due to the lack of studies. Kleinert *et al.* (2020) argue that grants can facilitate the success of equity CF, whereas Ahlers *et al.* (2015) report that government grants have no impact. There is almost no evidence on the interplay between government grants and BAs.

Government VC represents another significant tool at the disposal of governments to nurture the growth of new firms. Government VC can be structured as limited partnerships, wherein government investors receive financial returns only after private-sector limited partners achieve their predetermined hurdle rate of return. This configuration fosters positive synergies with private VC, attracting further investments into the industry as a whole (Cumming and Johan, 2014; Leleux and Surlemont, 2003). Alternatively, government VC initiatives can be organised as tax-subsidised mutual-fund-like entities aimed at attracting retail investors. However, such an approach can displace private VC funds (Cumming and MacIntosh, 2006, 2007).

Our comprehension of the interplay between government VC and other funding sources, such as incubators, accelerators, CF, BAs, and private debt, remains limited due to a paucity of research. According to Avnimelech and Teubal (2006), government VC and incubators constitute integral components of the success of the Israeli entrepreneurial ecosystem. Similarly, McCahery and Vermeulen (2014, 2016) argue that government programmes can use reward- and equity-based CF to leverage success. Moreover, Cumming and Johan (2010) observe that angel financing appears to be unrelated to the removal of tax-subsidised government VC programmes in Canada. Finally, government VC seems more likely to make use of debt finance (Cumming and Johan, 2014).

Further research on the interplay between public and private funding is warranted to assess how different types of government interventions affect other forms of finance. Indeed, public policies towards entrepreneurial finance may inadvertently create or exacerbate frictions among various investor types, harming the scale-up of entrepreneurial ventures (Cumming *et al.*, 2018).

8.3.2. *Multi-type co-investments*

In the dynamic landscape of entrepreneurial finance, simultaneous co-investments among diverse investor types are frequently observed. However, scholarly attention to this phenomenon has been relatively sparse.

Co-investments between VCs and BAs have garnered relatively more attention within academic discourse. For instance, an early study by Harrison and Mason (2000) presents survey-based evidence highlighting that co-investments between VCs and BAs in the UK accounted for 7% of all VC deals during the 1998–1999 period. This study asserts that such collaborations foster the implementation of complementary actions for value creation and business monitoring while acknowledging the potential introduction of internal conflicts in business management. Descriptive statistics on co-investments between BAs and VCs have been provided by other authors, although mixed syndications were not the main focus of the investigation (Croce *et al.*, 2018; Cumming and Zhang, 2019; Goldfarb *et al.*, 2013; Johnson and Sohl, 2012). Within the limited body of research focusing on co-investments, Bonnet and Wirtz (2012) argue that a simultaneous combination of BAs and VCs can lower the cost of capital for growth-oriented entrepreneurs in the realm of technology ventures. Contrasting findings emerge, however, from studies such as that by Goldfarb *et al.* (2013) and a more recent investigation by Hellmann *et al.* (2021), which identified a detrimental impact on performance when combining angel and VC funding compared to solo-VC investments. More recently, Verbouw *et al.* (2023) and Maus *et al.* (2023) have delved into the antecedents of multi-type co-investments, shedding light on the intricate dynamics shaping these collaborative investment strategies.

In the context of incubators, Cumming *et al.* (2019c) emphasise that when tech parks and VCs invest together, start-ups experience a slight reduction in their probability of being acquired, alongside a significant increase in the time taken to achieve acquisition due to conflicts of interest between tech parks and VCs.

A different stream of literature has focused on professional investors' active participation in CF campaigns. Indeed, VCs and angel investors frequently browse CF platforms in search of promising opportunities, allocating their money to projects they believe hold significant potential. Cumming *et al.* (2019b) examine the ownership structure of firms seeking equity CF and find that professional investors are more likely to invest in offerings that deliver voting rights above a certain investment threshold compared to those that provide voting rights to every investor. Furthermore, Wang *et al.* (2019) examine the effect of BAs' involvement in equity CF campaigns and find that angels play an essential role in funding large ventures. In addition, the visibility of BAs' funding behaviour acts as informative signals of venture quality to novice investors, reducing information asymmetry.

In summary, the existing academic literature recognises simultaneous interactions, wherein diverse investor types collaboratively engage in a single investment round. However, a notable gap exists for more thoroughly exploring these interactions. A comprehensive investigation into these simultaneous collaborations is crucial, promising to unveil intricate dynamics and illuminate their potential impact on the entrepreneurial landscape.

8.4. Directions for Future Research and Conclusions

Over the past decades, the entrepreneurial ecosystem has rapidly transformed due to the growth of start-up funding alternatives, technological advancements, and regulatory shifts, becoming significantly more complex and highly interconnected. Considering the intricate and evolving dynamics that have emerged among diverse financiers in the contemporary entrepreneurial ecosystem, numerous scholars have emphasised the importance of conducting research on the interactions between different sources of capital, breaking down the research segmentation in this field (Bellavitis *et al.*, 2017; Block *et al.*, 2017; Capizzi *et al.*, 2024a; Cosh *et al.*, 2009; Cumming *et al.*, 2019a; Cumming and Groh, 2018; Cumming and Vismara, 2017; Drover *et al.*, 2017a; Masiak *et al.*, 2017; Moritz *et al.*, 2016). However, the absence of a comprehensive literature map on the intricate interplays between diverse investor types has posed substantial limitations to researchers unfamiliar with this multifaceted research domain. The current chapter has provided a thorough systematisation of existing research on the relationship between different funding sources, considering both sequential interactions and co-investments. Building on the identified gaps in the existing literature, the following paragraphs summarise critical insights and delineate specific areas that warrant further research. With the growing accessibility of data sources, advancements in scraping algorithms, and the evolution of analysis methodologies, a pronounced opportunity emerges to address challenges in entrepreneurial finance research, particularly concerning the interplay among various investor types.

We can identify many avenues for future research within the domain of sequential interactions. The existing literature largely ignores the heterogeneity of start-ups; therefore, it becomes essential to investigate how a firm's inherent traits, as well as investors' characteristics and strategies, shape its financing trajectory.

First, academic research on the sequential relationships between incubators/accelerators and other funding sources is still scarce and inconclusive due to a lack of structured and large-scale data. Further research is needed to clarify how incubators and accelerators interact with follow-on equity and public financiers, their relationships with financial institutions and corporate partners, and the implications for accelerated start-ups. Moreover, future research should deepen the impact of programmes' heterogeneity, encompassing variations in services provided and affiliations, on the funding trajectories of supported start-ups.

Second, our comprehension of the factors influencing the correlation between CF and subsequent financing rounds remains limited, considering these factors may exhibit variations across different CF types. Furthermore, it is essential for forthcoming research to elucidate the synergistic or competitive dynamics between CF and alternative funding sources, as well as to ascertain whether CF adoption may also have a counter-signalling effect on start-ups in some circumstances.

Third, token fundraising represents an evolving financing avenue for start-ups, and additional research is imperative to delve into the factors influencing a venture's preference for ICOs compared to traditional financing channels. Moreover, there is a need to examine the sequential dynamics between token fundraising and alternative funding mechanisms throughout the successive financing rounds of a start-up's funding trajectory. These investigations should consider both the evolving landscape of token offerings, encompassing STOs, IEOs, and IDOs, and the escalating regulatory frameworks worldwide, progressively providing enhanced clarity and protection to investors.

Fourth, although the intricate interplay between VCs and BAs has occupied a dominant position within the scholarly discussion, it remains necessary to elucidate the nature of their relationship and how the latter is affected by institutional factors, the digital environment, and investors' specific characteristics such as VC affiliation or the heterogeneity of angel-investment organisations (clubs, groups, and networks). Additionally, no studies have explored the temporal overlap between a VC's entry and a BA's exit and the consequential shifts in the entrepreneur's relationship dynamics.

Fifth, our knowledge of the intricate relationship between banks and equity funding sources such as BAs or CF remains largely uncharted. Future studies could further explore their sequential interaction, mutual certification effect, cooperation strategies, potential conflicts, and how differences in institutional settings affect their relationship. For instance, how does the heterogeneity of banking systems influence the relationship between banks and BAs? How do different angel organisations (clubs, groups, and networks) interact with banks? What happens to the relationship between start-ups and banks after an unsuccessful CF campaign? Moreover, forthcoming research endeavours could elucidate the distinct ways banks contribute to entrepreneurial value compared to equity financiers, as well as explore the nuanced impact of different sectors, institutional factors, globalisation, or technological advancements.

Sixth, research opportunities on the interplay between public and private funding sources remain broad for researchers. The sequential interactions between public funding and equity sources such as CF, BAs, and private debt remain largely unexplored. Further enquiries should revolve around optimising start-up support programmes, considering the interplay between different investor types and how regulators should deal with these interactions. Researchers need to elucidate the effect of public policies on entrepreneurial finance, considering their overall impact on the broad spectrum of investor types. This approach will assist policymakers in conceiving public policies aimed at mitigating negative spillovers across different capital sources, thereby improving the scale-up of entrepreneurial ventures.

As for the domain of multi-type co-investments, it is imperative to understand how different investor types relate to each other, align their goals, foster a strong relationship, and cultivate learning opportunities over the investment process. Subsequent research efforts should focus on uncovering the underlying factors that drive multi-type co-investments and examining their impact on start-up performance. Finally, there is a pressing need to delve deeper into the dynamics surrounding multi-type co-investments within CF platforms.

References

Adhami, S., Giudici, G., and Martinazzi, S. (2018). Why do businesses go crypto? An empirical analysis of initial coin offerings. *Journal of Economics and Business*, 100, 64–75.

Aernoudt, R. (2004). Incubators: Tool for entrepreneurship? *Small Business Economics*, 23, 127–135.

Agrawal, A., Catalini, C., and Goldfarb, A. (2015). Crowdfunding: Geography, social networks, and the timing of investment decisions. *Journal of Economics and Management Strategy*, 24, 253–274.

Agrawal, A., Catalini, C., and Goldfarb, A. (2016). Are syndicates the killer app of equity crowdfunding? *California Management Review*, 58, 111–124.

Ahlers, G. K. C., Cumming, D., Günther, C., and Schweizer, D. (2015). Signaling in equity crowdfunding. *Entrepreneurship Theory and Practice*, 39, 955–980.

Andrieu, G. and Groh, A. P. (2012). Entrepreneurs' financing choice between independent and bank-affiliated venture capital firms. *Journal of Corporate Finance*, 18, 1143–1167.

Andrieu, G. and Groh, A. P. (2023). Crowdfunding vs. venture capital: Complements or substitutes? A theoretical analysis. *SSRN Electronic Journal*, 33, 1–38.

Avnimelech, G. and Teubal, M. (2006). Creating venture capital industries that co-evolve with high tech: Insights from an extended industry life cycle perspective of the Israeli experience. *Research Policy*, 35, 1477–1498.

Barry, C. B. and Mihov, V. T. (2015). Debt financing, venture capital, and the performance of initial public offerings. *Journal of Banking and Finance*, 58, 144–165.

Belitski, M. and Boreiko, D. (2022). Success factors of initial coin offerings. *The Journal of Technology Transfer*, 47, 1690–1706.

Bellavitis, C., Filatotchev, I., Kamuriwo, D. S., and Vanacker, T. (2017). Entrepreneurial finance: New frontiers of research and practice: Editorial for the special issue embracing entrepreneurial funding innovations. *Venture Capital*, 19(1), 1–16.

Benjamin, G. A. and Margulis, J. (2005). *Angel Capital: How to Raise Early-Stage Private Equity Financing*. John Wiley & Sons.

Berger, A. N. and Udell, G. F. (1998). The economics of small business finance: The roles of private equity and debt markets in the financial growth cycle. *Journal of Banking and Finance*, 22, 613–673.

Berger, A. N. and Udell, G. F. (2002). Small business credit availability and relationship lending: The importance of bank organisational structure. *Economic Journal*, 112, F32–F53.

Bessière, V., Stéphany, E., and Wirtz, P. (2020). Crowdfunding, business angels, and venture capital: An exploratory study of the concept of the funding trajectory. *Venture Capital*, 22, 135–160.

Blaseg, D., Cumming, D., and Koetter, M. (2021). Equity crowdfunding: High-quality or low-quality entrepreneurs? *Entrepreneurship Theory and Practice*, 45, 505–530.

Blaseg, D. and Koetter, M. (2016). Crowdfunding and bank stress. In P. Tasca, T. Aste, L. Pelizzon, and N. Pernoy (Eds.), *Banking Beyond Banks and Money: A Guide to Banking Services in the Twenty-First Century*. Springer.

Block, J. H., Cumming, D. J., and Vismara, S. (2017). International perspectives on venture capital and bank finance for entrepreneurial firms. *Journal of Industrial and Business Economics*, 44, 3–22.

Bonini, S. and Capizzi, V. (2019). The role of venture capital in the emerging entrepreneurial finance ecosystem: Future threats and opportunities. *Venture Capital*, 21, 137–175.

Bonini, S., Capizzi, V., Giudici, G., and Tenca, F. (2023). Business angels, crowdinvesting and the start-up financing funding gap. 4th Annual Boca-ECGI Corporate Finance and Governance Conference.

Bonini, S., Capizzi, V., Valletta, M., and Zocchi, P. (2018). Angel network affiliation and business angels' investment practices. *Journal of Corporate Finance*, 50, 592–608.

Bonnet, C., Capizzi, V., Cohen, L., Petit, A., and Wirtz, P. (2022). What drives the active involvement in business angel groups? The role of angels' decision-making style, investment-specific human capital and motivations. *Journal of Corporate Finance*, 77, 101944.

Bonnet, C. and Wirtz, P. (2012). Raising capital for rapid growth in young technology ventures: When business angels and venture capitalists coinvest. *Venture Capital*, 14, 91–110.

Bottazzi, L., Da Rin, M., and Hellmann, T. (2008). Who are the active investors? Evidence from venture capital. *Journal of Financial Economics*, 89, 488–512.

Bradley, S. R., Hayter, C. S., and Link, A. N. (2013). Proof of concept centers in the United States: An exploratory look. *Journal of Technology Transfer*, 38, 349–381.

Browne, O., Cumming, D., Hutchinson, M. C., Kirshner, S. N., and O'Reilly, P. (2024). Why avoid participating in an accelerator? Countersignalling by high-quality FinTech ventures. *British Journal of Management*, 0, 1–21.

Bruton, G. D., Filatotchev, I., Chahine, S., and Wright, M. (2010). Governance, ownership structure, and performance of IPO firms: The impact of different types of private equity investors and institutional environments. *Strategic Management Journal*, 31, 491–509.

Bruton, G., Khavul, S., Siegel, D., and Wright, M. (2015). New financial alternatives in seeding entrepreneurship: Microfinance, crowdfunding, and peer-to-peer innovations. *Entrepreneurship Theory and Practice*, 39, 9–26.

Bürer, M. J. and Wüstenhagen, R. (2009). Which renewable energy policy is a venture capitalist's best friend? Empirical evidence from a survey of international cleantech investors. *Energy Policy*, 37, 4997–5006.

Butticè, V., Croce, A., and Ughetto, E. (2021). Network dynamics in business angel group investment decisions. *Journal of Corporate Finance*, 66, 101812.

Butticè, V., Di Pietro, F., and Tenca, F. (2020). Is equity crowdfunding always good? Deal structure and the attraction of venture capital investors. *Journal of Corporate Finance*, 65, 101773.

Cao, Z., Cunningham, L. F., Gao, W., and Liu, Y. (2024). The downsides of specialization: The impact of business incubator's specialization on startups' R&D efficiency and venture capital financing. *R and D Management*, 54, 39–59.

Capizzi, V., Carta, N., Cavezzali, E., and Rigoni, U. (2023). Entrepreneurial firms and bank financing: Do business angels play a role?. *European Financial Management*.

Capizzi, V., Carta, N., Cavezzali, E., and Rigoni, U. (2024a). Il ruolo dei business angels alla luce dell'evoluzione dell'ecosistema delle start-up: Dinamiche e interazioni. *Bancaria*. https://onlinelibrary.wiley.com/doi/10.1111/eufm.12537.

Capizzi, V., Carta, N., Cavezzali, E., and Rigoni, U. (2024b). The angels and the crowd: Business angels' investment practices and follow-on crowdfunding in entrepreneurial firms. Unpublished working paper.

Capizzi, V., Croce, A., and Tenca, F. (2022). Do business angels' investments make it easier to raise follow-on venture capital financing? An analysis of the relevance of business angels' investment practices. *British Journal of Management*, 33, 306–326.

Cassar, G. (2004). The financing of business start-ups. *Journal of Business Venturing*, 19, 261–283.

Catalini, C. and Hui, X. (2018). Online syndicates and startup investment. Working Paper, Cambridge, MA.

Cavallo, A., Ghezzi, A., Dell'Era, C., and Pellizzoni, E. (2019). Fostering digital entrepreneurship from startup to scaleup: The role of venture capital funds and angel groups. *Technological Forecasting and Social Change*, 145, 24–35.

Caviggioli, F., Scellato, G., and Ughetto, E. (2020). Lenders' selection capabilities, patent quality, and the outcome of patent-backed loans. *Industrial and Corporate Change*, 29, 43–60.

Chemmanur, T. J. and Chen, Z. (2014). Venture capitalists versus angels: The dynamics of private firm financing contracts. *Review of Corporate Finance Studies*, 3, 39–86.

Chemmanur, T. J., Hull, T. J., and Krishnan, K. (2016). Do local and international venture capitalists play well together? The complementarity of local and international venture capitalists. *Journal of Business Venturing*, 31, 573–594.

Chemmanur, T. J., Krishnan, K., and Nandy, D. K. (2011). How does venture capital financing improve efficiency in private firms? A look beneath the surface. *Review of Financial Studies*, 24, 4037–4090.

Chen, Y. (2018). Blockchain tokens and the potential democratization of entrepreneurship and innovation. *Business Horizons*, 61, 567–575.

Choi, T. (2022). Financing product development projects in the blockchain era: Initial coin offerings versus bank loans. *IEEE Transactions on Engineering Management*, 69, 3184–3196.

Cholakova, M. and Clarysse, B. (2015). Does the possibility to make equity investments in crowdfunding projects crowd out reward-based investments? *Entrepreneurship Theory and Practice*, 39, 145–172.

Clayton, P. (2024). Different outcomes for different founders? Local organizational sponsorship and entrepreneurial finance. *Small Business Economics*, 62(1), 23–62.

Cohen, S. (2013). What do accelerators do? Insights from incubators and angels. *Innovations: Technology, Governance, Globalization*, 8, 19–25.

Cohen, S., Bingham, C., and Hallen, B. (2019a). The role of accelerator designs in mitigating bounded rationality in new ventures. *Administrative Science Quarterly*, 64, 810–854.

Cohen, S., Fehder, D. C., Hochberg, Y. V., and Murray, F. (2019b). The design of startup accelerators. *Research Policy*, 48, 1781–1797.

Cohen, S. and Hochberg, Y. V. (2014). Accelerating startups: The seed accelerator phenomenon. *SSRN Electronic Journal*, 1–16.

Cohen, L. and Wirtz, P. (2018). Characteristics of entrepreneurs, entrepreneurial finance, and growth paths. *SSRN Electronic Journal.*

Cole, R., Cumming, D., and Li, D. (2016). Do banks or VCs spur small firm growth? *Journal of International Financial Markets, Institutions and Money*, 41, 60–72.

Cole, R. A., Cumming, D. J., and Taylor, J. (2019). Does FinTech compete with or complement bank finance? *SSRN Electronic Journal.*

Cole, R. A. and Sokolyk, T. (2018). Debt financing, survival, and growth of start-up firms. *Journal of Corporate Finance*, 50, 609–625.

Colombo, M. G. and Delmastro, M. (2002). How effective are technology incubators? *Research Policy*, 31, 1103–1122.

Colombo, M. G. and Shafi, K. (2021). Receiving external equity following successfully crowdfunded technological projects: An informational mechanism. *Small Business Economics*, 56, 1507–1529.

Cosh, A., Cumming, D., and Hughes, A. (2009). Outside entrepreneurial capital. *The Economic Journal*, 119, 1494–1533.

Croce, A., Guerini, M., and Ughetto, E. (2018). Angel financing and the performance of high-tech start-ups. *Journal of Small Business Management*, 56, 208–228.

Croce, A., Schwienbacher, A., and Ughetto, E. (2023). Internationalization of business angel investments: The role of investors' experience and education. *International Business Review*, 32(1), 102033.

Croce, A., Tenca, F., and Ughetto, E. (2017). How business angel groups work: Rejection criteria in investment evaluation. *International Small Business Journal*, 35, 405–426.

Cumming, D., Deloof, M., Manigart, S., and Wright, M. (2019a). New directions in entrepreneurial finance. *Journal of Banking and Finance*, 100, 252–260.

Cumming, D. and Fischer, E. (2012). Publicly funded business advisory services and entrepreneurial outcomes. *Research Policy*, 41, 467–481.

Cumming, D., Grilli, L., and Murtinu, S. (2017). Governmental and independent venture capital investments in Europe: A firm-level performance analysis. *Journal of Corporate Finance*, 42, 439–459.

Cumming, D. and Groh, A. P. (2018). Entrepreneurial finance: Unifying themes and future directions. *Journal of Corporate Finance*, 50, 538–555.

Cumming, D. and Johan, S. (2009). Pre-seed government venture capital funds. *Journal of International Entrepreneurship*, 7, 26–56.

Cumming, D. and Johan, S. (2010). Phasing out an inefficient venture capital tax credit. *Journal of Industry, Competition and Trade*, 10, 227–252.

Cumming, D. and Johan, S. (2013). Technology parks and entrepreneurial outcomes around the world. *International Journal of Managerial Finance*, 9, 279–293.

Cumming, D. J. and Johan, S. A. (2014). *Venture Capital and Private Equity Contracting*. Elsevier.

Cumming, D. and Johan, S. (2017). Crowdfunding and entrepreneurial internationalization. In N. Dai and D. Siegel (Eds.), *Entrepreneurial Finance: Managerial and Policy Implications* (pp. 109–126). World Scientific Publishers.

Cumming, D., Johan, S., and Zhang, Y. (2018). Public policy towards entrepreneurial finance: Spillovers and the scale-up gap. *Oxford Review of Economic Policy*, 34, 652–675.

Cumming, D. and MacIntosh, J. (2006). Crowding out private equity: Canadian evidence. *Journal of Business Venturing*, 21, 569–609.

Cumming, D. and MacIntosh, J. (2007). Mutual funds that invest in private equity? An analysis of labour-sponsored investment funds. *Cambridge Journal of Economics*, 31, 445–487.

Cumming, D., Meoli, M., and Vismara, S. (2019b). Investors' choices between cash and voting rights: Evidence from dual-class equity crowdfunding. *Research Policy*, 48, 103740.

Cumming, D., Meoli, M., and Vismara, S. (2021). Does equity crowdfunding democratize entrepreneurial finance? *Small Business Economics*, 56, 533–552.

Cumming, D. and Vismara, S. (2017). De-segmenting research in entrepreneurial finance. *Venture Capital*, 19, 17–27.

Cumming, D., Werth, J. C., and Zhang, Y. (2019c). Governance in entrepreneurial ecosystems: Venture capitalists vs. technology parks. *Small Business Economics*, 52, 455–484.

Cumming, D. and Zhang, M. (2019). Angel investors around the world. *Journal of International Business Studies*, 50, 692–719.

Dai, N., Jo, H., and Kassicieh, S. (2012). Cross-border venture capital investments in Asia: Selection and exit performance. *Journal of Business Venturing*, 27, 666–684.

De Bettignies, J.-E. and Brander, J. A. (2007). Financing entrepreneurship: Bank finance versus venture capital. *Journal of Business Venturing*, 22, 808–832.

Deloof, M. and Vanacker, T. (2018). The recent financial crisis, start-up financing and survival. *Journal of Business Finance and Accounting*, 45, 928–951.

Drover, W., Busenitz, L., Matusik, S., Townsend, D., Anglin, A., and Dushnitsky, G. (2017a). A review and road map of entrepreneurial equity financing research: Venture capital, corporate venture capital, angel investment, crowdfunding, and accelerators. *Journal of Management*, 43, 1820–1853.

Drover, W., Wood, M. S., and Zacharakis, A. (2017b). Attributes of angel and crowdfunded investments as determinants of VC screening decisions. *Entrepreneurship Theory and Practice*, 41, 323–347.

Dunn, P. and Cheatham, L. (1993). Fundamentals of small business financial management for start up, survival, growth, and changing economic circumstances. *Managerial Finance*, 19, 1–13.

Ebben, J. J. and Johnson, A. C. (2011). Cash conversion cycle management in small firms: Relationships with liquidity, invested capital, and firm performance. *Journal of Small Business and Entrepreneurship*, 24, 381–396.

Etzkowitz, H. (2002). Incubation of incubators: Innovation as a triple helix of university-industry-government networks. *Science and Public Policy*, 29, 115–128.

Fehder, D. C. and Hochberg, Y. V. (2019). Spillover effects of startup accelerator programs: Evidence from venture-backed startup activity. Working paper.

Fisch, C. (2019). Initial coin offerings (ICOs) to finance new ventures. *Journal of Business Venturing*, 34, 1–22.

Fisch, C., Meoli, M., and Vismara, S. (2022). Does blockchain technology democratize entrepreneurial finance? An empirical comparison of ICOs, venture capital, and REITs. *Economics of Innovation and New Technology*, 31, 70–89.

Fraser, S., Bhaumik, S. K., and Wright, M. (2015). What do we know about entrepreneurial finance and its relationship with growth? *International Small Business Journal*, 33, 70–88.

Gafni, H., Marom, D., Robb, A., and Sade, O. (2021). Gender dynamics in crowdfunding (Kickstarter): Evidence on entrepreneurs, backers, and taste-based discrimination. *Review of Finance*, 25, 235–274.

Goldfarb, B., Triantis, A., Hoberg, G., and Kirsch, D. (2013). Are angels different? An analysis of early venture financing. Robert H. Smith School Research Paper RHS 06-072.

Goswami, K., Mitchell, J. R., and Bhagavatula, S. (2018). Accelerator expertise: Understanding the intermediary role of accelerators in the development of the Bangalore entrepreneurial ecosystem. *Strategic Entrepreneurship Journal*, 12, 117–150.

Grilli, L. and Murtinu, S. (2014). Government, venture capital and the growth of European high-tech entrepreneurial firms. *Research Policy*, 43, 1523–1543.

Gulbranson, C. A. and Audretsch, D. B. (2008). Proof of concept centers: Accelerating the commercialization of university innovation. *Journal of Technology Transfer*, 33, 249–258.

Hackober, C. and Bock, C. (2021). Which investors' characteristics are beneficial for initial coin offerings? Evidence from blockchain technology-based firms. *Journal of Business Economics*, 91, 1085–1124.

Hall, B. H. and Lerner, J. (2010). The financing of R&D and innovation. In *Handbook of the Economics of Innovation* (pp. 609–639). Elsevier.

Hallen, B., Cohen, S., and Park, S. H. (2023). Are seed accelerators status springboards for startups? Or sand traps? *Strategic Management Journal*, 44, 2060–2096.

Hanssens, J., Deloof, M., and Vanacker, T. (2016). The evolution of debt policies: New evidence from business startups. *Journal of Banking and Finance*, 65, 120–133.

Harrison, R. T. and Mason, C. M. (1999). An overview of informal venture capital research. *Venture Capital*, 1, 95–100.

Harrison, R. T. and Mason, C. M. (2000). Venture capital market complementarities: The links between business angels and venture capital funds in the United Kingdom. *Venture Capital*, 2, 223–242.

Harrison, R. T., Mason, C. M., and Girling, P. (2004). Financial bootstrapping and venture development in the software industry. *Entrepreneurship and Regional Development*, 16, 307–333.

Hayter, C. S. and Link, A. N. (2015). On the economic impact of university proof of concept centers. *Journal of Technology Transfer*, 40, 178–183.

Hellmann, T., Lindsey, L., and Puri, M. (2008). Building relationships early: Banks in venture capital. *Review of Financial Studies*, 21, 513–541.

Hellmann, T., Schure, P., and Vo, D. H. (2021). Angels and venture capitalists: Substitutes or complements? *Journal of Financial Economics*, 141, 454–478.

Hellmann, T. and Thiele, V. (2015). Friends or foes? The interrelationship between angel and venture capital markets. *Journal of Financial Economics*, 115, 639–653.

Hirsch, J. and Walz, U. (2019). The financing dynamics of newly founded firms. *Journal of Banking and Finance*, 100, 261–272.

Hochberg, Y. V., Serrano, C. J., and Ziedonis, R. H. (2018). Patent collateral, investor commitment, and the market for venture lending. *Journal of Financial Economics*, 130, 74–94.

Hornuf, L., Schmitt, M., and Stenzhorn, E. (2018). Equity crowdfunding in Germany and the United Kingdom: Follow-up funding and firm failure. *Corporate Governance: An International Review*, 26, 331–354.

Howell, S. T. (2017). Financing innovation: Evidence from R&D grants. *American Economic Review*, 107, 1136–1164.

Hsu, D. K., Haynie, J. M., Simmons, S. A., and McKelvie, A. (2014). What matters, matters differently: A conjoint analysis of the decision policies of angel and venture capital investors. *Venture Capital*, 16, 1–25.

Hu, Y., Xue, W., and Liu, Y. (2023). Value of initial coin offerings in the fashion industry. *IEEE Transactions on Engineering Management*, 70, 1343–1352.

Huyghebaert, N. and Van De Gucht, L. M. (2007). The determinants of financial structure: New insights from business start-ups. *European Financial Management*, 13, 101–133.

Ibrahim, D. (2013). Should angel-backed start-ups reject venture capital? *Michigan Business and Entrepreneurial Law Review*, 2, 251.

Islam, M., Fremeth, A., and Marcus, A. (2018). Signaling by early stage startups: US government research grants and venture capital funding. *Journal of Business Venturing*, 33, 35–51.

Johnson, W. C. and Sohl, J. (2012). Angels and venture capitalists in the initial public offering market. *Venture Capital*, 14, 27–42.

Jonsson, S. and Lindbergh, J. (2013). The development of social capital and financing of entrepreneurial firms: From financial bootstrapping to bank funding. *Entrepreneurship Theory and Practice*, 37, 661–686.

Kaminski, J., Hopp, C., and Tykvová, T. (2019). New technology assessment in entrepreneurial financing: Does crowdfunding predict venture capital investments? *Technological Forecasting and Social Change*, 139, 287–302.

Kerr, W. R., Lerner, J., and Schoar, A. (2014). The consequences of entrepreneurial finance: Evidence from angel financings. *Review of Financial Studies*, 27, 20–55.

Kleinert, S., Volkmann, C., and Grünhagen, M. (2020). Third-party signals in equity crowdfunding: The role of prior financing. *Small Business Economics*, 54, 341–365.

Koçak, Ö. and Can, Ö. (2014). Determinants of inter-firm networks among tenants of science technology parks. *Industrial and Corporate Change*, 23, 467–492.

Kolokas, D., Vanacker, T., Veredas, D., and Zahra, S. A. (2020). Venture capital, credit, and FinTech start-up formation: A cross-country study. *Entrepreneurship Theory and Practice*, 46, 1198–1230.

Kortum, S. and Lerner, J. (2000). Assessing the contribution of venture capital to innovation. *The RAND Journal of Economics*, 31, 674–692.

Landström, H. and Mason, C. M. (2016). *Handbook of Research on Business Angels*. Edward Elgar Publishing.

Leleux, B. and Surlemont, B. (2003). Public versus private venture capital: Seeding or crowding out? A pan-European analysis. *Journal of Business Venturing*, 18, 81–104.

Lerner, J. (2000). The government as venture capitalist: The long-run impact of the SBIR program. *The Journal of Private Equity*, 3, 55–78.

Lerner, J., Schoar, A., Sokolinski, S., and Wilson, K. (2018). The globalization of angel investments: Evidence across countries. *Journal of Financial Economics*, 127, 1–20.

Madill, J. J., Haines, G. H., and Riding, A. L. (2005). The role of angels in technology SMEs: A link to venture capital. *Venture Capital*, 7, 107–129.

Maia, C. and Claro, J. (2013). The role of a proof of concept center in a university ecosystem: An exploratory study. *Journal of Technology Transfer*, 38, 641–650.

Mäkelä, M. M. and Maula, M. V. J. (2008). Attracting cross-border venture capital: The role of a local investor. *Entrepreneurship and Regional Development*, 20, 237–257.

Mann, W. (2018). Creditor rights and innovation: Evidence from patent collateral. *Journal of Financial Economics*, 130, 25–47.

Masiak, C., Moritz, A., and Lang, F. (2017). Financing patterns of European SMEs: An updated empirical taxonomy and determinants of SME financing clusters. EIF Research and Market Analysis Working Paper 40.

Mason, C., Botelho, T., and Harrison, R. (2016). The transformation of the business angel market: Empirical evidence and research implications. *Venture Capital*, 18, 321–344.

Mason, C. and Harrison, R. T. (2015). Business angel investment activity in the financial crisis: UK evidence and policy implications. *Environment and Planning C: Government and Policy*, 33, 43–60.

Mason, C. and Stark, M. (2004). What do investors look for in a business plan? A comparison of the investment criteria of bankers, venture capitalists and business angels. *International Small Business Journal*, 22, 227–248.

Maus, C., Greven, A., Kurth, N., and Brettel, M. (2023). How do investor characteristics of business angels and venture capitalists predict the occurrence of co-investments? *Journal of Business Economics*, 94, 763–811.

McCahery, J. A. and Vermeulen, E. P. M. (2014). Conservatism and innovation in venture capital contracting. *European Business Organization Law Review*, 15, 235–266.

McCahery, J. A. and Vermeulen, E. P. M. (2016). Venture capital 2.0: From venturing to partnering. ECGI Working Paper Series in Law.

Miglo, A. (2022). Crowdfunding and bank financing: Substitutes or complements? *Small Business Economics*, 59, 1115–1142.

Mollick, E. (2014). The dynamics of crowdfunding: An exploratory study. *Journal of Business Venturing*, 29, 1–16.

Moritz, A., Block, J. H., and Heinz, A. (2016). Financing patterns of European SMEs: An empirical taxonomy. *Venture Capital*, 18, 115–148.

Peters, B. (2009). *Early Exits: Exit Strategies for Entrepreneurs and Angel Investors (but Maybe Not Venture Capitalists)*. Meteor Bytes Data Management Corp.

Phan, P. H., Siegel, D. S., and Wright, M. (2005). Science parks and incubators: Observations, synthesis and future research. *Journal of Business Venturing*, 20, 165–182.

Ribeiro, J., Higuchi, A., Bronzo, M., Veiga, R., and De Faria, A. (2016). A framework for the strategic management of science and technology parks. *Journal of Technology Management and Innovation*, 11, 80–90.

Robb, A. M. and Robinson, D. T. (2014). The capital structure decisions of new firms. *Review of Financial Studies*, 27, 153–179.

Robinson, D. (2012). New perspectives on entrepreneurial capital structure. In *The Oxford Handbook of Entrepreneurial Finance* (pp. 1–16). Oxford University Press.

Robinson, M. J. (2022). Factors impacting entrepreneurial success in accelerators: Revealed preferences of sophisticated mentors. *Review of Corporate Finance*, 2, 617–661.

Samila, S. and Sorenson, O. (2011). Venture capital, entrepreneurship, and economic growth. *The Review of Economics and Statistics*, 93, 338–349.

Schmalz, M. C., Sraer, D. A., and Thesmar, D. (2017). Housing collateral and entrepreneurship. *Journal of Finance*, 72, 99–132.

Schückes, M. and Gutmann, T. (2021). Why do startups pursue initial coin offerings (ICOs)? The role of economic drivers and social identity on funding choice. *Journal of Business Venturing Insights*, 15, 1027–1052.

Schwienbacher, A. (2009). Financing Commitments and Investors' Incentives in Entrepreneurial Firms. RICAFE Working Paper, London.

Seitz, N., Lehmann, E. E., and Haslanger, P. (2024). Corporate accelerators: Design and startup performance. *Small Business Economics*, 62(4), 1615–1640.

Shinkle, G. A. and Suchard, J. (2019). Innovation in newly public firms: The influence of government grants, venture capital, and private equity. *Australian Journal of Management*, 44, 248–281.

Signori, A. and Vismara, S. (2018). Does success bring success? The post-offering lives of equity-crowdfunded firms. *Journal of Corporate Finance*, 50, 575–591.

Sorenson, O., Assenova, V., Li, G.-C., Boada, J., and Fleming, L. (2016). Expand innovation finance via crowdfunding. *Science*, 354, 1526–1528.

Sørheim, R. (2005). Business angels as facilitators for further finance: An exploratory study. *Journal of Small Business and Enterprise Development*, 12, 178–191.

Stevenson, R. M., Kuratko, D. F., and Eutsler, J. (2019). Unleashing main street entrepreneurship: Crowdfunding, venture capital, and the democratization of new venture investments. *Small Business Economics*, 52, 375–393.

Takahashi, H. (2015). Dynamics of bank relationships in entrepreneurial finance. *Journal of Corporate Finance*, 34, 23–31.

Thies, F., Huber, A., Bock, C., Benlian, A., and Kraus, S. (2019). Following the crowd: Does crowdfunding affect venture capitalists' selection of entrepreneurial ventures? *Journal of Small Business Management*, 57, 1378–1398.

Ueda, M. (2004). Banks versus venture capital: Project evaluation, screening, and expropriation. *Journal of Finance*, 59, 601–621.

Vanacker, T., Collewaert, V., and Paeleman, I. (2013). The relationship between slack resources and the performance of entrepreneurial firms: The role of venture capital and angel investors. *Journal of Management Studies*, 50, 1070–1096.

Vanacker, T., Manigart, S., Meuleman, M., and Sels, L. (2011). A longitudinal study on the relationship between financial bootstrapping and new venture growth. *Entrepreneurship and Regional Development*, 23, 681–705.

Verbouw, J., Vanacker, T., and Manigart, S. (2023). Divide and Conquer: Investor Type Diversity in Entrepreneurial Ventures. Working Paper.

Wallmeroth, J., Wirtz, P., and Groh, A. P. (2018). Venture capital, angel financing, and crowdfunding of entrepreneurial ventures: A literature review. *Foundations and Trends in Entrepreneurship*, 14, 1–129.

Wang, W., Mahmood, A., Sismeiro, C., and Vulkan, N. (2019). The evolution of equity crowdfunding: Insights from co-investments of angels and the crowd. *Research Policy*, 48, 103727.

Winborg, J. and Landström, H. (2001). Financial bootstrapping in small businesses. *Journal of Business Venturing*, 16, 235–254.

Winston Smith, S. and Hannigan, T. J. (2014). Home run, strike out, or base hit: How do accelerators impact exit and VC financing in new firms? *Academy of Management Proceedings*.

Winton, A. and Yerramilli, V. (2008). Entrepreneurial finance: Banks versus venture capital. *Journal of Financial Economics*, 88, 51–79.

Wong, A., Bhatia, M., and Freeman, Z. (2009). Angel finance: The other venture capital. *Strategic Change*, 18, 221–230.

Woolley, J. L. and MacGregor, N. (2022). The influence of incubator and accelerator participation on nanotechnology venture success. *Entrepreneurship Theory and Practice*, 46, 1717–1755.

Xu, F., Guo, X., Xiao, G., and Zhang, F. (2018). Crowdfunding or bank financing: Effects of market uncertainty and word-of-mouth communication. *SSRN Electronic Journal.*

Zhang, Y. (2005). The science park phenomenon: Development, evolution and typology. *International Journal of Entrepreneurship and Innovation Management*, 5, 138.

Part 3

Modern Finance

https://doi.org/10.1142/9781800617032_0009

Chapter 9

The Geography of Cryptocurrencies: Drivers of the Adoption of Cryptocurrencies Around the World

Anita Quas

University of Milan, Milan, Italy

9.1. Introduction

Cryptocurrencies are digital financial assets, for which registrations and transfers of ownership are secured by an encryption system rather than by a bank or other trusted third party. The cryptocurrency market has evolved erratically and at an unprecedented speed since the first cryptocurrency, Bitcoin, was released to the public in January 2009 (see Figure 9.1). Overall, the market value of cryptocurrencies, as of 2023, stood at $1,900 billion, with daily trades of around $22 billion. The market value capped in November 2021, reaching $2,900. Since then, cryptocurrency markets have declined in value, influenced by multiple corporate bankruptcies, lawsuits, and regulatory threats.

Nevertheless, since the first alternative to Bitcoin (or Altcoin) appeared in 2011 with the name of Litecoin, the number of cryptocurrencies has also exponentially increased over time, at least until February 2022, as shown in Figure 9.2. As of May 2023,

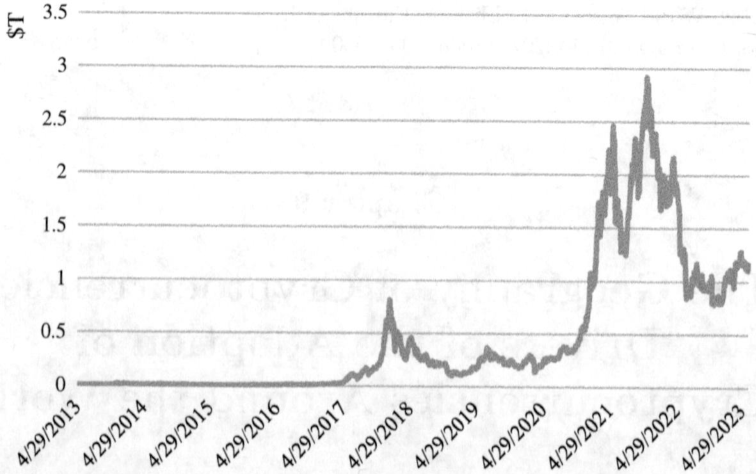

Figure 9.1. Market value ($bn) of cryptocurrencies in the world up to May 2023.
Source: coinmarketcap.com.

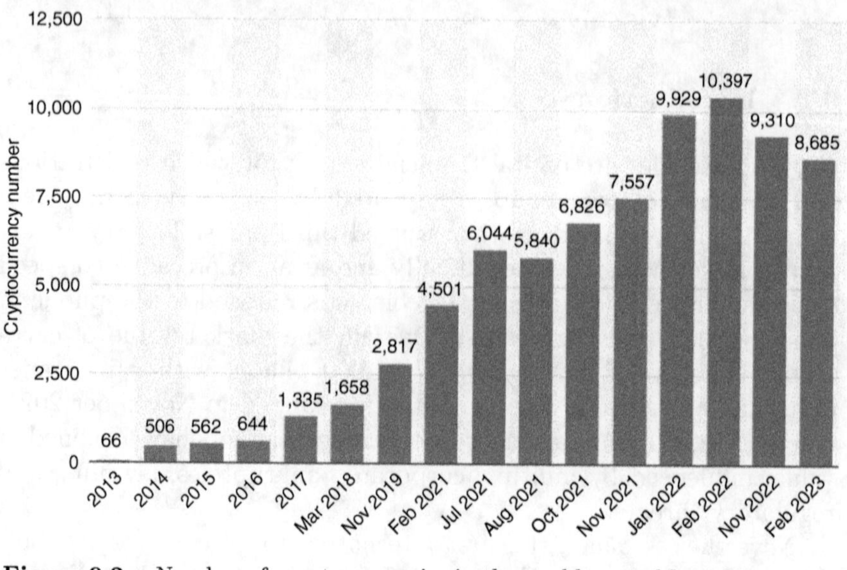

Figure 9.2. Number of cryptocurrencies in the world up to May 2023.
Source: Statista.

nearly 9,000 types of cryptocurrencies were in circulation, with different levels of innovation in terms of the underlying technology.

Figure 9.3 shows the distribution of current market value by cryptocurrency: Bitcoin is the cryptocurrency with the largest market share (about $522 billion), followed by Ethereum (launched in 2015, $219 billion in capitalisation), Tether (launched in 2014, $83 billion), BNB ($48 billion), and USD Coin ($30 billion).

Cryptocurrencies have attracted enormous academic interest across various disciplines. The number of articles mentioning the phenomenon has grown exponentially since 2011. In this chapter, I review several studies that have highlighted the opportunities and risks associated with the use of cryptocurrencies from a theoretical point of view. However, there are few studies that try to understand who uses cryptocurrencies, how, and why due to the difficulty in

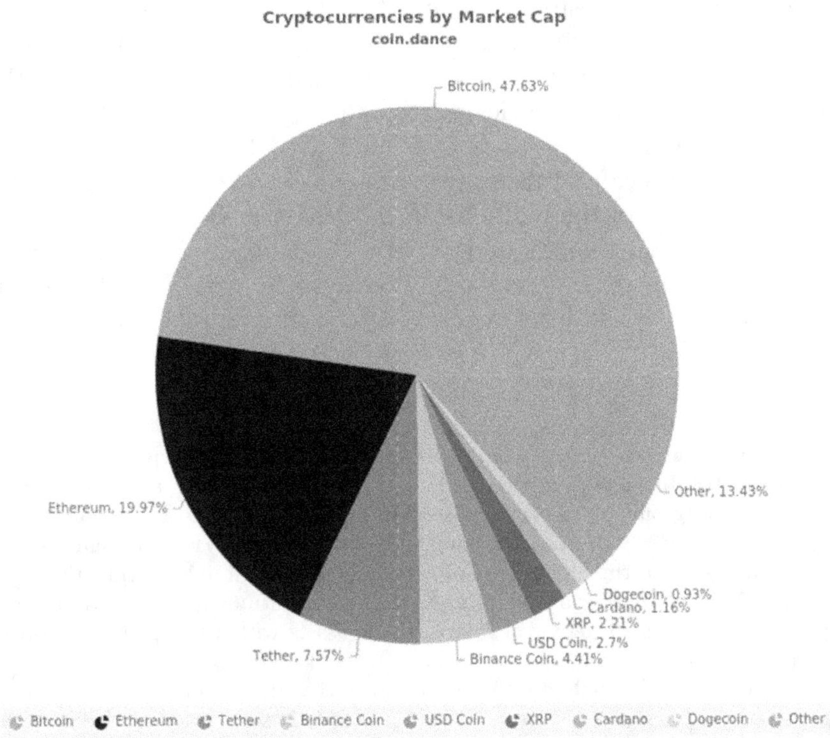

Figure 9.3. Breakdown of the market value of cryptocurrencies as of May 2023. *Source*: coin.dance.

finding data on actual users. In fact, cryptocurrency transactions allow the anonymity of the purchaser and the buyer; therefore, it is difficult to determine the personal characteristics of cryptocurrency users.

Cryptocurrencies are used in different ways and with varying prevalence in different countries of the world. While in some countries cryptocurrencies are banned (as in Algeria, Qatar, and Vietnam),[1] in others they have even been adopted as the official national currency (Venezuela or El Salvador).[2] Studies on the factors influencing the use of cryptocurrencies in different countries are mostly theoretical. In particular, some studies hypothesise that the use of cryptocurrencies may depend on the characteristics of the national context in which consumers operate, such as access to technology, and the availability and risks associated with undertaking investments and transactions through traditional channels. In the absence of data on the geographical position of the actual users, empirical evidence is so far largely preliminary. In this chapter, I intend to provide evidence on the use of cryptocurrencies in different countries of the world using original metrics which reflect the effective adoption of individual (retail) users as well as institutional ones.

More specifically, this study is based on a country-level econometric analysis of the relationship between the use of cryptocurrencies in a certain country and the key characteristics of the country itself, identified in the theoretical literature. In particular, I focus on the role of financial development, fraud risk, inflation, and exchange rate risk. Theory suggests that cryptocurrencies could be used by

[1]The Algerian government completely banned the use of cryptocurrencies as early as 2018. In some countries, such as Qatar, the ban limits the possibility of banks carrying out any services related to cryptocurrencies. In Vietnam, cryptocurrencies have been officially banned in 2017, despite Vietnam being one of the countries with the highest use of cryptocurrencies. In light of this, the Vietnamese Ministry of Finance set up a special research unit in 2020 to study and propose ways to manage and regulate virtual assets within the country. *Source*: https://freemanlaw.com/.

[2]The Bolivarian Republic of Venezuela was the first nation to issue a cryptocurrency, the Petro, as its national currency. Petro's price is tied to that of the country's oil reserves. In 2021, El Salvador was the first country to adopt Bitcoin as the official national currency, alongside the US dollar. *Source*: https://freemanlaw.com/.

potential investors, especially in regions where the risks of counterfeiting of the national currency, hyperinflation, and changes in exchange rates are greater or where access to 'traditional' investment opportunities is scarcer.

Understanding how institutional characteristics influence the use of cryptocurrencies in different countries helps to better characterise the reasons why consumers buy and exchange cryptocurrencies and to better understand a phenomenon that remains rather obscure.

The results presented in this chapter are also relevant from the point of view of a possible future regulation of the use of cryptocurrencies. According to Darlington (2014), cryptocurrencies have the potential to improve financial inclusion, i.e. the access of individuals and companies to useful and convenient financial products and services. Financial inclusion has been identified as necessary for the achievement of seven out of the 17 United Nations Sustainable Development Goals. According to the World Bank, a first step towards improving financial inclusion is the possibility of accessing a transaction account. At the same time, according to the latest data from Findex, almost a third of adults in the world – about 1.7 billion – are still without access to a bank (Demirgüç-Kunt *et al.*, 2022). Most of these people are located in developing countries with high corruption and nonexistent secure financial infrastructure. The development of mobile infrastructure is making mobile banking a possibility for many people. Cryptocurrencies could be a secure way to make payments via mobile phone.

9.2. Opportunities and Risks Related to the Use of Cryptocurrencies

The white paper by Nakamoto (2008), which originally presented the Bitcoin support technology (the blockchain), proposed cryptocurrencies as a payment mechanism that is not intermediated by financial institutions. The blockchain was meant to enable the digital transfer of money for payments or other financial activities, similar to the physical transfer of money. While financial intermediaries need to collect information between the selling party and the buyer, blockchain technology allows anonymous money transactions with lower transaction times and costs. According to some scholars (for a review, see Alzahrani and Daim, 2019), the great interest in cryptocurrencies is above all due to the fact that users appreciate the anonymity of their transactions. They seem to simply want more privacy around their financial transactions than what is allowed by traditional financial channels. Other reasons for using cryptocurrencies are the fascination for hi-tech or curiosity for a new fashionable phenomenon.

For many users, cryptocurrencies are of interest not so much as an anonymous and innovative means of payment but as a speculative investment. According to a survey launched by Coinbase and ARK Invest, 54% of users of the Coinbase site, one of the major cryptocurrency exchange platforms, used Bitcoin strictly for this purpose in 2016 (Burniske and White, 2017). Moreover, there are differences in the use of the main cryptocurrencies: some studies show that Bitcoins are more likely to be used as a short-term speculative investment than other currencies, such as Ethereum (Aspembitova *et al.*, 2021).

There is also a lively discussion about the origin of the sudden and unbridled appreciation of cryptocurrencies over time. For some scholars, it is related to the cost of 'mining', i.e. the energy and time spent on the computational efforts needed to record transactions or create new currencies. For others, it is a speculative bubble without any foundation. For most consumers, cryptocurrencies are difficult to understand due to their newness, technological complexity, and riskiness linked with the absence of third parties to monitor and act as guarantor (Giudici *et al.*, 2020).

The anonymity and cryptographic security of financial transactions carried out using cryptocurrencies have also attracted payment activities for criminal and, presumably, terrorist purposes. Böhme *et al.* (2015) show that, at the beginning of the Bitcoin era, most transactions were aimed at illicit activities, such as the purchase of drugs and medicines, but that the illegal share of Bitcoin activities is decreasing over time. These critical issues have increasingly motivated governments to regulate, limit, or even ban virtual currencies.[3]

Scepticism increased in the past couple of years, especially after the collapse in November 2022 of the cryptocurrency exchange FTX Trading Ltd. and subsequent arrest of its founder on fraud charges.

[3]For an analysis of the legislation on the use of cryptocurrencies in all countries of the world, see the Freeman Law website, https://freemanlaw.com/.

According to a survey conducted in 2023 in the US by Pew Research, the vast majority of Americans are not confident that current ways to invest in, trade, or use cryptocurrencies are reliable and safe (Faverio and Massart, 2023).

Finally, many cryptocurrency sceptics have also expressed concern about the energy consumption of cryptocurrency mining, which could lead to increased carbon emissions and climate change (Chenguel, 2022). In general, there is a general distrust of the value and sustainability of this opportunity.

9.3. Cryptocurrency Users

According to buybitcoinworldwide.com, as of May 2023, there were around 106 million Bitcoin users. Despite the widespread use of cryptocurrencies, little is known about the characteristics of the individuals who buy and trade them, i.e. their users. Many cryptocurrency companies and platforms do not share user data for a variety of reasons, including to protect privacy or because the nature of their services precludes data collection (for example, some virtual wallet managers rely on the use of a software to be downloaded to the device and do not require users to subscribe to a service).

A first relevant distinction needs to be made between retail users and institutional investors. In fact, while in the early years after the launch of Bitcoin institutional investors considered cryptocurrencies as a valueless digital resource and mostly used for illicit purposes, cryptocurrencies are now present in the portfolios of institutions such as family offices, hedge funds, and asset management funds, among which it is worth mentioning BlackRock, the largest asset manager in the world. According to estimates, $17 billion of institutional capital was invested in cryptocurrencies in 2021 (Wintermeyer, 2021). Cryptocurrencies have attracted institutional investors' attention with their exponential growth and the possibility of portfolio diversification. A recent study by Fidelity Digital Assets found that seven out of ten institutional investors expect to buy or invest in cryptocurrencies in the near future (Fidelity Digital Assets, 2021). More than half of the 1,100 respondents surveyed between December and April admitted they already own such investments. A survey conducted by Nickel Digital Asset Management (https://nickel.digital/)

came to a similar conclusion, with 82% of respondents planning to increase their cryptocurrency allocation over the next two years.

Institutional investors still represent a minority in terms of the amount of investments in cryptocurrencies. According to buybitcoinworldwide.com, as of February 2022, only 7.27% of the maximum available Bitcoins (21 million) were in the portfolios of institutional investors: 3.88% were in listed investment funds (ETFs), 1.3% were purchased by countries (Bulgaria, Ukraine, El Salvador, Finland, and Georgia), and the remainder by companies. The share of institutional investors has likely decreased since then, following the FTX scandal.

The majority of cryptocurrencies are therefore in the hands of non-professional retail investors. Information on the profile data of these users is very difficult to find. However, there are indirect approaches to identifying the typical retail user. An important source of information is represented by Google Trends, which shows the trend of Google searches about cryptocurrencies. There is an 80% correlation between the search intensity of the term 'Bitcoin' on Google and movements in the dollar value of Bitcoin (Schuh and Shy, 2015). Figure 9.4 shows how the peaks in interest for Bitcoin according to Google correspond to the speculative Bitcoin bubbles, most notably that of 2017, the year in which a Bitcoin reached the value of $20,000, before collapsing to $12,000 at the end of December. According to Figà-Talamanca and Patacca (2020), this parallelism between Google research on the subject of Bitcoins and actual cryptocurrency trade volumes allows us to hypothesise that the profile of those looking for information on Bitcoins is similar to the profile of the actual Bitcoin users. According to coindance.com, in May 2023, 85.77% of users who search for information on Bitcoin on Google are men, 41.35% are in the 25–24 age group, 20.16% are between 35 and 44 years old, and 16.65% are between 18 and 24 years old.

Another possible approach to studying the profile of the cryptocurrency user is to collect primary data through questionnaires. For example, the 2014–2015 Survey of Consumer Payment Choice (SCPC) indicates that about half of US consumers had heard of Bitcoin or about 700 other virtual currencies by the end of 2015. The study shows how awareness, adoption, and use of virtual currencies are related to various demographics and economic characteristics of consumers. A typical Bitcoin owner is a young man, of non-Caucasian ethnicity, and with a low level of education (Schuh and Shy, 2015).

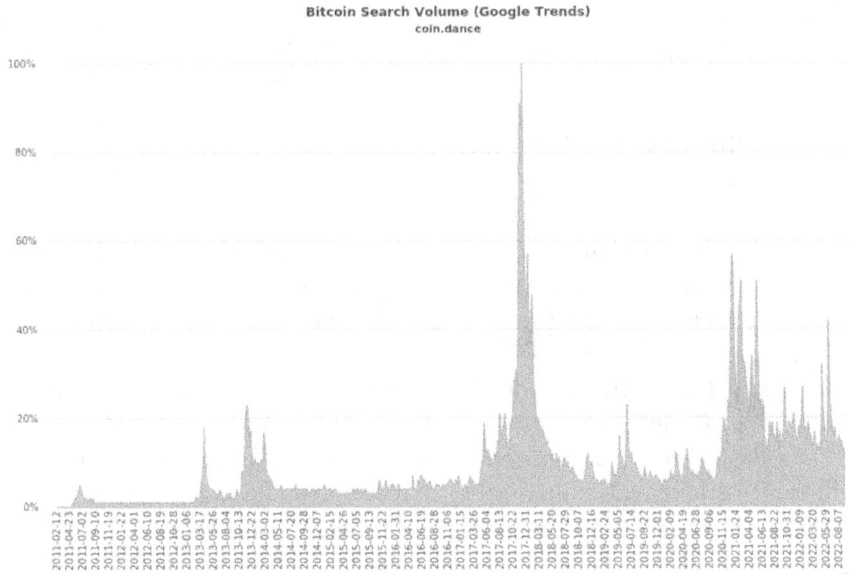

Figure 9.4. Number of searches on the topic 'Bitcoin' in Google as of May 2023.
Source: coin.dance.

The Cryptoasset Consumer Research Survey, a survey conducted in 2020 and 2021 in the UK by the Financial Conduct Authority (FCA), indicates that the average English user of cryptocurrencies is a man (78%), is over 35 years old (70%), and has managerial, administrative, or upper- or middle-professional occupation (45%). The survey also indicates that levels of retail investor knowledge and understanding of cryptocurrencies and the associated risks are low. Of UK retail cryptocurrency investors, 58% said that they have a 'good' level of understanding of risks, and only 10% remember being told about potential risks when buying cryptocurrencies.[4]

Pew Research conducted a cryptocurrency awareness study in September 2021, sampling 10,371 US adults. The survey showed that 16% had invested in, traded, or used cryptocurrency. The percentage

[4]In this regard, some financial authorities and regulators have launched information and training programs for investors aimed at highlighting potential risks linked with the use of cryptocurrencies. This issue has also been investigated by the International Organization of Securities Commissions (IOSCO, 2020).

is higher for males (22% vs. 10% for females), ages 18–39 (31%), and of Asian ethnicity (Faverio and Massart, 2022).

9.4. The Geographic Distribution of Cryptocurrency Users

Since the demographic profile of the cryptocurrency user is not visible, establishing an exact picture of where cryptocurrencies are used and in which countries the level of activity is highest is a challenging if not impossible task.

A key factor to consider is that the use of cryptocurrencies is banned in some countries. According to coin.dance, as of May 2023, the use of Bitcoin is allowed in 132 countries around the world, as shown in Figure 9.5. Currently, Bitcoin has been made illegal by the governments of Afghanistan, Algeria, Bangladesh, Bolivia, Pakistan, North Macedonia, and Vietnam (countries in black),[5] while there are restrictions on its use in American Samoa, China, Egypt, Morocco,

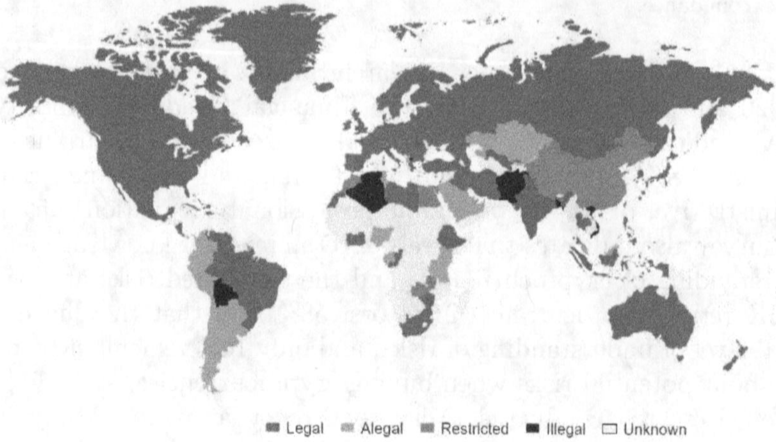

Figure 9.5. Legality of Bitcoin by country as of February 2022.
Source: coin.dance.

[5]There are actually different levels of illegality of cryptocurrencies. In Vietnam, the use of Bitcoin and other cryptocurrencies as a payment method is prohibited, but it is still permitted to own them as an investment.

Nepal, Qatar, and Zambia (countries in light grey). Other governments have fully embraced cryptocurrencies: in 2021, El Salvador was the first state to approve Bitcoin as an official currency, along with the US dollar. Some countries have bought cryptocurrencies themselves (Bulgaria, Ukraine, El Salvador, Finland, and Georgia).

There are also sources of information, albeit partial, which allow us to estimate the actual use of cryptocurrencies in various countries. As anticipated, one indicator is the number of searches on the topic through Google (Figure 9.6). Over the past five years, Nigeria had the highest number of searches on 'Bitcoin' with respect to the total number of searches in the country, followed by El Salvador, Austria, the Netherlands, and Switzerland. The geographical trends are very similar for terms such as 'cryptocurrency' or 'cryptocurrencies' but with much lower volumes.

Another relevant metric is the number of nodes per country that are mining Bitcoin. A node is a computer connected to other computers that follows the rules and shares information of the Bitcoin blockchain. Locating the nodes is possible since the Bitcoin network

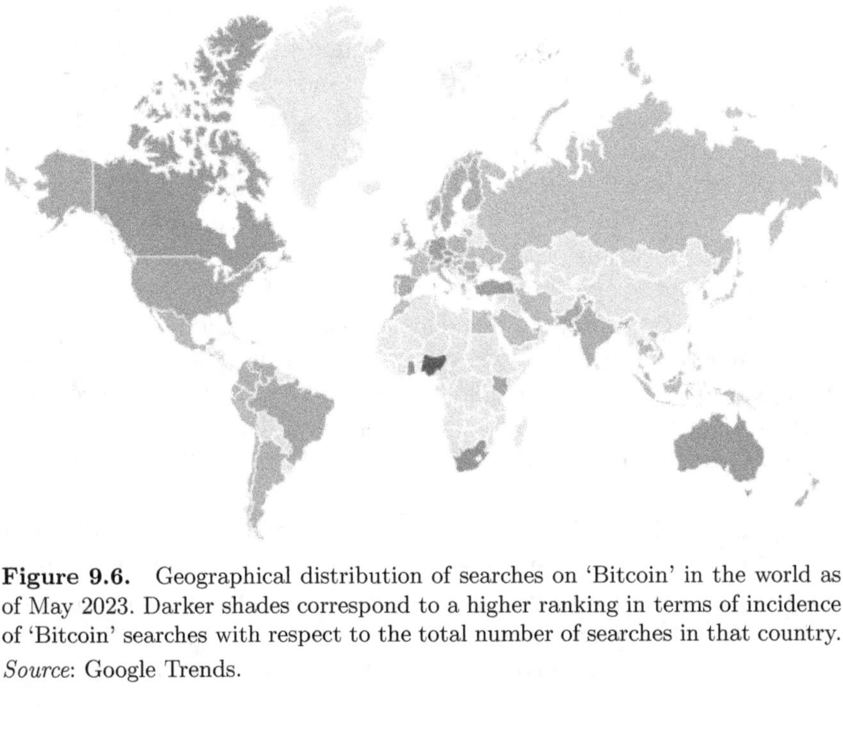

Figure 9.6. Geographical distribution of searches on 'Bitcoin' in the world as of May 2023. Darker shades correspond to a higher ranking in terms of incidence of 'Bitcoin' searches with respect to the total number of searches in that country. *Source*: Google Trends.

is open source. According to *bitnodes.io*, to date, the US, Germany, France, the Netherlands, and Canada are the top five countries in terms of the number of Bitcoin 'full nodes'. However, it should be noted that the origin of a full node can be obfuscated and that the geographic distribution of Bitcoin mining is not necessarily tied to the geographic distribution of Bitcoin transactions.

Data on the location of software downloads used for Bitcoin trading show a high incidence as a percentage of the population, especially in Scandinavian countries (Estonia, Iceland, Sweden, the Netherlands, and Denmark). However, the utility of the metric is limited by the fact that not all Bitcoin transactions are software-driven and not all software is tracked (Darlington, 2014).

LocalBitcoin was a cryptocurrency exchange platform that electronically connected users in 249 countries and which closed in February 2023. Exchange volumes were limited compared to other larger platforms (such as Binance or Coinbase Exchange), but LocalBitcoin provided the ability to identify the country of origin and destination of exchanges because they were carried out in physical ATMs distributed around the world. In early 2022, 94% of all known ATMs were located in the US (59%), Europe (20%), and Canada (15%), but there has been a rapid increase over time in emerging Asian countries (China, India, Malaysia, and Thailand), Latin America (Brazil, Chile, Colombia, Mexico, and Venezuela), Africa and the Middle East (Kenya, Nigeria, Saudi Arabia, Tanzania, and Turkey), and Eastern Europe (Russia and Ukraine) (Hileman and Rauchs, 2017).

Hileman and Rauchs (2017) analyse a proprietary database, which includes the location of customers of some wallet and payment platform providers, revealing that nearly 40% of cryptocurrency users are based in Asia, followed by Europe at 27%. The share for North America is surprisingly low and not in line with the figures mentioned above. However, it should be noted that these figures only represent data from a limited number of wallet and payment platform providers and do not take into account users of exchanges and mining pools.

Lastly, Park and Park (2020) investigate the geographic distribution of cryptocurrency information on the web by mapping the information network of cryptocurrency sites (the most important being bitcoin.org, bitcoin.com, and steemit.com). Results show that information production and consumption about coins are concentrated in

European and Asia-Pacific regions. Germany and technology start-up companies are the most central sources for cryptocurrency-related information in the network.

In conclusion, it seems that the adoption of cryptocurrencies is more advanced in North America and Europe; however, an increasing number of activities (and users) can be observed in other regions as well, with activities growing relatively rapidly in some emerging Asian countries, Latin America, Africa, and the Middle East. At the same time, it is currently more difficult to track the use of cryptocurrencies in these countries.

9.5. Use of Cryptocurrencies and Institutional Characteristics

In the absence of reliable data, some scholars have theorised about which countries are more likely to adopt cryptocurrencies. Although Bitcoin and other cryptocurrencies currently seem to dominate more developed and tech-savvy economies, the evolution of the phenomenon in the future could be very different. Darlington (2014) examines from a theoretical point of view how the characteristics of Bitcoin might help users counteract problems of inflation, currency exchange rate, monetary fraud, and poor accessibility to money. According to the study, cryptocurrencies could be used in relatively poor countries with developing economies, subject to unstable fiscal policies.

Hileman (2015) has developed the Bitcoin Market Potential Index (BMPI), a composite indicator that conceptualises and ranks the potential utility of Bitcoin across 178 countries. The index is based on a dataset with 40 variables grouped into seven sub-indices: technology penetration, international remittances, inflation, informal economy size, financial control, historical financial crises, and Bitcoin penetration. The results of the analysis indicate that the potential adoption of Bitcoin is higher in developing countries, such as the South Saharan region and Latin America.

Cryptocurrencies could be particularly useful in emerging markets, where a significant devaluation of the currency pushes users to buy cryptocurrency on P2P platforms to preserve their savings. Cryptocurrencies also offer advantages for making international transactions when currency exchange rate are unfavourable, both for individual remittances and for commercial use cases, such as buying goods to import and sell. Finally, many emerging markets limit the amount of national currency that citizens can move out of the country. Cryptocurrency offers citizens a way around those limits, so they can meet their financial needs (Chainalysis, 2021).

Finally, there are some studies that empirically analyse how the characteristics of countries influence the national use of cryptocurrencies. Ricci (2020) analyses the world's top 70 economies, revealing that high levels of international trade freedom combined with low inflation rates and low administrative requirements are key drivers of Bitcoin adoption at the national level. The number of Bitcoin transactions is also higher in countries with fewer capital controls and restrictions, a result that fuels suspicions of illegal behaviour, such as money laundering or terrorist financing, carried out through the use of cryptocurrencies. Based on Google Trends data, the Bitcoin node network, and the software download trend in each country, Sharma *et al.* (2021) indicate that the cryptocurrency market is more evolved in developed countries than in developing ones.

Current literature points out two fundamental issues: (1) the characteristics of the countries have, *a priori*, a fundamental role in the use of cryptocurrencies; and (2) the geographical distribution of cryptocurrency users is constantly evolving, and analyses based on data from a few years ago may not be relevant to explaining the future evolution of the use of cryptocurrencies.

In the light of these conclusions, in the following, I analyse the role of some country characteristics highlighted in the existing literature on the current use of cryptocurrencies and on the evolution of this use over time. The analysis is based on updated data and innovative indicators.

First, I consider the financial development of the sample countries. On the one hand, cryptocurrencies have the potential to improve access to finance in countries with underdeveloped financial markets (Darlington, 2014). More financially developed countries should enable their citizens to make payments and financial investments safely and at low cost and, therefore, should reduce the necessity of resorting to alternative currencies, such as cryptocurrencies. On the other hand, the population of countries with more developed financial markets could be more aware of the risks and opportunities offered by cryptocurrencies, and this could increase the appetite for their use. The empirical analysis will allow us to evaluate which of these two opposing effects between financial development and the use of cryptocurrencies prevails.

Second, high inflation is a factor that, according to scholars, should incentivise the use of cryptocurrencies (Darlington, 2014). Inflation and hyperinflation, due to unstable monetary policies and strong fluctuations in exchange rate, have historically led populations to adopt alternative currencies, rather than their own country's currency, or invest in naturally scarce resources, such as gold. Cryptocurrencies could therefore become more attractive when inflation is high because they can potentially reduce the financial risk to which investors are exposed. Indeed, the price variation of cryptocurrencies are *a priori* independent of the valuation fluctuations of official currencies since they are subject to decentralised regulation. Furthermore, cryptocurrencies are by nature largely immune to inflation. Indeed, the availability of many cryptocurrencies is fixed. In the case of Bitcoin, there are currently only 19 million units (tokens) in circulation, and every four years the amount of new Bitcoins that can be extracted (mined) halves; therefore, the overall availability tends to be a constant, i.e. 21 million unit. The scarcity of cryptocurrency supply means that it is less subject to inflation than other currencies whose quantity can increase as a result of expansive monetary policies. By investing in cryptocurrencies, citizens of countries prone to high inflation or hyperinflation can reduce their financial risk. A positive relationship is therefore expected between inflation and the use of cryptocurrencies at the national level.

A third factor that is considered in this study is the risk of financial fraud and illegal economic activity in general. On the one hand, thanks to their relative anonymity and lack of regulation, cryptocurrencies are an ideal medium for illegal purposes. As anticipated, Bitcoins were initially used mainly in illegal activities, such as trade in drugs and weapons, and therefore the use of Bitcoins should be greater in countries where informal markets (or black markets) are more developed (Hileman, 2015). Furthermore, cryptocurrencies could be used by people involved in illegal activities such as bribery and corruption, as well as terrorism, for the purposes of money laundering and circumvention of the control of law enforcement and other government agencies (Choo, 2015). On the other hand, cryptocurrencies could also represent the solution to monetary and financial fraud. In this sense, cryptocurrencies could be used in countries with a higher risk of fraud related to the forging of counterfeit money because they cannot be counterfeited or manipulated fraudulently (Darlington, 2014). For example, Bitcoin cannot be duplicated unless you are in control of over half of the Bitcoin blockchain network, which would require huge amounts of money and computing power (Kaplan, 2021).[6] It is therefore expected that there is a positive relationship between the use of cryptocurrencies and a tendency towards corruption and fraudulent action in general. This is not only because cryptocurrencies allow payments that finance such actions but also because they allow investors to insulate themselves from the negative consequences that such actions might have on the national currency.

Finally, the last factor that I consider in this study to be relevant in determining the widespread use of cryptocurrencies is the risk associated with currency exchange rate. Many countries, such as those in war-torn or tumultuous regions, have unstable currencies, leading to wildly fluctuating exchange rates. The population of these countries could protect themselves from currency fluctuations by converting their savings into cryptocurrencies or simply using cryptocurrencies to transact internationally (Darlington, 2014).

9.6. Method and Data

To answer the research questions and test the conjectures presented above, the study is based on a country-level econometric analysis of the relationship between the use of cryptocurrencies in a certain country and the institutional characteristics of the country itself.

The dependent variable is the adoption of cryptocurrencies in each country. I already acknowledged that there are no official sources for

[6]Kaplan (2021) highlights the potential of cryptocurrencies as a means of making payments efficiently and securely, thanks to blockchain technology and cryptography. The author suggests that governments should use blockchain technology to their advantage not only to facilitate payments but also to authorise and secure them, reducing fraud and corruption worldwide. However, this would require adding an identification number to each transaction, which does not make it anonymous.

this information. The aforementioned alternative sources of information, such as the number of Google searches on the topic, the number of 'nodes', the number of establishments that accept cryptocurrencies, software downloads, or trading volumes, have limitations due to the fact that they are usually based only on non-representative sub-samples of cryptocurrency networks.

The study is based on two alternative data sources that we believe overcome many of the limitations of the aforementioned metrics. The first is the indicator developed by the company Chainanalysis and made available in 2022 (Chainalysis, 2022). The index aims to identify countries with the highest adoption of cryptocurrencies by retail users who use cryptocurrencies for personal transactions and individual savings, rather than trading and speculation. The indicator is based on the volume of transactions in each country, corrected to avoid favouring countries with high levels of professional and institutional adoption of cryptocurrency, where volumes are high compared to the actual number of users. The trading volume is directly collected by the cryptocurrency blockchains and allocated to the different countries through weights that depend on the geographical origin of the users of the platforms used for the transactions. The indicator is based on five pillars: (1) the value of the cryptocurrency purchased in the country, weighted according to purchasing power (PPP) per capita; (2) the value of 'retail' cryptocurrency purchased in-country, defined as transactions with a value of less than $10,000, weighted by PPP; (3) the volume of exchanges through peer-to-peer (P2P) platforms and weighted on PPP and percentage of internet users; (4) the on-chain cryptocurrency transaction volume received from decentralised finance (DeFi) protocols, weighted by PPP per capita; and (5) the on-chain retail cryptocurrency transaction volume received from DeFi protocols, weighted by PPP per capita. The official Global Crypto Adoption Index indicator is the geometric mean of the rankings of each country on the basis of three parameters, normalised on a scale from 0 to 1.

The index is available for 146 countries and was calculated for 2020, 2021, and 2022 based on different methodologies, which therefore made the indexes incomparable across years. Figure 9.7 shows the country ranking based on the indicator in 2021. The index has high values for many emerging economies, including Kenya, Nigeria, Vietnam, and Venezuela. The result is largely due to the huge

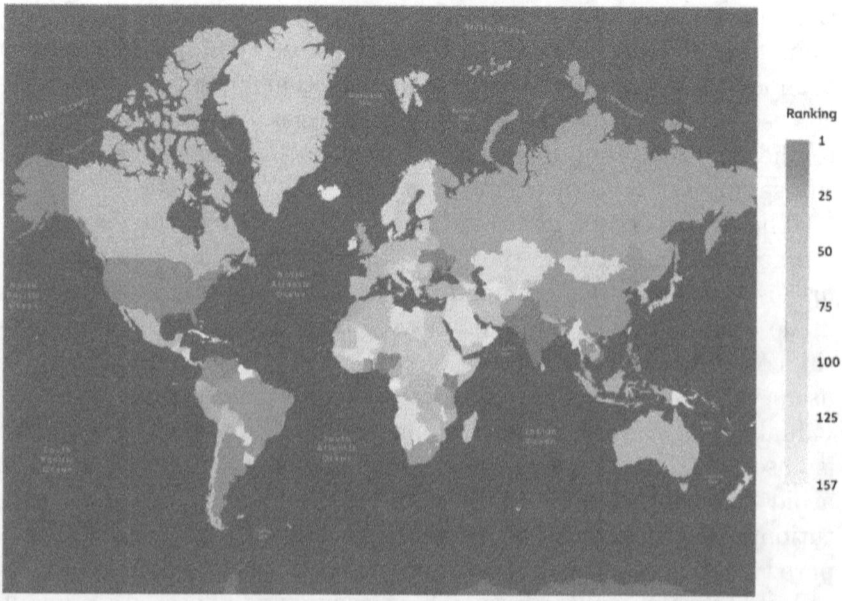

Figure 9.7. Ranking based on the Global Crypto Adoption Index 2021. *Source*: Chainalysis.com.

volumes of transactions on P2P platforms (the third component of the index). According to Chainanalysis, many users report choosing P2P platforms as their first gateway to cryptocurrency, often because they have no way to access centralised exchanges directly. Central and South Asia and Oceania, Latin America, and Africa send more web traffic to P2P platforms than regions whose countries tend to have larger economies, such as Western Europe and East Asia.

The second source of information on the use of cryptocurrencies in each country is provided by Statista (a German website that shares economic and public statistics, https://www.statista.com/). The indicator is available for the years 2019, 2020, and 2021 and is based on a survey, the Statista Global Consumer Survey, carried out in 56 countries around the world, which focuses on the consumption and use of different media. The survey is conducted online and targets populations in the 18–64 age range. Approximately 12,000 responses are collected in each country on a sample stratified by gender and age. Obviously, only the population that has access to the internet can participate in the survey. Among the questions, the survey enquires whether respondents own or use cryptocurrencies. Statista provides the percentage of respondents who answered affirmatively in 56 countries between 2019 and 2021. The data show particularly high percentages in 2021 in Africa, Asia, and South America. Nearly one in three respondents to the Statista survey in Nigeria, for example, said they own or use a digital currency, in contrast to six in 100 respondents in the US.

The two sources of data have complementary advantages and disadvantages. The Global Crypto Adoption Index is measured for several countries (146), but only in the year 2022. It is based on the actual volume of transactions, even if the allocation to the countries is inevitably imprecise. Furthermore, the calculation method of the indicator overcomes the limits of relying solely on the data of the cryptocurrency trading volume, which tends to give too much weight to rich countries with many internet users and a predominance of institutional investors.

The indicator from the Global Consumer Survey is available over three years and therefore allows us to analyse the trends in the use of cryptocurrencies over time, although for a smaller sample of countries (56). Being survey-based, the indicator can be subject to various response biases, primarily due to the non-representativeness of the sample of respondents compared to the reference population. (It is worth pointing out again that only individuals with internet access have the opportunity to answer the questionnaire.)

In the main empirical analysis, I use as dependent variables the Global Crypto Adoption Index measured in 2022, which I named $crypto_{2022}$, and its five components, which I normalised and named as follows: $crypto_{2022}\_all$ (the value of the cryptocurrency purchased in the country, weighted by PPP per capita); $crypto_{2022}\_retail$ (the value of 'retail' cryptocurrency purchased in-country, weighted by PPP per capita); $crypto_{2022}\_p2p$ (the volume of exchanges through P2P, weighted on PPP and percentage of internet users); $crypto_{2022}\_DeFi$ (the on-chain cryptocurrency transaction volume received from DeFi protocols, weighted by PPP per capita); and $crypto_{2022}\_DeFi\_retail$ (the on-chain retail cryptocurrency transaction volume received from DeFi protocols, weighted by PPP per capita). Each ranking was standardised and inverted in sign, so that higher values correspond to higher cryptocurrencies volumes.

As a robustness check, I also used the percentage of cryptocurrency users according to the Global Consumer Survey by Statista in the period 2019–2021, named $crypto_t$ (time variant), and employed a panel model to capture the dynamics of the cryptocurrency use over time.

The independent variables of the econometric models capture various country characteristics which, according to the research hypotheses, should influence the propensity to use cryptocurrencies.

To measure the financial development of each country, I use the financial development indicator created by the International Monetary Fund. The index has two main components that are used in the analysis: an index of development of financial markets (*Financial_markets*) and an index of development of financial institutions, such as banks and pension funds (*Financial_institutions*). The latest available data refer to 2020.

Inflation is measured by the percentage change in consumer prices (*Inflation*), as reported by the World Bank (last updated in 2021). The risk related to the change in the exchange rates of the national currency (*Exchange_risk*) is measured by the change in the exchange rates of the local currency against the USD with respect to the previous year (last updated in 2022), winsorised and divided by 100, also collected from the World Bank.

Finally, the risk of fraudulent action and illegal activity is inversely measured by the '*Corruption_control*' index in 2020, measured by the PRS group and part of the International Country Risk Guide. The index is lower in countries characterised by greater corruption within the political system, which has the potential to distort the economic and financial environment (for example by favouring the creation of black markets), reduce the country's efficiency by disfavouring meritocracy, and introduce political instability. The index measures various forms of corruption: demands for special payments and kickbacks related to import and export licences, exchange controls, tax assessments, police protection or loans, excessive clientelism, nepotism, job booking, secret financing of parties, and suspiciously close ties between politics and business.

In all analyses, I control for gross domestic product growth (*GDP_growth*), extracted from the World Bank database up to the year 2021.

Table 9.1 shows the descriptive statistics of the variables used in the cross-section analysis, while Table 9.3 shows the correlation matrix among them. Similarly, Tables 9.2 and 9.4 show the descriptive statistics and the correlation matrix of the variables used in the panel analysis.

It is worth mentioning the high correlation among the alternative independent variables that capture the use of cryptocurrencies, despite the fact that they are calculated using different metrics. In particular, $crypto_t$ measured in 2021 and $crypto_{2022}$ have a correlation of 39.6%.

Table 9.1. Descriptive statistics on the variables used in the cross-section analysis.

Variable	N	Mean	Std. dev.	Min	Max
crypto_{2022}	146	0.000	1.000	−1.714	1.714
crypto_{2022}_all	146	0.000	1.000	−1.714	1.714
crypto_{2022}_retail	146	0.000	1.000	−1.714	1.714
crypto_{2022}_p2p	146	0.000	1.000	−1.714	1.714
$crypto_{2022}\_DeFi$	146	0.000	1.000	−1.714	1.714
crypto_{2022}_DeFi_retail	146	0.000	1.000	−1.714	1.714
$\text{GDP\_growth}_{2020-21}$	146	5.909	6.228	−20.737	41.745
$\text{Financial\_markets}_{2020}$	137	0.268	0.279	0.000	0.922
$\text{Financial\_institutions}_{2020}$	137	0.470	0.204	0.089	0.953
Inflation_{2021}	133	6.796	16.596	−0.606	154.756
$\text{Exchange\_risk}_{2022}$	131	0.318	0.973	−0.681	5.4171
$\text{ControlCorruption}_{2020}$	124	0.476	0.192	0.083	1.000

Table 9.2. Descriptive statistics on the variables used in the panel analysis (2019–2021).

Variable	N	Mean	Std. dev.	Min	Max
crypto_t	168	0.111	0.058	0.030	0.420
GDP_growth_{t-1}	165	0.595	4.304	−11.325	8.528
$\text{Financial\_markets}_{t-1}$	165	0.506	0.247	0.017	0.922
$\text{Financial\_institutions}_{t-1}$	165	0.596	0.197	0.233	0.961
Inflation_{t-1}	162	2.532	3.018	−2.093	16.332
Exchange_risk_t	164	0.124	0.657	−0.681	4.482
$\text{ControlCorruption}_{2020}$	168	0.568	0.198	0.250	1.000

Table 9.3. Correlation matrix of the variables used in the cross-section analysis.

		1	2	3	4	5	6	7	8	9	10	11
1	$crypto_{2022}$	1.00										
2	$crypto_{2022}$_all	0.96	1.00									
3	$crypto_{2022}$_retail	0.96	1.00	1.00								
4	$crypto_{2022}$_p2p	0.22	−0.02	−0.02	1.00							
5	*$crypto_{2022}$_DeFi*	0.84	0.86	0.86	0.00	1.00						
6	$crypto_{2022}$_DeFi_retail	0.89	0.92	0.92	−0.04	0.95	1.00					
7	GDP_$growth_{2020-21}$	0.10	0.06	0.06	0.27	0.11	0.10	1.00				
8	Financial_$markets_{2020}$	0.28	0.34	0.34	−0.34	0.49	0.50	0.01	1.00			
9	Financial_$institutions_{2020}$	0.17	0.19	0.19	−0.15	0.37	0.37	0.11	0.77	1.00		
10	$Inflation_{2021}$	−0.10	−0.11	−0.11	0.04	0.06	−0.09	−0.40	−0.17	−0.13	1.00	
11	Exchange_$risk_{2022}$	0.12	0.13	0.13	−0.01	0.05	0.06	0.01	−0.09	−0.17	−0.06	1.00
12	$ControlCorruption_{2020}$	−0.06	−0.03	−0.03	−0.11	0.16	0.14	0.09	0.65	0.70	−0.21	−0.12

Table 9.4. Correlation matrix of the variables used in the panel analysis.

	1	2	3	4	5	6
1 $crypto_t$	1.00					
2 GDP_growth_{t-1}	−0.16	1.00				
3 $Financial\_markets_{t-1}$	−0.19	−0.21	1.00			
4 $Financial\_institutions_{t-1}$	−0.36	−0.18	0.82	1.00		
5 $Inflation_{t-1}$	0.32	0.22	−0.36	−0.48	1.00	
6 $Exchange\_risk_t$	0.19	0.18	−0.12	−0.12	0.07	1.00
7 $ControlCorruption_{2020}$	−0.40	−0.12	0.59	0.61	−0.45	−0.11

9.7. Results

Table 9.5 shows the results of the linear econometric analysis (ordinary least squares) with standard errors robust to the heteroskedasticity problem. The dependent variable is $crypto_{2022}$, i.e. the composite indicator that measures the adoption of cryptocurrencies based on trading volumes in 2022 (Global Crypto Adoption Index).

GDP growth and the financial development measures are included in the first column. The use of cryptocurrencies has a positive relationship with the development of financial markets, significant at the 99% level, but not with GDP growth or the development of financial institutions. In column II, the inflation measure is included, but its effect is not significant. In column III, the variable that captures the risk associated with exchange rate is added, and it is also not significant. The number of observations based on which the model is estimated decreases due to missing inflation data for some countries. Finally, in column IV, the variable that measures the control of corruption has a negative and significant coefficient (with a confidence level of 99%) in line with expectations, despite the reduction in the number of observations due to the fact that some countries are not included in the survey of the International Country Risk Guide. In this sample, the exchange risk variable has the expected positive sign, significant at the 95% level.

In columns V–IX, the fully fledged model is used to analyse, as alternative dependent variables, the five components of the crypto indicator: the use of cryptocurrencies in terms of total volumes ($crypto_{2022}\_all$), retail cryptocurrency transactions

Table 9.5. Results of ordinary least squares regression on the use of cryptocurrencies in each country.

	I	II	III	IV	V	VI	VII	VIII	IX
Dep. Var.	$crypto_{2022}$	$crypto_{2022}$	$crypto_{2022}$	$crypto_{2022}$	$crypto_{2022}$_all	$crypto_{2022}$_retail	$crypto_{2022}$_p2p	$crypto_{2022}$_DeFi	$crypto_{2022}$_DeFi_retail
$GDP\_growth_{2020-21}$	−0.007	−0.004	0.001	0.027	0.016	0.016	0.076***	0.051*	0.031
	(0.014)	(0.020)	(0.022)	(0.031)	(0.031)	(0.031)	(0.023)	(0.027)	(0.028)
$Financial\_markets_{2020}$	1.337***	1.326**	1.137**	1.692***	2.067***	2.067***	−1.760***	2.167***	2.190***
	(0.499)	(0.527)	(0.539)	(0.521)	(0.521)	(0.521)	(0.443)	(0.449)	(0.475)
$Financial\_institutions_{2020}$	−0.488	−0.669	−0.290	0.488	0.178	0.178	0.781	0.394	0.545
	(0.675)	(0.731)	(0.772)	(0.824)	(0.808)	(0.808)	(0.660)	(0.692)	(0.727)
$Inflation_{2021}$		−0.002	−0.002	−0.003	−0.004	−0.004	0.007**	0.012***	0.001
		(0.003)	(0.003)	(0.004)	(0.004)	(0.004)	(0.003)	(0.004)	(0.004)
$Exchange\_risk_{2022}$			0.092	0.147**	0.155***	0.155***	−0.007	0.112	0.112
			(0.071)	(0.070)	(0.059)	(0.059)	(0.134)	(0.083)	(0.085)
$ControlCorruption_{2020}$				−2.338***	−2.320***	−2.320***	0.555	−1.399***	−1.788***
				(0.545)	(0.519)	(0.519)	(0.615)	(0.464)	(0.500)
Constant	−0.054	0.053	−0.155	0.317	0.428	0.428	−0.628*	−0.410	−0.136
	(0.251)	(0.299)	(0.331)	(0.381)	(0.378)	(0.378)	(0.342)	(0.340)	(0.350)
N countries	136	126	118	105	105	105	105	105	105
F	5.418**	3.175**	2.843**	7.046***	10.035***	10.035***	6.053***	12.65***	13.618***
R^2	0.097	0.086	0.088	0.211	0.258	0.258	0.232	0.340	0.337

Note: The table shows the coefficients and, in parentheses, the robust standard errors of multivariate linear regressions whose dependent variable is reported in the table header. The levels of significance are as follows: *p-value <10%, **p-value <5%, ***p-value <1%.

($crypto_{2022}\_retail$), cryptocurrency transactions made through P2P platforms ($crypto_{2022}\_p2p$), DeFi cryptocurrency transactions ($crypto_{2022}\_DeFi$), and retail Defi cryptocurrency transactions ($crypto_{2022}\_DeFi\_retail$). Here, some interesting differences emerge when looking at the P2P and DeFi transactions: for both components, I find a positive and significant effect of GDP growth and the expected positive effect of inflation (significant at 95% or 99%). Instead, the exchange rate risk loses significance. Interestingly, the financial markets development index has a negative coefficient in the analysis of P2P transactions, suggesting a substitution effect between the two systems (p-value <1%).

Table 9.6 presents the results of the panel analysis in which the dependent variable is $crypto_t$, measured between 2019 and 2021 and representing the percentage of internet users who responded that they used cryptocurrencies during the year in the Global Consumer Survey.

Again, I gradually include our regressors in the analysis. GDP growth and the financial development measures included in the first column are all significant. GDP growth has a negative coefficient, significant at the 99% level. The use of cryptocurrencies has a positive relationship with the development of financial markets, significant at the 90% level (similarly to the cross-section estimates), but negative with the development of financial institutions, significant at the 99% level. In column II, the inflation measure is included, but its effect is not significant. The variable that captures the risk associated with exchange rates is added in column III and has a positive and significant coefficient (at the 90% level), similarly to the cross-section analysis. Finally, column IV confirms the positive association between corruption and use of cryptocurrencies, as the variable capturing corruption control has a negative and significant coefficient (with a confidence level of 90 %). In column V, as a robustness check, we include macro region dummy variables, which capture other unobservable differences across the different regions. We find that with respect to the baseline category, East Asia and Pacific, the use of cryptocurrencies is less spread in Europe, Central Asia, North America, and South Asia.

Table 9.6. Results of random effects panel model on the use of cryptocurrencies in each country in the 2019–2021 period.

	I	II	III	IV	
GDP_growth$_{t-1}$	−0.004***	−0.004***	−0.004***	−0.004***	−0.004***
	(0.001)	(0.001)	(0.001)	(0.001)	(0.001)
Financial_markets$_{t-1}$	0.063*	0.066*	0.067**	0.085**	0.095***
	(0.035)	(0.034)	(0.034)	(0.035)	(0.031)
Financial_institutions$_{t-1}$	−0.191***	−0.179***	−0.177***	−0.142***	−0.169***
	(0.055)	(0.052)	(0.053)	(0.048)	(0.048)
Inflation$_{t-1}$		0.002	0.002	0.001	0.001
		(0.003)	(0.002)	(0.002)	(0.002)
Exchange_risk$_t$			0.005	0.005	0.004
			(0.003)	(0.003)	(0.003)
ControlCorruption$_{2020}$				−0.091**	−0.060
				(0.045)	(0.039)
East Asia & Pacific					(omitted)
Europe & Central Asia					−0.037**
					(0.015)
Latin America & Caribbean					−0.016
					(0.021)
Middle East & North Africa					−0.031
					(0.022)
North America					−0.029*
					(0.015)
South Asia					−0.077***
					(0.022)
Sub-Saharan Africa					0.047
					(0.036)
Constant	0.114***	0.196***	0.182***	0.180***	0.204***
	(0.007)	(0.028)	(0.024)	(0.025)	(0.029)
N countries	55	55	54	54	54
N observations	165	165	162	161	161
χ^2	37.127***	46.984***	45.071***	55.603***	57.991***
R^2 overall	0.036	0.237	0.266	0.242	0.301

Note: The table shows the coefficients and, in parentheses, the robust standard errors, clustered at country level, of multivariate random effect panel regressions whose dependent variable is *crypto*$_t$. The levels of significance are as follows: $^*p$-value <10%, $^{**}p$-value <5%, $^{***}p$-value <1%.

9.8. Discussion and Conclusions

Despite the enormous diffusion of cryptocurrencies in the world and the growing academic interest in the phenomenon, our understanding of who adopts cryptocurrencies and why they do it is still partial. In particular, there is a lack of studies that analyse what determines the adoption of cryptocurrencies by the population in different countries of the world. This research gap is mainly due to the fact that it is very difficult to recover data on the geographical location of cryptocurrency users since they are exchanged in anonymous and encrypted transactions.

Some studies have theorised how cryptocurrencies could be particularly useful in emerging countries with problems of hyperinflation, volatile exchange rate, corruption, and limited access to money. However, many of the indicators used so far to describe the 'geography of cryptocurrency use' show a very different situation, with the US and Europe accounting for the majority of cryptocurrency use.

This chapter contributes to the knowledge of what determines the use of cryptocurrencies in a certain country by exploiting two new indicators that represent the actual geographical distribution of retail (and not only institutional) users of cryptocurrencies and which offer complementary advantages. The first measure covers virtually all the countries of the world and captures all the transactions that took place via blockchain, allocated to the various countries according to a reasonable criterion based on the origin of the web traffic of the platforms that allow the exchange of cryptocurrencies. In the indicator, the transaction volumes are weighted in order to limit the influence of exchanges between institutional investors and better represent the transactions of retail users. The second indicator uses data from an international survey in which a representative sample of the population in each country is asked whether they had bought or intended to buy cryptocurrencies during the year. The survey was repeated in the last three years, thus making it possible to analyse the evolution of the use of cryptocurrencies over time. Both metrics indicate more intense uses of cryptocurrencies in emerging countries, such as certain countries in Africa and South America.

The results obtained through the different measures and econometric specifications (specifically, cross-section and panel models) are consistent. The empirical analysis suggests that the adoption of cryptocurrencies is indeed linked to the level of development of financial markets and institutions, inflation, exchange rate risk, and the level of corruption in the country. In particular, where traditional financial markets, such as stock exchanges, are more developed, the population is more inclined to use cryptocurrencies (except those exchanged through P2P platforms), while the panel analysis suggests that the development of traditional financial institutions, such as banks and pension funds, reduces the adoption of cryptocurrencies. A possible explanation is that in countries with stronger financial markets, the population has a more developed knowledge of the concepts of risk and return and is therefore less reluctant to add investments in cryptocurrencies as well to their portfolio of investments in shares, bonds, and derivative instruments. In countries characterised by strong financial institutions, it is possible that the population has the option or preference to refer to traditional credit institutions to carry out financial transactions and investments and refrain from using cryptocurrencies.

I offer some empirical support to the notion that the level of inflation positively affects the use of cryptocurrencies exchanged through P2P platforms and DeFi protocols, consistent with the fact that the population uses them to reduce the financial risk of their investments. Support is also found for the positive relationship between cryptocurrency use and the variation in exchange rate, in line with the hypothesis that retail investors use cryptocurrencies to insulate themselves from exchange rate risk.

Finally, countries with a higher propensity to corruption use cryptocurrencies to a greater extent. Whether this is due to the fact that cryptocurrencies are used for illegal purposes (exploiting their anonymity in transactions) or, conversely, to protect themselves against monetary and financial fraud at the national level remains to be assessed.

The international adoption of cryptocurrencies is constantly evolving, as shown by the divergence in results based on metrics measured in different years. In the future, it will be necessary to continue monitoring this evolution to understand how the use of cryptocurrencies varies over time in terms of both quantity and purpose (for example investments, transactions, speculation, and illicit activities). Furthermore, future analyses should be based on indicators representative of the actual use of cryptocurrencies by the general public. Specifically, studies should compare different metrics and judge their suitability for research purposes in the absence of official data. The latter data will only be available if national and international governments decide for further regulation of cryptocurrencies, which allows their tracking, as suggested by some scholars (Kaplan, 2021). However, compromising anonymity in cryptocurrency transactions could substantially reduce their use, not only for illicit purposes.

Finally, the analysis of this study was carried out in peculiar years. The panel model encompasses the years 2019–2021, a period strongly affected by the COVID-19 pandemic, which may have changed the behaviour of cryptocurrency users (Demir *et al.*, 2020). The cross-section data refer to 2022, a year of volatile secondary markets, high inflation, and several fraud and failures in the cryptocurrencies segment (the 'crypto winter', see Duggan and Adams, 2023). As the particular circumstances make the study results not necessarily generalisable to normal settings, future research should replicate the analysis, ideally using longitudinal data spanning longer time horizons.

References

Alzahrani, S. and Daim, T. (2019). Evaluation of the cryptocurrency adoption decision using hierarchical decision modeling (HDM). *2019 Portland International Conference on Management of Engineering and Technology (PICMET)*. Institute of Electrical and Electronics Engineers Inc., pp. 1–7. doi: 10.23919/PICMET.2019.8893897.

Aspembitova, A. T., Feng, L., and Yue Chew, L. (2021). Behavioral structure of users in cryptocurrency market. *PLoS ONE*, 16(1 January), 1–19. doi: 10.1371/journal.pone.0242600.

Böhme, R. *et al.* (2015). Bitcoin: Economics, technology, and governance. *Journal of Economic Perspectives*, 29(2), 213–238. doi: 10.1257/jep.29.2.213.

Burniske, C. and White, A. (2017). *Bitcoin: Ringing the Bell for a New Assets Class.*

Chainalysis (2021). The 2020 Geography of Cryptocurrency Report, *Chainalysis*, (October).

Chainalysis (2022). The 2022 Geography of Cryptocurrency Report, *Chainalysis*, (October).

Chenguel, M.B. (2022). Blockchain and ecological impact: Between reality and accusation?', pp. 438–448. doi: 10.1007/978-3-030-93464-4_43.

Choo, K.K.R. (2015). Cryptocurrency and virtual currency: Corruption and money laundering/terrorism financing risks? *Handbook of Digital Currency: Bitcoin, Innovation, Financial Instruments, and Big Data.* Academic Press, pp. 283–307. doi: 10.1016/B978-0-12-802117-0.00015-1.

Darlington, J.K.I. (2014). *The Future of Bitcoin: Mapping the Global Adoption of World's Largest Cryptocurrency Through Benefit Analysis, TRACE: Tennessee Research and Creative Exchange*. Knoxville. doi: 10.2139/ssrn.3127327.

Demir, E. *et al.* (2020). The relationship between cryptocurrencies and COVID-19 pandemic. *Eurasian Economic Review*. Springer, 10(3), 349–360. doi: 10.1007/S40822-020-00154-1/FIGURES/5.

Demirgüç-Kunt, A. *et al.* (2022). *Financial Inclusion, Digital Payments, and Resilience in the Age of COVID-19, Global Findex Database 2021.*

Duggan, W. and Adams, M. (2023). *What Is Crypto Winter? — Forbes Advisor, Forbes.* Available at: https://www.forbes.com/advisor/investing/cryptocurrency/what-is-crypto-winter/ (Accessed: 30 May 2023).

Faverio, M. and Massart, N. (2022). *46% of Americans Who have Invested in Cryptocurrency Say It's Done Worse than Expected, Pew Research Center Logo.* Available at: https://www.pewresearch.org/short-reads/2022/08/23/46-of-americans-who-have-invested-in-cryptocurrency-say-its-done-worse-than-expected/ (Accessed: 25 May 2023).

Faverio, M. and Massart, N. (2023). *Majority of Americans aren't Confident in the Safety and Reliability of Cryptocurrency, Pew Research Center Logo2.* Available at: https://www.pewresearch.org/short-reads/2023/04/10/majority-of-americans-arent-confident-in-the-safety-and-reliability-of-cryptocurrency/ (Accessed: 21 May 2023).

Fidelity Digital Assets (2021). *The Institutional Investor Digital Assets Study.*

Figà-Talamanca, G. and Patacca, M. (2020). Disentangling the relationship between Bitcoin and market attention measures. *Journal of Industrial and Business Economics*, 47(1), 71–91. doi: 10.1007/s40812-019-00133-x.

Giudici, G., Milne, A., and Vinogradov, D. (2020). Cryptocurrencies: market analysis and perspectives. *Journal of Industrial and Business Economics.* Springer International Publishing, 47(1), 1–18. doi: 10.1007/s40812-019-00138-6.

Hileman, G. (2015). The bitcoin market potential index, *Lecture Notes in Computer Science (including subseries Lecture Notes in Artificial Intelligence and Lecture Notes in Bioinformatics)*, 8976, 92–93. doi: 10.1007/978-3-662-48051-9_7.

Hileman, G. and Rauchs, M. (2017). *Global Benchmarking Study, Cambridge Centre for Alternative Finance.*

IOSCO (2020). *Investor Education on Crypto-Assets Final Report The Board.*

Kaplan, A. (2021). Cryptocurrency and corruption: Auditing with blockchain, *Auditing Ecosystem and Strategic Accounting in the Digital Era*, 325–338. doi: 10.1007/978-3-030-72628-7_15.

Nakamoto, S. (2008). Bitcoin: A peer-to-peer electronic cash system. Satoshi Nakamoto Institute, *Bitcoin.Org*, 1–9.

Park, S. and Park, H. W. (2020). Diffusion of cryptocurrencies: Web traffic and social network attributes as indicators of cryptocurrency performance. *Quality and Quantity*. Springer Netherlands, 54(1), 297–314. doi: 10.1007/s11135-019-00840-6.

Ricci, P. (2020). How economic freedom reflects on the Bitcoin transaction network, *Journal of Industrial and Business Economics*. Springer International Publishing, 47(1), 133–161. doi: 10.1007/s40812-019-00143-9.

Schuh, S. and Shy, O. (2015). *U.S. Consumers' Adoption and Use of Bitcoin and other Virtual Currencies, Bank of Canada.*

Sharma, D., Verma, R., and Sam, S. (2021). Adoption of cryptocurrency: An international perspective. *International Journal of Technology Transfer and Commercialisation*. Inderscience Publishers, 18(3), 247. doi: 10.1504/ijttc.2021.118863.

Wintermeyer, L. (2021). Institutional money is pouring into the crypto market and its only going to grow, *Forbes*.

https://doi.org/10.1142/9781800617032_0010

Chapter 10

Exploring the Impact of Gender Dynamics in Equity Crowdfunding: A Social Role Theory Perspective

Scarlett Koster and Andrew Isaak

Manchot Graduate School, Heinrich Heine University, Düsseldorf, Germany

10.1. Introduction

Entrepreneurs often face challenges in financing their ventures due to the liabilities of newness (Stinchcombe, 1965) and size, with large firms assumed to have better survival prospects (e.g. Freeman and Hannan, 1983). Many entrepreneurs at the early stages of the venture encounter particular difficulties in securing the necessary funding from traditional sources, resulting in their start-ups' failure (Cumming *et al.*, 2021; Cumming and Vismara, 2017).

Fortunately, crowdfunding has emerged to support new business ideas and innovative ventures that respond to environmental, social, and economic issues (e.g. Lehner, 2013). Accordingly, many now see crowdfunding as a creative source of capital for new ventures, especially for those entrepreneurs who are disadvantaged when seeking funds from traditional investors (Bento *et al.*, 2019). Equity crowdfunding has promised to democratise entrepreneurial finance for underrepresented groups of potential entrepreneurs (Cumming *et al.*, 2021; Gorbatai and Nelson, 2015; Serwaah, 2022). It presents an alternative means of venture financing in which multiple investors contribute via an online platform in return for which they receive a small stake in the venture. This strategy has lower entry barriers (e.g. no collateral required) than bank loans or classic venture capital (e.g. Neuhaus *et al.*, 2022; Vismara, 2019). The global equity crowdfunding market has grown exponentially, making it an essential source of alternative financing for entrepreneurs (Butticè and Vismara, 2022).

Since Title III of the Jumpstart Our Business Startups (JOBS) Act was introduced in the United States in 2016, equity crowdfunding has steadily gained acceptance among the start-up community and surrounding stakeholders, and the COVID-19 pandemic has given it an additional boost in recent years (Brian, 2021). The continued growth of equity crowdfunding is an encouraging and optimistic sign for young ventures and private investors, as this new form of financing is more accessible to non-traditional stakeholders (Vu, 2021). US equity crowdfunding statistics underline this trend, with $494.0 million raised via Regulation Crowdfunding (Regulation C) across 33 active platforms (i.e. funding portals or broker-dealers) in 2022. The top three platforms (Wefunder, StartEngine, and Republic) accounted for 79.9% of total Regulation C dollars raised in 2022, at $394.5 million closed (Brian, 2023).

Various studies have noted that crowdfunding represents a successful tool for financing viable, long-term-oriented projects, such as campaigns associated with sustainable entrepreneurship (e.g. Calic and Mosakowski, 2016; Hörisch and Tenner, 2020; Lehner, 2013). Additionally, Schaltegger and Wagner (2011) point out that non-traditional entrepreneurship, such as sustainable or social entrepreneurship, is characterised by entrepreneurial activities that focus more on the personal initiative and skills of the entrepreneurial individual or team and less on management systems or technical procedures. This indicates that individual or team characteristics and perceptions are essential factors when it comes to entrepreneurial activities. Furthermore, entrepreneurial ventures offer women opportunities for empowerment, social inclusion, and economic security (Alkhaled and Berglund, 2018; Datta and Gailey, 2012). Since female entrepreneurship enhances women's empowerment and contributes to changing the social order (Haugh and Talwar, 2016), we believe that female entrepreneurship can be seen as a non-traditional form of entrepreneurship, similar to social or sustainable entrepreneurship (Singh *et al.*, 2022).

While work experience and gender have both been shown to play a role in successful crowdfunding (e.g. Duan *et al.*, 2020; Geiger and Oranburg, 2018; Li *et al.*, 2022; Vismara, 2016), little is known about the role of female team members and all-female teams in venture financing via crowdfunding. Significant gaps remain regarding the role of all-female and mixed-gender teams in equity crowdfunding in particular. Due to the predominance of male founders, female founders face a higher likelihood of inadequate financial support, resulting in male entrepreneurs outperforming their female counterparts in accessing formal financing. As a result of these systemic biases, women must engage more in obtaining alternative means (e.g. Malmström and Wincent, 2018). Thus, access to non-traditional and more inclusive forms of financing is crucial for female entrepreneurs. To shed further light on the interplay between alternative venture financing and team gender composition, we sought to examine how the female gender of team members (i.e. the number of female team members and all-female teams) affects the amount raised through equity crowdfunding and how the degree of previous work experience, as well as the chosen funding goal, moderate this relationship and, ultimately, affect the amount raised. Therefore, this study examines 361 US offerings based on data from two leading equity crowdfunding platforms, Wefunder and Republic, to investigate and discuss the relationship between gender and the amount of funding raised through equity crowdfunding.

10.2. Literature Review

10.2.1. *Female entrepreneurship and venture finance*

In 2015, the United Nations (2023) adopted the Sustainable Development Goals (SDGs) to achieve a better and more sustainable future for all. One of these goals involves the promotion of inclusive and sustainable economic growth, aiming for comprehensive, productive, and satisfactory employment opportunities for everyone (SDG No. 8). Another goal seeks to achieve gender equality by facilitating improved access to economic resources for women and fostering their active engagement in the economic, political, and social spheres (SDG No. 5). Aligning with previous research, we argue that one way to achieve economic growth and empower women is to encourage their access to and participation in entrepreneurial finance markets (Santos and Neumeyer, 2021; Serwaah and Shneor, 2021) because financial models that are more inclusive and supportive of women entrepreneurs can enhance economic development.

By contrast, insufficient resources and support for female entrepreneurs and their ventures create obstacles that hinder their chances of success, resulting in a notable underrepresentation of female-led economic ventures. Consequently, female entrepreneurs must actively seek and attract potential investors (Elitzur and Solodoha, 2021).

Female entrepreneurs are 63% less likely to raise equity funding than their male counterparts (Guzman and Kacperczyk, 2019). Thus, gender is an important variable that affects access to external capital (Cumming *et al.*, 2021). When seeking funding, female entrepreneurs face particular challenges, such as tighter financial constraints than their male counterparts (Blattman *et al.*, 2014; Dupas and Robinson, 2013; Faccio *et al.*, 2016; Gottlieb *et al.*, 2022), and gender-specific barriers such as discriminatory social norms (e.g. Jayachandran, 2021; Dean and Jayachandran, 2019).

Despite women's progress over the years, gender gaps and inequalities in business finance remain substantial and well documented in the literature. The entrepreneurship literature widely recognises differences in access to external equity based on gender (e.g. Brush *et al.*, 2004; Gicheva and Link, 2015; Greene *et al.*, 2001; Kanze *et al.*, 2018).

Even though some research suggests that female-led entrepreneurial ventures perform as well as, if not better, than male-led entrepreneurial ventures (e.g. Cowling *et al.*, 2020; Demartini, 2018; Kalnins and Williams, 2014), female entrepreneurs are generally less likely to secure funding than male entrepreneurs, as venture capitalists and traditional investor channels fund female-led ventures at a lower rate than those led by male entrepreneurs (e.g. Becker-Blease and Sohl, 2011; Brush *et al.*, 2018). Consequently, women are significantly less likely to seek financing than men (Kwapisz and Hechavarría, 2018).

Examining the interface between demand and supply of risk capital investments, Alsos and Ljunggren (2017) found that an entrepreneur's gender influences investment decisions. Due to the existence of gender-based discrimination in entrepreneurial activity

(Gupta *et al.*, 2019), female entrepreneurs face disadvantages when attempting to obtain external equity capital from initial public offerings (IPOs; Bigelow *et al.*, 2014), private equity and venture capital firms (Lins and Lutz, 2016; Malmström *et al.*, 2018), and angel investors (Edelman *et al.*, 2018; Poczter and Shapsis, 2018). Bigelow *et al.* (2014) have reported that IPOs led by women founders and CEOs are considered less attractive investments, even if they have identical personal qualifications and firm financials as men. Empirical evidence confirms that only a tiny proportion of women-led firms raise venture capital (Carter *et al.*, 2003) and that women receive a significantly lower share of venture capital financing than men (Lins and Lutz, 2016; Malmström *et al.*, 2018).

Thus, female entrepreneurs face a significant 'gender penalty' when seeking financial capital for their ventures (Brooks *et al.*, 2014). Even if female entrepreneurs successfully access funds, the sums raised are usually lower than those raised by male entrepreneurs (Kanze *et al.*, 2018). Researchers have also observed that the financial terms for the capital raised by female entrepreneurs are less favourable than those obtained by male entrepreneurs (Jennings and Brush, 2013; Madill *et al.*, 2006).

Some argue that these funding differences can be partly explained by the fact that women tend to use internal rather than external sources of financing (Bennett and Dann, 2000). However, studies have shown that women remain at a disadvantage relative to men in obtaining debt capital (i.e. bank loans) and that gender influences the evaluation criteria loan officers use in assessing applications (Carter *et al.*, 2007). Indeed, several studies have found evidence of gender-based differential treatment to the detriment of female entrepreneurs, whose legitimacy and credibility are often questioned (Aristei and Gallo, 2016). Consequently, many key financial figures indicate the differential treatment of women entrepreneurs. Due to the anticipation of being rejected, female entrepreneurs are less likely to apply for a bank loan (Moro *et al.*, 2017). When they do, they experience a higher rejection rate (Stefani and Vacca, 2015), obtain lower amounts (Eddleston *et al.*, 2016), are charged higher interest rates (Mascia and Rossi, 2017), and must provide more significant collateral than their male counterparts (Wu and Chua, 2012). Accordingly, women have less access to external capital and tend to rely on their savings, loans from family and friends, or micro-loans to finance their businesses (Coleman and Robb, 2009; Gicheva and Link, 2015).

The existing research offers many possible reasons for the gender penalty female entrepreneurs face. Some have claimed that traditional investors exhibit bias against female entrepreneurs, implicitly deeming that they lack the qualities necessary to engage in successful early-stage venturing (Lee and Huang, 2018). Others have argued that investors provide women with a smaller share of funds simply because female entrepreneurs seek and require less funding for their ventures in the first place (Brush *et al.*, 2018). Some have observed that women entrepreneurs' communication styles and investors' perceptions of long-term growth and scalability play a crucial role in investing decisions (Huang *et al.*, 2021).

These findings indicate that gender differences in access to external equity may be related to gender biases and stereotypes in entrepreneurship (Johnson *et al.*, 2018; Laguía *et al.*, 2019). Women tend to be associated with family and social roles rather than business or entrepreneurial roles (Eagly and Karau, 2002), and they are often considered to have fewer management and leadership skills than men, reducing their chances of attracting investors (Balachandra *et al.*, 2019). Thus, women who want to become entrepreneurs face many barriers to entry, and in addition to more challenges in accessing financial assets, female entrepreneurs also face gender role expectations (Sullivan and Meek, 2012). Women's limited access to external capital also relates to barriers based on personal characteristics, attitudes, cultural background, and the entrepreneurial environment (Audretsch *et al.*, 2017). Thus, equity crowdfunding has emerged as an alternative to traditional forms of venture financing, allowing innovative early-stage companies to obtain funding through small equity investments from a vast range of investors via online platforms (Block *et al.*, 2018; Butticè and Vismara, 2022).

10.2.2. *Equity crowdfunding*

Schwienbacher and Larralde (2010, p. 4) define crowdfunding as 'an open call, essentially through the Internet, for the provision of financial resources either in the form of donation or in exchange for some form of reward and voting rights to support initiatives for specific purposes'. Entrepreneurs turn to crowdfunding when they need financial assistance to realise a project. Depending on the crowdfunding type, entrepreneurs can acquire customers and validate their business models or ideas early on while retaining a high degree of independence from individual investors (Neuhaus *et al.*, 2022). The four main types of crowdfunding are reward-based, donation-based, lending-based, and equity-based (Neuhaus *et al.*, 2022; Vismara, 2019).

In this study, we examine the US equity crowdfunding market. To set this type of crowdfunding apart, Vismara (2016, p. 589) states that 'most importantly, whereas general crowdfunding platforms allow investors to deliver money to companies in exchange for products, rewards, or bond-like instruments, pure equity crowdfunding platforms allow investors to become shareholders of startups.' Entrepreneurs utilise equity crowdfunding to publicly offer a predetermined quantity of their company's equity shares for sale over the internet, employing online platforms to facilitate the transaction process (Butticè and Vismara, 2022). In equity crowdfunding, entrepreneurs seek funding from a relatively large crowd of potential investors in exchange for an equity stake in their company. This type of financing has recently emerged as a new player in entrepreneurial finance, allowing even early-stage companies to obtain funding through small equity investments from an extensive range of investors (Block *et al.*, 2018).

In contrast to reward-based crowdfunding, which essentially involves the pre-sale of goods and services, funders of equity crowdfunding receive a long-term stake in the venture. As such, raising capital through equity crowdfunding differs from reward-based crowdfunding in substantive ways (Geiger and Oranburg, 2018). Accordingly, investors of equity crowdfunding campaigns are primarily motivated by extrinsic factors such as profits. Research by Cholakova and Clarysse (2015) showed that only financial return motivations positively predict investment decisions in equity crowdfunding and that non-financial motives do not play a significant role in these decisions. Similarly, Vismara (2016) discovered that offering rewards to investors does not increase the probability of success of equity crowdfunding campaigns. These findings led Butticé and Vismara (2022) to conclude that equity crowdfunding is a fully-fledged new source of risk capital. Therefore, if profits primarily drive investors' incentives to participate in equity crowdfunding campaigns, the gender-related funding patterns for these campaigns may be similar to those of more traditional forms of venture finance.

Like traditional stock exchanges, the offerings listed by equity crowdfunding platforms are open to the public. Thus, crowdfunding platforms allow anyone to view projects posted online, creating a heterogeneous population of small investors (Cumming *et al.*, 2021). However, unlike traditional public offerings, equity crowdfunding is available to various types of early-stage firms and is substantially less costly for issuers (Butticé and Vismara, 2022).

Equity crowdfunding, as defined by the Securities and Exchange Commission (SEC, 2023b), involves raising funds online in exchange for securities. The Securities Act of 1933 and the Securities Exchange Act of 1934 imposed strict regulations on new ventures, prohibiting them from publicly soliciting investments without registering the securities offered and providing comprehensive audited financial statements (SEC, 2015). However, following the financial crisis of 2007–2008, the US government enacted the JOBS Act in 2012. The JOBS Act aimed to enhance capital accessibility for entrepreneurial ventures by alleviating the existing regulatory filing requirements associated with various types of fundraising for new ventures.

The emergence of equity crowdfunding has created a financing channel to facilitate entrepreneurs' access to external funding and allow new, more heterogeneous groups of investors to support young ventures. In this regard, equity crowdfunding is a powerful tool that aims to democratise entrepreneurial finance (e.g. Serwaah, 2022) by giving entrepreneurs historically underrepresented in traditional capital markets a better chance of attracting funding (Mollick and Robb, 2016). However, the existing evidence is mixed on whether crowdfunding meets these expectations and reduces economic friction associated with, for instance, the age, size, or ethnicity of the founder team (e.g. Cumming *et al.*, 2021; Greenberg and Mollick, 2017).

10.2.3. *Crowdfunding and female entrepreneurship*

Research has consistently demonstrated that female business owners face obstacles in accessing external capital (e.g. Brush *et al.*, 2018; Lins and Lutz, 2016). Considering these challenging circumstances, the rise of crowdfunding offers a promising opportunity to democratise early-stage investment in start-up companies.

Indeed, crowdfunding has been found to support new business ideas and innovative ventures that respond to environmental, social, and economic issues (Calic and Mosakowski, 2016; Hörisch and Tenner, 2020; Lehner, 2013). Nevertheless, the results regarding gender and crowdfunding are mixed. Some scholars have argued that female founders have advantages in alternative financing over traditional financing; for example, in online fundraising, women benefit particularly from their communication style, leading to advantages in financing (Gorbatai and Nelson, 2015). Analysing Indiegogo campaigns, Gorbatai and Nelson (2015) found that gender-specific language partially mediates the success of women in reward-based crowdfunding, as funders prefer female-specific linguistic patterns in pitches (e.g. using more positive emotion words and more inclusive language). However, although women may receive crowdfunding, they experience a disadvantage in the actual funding amount (Geiger, 2020). Therefore, other scholars have argued that male entrepreneurs benefit more from equity crowdfunding, as women receive significantly less funding than men (Geiger and Oranburg, 2018). Similarly, a recent study found that female entrepreneurs do not have a higher chance of successfully raising external capital through equity crowdfunding (Cumming *et al.*, 2021). Given these contrasting findings, more research is needed, particularly on equity crowdfunding and women's entrepreneurship and how this type of financing can help reduce the existing gender financing gap (Buttice and Vismara, 2022). Overall, the success or failure rates of crowdfunding campaigns led by female entrepreneurs depend more on contextual and external factors (Serwaah, 2022). This represents an opportunity for sustainable development projects because sustainable entrepreneurship (i.e. the application of entrepreneurial methods to achieve societal objectives and transform market environments) is characterised by activities that focus more on the personal initiative and skills of the entrepreneur and less on management systems or technical procedures (Schaltegger and Wagner, 2011).

The literature recognises that equity crowdfunding has the potential to narrow the gender gap by democratising access to finance for underrepresented groups of potential entrepreneurs, including women who are at a disadvantage compared to men in accessing traditional external finance (Cumming *et al.*, 2021). Preliminary empirical observations from crowdfunding research in Europe and the US suggest that investors appear more willing to support women in alternative, more informal financing settings (Barbi and Mattioli, 2019; Greenberg and Mollick, 2017; Johnson *et al.*, 2018; Zhao *et al.*, 2021). Yet, while female entrepreneurs can attract a similar number of investors as their male counterparts, they raise less capital on equity crowdfunding platforms (Vismara, 2016). Therefore, we differentiate between the various types of crowdfunding in the following section, which provides an overview of previous research on female entrepreneurship in crowdfunding.

Drawing on data from Kickstarter, the prominent reward-based crowdfunding platform in the US, Greenberg and Mollick (2017) present evidence indicating that women have a higher likelihood of achieving crowdfunding success than men, particularly in industries where they are underrepresented. The authors attribute this advantage to a phenomenon known as 'activist choice homophily', which suggests that individuals are not only drawn to others who resemble them but also perceive shared structural barriers arising from a common social identity based on group membership. These shared identities foster support and enhance women's crowdfunding prospects (Greenberg and Mollick, 2017). Moreover, Johnson *et al.* (2018) researched investor stereotypes and implicit biases in reward-based crowdfunding decisions on Kickstarter. Their findings indicate that the prevalent gender biases held by non-professional investors contribute to the perception of female entrepreneurs as trustworthy, subsequently increasing investors' willingness to fund early-stage ventures led by women (Johnson *et al.*, 2018).

Researchers have also explored the influence of gender in lending-based crowdfunding, indicating no funding inequalities. Pope and Sydnor (2011) examined the determinants of access to credit on the US-based peer-to-peer lending platform Prosper. They analysed how information cues such as race, age, and gender, conveyed through photographs, influenced the likelihood of receiving loan funding. Although the study did not reveal significant gender disparities, the results suggest a preference for men over women at high credit grades in the peer-to-peer lending market. In contrast, the results demonstrate that women may be more likely to obtain funding at lower credit grades than men. However, high-credit-grade borrowers are generally more likely to be financed than low-credit-grade borrowers (Pope and Sydnor, 2011).

Barasinska and Schäfer (2014) utilised data from a large German peer-to-peer lending platform to explore borrowing patterns. They found that female borrowers had a better chance of obtaining funds than males. The authors attributed this phenomenon to the collective wisdom of the lending crowd, suggesting that female discrimination was mitigated in this context (Barasinska and Schäfer, 2014).

Chen *et al.* (2020) recently examined the gender gap in the Chinese peer-to-peer lending market. The results reveal a gender gap in which lenders discriminate against female borrowers. Despite female borrowers' higher creditworthiness, they experienced lower success rates than their male counterparts in securing funding. Thus, female borrowers must offer lenders higher profitability to attain an equal likelihood of obtaining financing (Chen *et al.*, 2020).

By contrast, Singh *et al.* (2022) examined how an entrepreneur's gender affects venture funding through crowdlending platforms focusing on service businesses or those with a social cause. Their analysis of a large dataset of 917,307 loan records (cases) from male and female entrepreneurs from 102 countries obtained from KIVA, a non-profit-based crowdlending platform, suggests that while online crowdlending platforms exert a democratising influence on the funding of female entrepreneurial ventures, female-led service businesses still face challenges in obtaining funding, particularly for larger loans and longer loan terms. They were less able to secure financial backing than their male counterparts or non-service businesses (Singh *et al.*, 2022). Thus, the democratising effect of crowdfunding for female-led ventures remains absent in this setting.

Similarly, Vismara (2016) analysed a sample of 271 projects listed on the UK equity crowdfunding platforms Crowdcube and Seedrs, revealing that female founders, like their male counterparts, successfully attracted investors. However, female-led campaigns raised less funding than male-led campaigns, highlighting the disparity in funding between male and female founders (Vismara, 2016).

On the other hand, Malaga *et al.* (2018) conducted an exploratory analysis using a dataset comprising 6,234 equity crowdfunded offerings – legalised under Title II of the 2012 JOBS Act in the US – aggregated from 17 platforms. They found that the entrepreneurs' gender did not significantly impact the likelihood of women-owned companies successfully raising funds, suggesting a more equitable fundraising landscape across various platforms. The study nevertheless revealed that women-owned companies accounted for only 15.2% of the ventures seeking funding within this dataset (Malaga *et al.*, 2018). These findings provide empirical evidence that crowdfunding has had a limited effect in democratising access to capital for women-owned start-ups and small businesses. The data indicate that women-owned companies are even more underrepresented in Title II equity crowdfunding than angel and venture capital investments (Malaga *et al.*, 2018). This study underscores the importance of exploring the role of gender in equity crowdfunding in different countries to gain a comprehensive understanding of the dynamics at play. However, McGuire (2020) later examined the impact of Title II and observed a three-percentage-point reduction in the gender gap regarding external financing. This decrease in the funding gap between male- and female-founded firms reflects the effects of Title II legislation, which contributed to a relative increase in funding for female entrepreneurs compared to male entrepreneurs (McGuire, 2020). However, both these studies are based on Regulation D projects; in this chapter, we examine campaigns under Regulation C.

A recent study suggests that women have a positive influence on equity crowdfunding. Cicchiello *et al.* (2022) examined whether gender disparity impacts the likelihood of obtaining equity crowdfunding financing in Latin America. By analysing 492 projects from different equity crowdfunding platforms in Brazil, Chile, and Mexico from 2013 to 2017, the authors found that the involvement of at least one woman on the board of firms seeking equity financing significantly increased campaigns' success. The gender of team members did not impact projects' likelihood of experiencing overfunding, the other tested dependent variable (Cicchiello *et al.*, 2022). Similarly, by employing stereotype content theory and warm-glow theory, Zhao *et al.* (2021) discovered that female entrepreneurs are more likely to secure funding through equity crowdfunding than their male counterparts. Their results, based on a dataset of 259 projects from three equity crowdfunding platforms in China, demonstrated that lead investors and venture stage moderate the impact of gender (Zhao *et al.*, 2021).

Additionally, some empirical observations in the UK have revealed a funding advantage for women in equity crowdfunding. First, Vismara *et al.* (2017) examined a sample of 58 equity offerings on the UK crowdfunding platform Seedrs and found higher success rates for firms led by a female CEO. The authors confirmed a higher gender diversity in equity crowdfunding and showed that crowdfunding provides greater access to equity capital than traditional methods of entrepreneurial finance (Vismara *et al.*, 2017). Second, Barbi and Mattioli (2019) discovered that an entrepreneurial team's gender composition affects the success of campaigns on the UK equity crowdfunding platform Crowdcube. Using a sample of 521 funded companies between 2011 and 2017, their analysis demonstrated that having an additional woman on the team increased the total funding by approximately 6%. However, when analysing equity offerings on both Crowdcube and London's Alternative Investment Market, Cumming *et al.* (2021) recently found that female entrepreneurs did not have a higher chance of raising funds through equity crowdfunding.

Overall, these studies highlight the complex dynamics of gender and funding in equity crowdfunding, with some indicating a funding advantage for women-led ventures and others emphasising the influence of team composition and investor attraction. However, the existing research does not include empirical observations about female entrepreneurs leading Regulation C projects in the US-based equity market. With our study, we intend to contribute new insight to close this gap. Equity crowdfunding stands apart from other forms of online fundraising, making it crucial to investigate the influence of gender in this particular context.

10.2.4. *Gender-related differences in entrepreneurial teams*

The discourse surrounding the involvement of women in entrepreneurial endeavours has made notable progress within entrepreneurship research (Brush *et al.*, 2009). The impact of gender representation on entrepreneurial teams has garnered increasing interest in the scholarly literature, indicating that having a diverse gender composition might affect team performance (Zhou and Rosini, 2015). According to Harper (2008), an entrepreneurial team is a collective of entrepreneurs working towards a shared objective that necessitates the effective combination of individual entrepreneurial actions.

Entrepreneurial teams are essential in driving new business growth, as they can shape a business's trajectory (Kamm *et al.*, 1990). While gender diversity within groups can lead to increased relational conflicts (Chowdhury, 2005), the prevailing literature widely concurs that gender diversity (i.e. the increased presence of women) within entrepreneurial teams has a positive impact on both team and firm performance (Dai *et al.*, 2019).

Litz and Folker (2002) determined that a gender balance within management teams improves firm performance. Companies characterised by a higher gender balance in their management teams demonstrate superior profitability compared to those managed exclusively or disproportionately by a single gender. Similarly, Hellerstedt *et al.* (2007) found that entrepreneurial teams with elevated gender diversity experience better stability. Drawing on data from 534 IPO firms, Welbourne *et al.* (2007) observed that the presence of women on top management teams positively affects firms' short-term performance, stock price growth, and earnings per share. According to the authors, women, on average, exhibit higher performance than men, and diverse top management teams are characterised by enhanced innovation and problem-solving capabilities (Welbourne *et al.*, 2007).

Dautzenberg (2012) discovered that mixed entrepreneurial teams in very high-tech and high-tech manufacturing firms, where women are significantly underrepresented, exhibit a higher return on equity. These findings align with those of Godwin *et al.* (2006), who suggest that women in male-dominated industries may strategically choose male partners to enhance their chances of accessing resources for their ventures, thereby overcoming financing obstacles. Additionally, Vogel *et al.* (2014) demonstrated a positive correlation between mixed teams and investment decisions, with venture capitalists perceiving gender diversity within entrepreneurial teams as advantageous. According to the authors, mixed teams are more adept at understanding the diverse needs of potential customers across different gender-related social categories, and they benefit from a broader network of social connections.

Their findings revealed a significant positive association between task-oriented diversity, such as educational background and experience, and respondents' inclination to provide capital. Interestingly, the authors observed the same trend for relations-oriented diversity, which includes age and nationality. This implies that an entrepreneurial team's social capital holds greater importance in shaping funding decisions by external investors than the behavioural integration of the team's human capital. Consequently, entrepreneurial teams must balance the social costs associated with non-task-related diversity and the ability to access financial resources (Vogel *et al.*, 2014).

Dai *et al.* (2019) identified a positive correlation between gender diversity within new venture teams and the innovation performance of these ventures. The authors suggest that the presence of diverse genders enhances innovation performance by promoting the differentiation and integration of knowledge (Dai *et al.*, 2019). Although each study has limitations, these findings collectively highlight women's crucial role in entrepreneurial teams. However, studies examining gender composition in equity crowdfunding remain relatively limited, with only a few, such as Barbi and Mattioli (2019), addressing this aspect.

Cicchiello *et al.*'s (2020) research reaffirmed previous studies highlighting the advantages of gender diversity on entrepreneurial teams, particularly in securing financial resources, especially within male-dominated industries (Vogel *et al.*, 2014). Examining the role of gender in the equity crowdfunding market in Latin America, Cicchiello *et al.* (2020) predicted that the presence of women on entrepreneurial teams would increase the likelihood of obtaining equity crowdfunding financing and achieving fundraising goals. They identified a significant correlation between the founders' gender and the success of their crowdfunding campaigns. Specifically, they found that mixed-gender teams (including at least one woman) were more likely to be funded than all-male or all-female teams. However, contrary to their expectations, their overall results did not support the notion that the presence of women on the team increases the likelihood of overfunding (Cicchiello *et al.*, 2022).

10.3. Theoretical Foundations

Crowdfunding's unique approach to equity financing is seen as a way to democratise entrepreneurial finance, offering greater opportunities to underrepresented groups (Cumming *et al.*, 2021; Gorbatai and Nelson, 2015; Serwaah, 2022). Because platform-mediated interactions occur online, crowdfunding investors rarely personally meet the issuers from whom they purchase securities, in stark contrast to the hands-on approach that venture capitalists and angel investors typically take. The online dimension of equity crowdfunding differentiates it from other early-stage funding sources in different ways as well. Equity crowdfunding markets are arguably less equipped to overcome information asymmetry problems than other entrepreneurial finance settings (Butticé and Vismara, 2022). Equity crowdfunding investors have limited opportunities to perform due diligence and ongoing monitoring like professional investors and investment bankers do. Firms seeking equity funds through crowdfunding often lack a track record and may be launched by first-time entrepreneurs. Therefore, information about these companies from crowdfunding platforms is scarce. Yet, despite its scarcity, the information provided by online crowdfunding platforms likely plays a significant role for small investors (Butticé and Vismara, 2022). Therefore, information asymmetry remains a fundamental problem on crowdfunding platforms (Leboeuf and Schwienbacher, 2018), and equity crowdfunding, in particular, is characterised by high information asymmetry (Ahlers *et al.*, 2015).

Hence, the entrepreneur or entrepreneurial team plays a significant role in crowdfunding campaigns to raise funds. Additionally, various studies indicate that investors consider human and social capital factors when making investment decisions for a company (Ahlers *et al.*, 2015; Carter *et al.*, 2003). Human capital encompasses aspects such as educational attainment, professional experience, and management background, while social capital pertains to an entrepreneur's network of friends, family members, and professional acquaintances (Malaga *et al.*, 2018). Therefore, as our theoretical foundation, we chose a sociological and psychological framework positing that societal expectations, beliefs, and stereotypes about gender roles influence individuals' behaviour and ultimately guide their actions (Eagly, 1987; Eagly and Wood, 2012).

10.3.1. *Perception of social stereotypes*

People unconsciously rate others' implicit characteristics and behaviours (Borkenau, 1992), employing specific patterns and biases when forming impressions based on limited initial information about unfamiliar individuals (Pedersen, 1965). This results in the expectation of the co-occurrence of traits and behaviours. For example, people expect talkative people to be sociable (Borkenau, 1992).

Much of social perception is automated, occurring without conscious awareness (Bargh and Chartrand, 1999). Deliberately regulating one's behaviour, evaluations, decisions, and emotional states requires considerable effort and is relatively slow; therefore, conscious self-regulatory acts only occur briefly. On the other hand, unconscious or automatic processes occur unintentionally, effortlessly, and quickly and guide people safely through the day (Bargh and Chartrand, 1999).

Individuals hold varying implicit expectations when encountering strangers, leading them to unconsciously assess others' implicit traits and behaviours differently (Borkenau, 1992). However, despite these differences, individuals often perceive themselves and others in similar ways, and these perceptions tend to remain stable over time, contributing to the formation of group-specific stereotypes (Srivastava *et al.*, 2010).

Attribution plays an essential part in this formation process. Attribution theory is a social psychological framework that explores how individuals explain behaviour by attributing it to internal or external factors. Consequences, social desirability, and personal motivation can influence attribution. Psychologists have recognised biases, such as the fundamental attribution error, where people tend to attribute behaviour to dispositional factors rather than external ones. These interpretations shape people's reactions to behaviour and interactions with others, such as attributing strong and persuasive traits to a male entrepreneur based on gender stereotypes (Kelley and Michela, 1980). For instance, research has shown that project creators who communicate specific personality traits through their equity crowdfunding campaigns are more likely to attract funding (Neuhaus *et al.*, 2022). Therefore, potential investors' first impressions and perceptions of an entrepreneur, considering factors such as their gender and the sustainability orientation of their project, become relevant in an uncertain online funding environment, especially considering the influence of loss aversion.

This could be especially true for female entrepreneurs, who are linked to stereotypical behaviours (Bloodhart and Swim, 2020) and are generally assigned specific characteristics and personality traits that differentiate them from male entrepreneurs. For example, research has found that people expect women to be more concerned about environmental issues, such as climate change, while they expect men to be dismissive (Swim and Geiger, 2018). They also see women as more ethical and risk-averse than men, on average (Cumming *et al.*, 2015). Other studies have argued that to attract funding, women should focus on their physical attractiveness, friendliness, and warmth rather than their credibility and experience as men do (Duan *et al.*, 2020; Li *et al.*, 2022). However, some scholars contend that female entrepreneurs sending signs congruent with their stereotypical gender roles are more likely to succeed in equity crowdfunding (Kleinert and Mochkabadi, 2022), while others suggest that women are more successful in reward-based crowdfunding when they contradict stereotypes and launch campaigns in male-dominant categories (e.g. technology as a male-typed category vs. fashion as a female-typed category; Greenberg and Mollick, 2017; Seigner *et al.*, 2022). Overall, implicit personality associations can turn into stereotypical beliefs.

10.3.2. *Social role theory*

As mentioned earlier, identifiable differences exist between female and male entrepreneurs. Various research studies indicate advantages for women in some cases, while others show benefits for men. In all cases, however, the empirical findings demonstrate that the outcomes of crowdfunding campaigns can vary depending on the gender of the entrepreneur or entrepreneurial team. This raises an important question about the factors contributing to gender differences and similarities in behaviour. Therefore, it is crucial to examine social stereotypes related to gender. These stereotypes represent beliefs about the roles associated with each gender, formed when individuals observe the behaviours of men and women and draw conclusions about their inherent characteristics (Eagly and Wood, 2012). An often-used example that remains prevalent today is the notion that in industrial societies, women are more likely to assume caregiving responsibilities both at work and at home, leading to the perception that women possess communal and nurturing qualities (Eagly and Wood, 2012). While the origins of these gender roles are primarily rooted in physical sex differences that have evolved in humans, socialisation further reinforces these gender-typical role perceptions by shaping the development of appropriate personality traits and skills for men and women (Eagly and Wood, 2012).

One of the foundational ideas in the theory developed by Eagly (1987) is the role concept, which is described as a crucial integrative concept in the social sciences. Its significance lies in its ability to serve as an analytical bridge between individuals and their social environment. Hence, differences and similarities in behaviour between sexes are influenced by gender role beliefs, which represent society's perceptions of the social roles assigned to men and women. These beliefs emerge as people observe the behaviours of females and males and make inferences about their inherent dispositions (Eagly and Wood, 2012). Consequently, men and women are presumed to possess certain traits that make them suitable for the gender-typical roles commonly acknowledged and reflected in shared beliefs or gender stereotypes. Individuals then enact these traits within specific social roles, such as being a parent or an employee (Eagly and Wood, 2012).

As a result, role expectations exist in the minds of individuals and are shared with others, contributing to the formation of social consensus from which social structure and culture emerge (Eagly, 1987). However, gender roles, defined as expectations for male and female behaviour, are not as fixed or immutable as they were once thought to be. Instead, these expectations can evolve and change over time, influenced by factors such as the typical work and family roles of each gender and economic and technological developments (Eagly and Wood, 2012).

Social role theory can be used to understand behaviour in an organisational setting. In analysing organisational behaviour, research has found that for men, the managerial (or leadership) role and their gender role are similar in content. By contrast, these roles are incongruent for women. The incongruence of female managers' roles has several consequences, including prejudice against them as potential and actual managers (Eagly and Karau, 2002).

Gender roles have developed due to the division of labour and the distinct societal roles undertaken by men and women. These gender roles influence society's expectations regarding women's and men's characteristics and behaviours. Consequently, men are expected to embody traits associated with the male gender role, characterised by assertiveness. In contrast, women are expected to fulfil the female gender role, characterised by nurturing and communal attributes (Wood and Eagly, 2002).

In contemporary society, an increasing number of individuals are challenging traditional gender role expectations by assuming social roles traditionally associated with the opposite sex (e.g. male homemakers and female leaders). This includes men taking on domestic responsibilities and women occupying leadership positions. Consistent with social role theory, the perception of gender role orientation (masculine or feminine) is more closely linked to the specific social roles individuals adopt rather than their biological sex (Eagly *et al.*, 2000). For instance, individuals in leadership positions, regardless of their gender, are more likely to be seen as displaying action-oriented traits associated with the masculine gender role orientation. Conversely, individuals in caregiving roles, such as stay-at-home parents, are more likely to be perceived as exhibiting communal traits aligned with the feminine gender role orientation (Eagly *et al.*, 2000). However, deviations from traditional gender role norms can lead to negative attitudes due to societal norms that prescribe how men and women should behave and conform to gender expectations (Harrison and Lynch, 2005).

Gender roles, which are collective beliefs about the attributes associated with men and women, exist alongside specific roles shaped by factors such as familial connections (e.g. daughter, father) and occupational positions (e.g. nurse, engineer). In various real-life contexts, specific roles directly affect task execution, making them potentially more influential than gender roles (Eagly and Wood, 2012).

Harrison and Lynch (2005) also applied social role theory to investigate how people perceive athletes in terms of their gender role orientation across different sports. They hypothesised that the specific roles associated with the sport would have a more significant influence on perceptions than the athlete's gender. Consistent with their hypothesis, the study demonstrated that an athlete's gender has little impact on the overall perception of their gender role orientation. However, the athletic roles themselves play a significant role, as athletes in sports traditionally associated with masculine roles, such as football and basketball, are more likely to be perceived as having a masculine gender role orientation. Similarly, athletes in sports associated with feminine roles, such as cheerleading, are more likely to be perceived as having a feminine gender role orientation. Therefore, athletes' perceived gender role orientations are primarily shaped by the specific athletic roles they fulfil rather than their gender (Harrison and Lynch, 2005).

In summary, if individuals were to rely on stereotypes, they might seek assistance from a woman when facing challenges in their emotional relationships. In contrast, they would turn to a man for help confronting a demanding employer (Koenig and Eagly, 2014). These stereotypes manifest in descriptive, prescriptive, and proscriptive forms, describing how men and women are perceived to behave, how they are expected to behave, how they are allowed to act, and how they are discouraged from conducting themselves in ways that defy these norms (Eagly and Karau, 2002; Prentice and Carranza, 2002). Research indicates that gender stereotypes persist widely despite contradictory evidence (Eagly and Diekman, 2005). For instance, Madera *et al.* (2009) conducted two studies revealing biased letters of recommendation for men and women applying for academic positions. They found that women were depicted as more communal and less agentic than men, with communal characteristics negatively impacting hiring decisions in academia (Madera *et al.*, 2009). Despite their disadvantages in contemporary society and business, men and women often reinforce gender-stereotypical expectations through socialisation processes (Eagly *et al.*, 2000).

10.4. Hypotheses Development: The Influence of Female Team Members and 'All-Female' Campaigns on Equity Crowdfunding

In equity crowdfunding, the quality of a venture is often communicated through information cues about its human capital, particularly in the context of early-stage companies that are considered risky and lack transparency in the market. Given that the crowd of investors may have limited financial expertise, attributes such as education, professional experience, and the gender of team members significantly impact the amount of capital raised and the level of investor support received (Barbi and Mattioli, 2019). As crowd investors' behaviours may be based on implicit associations and stereotypical beliefs, first impressions and how potential investors perceive a crowdfunding project through the gender of the entrepreneurial individual or team member are likely to be highly relevant in an uncertain online funding situation characterised by loss aversion. This may particularly affect female entrepreneurs, who are linked to stereotypical behaviours (Bloodhart and Swim, 2020) and are generally perceived as having specific characteristics and personality traits that differentiate them from male entrepreneurs.

10.4.1. *Number of female team members*

Social role theory is a sociological and psychological framework positing that societal expectations, beliefs, and stereotypes about gender roles influence individuals' behaviour and shape their social interactions. According to this theory, society assigns specific roles, behaviours, and attributes to individuals based on their gender, and these roles become internalised and guide people's actions (Eagly, 1987; Eagly and Wood, 2012).

Social role theory differentiates between agentic (instrumental) and communal (expressive) roles and behaviours. Agentic characteristics are typically linked to leadership roles and encompass qualities such as assertiveness, dominance, independence, and task-oriented behaviours. In contrast, communal traits involve nurturance, agreeableness, cooperation, and relationship-oriented behaviours. While agentic roles are considered masculine, communal roles are typically associated with femininity (Eagly, 1987). Moreover, social role theory proposes that individuals conform to the expectations and norms of their assigned gender roles due to socialisation processes, which are influenced by factors such as family, education, and media (Eagly and Wood, 2012).

Thus, gender roles are shaped by abstract and widespread beliefs about the characteristics and behaviours associated with men and women, and these beliefs are often expressed through stereotypes. Social psychologists have commonly observed that people tend to make assumptions about individuals' inherent traits and qualities based on their behaviours (Eagly and Wood, 2012). Therefore, potential investors may assume that entrepreneurs or entrepreneurial team members are portraying their innate characteristics and attributes through their crowdfunding campaigns, which can reinforce stereotypical beliefs.

Founding a new venture or launching a crowdfunding campaign as a team rather than a solo entrepreneur can improve the venture's chances of succeeding. The entrepreneurial team's expertise, experience, and credibility are crucial to its crowdfunding success. Venture capitalists often evaluate a team's qualifications, track record, and ability to execute the proposed venture (Kamm *et al.*, 1990). A competent and experienced team enhances credibility and instils confidence in potential investors.

Entrepreneurial teams are more likely to succeed than individuals (Coakley *et al.*, 2022). A founder team sends a positive signal to potential investors, symbolising that their investment is backed by at least two individuals, increasing the chances of a financial return. It also indicates that the team's competencies are divided based on its members' strengths. Thus, each team member executes the tasks they are most capable of doing. Every venture, especially early-stage ones, will face difficulties and overcome challenges. Due to the quality of their human capital (Coakley *et al.*, 2022), an entrepreneurial team can display the confidence to succeed despite difficulties. The presence of both female and male members on an entrepreneurial team can be considered a sign of diversity and inclusiveness, as both genders work together to accomplish a common goal based on shared beliefs. Here, we are specifically interested in the effect of the number of female team members on the amount of funding received.

As noted above, social role theory has been used to show that women's expected gender role is incongruent with managerial role expectations, while men's gender expectations align more closely with a leadership role (Eagly and Karau, 2002). Furthermore, female leaders are more inclined to demonstrate care and concern for individuals, prioritising their well-being. By contrast, male leaders are often associated with traits that promote competition and emphasise a competitive approach (Eagly and Johnson, 1990; Eagly *et al.*, 1995). Based on social role theory, collaborative behaviours can be classified as communal since they involve more social interaction, nurturing, and agreeableness. Conversely, self-focused behaviours are more likely to be categorised as agentic (Eagly, 1987). Consequently, leadership behaviours are typically viewed as agentic, while collaborative behaviours are perceived as communal (Hmieleski and Sheppard, 2019). For instance, research applying social role theory has shown gender differences in ethical sensitivity and degree of risk aversion, with women being more ethical and risk-averse than men. Thus, Cumming *et al.* (2015) argue that women are more effective in male-dominated industries in reducing the frequency and severity of fraud. Women are also expected to be more concerned about environmental or social issues, such as climate change, while men are expected to be dismissive (Swim and Geiger, 2018).

Yet, according to social role theory, attributing these communal qualities to women perpetuates stereotypical beliefs about female characteristics, thus reinforcing the gender-typical belief that women are, above all, caring people (Eagly and Wood, 2012). As agentic and communal traits serve as indicators of behaviour, female team members, who traditionally display more prominent communal attributes, are expected to exhibit a greater inclination towards teamwork than their male counterparts, who tend to demonstrate more agentic traits (e.g. Madera *et al.*, 2009). Consequently, women are expected to do more of the caring and communicating work on the team (Koenig and Eagly, 2014). In caring about the well-being of their environment and the other team members, women tend to compromise more, which could lead them to be perceived as less influential, strong-willed, and competent. Therefore, female members are devalued compared to their male counterparts and are considered less likely to have played a leadership role in a given task (Heilman and Haynes, 2005).

According to social role theory, such communal characteristics and collaborative behaviours are typically associated with femininity and are expected from female team members. Thus, we posit that crowdfunding investors do not associate women with leadership behaviours because leadership behaviours are typically viewed as agentic and associated with masculinity (Eagly, 1987; Hmieleski and Sheppard, 2019). The stereotypical view of female team members as caring, agreeable, and less competitive may create a funding disadvantage, leading their teams to receive less equity financing. From a social role theory perspective, we predicted that investors would implicitly judge feminine ventures as less worthy of additional funding. As a result, we posited that an increased number of female team members would affect the team's financial success, resulting in less funding than campaigns with no women in their units. Thus, our first hypothesis is as follows:

H1a: A higher number of female team members on an entrepreneurial team will lead to less equity crowdfunding.

10.4.2. *All-female campaigns*

To influence behaviour in role-appropriate directions, gender roles work through a trio of biosocial mechanisms: biological processes involving hormonal changes, sociocultural factors of gender identity, and the stereotypic expectations of others (Wood and Eagly, 2010).

The third biosocial mechanism is essential for this study because one critical assumption of social role theory is that other people typically reward women and men for conforming to gender roles and penalise them for deviating. People often sanction behaviour that does not conform to gender roles; thus, these roles have a conservative effect by imposing costs on men and women who deviate from the norm (Eagly and Wood, 2012).

Gender roles are essential to any society's culture and social structure. Their power to influence behaviour stems from their actual quality, which reflects the inherent characteristics of women and men, their associated tendency to be relatively consensual, and the fact that people are aware of this consensus (Wood and Eagly, 2010). Due to the shared nature of gender roles, individuals tend to presume that others are more likely to respond positively to behaviour that aligns with traditional gender expectations than to behaviour that deviates from them (Eagly and Wood, 2012).

A study by Balachandra *et al.* (2019, p. 118) demonstrates the complexity of this detrimental bias, as potential investors are generally biased against entrepreneurs who 'display feminine-stereotyped behaviours'. This aligns with the emerging importance of social roles: the perception of gender role orientation (masculine or feminine) is more closely linked to the specific social roles individuals adopt rather than their biological sex (Eagly *et al.*, 2000).

As mentioned above, crowdfunding campaigns run by entrepreneurial teams consisting exclusively of men receive more funding than those with female team members. Equity crowdfunding projects led by female entrepreneurs are generally found to generate less funding than those run by their male counterparts (Cumming *et al.*, 2021; Geiger and Oranburg, 2018). Even if they can attract more investors, when considering the pure funding amount, women are less successful than men (Vismara, 2016). While some scholars have found that female entrepreneurs benefit more from crowdfunding, this mainly applies to reward-based crowdfunding. Research on equity crowdfunding often indicates the opposite and rarely finds significant advantages for women. Thus, the promised democratising effect has yet to appear in equity crowdfunding (e.g. Cumming *et al.*, 2021; Malaga *et al.*, 2018; Singh *et al.*, 2022). One of the main reasons may be that, although equity crowdfunding is an alternative financing means, it is similar to classical venture finance in its focus on financial returns. In reward-based crowdfunding, backers are intrinsically motivated and value their position as co-creators of something innovative or doing something socially impactful. By contrast, equity crowdfunding backers are investors in the crowd driven by financial motives, much like classic investors in traditional venture financing (Butticé and Vismara, 2022; Cholakova and Clarlysse, 2015). As a result of this similarity, the typical beliefs about males' advantages as successful entrepreneurs are also present in the equity crowdfunding setting. Thus, based on social role theory, we predicted that because of gender-based stereotypes and social roles in profit-driven investment decisions, female entrepreneurs would enjoy no funding advantages. As all-female campaigns are characterised by an increased salience of femininity, we assumed they would receive significantly less equity, leading us to hypothesise the following:

H1b: Campaigns led by all-female teams will receive less equity crowdfunding.

10.4.3. *Moderating effect of the campaign's target offering*

Women are commonly observed to be better listeners; consequently, they tend to seek advisors who are also good listeners, especially in financial matters (Cohen, 2014). This ability might allow them to make more realistic financial decisions than men, as they exhibit greater understanding and responsiveness. From a social role theory perspective (Eagly, 1987; Eagly and Wood, 2012), this could result from women's caring and communicative roles. So, making realistic and reasonable financial decisions is a behaviour associated with women. Especially in difficult economic times, with prices increasing and everyday items getting more expensive, budgeting and spending money wisely are crucial. The person responsible for the caring work in the household often takes on the role of budgeting for a range of items, from groceries to insurance. Women usually hold this position, inherently making and adjusting decisions to the current circumstances. While this character trait is essential and beneficial in everyday life, it can represent a disadvantage in business situations.

When launching a campaign on an equity crowdfunding platform, the issuer must set a target offering amount and a maximum offering amount for the project. Both numbers are shown on the campaign's homepage, making them available and clearly visible to potential investors. A funding target is a relative object factor that can influence investment decisions and, consequently, the funding success of a project (Geiger and Oranburg, 2018). While it may be realistic to set a lower, more achievable target offering amount and thus assure some funding success, a higher target offering amount may be a positive sign to potential investors, who may see the issuer as an ambitious, passionate, and big-thinking entrepreneur. As research has found female entrepreneurs to be less aggressive and competition-oriented in an organisational environment than their male counterparts (Eagly and Karau, 2002), social role theory would predict women to set lower target offering amounts and ask for less funding for their crowdfunding projects. Therefore, we considered the target offering amount as a moderator in our study. Considering our two gender-based variables – the number of female team members and all-female campaigns – we predicted that projects with more female influence would have lower funding amounts than those with less female influence.

H2a: A low funding target positively moderates the relationship between the number of female team members and the amount of equity crowdfunding. This relationship is more strongly negative in the case of low funding targets.

H2b: A low funding target positively moderates the relationship between campaigns led by all-female teams and the amount of equity crowdfunding. This relationship is more strongly negative in the case of low funding targets.

10.4.4. *Moderating effect of the issuer's work experience*

Recent research on crowdfunding and the influence of the entrepreneur's gender suggests that to attract more funding, women should focus on their friendliness and warmth rather than their credibility and experience as men do (Duan *et al.*, 2020; Li *et al.*, 2022). Accordingly, employers usually use factors such as education and experience to validate the profiles of job applicants to determine whether they fit the position and can execute the required task and fulfil expectations. However, these characteristics do not benefit women in investment situations. Instead, female entrepreneurs should focus on their soft skills to convince potential investors of their venture and entrepreneurial capabilities. Through the lens of social role theory, women presenting themselves as congruent with social stereotypes and emphasising their caring and agreeable characteristics are rewarded, while female entrepreneurs showing behaviour incongruent with stereotypes are penalised (Eagly and Wood, 2012; Eagly *et al.*, 2000; Harrison and Lynch, 2005).

This may be especially true in the case of equity crowdfunding, which more closely resembles traditional venture finance than other forms of crowdfunding, such as donation-based or reward-based crowdfunding. The challenges and disadvantages women in venture finance face are well documented in the literature and have significant consequences. The lack of resources and support for female entrepreneurs and their ventures not only lowers their chances of success but ultimately leads to the underrepresentation of female-led ventures in the economy (Elitzur and Solodoha, 2021). Due to this underrepresentation, society's image of a successful entrepreneur is still associated predominantly with males. Though women open and own more businesses than previously, women-owned companies tend to occupy lower-profitability sectors (Carter *et al.*, 2007; Eddleston *et al.*, 2016). This aligns with social role theory, which associates leadership and managerial attributes with masculinity. Thus, a woman as an entrepreneur plays a role that is incongruent with her gender role. The incongruence of female managers' roles has several consequences, including prejudice against women as potential and actual managers (Eagly and Karau, 2002), especially since female entrepreneurs sending information cues congruent with their stereotypical gender roles are more likely to succeed in equity crowdfunding (Kleinert and Mochkabadi, 2022). This is due to the similarities between equity crowdfunding and traditional venture finance, where social behaviour congruent with stereotypical views also leads to more funding. Thus, according to social role theory, women with work experience in their field violate society's belief about the social role of a successful entrepreneur, and incongruent behaviour leads to less funding. Here, we hypothesised that female team members' work experience in mixed-gender and all-female teams would reinforce investors' implicit assumptions that female companies are not a good investment.

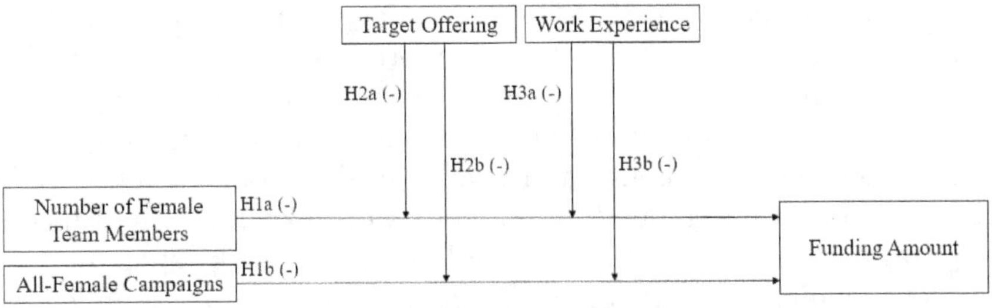

Figure 10.1 Research model.

H3a: Work experience positively moderates the relationship between the number of female team members and the amount of equity crowdfunding. This relationship is more strongly negative in the case of extensive work experience.

H3b: Work experience positively moderates the relationship between campaigns led by all-female teams and the amount of equity crowdfunding. This relationship is more strongly negative in the case of extensive work experience.

Our research model, including our six hypotheses, is presented in Figure 10.1.

10.5. Data and Methodology

We empirically tested our assertions using a dataset of 366 campaigns from two leading US-based equity crowdfunding platforms, Wefunder and Republic, from 2016 to 2020. First, we extracted the campaign descriptions, including comments, updates, and corresponding video pitch subtitles, from the platforms' homepages. Then, we added information from each project's SEC filing. These documents are freely available through the Electronic Data Gathering, Analysis, and Retrieval (EDGAR) system, the primary system for companies and others submitting documents under the Securities Act of 1933, the Securities Exchange Act of 1934, the Trust Indenture Act of 1939, and the Investment Company Act of 1940 (SEC, 2023b). As we were examining crowdfunding projects under Regulation C, we found the corresponding documents for all ventures on EDGAR's public database based on the company's name. Additionally, on the Republic platform, the 'Form C' filing is directly accessible on each campaign's site. The gathered information of interest included venture-related characteristics, such as the number of employees, company age, and location, and campaign-related factors, such as the target offering amount and campaign duration. Lastly, we collected information about the founder's work experience and media coverage, mainly through the social business network LinkedIn.

The equity crowdfunding platform Republic was founded in 2016 in the US by alums of AngelList, the largest online platform for private investing. Accredited and non-accredited investors meet entrepreneurs on the platform and can access high-growth potential deals across various private markets (Republic, 2023). The equity crowdfunding platform Wefunder claims that users can 'invest in founders you believe in'. Founded in 2012 by Y Combinator and Techstars alums, the platform has become the market leader with a 40% market share in Regulation C in 2022 (Wefunder, 2023). On both platforms, investments start at $100 and follow an 'all or nothing' approach. The two platforms are suitable sources for our sample, as they are among the leading emerging crowdfunding platforms in the US, and their campaign homepages have a similar structure. Thus, entrepreneurs and entrepreneurial teams present themselves and their ventures similarly on both platforms, making a comparative analysis of communication cues possible.

10.5.1. *Description of variables*

In our study of equity crowdfunding promotions, we identified five distinct categories of characteristics that potentially contribute to the appeal of fundraising ventures and thus affect their funding outcomes. To establish these categories, we drew inspiration from prior research (e.g. Cicchiello *et al.*, 2022; Prokop and Wang, 2022). To explore gender-based funding disparities in equity crowdfunding, we relied on publicly accessible campaign data from crowdfunding platforms. Our analysis involved determining the entrepreneurs' gender based on their first names and the images displayed on their campaign's homepage. Our study's two primary variables of interest were the presence of female team members and whether women exclusively led the campaign. Furthermore, as outlined in the following, we gathered various details related to the campaign, entrepreneur, promotion, venture, and industry from the platforms' websites and the venture's SEC filing.

The funding outcome is our dependent variable, measured as *funding amount.* We defined this campaign-related variable as the total funding a venture receives at the end of the crowdfunding campaign. As such, we retrieved the funding amount directly from the crowdfunding platform. We used the natural logarithm of the actual funding amount the venture raised for the analyses. Previous research in crowdfunding (e.g. Duan *et al.*, 2020; Johnson *et al.*, 2018; Singh *et al.*, 2022) often examined funding success based on a campaign's outcome – that is, being successfully funded or not. In contrast, like other studies on equity crowdfunding (e.g. Geiger and Oranburg, 2018; Kleinert and Mochkabadi, 2022), we decided to use the actual funding amount a project raised at the end of the campaign as our dependent variable. As mentioned above, equity crowdfunding is profoundly different from other types of crowdfunding, such as reward-based crowdfunding, and is more similar to classical venture financing (e.g. Butticé and Vismara, 2022; Geiger and Oranburg, 2018). Moreover, research in this field has shown that female entrepreneurs are disadvantaged in terms of several key financial figures. For example, women receive a significantly lower share of venture capital financing than men (Lins and Lutz, 2016; Malmström *et al.*, 2018), and the financial terms for the capital raised by female entrepreneurs are less favourable than those raised by male entrepreneurs (Jennings and Brush, 2013; Madill *et al.*, 2006). Thus, the actual funding amount raised is an essential factor.

When empirically examining the role of gender in crowdfunding, the variable reflecting the gender of the entrepreneur or entrepreneurial team is often defined based on the primary signatory of the crowdfunding campaign. In general, this is the founder or CEO of the venture launching the campaign, who is responsible for the legal and financial affairs related to the crowdfunding platform. The gender of the primary signatory is often based on their first name (e.g. using the tool genderize.io) and, in some unclear cases, the photo shown on the campaign site. Multiple studies have applied this approach to identifying female-led projects, such as in reward- or equity-based crowdfunding research. However, considering the structure of the campaigns' websites on the platforms and that the primary signatory is, in most cases, identified by the SEC filing, which needs to be explicitly accessed, we decided to use a different approach based on more visible, accessible information. As our study examines female entrepreneurship in crowdfunding through the lens of social role theory and, thus, social beliefs about gender stereotypes, we wanted to create more obvious gender-based variables in our study. Therefore, we focused on the number of female team members and whether a campaign is entirely female-led.

Our two main variables of interest are the number of female team members and whether a project is entirely female-led. As the independent variables in our models, *number of female team members* and *all-female campaign* were hand-coded based on the information given on the crowdfunding platform. Thus, *number of female team members* is the actual number of female team members, and *all-female campaign* is a dummy variable that equals 1 if the crowdfunding campaign is exclusively female-led and 0 otherwise.

Much is unknown about gender-related disparities and how they impact funding decisions; thus, the funding outcome can be a complex topic involving various factors. Therefore, we follow previous research (e.g. Geiger and Oranburg, 2018) and include several explanatory variables that may moderate the funding outcome of female entrepreneurs or female-led entrepreneurial teams.

The first moderator variable is the target amount of financing (in USD); *target offering* is displayed on the campaign's platform homepage, but this critical figure can also be found in the SEC filing (Pope and Sydnor, 2011). Conversely, a campaign with a comparatively low funding target is more likely to succeed, assuming all other factors remain constant. This success sends a positive signal to current and potential investors, encouraging additional investments (Block *et al.*, 2018). On the other hand, crowd investors may perceive a relatively low funding target as a lack of confidence among the entrepreneurs, potentially diminishing the venture's appeal as an investment opportunity (Prokop and Wang, 2022). With *work experience*, we include an entrepreneur characteristic as another moderator variable. To generate this variable, we hand-collected the founder's years of working experience before the venture incorporation based on information on their LinkedIn profile. In cases where the founder had no profile on LinkedIn, we used their description on the platform or the venture's homepage to gain information about their previous work experience. As previous studies have suggested that this is a potential factor leading to gender-related disparities (Li *et al.*, 2022; Duan *et al.*, 2020), we wanted to assess this characteristic as accurately as possible.

We also included a vector of control variables suggested in the literature to limit the degree of omitted variable bias. Perceived project quality shapes investors' overall impression of a crowdfunding campaign (Bi *et al.*, 2017), influencing the effect of communication cues or other campaign characteristics on crowdfunding success (Mollick, 2014).

Based on previous research (Barbi and Mattioli, 2019; Mollick, 2014; Vismara *et al.*, 2017), we controlled for the number of employees in the form of *employee count*, company age (*established company*), *year* of the crowdfunding campaign, location of the venture (*jurisdiction*), and *campaign duration.* Research on this topic also denotes other characteristics of the venture promotion, such as the *word count* of the campaign description and video text, media use (e.g. pictures, measured as *gallery*), and the number of *updates* as quality indicators (Bi *et al.*, 2017; Courtney *et al.*, 2017; Mollick, 2014). We used the natural logarithm of *word count.* As the industry is essential for venture funding, we also controlled *campaign category* (e.g. Elitzur and Solodoha, 2021; Geiger and Oranburg, 2018; Johnson *et al.*, 2018). Finally, we controlled for another entrepreneur-related factor regarding social media coverage (e.g. Cicchiello *et al.*, 2022). We hand-coded *connections* as a dummy variable, which equals 1 if the founder has more than 500 connections on LinkedIn and 0 otherwise. An overview of all variables and their descriptions is presented in Table 10.1.

After a careful review and verification of the completeness of the available information, we removed one campaign from the dataset. This specific campaign had no funding amount (0 USD), leading us to believe that the venture had withdrawn the project and the campaign had been aborted. Finally, we compiled a final dataset comprising 365 campaigns, forming the basis for our empirical investigation.

10.5.2. *Regulation C*

All crowdfunding campaigns in our dataset are under 'Regulation C', also known as Regulation Crowdfunding. The SEC enacted Regulation C in 2016 as part of the JOBS Act (Title III), allowing

Table 10.1 Description of variables.

Variable	Description	Data source
Dependent Variable		
Funding amount	Total amount of funding received at the end of the crowdfunding campaign.	Platform
Independent Variables		
Number of female team members	Number of female team members.	Platform
All-female campaign	Dummy variable, equals 1 if the crowdfunding campaign is exclusively female-led and 0 otherwise.	Platform
Moderator Variables		
Target offering	Target amount of financing (in USD).	Platform, SEC filing
Work experience	Founder's years of work experience before the venture incorporation.	LinkedIn
Control Variables		
Connections	Dummy variable, equals 1 if the founder has more than 500 connections on LinkedIn and 0 otherwise.	LinkedIn
Gallery	Number of pictures on the campaign page (without header and footer).	Platform
Employee count	Dummy variable based on the number of employees, equals 1 if the company has a high employee count and 0 otherwise.	SEC filing
Campaign duration	Calculated campaign duration (days between filing and deadline).	SEC filing
Word count	Word count of the homepage and video text.	Platform
Updates	Number of updates posted on the campaign page (by the founder or entrepreneurial team).	Platform
Established company	Dummy variable based on the company age at the beginning of the campaign, equals 1 if the company is older than five years and 0 otherwise.	SEC filing
Jurisdiction (state)	Company location (state).	SEC filing
Campaign category	Selected category of the crowdfunding campaign.	Platform
Year	Year of the crowdfunding campaign.	SEC filing

small businesses and start-ups to raise capital through crowdfunding (SEC, 2023a). Title II of the JOBS Act, commonly referred to as 'Regulation D', on the other hand, allows companies to solicit investment from accredited investors, that is, individuals or entities that meet certain wealth or income thresholds (SEC, 2022).

Ventures often launch campaigns under Regulation C due to the ease of compliance compared to other fundraising options. While Regulation C has specific disclosure requirements and limitations (SEC, 2023a), they are generally less burdensome than those associated with traditional fundraising methods, such as IPOs or private placements. This makes it relatively easy for ventures, in particular small businesses and start-ups, to comply with the regulations and engage in fundraising activities without being overwhelmed by complex legal and financial procedures.

Moreover, one of the critical goals of Regulation C is to democratise access to investment opportunities. By allowing accredited and non-accredited investors to participate, Regulation C opens up investment possibilities to a broader range of individuals who may not meet the standard accreditation requirements. This creates a more inclusive investment ecosystem, giving individuals from diverse backgrounds and financial situations a chance to invest in promising ventures and benefit from their success. Simultaneously, Regulation C aims to democratise funding opportunities and increase access to capital for a broader range of entrepreneurial ventures. Additionally, it provides an increased fundraising limit of up to $5 million in a 12-month period (SEC, 2023b).

10.5.3. *Statistical methods*

Considering the inherent attributes of our variables in this study, we utilised generalised linear model (GLM) regression to optimise our findings. Previous crowdfunding researchers have also adopted GLM (e.g. Cicchiello *et al.*, 2022; Seigner *et al.*, 2020), which allows for non-normally distributed dependent variables (McCullagh and Nelder, 2019). The histogram visually demonstrates that the dependent variable in our study is not normally distributed; moreover, the Shapiro–Wilk test resulted in $p < 0.01$ for *funding amount.* So, for this variable, we used the GLM from the Gaussian family with an identity link.

Next, we tested the assumption of homoscedasticity, which means that the residuals have equal variance (homoscedasticity) for every value of the fitted values and the predictors. Homoscedasticity is necessary to calculate accurate standard errors for parameter estimates. We used the Breusch–Pagan test (chi-square = 52.86). The chi-squared test's small p-value (<0.05) led us to reject the null hypothesis of homoscedasticity and infer that the error variance is non-constant. The correlation matrix for all variables in Table 10.2 shows that the highest correlation can be found between *updates* and *word count* (0.324) and *target offering* and *funding amount* (0.322). We found no signs of multicollinearity (mean VIF = 1.59).

10.6. Results

Starting with the descriptive statistics, we found that projects had a mean funding amount of just over $308,000 but with a considerable standard deviation, ranging from about $14,000 to over $2 million in funding achieved. Similarly, campaigns had an average of 590 investors but ranged from 20 to around 8,000 backers. Only seven out of 365 campaigns were not successfully funded, meaning they received less funding than targeted at the end of the campaign. Thus, we considered 358 crowdfunding projects in our dataset a funding success.

On average, the campaigns lasted around 90 days; one ran for about 14 months. Campaigns can be extended on both equity crowdfunding platforms, mainly if they are highly successful in the first round. Of the 28 campaign categories, software and services (84 campaigns), food and beverage (76), technology (27), health tech (21), financial services (20), and consumer products (13) were most frequently represented, followed by retail (12), media (11), consumer internet (11), and education (10); all other categories comprised fewer than 10 campaigns each. The distribution of projects is relatively representative in terms of industry composition. Including various campaign categories ensures that different industries are represented in the dataset and that a potential gender bias is minimised. Regarding the campaign communication data, we found that

Table 10.2 Correlation table.

Variables	(1)	(2)	(3)	(4)	(5)	(6)	(7)	(8)
(1) Funding amount (ln)	1.000							
(2) Number of female team members	−0.071	1.000						
(3) All female campaign	−0.120*	−0.001	1.000					
(4) Target offering	0.322*	−0.048	−0.081	1.000				
(5) Work experience	−0.031	0.034	−0.141*	0.104*	1.000			
(6) Connections	−0.007	0.142*	−0.020	−0.086	−0.017	1.000		
(7) Gallery	0.149*	0.058	−0.137*	0.230*	0.080	−0.082	1.000	
(8) Employee count	−0.241*	−0.160*	0.060	−0.153*	−0.034	0.041	−0.162*	1.000
(9) Campaign duration	0.007	0.000	0.080	−0.051	−0.027	0.109*	−0.112*	0.019
(10) Word count (ln)	0.246*	−0.114*	−0.065	0.197*	0.152*	−0.136*	0.277*	−0.085
(11) Updates	0.251*	−0.054	−0.017	0.103*	0.131*	0.006	−0.045	0.071
(12) Established company	0.092	−0.006	0.029	0.122*	0.088	−0.100	0.050	−0.261*
(13) Jurisdiction	−0.048	−0.087	−0.059	0.076	0.000	−0.210*	0.025	−0.029
(14) Campaign category	−0.009	0.089	−0.071	−0.081	−0.031	0.027	−0.088	−0.022
(15) Year	0.106*	−0.026	0.053	−0.001	0.054	−0.011	−0.219*	−0.066

(Continued)

Table 10.2 (*Continued*)

Variables	(9)	(10)	(11)	(12)	(13)	(14)	(15)
(1) Funding amount (ln)							
(2) Number of female team members							
(3) All female campaign							
(4) Target offering							
(5) Work experience							
(6) Connections							
(7) Gallery							
(8) Employee count							
(9) Campaign duration	1.000						
(10) Word count (ln)	−0.039	1.000					
(11) Updates	0.008	0.324*	1.000				
(12) Established company	−0.007	0.137*	0.096	1.000			
(13) Jurisdiction	0.007	0.038	−0.004	0.073	1.000		
(14) Campaign category	0.060	−0.087	−0.065	−0.072	−0.137*	1.000	
(15) Year	0.258*	0.013	0.212*	0.078	0.034	−0.019	1.000

Note: $^{***}p < 0.01$, $^{**}p < 0.05$, $^{*}p < 0.1$.

campaigns had an average of 38 images and 11 updates on the two platforms observed (WeFunder and Republic). The projects used over 6,000 words on average in their campaign descriptions and videos. Regarding venture-related results, about 20% were established companies (existing for over five years), and about 23% of the ventures had a high employee count (more than six employees).

Considering social media coverage, approximately two-thirds of founders had more than 500 connections on LinkedIn, indicating effective use of online social networking. Moreover, campaign founders had an average previous work experience of 12 years, while about 42% of founders had less than 10 years of work experience before launching the venture presented in the crowdfunding campaign. We found that projects had a mean target offering of just over $75,000 but with a considerable standard deviation, ranging to over $1 million as a funding goal. The summary statistics for our variables are presented in Table 10.3.

Regarding our two gender variables, we found that only 11 campaigns consisted of all-female teams, while over 70% had at least one female team member. Thus, 113 out of the 365 crowdfunding campaigns were run by entirely male groups. This reflects the general underrepresentation of female entrepreneurs in the economy. The results of our stepwise GLM regression models are presented in Tables 10.4 and 10.5.

10.6.1. *Number of female team members*

First, Model 1 regressed the control variables related to the hard facts of the campaign (e.g. *campaign category* and *duration*) and campaign communication (e.g. *word count* and the number of *updates* and *comments*) against our dependent variable, the final funding amount achieved by the campaign. Among the hard facts, having a high number of employees (*employee count*) was significant across all three models ($p < 0.01$), while the other campaign-related factors, such as *campaign duration* and campaign *year*, were not significant in the models. *Campaign category* was likely insignificant due to the high number of categories included. Regarding the campaign communication controls, we found that *word count* ($p < 0.05$) and the number of

Table 10.3 Summary statistics.

Variable	Obs.	Mean	Std. dev.	Min	Max
Funding amount (USD)	365	308,421.24	335,151.51	13,966	2,188,466
Investors (count)	365	592.5753	922.5982	20	8551
Number of female team members (count)	365	1.742	1.983	0	11
All-female campaign (categorical)	365	0.03	0.171	0	1
Target offering (USD)	365	75,166.498	85,274.164	0.01	1,070,000
Work experience (count)	365	12.405	8.589	0	42
Connections (categorical)	365	0.775	0.418	0	1
Gallery	365	38.414	21.01	1	159
Employee count (categorical)	365	0.764	0.425	0	1
Campaign duration	365	90.674	57.876	0	425
Word count (homepage & pitch)	365	6262.068	3166.691	736	30,830
Updates	365	11.488	11.744	0	96
Established company (>5 years)	365	0.2054795	0.4046062	0	1
Jurisdiction (state)	365	n/a	n/a	1	37
Campaign category	365	17.54	7.241	1	28
Year	365	n/a	n/a	2016	2020

Table 10.4 GLM regression models of number of female team members and funding level.

DV: Funding amount (ln)	Model 1 (H1a)	Model 2 (H2a)	Model 3 (H3a)
Independent Variable			
Number of female team members	-0.043^{*}	-0.050^{**}	-0.042^{*}
	(0.025)	(0.026)	(0.025)
Moderator Variables			
Target offering	0.000^{***}	0.000^{***}	0.000^{***}
	(0.000)	(0.000)	(0.000)
Work experience	-0.013^{***}	$-0.014{*}^{**}$	-0.010
	(0.005)	(0.005)	(0.006)
Moderator Terms			
Number of female team members # Target offering		-0.000^{***}	
		(0.000)	
Number of female team members # Work experience			-0.001
			(0.003)
Control Variables			
Connections	0.067	0.082	0.067
	(0.106)	(0.104)	(0.107)
Gallery	0.004	0.003	0.004
	(0.002)	(0.002)	(0.002)
Employee count	-0.506^{***}	-0.516^{***}	-0.502^{***}
	(0.112)	(0.112)	(0.112)
Campaign duration	0.000	0.000	0.000
	(0.001)	(0.001)	(0.001)
Word count (ln)	0.214^{**}	0.214^{**}	0.213^{**}
	(0.104)	(0.103)	(0.104)
Updates	0.017^{***}	0.016^{***}	0.017^{***}
	(0.004)	(0.004)	(0.004)
Established company	-0.047	-0.046	-0.047
	(0.110)	(0.110)	(0.110)
Jurisdiction	-0.008	-0.009^{*}	-0.007
	(0.005)	(0.005)	(0.005)
Campaign category	0.004	0.003	0.004
	(0.006)	(0.006)	(0.006)
Year dummies included	Yes	Yes	Yes
Observations	365	365	365

Note: Robust standard errors in parentheses, constant included but not shown, $^{***}p < 0.01$, $^{**}p < 0.05$, $^{*}p < 0.1$.

Table 10.5 GLM regression models of all-female campaign and funding level.

DV: Funding amount (ln)	Model 4 (H1b)	Model 5 (H2b)	Model 6 (H3b)
Independent Variable			
All-female campaign	−0.546**	−0.809	−0.940***
	(0.234)	(0.516)	(0.223)
Moderator Variables			
Target offering	0.000***	0.000***	0.000***
	(0.000)	(0.000)	(0.000)
Work experience	−0.014***	−0.014***	−0.014***
	(0.005)	(0.005)	(0.005)
Moderator Terms			
All-female campaign # Target offering		−0.000	
		(0.000)	
All-female campaign # Work experience			−0.058*
			(0.032)
Control Variables			
Connections	0.029	0.028	0.035
	(0.105)	(0.105)	(0.105)
Gallery	0.003	0.003	0.003
	(0.002)	(0.002)	(0.002)
Employee count	−0.461***	−0.462***	−0.465***
	(0.111)	(0.111)	(0.111)
Campaign duration	0.000	0.001	0.000
	(0.001)	(0.001)	(0.001)
Word count (ln)	0.229**	0.226**	0.220**
	(0.104)	(0.104)	(0.103)
Updates	0.016***	0.016***	0.016***
	(0.004)	(0.004)	(0.004)
Established company	−0.031	−0.026	−0.005
	(0.110)	(0.112)	(0.113)
Jurisdiction	−0.008	−0.008	−0.008
	(0.005)	(0.005)	(0.005)
Campaign category	0.002	0.002	0.003
	(0.006)	(0.007)	(0.007)
Year dummies included	Yes	Yes	Yes
Observations	365	365	365

Note: Robust standard errors in parentheses, constant included but not shown, $^{***}p < 0.01$, $^{**}p < 0.05$, $^{*}p < 0.1$.

campaign *updates* (reflecting entrepreneurs' effort to keep investors informed; $p < 0.01$) had significant effects. In contrast, the number of photos (*gallery*) did not reach significance. Similarly, venture-related factors, such as the company age (*established company*) and location (*jurisdiction*), as well as the founder's degree of social connections (mainly on LinkedIn), did not reach significance.

Next, Model 1 also regressed our three independent variables and supported our first hypothesis (H1a). Our first gender variable, *number of female team members*, had a significant negative effect on the amount funded ($ß = -0.043$, $p = 0.083$ in Model 1), as predicted in H1a. In addition, *target offering* and *work experience* also reached significance in Model 1 ($p < 0.01$).

Model 2 added the first moderator, *target offering*, to our gender variable. Here, *number of female team members* ($ß = -0.050$, $p = 0.049$ in Model 2), *target offering* ($ß = 0.000$, $p = 0.000$ in Model 2), and the interaction of both variables ($ß = -0.000$, $p = 0.008$, in Model 2) reached significance in terms of predicting the funding amount; therefore, we found support for H2a.

Finally, Model 3 presented the variable *work experience* as a potential moderator and showed that its interaction with *number of female team members* was negative but insignificant ($p > 0.1$); therefore, we had to reject H3a. In this model, its main effect was also negative but insignificant ($p > 0.1$). However, the main effect of *number of female team members* reached significance ($ß = -0.042$, $p = 0.094$ in Model 3).

10.6.2. *All-female campaigns*

Regarding the control variables in the GLM regressions with our second gender variable, *all-female campaign*, we found similar results as above. *Employee count* ($p < 0.01$), *word count* ($p < 0.05$), and the number of *updates* ($p < 0.01$) were significant in all three models. At the same time, the other campaign- and venture-related control variables did not reach significance in the models. In Model 1, the independent variables *target offering* ($ß = 0.000$, $p = 0.002$ in Model 4) and *work experience* ($ß = -0.014$, $p = 0.003$ in Model 4) were significant. The team characteristic *all-female campaign* significantly negatively affected the amount funded ($ß = -0.546$, $p = 0.019$ in

Model 4), as predicted in H1b. Thus, crowdfunding campaigns by all-female teams received significantly less equity funding than campaigns led by mixed-gender or all-male teams.

Model 5 presented the variable *target offering* as a potential moderation and showed that its interaction with *female team members* was negative but insignificant ($p > 0.1$); therefore, we had to reject H2b. The main effect of *target offering* was significant ($ß = 0.000$, $p = 0.002$ in Model 5). However, the main effect of *all-female campaign* did not reach significance ($p > 0.1$) but was negative. Model 6 analysed the moderation of *work experience* on the effect of our gender variable. Here, we found that *all-female campaign* ($ß = -0.940$, $p = 0.000$ in Model 6), *work experience* ($ß = -0.014$, $p = 0.005$ in Model 6), and the interaction of both variables ($ß = -0.058$, $p = 0.072$ in Model 6) reached significance in terms of predicting the funding amount, therefore supporting H3b.

Additional descriptive statistics for our variables are provided in Tables 10.6 and 10.7 for a more detailed look at the findings. These statistics are based on our two gender-related variables: *number of female team members* and *all-female campaign*. For example, the significant difference in Model 4 regarding the funding amount is visible in Table 10.6: all female campaigns received, on average, $150,000, which is only half of what the other campaigns (consisting of all-male teams or teams having at least one female team member) acquired.

Regarding the number of investors based on our gender-related variables, Table 10.7 shows that the average number of investors was similar between the different groups. Nonetheless, we found a difference when comparing the maximum numbers for all-female campaigns (2,553 investors) and all-male campaigns (4,411 investors), which underlines our statistical findings. The highest number of investors was found in mixed-gender campaigns (8,551 investors).

10.6.3. *Robustness checks*

To control for the robustness of our developed model, we performed a GLM regression with the number of investors as the dependent variable for both of our gender-based variables and a Poisson regression

Table 10.6 Funding amount based on gender-related variables.

	Funding amount				
Number of female team members	*N*	Mean	Std. dev.	Min	Max
0	113	307,828.6	309,330.5	13,966	1,579,625
1	96	309,189.8	362,285.9	22,250	2,188,466
2	64	337,821.8	372,675.9	27,602	1,699,901
3	37	348,227.6	355,224.5	26,110	1,270,983
4	30	273,107.9	312,680.8	46,798	1,070,000
5	3	169,436.3	133,632.5	70,954	321,554
6	8	170,811.8	134,383.6	39,408	429,119
7	2	232,803	123,609.3	145,398	320,208
8	8	307,929.5	345,911.3	31,695	1,070,000
9	1	114,858	—	114,858	114,858
10	2	44,272	20,183.66	30,000	58,544
11	1	401,401	—	401,401	401,401
Female Team Member (Categorical)					
0 (no)	113	307,828.6	309,330.5	13,966	1,579,625
1 (yes)	252	308,687	346,697.8	22,250	2,188,466
All-Female Campaign (Categorical)					
0 (no)	354	313,255.5	337,822.2	13,966	2,188,466
1 (yes)	11	152,844.6	180,729.5	25,467	516,200
Total	365	308,421.2	335,151.5	13,966	2,188,466

for *number of female team members* and *all-female campaign*. The Poisson regressions in Tables 10.8 and 10.9 confirm our previous results, showing that *number of female team members* ($\beta = -0.042$, $p = 0.091$ in Model 1) and *all-female campaign* ($\beta = -0.552$, $p = 0.017$ in Model 4) had a significant negative effect on a crowdfunding campaign's funding amount. Furthermore, as shown in Table 10.8, the significant interaction of *number of female team members* and *target offering* ($\beta = -0.000$, $p = 0.018$ in Model 2) predicting the funding amount was confirmed.

We also found support for the significant interaction of *all-female campaign* and *work experience* ($\beta = -0.055$, $p = 0.078$ in Model 6), as presented in the Poisson regression models in Table 10.9.

Table 10.7 Investors based on gender-related variables.

Number of female team members	Investors N	Mean	Std. dev.	Min	Max
0	113	560.858	747.2606	20	4411
1	96	634.583	1119.531	24	8551
2	64	528.609	799.876	22	4467
3	37	571.811	625.496	72	2553
4	30	737.067	1303.794	67	5492
5	3	457	539.756	130	1080
6	8	401.25	298.689	113	1062
7	2	430	141.421	330	530
8	8	1074.5	1656.730	121	4843
9	1	355	—	355	355
10	2	198.5	205.768	53	344
11	1	104	—	104	104
Female Team Member (Categorical)					
0 (no)	113	560.858	747.261	20	4411
1 (yes)	252	606.798	992.255	22	8551
All-Female Campaign (Categorical)					
0 (no)	354	592.828	922.360	20	8551
1 (yes)	11	584.455	975.580	40	2553
Total	365	592.5753	922.598	20	8551

10.7. Discussion

Crowdfunding is widely believed to have the potential to 'democratise' entrepreneurial finance, offering underrepresented groups a greater chance to secure funding since factors such as gender and age significantly influence one's ability to access external capital funding (Cumming *et al.*, 2021). Scholars have examined the impact of gender differences in organisational and entrepreneurship contexts and documented the challenges female business owners face when trying to access external capital (e.g. Balachandra *et al.*, 2019; Brush *et al.*, 2018; Eddleston *et al.*, 2016; Lins and Lutz, 2016). Due to this disparity, female entrepreneurs may encounter discrimination from external funding sources and often receive comparatively less financial support

Table 10.8 Poisson regression models of number of female team members and funding level.

DV: Funding amount (ln)	Model 1 (H1a)	Model 2 (H2a)	Model 3 (H3a)
Independent Variable			
Number of female team members	-0.042^{*}	-0.050^{*}	-0.041
	(0.025)	(0.026)	(0.025)
Moderator Variables			
Target offering	0.000^{***}	0.000^{***}	0.000^{***}
	(0.000)	(0.000)	(0.000)
Work experience	-0.013^{***}	-0.014^{***}	-0.010
	(0.005)	(0.005)	(0.006)
Moderator Terms			
Number of female team members # Target offering		-0.000^{**}	
		(0.000)	
Number of female team members # Work experience			-0.001
			(0.002)
Control Variables			
Connections	0.071	0.085	0.070
	(0.106)	(0.105)	(0.107)
Gallery	0.004	0.003	0.004
	(0.002)	(0.002)	(0.002)
Employee count	-0.507^{***}	-0.517^{***}	-0.503^{***}
	(0.112)	(0.113)	(0.111)
Campaign duration	0.000	0.000	0.000
	(0.001)	(0.001)	(0.001)
Word count (ln)	0.209^{**}	0.212^{**}	0.208^{**}
	(0.102)	(0.101)	(0.102)
Updates	0.017^{***}	0.016^{***}	0.017^{***}
	(0.004)	(0.004)	(0.004)
Established company	-0.057	-0.051	-0.056
	(0.110)	(0.110)	(0.111)
Jurisdiction	-0.008	-0.009^{*}	-0.008
	(0.005)	(0.005)	(0.005)
Campaign category	0.004	0.003	0.004
	(0.006)	(0.006)	(0.006)
Year dummies included	Yes	Yes	Yes
Observations	365	365	365

Note: Robust standard errors in parentheses, constant included but not shown, $^{***}p < 0.01$, $^{**}p < 0.05$, $^{*}p < 0.1$.

Table 10.9 Poisson regression models of all-female campaign and funding level.

DV: Funding amount (ln)	Model 4 (H1b)	Model 5 (H2b)	Model 6 (H3b)
Independent Variable			
All-female campaign	−0.552**	−0.781	−0.923***
	(0.232)	(0.522)	(0.216)
Moderator Variables			
Target offering	0.000***	0.000***	0.000***
	(0.000)	(0.000)	(0.000)
Work experience	−0.015***	−0.015***	−0.014***
	(0.005)	(0.005)	(0.005)
Moderator Terms			
All-female campaign # Target offering		−0.000	
		(0.000)	
All-female campaign # Work experience			−0.055*
			(0.031)
Control Variables			
Connections	0.034	0.033	0.040
	(0.105)	(0.105)	(0.105)
Gallery	0.003	0.003	0.003
	(0.002)	(0.002)	(0.002)
Employee count	−0.463***	−0.464***	−0.467***
	(0.110)	(0.110)	(0.110)
Campaign duration	0.001	0.001	0.000
	(0.001)	(0.001)	(0.001)
Word count (ln)	0.225**	0.222**	0.216**
	(0.102)	(0.102)	(0.102)
Updates	0.016***	0.016***	0.016***
	(0.004)	(0.004)	(0.004)
Established company	−0.040	−0.036	−0.014
	(0.111)	(0.112)	(0.114)
Jurisdiction	−0.008	−0.008	−0.008
	(0.005)	(0.005)	(0.005)
Campaign category	0.002	0.002	0.003
	(0.006)	(0.007)	(0.007)
Year dummies included	Yes	Yes	Yes
Obs	365	365	365

Note: Robust standard errors in parentheses, constant included but not shown, $^{***}p < 0.01$, $^{**}p < 0.05$, $^{*}p < 0.1$.

than their male counterparts (e.g. Bingelow *et al.*, 2014; Cumming *et al.*, 2021; Kanze *et al.*, 2018). However, our understanding of how gender affects the fundraising process in new forms of venture finance, such as equity crowdfunding, is incomplete as the extant results are somewhat mixed. Therefore, to shed further light on the interplay regarding the gender composition of teams in equity crowdfunding, we sought to understand how the female gender of one or all founding team members affects the amount raised in equity crowdfunding and how the degree of previous work experience as well as the chosen funding goal moderate this relationship.

First, we found that having female team members in an equity crowdfunding project led to a funding disadvantage. Compared to all-male teams, campaigns with female team members received less funding. Second, we found empirical evidence that all-female teams also have a significant financing disadvantage. Compared to all-male or mixed-gender teams, equity crowdfunding campaigns launched by entirely female funding teams generated comparatively less funding. The negative effect of all-female teams is stronger than the impact of female team members on a mixed-gender team. In all-female funding situations, stereotypes and social role incongruence (such as being an entrepreneur) appear to be more visible and robust, leading to a stronger reaction from the investors. Through the lens of social role theory, giving female entrepreneurs less capital acts as a punishment for incongruent behaviours. Additionally, experimental studies have found empirical evidence that, in contrast to their male counterparts, female team members experienced devaluation, with lower ratings regarding competence, influence, and likelihood of holding a leadership role in the task – even in cases when the work outcome is highly favourable (Heilman and Haynes, 2005). The findings above show that the women in our sample are in a similar situation – even successful campaigns faced a funding disadvantage, receiving significantly less capital from crowdfunding investors.

Third, we found different results for all-female and mixed-gender teams regarding the moderation of the chosen funding target and previous work experience. We saw a significant interaction between female team members and their campaigns' target offerings. The target offering negatively influenced the gender-related effect on funding success, leading to lower amounts raised by mixed-gender campaigns than by all-male projects. In contrast, the funding goal had surprisingly no significant effect on projects developed by entirely female teams.

Finally, our analysis showed a significant interaction (albeit a weak one) between all-female campaigns and previous work experience as an essential entrepreneurial characteristic. A founder's work experience influenced the impact of women-run crowdfunding projects. Thus, campaigns launched entirely by women received significantly less equity funding than all-male or mixed-gender teams. This result aligns with social role theory and confirms previous research on gender differences in equity crowdfunding.

We found that the informal funding situation on equity crowdfunding platforms did not increase the funding amount raised by female entrepreneurs. Even though campaigns with female team members or an all-female team were still successfully funded, the amount raised was significantly less when women were present. Therefore, we confirmed previous research on equity crowdfunding and gender-related financing differences that also found that women receive substantially less equity funding than men (Geiger and Oranburg, 2018; Vismara, 2016) and, thus, that female entrepreneurs do not have a higher chance of successfully raising external capital through equity crowdfunding (Cumming *et al.*, 2021).

Our results on Regulation C crowdfunding projects contrast with research on equity offerings under Regulation D of the JOBS Act. For example, Malaga *et al.* (2018) found that the gender of the entrepreneurs did not significantly impact the likelihood of women-owned companies successfully raising funds and thus suggested a more equitable fundraising landscape for women-owned companies across various platforms. Moreover, McGuire (2020) observed a three-percentage-point reduction in the gender gap regarding external financing.

In contrast to a recent study by Cicchiello *et al.* (2022), which found a positive influence of women in equity crowdfunding and revealed that the involvement of at least one woman on the board of firms seeking equity financing increases campaigns' success significantly, our results suggest the opposite. Similarly, Barbi and Mattioli (2019) discovered that the gender composition of an entrepreneurial team positively impacts the success of its campaigns. While their analysis demonstrated that having an additional woman on the team increased the total funding by approximately 6%, we could not confirm that the presence of female team members led to increased funding. However, our findings confirmed those of the study closest to ours (Geiger and Oranburg, 2018) regarding crowdfunding type and country context (US-based equity crowdfunding).

We conducted this study through the lens of social role theory. This sociological and psychological framework posits that societal expectations, beliefs, and stereotypes about gender roles influence individuals' behaviour and shape their social interactions. According to this theory, society assigns specific roles, behaviours, and attributes to individuals based on their gender, and these roles become internalised and guide people's actions (Eagly and Wood, 2012; Eagly, 1987). As the theory distinguishes between different roles and behaviours, it attributes agentic characteristics, which are typically linked to leadership roles and encompass qualities such as assertiveness, dominance, and independence, to masculinity. In contrast, communal traits, which involve nurturance, agreeableness, cooperation, and relationship-oriented behaviours, are typically associated with femininity (Eagly, 1987; Hmieleski and Sheppard, 2019). Furthermore, female leaders are more inclined to demonstrate care and concern for individuals, prioritising their well-being. On the other hand, male leaders are often associated with traits that promote competition and emphasise a competitive approach (Eagly and Johnson, 1990; Eagly *et al.*, 1995). In the context of equity crowdfunding, we found that societal expectations, beliefs, and stereotypes about female roles negatively influenced investment decisions. Some may conclude that investors penalise campaigns portraying femininity by awarding them less financing. Thus, projects with female team members or consisting of an entirely female team raise less funding.

The communal traits associated with women are found to be solid and robust. For instance, even in highly challenging situations, female teams are more sensitive to emotional concerns, such as the welfare of another team member (Kahn and Leon, 1994). Predominantly female teams act in a more other-regarding way and display greater generosity than predominantly male groups (Dufwenberg and Muren, 2006).

If a group includes more women, its 'collective intelligence' seems to rise. Research data show that intelligent groups listen to each other, and their team members share criticism constructively, have open minds, and are not autocratic (Woolley and Malone, 2011). All these characteristics can be associated with the communal traits typically attributed to women. Thus, having female team members can be beneficial. However, it appears that investors in equity crowdfunding are uneasy about this depth of collective insight and rely on easy-to-access social beliefs and stereotypes in their investment decisions. Even though research has proven that women exhibit leadership abilities in diverse and intricate ways that challenge traditional gender categorisations (Baxter, 2014), women experience prejudice against them as potential and actual leaders or managers (Eagly and Karau, 2002). Thus, performing a leadership role continues to present distinctively gendered challenges (Baxter, 2014).

We believe this chapter offers a timely contribution to the growing stream of research that seeks to explore the potential opportunities of equity crowdfunding to promote entrepreneurship for those struggling to obtain venture finance (Cumming *et al.*, 2021). Drawing from research on female entrepreneurs in equity crowdfunding and social role theory, our work fills a significant gap in the literature and answers the call for more research on equity crowdfunding and female entrepreneurship and how this financing type can help reduce the existing gender financing gap (Butticè and Vismara, 2022). We also contribute new insights into using social role theory in entrepreneurial finance as a social and psychological framework to analyse the investments of crowdfunding backers. From a practical point of view, our findings might help female entrepreneurs or entrepreneurial teams seeking funding regarding the choice of financing method and the impact of crucial crowdfunding campaign characteristics, such as the chosen target offering amount.

10.8. Limitations and Future Research

As with every study, ours also has limitations. First, our final dataset of 366 campaigns is relatively small. However, regarding internal validity in terms of representing the population under study, our sample represents about 10% of the US-based equity crowdfunding projects classified under Regulation C during the period observed (2016–2020). Moreover, we retrieved the campaigns from Wefunder and Republic, two of the top three equity crowdfunding platforms in the US (Brian, 2023).

Second, due to resource and data availability constraints, our analysis focuses only on US-based platforms, disregarding potential cross-national variation. However, using a sample from a single country contributes to the study's internal validity, as stereotypical beliefs and expectations linked to social roles may vary between countries. Regarding external validity, our study's focus on the US implies that its findings can be generalised reasonably well to other Anglo-Saxon regions with similar institutional contexts, such as Canada, Australia, New Zealand, and the UK.

Third, while we included various independent and control variables in our model, we mainly focused on the venture- and promotion-related campaign characteristics considered 'hard facts'. In future research, examining more 'soft facts' possessing a more intangible character might lead to a better understanding of the internal reaction of investors in the crowd. For instance, recent research has shown that personality traits can be portrayed through campaign communications and that different personality traits can influence investment decisions in equity crowdfunding (e.g. Creek *et al.*, 2019; Isaak *et al.*, 2021). Throughout our GLM regression models, the control variables for the campaigns' word count and the number of updates are consistently significant, indicating that communication-related factors are essential for crowdfunding projects. Therefore, future research could examine gender differences through campaign communication in equity crowdfunding based on softer and more individual characteristics, such as linguistic patterns or personality traits. For example, Gorbatai and Nelson (2015) have proposed that online settings might alleviate this gender classification through interaction by providing participants with a mediated (virtual) environment that grants them independence from their physical identities and diminishes the significance of gender as a social category. Thus, women can benefit from their communication style, as gender-specific language partially mediates women's success in reward-based crowdfunding (Gorbatai and Nelson, 2015).

Finally, we observed gender-related funding differences based only on women and men. Our gender composition did not include members of the LGBTQ community who do not identify as female or male. Thus, regarding the rising importance of entrepreneurship for underrepresented social groups, a more diverse and inclusive role theory approach (Anglin *et al.*, 2022) could be interesting for future researchers to study, thus further promoting entrepreneurship for those struggling to obtain venture finance.

References

Ahlers, G. K., Cumming, D., Günther, C., and Schweizer, D. (2015). Signaling in equity crowdfunding. *Entrepreneurship Theory and Practice*, 39(4), 955–980.

Alkhaled, S. and Berglund, K. (2018). "And now I'm free": Women's empowerment and emancipation through entrepreneurship in Saudi Arabia and Sweden. *Entrepreneurship and Regional Development*, 30(7–8), 877–900.

Alsos, G. A. and Ljunggren, E. (2017). The role of gender in entrepreneur-investor relationships: A signaling theory approach. *Entrepreneurship Theory and Practice*, 41(4), 567–590.

Anglin, A. H., Kincaid, P. A., Short, J. C., and Allen, D. G. (2022). Role theory perspectives: Past, present, and future applications of role theories in management research. *Journal of Management*, 48(6), 1469–1502.

Aristei, D. and Gallo, M. (2016). Does gender matter for firms' access to credit? Evidence from international data. *Finance Research Letters*, 18, 67–75.

Audretsch, D. B., Lehmann, E. E., and Wirsching, K. (2017). Female immigrant entrepreneurship in Germany. In A. N. Link (Ed.), *Gender and Entrepreneurial Activity* (pp. 46–68). Edward Elgar Publishing.

Balachandra, L., Briggs, T., Eddleston, K., and Brush, C. (2019). Don't pitch like a girl!: How gender stereotypes influence investor decisions. *Entrepreneurship Theory and Practice*, 43(1), 116–137.

Barasinska, N. and Schäfer, D. (2014). Is crowdfunding different? Evidence on the relation between gender and funding success from a German peer-to-peer lending platform. *German Economic Review*, 15(4), 436–452.

Barbi, M. and Mattioli, S. (2019). Human capital, investor trust, and equity crowdfunding. *Research in International Business and Finance*, 49, 1–12.

Bargh, J. A. and Chartrand, T. L. (1999). The unbearable automaticity of being. *American Psychologist*, 54(7), 462–479.

Baxter, J. (2014). "If you had only listened carefully...": The discursive construction of emerging leadership in a UK all-women management team. *Discourse & Communication*, 8(1), 23–39.

Becker-Blease, J. R. and Sohl, J. E. (2011). The effect of gender diversity on angel group investment. *Entrepreneurship Theory and Practice*, 35(4), 709–733.

Bennett, R. and Dann, S. (2000). The changing experience of Australian female entrepreneurs. *Gender, Work and Organization*, 7(2), 75–83.

Bento, N., Gianfrate, G., and Thoni, M. H. (2019). Crowdfunding for sustainability ventures. *Journal of Cleaner Production*, 237, 117751.

Bi, S., Liu, Z., and Usman, K. (2017). The influence of online information on investing decisions of reward-based crowdfunding. *Journal of Business Research*, 71, 10–18.

Bigelow, L. S., Lundmark, L., McLean Parks, J., and Wuebker, R. (2014). Skirting the issues: Experimental evidence of gender bias in IPO prospectus evaluations. *Journal of Management*, 40(6), 1732–1759.

Blattman, C., Fiala, N., and Martinez, S. (2014). Generating skilled self-employment in developing countries: Experimental evidence from Uganda. *The Quarterly Journal of Economics*, 129(2), 697–752.

Block, J. H., Colombo, M. G., Cumming, D. J., and Vismara, S. (2018). New players in entrepreneurial finance and why they are there. *Small Business Economics*, 50(2), 239–250.

Bloodhart, B. and Swim, J. K. (2020). Sustainability and consumption: What's gender got to do with it? *Journal of Social Issues*, 76(1), 101–113.

Borkenau, P. (1992). Implicit personality theory and the five-factor model. *Journal of Personality*, 60(2), 295–327.

Brian (2021). 2020 US equity crowdfunding stats: Year in review. CrowdWise LLC.

Brian (2023). 2022 Equity crowdfunding stats and top platforms. CrowdWise LLC.

Brooks, A. W., Huang, L., Kearney, S. W., and Murray, F. E. (2014). Investors prefer entrepreneurial ventures pitched by attractive men. *Proceedings of the National Academy of Sciences of the United States of America*, 111(12), 4427–4431.

Brush, C., de Bruin, A., and Welter, F. (2009). A gender-aware framework for women's entrepreneurship. *International Journal of Gender and Entrepreneurship*, 1(1), 8–24.

Brush, C., Carter, N. M., Gatewood, E. J., Greene, P. G., and Hart, M. (2004). Gatekeepers of venture growth: A Diana Project report on the role and participation of women in the venture capital industry. *SSRN Electronic Journal.*

Brush, C., Greene, P., Balachandra, L., and Davis, A. (2018). The gender gap in venture capital: Progress, problems, and perspectives. *Venture Capital*, 20(2), 115–136.

Butticè, V. and Vismara, S. (2022). Inclusive digital finance: The industry of equity crowdfunding. *The Journal of Technology Transfer*, 47(4), 1224–1241.

Calic, G. and Mosakowski, E. (2016). Kicking off social entrepreneurship: How a sustainability orientation influences crowdfunding success. *Journal of Management Studies*, 53(5), 738–767.

Carter, N., Brush, C., Greene, P., Gatewood, E., and Hart, M. (2003). Women entrepreneurs who break through to equity financing: The influence of human, social and financial capital. *Venture Capital*, 5(1), 1–28.

Carter, S., Shaw, E., Lam, W., and Wilson, F. (2007). Gender, entrepreneurship, and bank lending: The criteria and processes used by bank loan officers in assessing applications. *Entrepreneurship Theory and Practice*, 31(3), 427–444.

Chen, X., Huang, B., and Ye, D. (2020). Gender gap in peer-to-peer lending: Evidence from China. *Journal of Banking & Finance*, 112, 105633.

Cholakova, M. and Clarysse, B. (2015). Does the possibility to make equity investments in crowdfunding projects crowd out reward-based investments? *Entrepreneurship Theory and Practice*, 39(1), 145–172.

Chowdhury, S. (2005). Demographic diversity for building an effective entrepreneurial team: Is it important? *Journal of Business Venturing*, 20(6), 727–746.

Cicchiello, A. F., Kazemikhasragh, A., and Monferrà, S. (2022). Gender differences in new venture financing: Evidence from equity crowdfunding in Latin America. *International Journal of Emerging Markets*, 17(5), 1175–1197.

Coakley, J., Lazos, A., and Liñares-Zegarra, J. M. (2022). Equity crowdfunding founder teams: Campaign success and venture failure. *British Journal of Management*, 33(1), 286–305.

Cohen, D. L. (2014, January 17). Your practice: Financial advisers changing approaches for women. *Reuters.*

Coleman, S. and Robb, A. (2009). A comparison of new firm financing by gender: Evidence from the Kauffman Firm Survey data. *Small Business Economics*, 33(4), 397–411.

Courtney, C., Dutta, S., and Li, Y. (2017). Resolving information asymmetry: Signaling, endorsement, and crowdfunding success. *Entrepreneurship Theory and Practice*, 41(2), 265–290.

Cowling, M., Marlow, S., and Liu, W. (2020). Gender and bank lending after the global financial crisis: Are women entrepreneurs safer bets? *Small Business Economics*, 55(4), 853–880.

Creek, S., Allison, T. H., Sahaym, A., Hmieleski, K., and Maurer, J. (2019). The dark triad and entrepreneurial crowdfunding: A comparison of rewards-based vs equity campaigns. *Academy of Management Proceedings*, 2019(1), 15932.

Cumming, D., Leung, T. Y., and Rui, O. (2015). Gender diversity and securities fraud. *Academy of Management Journal*, 58(5), 1572–1593.

Cumming, D., Meoli, M., and Vismara, S. (2021). Does equity crowdfunding democratize entrepreneurial finance? *Small Business Economics*, 56(2), 533–552.

Cumming, D. and Vismara, S. (2017). De-segmenting research in entrepreneurial finance. *Venture Capital*, 19(1–2), 17–27.

Dai, Y., Byun, G., and Ding, F. (2019). The direct and indirect impact of gender diversity in new venture teams on innovation performance. *Entrepreneurship Theory and Practice*, 43(3), 505–528.

Datta, P. B. and Gailey, R. (2012). Empowering women through social entrepreneurship: Case study of a women's cooperative in India. *Entrepreneurship Theory and Practice*, 36(3), 569–587.

Dautzenberg, K. (2012). Gender differences of business owners in technology-based firms. *International Journal of Gender and Entrepreneurship*, 4(1), 79–98.

Dean, J. T. and Jayachandran, S. (2019). Changing family attitudes to promote female employment. *AEA Papers and Proceedings*, 109, 138–142.

Demartini, P. (2018). Innovative female-led startups: Do women in business underperform? *Administrative Sciences*, 8(4), 70.

Duan, Y., Hsieh, T.-S., Wang, R. R., and Wang, Z. (2020). Entrepreneurs' facial trustworthiness, gender, and crowdfunding success. *Journal of Corporate Finance*, 64, 101693.

Dufwenberg, M. and Muren, A. (2006). Gender composition in teams. *Journal of Economic Behavior and Organization*, 61(1), 50–54.

Dupas, P. and Robinson, J. (2013). Savings constraints and microenterprise development: Evidence from a field experiment in Kenya. *American Economic Journal: Applied Economics*, 5(1), 163–192.

Eagly, A. H. (1987). *Sex Differences in Social Behavior: A Social-Role Interpretation.* Lawrence Erlbaum.

Eagly, A. H. and Diekman, A. B. (2005). What is the problem? Prejudice as an attitude-in-context. In J. F. Dovidio, P. Glick, and L. A. Rudman (Eds.), *On the Nature of Prejudice: Fifty Years After Allport* (pp. 19–35). Blackwell Publishing.

Eagly, A. H. and Johnson, B. T. (1990). Gender and leadership style: A meta-analysis. *Psychological Bulletin*, 108, 233–256.

Eagly, A. H. and Karau, S. J. (2002). Role congruity theory of prejudice toward female leaders. *Psychological Review*, 109(3), 573–598.

Eagly, A. H., Karau, S. J., and Makhijani, M. G. (1995). Gender and the effectiveness of leaders: A meta-analysis. *Psychological Bulletin*, 117(1), 125.

Eagly, A. H. and Wood, W. (2012). Social role theory. In P. A. M. Van Lange, A. W. Kruglanski, and E. T. Higgins (Eds.), *Handbook of Theories of Social Psychology* (pp. 458–476). Sage Publications Ltd.

Eagly, A. H., Wood, W., and Diekman, A. B. (2000). Social role theory of sex differences and similarities: A current appraisal. *The Developmental Social Psychology of Gender*, 12(174), 9781410605245-12.

Eddleston, K. A., Ladge, J. J., Mitteness, C., and Balachandra, L. (2016). Do you see what I see? Signaling effects of gender and firm characteristics on financing entrepreneurial ventures. *Entrepreneurship Theory and Practice*, 40(3), 489–514.

Edelman, L. F., Donnelly, R., Manolova, T., and Brush, C. G. (2018). Gender stereotypes in the angel investment process. *International Journal of Gender and Entrepreneurship*, 10(2), 134–157.

Elitzur, R. and Solodoha, E. (2021). Does gender matter? Evidence from crowdfunding. *Journal of Business Venturing Insights*, 16, e00268.

Faccio, M., Marchica, M.-T., and Mura, R. (2016). CEO gender, corporate risk-taking, and the efficiency of capital allocation. *Journal of Corporate Finance*, 39, 193–209.

Freeman, J. and Hannan, M. T. (1983). Niche width and the dynamics of organizational populations. *American Journal of Sociology*, 88(6), 1116–1145.

Geiger, M. (2020). A meta-analysis of the gender gap(s) in venture funding: Funder- and entrepreneur-driven perspectives. *Journal of Business Venturing Insights*, 13, e00167.

Geiger, M. and Oranburg, S. C. (2018). Female entrepreneurs and equity crowdfunding in the US: Receiving less when asking for more. *Journal of Business Venturing Insights*, 10, e00099.

Gicheva, D. and Link, A. N. (2015). The gender gap in federal and private support for entrepreneurship. *Small Business Economics*, 45(4), 729–733.

Godwin, L. N., Stevens, C. E., and Brenner, N. L. (2006). Forced to play by the rules? Theorizing how mixed-sex founding teams benefit women entrepreneurs in male-dominated contexts. *Entrepreneurship Theory and Practice*, 30(5), 623–642.

Gorbatai, A. and Nelson, L. (2015). The narrative advantage: Gender and the language of crowdfunding. Haas School of Business UC Berkeley Working Paper, 1–32.

Gottlieb, J. D., Townsend, R. R., and Xu, T. (2022). Does career risk deter potential entrepreneurs? *The Review of Financial Studies*, 35(9), 3973–4015.

Greenberg, J. and Mollick, E. (2017). Activist choice homophily and the crowdfunding of female founders. *Administrative Science Quarterly*, 62(2), 341–374.

Greene, P. G., Brush, C. G., Hart, M. M., and Saparito, P. (2001). Patterns of venture capital funding: Is gender a factor? *Venture Capital*, 3(1), 63–83.

Gupta, V. K., Wieland, A. M., and Turban, D. B. (2019). Gender characterizations in entrepreneurship: A multi-level investigation of sex-role stereotypes about high-growth, commercial, and social entrepreneurs. *Journal of Small Business Management*, 57(1), 131–153.

Guzman, J. and Kacperczyk, A. (2019). Gender gap in entrepreneurship. *Research Policy*, 48(7), 1666–1680.

Harper, D. A. (2008). Towards a theory of entrepreneurial teams. *Journal of Business Venturing*, 23(6), 613–626.

Harrison, L. A. and Lynch, A. B. (2005). Social role theory and the perceived gender role orientation of athletes. *Sex Roles*, 52(3–4), 227–236.

Haugh, H. M. and Talwar, A. (2016). Linking social entrepreneurship and social change: The mediating role of empowerment. *Journal of Business Ethics*, 133(4), 643–658.

Heilman, M. E. and Haynes, M. C. (2005). No credit where credit is due: Attributional rationalization of women's success in male-female teams. *The Journal of Applied Psychology*, 90(5), 905–916.

Hellerstedt, K., Aldrich, H. E., and Wiklund, J. (2007). The impact of past performance on the exit of team members in young firms: The role of team composition. *Frontiers of Entrepreneurship Research*.

Hmieleski, K. M. and Sheppard, L. D. (2019). The yin and yang of entrepreneurship: Gender differences in the importance of communal and agentic characteristics for entrepreneurs' subjective well-being and performance. *Journal of Business Venturing*, 34(4), 709–730.

Hörisch, J. and Tenner, I. (2020). How environmental and social orientations influence the funding success of investment-based crowdfunding: The mediating role of the number of funders and the average funding amount. *Technological Forecasting and Social Change*, 161, 120311.

Huang, L., Joshi, P., Wakslak, C., and Wu, A. (2021). Sizing up entrepreneurial potential: Gender differences in communication and investor perceptions of long-term growth and scalability. *Academy of Management Journal*, 64(3), 716–740.

Isaak, A. J., Neuhaus, J., and Bostandzic, D. (2021). Success lies in the eye of the beholder: Personality traits, negativity bias and equity crowdfunding. *Academy of Management Proceedings*, 2021(1), 11151.

Jayachandran, S. (2021). Social norms as a barrier to women's employment in developing countries. *IMF Economic Review*, 69(3), 576–595.

Jennings, J. E. and Brush, C. G. (2013). Research on women entrepreneurs: Challenges to (and from) the broader entrepreneurship literature? *Academy of Management Annals*, 7(1), 663–715.

Johnson, M. A., Stevenson, R. M., and Letwin, C. R. (2018). A woman's place is in the... startup! Crowdfunder judgments, implicit bias, and the stereotype content model. *Journal of Business Venturing*, 33(6), 813–831.

Kahn, P. M. and Leon, G. R. (1994). Group climate and individual functioning in an all-women Antarctic expedition team. *Environment and Behavior*, 26(5), 669–697.

Kalnins, A. and Williams, M. (2014). When do female-owned businesses out-survive male-owned businesses? A disaggregated approach by industry and geography. *Journal of Business Venturing*, 29(6), 822–835.

Kamm, J. B., Shuman, J. C., Seeger, J. A., and Nurick, A. J. (1990). Entrepreneurial teams in new venture creation: A research agenda. *Entrepreneurship Theory and Practice*, 14(4), 7–17.

Kanze, D., Huang, L., Conley, M. A., and Higgins, E. T. (2018). We ask men to win and women not to lose: Closing the gender gap in startup funding. *Academy of Management Journal*, 61(2), 586–614.

Kelley, H. H. and Michela, J. L. (1980). Attribution theory and research. *Annual Review of Psychology*, 31(1), 457–501.

Kleinert, S. and Mochkabadi, K. (2022). Gender stereotypes in equity crowdfunding: The effect of gender bias on the interpretation of quality signals. *The Journal of Technology Transfer*, 47(6), 1640–1661.

Koenig, A. M. and Eagly, A. H. (2014). Evidence for the social role theory of stereotype content: Observations of groups' roles shape stereotypes. *Journal of Personality and Social Psychology*, 107(3), 371–392.

Kwapisz, A. and Hechavarría, D. M. (2018). Women don't ask: An investigation of start-up financing and gender. *Venture Capital*, 20(2), 159–190.

Laguía, A., García-Ael, C., Wach, D., and Moriano, J. A. (2019). "Think entrepreneur-think male": A task and relationship scale to measure gender stereotypes in entrepreneurship. *International Entrepreneurship and Management Journal*, 15(3), 749–772.

Leboeuf, G. and Schwienbacher, A. (2018). Crowdfunding as a new financing tool. In D. Cumming and L. Hornuf (Eds.), *The Economics of Crowdfunding: Startups, Portals, and Investor Behavior* (pp. 11–28). Palgrave Macmillan.

Lee, M. and Huang, L. (2018). Gender bias, social impact framing, and evaluation of entrepreneurial ventures. *Organization Science*, 29(1), 1–16.

Lehner, O. M. (2013). Crowdfunding social ventures: A model and research agenda. *Venture Capital*, 15(4), 289–311.

Li, Y., Sui, S., and Wu, S. (2022). The effect of gender fit on crowdfunding success. *Journal of Business Venturing Insights*, 18, e00333.

Lins, E. and Lutz, E. (2016). Bridging the gender funding gap: Do female entrepreneurs have equal access to venture capital? *International Journal of Entrepreneurship and Small Business*, 27(2–3), 347.

Litz, R. A. and Folker, C. A. (2002). When he and she sell seashells: Exploring the relationship between management team gender-balance and small firm performance. *Journal of Developmental Entrepreneurship*, 7(4), 341.

Madera, J. M., Hebl, M. R., and Martin, R. C. (2009). Gender and letters of recommendation for academia: Agentic and communal differences. *Journal of Applied Psychology*, 94(6), 1591–1599.

Madill, J. J., Riding, A. L., and Haines, G. H. (2006). Women entrepreneurs: Debt financing and banking relationships. *Journal of Small Business and Entrepreneurship*, 19(2), 121–142.

Malaga, R., Mamonov, S., and Rosenblum, J. (2018). Gender difference in equity crowdfunding: An exploratory analysis. *International Journal of Gender and Entrepreneurship*, 10(4), 332–343.

Malmström, M., Voitkane, A., Johansson, J., and Wincent, J. (2018). When stereotypical gender notions see the light of day, will they burst? Venture capitalists' gender constructions versus venturing performance facts. *Journal of Business Venturing Insights*, 9, 32–38.

Malmström, M. and Wincent, J. (2018). Bank lending and financial discrimination from the formal economy: How women entrepreneurs get forced into involuntary bootstrapping. *Journal of Business Venturing Insights*, 10, e00096.

Mascia, D. V. and Rossi, S. P. (2017). Is there a gender effect on the cost of bank financing? *Journal of Financial Stability*, 31, 136–153.

McCullagh, P. and Nelder, J. A. (2019). *Generalized Linear Models* (2nd ed.). Routledge, available at: https://doi.org/10.1201/9780203753736.

McGuire, E. (2020). Can equity crowdfunding close the gender gap in startup finance? *SSRN Electronic Journal*, available at SSRN: https://ssrn.com/abstract=3233809.

Mollick, E. (2014). The dynamics of crowdfunding: An exploratory study. *Journal of Business Venturing*, 29(1), 1–16.

Mollick, E. and Robb, A. (2016). Democratizing innovation and capital access: The role of crowdfunding. *California Management Review*, 58(2), 72–87.

Moro, A., Wisniewski, T. P., and Mantovani, G. M. (2017). Does a manager's gender matter when accessing credit? Evidence from European data. *Journal of Banking and Finance*, 80, 119–134.

Neuhaus, J., Isaak, A., and Bostandzic, D. (2022). Million dollar personality: A systematic literature review on personality in crowdfunding. *Management Review Quarterly*, 72(2), 309–345.

Pedersen, D. M. (1965). The measurement of individual differences in perceived personality-trait relationships and their relation to certain determinants. *The Journal of Social Psychology*, 65, 233–258.

Poczter, S. and Shapsis, M. (2018). Gender disparity in angel financing. *Small Business Economics*, 51(1), 31–55.

Pope, D. G. and Sydnor, J. R. (2011). What's in a picture? Evidence of discrimination from prosper.com. *Journal of Human Resources*, 46(1), 53–92.

Prentice, D. A. and Carranza, E. (2002). What women and men should be, shouldn't be, are allowed to be, and don't have to be: The contents of prescriptive gender stereotypes. *Psychology of Women Quarterly*, 26(4), 269–281.

Prokop, J. and Wang, D. (2022). Is there a gender gap in equity-based crowdfunding? *Small Business Economics*, 59(3), 1219–1244.

Republic (2023). The future of private investing. Republic.

Santos, S. C. and Neumeyer, X. (2021). Gender, poverty and entrepreneurship: A systematic literature review and future research agenda. *Journal of Developmental Entrepreneurship*, 26(3), 2150018.

Schaltegger, S. and Wagner, M. (2011). Sustainable entrepreneurship and sustainability innovation: Categories and interactions. *Business Strategy and the Environment*, 20(4), 222–237.

Schwienbacher, A. and Larralde, B. (2010). Crowdfunding of small entrepreneurial ventures. *SSRN Electronic Journal*, available at SSRN: https://ssrn.com/abstract=1699183.

Securities and Exchange Commission, SEC (2015). Final rule: Crowdfunding.

Securities and Exchange Commission, SEC (2022). Private placements under Regulation D: Investor Bulletin.

Securities and Exchange Commission, SEC (2023a). About EDGAR. US Securities and Exchange Commission.

Securities and Exchange Commission, SEC (2023b). Regulation crowdfunding.

Seigner, B. D. C., Milanov, H., and McKenny, A. F. (2022). Who can claim innovation and benefit from it? Gender and expectancy violations in reward-based crowdfunding. *Strategic Entrepreneurship Journal*, 16(2), 381–422.

Serwaah, P. (2022). Crowdfunding, gender and the promise of financial democracy: A systematic review. *International Journal of Gender and Entrepreneurship*, 14(2), 263–283.

Serwaah, P. and Shneor, R. (2021). Women and entrepreneurial finance: A systematic review. *Venture Capital*, 23(4), 291–319.

Singh, S. P., Sego, T. A., and Sarin, S. (2022). Overcoming bias against funding of female-led entrepreneurial initiatives: The democratizing influence of online crowdlending platforms. *Service Business*, 16(4), 907–933.

Srivastava, S., Guglielmo, S., and Beer, J. S. (2010). Perceiving others' personalities: Examining the dimensionality, assumed similarity to the self, and stability of perceiver effects. *Journal of Personality and Social Psychology*, 98(3), 520–534.

Stefani, M. L. and Vacca, V. (2015). Small firms' credit access in the Euro area: Does gender matter? *CESifo Economic Studies*, 61(1), 165–201.

Stinchcombe, A. (1965). Organization-creating organizations. *Society*, 2(2), 34–35.

Sullivan, D. M. and Meek, W. R. (2012). Gender and entrepreneurship: A review and process model. *Journal of Managerial Psychology*, 27(5), 428–458.

Swim, J. K. and Geiger, N. (2018). The gendered nature of stereotypes about climate change opinion groups. *Group Processes and Intergroup Relations*, 21(3), 438–456.

United Nations (2023). The 17 goals. Department of Economic and Social Affairs.

Vismara, S. (2016). Equity retention and social network theory in equity crowdfunding. *Small Business Economics*, 46(4), 579–590.

Vismara, S. (2019). Sustainability in equity crowdfunding. *Technological Forecasting and Social Change*, 141, 98–106.

Vismara, S., Benaroio, D., and Carne, F. (2017). Gender in entrepreneurial finance: Matching investors and entrepreneurs in equity crowdfunding. In A. N. Link (Ed.), *Gender and Entrepreneurial Activity* (pp. 271–288). Edward Elgar Publishing.

Vogel, R., Puhan, T. X., Shehu, E., Kliger, D., and Beese, H. (2014). Funding decisions and entrepreneurial team diversity: A field study. *Journal of Economic Behavior and Organization*, 107, 595–613.

Vu, F. (2021). Equity crowdfunding shows more growth than venture capital. *KingsCrowd.*

Wefunder. (2023). *Angel Investing for Everyone.* https://wefunder.com/wefunder.

Welbourne, T. M., Cycyota, C. S., and Ferrante, C. J. (2007). Wall Street reaction to women in IPOs. *Group and Organization Management*, 32(5), 524–547.

Wood, W. and Eagly, A. H. (2002). A cross-cultural analysis of the behavior of women and men: Implications for the origins of sex differences. *Psychological Bulletin*, 128(5), 699–727.

Wood, W. and Eagly, A. H. (2010). Gender. In S. Fiske, D. Gilbert, and G. Lindzey (Eds.), *Handbook of Social Psychology* (5th ed., Vol. 1, pp. 629-667). Oxford University Press.

Woolley, A. and Malone, T. (2011). What makes a team smarter? More women. *Harvard Business Review*, 89(6), 32–33.

Wu, Z. and Chua, J. H. (2012). Second-order gender effects: The case of U.S. small business borrowing cost. *Entrepreneurship Theory and Practice*, 36(3), 443–463.

Zhao, Y., Xie, X., and Yang, L. (2021). Female entrepreneurs and equity crowdfunding: The consequential roles of lead investors and venture stages. *International Entrepreneurship and Management Journal*, 17(3), 1183–1211.

Zhou, W. and Rosini, E. (2015). Entrepreneurial team diversity and performance: Toward an integrated model. *Entrepreneurship Research Journal*, 5(1), 31–60.

https://doi.org/10.1142/9781800617032_0011

Chapter 11

From Digitalisation to Artificial Intelligence: The New Frontiers of Entrepreneurial Finance

Luca Farè* **and Silvio Vismara**†

** University of Bergamo, Department of Management, Information and Production Engineering, Italy*
† University of Bergamo, Department of Management, IMT School for Advanced Studies Lucca, Italy

11.1. Introduction

Entrepreneurial finance has undergone significant transformations in the past decade (Block *et al.*, 2018). The pervasive influence of digitisation on the global economy, coupled with the rapid proliferation of artificial intelligence (AI), is propelling the financial industry towards novel frontiers. In this chapter, we shed light on some of the latest major developments in entrepreneurial finance, such as the establishment of financial technology (fintech) ventures, the diffusion of alternative sources of financing, including equity crowdfunding (ECF) and initial coin offerings (ICOs), and the financing of companies adopting AI technologies.

The transformation driven by digitisation has not only altered the traditional dynamics of finance but also led to alternative financing channels leveraging cutting-edge innovative fintech. Some examples in the dynamic realm of fintech are digital payments and lending, ECF, ICOs, blockchain technologies, and insurtech (Allen *et al.*, 2021). Notably, ECF and ICOs have experienced extraordinary growth over the past few years (e.g. Cumming *et al.*, 2024; Fisch, 2019). Fintech has emerged as a primary consequence of the diffusion of digital platforms, recognised as novel and distinct organisational forms exploiting digital tools to facilitate multi-side interactions between entrepreneurs and investors (Chen *et al.*, 2022). These platforms are dynamic and evolving systems, often allowing users to overcome the intermediation of traditional and institutional investors. Scholars have recently focused their attention not only on the market or network function of fintech platforms but also on their architectural design, stressing the need for a more comprehensive understanding of their governance structure (e.g. Ahlstrom *et al.*, 2017; Foss *et al.*, 2021; Gewer, 2022; McIntyre *et al.*, 2021). Fintech platforms are becoming increasingly sophisticated, designing advanced and diverse business models. Many of them have a signalling and certification role and function as a service provider (Block *et al.*, 2021). Interestingly, although fintech has often been presented as a disruptive force, in contrast to existing financing providers such as banks, private equity, or venture capital (VC), recent evidence challenges this view and shows that fintech primarily expands, rather than substitutes, the supply of financial services (e.g. Erel and Liebersohn, 2022).

Digitalisation also drives the rapid diffusion of AI adoption in established companies and the rise of new AI-based start-ups, which will produce further transformations in entrepreneurial finance. AI technologies and tools have existed for several decades, and their utilisation in finance has increased recently (OECD, 2021). However, the swift advancement in the pace of AI innovation and the introduction of content-generating capabilities, known as generative AI (GenAI), have sparked a renewed interest in this technological evolution. The introduction of conversational chatbot solutions, such as ChatGPT and Gemini, marked a breakthrough in the ongoing development of AI. Their user-friendliness and intuitive interface have accelerated the adoption speed of GenAI tools (OECD, 2023), allowing users to engage with complex technologies that align intuitively with human cognition. The easy and cost-effective (frequently free) access to some of these technologies has led to a surge in private and public adoption of AI models. Scholars have also recently called for leveraging AI in the design phase of academic studies (e.g. Matthews *et al.*, 2024; von Krogh *et al.*, 2023). However, despite the growing interest, how AI and GenAI will affect finance remains an open question. In this chapter, we seek to contribute to this conversation, providing some insights into the financing of AI-based companies and their access to ECF and ICOs.

11.2. The Digitisation of Finance

Digitisation has become a driving force in reshaping entrepreneurial finance, as it fundamentally altered entrepreneurial business models, enabling inherently digital products and services to compete globally (Monaghan *et al.*, 2020). Within the financial industry, digitisation has disrupted traditional services, including banking and insurance, ushering in a new era led by fintech and insurtech companies (Bollaert *et al.*, 2021; Girardone and Ricci, 2023; D'Acunto *et al.*, 2019). These entities seek to enhance customer experiences and streamline the delivery of financial services through technological innovation. Payment systems, which began their digitisation journey with the widespread adoption of credit and debit cards, have evolved into a competitive market where smaller, more agile players are introducing game-changing technologies. Further, an increasing number of start-ups leverage AI and machine learning (ML) to provide tailored management services and advanced trading tools (Chen *et al.*, 2019; Cong and He, 2019; Meoli and Vismara, 2022). The essence of finance and banking — lending and capital provision — has been profoundly affected, prompting traditional banks to explore previously uncharted territories and providing new opportunities in vulnerable ecosystems (Rawhouser *et al.*, 2024).

Amidst the altered finance landscape, alternative financing channels have rapidly surged. In particular, ECF and ICOs have emerged as viable options, complementing traditional VC and business angel (BA) funding. Equity underwriting has experienced simplification and disintermediation, enabling start-ups to access finance from a diverse crowd of small retail investors. These alternative means of financing not only simplify the funding process but also provide unique value propositions. Crowdfunding, for instance, offers start-ups the opportunity to obtain finance from the crowd, offering funding alternatives that may be particularly valuable when other sources are not readily available (Walthoff-Borm *et al.*, 2018). Additionally, with ICOs, firms can raise money on the internet by offering digital tokens, bypassing any screening or control from central entities and independent auditors (Giudici and Adhami, 2019).

At the forefront of the entrepreneurial finance evolution stands fintech, reshaping how finance is delivered and experienced. The advent of cutting-edge digital tools within the fintech sector has revolutionised business transactions, decreased transaction costs, and attracted novice investors (Philippon, 2016; Block *et al.*, 2018). The surge of new fintech ventures over the past decade exemplifies the vibrancy of entrepreneurial activity in this domain (Cumming *et al.*, 2023; Farè *et al.*, 2024a)). While the impact of fintech has been global, the driving forces behind the establishment and geographical diffusion of fintech ventures have been the subject of enquiry in recent academic studies. Extant research has explored factors ranging from VC and private sector credit availability to regulatory enforcement and the size of financial centres (e.g. Haddad and Hornuf, 2019; Kolokas *et al.*, 2022).

The relationship between fintech and traditional finance is nuanced and evolving, with mixed findings in existing research. Some studies suggest that fintech often serves as a complement to, rather than a substitute for, traditional banking services and existing financial intermediaries (Haddad and Hornuf, 2019). Conversely, other researchers point out that the influence of fintech companies on banks is heterogeneous, with their impact varying based on factors such as loan size and credit quality of borrowers (Tang, 2019). An intriguing aspect of the impact of fintech on traditional finance is its role in expanding the supply of financial services to small businesses that banks poorly serve. Erel and Liebersohn (2022) reveal that fintech is disproportionately used in locations with fewer bank branches, lower incomes, and more minority households and in industries with fewer banking relationships, suggesting that fintech primarily expands, rather than substitutes, the supply of financial services. These findings challenge conventional narratives that portray fintech as a disruptive force aiming to replace traditional banking services.

The digitalisation of the economic and financial sectors has also drawn the attention of practitioners and policymakers to the prominent role of qualified human capital in science, technology, engineering, and math (STEM) fields. The finance industry has become more STEM-intensive than other sectors, attracting graduates in STEM fields at an increasing rate (Marin and Vona, 2023). Governments worldwide have recently adopted policies to increase the number of STEM graduates, and more and more schools and universities are establishing STEM programmes. The America COMPETES Act of 2022 (USA), the STEM Futures Programme 2023 (UK), the China STEM Education 2029 Action Plan (China), the Indian Institutes of Information Technology Laws Bill of 2020 (India), and the European Union (EU) Digital Education Action Plan 2021–2027 (EU), to name a few, highlight the prominent role that STEM has been garnering in the policy agenda. However, while attracting growing interest, the connection between human capital and the diffusion of digital finance remains underresearched. For instance, only a few studies have addressed the intriguing question about the role of universities and technology parks in shaping the impact of digitalisation, presenting mixed evidence. Browne *et al.* (2024) document that fintech ventures have limited compatibility with accelerator programmes due to the wide array of external funding opportunities, which offer little motivation for high-quality ventures to participate. Conversely, Gazel and Schwienbacher (2021) show that the presence of incubators affects the location of new fintech start-ups and reveal that fintech start-ups developed in an incubator have a higher chance of survival. Considering the limited and mixed evidence, gaining a more comprehensive understanding of the interplay between human capital, accelerator programmes, and the development of digital finance represents a compelling goal for future research.

11.3. Fintech Platforms as a Novel Organisational Form

The rise of digital platforms is a major consequence of the digital revolution, and it is arguably one of the primary driving factors of the evolution of entrepreneurial finance. The industrial organisation view (e.g. Boudreau and Hagiu, 2009) conceptualises digital platforms primarily as marketplaces, facilitating the interactions between different agents, while the engineering view (e.g. Krishnan and Gupta, 2001) considers these platforms as advanced technological architectures to generate innovation. More recently, scholars have started embracing a new organisational perspective, which looks at digital platforms as a distinct organisational form or 'meta-organisation' (e.g. Cennamo and Santaló, 2019; Chen *et al.*, 2022; Gawer, 2014), fundamentally reshaping conventional business models. Digital platforms, including fintech ones, differ from traditional industries because they govern through digital design features, such as sharing digital resources and providing analytics-based information (Chen *et al.*, 2022). Acting as standardised digital interfaces, they utilise digital technologies to facilitate interactions among diverse parties, leading scholars to frequently categorise them as multi-sided (McIntyre *et al.*, 2021). Beyond conventional market mechanisms, digital platforms employ digital means to coordinate activities within their organisational boundaries.

The organisational perspective stresses the dynamic nature of digital platforms, emphasising the relevant role of their architectural design (Chen *et al.*, 2022; Kretschmer *et al.*, 2022). Unlike the industrial organisation and engineering perspectives, the organisational viewpoint redirects attention to the evolving structure of the platform, whereby the platform's constitutive agents play multiple roles that evolve over time (McIntyre *et al.*, 2021; McIntyre and Srinivasan, 2017). Notably, the owners and managers assume a central role in shaping the platform's performance (Chen *et al.*, 2021; Chen *et al.*, 2022), and governance competencies become crucial for value creation (Foss *et al.*, 2021). The organisational viewpoint involves changing how platforms are conceptualised, redirecting the focus from platforms as markets or networks to platforms as planned organisational forms and strategic levers by which owners and managers can proactively create value (Kretschmer *et al.*, 2022).

A growing body of research assumes the platform's governance viewpoint, instead of the structural features of the multi-sided market or network, as a cornerstone for an integrative approach towards digital platforms (Chen *et al.*, 2022). Therefore, there is a growing recognition that examining the digital platform organisational structure and its implications becomes critical to understanding their evolution (McIntyre *et al.*, 2021). Variations in governance strategies are indeed associated with platform-level factors (e.g. Kretschmer *et al.*, 2022; Rietveld *et al.*, 2020). As the attention shifts towards platform dynamics and organisational evolution, a growing interest arises in understanding the relationship between platform constitutive agents and other individuals (e.g. Chen *et al.*, 2022; Gewer, 2022). This nuanced perspective presents a comprehensive framework for exploring the evolving and dynamic nature of digital platforms in entrepreneurial finance.

11.4. Equity Crowdfunding

ECF is one of the most innovative financing channels connected with the evolution of digital platforms (Coakley and Lazos, 2021; Cumming *et al.*, 2025; Farè and Vismara, 2025; Mataigne *et al.*, 2025; Vismara and Wirtz, 2025). Following the 2008 financial crisis, crowdfunding emerged as one of the primary new advancements of entrepreneurial finance, allowing entrepreneurs to secure funding directly from the crowd through dedicated digital platforms. Figure 11.1 illustrates the impressive rise in crowdfunding platforms launched from 2008 to 2014. Although the crowdfunding market has consolidated, with fewer newcomers entering the market after 2015, new platforms have continued to be launched in recent years, and the creation process is still ongoing, which documents a vibrant activity

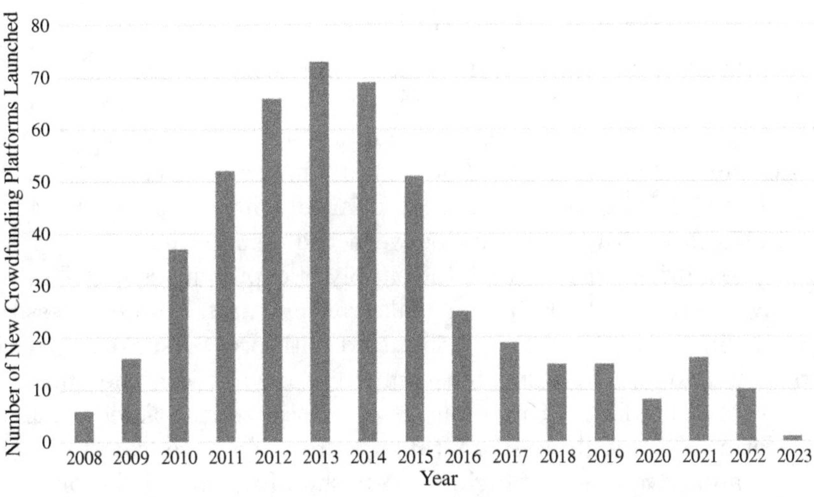

Figure 11.1. Number of crowdfunding platforms launched per year, 2008–2023.
Source: Dealroom.

in the field. As of 31 March 2025, Dealroom registered 651 worldwide crowdfunding platforms.

ECF differs from other types of crowdfunding, such as donation- and reward-based crowdfunding or peer-to-peer lending, in that it allows individuals to purchase equity securities and become shareholders. Through ECF, businesses can raise funds online from a diverse range of investors, offering primary market opportunities that resemble those of traditional public markets, such as initial public offerings (Ritter *et al.*, 2013). Equity-based crowdfunding is the most complex and risky among crowdfunding models, and it is characterised by high information asymmetries (Ahlers *et al.*, 2015). As such, entrepreneurial finance research has shown a primary interest in ECF, highlighting several factors of ECF's demand and supply sides, namely the entrepreneurs and the investors, respectively. In line with the emerging organisational perspective of digital platforms, which focuses on the platform itself instead of the agents that the platform connects, scholars have also recently started exploring platform-level factors, assuming the platform as the unit of observation (e.g. Cumming *et al.*, 2019a; Cumming *et al.*, 2024; Farè *et al.*, 2024b; Johan and Reardon, 2024; Vismara, 2022).

11.4.1. *The ECF demand side: Entrepreneurs and successful campaigns*

We first illustrate the main factors affecting the success or failure of ECF campaigns, providing a nuanced perspective on the evolving landscape of entrepreneurial funding. Scholars have emphasised the inclusion function of digital finance, especially of ECF. By democratising entrepreneurial finance (Cumming *et al.*, 2021) and facilitating the matching between the demand for capital from entrepreneurial ventures with the supply of capital investors (Butticè and Vismara, 2022), ECF can make raising capital more accessible for specific categories of disadvantaged entrepreneurs. For instance, younger and remotely located companies display a higher propensity to opt for ECF (Cumming *et al.*, 2021). Firms listed on ECF platforms are usually less profitable, more often have excessive debt levels, and have more intangible assets than firms not listed on these platforms (Walthoff-Borm *et al.*, 2018). ECF also provides a valuable financing source for family businesses (Rossi *et al.*, 2023), which might face difficulties in raising capital. Additionally, ECF represents a relevant source of financing for the often-disadvantaged category of small businesses. Despite their valuable contribution to innovation (Farè, 2022), small businesses usually face financing constraints and challenges in accessing traditional bank loans. ECF can provide them an alternative way to raise capital, thus reducing their liability of smallness.

However, making fundraising more accessible might also entail drawbacks, such as attracting low-quality entrepreneurs (Blaseg *et al.*, 2021). One of the major concerns for the development of the ECF market is that low-quality entrepreneurs seek financing through crowdfunding to take advantage of unsophisticated small investors (Cumming *et al.*, 2020). Crowdfunding might thus empower entrepreneurs to exploit inexperienced and uncoordinated investors with behavioural and herding biases.

Among the factors determining the success or failure of ECF campaigns, Cumming *et al.* (2019a) document that a higher separation between ownership and control rights significantly diminishes the probability of success for ECF offerings, while Vismara (2016) reveals that entrepreneurs who sell a smaller fraction of their companies at listing and possess more social capital are more likely to achieve success. In the same vein, Rossi *et al.* (2021) reveal that higher equity retention by original entrepreneurs positively affects the chances of success of the offerings and amount of capital raised. These findings emphasise the significance of both financial strategies and social networks in bolstering the prospects of ECF campaigns. Additionally, firms reaching the target capital quickly are more likely to launch follow-on offerings, evoking that success brings success (Signori and Vismara, 2018). Huang *et al.* (2022) delve into the psychological aspect of crowdfunding, demonstrating that the management team's confidence is positively associated with the fundraising amount. In the same line, Anglin *et al.* (2018) show that entrepreneurs conveying hope, optimism, resilience, and confidence experience superior fundraising performance. Stevenson *et al.* (2019) introduce an additional nuanced psychological dimension to ECF decision-making by exploring the concept of self-efficacy. High-self-efficacy funders, while seemingly advantageous, tend to exhibit a 'crowd bias', overweighting crowd opinions and increasing the likelihood of funding poor-quality ventures when favoured by the crowd. These findings highlight the relevant role of psychological factors in shaping entrepreneurs' fundraising success.

Research has also provided valuable insights into the role of signalling mechanisms in ECF. For instance, Ahlers *et al.* (2015) emphasise that effective signals, such as retaining equity and providing detailed information about risks, strongly impact the probability of funding success. In contrast, social and intellectual capital exhibit minimal or no impact on funding success. Digging deeper into the signalling theory in ECF, Kleinert *et al.* (2022) reveal that co-investment requirements, revenue generation, industry background, and signal accessibility matter for the platform's interpretation of quality signals. Additionally, expressing entrepreneurial ambitions may signal growth potential to early-stage investors. However, promising overly high growth ambitions might backfire for entrepreneurs, as they might be dismissed as cheap talk and even penalised due to investors' credibility concerns. Therefore, entrepreneurs may need to complement their high ambitions with costly signals, which can serve as credibility buffers and transform high ambitions from cheap talk into credible signals (Kleinert, 2024).

The country's regulatory framework also matters for ECF. Hornuf and Schwienbacher (2017) show that excessively strong investor protection may harm small firms and entrepreneurial initiatives, which contrasts with the traditional 'law and finance' view that stronger investor protection is better. Specifically, they demonstrate that optimal regulation depends on the availability of alternative early-stage financing, such as VC and angel finance.

11.4.2. *The ECF supply side: The determinants of investor decisions*

Along with increasing fundraising opportunities for entrepreneurs, ECF also provides investors with a broader range of investment choices. ECF enlarges the pool of potential investors, primarily attracting small and non-professional ones. Extant research has investigated the factors attracting investors to ECF and their behaviour. Among the several types of crowdfunding, equity-based crowdfunding is characterised by the highest levels of complexity, uncertainty, and information asymmetries (Ahlers *et al.*, 2015). As such, dealing with ECF investment decisions is particularly challenging. Investors in early-stage companies want to detect and select high-potential opportunities to maximise their long-term returns.

However, company information is often opaque in uncertain and risky early-stage investment contexts, and decision-making timeframes are compressed (Guarana *et al.*, 2022).

The dynamics of early-stage investments are intricate and influenced by various factors that shape investors' decisions and the overall success of crowdfunding campaigns. One critical aspect is the temporal dimension, with early bids playing a pivotal role in attracting subsequent investors and initiating information cascades (Vismara, 2018). The early stages of a campaign set the tone, creating a ripple effect that can significantly impact investment outcomes. Furthermore, the nature of the project itself is a crucial determinant of crowdfunding success. Highly innovative projects not only draw more attention from the crowd but also succeed in raising more capital, underscoring the importance of novelty and ingenuity in attracting investors (Le Pendeven and Schwienbacher, 2023).

Geographic considerations also come into play, with distance influencing investment decisions differently for home-country investors than overseas investors. Guenther *et al.* (2018) found a negative correlation between ECF investment probability and geographic distance for investors in their home country, while overseas investors are less sensitive to such distances. This evidence suggests that the geographical location of investors and campaigns can significantly impact the likelihood of the investment, emphasising the global nature of contemporary crowdfunding. Adding another layer of complexity, Kleinert and Mochkabadi (2021) shed light on the gender dimension of quality signals, showing that quality signals have varying effects on investment decisions, depending on whether they emanate from male or female entrepreneurs. They highlight the nuanced interplay between gender, signalling, and investor responses in the crowdfunding ecosystem.

Beyond these factors, the temporal aspect of investment decisions takes centre stage. Guarana *et al.* (2022) reveal that the timing of investment decisions, influenced by individual chronotypes and the time of day, can significantly impact the amount of information investors seek and, consequently, their investment decisions. Lark investors, for instance, make better decisions in the morning, while owl investors perform better in the evening, with information search efforts mediating this relationship. This research introduces a novel dimension to understanding investor behaviour, integrating the circadian process into the broader framework of early-stage investments. Research has also stressed the globalisation function of ECF in fostering cross-border investment opportunities. Maula and Lukkarinen (2022) theorise and empirically demonstrate how international investor attention influences cross-border ECF investments. In a realm where information is crucial, the withdrawal option available to investors within a cooling-off period becomes relevant. Additionally, Meoli and Vismara (2021) reveal that early withdrawals can influence campaign dynamics, mainly when platform members engage in this practice. Their investments and subsequent withdrawals create a dynamic environment, influencing subsequent bids and contributing to the overall narrative of crowdfunding success.

Taken together, the literature findings document that investments in ECF are shaped by many factors, ranging from the timing of bids and the nature of projects to geographic considerations, gender dynamics, and even the temporal aspects of decision-making.

11.4.3. *What about the ECF platforms?*

Recent studies have redirected the attention from the agents that the platform connects (i.e. entrepreneurs and investors) to the platform itself, trying to understand the driving factors of their birth and performance (Inceoglu *et al.*, 2024). As ECF platforms differ from one another in terms of spatial diffusion, services provided, and performance (e.g. Dushnitsky *et al.*, 2016; Rossi and Vismara, 2018; Cumming *et al.*, 2024), scholars have started exploring the determinants of such heterogeneity. Although studies employing the platform as the unit of observation are in the minority, their interesting findings are worthy of illustration.

The literature has first documented that country-level characteristics matter for creating crowdfunding platforms in a specific country. Dushnitsky *et al.* (2016) reveal that the main drivers of crowdfunding platform creation are the size of the national population, national entrepreneurial rates, and the presence of platforms operated by incumbent financial organisations (e.g. large banks, cooperative banks, and angel networks). Turning attention to financial literacy at the country level, Meoli *et al.* (2022) provide insights into a broader contextual factor. They establish a positive association between a country's financial literacy and the survival profiles of crowdfunding platforms. This indicates that the financial literacy landscape in a country plays a pivotal role in the long-term prospects of crowdfunding platforms, suggesting that a financially literate population contributes to the enduring presence of these platforms.

As regards the platform-level factors driving the success and survival profile of the ECF platforms, Rossi and Vismara (2018) reveal that platforms offering a higher number of post-campaign services, including exit assistance, periodical updates, advisory support for further funding, and general assistance, exhibit an increased annual number of successful campaigns. Interestingly, services provided before and during campaigns do not exert a similar influence, emphasising the unique impact of post-campaign support mechanisms on crowdfunding success. Along the same line, Cumming *et al.* (2019b) highlight the impact of the due diligence practice on campaign success and platform performance. Platforms implementing due diligence not only provide more services to project issuers and funders but also exhibit higher percentages of successful campaigns, increased numbers of fund contributors, and larger capital raised.

Platform governance also emerges as fundamental to platform performance. Rossi *et al.* (2019), for example, unveil that a large variety of governance mechanisms, including voting rights assignment, nominee structure, and involvement of accredited investors, significantly impact the platform's success. Specifically, the delivery of individual voting rights is associated with lower chances of success, shedding light on the nuanced interplay between governance structures and crowdfunding outcomes. The performance of ECF platforms is also connected with environmental, social, and governance (ESG) goals (Farè *et al.*, 2024b). Cumming *et al.* (2024) provide evidence that platforms with higher levels of ESG selection criteria attract more investors and thus survive longer. Moreover, governance emerges as the most influential component, signalling the paramount importance of robust governance structures in ensuring the sustainability of crowdfunding platforms. ESG criteria are more critical for platforms operating in countries with lower power distances.

In sum, the success and survival of crowdfunding platforms involve a spectrum of factors, ranging from post-campaign services and financial literacy at the country level to corporate governance mechanisms, due diligence practices, and the integration of ESG goals.

11.5. Initial Coin Offerings

Along with ECF, ICOs are the major alternative financing channel that have profoundly changed the entrepreneurial finance system. ICOs have emerged as a transformative mechanism for entrepreneurial ventures to raise capital by selling tokens to a crowd of investors using distributed ledger technologies, such as blockchain technology (Bongini *et al.*, 2025; Fisch, 2019; Huang *et al.*, 2020; Lo Monaco *et al.*, 2025). The remarkable ascent (followed by a partial downturn) of ICOs, marked by a global volume that surged from $7 billion in 2017 to $20 billion in 2018 (PWC, 2020) and subsequently declined to $3 billion in 2019 (Haffke and Fromberger, 2020), has unequivocally demonstrated the potential for a comprehensive digitisation of not only funding but also developing a company in a decentralised setting. Through ICOs, entrepreneurs have successfully overcome conventional constraints by bypassing intermediaries and regulators and directly engaging with individual investors. This phenomenon has prompted an enquiry into the extent to which ICOs are eradicating the boundaries of sovereign regulations. On the one hand, the decentralised nature of blockchain-based tokens appears to be incongruent with the regulations of any particular country. On the other, the country of investors may assert the right to impose constraints on investors within its jurisdiction. Despite its short history, there have been dramatic changes and shifts in the number of ICOs, the amount of money raised, the geographic distribution of ICOs, and their regulation (Bellavitis *et al.*, 2021).

At the macro-level, Huang *et al.* (2020) investigate the global landscape of ICOs, shedding light on the factors influencing their prevalence across countries. Their study reveals a correlation between the frequency of ICOs and the presence of developed financial systems, public equity markets, and advanced digital technologies. The availability of investment-based crowdfunding platforms is also positively associated with the emergence of ICOs, while debt and private equity markets do not provide similar effects. Additionally, countries with ICO-friendly regulations have more ICOs, whereas tax regimes are not clearly related to ICOs. The relationship between ICOs and regulation is also the subject of enquiry by Bellavitis *et al.* (2021). Drawing on institutional theory, they show that regulatory spillovers (i.e. when the regulation in one country affects either the expected regulatory approach or entrepreneurial finance markets in other countries) have both short- and long-term effects on the number and quality of ICOs. Specifically, a regulatory ban on ICOs in one country causes a short-term increase in the number of low-rated ICOs in other countries and a long-term drop in the number of ICOs, especially low-rated ones, which increases the average ICO rating. A restrictive regulation triggers a process of increased market selection. Masiak *et al.* (2020) investigate the market cycles of ICOs, showing that they exist and that shocks to the growth rates of ICO volumes are persistent. Additionally, shocks in cryptocurrency returns have a substantial and positive effect on ICO volumes. In contrast, the volatility of cryptocurrency returns does not significantly affect ICO volumes.

At the micro-level, Fisch (2019) offers a pioneering investigation of the dynamic of ICOs, assessing the determinants of the amount raised through this novel means of financing. Focusing on the role of signalling ventures' technological capabilities in ICOs, the study documents that technical white papers and high-quality source codes increase the amount raised, while patents are not associated with increased amounts of funding. Following these findings, Thewissen *et al.* (2022) unpack the black box of ICO white papers to analyse their information value to investors. Using a sentence-based topic modelling algorithm, they show that the algorithm produces a semantically meaningful set of topics, which significantly improves the model performance in identifying successful projects, and that the most value-relevant topics are concerned with the technical features of the ICO. Credibility-enhancing mechanisms, such as regulations and ICO analysts, reinforce the information value of ICO white papers. However, the informativeness of white papers substantially diminishes after listing the token. Philippi *et al.* (2021) corroborate the evidence that vehicles for technological capabilities determine the fundraising success of ICOs, indicating that start-ups raise funds more successfully when they publish their source code.

Giudici and Adhami (2019) study the relationship between governance issues and the fundraising success of ICOs, examining the governance signals of ICO-backed projects, such as token rights, institutional setting, and team quality. They document that the project team and advisory committee size are positively and significantly correlated with the ICOs' success and that past managerial experience is a valuable asset for contributors, as well as a credible governance signal. Related to governance issues, Mansouri and Momtaz (2022) show that ESG goals increase start-ups' funding amount through ICOs. Along with governance, ownership can also shape ICO success. This finding is consistent with the evidence from ECF markets that a sustainable orientation matters in digital finance markets (Vismara, 2019). More broadly, Billio *et al.* (2024) consider the relationship between digital and sustainable finance.

Huang *et al.* (2022) introduce a psychological dimension to ICOs. Using an experimental approach involving the assessment of management team confidence based on participants' appraisal of images, the study establishes a positive association between management confidence and the amount of capital raised. Colombo *et al.* (2022) apply insights from research in social psychology and labour economics to the domain of entrepreneurial finance and investigate how the facial attractiveness of founder chief executive officers influences firm valuation. They document a pronounced founder CEO beauty premium, with a positive relationship between founder CEO attractiveness and firm valuation at the ICO.

Fisch and Momtaz (2020) highlight the importance of institutional investors in the ICO context. They stress that institutional investors' superior screening (selection effect) and coaching abilities (treatment effect) enable them to partly overcome the information asymmetry of the ICO context and extract informational rents from their ICO investments. In line with this prediction, they find that institutional investor backing is indeed associated with higher post-ICO performance. Focusing on the investor side, Fisch *et al.* (2021) reveal that ICO investors are driven, in order of importance, by technological, financial, and ideological motives. They also show significant differences across motives about investors' risk perception, sources of information, and demand for strict regulation. Boreiko and Risteki (2021) provide further evidence regarding investor behaviour in ICOs, their investment patterns, and their role in the success of campaigns. They document the presence of serial investors investing in more than one campaign, who usually contribute earlier. However, serial investors are not more informed and fail to pick better-quality ICOs. Only large serial investors who invest more in campaigns that raise more funds and attract more contributors are more likely to reach their hard caps and distribute tokens that are listed on a crypto exchange.

Research has also highlighted some drawbacks of ICOs. A defining feature of ICOs is that entrepreneurs bear the full marginal investment cost but profit only partially from the marginal investment payoff. This design may exacerbate agency conflicts inherent in corporate finance and asymmetric information between entrepreneurs and investors, which can be reduced by signals of entrepreneurial quality, such as CEO loyalty (Momtaz, 2021a). In the same line, Momtaz (2021b) provides evidence of a moral hazard in signalling in ICOs, showing that token issuers systematically exaggerate information disclosed in white papers. Exaggerating entrepreneurs raise more funds in less time, suggesting investors do not see through this practice initially. This evidence suggests that the absence of institutions that verify endogenous signals may induce a moral hazard in signalling.

Although ECF and ICOs initially appear to be similar, they exhibit some differences in stakeholders, micro-structures, regulatory environments, and market development (Block *et al.*, 2021). Moreover, while ECF has experienced gradual, fast, and steady growth, ICOs have shown extraordinary growth followed by a significant contraction (Figure 11.2). The main differences between ECF and ICOs can be summarised as follows. While ECF involves the issuance of equity or equity-like securities to a crowd of investors via an online platform, ICOs involve the sale of blockchain-based tokens that can

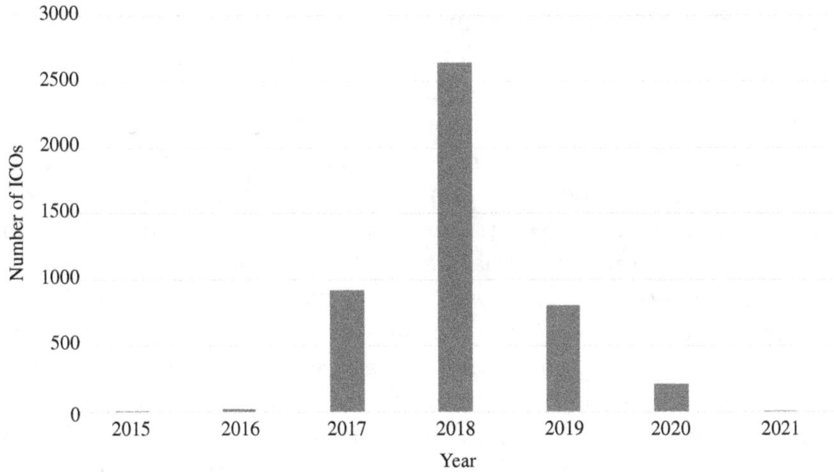

Figure 11.2. Number of ICOs per year, 2015–2021.
Source: The Token Offerings Research Database (TORD).

provide utility or financial rights to a crowd of investors without intermediaries. Regarding proponents, ECF is limited to firms, and it is mainly used by ventures operating in traditional sectors that are not overly complex or innovative. In contrast, ICOs can be initiated by firms or individuals, and they are mostly used by ventures based on blockchain technology, which is more complex and innovative. Investors in ECF are primarily motivated by financial returns. They may have some monitoring and governance rights over the funded ventures. At the same time, those in ICOs are more interested in the technological aspects of the projects and have less incentive and ability to monitor and influence the entrepreneurs. ECF platforms act as intermediaries that screen, certify, and match projects with investors, while ICO platforms are less developed and do not provide many services or guarantees. Regarding regulation, ECF is regulated by securities law in most jurisdictions, whereas ICOs face a more uncertain and heterogeneous regulatory environment depending on the nature and characteristics of the tokens issued.

11.6. Alternative and Traditional Finance: Complements or Substitutes?

The rapid diffusion of alternative sources of financing, such as ECF and ICOs, has resulted in remarkable segmentation of the entrepreneurial finance literature (e.g. Cumming and Vismara, 2017). Notably, whether these new developments complement or substitute other more traditional forms of finance is still a matter of contention. For example, how does ECF interact with other early-stage financing providers like BAs or VCs? Answering this question is not straightforward, as there may be both complementarities and frictions between ECF and BAs or VCs (Cumming *et al.*, 2018). On the one hand, BAs and VCs could potentially find it beneficial to get involved in ECF to expand their deal-sourcing methods, creating an additional revenue stream. They could be interested in forging relationships with start-ups at a more nascent stage, which could lead to more robust investments in the future. ECF can indeed be useful in gauging the market relevance and potential success of a new start-up. Additionally, ECF might have some complementarities with other sources of entrepreneurial finance. For instance, entrepreneurs can enhance their chances of successful ECF through the social capital gained from associations with government agencies and incubators, thereby creating a positive synergy between incubators, government grant programmes, and ECF (e.g. Vismara, 2016). Further evidence suggesting the existence of complementarities is that successful ECF campaigns also have a higher chance of securing VC funding in the future and that VC subsequent funding is more likely with ECF backing than with BA backing (Signori and Vismara, 2018). Signori and Vismara (2018) reveal that a non-negligible proportion of their sample of successfully funded initial ECF offerings pursued one or more equity offerings in the form of private equity and that companies initially backed by qualified investors have better chances of survival.

On the other hand, there exists some tension between ECF, BAs, and VCs investment, evoking a substitution effect between ECF and more traditional forms of financing. For example, ECF is often used as a 'last resort' by ventures that are unable to raise bank financing or by lower-quality ventures that do not have the chance to secure alternative funding (e.g. Blaseg *et al.*, 2021; Walthoff-Borm *et al.*, 2018). Additionally, sophisticated investors should do better in performing due diligence and negotiating investor protection compared to the crowd. A further element of friction is that the involvement of BA investor syndicates in online crowdfunding platforms tends to compromise the initial aims of crowdfunding markets, as these angel groups utilise unique investment strategies. As such, while crowdfunding is meant to democratise funding access for entrepreneurs, when online BAs investor syndicates are involved, the focus tends to shift from crowdfunding the entrepreneurs to primarily supporting the main investors in these angel syndicates, as the crowd often prefers to back esteemed lead investors. As it emerges from the literature, the interplay of new digital finance developments and more traditional forms is still highly debated, and it represents an intriguing avenue for future research. Notably, scholars could investigate whether there has been a rise or decline in collaborations with traditional finance as the digital finance industry matures.

11.7. The Financing of AI-Based Companies

AI is among the most significant transformations of the digital era, quickly becoming 'a key driver of the Fourth Industrial Revolution'

(World Economic Forum, 2021, p. 54). AI has emerged as one of the most promising and disruptive general purpose technologies (GPTs), with the potential to change every aspect of our lives and spur economic growth (Acemoglu and Restrepo, 2018; Aghion *et al.*, 2018; Cockburn *et al.*, 2018; Trajtenberg, 2018). As technological change is a key driver of investment opportunities (Romer, 1990; Aghion and Howitt, 1992), AI could reshape the landscape of finance in unprecedented ways (e.g. Babina *et al.*, 2024; Grennan and Michaely, 2020; Gofman and Jin, 2024). Integrating AI technologies enhances decision-making processes, risk assessment, and overall efficiency within financial systems. In entrepreneurial finance, AI algorithms can be employed for market analysis, providing entrepreneurs and investors with valuable insights into investment opportunities and potential risks. Moreover, AI-driven tools can revolutionise the underwriting process by automating the evaluation of creditworthiness and streamlining lending decisions. This not only expedites the financing process for entrepreneurs but also ensures a more data-driven and granular approach to risk assessment. Additionally, AI is contributing to the development of innovative financial products and services, such as robo-advisors, which offer automated investment advice based on sophisticated algorithms. As AI continues to evolve, its role in entrepreneurial finance is likely to expand further.

AI is likely to strongly influence entrepreneurial finance, if anything, for two main reasons. First, the number of AI-based companies has dramatically increased over the recent years, as has the number of firms investing in AI (Babina *et al.*, 2024). As most of the new AI-based ventures are start-ups that need early-stage investment to finance their projects, AI-based ventures have attracted and will attract a considerable amount of public and private funding. According to the AI Index 2023 Annual Report (Maslej *et al.*, 2023), as depicted in Figures 11.3(a) and 11.3(b), private investment in global AI-based start-ups has increased over the past decade, reaching a record in 2021, especially in the US. While investment activity has decreased since 2021, it is still 18 times higher than it was in 2013. A similar trend is depicted in Figure 11.4(a), illustrating that the number of newly funded AI-based companies worldwide increased from 495 in 2013 to 3,538 in 2022. The US continues to outpace the EU, the UK, and China (Figure 11.4(b)). However, the

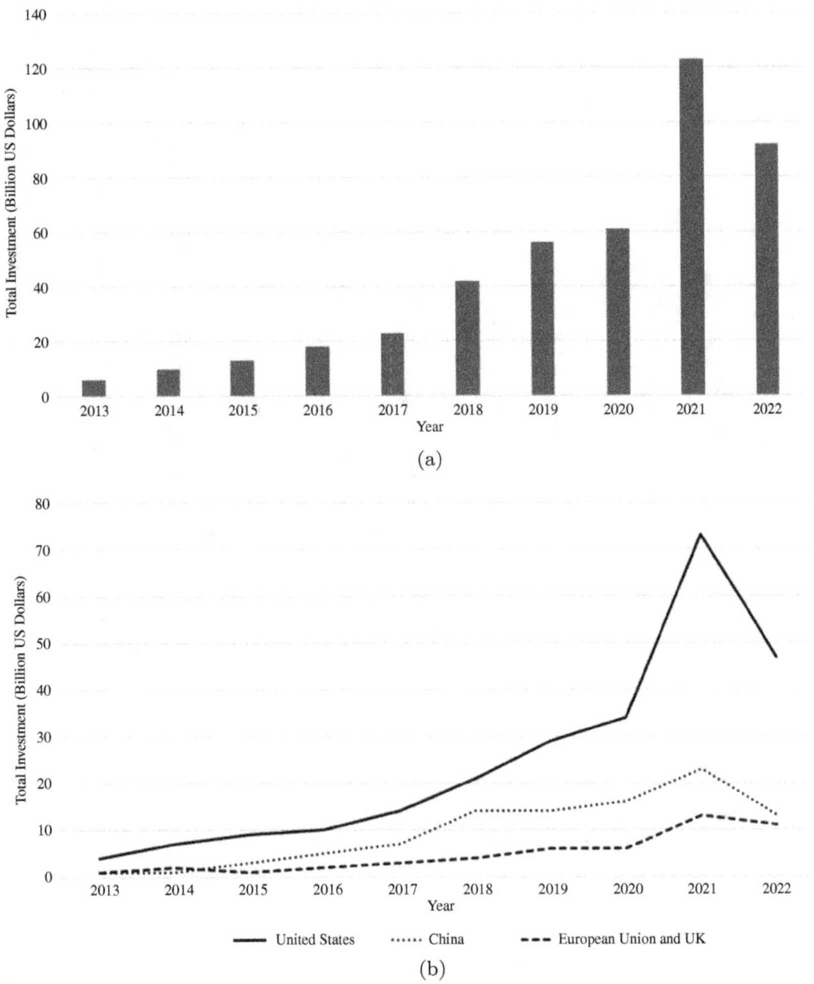

Figure 11.3. (a) Global private investment in AI start-ups. (b) Private investment in AI start-ups by geographic region.
Source: (a) Stanford University AI Index Report (2023); (b) Stanford University AI Index Report (2023).

growth rates of the different regions are relatively similar. Many factors can explain the US leadership in AI financing, such as the economic, financial, and economic development. Gofman and Jin (2024) introduce a further dimension by revealing that academic knowledge of AI is an important factor in start-ups' successful fundraising, as

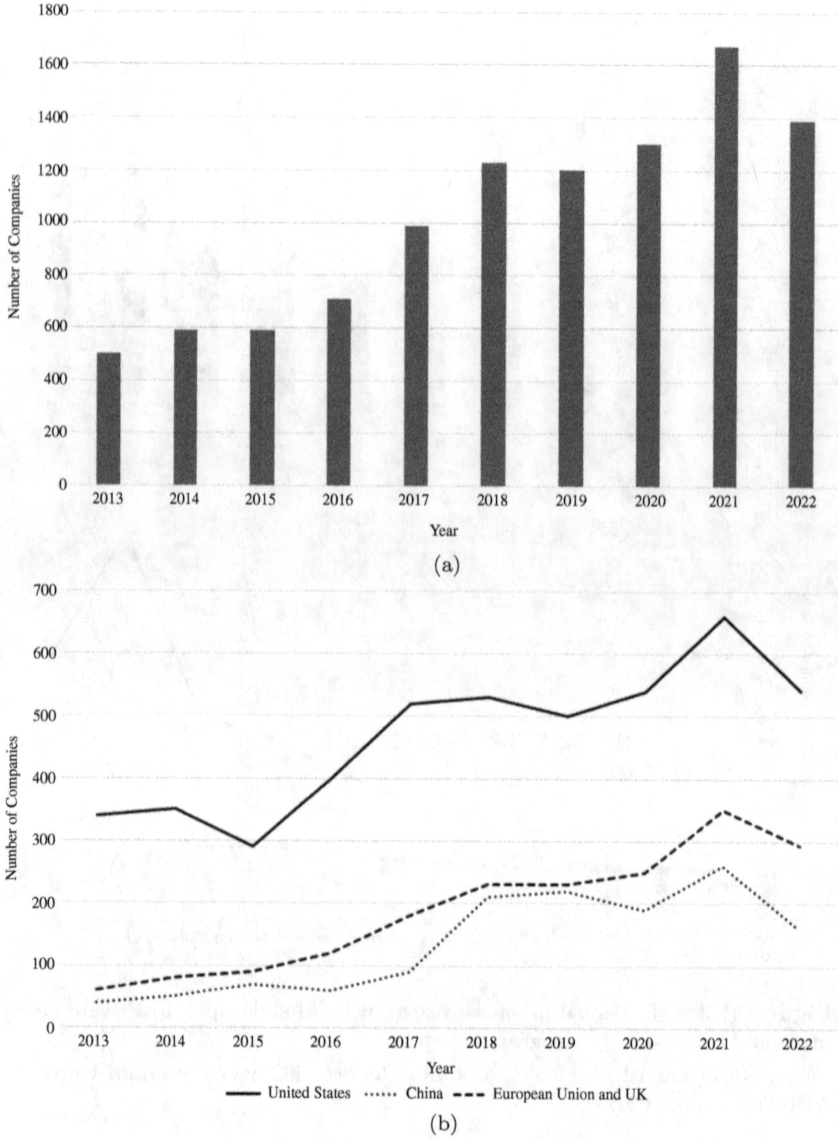

Figure 11.4. (a) Global newly funded AI companies. (b) Newly funded AI companies by geographic region.
Source: (a) Stanford University AI Index Report (2023); (b) Stanford University AI Index Report (2023).

the funders' formal education is positively associated with the funding they receive. The US leadership in academic AI expertise can thus explain the larger amount of AI investments and newly funded companies.

The OECD AI observatory provides an interesting comparison of VC investments in AI-based start-ups. Figure 11.5 illustrates a notable increment in VC funds flowing to US start-ups, growing from \$33.8 billion in 2018 to \$114.4 billion in 2021, before taking a year break in 2022 with \$57.2 billion and then rising back to \$67.3 billion in 2023. VC investments in the EU start-ups increased as well, going from \$2.2 billion in 2018 to \$4.3 billion in 2020, \$13.2 billion in 2021, and \$15.7 billion in 2022, before decreasing to \$6.1 billion in 2023. However, the volume of VC investments in AI-based start-ups in the EU is still far from that in the US, and the gap has significantly increased. Conversely, the EU has closed the gap with China, where VC investments decreased from \$32.7 billion in 2018 (very close to the US) to \$14.9 billion in 2023, after reaching a peak of \$49.2 billion in 2021. Interestingly, the volume of VC investments in the UK was equal to that of the entire EU until 2020, when the EU began to outpace the UK.

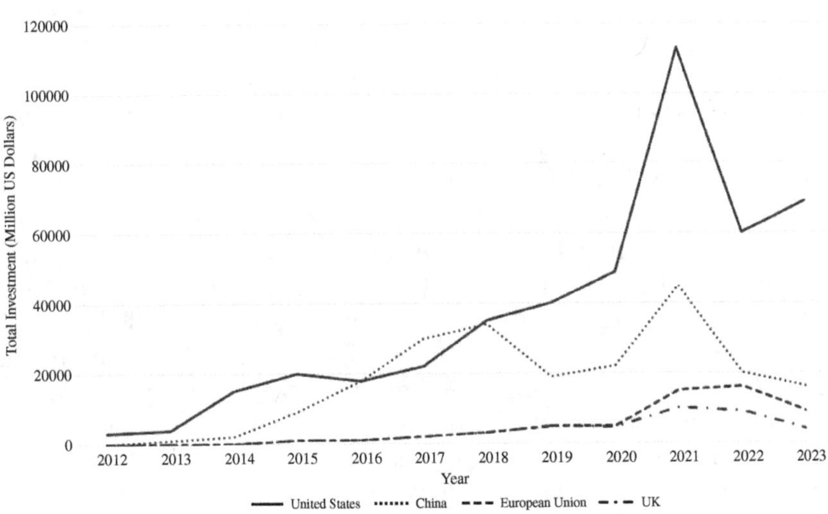

Figure 11.5. Venture capital investments in AI-based start-ups by geographic region.
Source: OECD.

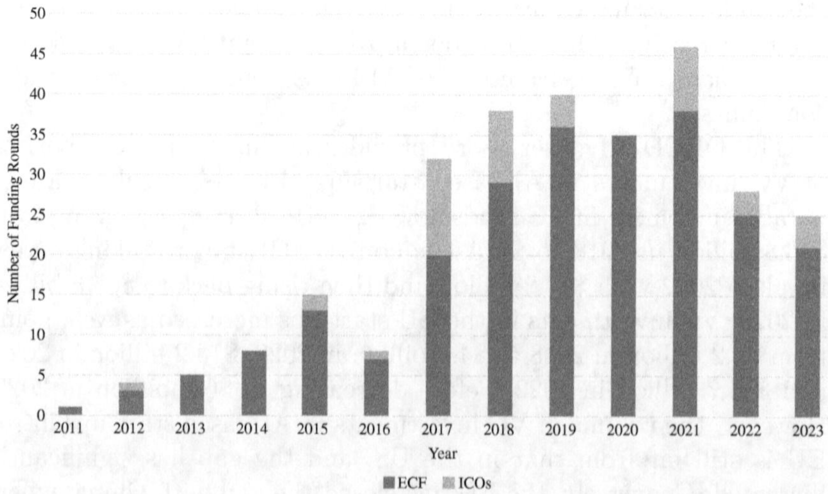

Figure 11.6. Number of ECF and ICO funding rounds of AI companies per year, 2011–2023.
Source: Crunchbase.

AI-based companies also raise capital through ECF and ICOs. As of 31 December 2023, Crunchbase registered 240 funding rounds of ECF and 44 ICOs of AI-based companies. Figure 11.6 shows the number of funding rounds in ECF or ICOs from 2011 to 2023, documenting a remarkable increase, particularly after 2016. The slowdown in the last two years might be due to the fact that Crunchbase collects some of the information with a time lag (Haddad and Hornuf, 2019). ECF, especially, has become a valid source of financing for AI-based companies. Interestingly, while Europe lags behind in the amount of private investment (Figure 11.3(b)) and the number of newly funded AI-based start-ups (Figure 11.4(b)), it takes the lead in the number of AI-based companies funded through ECF or ICOs, counting 135 rounds (Figure 11.7). Compared to the US, Europe has a less developed equity market. Thus, this evidence might evoke a negative relationship between the financing for AI-based start-ups through digital finance and the development of the traditional equity market. We delve deeper into this intuition by correlating at the geographic regional level the number of ECF and ICO rounds with the market capitalisation of domestic companies as a measure of equity market development. We found a large and statistically significant negative correlation coefficient $(-0.58, p < 0,01)$, suggesting that AI-based start-ups tend to use more digital finance

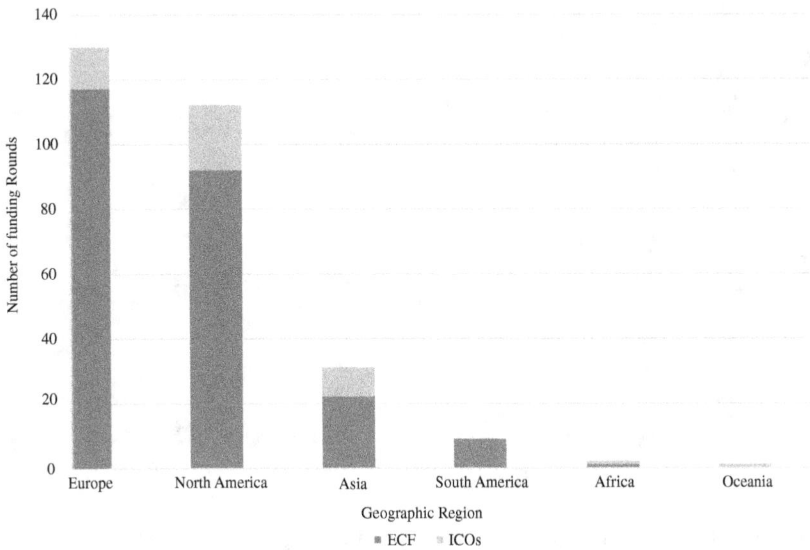

Figure 11.7. Number of ECF and ICO funding rounds of AI companies by geographic region.
Source: Crunchbase.

to compensate for the lack of a sound traditional equity market. Figure 11.8, reporting the top 10 countries in terms of rounds, surprisingly shows Spain and Italy at third and fourth places, following the US and the UK. London is by far the city with the largest number of rounds, with more than 50 ECF or ICO financing deals, followed by San Francisco and Boston (Figure 11.9). The presence of Barcelona and Madrid among the top 10 cities confirms the vibrant activity of Spain.

The second reason why AI is likely to exert a stronger influence on entrepreneurial finance is that AI tools can change the functioning of existing forms of financing or introduce new ones. Ingenious players have already started using AI to provide tailored management services and advanced trading tools in areas previously simply nonexistent, such as, for instance, bond trading. As of 31 March 2025, Futurepedia, an online platform registering AI tools, counted over 2,318 AI tools classified into 10 categories, ranging from productivity tools (e.g. website builders, marketing, finance, project management, social media) to text, image, video, and code generators. All these tools are potentially available for entrepreneurs, investors, and financial service providers. For instance, entrepreneurs might adopt AI to design a campaign to improve attractiveness and promotion.

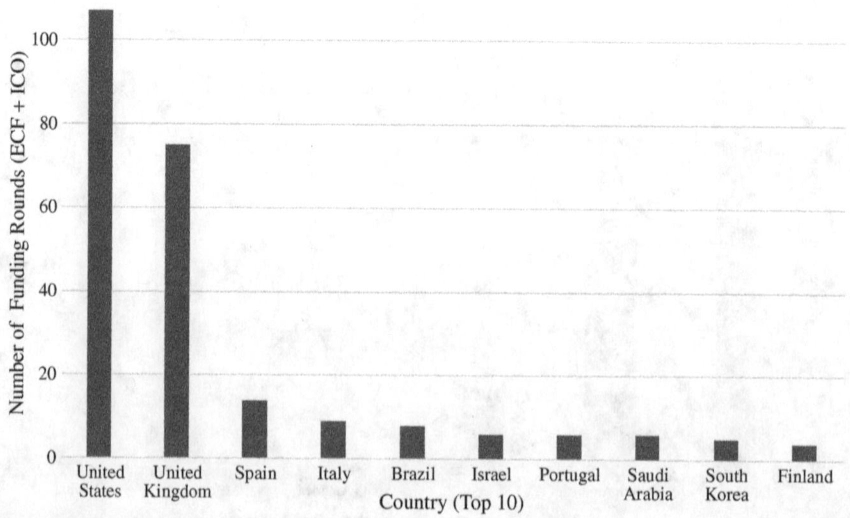

Figure 11.8. Number of ECF and ICO funding rounds of AI companies by country (top 10).
Source: Crunchbase.

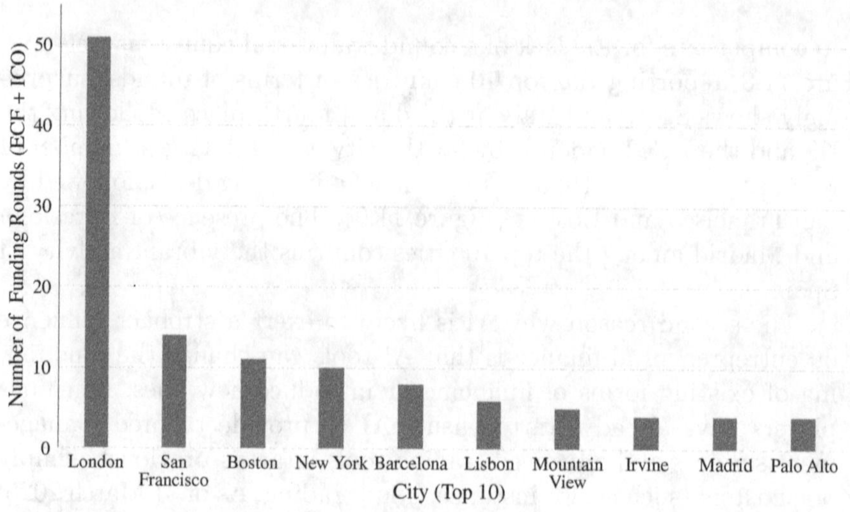

Figure 11.9. Number of ECF and ICO funding rounds of AI companies by city (top 10).
Source: Crunchbase.

Matthews *et al.* (2024) deploy a randomised experiment that uses AI to manipulate founder age in fundraising appeals, revealing that entrepreneurs benefit from appearing older (but not too much) when seeking funding. Investors may take advantage of the greater amount of information the AI can provide to reduce information asymmetries, thus reducing uncertainty and risks in their investment decisions. By processing a large amount of data faster, AI can also benefit financial service providers, particularly fintech platforms, in their due diligence and screening process.

11.7.1. *Generative AI and finance*

Among the different types of AI, GenAI is a subset that can create new content in response to prompts based on the data it has been trained on. It can generate text, images, audio, code, and other media types, often with human-like quality and creativity. GenAI has attracted considerable attention in recent years, especially with the development of large language models (LLMs) such as ChatGPT, Gemini, and Claude, which can engage in natural language processing (NLP) tasks such as conversation, summarisation, translation, and writing. GenAI has also been used for visual and audio synthesis, such as creating realistic images, videos, and speech. The use of GenAI in finance is still at an early stage, and we need to further understand the nature of the relationship. To date, there is a growing recognition that GenAI offers various opportunities for efficiency, productivity, and innovation (OECD, 2023). GenAI can be used for information management, data analysis, reporting, code generation, financial research, customer support, marketing, expense management, and financial advice. It can also support sustainable finance, ESG investing by providing real-time assessments and insights.

However, the use of GenAI in finance also entails significant risks and challenges that need to be addressed by policymakers and regulators (OECD, 2023). Some of these risks are common to other forms of AI, such as bias, discrimination, lack of explainability, data quality, privacy, security, model robustness, resilience, and reliability. GenAI also poses specific risks related to the generation of false, deceptive, or misleading content, which can undermine the credibility and trustworthiness of financial market participants and potentially harm consumers and investors. Moreover, GenAI can amplify existing risks in financial markets, such as market manipulation, cyberattacks, fraud, financial stability, competition, and concentration. To mitigate these risks and foster the safe and responsible adoption of GenAI in finance, policymakers may need to consider several actions, such as strengthening data governance practices, encouraging efforts to improve the levels of explainability of GenAI models, fostering transparency and disclosure requirements, strengthening model governance, and promoting accountability mechanisms as well as international multi-disciplinary and multi-stakeholder collaboration.

11.8. Directions for Future Research

The dynamic evolution of entrepreneurial finance opens fascinating avenues for future studies, with numerous intriguing issues yet to be fully grasped. We propose in Table 11.1 a selection of research areas and related questions that we believe could enrich our knowledge on raising financing in the era of digitalisation and AI.

11.9. Conclusions

This chapter delves into the latest evolution of entrepreneurial finance amidst the digital transformation and the breakthrough of AI. We analyse the main findings that academic research has highlighted about the rise of fintech, its interplay with traditional finance providers, and two major innovative channels that entrepreneurs have been recently deploying to raise capital: ECF and ICOs. We provide insights into the financing of AI-based companies, showing that AI-based start-ups are attracting an increasing volume of private funding and using ECF and ICOs to raise capital. Our findings suggest that digital finance provides a valuable source of financing for AI-based start-ups, especially where the traditional equity market is less developed. For instance, while the US leads the ranking of private and VC investments in AI-based companies., the European Union has the largest number of ECF and ICO rounds. Additionally, we found a negative correlation between access to digital finance and equity market development at the geographic regional level. Alternative equity financing channels seem to be more relevant for AI-based ventures when traditional investment sources such as VC and private equity

Table 11.1. Directions for future research.

Research areas	Research questions
New developments of entrepreneurial finance	• How is entrepreneurial finance evolving around the world? Are there regional differences in the way new financing providers like fintech ventures develop and grow? • How do different forms of fintech financing (e.g. crowdfunding, ICOs, peer-to-peer lending, robo-advisors) interact with each other? • How do human capital creators like universities and incubators affect the diffusion of digital finance?
Digital versus traditional finance	• As digital finance matures, have collaborations and interactions with traditional forms of financing increased or decreased? • Will AI make digital and traditional finance more complementary or substitutive? • Which factors could promote a convergence between digital and traditional finance?
AI and finance	• What are the main advantages and risks of AI adoption in raising financing? • Will AI help or hurt the competitive position of the different forms of financing? • How do AI start-ups make use of alternative and traditional equity financing channels? Are they complements or substitutes?
GenAI and fundraising	• What is the nature of the relationship between GenAI and finance? What are the potential intersections? • How can firms adoption of GenAI tools transform their fundraising outcomes? • How do human capital and GenAI interact in firms financing practices?

are less diffused. We acknowledge that this conjecture needs to be subjected to more rigorous empirical scrutiny, which would represent an intriguing avenue for future research. We document that the interplay between entrepreneurial finance, fintech, and AI presents a multifaceted and rapidly evolving landscape marked by innovation, disruption, and interactions between the traditional and non-traditional finance industries. We encourage researchers to further navigate through the complexities of this landscape, with particular attention to understanding how AI adoption will shape the future of finance.

References

Acemoglu, D. and Restrepo, P. (2018). Artificial intelligence, automation, and work. In *The Economics of Artificial Intelligence: An Agenda* (pp. 197–236). University of Chicago Press.

Aghion, P., Benjamin J., and Charles J. (2018). Artificial intelligence and economic growth. In *The Economics of Artificial Intelligence: An Agenda* (pp. 237–282). University of Chicago Press.

Aghion, P. and Howitt, P. (1992). A model of growth through creative destruction. *Econometrica*, 60, 323–351.

Ahlers, G. K., Cumming, D., Günther, C., and Schweizer, D. (2015). Signaling in equity crowdfunding. *Entrepreneurship Theory and Practice*, 39(4), 955–980.

Ahlstrom, D., Cumming, D. J., and Vismara, S. (2017). Corporate governance implications of new methods of entrepreneurial firm formation. *Corporate Governance: An International Review*, 25(1), 41–57.

Allen, F., Gu, X., and Jagtiani, J. (2021). A survey of fintech research and policy discussion. *Review of Corporate Finance*, 1(3-4), 259–339.

Anglin, A. H., Short, J. C., Drover, W., Stevenson, R. M., McKenny, A. F., and Allison, T. H. (2018). The power of positivity? The influence of positive psychological capital language on crowdfunding performance. *Journal of Business Venturing*, 33(4), 470–492.

Babina, T., Fedyk, A., He, A., and Hodson, J. (2024). Artificial intelligence, firm growth, and product innovation. *Journal of Financial Economics*, 151, 103745.

Bellavitis, C., Fisch, C., and Wiklund, J. (2021). A comprehensive review of the global development of initial coin offerings (ICOs) and their regulation. *Journal of Business Venturing Insights*, 15, e00213.

Billio, M., Murgia, M., and Vismara, S. (2024). Sustainable and climate finance: An integrative framework from corporates to markets and society. *Review of Corporate Finance*, 4(1-2), 1–16.

Blaseg, D., Cumming, D., and Koetter, M. (2021). Equity crowdfunding: High-quality or low-quality entrepreneurs? *Entrepreneurship Theory and Practice*, 45(3), 505–530.

Block, J. H., Colombo, M. G., Cumming, D. J., and Vismara, S. (2018). New players in entrepreneurial finance and why they are there. *Small Business Economics*, 50, 239–250.

Block, J. H., Groh, A., Hornuf, L., Vanacker, T., and Vismara, S. (2021). The entrepreneurial finance markets of the future: A comparison of crowdfunding and initial coin offerings. *Small Business Economics*, 57(2), 865–882.

Bollaert, H., Lopez-de-Silanes, F., and Schwienbacher, A. (2021). Fintech and access to finance. *Journal of Corporate Finance*, 68, 101941.

Bongini, P. A., Mattassoglio, F., Pedrazzoli, A., and Vismara, S. (2025). Crypto ecosystem: Navigating the past, present, and future of decentralized finance. *The Journal of Technology Transfer*, 1–22.

Boreiko, D. and Risteski, D. (2021). Serial and large investors in initial coin offerings. *Small Business Economics*, 57, 1053–1071.

Boudreau, K. J. and Hagiu, A. (2009). Platform rules: Multi-sided platforms as regulators. In A. Gawer (Ed.), *Platforms, Markets and Innovation*, 1, 163–191. Cheltenham, UK: *Edward Elgar Publishing*.

Browne, O., Cumming, D., Hutchinson, M. C., Kirshner, S. N., and O'Reilly, P. (2024). Why avoid participating in an accelerator? Countersignalling by high-quality FinTech ventures. *British Journal of Management*, 35, 1822–1842.

Butticè, V. and Vismara, S. (2022). Inclusive digital finance: The industry of equity crowdfunding. *The Journal of Technology Transfer*, 47(4), 1224–1241.

Cennamo, C. and Santaló, J. (2019). Generativity tension and value creation in platform ecosystems. *Organization Science*, 30(3), 617–641.

Chen, L., Tong, T. W., Tang, S., and Han, N. (2022). Governance and design of digital platforms: A review and future research directions on a meta-organization. *Journal of Management*, 48(1), 147–184.

Chen, M. A., Wu, Q., and Yang, B. (2019). How valuable is FinTech innovation? *The Review of Financial Studies*, 32(5), 2062–2106.

Chen, Y., Richter, J. I., and Patel, P. C. (2021). Decentralized governance of digital platforms. *Journal of Management*, 47(5), 1305–1337.

Coakley, J. and Lazos, A. (2021). New developments in equity crowdfunding: A review. *Review of Corporate Finance*, 1(3-4), 341–405.

Cockburn, I. M., Henderson, R., and Stern, S. (2018). The impact of artificial intelligence on innovation: An exploratory analysis. In *The Economics of Artificial Intelligence: An Agenda* (pp. 115–146). *University of Chicago Press.*

Colombo, M. G., Fisch, C., Momtaz, P. P., and Vismara, S. (2022). The CEO beauty premium: Founder CEO attractiveness and firm valuation in initial coin offerings. *Strategic Entrepreneurship Journal*, 16(3),
491–521.

Cong, L. W. and He, Z. (2019). Blockchain disruption and smart contracts. *The Review of Financial Studies*, 32(5), 1754–1797.

Cumming, D., Johan, S., and Reardon, R. (2023). Global fintech trends and their impact on international business: A review. *Multinational Business Review*, 31(3), 413–436.

Cumming, D. J., Johan, S., and Reardon, R. S. (2025). Institutional quality and success in US equity crowdfunding. *Research Policy*, 54(1), 105114.

Cumming, D., Johan, S., and Zhang, Y. (2018). Public policy towards entrepreneurial finance: Spillovers and the scale-up gap. *Oxford Review of Economic Policy*, 34(4), 652–675.

Cumming, D., Johan, S., and Zhang, Y. (2019a). The role of due diligence in crowdfunding platforms. *Journal of Banking & Finance*, 108, 105661.

Cumming, D., Johan, S., and Zhang, Y. (2019b). The role of due diligence in crowdfunding platforms. *Journal of Banking & Finance*, 108, 105661.

Cumming, D., Meoli, M., and Vismara, S. (2021). Does equity crowdfunding democratize entrepreneurial finance? *Small Business Economics*, 56, 533–552.

Cumming, D., Meoli, M., Rossi, A., and Vismara, S. (2024). ESG and crowdfunding platforms. *Journal of Business Venturing*, 39(1), 106362.

Cumming, D. and Vismara, S. (2017). De-segmenting research in entrepreneurial finance. *Venture Capital*, 19(1-2), 17–27.

Cummings, M. E., Rawhouser, H., Vismara, S., and Hamilton, E. L. (2020). An equity crowdfunding research agenda: Evidence from stakeholder participation in the rulemaking process. *Small Business Economics*, 54, 907–932.

Dushnitsky, G., Guerini, M., Piva, E., and Rossi-Lamastra, C. (2016). Crowdfunding in Europe: Determinants of platform creation across countries. *California Management Review*, 58(2), 44–71.

D'Acunto, F., Prabhala, N., and Rossi, A. G. (2019). The promises and pitfalls of robo-advising. *The Review of Financial Studies*, 32(5), 1983–2020.

Erel, I. and Liebersohn, J. (2022). Can FinTech reduce disparities in access to finance? Evidence from the Paycheck Protection Program. *Journal of Financial Economics*, 146(1), 90–118.

Farè, L. (2022). Exploring the contribution of micro firms to innovation: Does competition matter? *Small Business Economics*, 59(3), 1081–1113.

Farè, L., Meoli, M., and Vismara, S. (2024a). STEM and new fintech ventures. *The European Journal of Finance*, 1–17.

Farè, L., Meoli, M., and Vismara, S. (2024b). Sustainable crowdfunding and cultural contexts: Evidence from a longitudinal multi-country analysis. *Finance Research Letters*, 70, 106345.

Farè, L. and Vismara, S. (2025). Internationalization of Equity Crowdfunding Platforms. *The British Accounting Review*, 101627.

Fisch, C. (2019). Initial coin offerings (ICOs) to finance new ventures. *Journal of Business Venturing*, 34(1), 1–22.

Fisch, C., Masiak, C., Vismara, S., and Block, J. (2021). Motives and profiles of ICO investors. *Journal of Business Research*, 125, 564–576.

Fisch, C. and Momtaz, P. P. (2020). Institutional investors and post-ICO performance: An empirical analysis of investor returns in initial coin offerings (ICOs). *Journal of Corporate Finance*, 64, 101679.

Foss, N. J., Klein, P. G., Lien, L. B., Zellweger, T., and Zenger, T. (2023). Ownership competence: The enabling and constraining role of institutions. *Strategic Management Journal*, 44(8), 1955–1964.

Gawer, A. (2014). Bridging differing perspectives on technological platforms: Toward an integrative framework. *Research Policy*, 43(7), 1239–1249.

Gazel, M. and Schwienbacher, A. (2021). Entrepreneurial fintech clusters. *Small Business Economics*, 57, 883–903.

Girardone, C. and Ricci, O. (2023). Emerging issues in banking. *Review of Corporate Finance*, 3(3), 245–273.

Giudici, G. and Adhami, S. (2019). The impact of governance signals on ICO fundraising success. *Journal of Industrial and Business Economics*, 46(2), 283–312.

Gofman, M. and Jin, Z. (2024). Artificial intelligence, education, and entrepreneurship. *The Journal of Finance*, 79(1), 631–667.

Grennan, J. and Michaely, R. (2020). Artificial intelligence and high-skilled work: Evidence from analysts. *Swiss Finance Institute Research Paper*, (20-84).

Guarana, C. L., Stevenson, R. M., Gish, J. J., Ryu, J. W., and Crawley, R. (2022). Owls, larks, or investment sharks? The role of circadian process in early-stage investment decisions. *Journal of Business Venturing*, 37(1), 106165.

Guenther, C., Johan, S., and Schweizer, D. (2018). Is the crowd sensitive to distance? How investment decisions differ by investor type. *Small Business Economics*, 50, 289–305.

Haddad, C. and Hornuf, L. (2019). The emergence of the global fintech market: Economic and technological determinants. *Small Business Economics*, 53(1), 81–105.

Haffke, L. and Fromberger, M. (2020). ICO market report 2019/2020 – Performance analysis of 2019's initial coin offerings. *Journal of Banking Regulation*, 21(2), 125–138.

Hornuf, L. and Schwienbacher, A. (2017). Should securities regulation promote equity crowdfunding? *Small Business Economics*, 49, 579–593.

Huang, W., Meoli, M., and Vismara, S. (2020). The geography of initial coin offerings. *Small Business Economics*, 55, 77–102.

Huang, W., Vismara, S., and Wei, X. (2022). Confidence and capital raising. *Journal of Corporate Finance*, 77, 101900.

Johan, S. and Reardon, R. S. (2024). The role of platform stakes in equity crowdfunding success. *Finance Research Letters*, 69, 106097.

Inceoglu, I., Vanacker, T., and Vismara, S. (2024). Digitalization and resource mobilization. *British Journal of Management*, 35, 567–593.

Kleinert, S. (2024). The promise of new ventures' growth ambitions in early-stage funding: On the crossroads between cheap talk and credible signals. *Entrepreneurship Theory and Practice*, 48(1), 274–309.

Kleinert, S., Bafera, J., Urbig, D., and Volkmann, C. K. (2022). Access denied: How equity crowdfunding platforms use quality signals to select new ventures. *Entrepreneurship Theory and Practice*, 46(6), 1626–1657.

Kleinert, S. and Mochkabadi, K. (2021). Gender stereotypes in equity crowdfunding: The effect of gender bias on the interpretation of quality signals. *The Journal of Technology Transfer*, 1–22.

Kolokas, D., Vanacker, T., Veredas, D., and Zahra, S. A. (2022). Venture capital, credit, and fintech start-up formation: A cross-country study. *Entrepreneurship Theory and Practice*, 46(5), 1198–1230.

Kretschmer, T., Leiponen, A., Schilling, M., and Vasudeva, G. (2022). Platform ecosystems as meta-organizations: Implications for platform strategies. *Strategic Management Journal*, 43(3), 405–424.

Krishnan, V. and Gupta, S. (2001). Appropriateness and impact of platform-based product development. *Management Science*, 47(1), 52–68.

Le Pendeven, B. and Schwienbacher, A. (2023). Equity crowdfunding: The influence of perceived innovativeness on campaign success. *British Journal of Management*, 34(1), 280–298.

Lo Monaco, V., Momtaz, P., and Vismara, S. (2025). Distributed governance and value creation in decentralized autonomous organizations: Evidence from a regression discontinuity design. *Economics Letters*, 112233.

Mansouri, S. and Momtaz, P. P. (2022). Financing sustainable entrepreneurship: ESG measurement, valuation, and performance. *Journal of Business Venturing*, 37(6), 106258.

Marin, G. and Vona, F. (2023). Finance and the reallocation of scientific, engineering, and mathematical talent. *Research Policy*, 52(5), 104757.

Masiak, C., Block, J. H., Masiak, T., Neuenkirch, M., and Pielen, K. N. (2020). Initial coin offerings (ICOs): Market cycles and relationship with bitcoin and ether. *Small Business Economics*, 55, 1113–1130.

Maslej, N., Fattorini, L., Brynjolfsson, E., Etchemendy, J., Ligett, K., Lyons, T., Manyika, J., Ngo, H., Niebles, J. C., Parli, V., Shoham,

Y., Wald, R., Clark, J., and Perrault, R. (2023). The AI Index 2023 Annual Report. AI Index Steering Committee, Institute for Human-Centered AI, Stanford University, Stanford, CA, April 2023.

Mataigne, V., Meoli, M., Vanacker, T., and Vismara, S. (2025). False signaling by platform team members and post-campaign venture outcomes: Evidence from an equity crowdfunding platform. *Journal of Business Venturing*, 40(1), 106457.

Matthews, M. J., Anglin, A. H., Drover, W., and Wolfe, M. T. (2024). Just a number? Using artificial intelligence to explore perceived founder age in entrepreneurial fundraising. *Journal of Business Venturing*, 39(1), 106361.

Maula, M. V. and Lukkarinen, A. (2022). Attention across borders: Investor attention as a driver of cross-border equity crowdfunding investments. *Strategic Entrepreneurship Journal*, 16(4), 699–734.

McIntyre, D. P. and Srinivasan, A. (2017). Networks, platforms, and strategy: Emerging views and next steps. *Strategic Management Journal*, 38(1), 141–160.

McIntyre, D., Srinivasan, A., Afuah, A., Gawer, A., and Kretschmer, T. (2021). Multisided platforms as new organizational forms. *Academy of Management Perspectives*, 35(4), 566–583.

Meoli, M., Rossi, A., and Vismara, S. (2022). Financial literacy and security-based crowdfunding. *Corporate Governance: An International Review*, 30(1), 27–54.

Meoli, M. and Vismara, S. (2021). Information manipulation in equity crowdfunding markets. *Journal of Corporate Finance*, 67, 101866.

Meoli, M. and Vismara, S. (2022). Machine-learning forecasting of successful ICOs. *Journal of Economics and Business*, 121, 106071.

Momtaz, P. P. (2021a). Initial coin offerings, asymmetric information, and loyal CEOs. *Small Business Economics*, 57(2), 975–997.

Momtaz, P. P. (2021b). Entrepreneurial finance and moral hazard: Evidence from token offerings. *Journal of Business Venturing*, 36(5), 106001.

Monaghan, S., Tippmann, E., and Coviello, N. (2020). Born digitals: Thoughts on their internationalization and a research agenda. *Journal of International Business Studies*, 51, 11–22.

OECD. (2021). Artificial Intelligence, Machine Learning and Big Data in Finance: Opportunities, Challenges and Implications for Policy Makers. Retrieved from https://www.oecd.org/finance/financial-markets/Artificial-intelligence-machine-learning-big-data-in-finance.pdf.

OECD. (2023). Generative Artificial Intelligence in Finance. Retrieved from https://www.oecd-ilibrary.org/finance-and-investment/generative-artificial-intelligence-in-finance_ac7149cc-en.

Philippi, S., Schuhmacher, M. C., and Bastian, N. (2021). Attracting investors in initial coin offerings: The relevance of specific technological capabilities for fundraising success. *Review of Corporate Finance*, 1(3-4), 455–485.

Philippon, T. (2016). The FinTech opportunity. Unpublished working paper. *National Bureau of Economic Research.*

PWC. (2020). 6th ICO/STO Report: A Strategic Perspective. Retrieved from https://www.pwc.com/ee/et/publications/pub/Strategy&_ICO_STO_Study_Version_Spring_2020.pdf.

Rawhouser, H., Vismara, S., and Kshetri, N. (2024). Blockchain and vulnerable entrepreneurial ecosystems. *Entrepreneurship & Regional Development*, 36(1-2), 10–35.

Rietveld, J., Ploog, J. N., and Nieborg, D. B. (2020). Coevolution of platform dominance and governance strategies: Effects on complementor performance outcomes. *Academy of Management Discoveries*, 6(3), 488–513.

Ritter, J., Signori, A., and Vismara, S. (2013). Economies of scope and IPO volume in Europe. In M. Levis & S. Vismara (Eds.), *Handbook of Research on IPOs* (pp. 11–34). Cheltenham, UK: *Edward Elgar.* ISBN: 978 1 78195 536 9.

Romer, P. M. (1990). Endogenous technological change. *Journal of Political Economy*, 98(5, Part 2), S71–S102.

Rossi, A., Vanacker, T. R., and Vismara, S. (2020). Equity crowdfunding: New evidence from US and UK markets. *Review of Corporate Finance*, 1(3–4), 407–453.

Rossi, A., Vanacker, T., and Vismara, S. (2023). Unsuccessful equity crowdfunding offerings and the persistence in equity fundraising of family business start-ups. *Entrepreneurship Theory and Practice*, 47(4), 1327–1355.

Rossi, A. and Vismara, S. (2018). What do crowdfunding platforms do? A comparison between investment-based platforms in Europe. *Eurasian Business Review*, 8, 93–118.

Rossi, A., Vismara, S., and Meoli, M. (2019). Voting rights delivery in investment-based crowdfunding: A cross-platform analysis. *Journal of Industrial and Business Economics*, 46, 251–281.

Signori, A. and Vismara, S. (2018). Does success bring success? The post-offering lives of equity-crowdfunded firms. *Journal of Corporate Finance*, 50, 575–591.

Stevenson, R. M., Ciuchta, M. P., Letwin, C., Dinger, J. M., and Vancouver, J. B. (2019). Out of control or right on the money? Funder self-efficacy and crowd bias in equity crowdfunding. *Journal of Business Venturing*, 34(2), 348–367.

Tang, H. (2019). Peer-to-peer lenders versus banks: Substitutes or complements? *The Review of Financial Studies*, 32(5), 1900–1938.

Thewissen, J., Shrestha, P., Torsin, W., and Pastwa, A. M. (2022). Unpacking the black box of ICO white papers: A topic modeling approach. *Journal of Corporate Finance*, 75, 102225.

Trajtenberg, M. (2018). AI as the next GPT: A political-economy perspective (No. w24245). *National Bureau of Economic Research.*

Vismara, S. (2016). Equity retention and social network theory in equity crowdfunding. *Small Business Economics*, 46, 579–590.

Vismara, S. (2018). Information cascades among investors in equity crowdfunding. *Entrepreneurship Theory and Practice*, 42(3), 467–497.

Vismara, S. (2019). Sustainability in equity crowdfunding. *Technological Forecasting and Social Change*, 141, 98–106.

Vismara, S. (2022). Expanding corporate finance perspectives to equity crowdfunding. *The Journal of Technology Transfer*, 47(6), 1629–1639.

Vismara, S. and Wirtz, P. (2025). Fundraising, Governance and Environmental Ethics: Evidence from Equity Crowdfunding. *Journal of Business Ethics*, 1–25.

von Krogh, G., Roberson, Q., and Gruber, M. (2023). Recognizing and utilizing novel research opportunities with artificial intelligence. *Academy of Management Journal*, 66(2), 367–373.

Walthoff-Borm, X., Schwienbacher, A., and Vanacker, T. (2018). Equity crowdfunding: First resort or last resort? *Journal of Business Venturing*, 33(4), 513–533.

World Economic Forum. (2021). Centre for the Fourth Industrial Revolution — Annual Report 2019–2020. Retrieved from https://www3.weforum.org/docs/WEF_Annual_Report_2019_2020.pdf.

https://doi.org/10.1142/9781800617032_0012

Chapter 12

Innovative Banking and Systemic Risks: The Silicon Valley Bank Case and Entrepreneurial Finance Dynamics

Shaen Corbet[*,†] **and Charles Larkin**[‡,§,**]

[*]*DCU Business School, Dublin City University, Dublin, Ireland*
[†]*School of Accounting, Finance and Economics, University of Waikato, Hamilton, New Zealand*
[‡]*Institute for Policy Research, University of Bath, UK*
[§]*Krieger School of Arts and Sciences, Johns Hopkins University, Baltimore, MD, USA*
[**]*Trinity Business School, Trinity College Dublin, Dublin, Ireland*

12.1. Introduction

Silicon Valley Bank (SVB), established in 1983 by Bill Biggerstaff and Robert Medearis, emerged from a profound understanding of Silicon Valley's startup culture. The bank was tailored to cater to the unique financial needs of innovative startups, particularly in technology and life sciences, which traditional financial institutions often neglected. This specialisation allowed SVB to provide distinctive banking services, focusing on the future growth potential and intellectual properties of these companies rather than traditional financial metrics. The evolution of the bank into SVB Financial Group marked a strategic expansion. This transition involved diversifying its offerings beyond commercial banking to become a comprehensive financial services provider. This included acquisitions and an expansion into private banking and wealth management, targeting high-net-worth individuals and private equity (PE) firms (Nguyen, 2024). SVB Financial Group's growth paralleled the technology sector's expansion, positioning the bank as a preferred choice for tech startups and venture capital (VC) firms. This evolution reflected its unique business philosophy, centralised in agility, risk awareness, and a deep connection with the startup ecosystem (Corbet and Larkin, 2023).

This chapter examines SVB's growth toward becoming a cornerstone in entrepreneurial finance, its subsequent collapse, and the resultant ramifications for the tech sector and associated regulatory frameworks. We assess the immediate and longer-term impacts of SVB's failure on the startup ecosystem, VC, and the banking industry, identifying several vulnerabilities within niche banking practices and proposing recommendations for strengthening financial oversight, diversification in risk management, and the strategic adaptation of banks serving specialised markets. SVB's origins played a significant role in shaping its business philosophy and operations. The bank's services and products, such as venture debt, were tailored to the unique cycle and needs of startups and venture capitalists, reflecting an in-depth understanding of the tech sector's trends and dynamics. This alignment of services with the needs of the tech sector not only drove SVB's growth but also positioned it as a pivotal player in the entrepreneurial finance landscape (Nguyen, 2024).

SVB's significance in entrepreneurial finance can be attributed to its unique approach to banking, as mentioned above. Its evaluation of creditworthiness, based on intellectual property and growth potential, provided a lifeline to many tech startups that would have otherwise struggled to secure funding through traditional means. This represents a standard feature of entrepreneurial finance, unlike corporate finance, which looks at existing firms with the primary goal of improving returns and enhancing shareholder value. The focus on the study of a startup firm's potential value is at the core of entrepreneurial finance, positioning it on par with VC. This approach enabled SVB to fill a crucial gap in the market, supporting the growth and development of numerous startups and tech companies (Leach and Melicher, 2012). The bank's close relationships with VC firms and understanding of the venture funding cycle allowed it to offer specialised banking services aligned with startup growth stages. This integration into the startup ecosystem and its tailored financial products positioned SVB as a key player in entrepreneurial finance, fostering innovation and growth within the tech sector. SVB's services were specifically designed to cater to the distinctive requirements of startups and VC firms. The bank's credit facilities, such as lines of credit, were structured to align with the funding stages of startups, providing crucial financial support during critical growth phases.

Additionally, SVB's risk management strategy, which involved engaging with startups backed by reputable VC firms, allowed it to manage risks effectively while supporting businesses with high growth potential. This strategic approach enabled SVB to develop a deep understanding of the trends and needs of the tech sector, further enhancing its role as a critical financial partner for startups and venture capitalists. However, it also increased the bank's overall risk exposure (Gompers, 2023).

The collapse of SVB, reverberated throughout the entrepreneurial ecosystem, impacting various forms of finance in nuanced ways. An understanding of these dynamics is crucial for comprehending the broader economic implications, particularly in terms of how alternative financial instruments serve as either complements to or substitutes for traditional bank financing. First, VC and PE funding, which are prevalent sources of finance for startups and growth-stage companies, often act as substitutes for traditional bank loans. In the wake of a bank's failure, as traditional lending tightens due to increased risk aversion and regulatory scrutiny, entrepreneurs and businesses may increasingly turn towards these non-bank financial entities. The lack of bank loans could lead to a surge in demand for VC and PE funding, potentially increasing the availability of capital for innovative but higher-risk ventures that banks typically avoid. Conversely, angel investments and crowdfunding platforms, which also serve the startup ecosystem, could experience mixed effects. These platforms often complement bank financing by providing seed funding that subsequent stages of bank loans can leverage. With the collapse of a significant bank like SVB, early-stage companies might struggle to secure initial funding, leading to a cascading effect that jeopardises subsequent rounds of funding, including more substantial bank loans or larger VC investments. The potential disruption during the initial funding stages could deter the overall flow of capital into new ventures, thereby stifling innovation and growth.

Additionally, the role of fintech companies, particularly those offering alternative lending solutions, must be examined. Fintech platforms can swiftly act as substitutes by filling the void left by traditional banks. These platforms often employ innovative credit models and data analytics to assess risk differently from banks, potentially making them more willing to lend during periods of financial instability. As such, the failure of a bank might accelerate the adoption and reliance on fintech solutions by entrepreneurs. Lastly, the interplay among different forms of finance in the aftermath of a bank failure could reshape the entrepreneurial landscape. Regions or sectors heavily reliant on the failed bank for financing might temporarily experience a slowdown in entrepreneurial activity. In contrast, those with more diversified financial ecosystems might experience minimal disruption. This differential impact could shift where and how new ventures are developed and funded, influencing economic recovery and growth patterns following the bank failure.

SVB's foundational philosophy and its evolution into SVB Financial Group were central to its role in entrepreneurial finance. SVB, therefore, became one of the leading lenders for the tech sector; however, its specialisation was both a unique selling point and the primary risk for the bank. In the following section, we highlight how SVB rapidly expanded between 2019 and 2021, tripling in size from $71 billion to $211 billion as the result of a rapid inflow of VC money.

12.2. The Rise of SVB

SVB was established in 1983 with a vision that diverged from traditional banking norms. The core founding principle was to serve what was then a niche market: high-tech startups and VC firms. This focus emerged from recognising the expanding tech industry's unique financial needs and potential, especially in Silicon Valley. SVB aimed to fill a significant gap in the market by providing tailored financial solutions to companies often overlooked by conventional banks due to their high risk and lack of tangible collateral. SVB's approach was characterised by a deep understanding of the technology sector's dynamics, embracing the risk and innovation inherent in its client base. This alignment with the tech ecosystem's unique demands differentiated SVB from traditional financial institutions, setting the foundation for a banking model that was both innovative and adaptive.

The early challenges faced by SVB were multifaceted, as outlined in Table 12.1. First, the bank had to establish credibility and trust in a sector that saw limited engagement from traditional financial institutions. Convincing startups and venture capitalists of the benefits of a bank tailored to their specific needs required innovative financial products and a new approach to banking relationships. Assessing the creditworthiness of startups, which typically lacked traditional financial metrics such as consistent revenue streams or collateral, presented a significant challenge. SVB had to develop novel risk assessment models capable of accurately evaluating the potential and viability of high-tech startups. This involved a deeper understanding of technology markets, the life cycle of startups, and the nature of VC funding. The bank attracted startups and venture capitalists by offering them venture debt to minimise equity dilution. SVB also specialised in managing dynamic cash flows and provided cash management and foreign exchange services to effectively navigate international markets (Hyun and Lee, 2022). Its bespoke banking solutions, including lines of credit and equipment financing, addressed the unique needs of the tech sector, enabling fast-growing companies to scale efficiently.

Since its inception, SVB had positioned itself uniquely in the banking sector by focusing on relationship-based banking, underpinned by a deep understanding of the tech industry. Unlike traditional banks, SVB's model was built around the needs and potential of high-risk, high-innovation companies. This involved offering financial services, strategic advice, networking opportunities, and industry insights. SVB's approach also entailed tailoring its financial products, such as venture debt, to suit the specific needs of startups. This venture debt allowed startups to grow while minimising equity dilution, a crucial aspect for founders and investors (Gompers, 2023; Nguyen, 2024). By focusing on these unique services, SVB became an integral part of the startup ecosystem, facilitating the growth and success of numerous high-tech companies.

Table 12.1. Key dates during the growth and collapse of Silicon Valley Bank.

Date	Event	Detail
Early 2020	Rapid Growth	SVB's deposits doubled from $62 billion in March 2020 to $124 billion in March 2021, driven by the tech boom during the COVID-19 pandemic. The bank invested these funds in long-term Treasury bonds, aiming for higher returns.
April 2022	Chief Risk Officer Steps Down	As interest rates began to rise, SVB's Chief Risk Officer stepped down, leaving a critical position unfilled during a key period of increasing interest rate risk.
End of 2022	Unrealised Losses	By the end of 2022, SVB held a $117 billion bond portfolio with over $15 billion in unrealised losses, exacerbated by the failure to hedge against rising interest rates effectively.
In early 2023	Moody's Warning	Moody's Investors Service signalled SVB was at risk of a downgrade due to significant unrealised losses, highlighting the bank's financial instability.
8 March 2023	Emergency Measures Announced	SVB announced the need to raise over $2 billion to shore up its balance sheet, revealing significant financial distress.
9 March 2023	Bank Run Begins	Influential VC firms and their portfolio companies began withdrawing their deposits *en masse*, precipitating a liquidity crisis. SVB's attempts to stabilise, including selling off investments at a loss, failed to stem the outflow.
10 March 2023	Regulatory Closure	Facing a negative cash balance and unable to meet withdrawal demands, SVB was closed by California regulators and placed under FDIC receivership, marking the largest bank failure since the 2008 financial crisis.
11 March 2023	VC Community Reaction	The VC community issued statements of support for SVB after its closure, even as the bank's failure sparked debates within the sector.
12 March 2023	Government Response	The Federal Reserve announced that all SVB depositors, including those with uninsured funds, would be fully protected to stabilise the banking sector and protect the broader economy.
13 March 2023	Acquisition of SVB UK	HSBC acquired SVB's UK arm in a last-minute deal, ensuring the safety of depositors' funds and providing some stability to the UK tech sector.

SVB implemented several key strategies for growth and diversification, crucial for its evolution and prominence in the tech sector. These strategies can be categorised into three main areas: specialisation, geographic expansion, and service diversification. SVB honed its specialisation in banking services for technology and life sciences companies, VC firms, and PE, driven by its insights into these sectors' unique needs. Recognising the global nature of the tech industry, SVB also expanded its operations beyond Silicon Valley. This included establishing branches in major tech hubs across the United States and later expanding to key international markets like Europe and Asia. This geographical diversification allowed SVB to capture a broader market and cater to the international financing needs of its clients (Nguyen, 2024).

SVB precisely identified and addressed the unique needs of the tech and startup sectors, which were markedly different from those of more established industries; however, providing such different services also introduced unique risks. An example is the previously mentioned venture debt financing, which was commonly sought by startups for substantial early-stage funding while avoiding equity dilution (Ibrahim, 2010; De Rassenfosse and Fischer, 2016). SVB offered venture debt and financing that provided necessary capital without requiring startups to raise significant equity stakes. Recognising the value of networks in the tech ecosystem, SVB facilitated connections between startups, investors, and industry experts. This networking support extended beyond mere banking services, playing a crucial role in the growth and success of startups. Further, considering the rapid and unpredictable growth trajectories often experienced by tech startups, SVB provided flexible banking solutions, including cash management services and credit facilities that could scale with the company (Morse, 2024).

This approach, essentially a debt-financed monoline banking model, was similar to the model adopted by the Irish banking sector during its long boom from the early 1990s to 2008. The dangers of this approach, evident in the nationalisation of the Anglo-Irish Bank and the Irish Nationwide Building Society – the two primary components of the Irish Bank Resolution Corporation – are often cited when applied to the property and commercial development market rather than the technology sector. More details can be found in the works of Corbet (2016), Ahuja *et al.* (2019), and Barrett *et al.* (2019).

SVB's growth and strategic alignment with the technology and startup sectors were significantly propelled by its targeted investments and acquisitions aimed at expanding its services, entering new markets, and incorporating emerging technologies. Key acquisitions, such as Boston Private Financial Holdings, enhanced its wealth management and private banking offerings, enabling SVB to cater to tech sector entrepreneurs' and investors' comprehensive financial needs (Nguyen, 2024). This created a leading client list according to *Forbes* at the time of the collapse of SVB: Circle: $3.3 Billion, Roku: $487 million, Block-Fi: $227 million, Roblox: approximately $150 million, Ginkgo Bioworks Holdings: $74 million, iRhythm Technologies: $54.5 million, Rocket Lab: $38 million, Sangamo Therapeutics: $34.4 million, LendingClub: $21 million, Payoneer Global Inc: $20 million, Protagonist Therapeutics: $13 million, Oncorus: $10 million, Eiger Biopharmaceuticals: $8.3 million, Compugen LTD, and QuantumScape Corp Tellez (2023).

SVB Capital, the bank's VC arm, managed a diverse portfolio of funds, strengthening SVB's foothold in the startup ecosystem and providing valuable market insights that informed its banking strategies and financial advisory services. Additionally, SVB's investments in fintech startups and technology initiatives highlighted its commitment to innovation. The bank's international expansion strategy supported its clients' international ventures and allowed access to emerging tech markets through acquisitions and partnerships in global tech hubs. This strategy, alongside VC activities, reinforced SVB's specialised service model for the tech and startup sectors, enhancing its service offerings and geographic reach.

Subsidiaries of SVB, namely SVB Capital and SVB Securities, played pivotal roles in the bank's ecosystem, facilitating mergers, acquisitions, and capital market transactions and in expanding its service offerings. While these entities supported SVB's growth and the startup ecosystem, they also presented strategic challenges, especially in risk management within the volatile tech sector. The Federal Reserve's investigation into SVB's collapse underlined the importance of balancing aggressive growth strategies with robust risk management, highlighting the complexity of SVB's business model in dynamic sectors. More specifically, the investigation into SVB's collapse highlighted the execution of these strategies and the importance of robust risk management. Morse (2024) puts it best:

> *The cause of SVB's collapse relates to a perfect storm of reasons: large stores of uninsured deposits, asset-liability duration mismatch, the rise in interest rates, liquidity needs of innovation economy clients, and many SVB agency and regulation governance shortfalls.*

While these strategies propelled SVB's growth and sector alignment, the investigation revealed risks tied to rapid expansion and managing a diverse investment portfolio in the volatile technology market (Morse, 2024).

Recent research has focused on the specific complexity of contagion effects stemming from the collapse. Bhagat and Laurion (2023) critique the systemic flaws in executive compensation and bank capital structures that exacerbated the failures of financial institutions, including SVB. They suggest that incentives should prioritise long-term stability over short-term gains, proposing compensation structures including restricted stock and options that vest post-retirement. Additionally, they recommend increasing the minimum equity-to-total-assets ratio to 20% to bolster financial resilience. This parallels the lessons from the 2008 financial crisis, underlining the need for comprehensive reforms in incentive systems and capital frameworks. Similarly, Corbet and Larkin (2023) examine the rapid downfall of SVB, attributing it to an erosion of investor confidence and a massive withdrawal of deposits following the announcement of substantial losses from securities sales. They emphasise the need for stricter regulatory oversight, especially for banks with significant industry exposure like SVB, and call for a reevaluation of deregulatory measures to prevent similar collapses in the future. Further research by Van Vo and Le (2023) delves into SVB's internal mismanagement and risky investment strategies, which became liabilities as interest rates rose. Aharon *et al.* (2023) and Martins (2024) explore the broader market implications of SVB's collapse, noting significant negative reactions in global equity markets and contagion effects on other U.S. banks, respectively. These studies highlight the interconnectedness and systemic risks inherent in the global financial system and stress the importance of managing information asymmetries and maintaining robust liquidity. Semeyutin *et al.* (2023) investigate the role of CEO risk culture in bank stability, advocating for textual analysis of earnings calls as early warning signs of bank distress.

Finally, Bales and Burghof (2024) focus on the role of social media in SVB's trading dynamics, finding that heightened public attention and negative sentiment on platforms such as X (formerly Twitter) significantly accelerated the bank's collapse. Collectively, these studies comprehensively analyse the factors leading to SVB's failure and offer insights into preventing similar financial crises in the future.

12.3. The Collapse of SVB

The collapse of SVB resulted from its concentrated investment strategy, sensitivity to interest rate fluctuations, and broader economic shifts, particularly within the tech and startup sectors it predominantly served. The bank's significant holdings of long-term Treasury bonds were adversely affected as interest rates rose, leading to substantial unrealised losses. This, combined with a sector-specific downturn, heightened its vulnerability to a liquidity crisis, ultimately triggering a bank run as clients rapidly withdrew their funds following the announcement of these losses. The scale of the decline is evident in the collapse of the company's share price, as presented in Figure 12.1, along with the associated elevated price volatility and liquidity, presented in Figures 12.2 and 12.3, respectively.

The Federal Reserve's investigation into SVB's collapse highlighted several critical weaknesses in the bank's risk management and governance frameworks.[1] Notably, SVB's strategy of financing long-term investments with short-term deposits, without sufficient hedging against interest rate risks, left it exposed to market volatility. The investigation also pointed to a lack of diversification, with an over-reliance on the tech sector, and identified significant gaps in stress testing, contingency planning, and the overall recognition of the risks tied to its business model and asset portfolio.[2]

Complicating SVB's stability were external economic forces and a tightening monetary policy, which exacerbated the bank's vulnerabilities. Additionally, deficiencies in oversight and shifts in governance for mid-sized banks like SVB were spotlighted, raising concerns about

[1]Provided by the Federal Reserve Board and found in https://www.federalreserve.gov/publications/files/svb-review-20230428.pdf.

[2]Review of the Federal Reserve's Supervision and Regulation of Silicon Valley Bank, Federal Reserve Board of Governors, 2023.

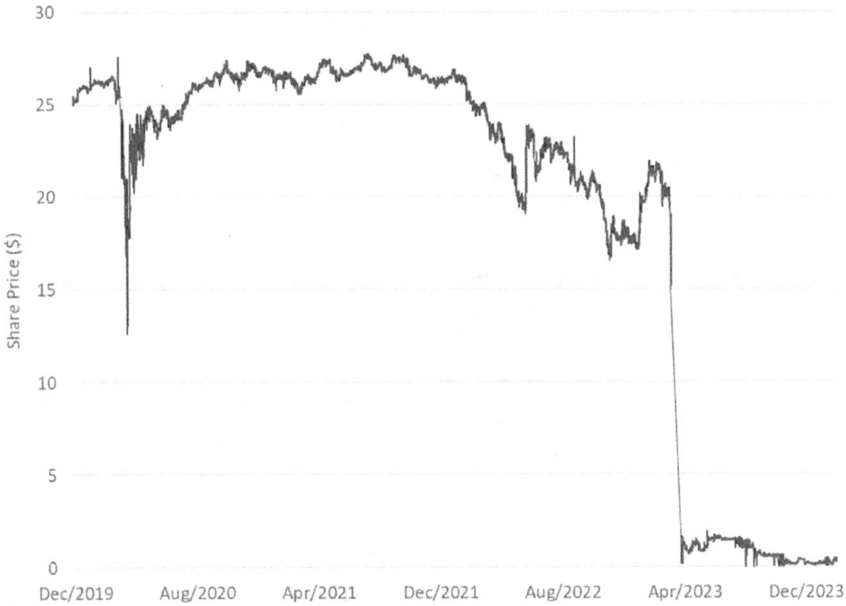

Figure 12.1. Silicon Valley Bank (SBV) share price.
Source: Data obtained from Thomson Reuters Eikon, spanning 2 December 2019 through 31 January 2024.

the adequacy of regulatory frameworks to address the unique challenges posed by banks with concentrated sector exposures.

In response to SVB's collapse, the government's intervention was swift and comprehensive, with the Federal Deposit Insurance Corporation (FDIC) taking control to protect insured deposits and announcing that all depositors would have access to their funds, including those exceeding insured limits. This move and the Federal Reserve's emergency lending programme were crucial in restoring confidence in the banking system and preventing a wider financial crisis. However, this intervention sparked discussions on moral hazards and the importance of rigorous risk management practices[3] within banks.[4]

[3]Report on the 2023 banking turmoil, Basel Committee on Banking Supervision, 2023, Bank for International Settlements.

[4]Concerns over SVB's financial health were amplified following the bank's disclosure of a substantial loss from its bond portfolio sale and plans for an equity raise. This disclosure, coupled with ineffective communication strategies and the rapid

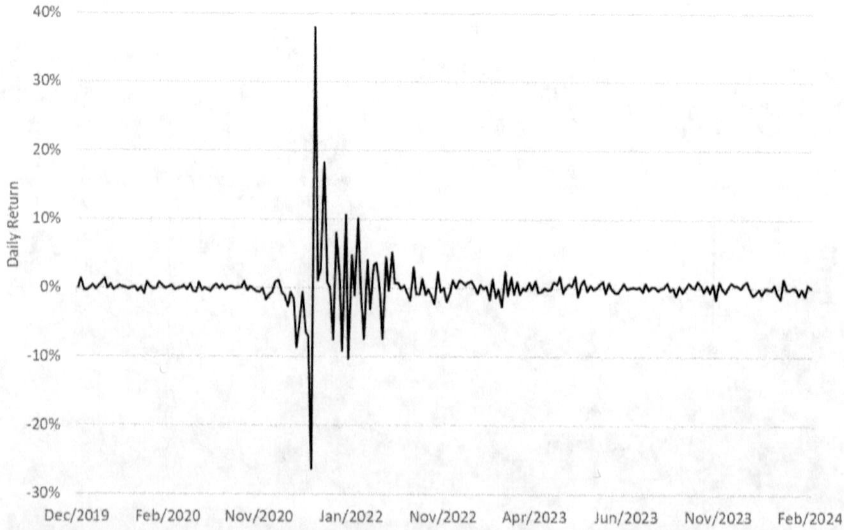

Figure 12.2. Silicon Valley Bank (SBV) daily share price volatility.
Source: Data obtained from Thomson Reuters Eikon, spanning 2 December 2019 through 31 January 2024.

In essence, the SVB crisis was precipitated by a combination of internal management decisions, market dynamics, and regulatory policies, underscoring the need for financial institutions to maintain vigilant oversight and adaptability (Morse, 2024). The Federal Reserve's thorough review provides essential insights into these dynamics, highlighting the importance of robust risk management and a regulatory framework capable of addressing the complexities

dissemination of concerns through social media, eroded depositor confidence, precipitating a swift and widespread bank run. In response to the unfolding crisis, the government, through various federal agencies, executed a comprehensive and multi-pronged intervention strategy. The FDIC's takeover protected insured deposits up to $250,000, a crucial step in averting further destabilisation. In a remarkable move, the government guaranteed full access to funds for all depositors, including those holding amounts above the insured limit, aiming to quell panic and restore faith in the banking system. Additionally, the Federal Reserve introduced an emergency lending programme to bolster liquidity across banks, a pivotal action in stabilising the banking sector and mitigating the risk of contagion.

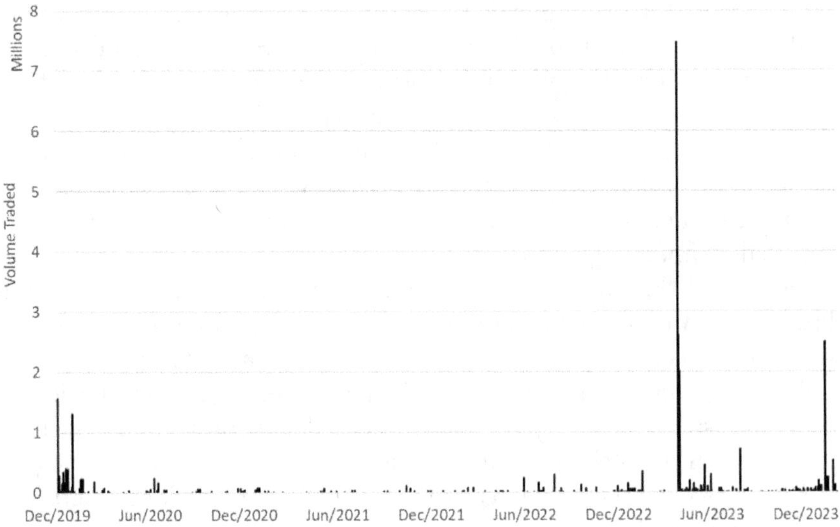

Figure 12.3. Silicon Valley Bank (SBV) daily volume traded.
Source: Data obtained from Thomson Reuters Eikon, spanning 2 December 2019 through 31 January 2024.

of managing growth within volatile sectors. The government's effective response to the crisis, while pivotal in stabilising the banking sector, also emphasises the ongoing need for strategic regulatory and management practices to mitigate such risks in the future.

12.4. Impact on the Tech and Startup Ecosystem

The sudden demise of SVB profoundly impacted its clients, investors, and the wider tech and startup ecosystem. Startups and tech companies, in particular, faced significant cash flow interruptions, impairing their ability to manage operational costs and fulfil payroll obligations. This event introduced uncertainty among VC investors regarding the stability of banking services and the potential devaluation of startup investments, contributing to volatility across financial markets.

This incident caused a significant reevaluation of banking relationships within tech and startup communities, highlighting the critical need for diversification and enhanced financial risk management, especially in the context of venture debt. It led to heightened scrutiny over the health of financial institutions, focusing on their stability and risk management practices. Furthermore, SVB's collapse spurred discussions around regulatory reforms to bolster oversight for banks serving specialised sectors, aiming to avert similar crises in the future.

For the VC and banking sectors, the ramifications of their reliance on SVB were significant, prompting many to reevaluate risks and reconsider their financial strategies by shifting towards larger, more diversified financial institutions to mitigate those risks. This event underscored the importance of stringent risk management and regulatory scrutiny for banks operating within niche markets, driving a move towards more prudent financial practices and reinforcing robust risk management strategies. The Federal Reserve's examination of the collapse focused on the interconnected nature of financial institutions with the tech and startup ecosystem, stressing the necessity of balancing specialised services with comprehensive risk management in the banking sector.

12.4.1. *What key lessons can be learnt from SVB's collapse?*

SVB's collapse provides pivotal lessons for the banking sector, highlighting the importance of various practices such as addressing niche market risks, managing asset–liability ratios, adhering to regulatory compliance, integrating technology, ensuring effective crisis communication, preparing for economic shifts, enforcing corporate governance, and applying sector-specific insights. This event demonstrated the need for banks, especially those operating in volatile niche markets, to adopt diversified risk management strategies encompassing market, liquidity, operational, and strategic risks alongside credit risk.

The asset–liability mismatch revealed by SVB's downfall underscores the essential need for rigorous asset–liability management practices. The Federal Reserve's investigation identified significant lapses in regulatory compliance, making it clear that maintaining solid capital buffers and liquid assets is essential to withstand financial adversities. Moreover, the collapse highlighted the role of technology in enhancing risk assessment, customer service, and operational efficiency, as well as the importance of transparent crisis management and communication strategies.

The presence of broader economic factors contributing to SVB's challenges, such as rising interest rates, should have prompted the bank to be better prepared for economic fluctuations. Strong corporate governance and oversight are also critical in ensuring that management decisions are aligned with the bank's risk appetite and regulatory requirements.

12.4.2. *How can these lessons inform future practices in entrepreneurial finance?*

SVB's collapse provides essential insights for those involved in entrepreneurial finance, particularly concerning strategic adaptability, advanced risk management, and strict regulatory compliance. The importance of implementing comprehensive risk assessment frameworks that acknowledge the unique uncertainties of the startup sector is clear; a balanced approach to investment portfolios and banking services is necessary to mitigate sector-specific risks. The Federal Reserve's examination of SVB's collapse underlines the critical need for strict regulatory compliance and proficient liquidity management. Key aspects of this report are outlined in Table 12.2. Institutions engaged in entrepreneurial finance must ensure adherence to regulations, particularly those concerning capital adequacy and liquidity, to navigate financial challenges successfully.

Economic adaptability is crucial in entrepreneurial finance, with institutions and investors required to remain responsive to shifts in interest rates, investment trends, and the economic climate. Integrating advanced technologies into financial services emerges as a key lesson, enhancing service quality, risk assessment, and operational efficiency. Effective corporate governance and strong internal controls are paramount: regular risk management oversight is essential, and management decisions must align with the institution's risk tolerance and regulatory demands. These governance practices are essential for building investor and client confidence and are pivotal in the entrepreneurial finance sector (Corbet and Larkin, 2023).

SVB's collapse offers us a comprehensive guide for navigating the complexities of entrepreneurial finance, marking key checkpoints such as risk management, diversification, regulatory compliance, adaptability, technology use, and governance integrity. These principles are crucial for guiding strategic and operational decisions, especially for

Table 12.2. Critical weaknesses in the SVB's risk management and governance frameworks as highlighted by the Federal Reserve.

Key point	Detail
Management and Board Oversight Failure	SVB's board and senior management failed to effectively oversee risks inherent in the bank's business model and strategies, not adapting governance and risk management frameworks to keep pace with rapid growth and emerging risks.
Rapid Growth Without Adequate Supervision	The bank experienced unchecked rapid growth from $71 billion to over $211 billion in assets between 2019 and 2021 without being subjected to heightened supervisory or regulatory standards, contributing to its vulnerabilities.
Liquidity Management Weaknesses	SVB showed foundational weaknesses in liquidity risk management, failing its internal liquidity stress tests and lacking viable plans to access liquidity during times of stress, which was critical given its reliance on uninsured deposits.
Interest Rate Risk Mismanagement	The bank's management focused on short-term profits and failed to manage interest rate risk effectively, removing hedges and making counter-intuitive modelling assumptions that exacerbated its vulnerabilities to rising rates.
Inadequate Capital Planning	SVB's capital planning was found inadequate, with the bank not having sufficient buffers to absorb the shock of rapid interest rate hikes and large-scale client withdrawals.
Supervisory Delays and Underappreciation of Risks	Federal Reserve supervisors did not fully appreciate the extent of SVB's vulnerabilities as they grew in size and complexity, and when vulnerabilities were identified, supervisory actions were delayed.
Regulatory Tailoring and Reduced Standards	The tailoring approach in response to regulatory relief acts and a shift in supervisory policy led to reduced standards, increased complexity, and a less assertive supervisory approach, impeding effective oversight.
Unrealised Losses on Securities	SVB did not adequately account for unrealised gains or losses on available-for-sale securities, which led to the bank's capital requirements being misaligned with its financial position and risks.
Failure to Address Identified Deficiencies	Even when critical deficiencies in governance, liquidity, and interest rate risk management were identified, the bank remained well-rated, indicating a failure to address problems as they were recognised.

Table 12.2. (*Continued*)

Key point	Detail
Impact of Social Media and Technology on Bank Runs	The combination of social media and technology changed the dynamics and speed of bank runs, as seen with SVB, where concerns spread quickly, leading to massive, rapid withdrawals.
Systemic Risk Underestimation	SVB's distress demonstrated that systemic consequences through contagion could arise even if the firm is not extremely large or highly interconnected, indicating an underestimation of systemic risk.
Incentive Compensation Misalignment	SVB's incentive compensation did not encourage senior management to manage risks effectively, focusing on short-term earnings and equity returns without incorporating risk metrics.
Over-reliance on Uninsured Deposits	The bank's reliance on uninsured deposits, particularly from the tech sector, made it vulnerable to sudden and large-scale withdrawals, highlighting the need for better management of deposit base stability.
Changing Economic and Financial Environment	SVB and its management could not effectively navigate the changing economic and financial environment marked by rising interest rates and slowing activity in the tech sector, exacerbating its financial condition.
Failure of Contingent Funding Plans	In the days leading to its collapse, SVB's inability to execute its contingent funding plans revealed operational weaknesses, particularly its preparedness to access emergency liquidity.

Note: The Federal Reserve's investigation into SVB's collapse highlighted several critical weaknesses in the bank's risk management and governance frameworks. Found in https:// www.federalreserve.gov/publications/files/svb-review-20230428.pdf.

firms operating in specialised and dynamic markets like technology and startups, thereby offering a blueprint for resilience and strategic foresight in entrepreneurial finance.

12.5. SVB Financial Group's Bankruptcy and Aftermath

The Chapter 11 bankruptcy filing of SVB Financial Group resulted from a complex interplay of factors that underscored the vulnerabilities inherent in the banking sector, especially for institutions with a concentrated focus on specific industries.[5] At the heart of

[5]SVB, SVB Financial Group (SVB Financial), filed for Chapter 11 bankruptcy relief in U.S. Bankruptcy Court for the Southern District of New York on Friday,

SVB's downfall was a severe liquidity crisis precipitated by substantial deposit withdrawals as clients grew increasingly concerned about the bank's financial stability. This situation was aggravated by SVB's significant investments in long-term assets that experienced rapid depreciation amid rising interest rates and a tightening capital environment, particularly in the tech and startup sectors. The bank's inability to quickly liquidate these assets without incurring heavy losses and its deep exposure to sector-specific downturns ultimately led to its bankruptcy filing. These conditions strained SVB's liquidity and severely restricted its capital-raising capabilities, pushing the bank into a precarious financial position.

The fallout from SVB's collapse sent ripples across the financial industry, shifting attention to several critical areas for introspection and improvement. The incident laid bare the inherent risks of niche banking, driving financial institutions to reassess their risk management frameworks and strategies. It prompted a surge in regulatory scrutiny aimed at banks with concentrated exposures to specific sectors, with regulators and stakeholders calling for enhanced measures to safeguard against similar crises. Moreover, SVB's downfall profoundly impacted investor confidence, highlighting the need for transparency and robust communication to maintain trust. The event has also reinforced the importance of contingency planning and corporate governance within the financial sector. It showed that effective risk management and strategic oversight are pivotal when navigating the complexities of the financial landscape.

In the aftermath of its collapse and subsequent Chapter 11 bankruptcy filing, SVB Financial Group's focus on restructuring and the sale of its subsidiaries were crucial to its recovery efforts. This strategic redirection aimed to address the financial challenges faced by the group, with a particular emphasis on greater realignment of its operations and management with the prevailing market conditions and financial realities. The restructuring efforts included

17 March 2023, Case No. 23-10367. https://www.govinfo.gov/app/details/USCOURTS-nysb-1_23-bk-10367/summary. SVB Securities and SVB Capital are not included in the Chapter 11 filing and operate normally. SVB is now operating as Silicon Valley Bridging Bank, NA, under the jurisdiction of the FDIC as Receiver.

significant operational overhauls, such as scaling back non-core operations, focusing on key competencies, and streamlining management processes to enhance efficiency and reduce costs. The sale of various subsidiaries generated the necessary funds to repay creditors while preserving the entities' value and operational integrity. Furthermore, SVB Financial Group's post-bankruptcy strategy shifted towards more sustainable, risk-averse business practices, with a renewed focus on regulatory compliance, financial stability, and strategic partnerships. These initiatives reflect a concerted effort to navigate the complexities of the financial landscape, prioritising sustainability and risk management.

12.6. Regulatory and Policy Lessons from SVB's Failure

The failure of SVB attracted significant attention to the regulatory and policy frameworks governing the financial industry, offering crucial lessons for enhancing the stability and resilience of the banking sector. A primary lesson from SVB's downfall is the critical importance of advanced risk management practices. The bank's concentrated exposure to the tech and startup sectors and asset–liability mismatches were indicative of the vulnerabilities inherent in specialised banking. Addressing such vulnerabilities requires a robust risk management framework, encompassing various risks associated with market fluctuations, liquidity constraints, and sector-specific downturns.

Strengthening bank liquidity management through regulatory mandates for higher liquidity buffers and strategies for handling sudden, large-scale withdrawals is essential to prevent crises like the one that caused SVB's collapse. Furthermore, the bank's failure revealed potential gaps in the current stress-testing frameworks, especially for mid-sized banks with unique business models or sector concentrations. These frameworks may require revision to better capture the full spectrum of risks such institutions face.

Another critical area for regulatory focus is enhancing transparent communication between banks and their stakeholders. Improved disclosure requirements could help mitigate misinformation and prevent the panic that led to SVB's rapid deposit withdrawals.

Additionally, the bank's significant sector concentration raised questions about whether sector-specific regulations, including tailored capital and liquidity requirements, might be necessary for banks with high exposure to particular industries. Finally, SVB's collapse highlighted the need for improved supervisory oversight. Banks with unique risk profiles may benefit from more frequent and detailed regulatory examinations and audits, ensuring they adhere to sound risk management practices and maintain financial stability.

12.6.1. *Preventing future bank failures: Lessons from SVB's collapse with a focus on entrepreneurship in finance*

The collapse of SVB has shed light on the intersection of banking and entrepreneurship by emphasising the need for strategic adaptation, innovative funding strategies, and the integration of technological advancements in financial services. Banks operating within the entrepreneurial finance sector should review their relationships with fintech companies. Partnerships that bolster technological capabilities can lead to better risk assessment tools and more efficient client service platforms, which are crucial for keeping pace with the rapid evolution of the tech sector. Innovative funding strategies that extend beyond traditional lending, such as equity investments in startups, venture debt offerings, and support for crowdfunding platforms, can diversify banks' revenue streams and distribute risk more evenly. Moreover, given the global nature of the tech sector, there is a pressing need for regulatory alignment across jurisdictions to manage cross-border risks effectively and ensure a stable financial environment for entrepreneurial ventures.

12.6.2. *The future of specialised banking in entrepreneurial finance*

The failure of SVB has served as a watershed moment for specialised banking, particularly in entrepreneurial finance. This event has necessitated a thorough reevaluation of how banks approach risk management, regulatory compliance, and their strategic focus on specific sectors, such as technology and life sciences. Diversification will be key to mitigating the risks of over-concentration in any one sector as we advance. Banks will likely broaden their investment portfolios and seek a more balanced approach to sector specialisation. Additionally, integrating technological solutions will enhance risk assessment, improve customer service, and boost operational efficiencies. Adopting big data, artificial intelligence, and machine learning technologies can significantly refine banks' ability to navigate the complexities of the financial landscape. Regulatory compliance will also come under sharper focus, with banks striving to align more closely with the standards and requirements set forth by oversight bodies. This includes maintaining adequate capital buffers and liquidity to withstand financial stressors. Nonetheless, developing innovative financial products that meet the evolving needs of startups and entrepreneurs will remain crucial for banks looking to support the growth of these dynamic sectors.

In balancing risk and specialisation, banks must employ a multifaceted strategy that includes comprehensive due diligence, robust risk management frameworks, continuous market and regulatory monitoring, strengthened capital reserves, sustainable growth approaches, and active client education and engagement. These strategies, informed by the lessons learnt from SVB's collapse, are essential for building a more resilient and adaptive banking sector capable of supporting the vibrant landscape of entrepreneurial finance.

12.7. Concluding Thoughts: Balancing Risk and Specialisation in Banking

The collapse of SVB serves as a poignant case study of the vulnerabilities inherent in highly specialised banking models that primarily cater to niche sectors such as technology and startups. Specialisation allows banks to offer tailored financial solutions, fostering innovation and growth within specific sectors; however, it simultaneously concentrates risk, making these institutions particularly susceptible to sector-specific downturns and broader economic shifts. This duality presents a critical challenge for banks in maintaining a balance that safeguards their operational integrity and the financial system.

Moreover, the insights derived from SVB's failure highlight the importance of regulatory frameworks that are attuned to the complexities of specialised banking. Regulators must foster an environment that encourages innovation, all the while making certain that banks possess adequate capital buffers, liquidity, and risk mitigation strategies to withstand adverse conditions. This balance is crucial for maintaining the financial system's stability and protecting the interests of depositors and other stakeholders.

The collapse of SVB will have profound implications for future strategies in entrepreneurial finance and the banking sector. For one, there is a clear need for diversified banking practices that mitigate the risks of over-reliance on specific sectors. Banks should explore avenues for broadening their portfolio of services and clientele to include a wider range of industries, thereby distributing risk more evenly.

References

Aharon, D. Y., Ali, S., and Naved, M. (2023). Too big to fail: The aftermath of Silicon Valley Bank (SVB) collapse and its impact on financial markets. *Research in International Business and Finance*, 66, 102036.

Ahuja, R., Barrett, S., Corbet, S., and Larkin, C. (2019). A way forward: The future of Irish and European Union financial regulation. *Economic Analysis and Policy*, 64, 346–360.

Bales, S. and Burghof, H.-P. (2024). Public attention, sentiment and the default of silicon valley bank. *The North American Journal of Economics and Finance*, 69, 102026.

Barrett, S., Corbet, S., and Larkin, C. (2019). Sustainability, accountability and democracy: Ireland's troika experience. *Finance Research Letters*, 28, 53–60.

Bhagat, S. and Laurion, H. (2023). Silicon valley bank demise: Causes and the path forward. *Review of Corporate Finance*, 4(3), 337–374.

Corbet, S. (2016). Turning tigers into PIIGS: The role of leverage in the Irish economic collapse. In *Lessons from the Great Recession: At the Crossroads of Sustainability and Recovery*, Vol. 18. Emerald Group Publishing Limited, pp. 21–55.

Corbet, S. and Larkin, C. J. (2023). The implications of the Silicon Valley Bank collapse. Available at *SSRN* 4640800.

De Rassenfosse, G. and Fischer, T. (2016). Venture debt financing: Determinants of the lending decision. *Strategic Entrepreneurship Journal*, 10(3), 235–256.

Gompers, P. (2023). Silicon valley bank's focus on startups was a double-edged sword. *Harvard Business Review.*

Hyun, S. and Lee, H. S. (2022). Positive effects of portfolio financing strategy for startups. *Economic Analysis and Policy*, 74, 623–633.

Ibrahim, D. M. (2010). Debt as venture capital. *University of Illinois Law Review*, 1169.

Leach, J. C. and Melicher, R. W. (2012). *Entrepreneurial Finance.* Cengage Learning.

Martins, A. M. (2024). The collapse of silicon valley bank and credit Suisse and their impact on other us banks. *Applied Economics Letters*, 1–5.

Morse, A. (2024). *Venture Debt.* Technical Report, National Bureau of Economic Research.

Nguyen, X.-T. (2024). *Silicon Valley Bank: The Rise and Fall of a Community Bank for Tech.* Cambridge University Press.

Semeyutin, A., Kaawach, S., and Kara, A. (2023). CEO risk-culture, bank stability and the case of the Silicon Valley Bank. *Economics Letters*, 233, 111373.

Tellez, A. (13 March 2023). Coinbase, circle, paxos: Here are the major firms with funds tied up in SVB and Signature Bank. *Forbes.* Available at: https://www.forbes.com/sites/anthonytellez/2023/03/13/coinbase-circle-paxos-here-are-the-major-firms-with-funds-tied-up-in-svb-and-signature-bank/?sh=369892e54574.

Van Vo, L. and Le, H. T. T. (2023). From hero to zero: The case of silicon valley bank. *Journal of Economics and Business*, 127, 106138.

Part 4

Green Finance

https://doi.org/10.1142/9781800617032_0013

Chapter 13

Green Bonds: A Governance Perspective*

Gaoguang Zhou

Department of Accountancy, Economics and Finance, Hong Kong Baptist University, Hong Kong

13.1. Introduction

Growing concerns about the global risks of climate change led to the creation of the 2015 Paris Agreement, which set a goal of holding 'the increase in the global average temperature to well below 2°C above pre-industrial levels'.[1] The agreement is a legally binding international treaty, and so far 194 parties (including 193 countries and the European Union) have joined it. Most of the participating countries have pledged to achieve net-zero emission targets; this commitment has driven their governments to take actions to mitigate emissions. The Paris Agreement also recognises the necessity of massive investments in low-carbon, climate-resilient infrastructure and hence the role of financing in climate change mitigation and adaptation. As such, the Paris Agreement calls for mobilising financing from various channels to support investment in green projects. Recently, after reviewing current progress on addressing

*I would like to thank Di Guo, Eric Luk, and Weiqiang Tan for their valuable comments.

[1]https://unfccc.int/process-and-meetings/the-paris-agreement.

climate change, the Intergovernmental Panel on Climate Change (IPCC, 2023) highlighted the lack of financing as a barrier to climate change mitigation and adaptation and called for more financing to support emission reduction projects to meet emissions targets by 2030.[2] The failure to meet climate targets to date and the demand for financing for green projects have spurred the development of innovative financial instruments.

One such instrument is the green bond: the issuer of such a bond promises that the bond proceeds will be (either partly or wholly) used to finance or refinance eligible green projects such as renewable energy, green construction projects, energy-saving efforts, or pollution prevention and control (Green Bond Principles [GBP], 2021). The first green bond was issued in 2007, and the following decades have witnessed the rapid development of the market for green bonds. Because of their importance as a source of financing for green projects, the former general secretary of the United Nations, Ban Ki-Moon, called them 'one of the most significant developments in the financing of low-carbon, climate resilient investment opportunities'[3] and called on banks to scale up green bond markets.[4]

Despite the rapid development of green bonds, the green bond market remains an insignificant fraction of the global bond market (the International Capital Market Association [ICMA], 2020). One of the major barriers to the development of green bonds is the phenomenon of greenwashing, in which green bond issuers label their bonds 'green bonds' without planning to invest in authentic green projects (e.g. Freeburn and Ramsay, 2020). Given the benefits of issuing green bonds, including enhancing the issuer's reputation for social responsibility, lower bond yield spreads, and potential government subsidies, issuers may have strong incentives to label their bonds as green bonds even if they do not plan to fulfil their promises of investing in green projects. This problem is exacerbated by dispersed

[2]https://report.ipcc.ch/ar6syr/pdf/IPCC_AR6_SYR_LongerReport.pdf.

[3]'Climate Bonds Standard & Certification Scheme', March 2018, https://www.climatebonds.net/files/files/Climate%20Bonds%20Standards%20and%20Certification%20Scheme%20Brochure%202018.pdf.

[4]https://www.un.org/sustainabledevelopment/blog/2016/01/ban-ki-moons-remarks-at-investor-summit-on-climate-risk/.

bond ownership, which lowers investors' monitoring incentives (Park, 2019).

Several parties govern the green bond market by setting green bond standards and monitoring whether supposedly green projects are indeed green and whether the proceeds are appropriately allocated. In the green bond domain, public governance parties include the government, regulators, stock exchanges, and other institutions, while private governance[5] bodies include private standard setters, underwriters, investors, and financial information intermediaries. Although the sustainable development of green bonds requires both public and private governance, private governance plays a more direct and important role in governing green bonds because of its timelier responsiveness and lower transaction costs (Park, 2018). In this regard, green bond governance is an example of how private governance fills the gap in international governance left by public governance because public governance regulators have less expertise, knowledge, and experience than private governance regulators when dealing with international business (Park, 2019; Abbott and Snidal, 2009, 2021). Despite the success of private governance in fostering the early development of the green bond market, several critics have questioned its effectiveness as a monitoring system because it may only reflect the narrow economic interests of private parties and be vulnerable to pressure from interest groups (Park, 2018; Abbott and Snidal, 2009, 2021). Additionally, private governance relies on market-based mechanisms such as reputation and competition, which may not be effective without the help of public governance (Abbott and Snidal, 2009, 2021). As a result, both public and private governance need to work together to improve the governance of green bonds and foster the development of the green bond market.

This study analyses green bonds from a governance perspective. In line with the paradigm of governance outcome that is widely adopted in the corporate governance literature (e.g. Gompers *et al.*, 2003), the outcomes of green bonds at both country and bond levels (the amount of green bond issuance at country level and green bond premium, or greenium, at bond level) are regarded as the function of

[5]Private governance mechanisms include investor-based standards, certification schemes, green bond indices, and external assurance (Park 2018).

green bond governance (which is a combination of private and public governance). Specifically, both public and private governance bodies provide governance mechanisms, including standard setting, regulations, external review schemes, and monitoring, which influence the outcomes of green bonds both at the country and bond levels. Figure 13.1 illustrates the framework that guides my examination of the development of the green bond market; I use it to synthesise previous empirical findings concerning green bond premium and to organise my discussion of the development of green bonds.

The rest of this chapter is organised as follows. I begin by giving an account of the history of the green bond market. Based on this history, I summarise the factors that influence green bond market development. A major challenge in green bond issuance is ensuring the credibility of a bond's greenness and preventing greenwashing. I discuss several green bond governance mechanisms that can enhance green credibility. Understanding green bonds requires both descriptions and more comprehensive analyses. Given that effective green bond governance mechanisms reduce investors' greenwashing concerns and result in lower bond spreads than conventional bonds (referred to as 'the greenium'), I comprehensively review the literature on the greenium and synthesise the findings on the effectiveness of various green bond governance mechanisms. Next, I propose an integrated governance model and discuss how various governance mechanisms should be developed and integrated to foster green bond market development. Last, I summarise my conclusions.

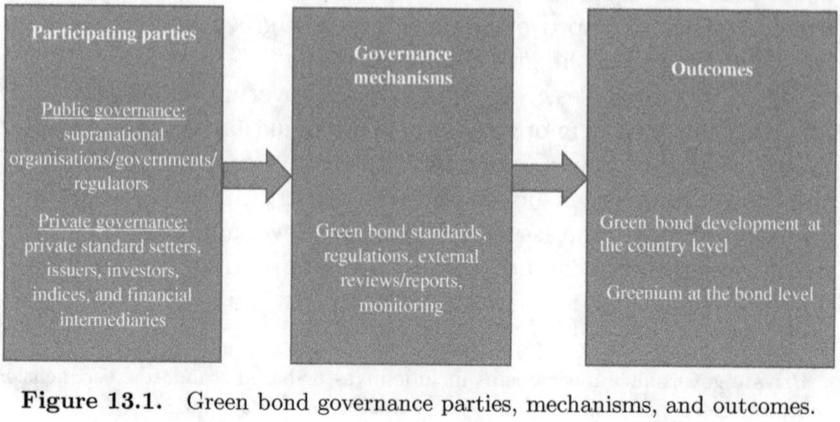

Figure 13.1. Green bond governance parties, mechanisms, and outcomes.

13.2. Green Bonds: Development and Current Status

13.2.1. *A brief history of green bonds*

In 2007, the European Investment Bank and the World Bank issued the first green bond – the Climate Awareness Bond, with a total issuance of $0.9 billion. The European Investment Bank issued its next Climate Awareness Bond in 2009 and launched new Climate Awareness Bonds with a total value of €543 million in four currencies in 2010. In November 2013, Vasakronan, a Swedish company, issued the first corporate green bond (Park, 2019). Although several green bonds were issued in 2007 and 2013 and gained increasing recognition from the investment community, green bond issuance was largely restricted to multilateral development banks and other public development organisations (Park, 2018). Because of the early dominance of these organisations in the green bond market, they had a major influence on green bond practices during this period.

In 2014, the promulgation of the GBP by the ICMA, an international not-for-profit association initially consisting of four major investment banks,[6] marked an important development of the green bond market. The GBP was the first set of international standards to establish guidelines and recommendations for green bond practices. The GBP became the foundation for many international green bond standards (Ehlers and Packer, 2017), which in turn ultimately drove the growth of the green bond market (Cortellini and Panetta, 2021). In 2014, the Climate Bonds Initiative (CBI), another not-for-profit organisation established in 2009, adopted and modified the GBP, releasing the first version of the Climate Bonds Standard (CBS), which differs from the GBP in several respects.

Following the release of the GBP, governments and other agencies entered the green bond market (Cortellini and Panetta, 2021). While the GBP and the CBS were developed by nongovernmental organisations (NGOs), several governments such as the Chinese government have taken these standards as a basis and developed their own green bond standards. Many governments, including those of China and Singapore, also provide subsidies to green bond issuers to

[6] As of March 2020, ICMA had 600 members from 62 countries, including banks, law firms, and investment funds (Cortellini and Panetta, 2021).

foster the development of green bonds. In addition, stock exchanges facilitate green bond development by regulating green bonds and providing investors with easy access to them. By 2015, the London, Oslo, and Stockholm stock exchanges provided platforms for green bond trading (Organisation for Economic Co-Operation and Development [OECD], 2015). Since then, several stock exchanges have allowed investors to trade green bonds.[7] Stock exchanges also support green bond indices, which can help institutional investors required to invest in green assets choose green securities.

In response to the demand for green bond certification, green-bond-related information intermediaries also emerged and developed. One such group of information intermediaries includes established rating agencies (such as Standard & Poor's [S&P], Moody's, and Fitch) and audit firms. Another is newly established environmental, social, and governance (ESG) experts, such as ISS-Oekom, Sustainalytics, and Vigeo Eiris. In short, although both public and private governance bodies participate in green bond governance, private governance plays a more direct and important role in governing the green bond market after 2014 (Park, 2019).

The demand for green bonds to finance green projects, coupled with the efforts of several parties in response to this demand, has fuelled the rapid expansion of the green bond market. The CBI (2021) reports that green bonds meeting the CBI definition have been issued in around 80 countries and the total amount of green bonds issued increased from $37.1 billion in 2014 to $578.4 billion in 2021 (see Table 13.1). As shown in Table 13.1, during the 2014–2021 period, the total amount of green bonds issued grew monotonically at an impressive rate. Among the various types of green bonds,[8] corporate green bonds (including financial and nonfinancial corporate bonds) predominate (representing around 53% of all green bonds in 2021). Compared with other types of green bonds, corporate green bonds also have much higher growth rates. For example, this type of bond grew by 53% during the 2018–2019 period and

[7] https://www.climatebonds.net/green-bond-segments-stock-exchanges.

[8] These types of bonds include asset-backed security, development bank, financial corporate, government-backed entity, local government, nonfinancial corporate, loan, and sovereign green bonds.

Table 13.1. Green bond issuance by issuer type, 2014–2021 (in $ billion).

Issuer type	2014	2015	2016	2017	2018	2019	2020	2021
Asset-backed security	2.4	2.4	8.7	35.6	26.3	32.6	23.4	29.4
Development bank	15	15.1	22.6	22.1	16.1	29.5	26.4	43
Financial corporate	2.8	10.2	16	26.2	50.5	59.7	55.9	147.9
Government-backed entity	2	6	14.2	18.7	19.5	36.3	65.1	85.8
Local government	3.7	5.3	7.6	12.9	7.3	12	18.5	15.1
Nonfinancial corporate	11.2	7.2	14.6	29.9	29.4	62.6	67.6	151.2
Green loans			0.1	3.5	6	14.2	11.1	19.8
Sovereign			0.8	10.8	17.6	24.7	37.9	86.2
Total	37.1	46.2	84.6	159.7	172.7	271.6	305.9	578.4

Note: This table presents the amounts (in $ billion) of various types of green bond issued during 2014–2021.
Source: https://www.climatebonds.net/market/data/.

Table 13.2. Green bond issuance by region, 2014–2021 (in $ billion).

Region	2014	2015	2016	2017	2018	2019	2020	2021
Africa	0.1		0.2	0.3	0.2	0.9	1.2	0.4
Asia-Pacific	1.6	3.9	26.6	35.5	50.4	67.2	56.5	147.7
Europe	18.3	20	25	61.2	68	122.2	164.2	288.5
Latin America	0.2	1.1	1.6	4.2	1.6	4.9	9.1	8.9
North America	7.4	12.8	20.9	49	39.7	61.6	60.9	102
Supranational	9.4	8.4	10.2	9.5	12.7	14.6	13.8	30.9
Total	37	46.2	84.5	159.7	172.6	271.4	305.7	578.4

Note: This table presents the amounts (in $ billion) of green bond by regions during 2014–2021.
Source: https://www.climatebonds.net/market/data/.

142% during the 2020–2021 period, suggesting that corporate green bonds have robust growth potential. To better understand the global green bond market, I also report green bond markets by region during the 2014–2021 period in Table 13.2. In 2014, Europe issued the largest amount of green bonds. After 2014, Europe continued to lead the green bond market except in 2016, when the amount of green bonds in Asia-Pacific exceeded that in Europe. While Asia-Pacific issued a relatively small amount of green bonds in 2014 and 2015, the green bond market experienced strong annual growth, especially during the 2015–2016 (582% growth rate) and 2020–2021 periods

(161% growth rate). Among all of the regions, Africa had the lowest amount of green bonds during the period. It is also worth noting that supranational organisations, such as the World Bank and the European Investment Bank, have issued a considerable amount of green bonds. For example, in 2021, these organisations issued green bonds with a total value of $30.9 billion, which is far greater than the sum of all green bonds issued in Africa and Latin America. Altogether, Table 13.2 shows an uneven development of green bond markets across different regions. I also report green bond issuance in major economies in 2021 in Figure 13.2. While the US, China, and Japan were the leading countries in green bond issuance in 2021, the US maintained its leading status. Among the 12 economies that issued the largest amount of green bonds globally, China was the only developing economy.

The development of green bonds is not only manifested by the amount but also by the variety of green bonds. ICMA (2021a) identifies four types of green bonds: Standard Green Use of Proceeds

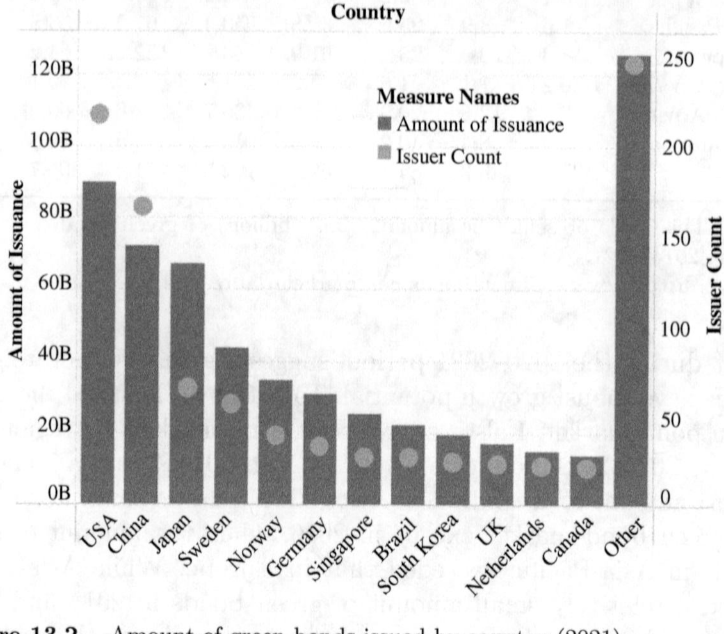

Figure 13.2. Amount of green bonds issued by country (2021).
Note: Amount of issuance in $ billion.

Table 13.3. Types of green bonds (ICMA, 2021a).

Type of green bond	Definition
Standard green use of proceeds bond	An unsecured debt obligation with full recourse-to-the-issuer only and aligned with the GBP.
Green revenue bond	A non-recourse-to-the-issuer debt obligation aligned with the GBP, in which the credit exposure of the bond is to the pledged cash flows of the revenue streams, fees, taxes, etc., and whose proceeds go to related or unrelated Green Project(s).
Green project bond	A project bond for a single or multiple Green Project(s) for which the investor has direct exposure to the risk of the project(s) with or without potential recourse to the issuer; it is aligned with the GBP.
Secured green bond	A secured bond where the net proceeds will be exclusively applied to financing or refinancing either: i. The Green Project(s) securing the specific bond only (a 'Secured Green Collateral Bond'); or ii. The Green Project(s) of the issuer, originator, or sponsor, where such Green Projects may or may not be securing the specific bond in whole or in part (a 'Secured Green Standard Bond'). A Secured Green Standard Bond may be a specific class or tranche of a larger transaction.

Note: This table summarises four types of green bonds and their definitions based on ICMA (2021a).

Bonds, Green Revenue Bonds, Green Project Bonds, and Secured Green Bonds (see Table 13.3). Green bonds can either be secured (e.g. Green Revenue Bonds) or unsecured (e.g. Standard Green Use of Proceeds Bonds). The variety of green bonds gives both issuers and investors more choice and, therefore, can further fuel the development of green bonds. The green bond experience also spurs the creation of related bonds, such as social- and sustainability-linked bonds.

Despite the rapid growth of green bond markets, they remain an insignificant fraction of the global bond market worth over \$120 trillion (ICMA, 2020). HSBC (2021) estimates that in 2021, labelled green bonds took up merely 1% of the overall bond market in China, which has experienced the highest global growth rate in green bond markets and represents the second-largest green bond market around the world. A recent CBI report suggests that the volume of green bonds is far lower than McKinsey's estimate that $9 trillion in annual demand for green investments is required to achieve the net-zero target by 2050[9]; this suggests the urgency of accelerating the development of green bond markets.

13.2.2. *Drivers of green bond issuance*

As mentioned earlier, while the green bond market has emerged and developed rapidly, its market size is still small compared with the conventional bond market. Additionally, the development of green bonds exhibits large variations across regions and countries. An interesting question is why green bond issuance varies with different issuers and countries. In this section, I discuss the drivers of green bond issuance from three aspects.

13.2.2.1. *Demand side*

From the demand side, investors' preferences are an important factor in green bond issuance. Because of increasing social concerns about social and environmental issues, individual investors' preferences for ESG, and more prudential investment regulations, many institutional investors make ESG an important criterion for their investment decisions (Matos, 2020). In 2018, more than $30 trillion wase managed globally following responsible investment criteria (Global Sustainable Investment Alliance, 2019). Several institutional investors have committed themselves to ESG by becoming signatories to ESG investment principles. The Principles for Responsible Investment, the world's leading network of institutional investors committed to impact investing, report that the assets under management of their 3,826 signatories had reached $121 trillion as of 31 March 2021.[10] Green bonds that are classified as green assets and

[9]https://www.climatebonds.net/2022/01/500bn-green-issuance-2021-social-and-sustainable-acceleration-annual-green-1tn-sight-market.

[10]https://www.unpri.org/annual-report-2021/how-we-work/building-our-effectiveness/enhance-our-global-footprint.

have low volatility (Veys, 2010) are attractive to the institutional investors.

However, despite the global trend in institutional investors' preferences for green bonds, this trend varies across countries. Dyck *et al.* (2019) show that in countries with strong social and environmental norms, investors are more inclined to invest in firms with good ESG performance, which also explains the variation in green bond market development across countries.

13.2.2.2. *Supply side*

From the supply side, issuers have several incentives to issue green bonds. First, green bonds have advantages over conventional bonds for financing green projects. While issuers can use conventional bonds to finance such projects, green bonds can attract a wider range of investors (Asian Development Bank, 2018), especially those with ESG commitments. Additionally, because many green projects are long-term and require high upfront capital costs, green bonds are better suited to such projects than conventional bonds (OECD, 2015).

Second, the issuance of green bonds can provide issuers with several financial benefits. Investors are willing to accept a lower return from green bonds; therefore, green bond issuers are likely to experience oversubscription and have lower financing costs (Dorfleitner, Utz, and Zhang, 2022; Flammer, 2021; Dorfleitner and Utz, 2014; Höchstädter and Scheck, 2015). The benefits of green bond issuance can also spill over to issuers' stock market performance, such as higher firm value and stock liquidity (Tang and Zhang, 2018). As a result, firms have strong economic incentives to issue green bonds.

Third, green bond issuance can demonstrate issuers' commitment to ESG and gain stakeholders' support. In response to climate change, several intergovernmental bodies, governments, NGOs, and investors have urged firms to commit to ESG. For example, prior studies show that investors pressure firms to care about the environment by actively intervening in their operations or selling stocks of polluting firms (Dyck *et al.*, 2019; Choi *et al.*, 2020). Green bond issuance signals companies' environmental commitment (Lyon and Maxwell, 2011; Lyon and Montgomery, 2015; Flammer, 2021; Allman and Lock, 2022; Larcker and Watts, 2020), which can enhance their ESG reputation and gain support from a variety of stakeholders, including investors, employees, and consumers[11] (e.g. Freeman, 1984; Deschryver and De Mariz, 2020).

Finally, interestingly, firms may choose to issue green bonds because of peer pressure. For example, in 2019, PepsiCo issued green bonds after Starbucks' issuance of green bonds in 2016 and Coca-Cola's amendment of loan to include a sustainability element in 2019 (Deschryver and De Mariz, 2020).

13.2.2.3. *Governments and regulations*

Governments and regulations can affect green bond issuance by influencing both the demand and supply sides. Green bond issuance is subject to bond market regulations. Regulations can affect green bond issuance by affecting market participation (Barua and Chiesa, 2019). Additionally, more relaxed supervision of the use of bond proceeds encourages issuers to issue green bonds (Dou and Qi, 2019; Deng *et al.*, 2020; Chiesa and Barua, 2019). Greater flexibility in green bond practice can increase the available options for financing, leading to more green bond issuance.

Governments can also foster the development of green bonds by providing support to issuers and setting green bond standards. For example, the Chinese government provides economic benefits to green bond issuers, such as tax reductions or direct subsidies (OECD, 2015). In the US, the Clean Renewable Energy Bonds and Qualified Energy Conservation Bonds programmes support government agencies and other designated public bodies to finance clean energy projects by giving tax credits (Herrick and Elias, 2011). In Singapore, the Monetary Authority of Singapore promulgated a grant scheme to subsidise green bond issuance for three years in 2017[12] (Azhgaliyeva and Kapsalyamova, 2021). To better cultivate green bond markets, several governments from China, the EU, and Vietnam have set green bond standards to facilitate green bond issuance.

[11] Deschryver and De Mariz (2020) consider green bonds as a powerful instrument to increase employee morale.

[12] This includes external review fees of up to $0.075 million for green bonds issued and listed on the Singapore Stock Exchange with a minimum tenure of three years (Azhgaliyeva and Kapsalyamova, 2021).

13.3. The Governance of Green Bonds

Despite the explosive growth of green bonds, the most persistent and common problem of the green bond market is 'greenwashing' (Freeburn and Ramsay, 2020). This phenomenon occurs when green bond issuers, who wish to obtain the benefits of green bonds, label their bonds as green bonds even though they do not plan to invest in green projects. Greenwashing undermines investors' confidence in the green credentials of green bonds (Grene, 2015; Deschryver and de Mariz, 2020; Freeburn and Ramsay, 2020; Dorfleitner *et al.*, 2022; Sangiorgi and Schopohl, 2021) and is therefore reminiscent of the lemons problem (Akerlof, 1970): failure to address the asymmetric information problem results in market collapse. As such, the green bond market, like other capital markets, cannot develop in a sustainable manner without proper governance to mitigate the greenwashing problem.

Unlike the conventional bond market, where public governance is more important than private governance, the green bond market is largely governed by private governance (Park, 2019) because this market was originally developed by private agencies and includes important cross-border elements. Green bond governance takes various forms, including green bond standards, regulations, external reviews, monitoring, and enforcement. In this section, I describe how various governance parties participate in different forms of green bond governance.

13.3.1. *Green bond standards*

In the early years (2007–2013), green bond issuance was largely unregulated and there was no clear guidance. To overcome this problem, ICMA promulgated its first version of the GBP in 2014, which provided a general framework for subsequent standards, including another international green bond standard, the CBS, and country-level green bond standards.

13.3.1.1. *GBP*

ICMA established the GBP in 2014 as a set of voluntary guidelines for broad use by green bond market participants, including issuers, investors, and underwriters (ICMA, 2021a). For issuers, the GBP provides 'guidance on the key components involved in launching a credible Green Bond' (ICMA, 2021a, 4). The GBP consists of four core components (ICMA, 2021a): (i) use of proceeds,[13] (ii) process for project evaluation and selection, (iii) management of proceeds, and (iv) reporting. Furthermore, the GBP recommends that issuers assess alignment with the core components of the GBP during the pre-issuance stage, supplemented by using an external auditor or other third party to assess the management, tracking, and allocation of proceeds in the post-issuance stage (ICMA, 2021a). Under the GBP, there are broadly four types of external reviews: (i) second-party opinion (SPO), (ii) verification, (iii) rating/scoring, and (iv) verification/assurance. Although ICMA issued guidelines for the external review of green bonds, the GBP does not prescribe any form of external review nor recommend or approve any external reviewers. Instead, the GBP adopts a market-oriented approach and encourages external review providers to disclose their credentials, their relevant expertise, and the scope of their external review services. Furthermore, the principles recommend that issuers make their external review reports publicly available. Under the GBP, each issuer has discretion to choose both the type(s) of external review(s) and external review provider(s). Since 2014, the GBP has become the most widely accepted green bond standard among issuers, underwriters, investors, and regulators (OECD, 2015).

13.3.1.2. *CBS*

The CBI, an NGO established in 2010, adapted the GBP to create the first version of its CBS in 2014. Similar to the GBP, the CBS includes four core components in both pre- and post-issuance stages. Compared with the GBP, the CBS has three distinct features: more detailed requirements for green bond issuers, a more rigorous certification scheme, and sector-specific criteria for green projects

[13]ICMA lists eligible green project categories: renewable energy, energy efficiency, pollution prevention and control, environmentally sustainable management of living natural resources and land use, terrestrial and aquatic biodiversity, clean transportation, sustainable water and wastewater management, climate change adaptation, circular economy-adapted products, production technologies and processes, and green buildings.

(taxonomy). The CBI develops its certification scheme to provide an arguably higher level of assurance than the GBP and a more environmentally rigorous assessment of the authenticity of green bonds. The CBS incorporates science-based criteria for compatibility with the Paris Climate Agreement. In terms of external review, the CBS requires issuers to obtain independent verification of CBS compliance during both pre- and post-issuance stages. Issuers need to choose certification providers from the list of 57 approved providers as of 2021 (CBI, 2021b),[14] and verifiers need to fulfil criteria such as competence and experience in debt instruments, carbon projects, and assurance services. Additionally, the CBI considers verifiers' geographic coverage and technical scope in determining their qualifications.[15] The CBS requires that green bond assurance be conducted following the International Standard on Assurance Engagements 3000. To illustrate the differences between these two standards, I summarise them in Table 13.4. I also summarise the differences between the four core principles of the GBP and the CBS in Table 13.5.

Table 13.4. Overview of the differences between the GBP and the CBS.

Agency	GBP	CBS
Standards (versions)	2014 (V1) 2018 (V2) 2021 (V3)	2014 (V1) 2015 (V2) 2017 (V2.1) 2019 (V3) 2023 (V4)
External reviews	Voluntary	Mandatory
Type of external reviews	SPO, third-party assurance, certification, and green bond rating	Certification (both pre- and post-issuance)
Verified external reviewer	Voluntary	Approved by the CBI
Taxonomy	Loosely defined, no formal taxonomy	Climate bonds taxonomy (CBT)

Note: This table summarises the differences between the GSB and the CBS.

[14]https://www.climatebonds.net/certification/approved-verifiers CBI. (2021b). *Approved Verifiers under the Climate Bonds Standard.* Retrieved December 31, 2021, from https://www.climatebonds.net/certification/approved-verifiers.

[15]https://www.climatebonds.net/certification/become-a-verifier.

Table 13.5. Main differences in the four core components between the GBP and the CBS.

	GBP	CBS
Use of proceeds	• Issuers should use the proceeds of green bonds in green projects and disclose this in the legal documentation for the green bonds.	*Pre-issuance* • Proposed financed projects and assets should be clearly documented, listed, and should not be nominated for other green bonds unless reasonable demonstration is made otherwise. *Post-issuance* • Use of bond proceeds should be allocated to eligible proposed projects and assets, appropriately documented and tracked during the internal process.
Process for evaluation and selection of projects and assets	• Issuers need to communicate to investors the environmental objectives of their green projects and the decision-making process for determining eligible green projects.	*Pre-issuance* • The issuer should establish, maintain, and document the decision-making process that determines the eligibility of financed projects and assets. *Post-issuance* • The decision-making process of continuing eligibility of financed projects and assets should be documented and maintained.
Management of proceeds	• Issuers should create a subaccount to manage the proceeds. • Issuers should maintain a high degree of transparency. • Issuers should involve an auditor or other third party to verify the tracking method and allocation of proceeds after issuance.	*Pre-issuance* • The process of proceed management, including tracking the proceeds, managing unallocated proceeds, and earmarking funds to nominated projects, should be disclosed to the verifier. *Post-issuance* • Issuers should create a subaccount to manage the proceeds. • Net proceeds of bonds should be identified and documented. • Allocate net proceeds to nominated projects and assets.

Table 13.5. (*Continued*)

	GBP	CBS
Reporting	• Issuers should report the use of proceeds annually until full allocation. • Report material developments, if any, in a timely manner.	*Pre-issuance* • The green bond framework should be prepared and made available to the public. • Report disclosure documentation, including investment areas, verifier involved, intended investments, and the CBI disclaimer in the certification agreement. *Post-issuance* • The update report that includes allocation reporting, eligibility reporting, and impact reporting, should be updated at least annually. • The verifier's report and relevant material that supports the update report should be made available to the public. • Information regarding nominated projects and management of proceeds should be reported to the verifier and the CBS board for their assessment of CBS compliance.

Note: This table summarises the main differences in the four core components between the GBP and the CBS.

While these two standards are designed to enhance the credibility of green bonds, some criticisms question their effectiveness. First, compliance with these standards is voluntary, so self-labelled green bonds remain a concern for investors (Simeth, 2022). Second, due to the voluntary nature of guidelines, green bond issuers can choose less stringent standards that are favourable to their interests. Third, due to the lack of a universal certification system, investors are likely to be confused and their investments are at risk (Grene, 2015; Deschryver and de Mariz, 2020). Finally, both ICMA and CBI are not-for-profit organisations, so they lack the authority to enforce or punish issuers with potential or confirmed greenwashing or green defaults (Park, 2018). As a result, whether these two standards can attain their desired goals remains debatable.

Despite their limitations, these two sets of standards, especially the GBP, have had a major influence on regional green bond standards. Several countries and regions have adapted these two standards and established their own green bond standards. In 2015, the People's Bank of China (PBC) issued the China Green Financial Bond Guidelines for green bonds issued by financial institutions. The Securities and Exchange Board of India released its green bond requirement in 2016. The ASEAN Capital Market Forum issued the ASEAN Green Bond Standards in 2018. The EU released its Green Bond Standard in 2019. However, these regional standards exhibit large variations and are not easily comparable.

13.3.2. *Taxonomy*

A key challenge of the green bond market is establishing a widely accepted definition of green projects. Because green bond issuers can set their own standards, defining green projects according to their own interests, these definitions may not be accepted among regulators, investors, and other stakeholders. International NGOs need to create a taxonomy of green projects. In an attempt to create a widely accepted set of definitions, the CBI published its Climate Bonds Taxonomy (CBT) in 2013, which provides a set of definitions for green projects. To increase its legitimacy, the CBI established the CBT based on 'the latest climate science and ... an extensive multi-stakeholder approach'.[16] To keep pace with the development of a green taxonomy, the CBI regularly updates the CBT by incorporating the latest climate science, information on new technologies, and the CBS Sector Criteria. The CBT has become recognised and applied globally. In addition to the CBI, the group of multilateral development banks, pioneers of green finance and important green bond issuers, worked in 2015 with the International Development Finance Club to develop two sets of principles for defining green

[16] https://www.climatebonds.net/standard/taxonomy.

projects.[17] The International Organization for Standardization (ISO) is also working on 'Environmental performance evaluation – Green debt instruments', which aims to provide guidance for related parties to designate and verify green bonds (ISO 14030-1) and loans (ISO 14030-2). ISO plans to complement these two sets of standards with a taxonomy (ISO 14030-3) and verification programme requirements (ISO 14030-4). While the GBP has not formally issued a taxonomy, the principles provide guidance on the mapping between GBP project categories and the related taxonomies offered by the CBI, the common principles of multilateral development banks and the International Development Finance Club, and the China Green Bond Catalogue (ICMA, 2021b).

Several governments have also set their own taxonomies. China has taken the lead in developing a green taxonomy. In 2015, the PBC published the China Green Bond Endorsed Project Catalogue (2015 Edition) (Green Finance Committee, 2015), the first green taxonomy for green bonds issued by banks and other financial institutions.[18] In 2019, China's seven authorities[19] jointly released the 2019 Green Industry Guidance Catalogue, or 2019 Industry Catalogue, which can be used by various authorities to create green policies, including tax incentive policies, public policies, and industry certifications. More recently, the PBC released a new green catalogue in 2021, which covers green bond issuance. To foster the development of sustainable finance, the EU formed a High-Level Expert Group on Sustainable Finance in 2016, whose recommendations laid the foundations for the EU Action Plan for Financing Sustainable Growth in 2018. Green taxonomy was identified as a priority plan under these two documents. A Technical Expert Group on Sustainable Finance was established to develop a green taxonomy in May

[17]These two sets of principles are the Common Principles for Climate Mitigation Finance Tracking and the Common Principles for Climate Change Adaptation Finance Tracking.

[18]https://www.oecd-ilibrary.org/sites/5abe80e9-en/index.html?itemId=/content/component/5abe80e9-en.

[19]These authorities include the Ministry of Industry and Information Technology, the Ministry of Natural Resources, the Ministry of Ecology and Environment, the Ministry of Housing and Urban-Rural Development, the National Development and Reform Commission, the PBC, and the National Energy Administration.

2018. In 2020, the EU released the Taxonomy Regulation, which provides a taxonomy for environmentally sustainable activities. In continental Europe, France and the Netherlands also developed their own taxonomies. In 2017, the Ministry of the Environment of Japan released Japan's green bond guidelines, which were revised in 2020 after incorporating the GBP.

A few countries, including Mongolia, Singapore, and South Africa, also developed their own taxonomies, influenced by the EU and Chinese taxonomies. However, because different countries have different environmental challenges and priorities, their taxonomies exhibit wide variations. To harmonise international taxonomies, several organisations, including the EU's Technical Expert Group on Sustainable Finance, the World Bank, and the OECD, have issued principles and guidance to help countries develop their own taxonomies (OECD, 2020; The World Bank, 2020). Another harmonisation effort has taken place through bilateral negotiation and recognition. In 2020, the EU and China set up a working group to assess the differences in taxonomies in these two jurisdictions. This working group published two versions of the Common Ground Taxonomy in July 2020 and June 2022, with the second version covering 72 climate mitigation activities recognised by both the EU and China.

13.3.3. *Stock exchanges*

Stock exchanges promote green bonds by regulating them and providing investors with easy access to them. Several exchanges have created green bond lists or dedicated segments to help investors trade green securities. The Luxembourg Stock Exchange (LuxSE) is a pioneer in this area. In 2007, the LuxSE established the first green bond list in the world. In September 2016, it created the Luxembourg Green Exchange (LGX), the first platform dedicated entirely to green securities. Like the LGX, many exchanges have set guidelines to regulate green bonds. For example, in 2016, the Shanghai Stock Exchange and Shenzhen Stock Exchange promulgated green bond guidelines that cover disclosure, taxonomy, eligibility of green bond issuers and external review providers, and proceed management. Information on the green bond segments of stock exchanges is presented in Table 13.6.

Table 13.6. Green bond segments of stock exchanges.

Stock exchange	Type of dedicated section	Launch date
Oslo Stock Exchange	Green bonds	January 2015
Stockholm Stock Exchange	Sustainable bonds	June 2015
London Stock Exchange	Sustainable bonds	July 2015
Shanghai Stock Exchange	Green bonds	March 2016
Mexico Stock Exchange	Green bonds	August 2016
Luxembourg Stock Exchange	Green bonds	September 2016
Borsa Italiana	Green and social bonds	March 2017
Taipei Exchange	Sustainable bonds	May 2017
Johannesburg Stock Exchange	Green bonds	October 2017
Japan Exchange Group	Green and social bonds	January 2018
Vienna Exchange	Green and social bonds	March 2018
NASDAQ	Sustainable bonds	May 2018
Swiss Stock Exchange	Green and sustainable bonds	July 2018
International Stock Exchange	Sustainable bonds	November 2018
Frankfurt Stock Exchange	Green bonds	November 2018
Santiago Stock Exchange	Green and social bonds	July 2019
Euronext	Green, sustainable, and social bonds	November 2019
Bombay Stock Exchange	Green bonds	June 2019
Argentina Stock Exchange	Green, sustainable, and social bonds	September 2019
Brazil Stock Exchange	Green bonds	September 2019
Nigerian Stock Exchange	Sustainable bonds	October 2019
Hong Kong Exchange	Green, sustainable, and social bonds	June 2020
Korea Exchange	Green, sustainable, and social bonds	June 2020
Toronto Stock Exchange	Sustainable bonds	November 2020
Singapore Stock Exchange	Green, sustainable, and social bonds	n.a.
Bolsas Mercados Españoles	Green, sustainable, and social bonds	n.a.

Note: This table presents green bond segments created by the stock exchanges, the types of dedicated sections, and their launch dates around the world.

Stock exchanges also support green bond indices, which have emerged in response to the demand for benchmarks for green bond performance. These indices adopt methodologies that are used to set the eligibility threshold for green bonds and track the performance of a specific group of green bonds. These indices thus help investors to monitor and evaluate green bond performance. Because green bond indices can increase transparency and reduce greenwashing risks and transaction costs, they can help institutional investors committed to ESG by investing in green bonds.

As of 2022, there were seven well-known, active international green bond indices, most of them developed and maintained by private agencies. I summarise the latest eligibility criteria for these indices in Table 13.7.

As shown in Table 13.7, each index has its own methodology and eligibility criteria, including bond size, currency, credit rating, maturity, coupon, and green criteria. Note that while bond size is an important criterion, I omit it in the table for brevity because green bond indices use multiple currencies to define bond size.[20] While the majority of green bond indices, including FTSE, S&P Dow Jones, iBoxx, Solactive, and ICE, use internationally recognised standards (the GBP or CBS) to screen for green bond eligibility, Barclays and MSCI and Bank of America Merrill Lynch adopt their own ESG methodologies to select green bonds. The inconsistency of eligibility standards makes it difficult for investors to compare and assess the performance of green bonds. At present, these global green bond indices focus on developed economies; however, a few emerging economies, such as China and Vietnam, have also developed their own green bond indices.[21]

13.3.4. *External reviews and service providers*

To the extent that external reviews can increase the integrity of green bonds, both private and public agencies recommend or mandate that green bond issuers provide external reviews. As discussed earlier, ICMA recommends and the CBI requires external reviews. Regulatory bodies such as stock exchanges also require external reviews for green bonds. For example, the LGX mandates pre-issuance external

[20]For example, the Barclays and MSCI green bond index defines green bond size using 17 currencies. https://www.msci.com/documents/10199/242721/Barclays_MSCI_Green_Bond_Index.pdf/.

[21]For example, China has ChinaBond China Green Bond Index Series, ChinaBond China Climate–aligned Bond Index, and CUFE-CNI Green Bond Index Series.

Table 13.7. Eligibility standards of seven international green bond indices.

Green bond index service provider	Bond sector	Currency	Credit quality	Maturity	Coupon	Green criteria
Bank of America Merrill Lynch	Corporate, quasi-government	Multicurrency	Investment grade based on average ratings from Moody's, S&P, and Fitch	At least 18 months	Fixed, fixed-for-floating	Bonds qualified as 'green' (no standards explicitly mentioned)
Barclays and MSCI	Corporate, municipal, government, treasury, securitised bonds	Multicurrency	Investment grade using middle ratings from Moody's, S&P, and Fitch (other sources are also considered)	No minimum limit of 1 year (bonds mature in the index)	Fixed, fixed-for-floating, step-up	Self-labelled and labelled bonds evaluated by MSCI ESG Research (reflecting the GBP)
Solactive	Corporate, government, supranational, and others	Currencies eligible for listing on the Luxemburg Stock Exchange	No requirements	At least 1 month	No requirements	Bonds complying with the GBP; must have at least one external review and one post-issuance report

(*Continued*)

Table 13.7. (*Continued*)

Green bond index service provider	Bond sector	Currency	Credit quality	Maturity	Coupon	Green criteria
S&P Dow Jones	Corporate, quasi-government, government	Multicurrency	Investment or subinvestment grade	At least 1 month	Fixed, fixed-for-floating, step-up, zero	Bonds labelled as 'green' by the CBS and verified by the GBP
FTSE	Corporate, government, government-sponsored, supranational	Multicurrency (local currencies for government)	Investment grade, high yield (depends on subindex)	At least 1 year	Fixed, fixed-for-floating, zero	Bonds labelled as 'green' by the CBS among projects categorised by the GBP
iBoxx	Corporate, sovereign, subsovereign	Multicurrency	Investment or subinvestment grade	At least 18 months	Fixed, fixed-for-floating, zero	Labelled bonds complying with the GBP
ICE	Corporate, quasi-government, sovereign	Multicurrency	Investment grade based on average ratings from Moody's, S&P, and Fitch	At least 18 months	Fixed, fixed-for-floating, zero	Bonds complying with the GBP

Note: This table presents the eligibility standards of seven international green bond indices.

reviews and encourages post-issuance external reviews.[22] Furthermore, the London Stock Exchange (LSE) sets stringent requirements for the qualifications of green assurance providers, including independence, avoidance of conflicts of interest, and expertise in providing external reviews on green bonds (LSE, 2016).

Although green bond standards and regulations require external reviews, green bond issuers have discretion to choose an external review provider. Because few regulations and public enforcement mechanisms punish external review providers, market-based mechanisms, such as competition and the desire to maintain one's reputation, play an important role in forcing external review providers to provide high-quality services. In the following section, I discuss each type of external review and the corresponding service providers.

13.3.4.1. *SPO*

SPO providers can leverage their expertise to help issuers establish a green project evaluation process and assess green projects for green bond issuance against green bond standards (ICMA, 2021a; Dorfleitner *et al.*, 2022). Experts and research institutes in environmental sustainability, such as CICERO, ISS-Oekm, Sustainalytics, Vigeo Eiris, and DNV GL, are the main SPO service providers. SPOs dominate the external review market, with an adoption rate of over 80% for green bond external reviews (Allman and Lock, 2022; Simeth, 2021; Dorfleitner *et al.*, 2022). Despite the popularity of SPOs, the OECD (2015) points out several concerns. For example, the reviews provided by SPO providers can lack standardisation across or within SPOs. To the extent that SPO providers both engage in green-bond-related consultancy and the provision of external reviews, SPOs are subject to independence concerns. Additionally, SPO providers often provide limited information on issuers' environmental performance standards, which makes it difficult for investors to assess issuers' environmental performance.

13.3.4.2. *Third-party assurance*

Green bond issuers can also hire qualified third parties or auditors to independently verify or audit certain aspects of the green

[22]https://www.luxse.com/discover-lgx/how-to-join-lgx?tab=0.

bond process, such as the internal tracking of fund use. Third-party assurance provides investors with a high level of confidence that the green bond issuer's processes for managing proceeds and reporting on outcomes are in line with green bond standards. While the GBP only recommends that the issuer seek assurance after green bond issuance, the CBS requires green bond issuers to conduct pre- and post-issuance verification. In addition, the CBI imposes stringent standards on the eligibility of verifiers, including competence and experience in debt instruments, carbon projects, and assurance services.

13.3.4.3. *Scoring/rating*

External reviews also include issuers' environmental performance relative to the GBP or a score/rating (ICMA, 2022). Rating agencies are important players that provide external reviews of green bonds. Moody's was the first rating agency to establish a green bond rating methodology and service. In 2016, Moody's published the first assessment methodology for rating green bonds, called Green Bond Assessment (GBA), which was mostly aligned with the GBP, with the aim of enhancing transparency and replicability. Moody's GBA uses quantifiable factors to estimate the relative likelihood of the proceeds of a green bond being used in environmentally friendly projects (Ehlers and Packer, 2017). The GBA ranks green bonds from GB1 (excellent) to GB5 (poor) based on five pillars that are highly similar to those of the GBP, including use of proceeds, ongoing reporting, organisation, proceed management, and disclosure of use of proceeds. Similar to a credit score refresh, the GBA provides rating updates and refreshes through regular review.

In 2017, S&P started providing ESG ratings through the introduction of Green Evaluation (GE). S&P GE has a broader focus than Moody's GBA, as it considers environmental impact, governance, and transparency (Elhers and Packer, 2017). GE ranks green bonds on a scale from 0 to 100 based on an evaluation of the environmental impact of the projects they invest in. Unlike the GBA, S&P GE does not provide an ongoing assessment of bond proceeds. The score provided is an evaluation given for a specific time point and is removed from the S&P website after 18 months.

Among the Big Three credit rating agencies, Fitch was the last to launch ESG ratings for green bonds. In 2022, Sustainable Fitch, a unit of Fitch, announced that it would provide ESG ratings for globally labelled structured bonds and covered bonds. Sustainable Fitch also provides ratings for green bonds.

In addition to the three international rating agencies, regional rating agencies such as R&I (Japan), RAM Holdings (Malaysia), and China Bond Rating provide ratings for green bonds. These rating agencies can foster the development of the green bond market by providing credible ESG ratings, as they integrate their expertise and knowledge into ESG ratings and leverage their established reputation in capital markets.

13.3.4.4. *Verification*

Under the GBP, an issuer may procure verification against a set of environmental criteria. While the GBP only provides guidelines for verifier qualifications, the CBI requires certification providers to fulfil its criteria, such as competence and experience, and obtain CBI approval. As of 2021, the CBI had 57 approved certification providers. ESG experts such as BLX Group and FSG Sustainable provide certifications to green bond issuers according to the GBP. CBI verifiers include several types of certification providers, including audit firms such as Deloitte, Ernst & Young, KPMG, and PWC, rating firms, ESG consulting firms, and scientific experts.

The CBI summarises different types of external reviews and external review providers (see Table 13.8). Note that verification under the GBP is usually associated with third-party assurance. MacAskill *et al.* (2021) show that the percentage of green bond issuers who hire related parties to provide external reviews increased from 53% in 2014 to 83% in 2018. The CBI (2021b, p. 22) reports the volume of green bonds issued during the 2015–2020 period by type of external review. The report shows that the number of bonds using external reviews exhibited an increasing trend up to 2019, the year before the COVID-19 outbroke. Among green bonds with external reviews, the majority chose SPOs and a small proportion chose multiple external reviews.

Table 13.8. Green bond external reviews and their providers.[23]

Type of review	Providers
Third-party assurance	Accounting/audit firms such as KPMG, Deloitte, Ernst & Young, and PWC, and consulting firms such as CECEP
SPO	ESG service providers (such as ISS-Oekom, Sustainalytics, Vigeo Eiris, DNV GL), scientific experts (such as CICERO, CECEP Consulting), and other environmental consultants and assessment organisations
Green bond rating	Rating agencies such as Moody's, S&P Global Ratings, Fitch, JCRA, R&I, and RAM Holdings
Verification	There are no specific requirements under the GBP. Verifiers should obtain CBI approval. CBI verifiers include audit firms such as Deloitte, Ernst & Young, KPMG, and PWC; rating firms; ESG consulting firms; and scientific experts

Note: This table presents the types of green bond external reviewers and their providers.

Due to a lack of publicly available market share data for the corporate green bond market, I cite the data from Allman and Lock (2022) to outline the market shares. Allman and Lock (2022) study a global sample of 1,242 corporate green bonds between 2013 and 2022 and show that 72.3% of corporate green bonds undergo external reviews and that the external review market is dominated by SPOs (57.2% with SPOs) during the sample period; these results are similar to those reported by the CBI and MacAskill *et al.* (2021). Around 9.6% of green bonds have a rating, followed by assurance (8.3%) and CBI certification (8.2%). In the SPO market, the top four reviewers with more than 10% market share are Sustainalytics (38.34%), Vigeo Eiris (23.67%), ISS-Oekom (16.6%), and CICERO (11.38%). While consulting firms also provide assurance reports for green bonds, auditors dominate this market, with the top two assurance providers being the Big Four auditors (Deloitte: 50.04%; Ernst & Young: 44.04%). Consulting firms such as CECEP also provide assurance (1.64%). Similar to the credit market share, Moody's and S&P hold 38.8% and 23.08% market share, respectively, in the green bond rating market. The other rating agencies with more than 10% market share are JCR

[23] https://www.climatebonds.net/market/second-opinion.

(11.08%) and R&I (Japan) (11.52%). The market share of CBI verifiers is quite different: both auditor and nonauditor ESG experts are dominant players in the market. Allman and Lock (2022) show that the top verifiers are ISS-Oekom (33.94%), Sustainalytics (24.52%), and Ernst & Young (15.32%).

13.4. The Effectiveness of Governance Mechanisms: A Literature Review on the Greenium

The preceding sections provide a overview of the development of green bonds. Specifically, I discuss various governance mechanisms and parties involved in the green bond market. Nevertheless, our understanding of green bonds is incomplete without deeper and more comprehensive analyses. As such, a literature review can give readers a better understanding of the effectiveness of green bond governance mechanisms. To this end, I present a systematic review of the literature on green bonds. While there are three previous review papers, Liaw (2020), MacAskill *et al.* (2021), and Cortellini and Panetta (2021), my study differs from these in that it incorporates more recent studies and focuses on how governance mechanisms affect the outcomes of green bonds. While the success of green bonds can be measured in several ways, I focus on the pricing of green bonds relative to conventional bonds (i.e. greenium), as this can capture whether investors have fewer greenwashing concerns. Although I confine my review to the greenium effect, I note that studies on the determinants of country-level green bond market development can also inform us about the effectiveness of governance mechanisms.

I searched academic papers on green bonds as of 1 March 2023. To include as many papers as possible in this review, I searched for the keyword 'green bond' on Scopus and the Web of Science, the two largest databases for academic research and citation analysis. These two databases are used by researchers to access the scholarly literature and track the impact of their research. In addition to these two databases, I searched Google Scholar to find relevant working papers on green bonds. After obtaining these papers, I screened them and retained empirical studies of the green bond premium (i.e. greenium). Despite my efforts, I acknowledge that the review may not include all of the relevant papers. In the following, after reviewing the literature, I summarise it and discuss possible future research directions.

13.4.1. *Green bond premium*

The green bond premium (i.e. greenium) refers to whether green bonds are traded at a premium compared with risk-paired conventional bonds (e.g. MacAskill *et al.*, 2021). The greenium can be reflected in both the primary and secondary green bond markets. When green bonds are initially issued in the market, the greenium can be manifested as the higher price of a green bond compared with that of a conventional bond. In later stages, when green bonds are traded in the market, the greenium is usually measured as the difference between the green bond yield and the conventional bond yield. As such, examining the greenium can be conducted in both primary and secondary green bond markets. Proponents of the existence of a greenium attribute it to investors' willingness to forgo financial gains for environmentally friendly projects (Friedman and Heinle, 2016) and low-risk green projects. In contrast, sceptics argue that investors care more about economic returns and therefore a greenium should not exist. As a result, whether a greenium exists is an interesting empirical question that has attracted much research attention over the past two decades. Based on a review of 30 empirical studies conducted between 2007 and 2019, MacAskill *et al.* (2021) report that the majority of prior studies support the existence of a greenium. Specifically, they report that 56% of prior studies confirm the existence of a greenium in the primary market and 70% confirm the existence of a greenium in the secondary market.

Because of these mixed results, much research focuses on how governance mechanisms affect this greenium. These studies primarily focus on private governance mechanisms, with a few examining the role of public governance mechanisms. A strand of the literature examines how governance mechanisms affect the greenium based on global green bond samples. Ehlers and Packer (2017) study a sample of global green bonds and find that green bonds trade at a higher price and lower yield (mean difference of 18 basis points [bps] in credit spread) than their comparable nongreen counterparts. Similarly, using a propensity-matched sample, Hyun *et al.* (2021) show that labelled green bonds enjoy lower yields than unlabelled green bonds, suggesting that compliance with the GBP can reduce investors' greenwashing concerns. Hyun *et al.* (2020) use the liquidity-adjusted ask–yield spread between green bonds and conventional bonds as a greenium measure and show that green bonds with an external reviewer have a lower spread (about 6 bps). Additionally, they find that green bonds with a CBI certificate have a larger discount (about 15 bps), suggesting that CBI certification can effectively signal the greenness of green bonds. Kapraun *et al.* (2021) also provide evidence confirming the role of third-party certification in increasing the credibility of green bonds. Bachelet *et al.* (2019) empirically show that the issuer's reputation and external reviews are two important factors that can reduce investors' greenwashing concerns and result in lower spreads. Immel *et al.* (2022) show that green bond issuers with good ESG ratings, especially corporate governance ratings, have lower yield spreads. While several studies examine the effect of external reviews, Simeth (2022) is probably the first to examine how different types of external reviews (SPO, verification/assurance, and rating/scoring) affect green bond pricing. Based on a global sample of 121 green bonds during the 2010–2018 period, the results show that the yield spread is 9 bps lower if a green bond is accompanied by an SPO. For a subsample of 45 financial institutions, which tend to obtain at least one type of external review, an SPO, verification/assurance, and rating/scoring can lower the yield spread by 6–9 bps, 3 bps, and 10 bps, respectively. Simeth (2022) therefore shows that an SPO is the most effective way to signal the credibility of a bond's greenness in the green bond market.

One strand of the literature examines how governance mechanisms affect the greenium in China, one of the world's largest green bond markets. Wang *et al.* (2019) provide a comprehensive analysis of the determinants of the greenium based on Chinese data. They show that multilevel factors (bond, issuer, and macroeconomy), including third-party certification, bond size, issuer and bond credit ratings, issuer profitability, and market interest rate, are significantly associated with the greenium. Wang *et al.* (2020) examine the greenium in China's primary green bond market. Based on 159 green bonds during the 2016–2019 period, they find that labelled green bonds trade at at-issue yield spreads lower by 33.9 bps on average than their comparable nongreen counterparts. Furthermore, for a subsample of 25 CBI-certified green bonds, the greenium effect is greater at 51.9 bps.

Moreover, the greenium is greater for issuers and underwriters with high ESG ratings (at lower yield spreads of 92.5 bps and 93.1 bps, respectively), whereas the greenium is not statistically significant for green bonds from issuers and underwriters with low or null ESG ratings. Deng *et al.* (2020) find that Chinese green bonds that are verified by a third party have lower yield spreads, and such an effect is more pronounced for more reputable third parties. The role of third-party certification in lowering the green bond yield spread is further confirmed by Xu *et al.* (2022)[24], while Sun *et al.* (2022), while Chang *et al.* (2021) find that issuers' credit rating and stock market liquidity are significantly and negatively associated with green bond yield spreads. Li *et al.* (2020) find that issuers' credit ratings, ESG performance, and green certification are significantly and positively associated with the greenium. Hu *et al.* (2022) show that the green bond greenium is more salient for issuers with less information asymmetry, namely, listed companies. Although these studies are based on Chinese data, which has many unique institutional features, the findings are largely consistent with those based on global data.

While several of the studies mentioned above focus on private governance, a handful of studies examine the effect on the greenium of public governance mechanisms and their interaction with private governance. Using a sample of global green bonds, Kapraun *et al.* (2021) document that investors are more likely to pay a premium for a green bond listed on an exchange with a dedicated green bond segment and strict listing requirements. More recently, Allman and Lock (2022) examine the effect on the corporate green bond greenium of several governance mechanisms at the micro and macro levels. While they find no evidence that external reviews can reduce green bond spreads, they show that external reviews influence at-issue bond prices when green bond issuers are domiciled in common law countries. They also find that green bond assurance providers, especially the Big Four audit firms, and rating agencies that serve as external reviewers significantly reduce the cost of green bonds relative to green bonds not reviewed externally, and such an effect is only present in common law countries. As such, Allman and Lock (2022)

[24]However, Xu *et al.* (2022) show that green bonds have higher credit spreads than conventional bonds.

show that the effectiveness of private governance in reducing greenwashing concerns in the green bond market hinges on legal protection, an important public governance mechanism, which suggests the supplementary effect of these two types of governance mechanisms.

Although prior studies show that issuers' characteristics (e.g. their ESG reputation), private governance mechanisms such as external reviews, and public governance mechanisms are key factors that affect the success of green bonds (summarised in Table 13.9), several governance mechanisms are omitted in these empirical studies.

Table 13.9. Empirical studies of the effect of governance mechanisms on the greenium.

Governance	Publication
Private governance	
External reviews/label	Ehlers and Packer (2017)
	Bachelet *et al.* (2019)
	Wang *et al.* (2019)
	Deng *et al.* (2020)
	Hyun *et al.* (2020)
	Li *et al.* (2020)
	Hyun *et al.* (2021)
	Simeth (2022)
Third-party verification	Deng *et al.* (2020)
	Allman and Lock (2022)
	Sun *et al.* (2022)
	Xu *et al.* (2022)
Issuers' ESG governance, corporate governance, and credit ratings	Bachelet *et al.* (2019)
	Wang *et al.* (2019)
	Immel *et al.* 2020)
	Li *et al.* (2020)
	Chang *et al.* (2021)
	Hu *et al.* (2022)
Bond credit ratings	Wang *et al.* (2019)
Underwriters	Wang *et al.* (2020)
Public governance	
	Kapraun *et al.* (2021)
Interplay between public and private governance	
Legal system and external reviews	Allman and Lock (2022)

Note: This table summarises the empirical studies of the effect of governance mechanisms on the greenium.

For example, given that lenders are important delegated monitors (Diamond, 1984), Park (2019) suggests appointing a trustee as a delegated monitor to alleviate greenwashing concerns and green defaults. So far, however, no empirical studies have examined the effect of delegated monitors on the greenium. Future studies may also consider the role of financial analysts in alleviating greenwashing problems in green bond markets. Given the increasing relevance of ESG information for firm value, financial analysts have incorporated ESG information into their reports to investors (Luo *et al.*, 2015). While studies show that financial analysts increase the value relevance of ESG reporting (Tsang *et al.*, 2022), little is known about whether they can alleviate the greenwashing problems in green bond markets. Future studies may also examine the effect of governance mechanisms within issuers because the issuers manage green bonds, including hiring external reviewers, allocating the proceeds to green projects, and reporting the use of proceeds. While Bachelet *et al.* (2019) and Li *et al.* (2020) show that issuers' ESG reputation matters, it is worth examining the effect of green bond issuers' corporate governance in general and their environmental governance mechanisms in particular.

13.5. Toward An Integrated Governance Model

As discussed earlier, despite the rapid expansion of the green bond market, several barriers have hindered its global development. The OECD (2015) points out several challenges to such development.[25] It is worth further examining the barriers that continue to impede the development of green bonds. This study focuses in particular on the governance mechanisms that affect the development of green bonds. Inspired by the notion of the governance triangle, which comprises firms, NGOs, and states (Abbott and Snidal, 2009, 2021) and previous empirical studies, I propose an integrated green bond governance

[25] These challenges include: a lack of awareness of the benefits of green bonds; costs of green bond issuance; insufficient supply of green bonds; lack of domestic green bond investors; absence of local green bond standards; lack of green bond ratings, listings, and indices; and inability of international investors to obtain access to local markets.

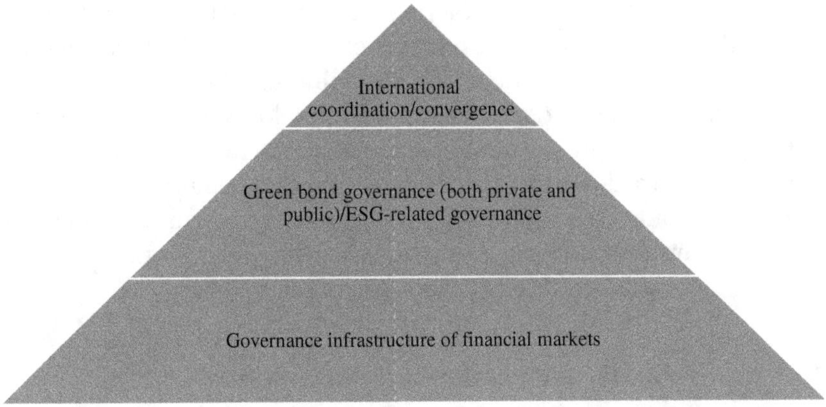

Figure 13.3. An integrated governance model of green bonds.

model that includes both private and public governance. The model is graphically represented in Figure 13.3. In this model, the governance infrastructure of financial markets serves as the foundation for the green bond market because green bonds, by nature, are a type of fixed-income instrument. Consistent with this notion, the green bond market is better developed in developed countries with solid financial market infrastructure. Given the backbone of this infrastructure, both private and public governance mechanisms need to be present to govern the green bond market because of their respective merits (Abbott and Snidal, 2009, 2021; Park, 2018). Because ESG-related regimes, including environmental regulations and ESG reporting standards, can punish polluting projects and increase the credibility of firms' environmental disclosure, they can supplement green-bond-specific governance mechanisms to monitor green bonds. Finally, I add international coordination and convergence at the top of the model because of the possible cross-border regulatory arbitrage problem. Having outlined the architecture of this model, I discuss each governance mechanism in turn in this section.

13.5.1. *The governance infrastructure of financial markets*

The green bond market is built on existing financial markets; therefore, the development of the green bond market also hinges on the financial market having a functioning infrastructure. Legal protection and enforcement are important elements of this infrastructure. As a result, debt market development exhibits large variations across countries, with more developed (underdeveloped) bond markets in developed (emerging) economies (e.g. La Porta *et al.*, 1998). In a similar vein, to develop a green bond market, emerging economies face more challenges than developed countries because of their lack of solid governance infrastructure for their financial markets (OECD, 2015).

13.5.2. *Private governance of green bonds*

We have already discussed several private governance mechanisms, including investor-based standards, certification schemes, green bond indices, and external assurance, in green bond markets (Park, 2018). Over the past decade, as an important private governance party, private standard setters such as ICMA and the CBI have established global green bond standards that provide guidance for green bond certification and criteria for green bond index inclusion. Despite the success of these private standard setters, concerns about possible regulatory capture remain (Park, 2018; Abbott and Snidal, 2009, 2021). As such, these agencies need to improve their governance and gain legitimacy (Park, 2018).

The implementation of green bond standards and the success of green bond indices require competent and responsible information intermediaries. The assessment of greenness requires an in-depth understanding of firms' ESG strategies, green bond standards, green taxonomy, and the use of proceeds. As a result, these agencies should have both financial and green knowledge to qualify as financial intermediaries. The shortfall of professionals with ESG knowledge therefore threatens the professionalism of information intermediaries. In addition, Banahan (2018) points out that several governance problems that were revealed during the 2008 financial crisis continue to impair the functioning of information intermediaries in green bond markets. For example, the issuer-paid model can result in conflict of interest that could threaten the independence of financial intermediaries and therefore the credibility of green bonds. This issue can manifest itself in several ways. For example, external review providers such as rating firms and auditors who provide multiple services to green bond issuers may issue favourable review reports because of their economic reliance on these clients. Consistent with this concern, Banahan (2018) observes that none of the top four green bond certifiers[26] had given a negative evaluation for a green bond as of 2019. Despite these problems, regulation of financial intermediaries in green bond markets is largely nonexistent. The CBI sets fairly rigorous standards for recognising verifiers; however, there are no continuous assessment rules or punishment mechanisms (e.g. blacklisting). To develop green bond markets, more efforts need to be made to increase the competence and credibility of information intermediaries.

13.5.3. *Public governance of green bonds*

Around the world, green bond markets are largely governed by private governance (Park, 2018). While private governance has several advantages, including expertise and responsiveness, it is vulnerable to pressure from interest groups and a lack of strong enforcement (Abbott and Snidal, 2009, 2021). For example, ICMA and the CBI are the most prominent international private agencies that govern green bonds by setting standards. While ICMA recommends external reviews of the use of proceeds for green projects, the CBI requires green bond certifiers to assess and report nonconformance. Although an overwhelming majority of green bonds follow the GBP, these principles are largely voluntary and do not punish green defaults. The CBI deprives nonconforming issuers of certification, which imposes costs on them. The punishment for green defaults is therefore largely a loss of certification, which may not be strong enough to deter such defaults. Because green defaults receive limited punishment, green bond issuers may have little incentive to fulfil their promises. In this regard, public governance should step in because it can provide stronger enforcement than private governance (Abbott and Snidal, 2009, 2021). However, it should be noted that some emerging economies may not have sufficient capacity to set green bond standards and monitor the market (Abbott and Snidal, 2009, 2021). As

[26]These four green bond certifiers are Ernst & Young, ISS-ESG, CICERO, and Vigeo Eiris.

such, public governance parties in these economies may consider collaborating with their private governance counterparts to govern their domestic green bond markets.

13.5.4. *ESG-related institutions*

The development of green bonds requires support from other related regimes. While fundamental regimes such as the rule of law are extremely difficult to improve, several ESG-related regimes are easier to improve. One notable area is environmental governance. So far, governments, NGOs, and firms have made a global effort to govern environmental issues. For example, China has established a stringent top-down, target-based environmental management system and tied government officers' promotions to environmental performance; this system has been shown to result in lower emission levels (Fan *et al.*, 2019). In the US, the Environmental Protection Agency, an independent agency of the federal government, works with industries to monitor their activities and enforce environmental regulations. Effective environmental governance can help detect and punish green bond issuers who use their proceeds to invest in polluting projects. Another way to alleviate greenwashing problems in green bonds is to provide more credible ESG reports. While ESG reports are voluntary in many countries, several jurisdictions such as China, Europe, and South Africa mandate ESG disclosures. In South Africa, ESG assurance is mandatory, which can further improve the credibility of ESG reports. With more transparent and credible ESG information, green bond investors can better assess the greenness of green bonds and monitor their allocation of proceeds.

13.5.5. *Convergence of international governance*

The absence of a commonly accepted green taxonomy and green bond standards, both within a country and internationally, is an important barrier to the development of the green bond market. So far, only a handful of jurisdictions such as the EU, China, and Japan, have developed their own green taxonomies, leaving several countries without uniform domestic green taxonomies. Internationally, there is no commonly accepted green taxonomy and green bond standards, which increases the information costs for investors and impedes the development of the global green bond market. Green bond issuers may take advantage of this and choose a jurisdiction where the regulatory framework is likely to be conducive to their interests, creating a regulatory arbitrage problem. Another problem is cross-border enforcement. For example, green bond issuers can circumvent regulations by issuing green bonds in jurisdictions where enforcement is less feasible or more lenient. Without extraterritorial enforcement and uniform standards, issuers may take advantage of governance gaps and engage in greenwashing without worrying about punishment from other countries. As a result, the convergence of green bond standards is a necessary condition for the development of the green bond market.

13.6. Conclusion

Increasing concerns about climate change among governments and other stakeholders have induced firms to invest in green projects. Individuals and institutional investors are also searching for green investment opportunities. Due to the growth of green investment needs and investors' keen interest in green assets, green bonds were created as an innovative financial instrument to finance green projects. Against this backdrop, regulators, researchers, and practitioners are increasingly interested in understanding the development of the green bond market and the potential barriers to this development.

This study provides a comprehensive understanding of the green bond market and discusses the governance model for green bonds. I first provide a brief history of green bond market development and discuss the drivers and current status of the global green bond market. A key observation is that while the green bond market has experienced rapid growth, its scale remains much smaller than that of the conventional bond market and cannot satisfy the financing demand for green projects that is necessary to achieve the net-zero target by 2050. An important problem impeding the development of the green bond market is greenwashing because it undermines investors' confidence in the green credentials of green bonds. As a result, green bond governance has attracted increasing attention from both practitioners and researchers. To better understand green bond governance, I describe how different governance parties govern green bonds and summarise the empirical findings on the relationship between governance mechanisms and the greenium.

After reviewing the current green bond governance mechanisms and synthesising the related empirical studies, I propose an integrated green bond governance model that not only includes several existing green bond governance mechanisms but also incorporates the notion of the governance triangle (Abbott and Snidal, 2009, 2021) and related governance mechanisms. First, well-functioning green bond governance should be built on the governance infrastructure of financial markets. Second, both private and public governance mechanisms should be present to govern green bond markets. Third, ESG-related regimes, including environmental regulations and ESG reporting standards, can supplement the governance mechanisms of green bond markets. Finally, due to possible cross-border regulatory arbitrage problems, international coordination and convergence are necessary to effectively govern the green bond market. In short, the tenet of this model is the integration of various governance mechanisms, including both private and public, green-bond-specific and related, and domestic and cross-border mechanisms. I also discuss the role and problems of each aspect of governance in the model and provide suggestions for improvement. The model should benefit practitioners and regulators to make relevant decisions. Researchers can help advance the state-of-the-art in green bond governance. More specifically, while prior studies certainly recognise the importance of individual governance mechanisms, the integrated model developed in this chapter can provide a broad and novel perspective for future research.

References

Abbott, K. W. and Snidal, D. (2009). Strengthening international regulation through transmittal new governance: Overcoming the orchestration deficit. *Vanderbilt Journal of Transnational Law*, 42(3), 501–543.

Abbott, K. W. and Snidal, D. (2021). The governance triangle: Regulatory standards institutions and the shadow of the state. *Journal of International Law*, 32(2), 52–91.

Akerlof, G. A. (1970). The market for 'lemons': Quality uncertainty and the market mechanism. *The Quarterly Journal of Economics*, 84(3), 488–500.

Allman, E. and Lock, B. (2022). External reviews and green bond credibility. *Journal of Financial Economics*, forthcoming.

Asian Development Bank. (2018). Promoting green local currency bonds for infrastructure development in ASEAN+3. Asian Development Bank, Manila, Philippines.

Azhgaliyeva, D. and Kapsalyamova, Z. (2021). Policy support in promoting green bonds in Asia. *Asian Development Bank Institute Working Papers*, 1275, 1–24.

Bachelet, M. J., Becchetti, L., and Manfredonia, S. (2019). The green bonds premium puzzle: The role of issuer characteristics and third-party verification. *Sustainability*, 11(4), 1098–1112.

Banahan, C. M. (2018). The bond villains of green investment: Why an unregulated securities market needs government to lay down the law. *Vermont Law Review*, 43(4), 841–868.

Barua, S. and Chiesa, M. (2019). Sustainable financing practices through green bonds: What affects the funding size? *Business Strategy and the Environment*, 28(6), 1131–1147.

Chang, K., Feng, Y. L., Liu, W., Lu, N., and Li, S. Z. (2021). The impacts of liquidity measures and credit rating on corporate bond yield spreads: Evidence from China's green bond market. *Applied Economics Letters*, 28(17), 1446–1457.

Chiesa, M. and Barua, S. (2019). The surge of impact borrowing: The magnitude and determinants of green bond supply and its heterogeneity across markets. *Journal of Sustainable Finance and Investment*, 9(2), 138–161.

Choi, D., Gao, Z., and Jiang, W. (2020). Attention to global warming. *The Review of Financial Studies*, 33(3), 1112–1145.

Climate Bond Initiative. (2021a). Sustainable debt global state of the market 2021. Technical report, Climate Bond Initiative.

Climate Bond Initiative. (2021b). How to issue green bonds, social bonds and sustainability bonds. Climate Bond Initiative.

Cortellini, G. and Panetta, I. C. (2021). Green bond: A systematic literature review for future research agendas. *Journal of Risk and Financial Management*, 14(12), 589–612.

Deng, Z., Tang, D. Y., and Zhang, Y. (2020). Is 'greenness' priced in the market? Evidence from green bond issuance in China. *The Journal of Alternative Investments*, 23(1), 57–70.

Deschryver, P. and De Mariz, F. (2020). What future for the green bond market? How can policymakers, companies, and investors unlock the potential of the green bond market? *Journal of Risk and Financial Management*, 13(3), 61–82.

Diamond, D. W. (1984). Financial intermediation and delegated monitoring. *The Review of Economic Studies*, 51(3), 393–414.

Dorfleitner, G. and Utz, S. (2014). Profiling German-speaking socially responsible investors. *Qualitative Research in Financial Markets*, 6(2), 118–156.

Dorfleitner, G., Utz, S., and Zhang, R. (2022). The pricing of green bonds: External reviews and the shades of green. *Review of Managerial Science*, 16(3), 797–834.

Dou, X. and Qi, S. (2019). The choice of green bond financing instruments. *Cogent Business and Management*, 6(1), 1652227.

Dyck, A., Lins, K. V., Roth, L., and Wagner, H. F. (2019). Do institutional investors drive corporate social responsibility? International evidence. *Journal of Financial Economics*, 131(3), 693–714.

Ehlers, T. and Packer, F. (2017). Green bond finance and certification. *BIS Quarterly Review*, September, 89–104.

Fan, H., Zivin, J. S. G., Kou, Z., Liu, X., and Wang, H. (2019). Going green in China: Firms' responses to stricter environmental regulations. *NBER Working Paper*, No. w26540.

Flammer, C. (2021). Corporate green bonds. *Journal of Financial Economics*, 142(2), 499–516.

Freeburn, L. and Ramsay, I. (2020). Green bonds: Legal and policy issues. *Capital Markets Law Journal*, 15(4), 418–442.

Freeman, R. E. (1984). Strategic management: A stakeholder approach. Cambridge University Press.

Friedman, H. L. and Heinle, M. S. (2016). Taste, information, and asset prices: Implications for the valuation of CSR. *Review of Accounting Studies*, 21(3), 740–747.

Global Sustainable Investment Alliance. (2019). Global sustainable investment review for 2018. GSIA Report.

Gompers, P., Ishii, J., and Metrick, A. (2003). Corporate governance and equity prices. *The Quarterly Journal of Economics*, 118(1), 107–156.

Grene, S. (2015). The dark side of green bonds. *Financial Times*, June 14.

Herrick, J. A. and Elias, C. S. (2011). Federal incentives for clean energy after Solyndra: A post-recovery act precipice. *North Dakota Law Review*, 87(4), 625–652.

Höchstädter, A. K. and Scheck, B. (2015). What's in a name: An analysis of impact investing understandings by academics and practitioners. *Journal of Business Ethics*, 132(2), 449–475.

Hongkong and Shanghai Banking Corporation Limited. (2021). HSBC green bonds report. HSBC.

Hu, X., Zhong, A., and Cao, Y. (2022). Greenium in the Chinese corporate bond market. *Emerging Markets Review*, 53, 100946.

Hyun, S., Park, D., and Tian, S. (2020). The price of going green: The role of greenness in green bond markets. *Accounting and Finance*, 60(1), 73–95.

Hyun, S., Park, D., and Tian, S. (2021). Pricing of green labeling: A comparison of labeled and unlabeled green bonds. *Finance Research Letters*, 41, 101816.

Immel, M., Hachenberg, B., Kiesel, F., and Schiereck, D. (2022). Green bonds: Shades of green and brown. In *Risks Related to Environmental, Social and Governmental Issues (ESG)*, 21–34. Palgrave Macmillan.

International Capital Market Association. (2020). Bond market size. *ICMA Report.*

International Capital Market Association. (2021a). The green bond principles 2021. *ICMA Report.*

International Capital Market Association. (2021b). Overview and recommendations for sustainable finance taxonomies. *ICMA Report.*

International Capital Market Association. (2022). Guidelines for green, social, sustainability and sustainability linked bonds external reviews. ICMA Report.

Kapraun, J., Latino, C., Scheins, C., and Schlag, C. (2021). (In)-credibly green: Which bonds trade at a green bond premium? *Proceedings of Paris December 2019 Finance Meeting EUROFIDAI-ESSEC.*

La Porta, R. L., Lopez-de-Silanes, F., Shleifer, A., and Vishny, R. W. (1998). Law and finance. *Journal of Political Economy*, 106(6), 1113–1155.

Larcker, D. F. and Watts, E. M. (2020). Where's the greenium? *Journal of Accounting and Economics*, 69(2), 101312.

Li, Z., Tang, Y., Wu, J., Zhang, J., and Lv, Q. (2020). The interest costs of green bonds: Credit ratings, corporate social responsibility, and certification. *Emerging Markets Finance and Trade*, 56(12), 2679–2692.

Liaw, K. T. (2020). Survey of green bond pricing and investment performance. *Journal of Risk and Financial Management*, 13(9), 193–215.

London Stock Exchange. (2016). London stock exchange green bonds listing process. *LSE Report.*

Luo, X., Wang, H., Raithel, S., and Zheng, Q. (2015). Corporate social performance, analyst stock recommendations, and firm future returns. *Strategic Management Journal*, 36(1), 123–136.

Lyon, T. P. and Maxwell, J. W. (2011). Greenwash: Corporate environmental disclosure under threat of audit. *Journal of Economics and Management Strategy*, 20(1), 3–41.

Lyon, T. P. and Montgomery, A. W. (2015). The means and end of greenwash. *Organization and Environment*, 28(2), 223–249.

MacAskill, S., Roca, E., Liu, B., Stewart, R. A., and Sahin, O. (2021). Is there a green premium in the green bond market? Systematic literature review revealing premium determinants. *Journal of Cleaner Production*, 280, 124491.

Matos, P. (2020). ESG and Responsible Institutional Investing around the World: A Critical Review. CFA Institute Research Foundation. ISBN 978-1-944960-97-1. https://doi.org/10.2139/ssrn.3668998.

OECD. (2015). Green Bonds: Country Experiences, Barriers, and Options. Available from: https://www.oecd.org/environment/cc/Green_Bonds_Country_Experiences_Barriers_and_Options.pdf.

OECD. (2020). Developing Sustainable Finance Definitions and Taxonomies. Paris: OECD Publishing. Retrieved from https://doi.org/10.1787/134a2dbe-en.

Park, S. K. (2018). Investors as regulators: Green bonds and the governance challenges of the sustainable finance revolution. *Stanford Journal of International Law*, 54(1), 1–47.

Park, S. K. (2019). Green Bonds and Beyond. In B. Sjåfjell and C. M. Bruner (Eds.), *The Cambridge Handbook of Corporate Law, Corporate Governance and Sustainability* (pp. 596–610). Cambridge University Press. Cambridge, U.K.

Sangiorgi, I. and Schopohl, L. (2021). Why do institutional investors buy green bonds: Evidence from a survey of European asset managers. *International Review of Financial Analysis*, 75, 101738.

Simeth, N. (2022). The value of external reviews in the secondary green bond market. *Finance Research Letters*, 46, 102306.

Sun, Z., Feng, J., Zhou, R., Yu, Y., and Deng, Y. (2022). Can labeled green bonds reduce financing cost in China? *Sustainability*, 14(20), 13510.

Tang, D. Y. and Zhang, Y. (2018). Do shareholders benefit from green bonds? *Journal of Corporate Finance*, 61, 104727.

Tsang, A., Wang, K. T., Wu, Y., and Lee, J. (2022). Nonfinancial corporate social responsibility reporting and firm value: International evidence on the role of financial analysts. *European Accounting Review*, forthcoming.

Veys, A. (2010). The sterling bond markets and low carbon or green bonds. *E3G Report.*

Wang, J., Chen, X., Li, X., Yu, J., and Zhong, R. (2020). The market reaction to green bond issuance: Evidence from China. *Pacific-Basin Finance Journal*, 60, 101294.

Wang, Q., Zhou, Y., Luo, L., and Ji, J. (2019). Research on the factors affecting the risk premium of China's green bond issuance. *Sustainability*, 11(22), 6394.

World Bank. (2020). Developing a national green taxonomy: A World Bank guide. The World Bank.

Xu, G., Lu, N., and Tong, Y. (2022). Greenwashing and credit spread: Evidence from the Chinese green bond market. *Finance Research Letters*, 48, 102927.

https://doi.org/10.1142/9781800617032_0014

Chapter 14

Financing Choices and Transition Risk: Economic and Social Implications

Geeta Duppati*, Ruwani Fernando†, and Sonono Energy‡

**College of Business Administration, Prince Mohammad University, Khobar, Saudi Arabia*

†Faculty of Commerce and Management Studies, University of Kelaniya, Sri Lanka

‡NWU School of Mathematical Sciences, North-West University, Vanderbijlpark Campus, South Africa

The transition to a low-carbon economy is a multifaceted and challenging process that requires careful assessment of financing options and transition risk. Companies must handle the financial consequences of transitioning to sustainable practices while mitigating the related risks. Transition risk may lead to job losses in carbon-intensive industries, resulting in unemployment and displeasure with the government. Economic collapse in fossil-fuel-dependent economies could result in poverty and inequality. Green technology and infrastructure investments can stimulate economic growth and job creation. A good transition minimises pollution and health risks, which benefits public health.

Financing decisions have a significant impact on how successfully businesses can manage the financial difficulties of this change. Equity finance allows businesses to raise funds without the immediate repayment responsibilities that debt financing requires. This can be especially beneficial for organisations going through big transformations because it allows them to share the risks with investors. However, the dilution of ownership and the greater cost of financing associated with equity are possible disadvantages. Debt financing, on the other hand, gives stability and tax benefits, but it also imposes payback responsibilities that might put pressure on resources, especially if the shift does not produce immediate financial returns. Green bonds have evolved as a unique financing option for sustainable initiatives. These bonds are useful since they provide specific cash for environmentally friendly efforts and can help a company's reputation with investors who value sustainability. However, the use-of-proceeds criteria and greater issuing costs may present difficulties.

This chapter therefore discusses the challenges and risks associated with the financing choices and transition risk from the perspective of the institutional investors, regulators, and political constructs. It also examines country-level approaches to mitigate carbon emissions from carbon taxes that have implications for business entrepreneurs, wider societies, and economies.

Understanding the relationship between financing options and transition risk is critical for businesses seeking long-term financial and operational resilience in a low-carbon economy. Companies can better negotiate the specifics of this important economic shift by strategically leveraging various financing choices and managing the related risks in advance. Another important consideration is market risk, which is being driven by shifting customer demand for sustainable products and services. Companies that fail to meet these demands risk losing market share. Diversifying product lines to include green alternatives and investing in innovation can help reduce this risk. Given the high pace of technological change in the green economy, technology risk is another source of concern. Companies can reduce this risk by investing continuously in R&D and forming relationships with technology providers. The term 'transition risk' refers to a variety of potential consequences of the transition to low-carbon economies. Regulatory risk is significant because changes in environmental regulations can impose large costs on businesses. For example, stricter pollution limits may necessitate large expenditures in new technology or processes. Companies can reduce this risk by investing in sustainable practices and aggressively working with lawmakers to support favourable policies.

Financing alternatives are changing substantially in comparison to traditional approaches, mainly due to the increased emphasis on environmental responsibility and the need to address climate change concerns. Primarily, a shift in legal frameworks and investor expectations towards green financing is critical in mobilising capital for ecologically friendly ventures and hastening the transition to a cleaner economy. Green financing supports innovation, resilience, and long-term prosperity by aligning financial incentives with environmental goals while also addressing global challenges such as climate change and resource scarcity. Similarly, loans were typically made primarily on standard credit criteria, with little emphasis on environmental or social effect factors.

Extreme weather and climatic disasters, such as floods, wildfires, and hurricanes, can have an influence on GDP by destroying property and physical capital required to generate goods, as well as on investments and financial institutions. In 2019, total economic losses from extreme events amounted to 1% of GDP in the euro area; without action, these costs are expected to rise over time. Recent research provides insight into institutional investors' perceptions of climate risk. Institutional investors believe that climate risks have financial consequences for their portfolio companies and that these risks, particularly regulatory threats, have already begun to manifest. Many investors, particularly long-term, large-scale, and ESG-oriented ones, believe that risk management and involvement, rather than divestment, are the best approaches to addressing climate threats (Krueger *et al.*, 2020). To finance the shift to a green economy, more institutional investors are implementing sustainable investment strategies. Choosing low emitters may not be one of these strategies. Rather, for eliminating carbon-intensive industries, they use screening, passive exclusion, and progressively more sophisticated active models.

Carbon pricing in large developing countries could catalyse and efficiently allocate private sector finance but is less urgent in low-income, low-emitting countries. A carbon tax of $70 per tonne would raise estimated revenues of around 1–3% of GDP for most countries (Argentina, Australia, Canada, China, Colombia, Costa Rica, Ethiopia, France, Germany, India, Indonesia, Iran, Jamaica, Japan, Kazakhstan, Macedonia, Mexico, Pakistan, Philippines, Russia, Saudi Arabia, South Africa, Tanzania, Turkey, UAE, UK, US, and Vietnam) and substantially more in a few cases (Iran, Kazakhstan,

Russia, Saudi Arabia, and South Africa). Further, revenues are about 70–85% higher under the $70 per ton carbon price compared with the $35 price (they are less than double, due to tax base erosion). Higher energy costs tend to reduce employment and investment at the economy-wide level, which will lower revenues from broader taxes, for example on labour and capital (IMF, 2019).

Understanding the effects of climate change across longer time horizons has become essential for banks and investors, as it increasingly affects economic and financial systems. Prior literature (Ho *et al.*, 2008) contributes to the topic of carbon price policies by investigating the potential negative implications on domestic industries, with an emphasis on specific sector-level research. The predicted policy scenario calls for a unilateral \$10/ton CO_2 price across the economy, with no additional border tax changes or any complementing policies. Their study adopts four modelling methodologies: short- to long-term time horizons for enterprises to pass through additional costs, change input mix, adopt new technologies, and reallocate capital. Their study findings show that certain industries are more severely impacted by reduced output, and the burdens on different industries remain consistent over all four time frames. Over longer time horizons, output recovers significantly, and the negative effects on profitability fade even faster in most circumstances. Over the short term, employment losses match output drops, whereas improvements in other industries fully offset the losses over the long term. At the same time, some sectors experience substantial losses outside, especially when exports are reduced.

The European Central Bank has intensified its quantitative work aimed at identifying climate-related risks to financial stability. This involves evaluating the financial system's exposure to climate-related risks, upgrading banking sector scenario analysis, and monitoring progress in green transition funding from investors. The effect of carbon pricing on industrial sectors is contingent upon various factors, including fuel use, emissions levels, and the degree to which lower-carbon fuels can be used in place of higher-carbon ones. Certain industries such as chemicals, cement, and iron and steel are more impacted than others because of their higher energy requirements and emissions. Technological developments and increasing efficiencies over time can allow sectors to react and potentially mitigate the initial cost increases (Konradt *et al.*, 2024).

As climate change increasingly affects economic and financial systems, understanding its impact over longer time horizons has become crucial for investors and banks. Both long-term exposure and climate risk exposure rating are important for several reasons.

14.1. Carbon Pricing Exposure

A carbon price incentivises families, corporations, and governments to reduce emissions cost-effectively. Long-term, growing carbon prices drive innovation to reduce pollution costs. Static and dynamic efficiency impacts are independent of policy design, given the price signal is robust and long-lasting. Carbon pricing aims at attaining emissions targets while simultaneously encouraging universal co-ownership of natural resources. As part of a climate policy strategy, carbon pricing imposes fees on carbon dioxide (CO2) emitters for each ton of emissions they are accountable for producing, raising the cost of all goods that contribute to CO2 emissions. The economy as a whole will probably be affected by a carbon price, but the ways in which different sectors respond will vary based on factors such as their carbon intensity and their ability to switch from high-carbon to lower-carbon fuels. This explainer goes over how the building, transportation, industrial, and electricity sectors are affected, or could be affected, by carbon pricing (Hayes and Hafstead, 2020).

The EU Emissions Trading System (EU ETS) indicates that polluters must pay for their greenhouse gas (GHG) emissions, which helps reduce emissions and generates revenue to fund the EU's green transition. It is effective in all EU nations, as well as Iceland, Liechtenstein, and Norway (EEA-EFTA states). It includes emissions from approximately 10,000 installations in the energy and manufacturing industries, as well as aircraft operators flying within the EU and departing to Switzerland and the UK – accounting for approximately 40% of the EU's emissions – and included emissions from maritime transport from 2024 onwards[1] (EU-ETS). On 19 February 2021, the European Commission stated that it was revising its aim for decreasing net GHG emissions by 2030 from 40% to at least 55% of 1990 levels (EUS, 2021).

[1]https://climate.ec.europa.eu/eu-action/eu-emissions-trading-system-eu-ets/what-eu-ets_en.

Carbon prices have experienced significant hikes, and recent policy promises indicate that they must increase even more in order to achieve global climate objectives. As per the World Bank's annual study 'State and Trends of Carbon Pricing', which was released today, the combined revenue from carbon taxes and ETS has reached a new record high of approximately $95 billion. This is true even if governments are dealing with difficult circumstances, including high inflation, tight budgetary constraints, and energy shortages (Bibao, 2023). A recent study (Konradt *et al.*, 2024) shows that an increase in effective carbon prices from around €40 per ton of CO_2 in 2021 to around €150 by 2030 could raise annual euro area inflation by between 0.2 and 0.4 percentage points. It is noteworthy that the increases in energy prices brought about by the effective carbon price rising to €150 are far less than the spike in energy prices that occurred in 2022 after the invasion of Ukraine.

The financial system is exposed to transition risk arising, for example, from exposures to firms with high carbon emissions throughout their value chains. Climate-related risk drivers refer to climate-related changes that affect economies. They can be grouped into two broad categories: physical risk and transition risk.

14.2. Physical Climate Risk and Insurance Costs

Physical risk arises from changes in climate that impact the economy. It can be considered acute, such as extreme weather events including lethal heatwaves, floods, wildfires, and storms, or chronic, such as rising sea levels, rising average temperatures, and ocean acidification. Extended periods of increased average temperature can negatively impact the ecosystem and agriculture, resulting in higher levels of migration and an increased risk of humanitarian crisis. Only a third of climate-related economic losses in the euro area are insured, and climate change is expected to cause this protection gap to widen. Insurers play an important role in mitigating the macroeconomic effects of catastrophes which may be precipitated by climate change. Estimates suggest that uninsured losses have a negative aggregate impact on a country's GDP, while this is not the case if the event is insured.

California already has one of the most alarming real estate markets in the US because to its exorbitant home prices and low supply. It is now becoming worse due to difficulties obtaining and paying for house insurance in the state that is prone to wildfires. Prospective purchasers are undergoing drawn-out, extensive searches and a fair degree of price shock for a product that was previously something of an afterthought due to the pressure of an approaching closing date. Lenders have had to adapt, frequently collaborating extensively with customers to secure insurance so that it doesn't become a barrier to loan acceptance. 'Up until the past year and a half, I really never even discussed insurance', according to Julee Felsman, senior vice president of mortgage lending at Guaranteed Rate, one of the biggest home lenders in the nation based on volume. 'Now that the borrower is eligible for the loan, it will have a big impact on them'. This is due to the fact that premiums are so expensive – up 55% nationwide from five years ago, per a Guaranteed Rate report – that they take up funds from a household's budget that could be used for a mortgage payment (Lopez and Smith, 2024).

Transition risk, on the other hand, is related to the societal changes arising from transitioning into a low-carbon economy, such as changes in public sector policies, innovation, technology, or investor and consumer sentiment towards a greener environment. These significant transitions are expected to be quite challenging, as firms, banks, and investors will be dealing with high levels of uncertainty arising from technology development, innovation, and the behaviour of competitors. (Haas *et al.*, 2023).

14.3. Regulatory Environment and National Policy towards Carbon Emission Tax

Carbon taxes are regarded by economists as a cost-effective method of reducing GHG emissions, making them appealing to countries with strong economic underpinnings and a dedication to efficient policies. The Kyoto Protocol defines binding emissions reduction targets for the European Union, 37 industrialised countries, and economies in transition. In entirety, these objectives result in an average reduction of 5% in emissions compared to 1990 levels during the five-year period of 2008–2012 (the initial commitment period).

Table 14.2 summarises the national carbon taxes enacted in countries until 2012, which is described as the initial commitment period of the Kyoto Protocol. The jurisprudence emissions (JEs) covered indicate the proportion of emissions covered by the tax within the jurisdiction, as well as a percentage of global emissions (GEs). The JEs and GEs displayed in Table 14.1 show considerable heterogeneity across countries.

Table 14.1. National carbon tax enactment and jurisdiction emissions covered by carbon tax (1990–2005).

S. No.	Country	Instrument name	Type	Status	Share of jurisdiction emissions covered
1	Denmark	Denmark carbon tax	National carbon tax	1992	48% of jurisdiction emissions, 0.04% of global emissions
2	Estonia	Estonia carbon tax	National carbon tax	2000	10% of jurisdiction emissions, 0.0026% of global emissions
3	EU	EU ETS	Regional ETS	2005	38% of jurisdiction emissions, 0.05% of global emissions
4	Finland	Finland carbon tax	National carbon tax	1990	45% of jurisdiction emissions, 0.05% of global emissions
5	Latvia	Latvia carbon tax	National carbon tax	2004	2% of jurisdiction emissions, 0.0004% of global emissions
6	Norway	Norway carbon tax	National carbon tax	1991	65% of jurisdiction emissions, 0.08% of global emissions
7	Poland	Poland carbon tax	National carbon tax	1990	24% of jurisdiction emissions, 0.18% of global emissions
8	Slovenia	Slovenia carbon tax	National carbon tax	1996	45.7% of jurisdiction emissions, 0.02% of global emissions
9	Sweden	Sweden carbon tax	National carbon tax	1991	40% of jurisdiction emissions, 0.05% of global emissions

Source: Data sourced from the World Bank Carbon Pricing Dashboard.

Kyoto protocol: First commitment period 2007–2012: It is evident from Tables 14.2–14.5 that some nations have enacted and implemented a carbon tax, while others are still considering the prospect for a range of economic, political, social, and environmental reasons. Early adopters of carbon taxes, such as Sweden and Canada,

Table 14.2. National carbon tax enactment and jurisdiction emissions covered by carbon tax (2007–2012).

S. No.	Country	Instrument name	Type	Enacted	Share of JE covered
1	Albania	Albania carbon tax	National carbon tax	2008	73% of JE, 0.01% of GE
2	Alberta	Alberta TIER	Province ETS	2007	
3	British Columbia	BC carbon tax	Province carbon tax	2008	80% of JE, 0.09% of GE
4	California	California CaT	Province ETS	2012	76% of JE, 0.56% of GE
5	Iceland	Iceland carbon tax	National carbon tax	2010	36% of JE, 0.0032% of GE
6	Ireland	Ireland carbon tax	National carbon tax	2010	34% of JE, 0.04% of GE
7	Japan	Japan carbon tax	National carbon tax	2012	80% of JE, 1.76% of GE
8	Liechtenstein	Liechtenstein-carbon tax	National carbon tax	2008	72% of JE, 0.0002% of GE
9	New Zealand	New Zealand ETS	National ETS	2008	48% of JE, 0.07% of GE
10	RGGI	RGGI	Province ETS	2009	
11	Saitama	Saitama ETS	Subnational city ETS	2011	18% of JE, 0.01% of GE
12	Switzerland	Switzerland ETS	National ETS	2008	12% of JE, 0.01% of GE
13	Switzerland	Switzerland carbon tax	National carbon tax	2008	35% of JE, 0.03% of GE
14	Tokyo	Tokyo CaT	Subnational city ETS	2010	18% of JE, 0.02% of GE
15	Ukraine	Ukraine carbon tax	National carbon tax	2011	32% of JE, 0.12% of GE

Source: Data sourced from the World Bank Carbon Pricing Dashboard.

Table 14.3. National carbon tax enactment and jurisdiction emissions covered by carbon tax (2013–2020).

S. No.	Country	Instrument name	Type	Enacted	Share of JE covered
1	Alberta	Alberta carbon tax	Subnational – state/province carbon tax	2017*	38% of JE, 0.27% of GE
2	Argentina	Argentina carbon tax	National carbon tax	2018	GE
3	Baja California	Baja California carbon tax	Subnational – state/province carbon tax	2020**	24% of JE, 0.06% of GE
4	Beijing	Beijing pilot ETS	Subnational – city ETS	2013	GE
5	British Columbia	BC OBPS	Subnational – state/province ETS	2016	0% of JE, 0% of GE
6	Canada	Canada federal OBPS	National ETS	2019	1% of JE, 0.01% of GE
7	Canada	Canada federal fuel charge	National carbon tax	2019	31% of JE, 0.44% of GE
8	Chile	Chile carbon tax	National carbon tax	2017	55% of JE, 0.14% of GE
9	Chongqing	Chongqing pilot ETS	Subnational – city ETS	2014	20% of JE, 0.08% of GE
10	Colombia	Colombia carbon tax	National carbon tax	2017	40% of JE, 0.32% of GE
11	France	France carbon tax	National carbon tax	2014	51% of JE, 0.28% of GE
12	Fujian	Fujian pilot ETS	Subnational – state/province ETS	2016	GE
13	Guangdong (except Shenzhen)	Guangdong pilot ETS	Subnational – state/province ETS	2013	40% of JE, 0.52% of GE
14	Hubei	Hubei pilot ETS	Subnational – state/province ETS	2014	47% of JE, 0.29% of GE
15	Kazakhstan	Kazakhstan ETS	National ETS	2013	GE

Table 14.3. (*Continued*)

S. No.	Country	Instrument name	Type	Enacted	Share of JE covered
16	Korea, Rep.	Korea ETS	National ETS	2015	89% of JE, 1.2% of GE
17	Massachusetts	Massachusetts ETS	Subnational – state/province ETS	2018	9% of JE, 0.01% of GE
18	Mexico	Mexico carbon tax	National carbon tax	2014	29% of JE, 0.44% of GE
19	Mexico	Mexico pilot ETS	National ETS	2020	40% of JE, 0.61% of GE
20	New Brunswick	New Brunswick carbon tax	Subnational – state/province carbon tax	2020***	38% of JE, 0.01% of GE
21	Newfoundland and Labrador	Newfoundland and Labrador OBPS	Subnational – state/province ETS	2019	GE
22	Newfoundland and Labrador	Newfoundland and Labrador carbon tax	Subnational – state/province carbon tax	2019***	38% of JE, 0.01% of GE
23	Northwest Territories	Northwest Territories carbon tax	Subnational – state/province carbon tax	2019	76% of JE, 0.0018% of GE
24	Nova Scotia	Nova Scotia OBPS	Subnational – state/province ETS	2019	87% of JE, 0.02% of GE
25	Ontario	Ontario CaT	Subnational – state/province ETS	2017#	40% of JE, 0.04% of GE
26	Portugal	Portugal carbon tax	National carbon tax	2015	GE
27	Prince Edward Island	Prince Edward Island carbon tax	Subnational – state/province carbon tax	2019***	78.5% of JE, 0.11% of GE
28	Quebec	Quebec CaT	Subnational – state/province ETS	2013	43% of JE, 0.05% of GE

(*Continued*)

Table 14.3. (*Continued*)

S. No.	Country	Instrument name	Type	Enacted	Share of JE covered
29	Saskatchewan	Saskatchewan OBPS	Subnational – state/province ETS	2019	36% of JE, 0.16% of GE
30	Shanghai	Shanghai pilot ETS	Subnational – city ETS	2013	30% of JE, 0.03% of GE
31	Shenzhen	Shenzhen pilot ETS	Subnational – city ETS	2013	GE
32	Singapore	Singapore carbon tax	National carbon tax	2019	79% of JE, 0.1% of GE
33	South Africa	South Africa carbon tax	National carbon tax	2019	82% of JE, 0.81% of GE
34	Spain	Spain carbon tax	National carbon tax	2014	1.9% of JE, 0.01% of GE
35	Tianjin	Tianjin pilot ETS	Subnational – city ETS	2013	35% of JE, 0.12% of GE

Notes: #Abolished in 2018; *Abolished in 2019; **Abolished in 2021; ***Abolished in 2023.
Source: Data sourced from the World Bank Carbon Pricing Dashboard.

have implemented them in part because they provide a new source of government revenue that can be used to fund public services or lower other taxes.

Prior literature documents the positive effects of carbon tax on increasing revenue potential and suggests economic implications. For instance, British Columbia became the first North American jurisdiction to impose a major carbon fee in 2008. A tax rate of $30 per ton CO_2 is applied to nearly all fossil fuel consumption in the province. Likewise, a study on the Republic of Ireland (Callan *et al.*, 2009) shows the effects of carbon tax and revenue recycling across the income distribution in the Republic of Ireland. In absolute terms, a carbon tax of €20/tCO_2 would cost the poorest households less than €3/week and the richest households more than €4/week. Consequently, a carbon price is regressive. Their research shows that if tax revenue is used to improve social benefits and tax credits, households across the income spectrum can benefit without using up all carbon tax revenue.

Table 14.4. National carbon tax enactment and jurisdiction emissions covered by carbon tax (2021–2024).

S. No.	Country	Instrument name	Type	Enacted	Share of JE covered
1	Australia	Australia safeguard mechanism	National ETS	2023	26% of JE, 0.28% of GE
2	Austria	Austria ETS	National ETS	2022	40.3% of JE, 0.06% of GE
3	China	China national ETS	National ETS	2021	31.87% of JE, 9.3% of GE
4	Durango	Durango carbon tax	Province carbon tax	2024	
5	Germany	Germany ETS	National ETS	2021	39% of JE, 0.57% of GE
6	Guanajuato	Guanajuato carbon tax	Province carbon tax	2023	42.7% of JE, 0.03% of GE
7	Hungary	Hungary carbon tax	National carbon tax	2023	32.3% of JE, 0.04% of GE
8	Indonesia	Indonesia ETS	National ETS	2023	26% of JE, 0.6% of GE
9	Luxembourg	Luxembourg carbon tax	National carbon tax	2021	72% of JE, 0.01% of GE
10	Montenegro	Montenegro ETS	National ETS	2022	42.94% of JE, 0.0029% of GE
11	Netherlands	Netherlands carbon tax	National carbon tax	2021	45% of JE, 0.14% of GE
12	New Brunswick	New Brunswick OBPS	Province ETS	2021	52% of JE, 0.01% of GE
13	Ontario	Ontario EPS	Province ETS	2022	26% of JE, 0.07% of GE
14	Queretaro	Queretaro carbon tax	Province carbon tax	2022	18% of JE, 0.01% of GE
15	State of Mexico	State of Mexico carbon tax	Province carbon tax	2022	47% of JE, 0.1% of GE
16	Taiwan, China	Taiwan carbon fee	Province carbon tax	2024	80% of JE, 0.46% of GE

(Continued)

Table 14.4. (*Continued*)

S. No.	Country	Instrument name	Type	Enacted	Share of JE covered
17	Tamaulipas	Tamaulipas carbon tax	Province carbon tax	2022*	
18	United Kingdom	UK ETS	National ETS	2021	28% of JE, 0.22% of GE
19	Uruguay	Uruguay CO2 tax	National carbon tax	2022	4.5% of JE, 0.0035% of GE
20	Washington	Washington CCA	Province ETS	2023	70% of JE, 0.11% of GE
21	Yucatan	Yucatan carbon tax	Province carbon tax	2022	32.2% of JE, 0.01% of GE

Note: *Abolished in 2023.
Source: Data sourced from the World Bank Carbon Pricing Dashboard.

Prior research (Beck *et al.*, 2015) employs a computable general equilibrium model and investigates the influence of tax on household income distribution. It discovers that the carbon price has a disproportionate impact on wealthy households in British Columbia, implying that the tax is extremely progressive. This discovery has significant implications for the societal acceptability of carbon prices as a GHG reduction policy. First, the carbon tax implemented by British Columbia, as a standalone policy without supporting revenue recycling measures, is quite progressive. This outcome is mostly due to general equilibrium changes in factor prices that precede the implementation of the carbon tax rather than changes in energy prices. Real wages fall, which disproportionately affects higher-income households because they rely more on labour for income. Second, a revenue recycling programme, such as that developed in British Columbia, can have an impact on tax incidence. In the case of revenue-recycling measures used in conjunction with the carbon tax in British Columbia, the programme increases the progressive incidence of the carbon tax (Ben *et al.*, 2015). New Zealand was a party to the United Nations Framework Convention on Climate Change (UNFCC) and a signatory to the Kyoto Protocol. It assumed responsibility for its emissions reduction target for the first commitment period during 2008–2012 to reduce GHG emissions to their

Table 14.5. National carbon tax enactment under consideration.

S. No.	Country	Instrument name	Type	Status of Enactment
1	Argentina	Argentina ETS	National ETS	Under consideration since 2024
2	Botswana	Botswana carbon tax	National carbon tax	Under consideration since 2022
3	Botswana	Botswana carbon tax	National carbon tax	Under consideration since 2022
4	Brazil	Brazil ETS	National ETS	Under consideration since 2022
5	Brunei Darussalam	Brunei Darussalam undecided	National undecided	Under consideration since 2021
6	Canada	Canada ETS	National ETS	Under development since 2024
7	Catalonia	Catalonia carbon tax	Subnational – state/province carbon tax	Under development since 2018
8	Chile	Chile ETS	National ETS	Under consideration since 2016
9	Colima	Colima carbon tax	Subnational – state/province carbon tax	Under consideration since 2024
10	Colombia	Colombia ETS	National ETS	Under development since 2016
11	Colorado	Colorado ETS	Subnational – state/province ETS	Under development since 2024
12	Côte d'Ivoire	Côte d'Ivoire carbon tax	National carbon tax	Under consideration since 2018
13	LU27+	EU ETS2	Regional ETS	Under development since 2023
14	Gabon	Gabon ETS	National ETS	Under consideration since 2022
15	Hawaii	Hawaii carbon tax	Subnational – state/province carbon tax	Under consideration since 2021
16	Hawaii	Hawaii carbon tax	Subnational – state/province carbon tax	Under consideration since 2021
17	India	India ETS	National ETS	Under development since 2024

(*Continued*)

Table 14.5. (*Continued*)

S. No.	Country	Instrument name	Type	Status of Enactment
18	Indonesia	Indonesia carbon tax	National carbon tax	Under consideration since 2021
19	Israel	Israel carbon tax	National carbon tax	Under consideration since 2021
20	Jalisco	Jalisco carbon tax	Subnational – state/province carbon tax	Under consideration since 2020
21	Japan	Japan ETS	National ETS	Under development since 2016
22	Kenya	Kenya carbon tax	National carbon tax	Under consideration since 2024
23	Malaysia	Malaysia ETS	National ETS	Under consideration since 2021
24	Manitoba	Manitoba ETS	Subnational – state/province ETS	Under consideration since 2018
25	Manitoba	Manitoba carbon tax	Subnational – state/province carbon tax	Under consideration since 2018
26	Manitoba	Manitoba carbon tax	Subnational – state/province carbon tax	Under consideration since 2018
27	Maryland	Maryland ETS	Subnational – state/province ETS	Under consideration since 2024
28	Mauritania	Mauritania carbon tax	National carbon tax	Under consideration since 2024
29	Morocco	Morocco carbon tax	National carbon tax	Under consideration since 2022
30	New York State	New York State ETS	Subnational – state/province ETS	Under development since 2023
31	New Zealand	New Zealand carbon tax	National carbon tax	Under consideration since 2022
32	Nigeria	Nigeria ETS	National ETS	Under consideration since 2022
33	Oregon	Oregon ETS	Subnational – state/province ETS	Under development since 2016

Table 14.5. (*Continued*)

S. No.	Country	Instrument name	Type	Status of Enactment
34	Pakistan	Pakistan ETS	National ETS	Under consideration since 2021
35	Paraguay	Paraguay carbon tax	National carbon tax	Under consideration since 2024
36	Pennsylvania	Pennsylvania ETS	Subnational – state/province ETS	Under development since 2019
37	Philippines	Philippines undecided	National undecided	Under consideration since 2024
38	Sakhalin	Sakhalin ETS	Subnational – state/province ETS	Under development since 2021
39	San Luis Potosi	San Luis Potosi carbon tax	Subnational – state/province carbon tax	Under development since 2024
40	Senegal	Senegal carbon tax	National carbon tax	Under consideration since 2019
41	Taiwan, China	Taiwan, China ETS	Subnational – state/province ETS	Under consideration since 2016
42	Thailand	Thailand ETS	National ETS	Under consideration since 2016
43	Turkey	Turkey ETS	National ETS	Under development since 2016

Source: Data sourced from the World Bank Carbon Pricing Dashboard.

1990 levels.[2] Further, it reiterated its commitment to the Kyoto Protocol by signing the Doha Amendment agreement on 30 November 2015, described as the second commitment period. New Zealand aims to reduce emissions to 30% below 2005 levels by 2030.

Global forums warn the adversaries of not reducing the GHG emissions on climate change. Therefore, urgent action by all the nations for saving our planet is vital. The emphasis is on setting up targets globally at the national level for carbon emissions, which

[2]https://environment.govt.nz/what-government-is-doing/international-action/nz-united-nations-framework-convention-climate-change/.

is one aspect of these green efforts to reduce carbon emissions. The Kyoto Protocol international treaty of 1997 came into force in 2005 as the United Nations Framework Convention on Climate Change (UNFCC). It urged the signatories to reduce the emission of six GHGs in 41 countries plus the European Union to 5.2% below 1990 levels. The signatories assumed mandatory emissions-reduction targets, depending on the unique circumstances of each country. At the same time, restrictions on emissions to developing countries, who are signatories to the UNFCC, were relaxed. New Zealand announced an unconditional target of −5% (below 1990 levels) by 2020, equivalent to a 2013–2020 QELRO (quantified emission limitation and reduction objectives) of 96.8 on 1990 emissions. New Zealand will apply the Kyoto Protocol framework of rules to its target to ensure actions are transparent and have integrity. New Zealand's conditional Copenhagen target range of reducing emissions between 10% and 20% by 2020 remains on the table, pending meeting those conditions (Duppati *et al.*, 2023).

Kyoto protocol: Second commitment period 2013–2020: Table 14.3 summarises the national carbon taxes enacted in countries until 2013–2020, a period that is described as the second commitment period of the Kyoto Protocol. In Doha, Qatar, on 8 December 2012, the Doha Amendment to the Kyoto Protocol was adopted for a second commitment period, starting in 2013 and lasting until 2020. As of 28 October 2020, 147 parties deposited their instruments of acceptance; therefore, the threshold of 144 instruments of acceptance for entry into force of the Doha Amendment was achieved. The amendment entered into force on 31 December 2020.[3]

14.4. Understanding Bank Loan Exposure and Non-Bank Financial Institutions Exposure

The financial sector is vulnerable to transition risk, which arises from exposures to companies with significant carbon emissions throughout their value chains. Physical assets represent around 50% of

[3]https://unfccc.int/kyoto_protocol#:~:text$=$The%20Kyoto%20Protocol%20also%20established,of%20the%20trades%20carried%20out.

the collateral value used to secure exposures to firms subject to high or increasing physical risks, but that share differs across sectors. Non-financial company (NFC) emissions are divided into three categories: direct, energy-related, and indirect emissions, which are connected with all other steps in the value chain, such as the consumption of items supplied. The universe of NFCs reporting GHG emissions is limited to primarily major publicly traded corporations, with indirect emissions providing the least coverage of all disclosures. Using simulated GHG emissions based on self-reported data from firms, it is found that €4 trillion in eurozone bank loans has exposures.

Around 30% of the euro area banking system's credit exposures to NFCs are to firms subject to high or increasing risk due to at least one physical risk driver, such as hurricanes, heat waves, floods, and wildfires. Looking at individual hazards, around 10% of loan exposures involve firms at high or increasing risk of floods, heat stress, or water stress. Taken together, around 80% of loan exposures are to firms with at least some exposure to physical risks. This may become increasingly relevant if emissions are not effectively reduced in the long run and if firms and economies fail to adapt to climate change. In addition, almost 10% of loan exposures to NFCs are subject to multiple high or increasing physical risk drivers (Alogoskoufis *et al.*, 2021).

Investment funds, insurance firms, and pension funds (ICPFs) invest around €1.3 trillion and €0.3 trillion, respectively, in securities issued by high emitters, primarily in the industrial, energy, and materials sectors (ESMA, 2021). While the proportional share of high-emitting enterprises in non-bank portfolios has been largely consistent at around 30% over the previous seven years, the absolute amount has doubled, from €0.8 trillion in 2013 to €1.6 trillion in 2019, almost in line with the growth of non-bank assets. At the same time, an increasing number of institutional investors are implementing sustainable investing methods to finance the green transition. These approaches do not always mean investing in current low emitters. Instead, they range from passive exclusion or screening procedures for carbon-intensive industries to more sophisticated and active models. These include the integration of environmental, social, and governance (ESG) considerations, as well as impact investing, which tries to involve enterprises in greening their activities by raising their

ESG score in comparison to the rest of the industry (Krueger *et al.*, 2020).

While manufacturing sector exposures are large and also linked to high indirect emissions, bank loan portfolios are exposed to the four sectors with the greatest emissions to varied degrees. Approximately 5% of banks' loan exposure is made up of companies in the mining and energy sectors. Despite being some of the creditors with the highest carbon footprints in bank loan portfolios, their small percentage of loans indicates that banks are not at a significant risk. Consequently, the impact of climate change on the financial industry has prompted significant concern worldwide, forcing regulatory agencies such as the Basel Committee on Banking Supervision (BCBS) to develop frameworks addressing the possible risks facing banks.

14.5. Role of Regulatory Frameworks: Basel Committee

14.5.1. *Establishing climate-change financial risk management and supervisory principles*

The BCBS has been instrumental in creating the fundamental concepts of climate-change risk management to support the committee's objective of enhancing the regulation, supervision, and practices of banks globally in order to improve financial stability. The process commenced with a comprehensive assessment of the current regulatory and supervisory measures implemented by the member jurisdictions of the committees. The findings of the inventory audit were recorded and released in April 2020 (BCBS, 2020). The committee then performed an analysis to better understand the risk characteristics of climate change and its potential consequences for individual banks. Two reports were then released to identify climate-change risk drivers and transmission channels, as well as challenges with climate-related financial risk quantification and techniques (BCBS, 2021).

In its most recent initiatives, the committee focused on examining the reliability of the existing framework in addressing climate-related financial risks by identifying potential gaps in the current framework and considering possible measures to address any identified gaps. The work was then complemented by the publication of the Principles for Effective Management and Supervision of Risk

Management and Supervisory Practices related to climate-related financial risks. Through this publication, the committee introduces 18 high-level principles to provide banks with guidance on effective management and supervision of climate-related financial risk. The key principles included the following:

- *Identification and assessment*: The first principle is to identify and assess climate-related financial risks, including physical risks (e.g. extreme weather events) and transition risks (e.g. policy and technological changes). This involves understanding the potential impact of climate change on financial institutions' balance sheets, income, and liquidity.
- *Governance and strategy*: Establishing effective governance structures and strategies is crucial. This includes integrating climate risk considerations into overall risk management frameworks, setting clear objectives, and ensuring accountability for managing climate-related financial risks.
- *Risk measurement and disclosure*: Adequate risk measurement methodologies are needed to assess and quantify climate-related financial risks. This involves developing appropriate models, scenarios, and stress tests to evaluate potential climate risk impacts. Additionally, promoting transparency through effective disclosure practices allows stakeholders to make more informed decisions.
- *Scenario analysis and stress testing*: Conducting scenario analysis and stress testing helps assess the resilience of financial institutions to climate-related risks under different future scenarios. These exercises can help identify vulnerabilities, guide risk management decisions, and inform supervisory oversight.
- *Integration of climate risk considerations*: Integrating climate-related considerations into financial institutions' day-to-day decision-making processes is crucial. This includes incorporating climate risk factors into credit risk assessments, investment decision-making, and strategic planning.
- *Supervisory review and cooperation*: Effective oversight and supervision play a critical role. Supervisory authorities should review and provide guidance on the adequacy of financial institutions' climate risk management practices, collaborate with other relevant authorities, and ensure consistency in the approach to climate risk management.

Basel Framework for Assessing Risk: Measuring climate risk exposure involves assigning a rating or score to a project. The analysis of the climate-related opportunities and risks for companies that the bank finances or is considering financing (e.g. considering the company's carbon footprint, climate change adaptation solutions, and strategic positioning). The intention of such an analysis is to provide the bank's credit officers with elements that may be useful to inform the credit decision. Rating or scoring approaches for clients or exposures are frequently used by banks. Such ratings derive from either in-house bank expertise or external ratings from specialised providers or traditional rating agencies.

The European Central Bank (ECB) will limit its purchases of longer-term debt issued by corporations that perform poorly under a new rating system designed to identify polluters and combat climate change. The maturity limit will reduce the Eurosystem's 'longer-term exposure to transition risks' (Schwartzkopf, 2022). The ECB will also provide 'special treatment' to green bonds that meet 'stringent' conditions and purchase more assets from top performers. It is the first detailed look at how the organisation intends to reinvest 'sizable redemptions' in the future years. Each year, about €30 billion ($30 billion), or 10% of its corporate-bond holdings, will be reinvested in what has been dubbed the 'most ambitious' initiative by a central bank to fight climate change (Schwartzkopf, 2022).

The ECB stated that the asset-allocation programme will help it achieve its dual aims of lowering financial risk associated with climate change and promoting 'the green transition of the economy in line with the European Union's climate-neutrality objectives'. The damage caused by rising temperatures is being highlighted by unusual fires, droughts, and floods, which has put pressure on central banks worldwide to do more to ensure the Paris Agreement is met. This month, in response to worries that businesses are inflating their claims, a dozen charity organisations, urged the ECB to man date science-based emission-reduction objectives. Later, the ECB said that issuers will score higher under its new methodology if their decarbonisation plans are supported by research and independently confirmed. More purchases will result from higher rankings (*Bloomberg News*, 2022).

According to Bloomberg News, Matua (2024) states that Deutsche Bank, for the first time, offered bonds intended to finance social projects, and investor demand was quite high. In accordance with the bank's sustainable instruments framework, proceeds will be utilised to refinance social assets, which may include providing suitable and affordable homes for underprivileged individuals or communities. According to the framework, the lender hopes to produce a total of €500 billion in sustainable financing and investments by the end of 2025, excluding its investment arm, DWS Group. $97.5 billion in social bonds have been borrowed by governments and businesses worldwide so far this year, a 14.9% increase over the same period last year. Table 14.6 presents the green, social, sustainability, and sustainability-linked corporate and government bond sales in the first week of July 2024.

14.5.2. *Theoretical considerations of transition risk*

Political will and popular support are critical for establishing and executing a carbon tax. Environmental initiatives enjoy widespread political support in countries such as Norway and New Zealand. Leaders in these countries frequently prioritise climate change mitigation. These countries' inhabitants are often more environmentally conscious and supportive of efforts to reduce carbon emissions. Prior research on New Zealand has demonstrated the effects of CO_2 emissions, renewables, fossil fuels, Brent, and Australian coal on economic growth. This study demonstrates that the crossing points between Brent and Australian coal have implications for New Zealand's cleaner economic growth. A negative shock in Brent benefits renewable energy while harming fossil fuels and CO_2 emissions. These impacts lead observers to assume that New Zealand's economic development is sensitive to fluctuations in oil and coal commodity prices and can therefore be tempered by reducing reliance on coal consumption and increasing renewable energy potential.

This study gives empirical insights into green policy initiatives, which will aid in the refinement of early mitigation actions as well as a transparent public debate regarding long-term desirable and achievable mitigation paths (Duppati *et al.*, 2023). According to

Table 14.6. Green, social, sustainability and sustainability-linked corporate and government bond sales.

Issuer	Type	Currency	Size (in millions)
Deutsche Bank AG	Social	EUR	500000000
European Investment Bank	Green	USD	4000000000
China Citic BK/London	Green	USD	300000000
DZ HYP AG	Green	EUR	500000000
Ulker Biskuvi Sanayi As	Sustainability linked	USD	550000000
Cmt Mtn Pte Ltd	Green	SGD	300000000
Taizhou Urban Const Inv	Sustainability linked	USD	500000000
Nomura real estate hldgs	Green	JPY	30000000000
NEC corporation	Sustainability linked	JPY	20000000000
Tongwei Co Ltd	Green	CNY	500000000
Mori Building Co	Green	JPY	10000000000
CHN New Energy Co	Green	CNY	1000000000
Japan Exp Hld/Debt Repay	Social	JPY	42000000000
JPN Housing Fin Agency	Green	JPY	10000000000
Asian Development Bank	Green	HKD	100000000
Japan Exp Hld/Debt Repay	Social	JPY	15000000000
China Merchants B/Sydney	Green	USD	400000000
Mena Warba Sukuk Ltd	Green	USD	500000000

Notes: Green, social, sustainability, and sustainability-linked corporate and government bond sales total $620.1 billion year-to-date, up 7.9% compared with the same period last year. Of this, green bond sales reached $303.2 billion, the data show.
Source: This information is sourced from Bloomberg for the first week of July 2024.

the carbon pricing theory, businesses with high carbon intensity will incur greater manufacturing expenses, which could lower their profitability, when the cost of producing carbon rises because of regulatory measures, such as carbon taxes or emissions trading programmes (IPCC, 2018). Those companies that can lower their carbon footprint or switch to greener technologies might save money and become more profitable (Cumming *et al.*, 2024). However, policymakers are concerned that rising carbon pricing will have a negative impact on economic activity and reduce the competitiveness of domestic enterprises (Stiglitz, 2019).

According to resource dependence theory (RDT), businesses require resources in order to exist for a long time into the future. RDT posits that enterprises that rely on carbon-intensive resources or industries are likely to suffer higher operational risks and costs when regulations and market preferences shift towards sustainability. Further, the risks and prospects that come with transitioning to a low-carbon economy have an impact on businesses. Because a high carbon risk means that profits will change more often, it is important to look at how carbon risk affects how companies act and what they do. Not doing anything to stop climate change will cost more than reducing carbon pollution.

14.5.3. *Traditional sources of financing and the choice between equity and debt*

In the changing landscape of business finance, choosing the right financing strategy is crucial for sustainable growth. As businesses explore options, the debate between contemporary financing and traditional sources of finance such as bank loans takes centre stage. Let's examine the objectives of traditional sources of financing and the theoretical foundations for choices between those strategies. In traditional finance, a long-standing question is whether to use equity or debt for company financing needs targeting survival and growth. There are many theories justifying the use of debt as the source of long-term financing compared to equity. However, companies typically move with equity if the actual debt level is higher than the target leverage, whereas if the actual is below the target, companies prefer to go with debt.

Modigliani and Miller (1958) posit that the value of the firm is not affected by capital structure decisions under the no-tax conditions. However, if the tax is available, there are tax advantages in using debt in the capital structure, and thus the companies are biased towards debt. Further, the tax savings would reduce the weighted average cost of capital while maximising the firm value. However, there are some considerations of the benefits of taxes over the nature of the tax advantage and size.[4] Thus, traditionally, the choice between debt and equity focuses on wealth maximisation. However, the trade-off theory counterargued that the tax advantages of debt are outweighed by the costs associated with bankruptcy and financial distress. The cost associated with bankruptcy or financial distress is immense compared to the tax benefits derived from the finance cost of the debt instruments.

Later, the pecking-order theory argued that the choice between equity and debt financing is largely affected by the costs associated with information asymmetry. Thus, the cost of external financing is higher than the cost of internal financing. Due to the information asymmetry, managers' actions also provide certain signals to the fund providers, and accordingly, the capital structure decisions are made. Further, studies have shown that small companies with high P/E ratios and high gearing tend to use equity financing (Cragg and Baxter, 1967; Martin and Scott, 1974). The reason for equity financing is that with the high P/E ratio, managers believe that issuing shares would generate sufficient cash when the market conditions are in favour of the company. Moreover, Cragg and Baxter also pointed out that companies with high market capitalisation also tend to go with equity financing rather than debt based on timing considerations. Companies with high payouts and low profitability tend to use more debt financing (Martin and Scott, 1974) due to the low-risk nature of the companies with high payout ratios.

Later, companies started to focus on and maintain a target capital structure, considering factors such as profitability, growth, size, tangibility, depreciation, research and development, industry leverage, and macroeconomic conditions. Extant studies support the idea that firms follow a target capital structure in choosing their sources of finance. Further, companies with high operating risk (business risk) have a tendency towards a low debt ratio and more short-term debt compared to long-term debt.

[4]Farrar and Selwyn (1967), with Miller (1977) claim that, in equilibrium, even though there is an optimal debt level for the corporate sector overall, one debt level will be as good as another at the level of the individual firm.

14.5.4. *The choice of sources of finance by developed and developing countries*

There are important differences between the choice of sources of finance among the developed and developing countries. Atkin and Glen (1992) show that there is a tendency for developed countries to use more internally generated funds than externally generated ones used by developing countries, such as bank loans and equity.[5] Thus, a challenge exists for developing countries to choose the optimal capital structure due to the unstable market conditions and institutional constraints on fund requests by companies in developing countries. Agarwal and Mohtadi (2004). As per Glen and Sigh (2004) emerging market firms tend to show lower levels of leverage than their developed market counterparts, and leverage has declined during the period 1994–2000. This is because emerging market firms employ a higher level of fixed assets, have lower levels of returns on assets and equity, and are significantly affected by country-specific factors. Glen and Singh (2004).

Further, emerging markets have more bank-based financial systems, whereas developed markets have more market-based financial systems. Thus, emerging markets tend to use bank loans as their primary sources of finance, as they have underdeveloped capital markets. Demirgüç-Kunt and Levine (2001). In general, banks, other financial intermediaries, and stock markets are larger and more active in wealthier countries, leading to the development of the financial sector. Thus, firms in developed countries easily find capital through the issue of equity.

14.5.5. *Credit quality assessments by financial institutions*

Considering the debt financing, the borrower is assessed by the fund providers to make sure of the repayment of the borrowed money or

[5]For example, as a fraction of total finance, internally generated finance was found to be between 52% and 100% in the G7 nations and 12% and 58% in the developing countries (Atkin and Glen, 1992).

the credit risk. Credit risk measurement for banks is a highly emphasised category under the Basel Capital Accord II. The BCBS introduced the Basel Accord, encompassing a series of regulations. Over the past few decades, credit screening and pricing models have been refined primarily based on financial information, such as accounting ratios and share price-related measures. Li and Miu (2010). These models generally rely on either accounting information or market information.

Initial studies on default prediction primarily relied on accounting information, exemplified by Beaver (1966) and Altman (1968). Altman's Z-Score model, based on five accounting ratios, became a significant milestone in credit risk modelling. Later, researchers began incorporating cash flow-based ratios, moving away from purely accrual-based accounting. However, accounting information-based models predict a firm's financial condition by assuming that it will continue as a going concern, while bankruptcy violates this fundamental accounting concept. Additionally, the use of accounting ratios can introduce biases related to industry-specific and macroeconomic factors. Agarwal and Taffler (2008) highlighted the importance of market-based information in default prediction. Market information, grounded in robust theoretical foundations, is free from the distortions of accounting accrual adjustments. However, its validity hinges on market efficiency. For instance, insider dealings can undermine the reliability of market-based models.

Recent studies, however, indicate that credit decisions depend not only on financial or quantitative information but also on qualitative or soft information. Gropp *et al.* (2012). Financial information has certain limitations; for instance, past performance reported in a firm's accounting reports may not be predictive of future performance due to potential accounting manipulations by managers, which can compromise the quality of financial reporting (Agarwal and Taffler, 2008). Market information may provide up-to-date insights about the borrowing firm that are not yet reflected in accounting ratios, though this relies on the assumption of market efficiency. The literature characterises internal credit rating models of banks as a combination of financial and non-financial information (e.g. Brunner *et al.*, 2000). Accordingly, recent studies highlight the importance of corporate governance as an alternative non-financial information source for bankruptcy prediction. These studies suggest that, in addition to financial information, non-financial information plays a crucial role in making credit decisions.

Models based on market information highlight the limitations of accounting information, whereas models incorporating both accounting and market information reveal the flaws in each type and underscore the benefits of integrated approaches. Hillegeist *et al.* (2004). Similarly, research on corporate governance emphasises the importance of non-financial information in credit decisions. Liang *et al.* (2016).

Therefore, in order to gain a deeper understanding on the topics of carbon pricing, political connections to the implementation of green growth initiatives, and the allocation of costs and benefits across socioeconomic categories, the conceptual and theoretical framework as well as the empirical data presented and reviewed above on the financing choices and transition risk conventional and green growth are essential for understanding and interpreting the topics on carbon pricing, political connectedness to green growth initiative execution, and the distribution of costs and benefits across socioeconomic categories. This work has implications for future studies and provides deeper insights into understanding the emergence of the new financing instruments, thereby expanding the scope of financing options. Against the backdrop of new pledges from the largest GHG-emitting countries to aim for future carbon neutrality, EU sustainable debt markets continued to expand at a brisk pace in 2020 (+32% from 1H20, €508 billion), linked to robust supply from the corporate sector and massive public-sector financing needs to support the EU's economic recovery. Within the EU financial sector, investment funds are more exposed to climate-sensitive economic sectors than banks, insurers, and pension funds.

Funds whose portfolios are tilted towards more polluting assets (brown funds) distribute their portfolios over a larger number of companies than funds with cleaner portfolios (green funds). This apparent diversification hides a concentration risk: brown funds are more closely connected with each other (have more similar portfolios) than green fund portfolios, which tend to 'herd' less (have less similar portfolios to those of other green funds). This suggests that widespread climate-related financial shocks are likely to disproportionately affect brown funds. In addition, brown funds have more systemic impact: they contribute more to total system-wide losses (by virtue of their greater interconnections within the fund universe) than green funds. These findings (ESMA, 2021) provide support for ongoing EU regulatory and supervisory initiatives on sustainable finance.

References

Agarwal, S. and Mohtadi, H. (2004). Financial markets and the financing choice of firms: Evidence from developing countries. *Global Finance Journal*, 15(1), 57–70.

Agarwal, V. and Taffler, R. (2008). Comparing the performance of market-based and accounting-based bankruptcy prediction models. *Journal of Banking and Finance*, 32(8), 1541–1551.

Alogoskoufis, S., Carbone, S., Coussens, W., Fahr, S., Giuzio, M., Kuik, F., and Spaggiari, M. (2021). Climate-related risks to financial stability. *Financial Stability Review*, 1, 1–28.

Altman, E. I. (1968). Financial ratios, discriminant analysis and the prediction of corporate bankruptcy. *The Journal of Finance*, 23(4), 589–609.

Atkin, M. and Glen, J. (1992). Comparing corporate capital structures around the globe. *The International Executive*, 34(5), 369–384.

Beck, M., Rivers, N., Wigle, R., and Yonezawa, H. (2015). Carbon tax and revenue recycling: Impacts on households in British Columbia. *Resource and Energy Economics*, 41, 40–69.

BCBS. (2020). Basel Committee on Banking Supervision, Climate-related financial risks: A survey on current initiatives. Basel Committee Report.

BCBS. (2021). Climate-related risk drivers and their transmission channels. Basel Committee Report.

Bilbao. (2023). Record high revenues from global carbon pricing near $100 billion. World Bank Group Report.

Boyce, J. K. (2018). Carbon pricing: effectiveness and equity. *Ecological Economics*, 150, 52–61.

Callan, T., Lyons, S., Scott, S., Tol, R. S., and Verde, S. (2009). The distributional implications of a carbon tax in Ireland. *Energy Policy*, 37(2), 407–412.

Cragg, J. G. and Baxter, N. D. (1970). The issuing of corporate securities. *Journal of Political Economy*, 78(6), 1310–1324.

Cumming, D., Duppati, G., Fernando, R., Singh, S. P., and Tiwari, A. K. (2024). Dynamics of carbon risk, cost of debt and leverage adjustments. *The British Accounting Review*, forthcoming.

Demirgüç-Kunt, A. and Levine, R. (2001). Bank-based and market-based financial systems: Cross-country comparisons. World Bank Working Paper.

Duppati, G., Tiwari, A. K., and Matlani, N. (2023). Effects of CO2, renewables and fuel prices on the economic growth in New Zealand. *International Journal of Energy Economics and Policy*, 13(4), 555–562.

ESMA. (2021). Report on trends, risks and vulnerabilities. European Securities and Markets Authority.

EUS. (2021). Speech by President von der Leyen at the Special Edition 2021 of the Munich Security Conference. European Union.

Glen, J. and Singh, A. (2004). Comparing capital structures and rates of return in developed and emerging markets. *Emerging Markets Review*, 5(2), 161–192.

Gropp, R., Gruendl, C., and Guettler, A. (2012). Does discretion in lending increase bank risk? Borrower self-selection and loan officer capture effects. *European Banking Center Discussion Paper*, No. 2012-010.

Haas, C., Jahns, H., Kempa, K., and Moslener, U. (2023). Deep uncertainty and the transition to a low-carbon economy. *Energy Research and Social Science*, 100, 103060.

Hayes, K. and Hafstead, M. (2020). Carbon pricing 103: Effects across sectors. Resources for the Future Report.

Hillegeist, S. A., Keating, E. K., Cram, D. P., and Lundstedt, K. G. (2004). Assessing the probability of bankruptcy. *Review of Accounting Studies*, 9(1), 5–34.

Ho, M. S., Morgenstern, R. D., and Shih, J. S. (2008). Impact of carbon price policies on US industry. Resources for the Future Working Paper.

IMF. (2019). Fiscal policies for Paris climate strategies — from principle to practice. International Monetary Fund Report.

Konradt, M., McGregor, T., and Toscani, F. (2024). Carbon prices and inflation in the Euro Area. *IMF Working Paper*, forthcoming.

Krueger, P., Sautner, Z., and Starks, L. T. (2020). The importance of climate risks for institutional investors. *The Review of Financial Studies*, 33(3), 1067–1111.

Li, M.-Y. L. and Miu, P. (2010). A hybrid bankruptcy prediction model with dynamic loadings on accounting-ratio-based and market-based information: A binary quantile regression approach. *Journal of Empirical Finance*, 17(4), 818–833.

Liang, D., Lu, C. C., Tsai, C. F., and Shih, G. A. (2016). Financial ratios and corporate governance indicators in bankruptcy prediction: A comprehensive study. *European Journal of Operational Research*, 252(2), 561–572.

Lopez, N. and Smith, P. (2024). Home insurance at $10,000 a year shows California buyers' pain. *Bloomberg News Report.*

Modigliani, F. and Miller, M. H. (1958). The cost of capital, corporation finance and the theory of investment. *The American Economic Review*, 48(3), 261–297.

Martin, J. D. and Scott Jr, D. F. (1974). A discriminant analysis of the corporate debt-equity decision. *Financial Management*, 3(4), 71–79.

Mutua, C. (2024). ESG bond weekly: Buyers flock to Deutsche Bank debut social bond. *Bloomberg First Word Report.*

Schwartzkopf, F. (2022). ECB to avoid climate laggards' longer debt in historic tilt. *Bloomberg News Report.*

https://doi.org/10.1142/9781800617032_bmatter

Index

www.ingramcontent.com/pod-product-compliance
Lightning Source LLC
LaVergne TN
LVHW010539300926
849162LV00002B/180
* 9 7 8 1 8 0 0 6 1 7 0 2 5 *